DATE DUE

THE
VIETNAM WAR
IN
AMERICAN MEMORY

A VOLUME IN THE SERIES

Culture, Politics, and the Cold War

EDITED BY

Christian G. Appy

THE
VIETNAM WAR
IN
AMERICAN MEMORY

Veterans, Memorials, and the
Politics of Healing

Patrick Hagopian

University of Massachusetts Press

AMHERST

LC 2008053928
ISBN 978-1-55849-693-4

Designed by Dennis Anderson
Set in Dante by House of Equations, Inc.
Printed and bound by Sheridan Books, Inc.

Library of Congress Cataloging-in-Publication Data

Hagopian, Patrick.
The Vietnam War in American memory : veterans, memorials, and the
politics of healing / Patrick Hagopian.
p. cm.
Includes bibliographical references and index.
ISBN 978-1-55849-639-4 (cloth : alk. paper)
1. Vietnam War, 1961–1975—Veterans—United States. 2. Vietnam War, 1961–1975—
Social aspects—United States. 3. Vietnam War, 1961–1975—United States—Psychological
aspects. 4. Veterans—United States—Political activity. 5. Veterans—United States—
Public opinion. 6. Memory—Social aspects—United States. 7. War memorials—Social
aspects—United States. 9. Mental healing—Social aspects—United States. 9. Mental
healing—Political aspects—United States. 10. Public opinion—United States. I. Title.

DS559.73.U6H34 2009
959.704′31—dc22
2008053928

British Library Cataloguing in Publication data are available.

CONTENTS

ILLUSTRATIONS

ACKNOWLEDGMENTS

THIS RESEARCH was completed with the support of grants and fellowships from the American Historical Association's Albert J. Beveridge Society; the Arts and Humanities Research Board (UK); Beyond the Wall (a nonprofit organization); the British Academy; the College of William and Mary's Commonwealth Center for the Study of American Culture; the University of Glamorgan; Lancaster University; the Pennsylvania Historical and Museum Commission; Johns Hopkins University's Program in Atlantic History and Culture; Johns Hopkins University's Frederick Jackson Turner Society; the Smithsonian Institution; and the United States Air Force Historical Research Agency.

The research was assisted by numerous librarians, archivists, and scholars. Jim Roan of the National Museum of American History's library actively searched out relevant materials rather than adopting the more conventional librarian's role of waiting for requests. John Baky of the Connelly Library, LaSalle University, Philadelphia, has assembled an important special collection of Vietnam War–related material, "Imaginative Representations of the Vietnam War." The research was also supported by Lisa Jones, archivist at the Reagan Presidential Library in Simi Valley, California; Fred Bauman, Ron Cogan, Ernie Emrich, Nan Ernst, Jeff Flannery, Mike Klein, Katie McDonough, Jeff Monagle, Mary Wolfskill, and Joe Sullivan of the Manuscript Division of the Library of Congress; the staff of the Division of Prints and Photographs of the Library of Congress; Hope Y. Yelich of the College of William and Mary's Earl Gregg Swem Library; Sue Clarke, at the Lancaster University library; Pacifico C. Lazo, a research analyst at the Government Accountability Office; and the staff of public libraries in all fifty states who assisted me in my questionnaire survey about Vietnam veterans memorials. I was assisted in research queries by Christy Thornton of NACLA Reports on the Americas, and by Oliver Trager of Facts on File. Elizabeth Mock of the University of Massachusetts, Boston's Healey Library gave me access to the special collection on the PBS documentary *Vietnam: A Television History*. Gene Michaud of the Joiner Center for the Study of War and Social Consequences helped me with numerous research leads and was a valued source of advice over many years. Philip Brookman and Susan Ades of the Washington Project for the Arts allowed me to study the records and transcripts of the "War and Memory: In the Aftermath of Vietnam" exhibition; staff of the National Museum of American Art gave me further access to the collection once it was deposited in their archives.

Hunter Hollins, coordinator of museum services at the U.S. Department of the Interior, helped me track down photo documentation of Frederick Hart's maquette of the statue *Three Infantrymen*.

Michael Rossman of the AOUON [All of Us or None] Archive, Berkeley, California, and Carol Wells of the Center for the Study of Political Graphics, Los Angeles, allowed me to photograph antiwar posters in their excellent collections. David Kunzle allowed me to duplicate his visual documentation of his "Posters of Protest" collection, now a part of the collection of the Center for the Study of Political Graphics. Larry Bird and Edith Mayo of the Division of Political History (now the Division of Politics and Reform) of the National Museum of American History, Smithsonian Institution, allowed me to photograph the museum's collection of protest posters. Eve Sinaiko, Sondra Varco, and Lucy Lippard assisted my research on visual arts of the Vietnam War. Dan Hallin helped me to obtain copies of documentaries about the Vietnam War. William Withuhn, a Vietnam veteran and curator at the National Museum of American History, gave invaluable support to the project at an early stage and introduced me to Jack Wheeler. Mina Marefat, senior architectural historian at the National Museum of American History, arranged my introduction to Paul Spreiregen.

I appreciate the assistance of the National Park Service's Duery Felton, David Guynes, and Pamela Beth West, who gave me access to the Vietnam Veterans Memorial Collection. The National Museum of American History's Jennifer Locke Jones informed me about the selection and installation of materials in the museum's exhibit, "Personal Legacy: The Healing of a Nation" and subsequently supported my research in numerous other ways. Cara Sutherland, of the Museum of Our National Heritage, informed me about the installation of materials in the "Gathered at the Wall" exhibition. Carole Page gave me invaluable assistance by sending me copies of the *From the Heart* newsletter. She and several contributors to Laura Palmer's *Shrapnel in the Heart*, including Dana Shuster and Dan Doyle, embraced my interest in their reunions at the Vietnam Veterans Memorial. Sue (Xuan) Burns gave me valuable insights into her journeys from Vietnam to Oregon and from there to the Vietnam Veterans Memorial. Others who responded to requests for information and materials are cited in the book's references.

A number of therapists increased my understanding of post-traumatic stress disorder and the treatment thereof. Dwight Edwards gave me permission to visit and meet some of the veteran clients at the Vet Center in Olney, Pennsylvania, when this research was at an early stage. Ray Scurfield, Gene DeWeese, and Steve Tice assisted me during my visit to the American Lake PTSD treatment center in Washington State. Irwin Noparstak granted me an interview to discuss his work as an in-country psychiatrist and a therapist after the war.

Numerous Vietnam veterans and others assisted me by giving me access to documents or by granting me interviews and often graciously invited me to their homes. Their generosity assisted me in understanding the design and construction histories of several Vietnam veterans memorials and, equally significantly, the motivations of people who devoted themselves to creating the memorials. In particular, I am grateful for the help of Don Drumheller, B .T. Collins, and Michael Kelley of the California Vietnam Veterans Memorial Commission, and Michael Larson, one of the memorial's designers. Michael Kelley was the first Vietnam veteran who informed me about the lore and legends surrounding Vietnam veteran status, including the "wannabe" phenomenon. Over the years, he has been an invaluable source of knowledge and insights. Jan Scruggs gave me permission for access to the Vietnam Veterans Memorial Collection in the Library of Congress before the collection became open to all, assisted with further queries, and generously donated copies of memorial-related publications. Lisa Gough responded to my queries about the Vietnam Veterans Memorial. Sue Kohler and Charles Atherton of the Commission of Fine Arts assisted me in my research of the commission's records.

Diane Carlson Evans of the Vietnam Women's Memorial Project sent me a copy of the videotape of the memorial's dedication ceremony; she and Diana Hellinger gave me access to the slide documentation of their design competition as well as other relevant materials. Rodger Brodin sent me information about his statue, *The Nurse*. At Cheryl "Nicki" Nicol's home, I saw one of the four scale models that toured the country. Glenna Goodacre allowed me to document versions of the maquette of the Vietnam Women's Memorial sculpture at her studio in Santa Fe, New Mexico.

Marc Leepson gave me access to the documentation and photographs of Vietnam Veterans Memorials gathered by Vietnam Veterans of America. He also allowed me to read Pegi Donovan's unpublished research on memorials around the United States. Nguyen Manh Hung of the Indochina Institute, George Mason University, gave me access to the raw questionnaire data gathered by the Project for the Vietnam Generation for its survey of Vietnam veterans memorials. Gary Ford generously sent me the unpublished research he produced leading to his article on Vietnam War memorials published in *Southern Living* magazine. Marcia Landau and Zack Burkett made available a wealth of documents about the Vietnam Veterans Leadership Program. Paul Spreiregen, who organized the design competition for the Vietnam Veterans Memorial, and George Dickie, the landscape designer for the Vietnam Women's Memorial, granted me interviews. Interviews with Edwin Meese III and Tom Shull gave me important insight into the actions of the Reagan White House. Lydia Fish gave me permission to quote from posts to the vwar-l email discussion list.

In Kentucky, my research was assisted by interviews with Ronald Ray, Jim Halvatgis, Helm Roberts, and William Black Jr., who gave me access to relevant documents and other materials. In New York, the research was similarly assisted by Bernard Edelman, Jim Hebron, and Robert Santos. In Portland, Oregon, I was helped by Doug Macy, Jerry Pero, Mike Goldade, Doug Bomarito, Ben Stanley, Frank and Fran Rauschkolb, Terence O'Donnell, and James G. Phillips. Mike Kaprielian sent me a collection of documents concerning the Rhode Island Vietnam Veterans Memorial, including documentation of contacts with other memorials around the country. T .J. McGarvey sent me materials concerning the Pittsburgh/Allegheny County Vietnam Veterans Memorial. Victor Westphall, Linda Vaughan, Susan Knutson, Ted

Luna, Bob Lenham, and Tom Turnbull assisted my research about the memorial at Angel Fire, New Mexico. Paul Russell, B .G. "Jug" Burkett, Richard Martratt, Gary Garmon, and Alexander "Russ" Bolling III assisted my research about the Texas Vietnam Veterans Memorial in Dallas. Bob Waechter, George Biswell, Art Fillmore, Norman Fretwell, Craig Gay, and the memorial's designer, David Baker, granted me interviews assisting my research about the Kansas City (Missouri) Vietnam Veterans Memorial. My research in Mississippi was assisted by Ed Horstman, Bob Landry, Stanley Parish, Henry Phan, and Bill Stallworth. John Devitt allowed me an interview and access to documents regarding the "Moving Wall," and showed me the warehouse in which offerings left at the Moving Wall are conserved. Alan Berolzheimer Teva told me about the controversy about the memorial in Thetford, Vermont. James Masland, Robert Bacon, Robert Pulaski, and Timothy Beebe assisted me with my research in Thetford. Although I devote more space in this book to some of these memorials than to others, the research at all of these sites was valuable, and at every site I found at least one lead or nugget of information that turned out to be crucial. I appreciate the generosity of all those I met and interviewed in giving me their time. Of course, none of them is responsible for my interpretations of the evidence.

Although I encouraged the Vietnam veterans who had custody of memorial-related documents to place them in archives and libraries, in many cases this has not, to the best of my knowledge, been done. Often, the materials were held in private collections, deposited in convenient file drawers in the premises of businesses or public institutions, or simply boxed in people's garages. Some of the materials may never be formally archived. In one case, an informant had thrown a box of records in the trash a week before I arrived to do my research. My research trips resulted in the preservation of some seventeen linear feet of memorial-related documents. They consist of photocopied materials such as the minutes and correspondence of the organizations that created the memorials discussed in this book, as well as photographs of and documents about dozens of other memorials that were not discussed in the book for reasons of space. These records, along with press clippings, videotapes of dedication ceremonies, and related materials, remain in my custody. It is my wish to place them in a suitable archive or archives. Anyone who wishes to discuss securing this material should contact me through the University of Massachusetts Press. Disappointingly, the Vietnam Veterans Leadership Program's records have not been collected and preserved by the National Archives and Records Administration, so there is a significant risk that the activities of the important federally funded organization might be lost to history.

Friends and colleagues, John Baky, Johanna Blakley, Stefan Cornelis, Elisabeth Dahl, Jennie Levy, Gene Michaud, Maureen Moynagh, H. Dieter Rickford, Kirk Savage, Ted Swedenberg, and Alan Berlozheimer Teva offered me hospitality during various research trips. Their spare rooms, sofas, and company provided welcome relief from the usual motel rooms and bed and breakfasts.

The book was read in whole or in part by a number of mentors, colleagues, and reviewers, beginning with my doctoral dissertation supervisor, Ronald G. Walters, who persuaded me that the topic counted as history, and who supported me stead-fastly through the period of dissertation research and writing. Toby Ditz, Neil Hertz, and David William Cohen gave me suggestions and advice that started me on the road to revision and that I still recall these many years later. Elisabeth Dahl made numerous editorial suggestions. H. Bruce Franklin, Ed Linenthal, and Marilyn Young were incisive, critical, and immensely supportive peer reviewers. Marilyn Young was generous enough to read the whole of two early versions of the book. Clark Dougan at the University of Massachusetts Press encouraged me to prepare the book for publication and made a significant contribution to the content. Chris Appy, the editor of the series in which this book appears, gave invaluable advice as an expert on the Vietnam War and the veterans' experience which helped shape the structure of the book and sharpened its arguments. Copy editor Deborah Smith helped hone the final draft. Carol Betsch managed the logistics of the editorial process with smooth efficiency. Jack Harrison skillfully handled the complexities of design and production. Mary McClintock prepared the index.

I presented versions of several chapters at a number of forums and benefited from the comments by participants. I particularly appreciate the comments of Nicola Caldwell, Sam Edwards, Nick Gebhardt, Michael Heale, Tim Hickman, and Jonathan Munby, colleagues in the American Studies reading group at Lancaster University; Sharon Ghamari-Tabrizi, Grey Gundaker, George Henderson, Robert Haywood, Alan Wallach, Chandos Brown, Robert Gross, and members of the Commonwealth Center seminar series at the College of William and Mary; Jeanne Houck, Jerma Jackson, Ruth Oldenziel, and participants in the Smithsonian Institution National Museum of American History seminars in American History; and participants in the Seminar on Remembering and Forgetting, Commonwealth Center for Literary and Cultural Change, University of Virginia.

Earlier versions of two chapters were published in *Prospects: An Annual of American Cultural Studies*, and the *Dumbarton Oaks Colloquium on the History of Landscape Architecture* and the conclusion draws on a chapter in *Contested Spaces: Sites, Representations and Histories of Conflict*, ed. Louise Purbrick, Jim Aulich, and Graham Dawson (Palgrave Macmillan, 2007). I am grateful to the editors for per-mission to reproduce and expand on those arguments in this volume. Excerpt taken from *A Rumor of War* by Philip Caputo. Copyright © 1977, 1996 by Philip Caputo. Reprinted by permission of Henry Holt and Company, LLC, and by The Aaron M. Priest Agency, 2008.

Every reasonable effort has been made to trace the ownership of copyrighted materials. Any omissions of acknowledgment are accidental and will be corrected in future editions if the publisher is notified.

Any mistakes in the book are, of course, mine alone.

THE
VIETNAM WAR
IN
AMERICAN MEMORY

INTRODUCTION

A "Noble Cause"

★

ON THE AFTERNOON of May 27, 1968, Victor Westphall was operating a mechanical digger, a backhoe, on Val Verde, his ranch in northern New Mexico. A pair of Marine Corps captains in dress uniforms were searching for the ranch, bearing bad news. They drove through the Moreno Valley, in the green foothills of Wheeler Peak, asking Westphall's neighbors for directions. When they found him, they told Westphall what every parent who sends a child to war dreads to hear: his son David, a lieutenant in the Marine Corps, had been shot and killed while leading his platoon in combat. Victor broke the news to his wife, Jeanne, at home nearby and telephoned David's brother, Douglas.

The family was determined to mark David's death in some special way, unwilling to allow it to be lost among the thousands of other all too ordinary wartime events, the death of young men in battle. Jeanne proposed that the family create a memorial to David and others who died in the war. By the time she began to have second thoughts, Victor and Douglas had committed themselves to the project. They hired an architect and began to outline the concept for a memorial, in Victor's words, "not only for David, but for all the veterans of Vietnam." He later recalled, "I just couldn't imagine, back then, that these young men would be damn near forgotten by this nation."[1]

Victor Westphall began construction of the memorial in late summer 1968, naming it the Vietnam Veterans Peace and Brotherhood Chapel. The memorial was completed in 1971 and dedicated on the third anniversary of David Westphall's death. David's life insurance policy had partially paid for construction, but as members of the public heard about the memorial, they sent in small donations, sometimes just a dollar or two.

On a hill near the towns of Angel Fire and Eagle Nest, two white stucco walls ascend, curving up to the apex fifty feet above the ground (fig. 1). (Stucco is a traditional Native American building material and is used by mission churches in the

1

Figure 1. Vietnam Veterans Memorial Chapel, Angel Fire, New Mexico; Ted Luna, designer,
dedicated May 22, 1971. Photo by author.

local pueblos.) Where the walls converge, a tall window looks out onto the scrubby
landscape dotted with pine trees and wild flowers—asters, gentians, and iris. Sudden
storms can blow up, bringing hail and fierce winds strong enough to shred flags flying
at the site. On fine days, set against the clear blue New Mexico sky, the sweeping
walls resemble a bird's wings, their light color suggesting a dove or a seabird; but
the location near Angel Fire makes some visitors think of angel wings. The roofline
curves down from the meeting point of the walls, splaying out to form a building
with a roughly triangular plan when they join an eight-foot-high rear wall. Here the
public enters and leaves the building. Inside, the play of light on the rough adobe continually creates subtle shifts in the walls' color tones. Banked seating slopes down to
the tall window, in front of which stands a simple cross (fig. 2). Photographs of those
who died in Vietnam, with David's at the center, form a gallery on the rear wall.[2]

Victor Westphall sometimes said his whole life had prepared him to create the
chapel.[3] He was a man with an extraordinary range of accomplishments in diverse
fields, all of which seemed to converge on his work of commemoration.[4] A builder,
a historian, an athlete, he wrote philosophical tracts espousing the cause of world
peace and calling on individuals to take responsibility for societal problems. He
was guided by his dreams and believed that the memorial tapped into a pipeline
of metaphysical forces that came from the nearby Blue Lake, sacred to the Taos
Pueblo Indians.[5] He sometimes felt that mysterious lines of fate had led him to create the memorial, reflecting that it was "as if some greater destiny, larger than all
of us, assigned [the job] to me."[6] He plastered the memorial himself, with the aid

Figure 2. Vietnam Veterans Memorial Chapel, interior. Photo by author.

of Vietnam veterans, glazed it with his own hands, laid the floor, and installed the electrical wiring.[7] A lifetime of manual labor and strenuous exercise, along with a deep sense of obligation, gave him the physical and moral capacity to proceed with single-minded devotion.[8] His unresolved relationship with his son added to his drive. For the next thirty years, Westphall devoted his life to the memorial, eventually moving into a visitors' center constructed at the site.

Westphall dated his activism to 1946 when, after naval service in World War II, he wrote an antiwar letter to President Harry Truman and began to work, as he said, "with the fervor of a zealot" to persuade the leaders of the United States to work for peace.[9] Later, as a father who had lost a son in war, Westphall wrote to U.S. presidents Richard Nixon and Gerald Ford, to senators and congressmen, to Governor Bruce King of New Mexico, to Pope Paul VI, and others, assuming the authority to moralize about war and peace. He proposed, for example, that the U.S. government create a department of peace. President Nixon replied to one of his letters, saying, "Your labor of love is far more than the sheer building of a monument; it is a symbol of the love which all fathers have for their sons."[10] Indeed, one of the reasons that Westphall stood out was that, among Americans bereaved by the Vietnam War, women were usually the ones who gave a voice and face to mourning; fathers were often silent and invisible in their grief.[11]

For Westphall, the Vietnam War heralded a "dangerous new epoch" characterized by lassitude, hedonism, irresponsibility, and waste. Addressing the people of America in a book published in 1981, Westphall warned that those who forgot Vietnam did so at their peril. The United States engaged in a futile war, he said, lied to itself, and brutalized a weaker country, "thrashing about in a vain effort to disengage rather than admitting we shouldn't be there," in the process creating a "shame of vast proportions." None of this, in Westphall's view, was the fault of those who fought. They were misled and therefore should not suffer the shame of a nation. What was vital, though, was that Americans honorably face up to that shame. If Americans ignored the lessons of the Vietnam War, he concluded, Vietnam could become the "saddest chapter" in American history.[12]

"All those wasted lives," Westphall said once, referring to the more than fifty-eight thousand Americans who died in military service in Vietnam. "I pray to God their sacrifices will give each of us the firm resolve to prevent future wars and establish brotherhood."[13] Westphall hoped that by being memorialized, his son would become a symbol that would arouse humankind, and that he would therefore not have died in vain.[14] His refusal to accept the catastrophe of a pointless, meaningless death is an impulse we see echoed often, as the bereaved comfort themselves with the thought that some redemptive purpose might be found in the death of a loved one in Vietnam—or, when no such consolation can be found, when they try to mitigate the blank awfulness of loss by making sure that, at least, the dead are not forgotten. What makes Victor Westphall unique is the unyielding strength of will with which he undertook his mission.

This powerful urge to memorialize his son was motivated in part by a feeling that he was at least indirectly to blame for David's death. As Westphall explains in another tribute to his son, the biography *David's Story*, David had quit college and joined the marines after Westphall disrupted his football career by giving the team coach unwanted advice.[15] Westphall's sense of responsibility was misplaced, though: David went to Vietnam only after leaving the marines and then re-enlisting, a decision in which Westphall played no part. Westphall's placing himself too close to the center of the story is typical of the phenomenon of "survivor guilt," in which survivors unconsciously reduce their own sense of powerlessness by assuming responsibility for events beyond their control. Westphall also devoted himself to David's memory to make up for the affection he had not shown his son while he was alive.[16] Their relationship was sometimes strained because David found it hard to live up to his demanding father's expectations. By creating the memorial, Westphall could show the world how proud he was of David and how much he loved his son. But here lies a paradox: the more complete his self-abnegating devotion to David's memory, the more Westphall drew attention to himself.[17] And Westphall's rousing appeals in the cause of peace contrast with David's own sentiments about the war: at the University of Montana, where he studied between his two stints as a marine, David espoused very conservative political views, vehemently denouncing liberals and Communists; a week before he died, he wrote to his brother that the only language Communists understand is force.[18] At Angel Fire, the causes that Victor Westphall dignified with a father's grief were not his son's but his own. Unique as it may be, this story of a father martyring himself to the memory of his fallen son illustrates something that is true of all commemorations: they are as much—sometimes more—about those who remember as they are about the objects of remembrance.

The memorial dedicated to peace and brotherhood touched a chord in the emotions of Americans affected by the Vietnam War.[19] A serviceman sent a small contribution in April 1970, thanking Victor Westphall in "the hope that one day soon, we may give peace a chance." Seven years later, after the war had ended, a man from Cambridge, Massachusetts, wrote to thank Westphall for ensuring that those who died in Vietnam would be remembered. The "war was useless," he added, "and maybe their sacrifice was in vain. But what you have built to honor them makes up for a lot of things that shouldn't have been allowed to happen." A woman from a small town in Virginia said that having a peace memorial, not a war memorial, "rings like a benediction." In 1979, another woman said that the memorial was one of the few beautiful things to come out of the war. She told of losing her husband to the war, even though he returned without physical wounds. For four years she searched his eyes for the spark she had known in them before he went to Vietnam. But he was only going through the motions of living, overwhelmed by pain and anger. Eventually, after they divorced, he moved away and she lost touch with him. She called him one of the "missing in action" and applauded Victor Westphall for turning his own loss into growth and love, not bitterness.[20]

The memorial at Angel Fire was among the first of the 461 Vietnam War memorials erected around the United States up to the present.[21] Although the vast majority of the memorials were dedicated in the 1980s, numerous memorials created around the country during the war years demonstrate a widespread impulse to commemorate the war even then.[22] The first, a park that honors a soldier posthumously awarded the Medal of Honor, was dedicated in Chicago in 1966. Most memorials dedicated during the war simply honored troops who had died, but others, like the Angel Fire memorial, questioned the purpose for which Americans were fighting and dying.[23]

The Angel Fire memorial's 1971 dedication ceremony reflected the widespread opposition to the war at the time. John Kerry, the national president of Vietnam Veterans Against the War (VVAW), spoke at the dedication, along with the leader of the New Mexico VVAW chapter. Antiwar protest songs played in the chapel and in its early years the VVAW flag flew there. In his speech, Kerry repeated part of the statement he had made before the Senate Foreign Relations Committee a month before, saying there is no answer when a man dying in Vietnam looks up and asks, "Why?"[24]

A memorial erected in Auburn, California, in 1967 poses the same question Kerry evoked (fig. 3). A precursor of the many sculptural memorials examined in this study, it depicts a soldier holding up the body of a dead comrade. It was commissioned by veterans of World War I and was intended to honor not just the dead from Placer County but "all the fighting men of the United States, past, present, and future." Clearly, though, it refers principally to the Vietnam War: the uniforms on the figures are of the Vietnam War era. Positioned in front of the Placer County Administration Center, the statue faces a cemetery in which the dead from other wars are buried. Behind the statue a gas torch burned, intended as an eternal flame, like the one that burns at President Kennedy's grave in Arlington National Cemetery. "I figured that if John F. Kennedy deserved it," the sculptor, Kenneth Fox, said, "so did every boy who died for our country."[25]

The Auburn memorial caused a local furor because of its plaque, inscribed with the single word "Why." Although no question mark follows the word, the memorial seemed to be questioning the reasons for the loss of the young men dying in Vietnam. In 1968, a majority of Americans had decided that the U.S. government had been wrong to enter the Vietnam War, after the January 1968 Tet Offensive proved that the achievement of U.S. goals, if they were attainable at all, was years away. In this political context, a statue of a soldier holding a dead comrade, captioned by the word "Why," suggested to many that the memorial was a protest against the war. Fox, however, steadfastly denied any such intention. He insisted that it was his prerogative as an artist to name the work; and, recalling the events years later, he said, "'Why?' is a legitimate question throughout the universe."[26]

In 1970, even as public support for the war waned and antiwar demonstrations took place on streets and college campuses across the country, the supervisors of Placer County decided that the inscription was unacceptable and they removed the plaque. When World War I veterans and local people gathered for a public meeting to discuss the matter, the threat of public disorder was sufficient for the police to be called out. As a result of the public outcry, the plaque was restored and Fox told the supervisors that if they wanted to remove it, they would have to remove the whole monument. Accordingly, the Placer County supervisors approved a mandate to move the whole monument, plaque, statue, and all, to the Veterans Memorial

Hall within ninety days, but somehow this was never done. The memorial instead began to suffer from official neglect. The "eternal flame" burned out, the gas supply disconnected, even though Fox offered to pay the utility bill.[27] The memorial languished, largely ignored, for the next twenty years.

Fox questioned the reasons for the war and Victor Westphall espoused peace in a period when the majority of Americans had turned against the war. Westphall,

Figure 3. *Why*. Placer County, California, soldier memorial; Kenneth Fox, sculptor, dedicated November 11, 1967. Photo by Rebecca Ford Soren, Ford Family Photography.

listening to an inner voice that chimed with popular opinion, wrote in 1972, "War itself is the enemy to be overcome."[28] The urgency of antiwar sentiments declined, however, once President Nixon's "Vietnamization" policy reduced U.S. troop numbers in Vietnam, and it dwindled further when the Paris Peace Accords of January 1973 led to the departure of the last U.S. combat troops. Later that year a former member of VVAW complained to Westphall that he was disappointed that the American people paid Vietnam veterans like himself very little attention, although they lavished attention and praise on the returning American prisoners of war who had been held captive in North Vietnam. Americans seemed to him to be thinking, "Let us now try and forget the whole thing and go on with the conduct of business as usual." Another correspondent, who supported amnesty for war resisters, wrote to Westphall in 1974 that the nation had unfinished business that it seemed to be evading: "Our country has still to face the Vietnam war—and to become, as it should and could, a leader for peace, instead of hurrying in the opposite direction."[29]

From 1973 until 1977, Victor Westphall struggled to maintain the memorial in good repair and to keep it open to the public. Visitation, which peaked at twenty-five thousand people a year in 1973, reduced to a trickle in 1977. Westphall speculated that few visitors came because Americans felt ashamed of the war and wanted to forget about Vietnam.[30] Observers refer to this immediate postwar period as one of "collective amnesia," when it looked as if Americans were determined to erase the memories of the war.[31] New Mexico senator Pete Domenici, speaking at a Memorial Day ceremony at the chapel in 1977, urged Americans who might want to wipe out the "unpleasant memory" of the Vietnam War not to forget those who fought.[32] Congress failed to pass a bill Domenici repeatedly proposed declaring the Angel Fire memorial a national monument and requiring the National Park Service to maintain it. The Park Service pointed out that the only war memorials it administered outside Washington, DC, were in historic battlefields, and the bill stalled in congressional committees.[33]

Victor Westphall decided that David's photograph in the memorial should be flanked by those of others who had died in Vietnam—twelve others, the number of marines who had died in the battle when David was killed. He solicited photographs of the dead from survivors around the country. Eventually, he gathered enough photos to allow twelve from each state in turn to be arrayed alongside David's, with the corresponding state flag flying at the site during each month-long display. Westphall frequently said that, to commemorate the dead on both sides, he would be happy to add photographs of Vietnamese Communist troops to the gallery. In an extraordinary gesture of magnanimity, he even said that, if the Vietnamese soldier who killed his son later died in combat, he would be willing to display that soldier's photo. In November 1979, a *Parade* magazine article reported to a nationwide audience that Victor Westphall had built a memorial to all the dead on both sides of the war. A correspondent from Massachusetts responded favorably and asked whether Westphall had solicited the names of casualties from Vietnam.[34] Indeed, ten years earlier, Westphall had written to Ho Chi Minh, the president of North Vietnam, soliciting photographs of Communist soldiers who had died in combat.[35]

The suggestion that the memorial at Angel Fire might commemorate the dead on both sides sets it apart from almost every other U.S. memorial to the Vietnam War. In letters to Victor Westphall, some Americans objected to the proposition that the memorial might honor their former enemies.[36] The vast majority of correspondents, though, found nothing objectionable in this proposal. Both of New Mexico's U.S. senators, Republican politicians not known for being "soft on Communism," responded favorably to the *Parade* article; one even read it into the *Congressional Record*. A correspondent from Los Angeles said that representing the "other side" would hasten the day when there would be no "sides" and the world would live in peace. Julie Urban, from Watertown, Massachusetts, wrote, "I support your effort to maintain the chapel and I hope that your effort to get it recognized as a national memorial [succeeds]. The effort may be small but maybe if enough people band together to preserve the chapel and the lessons it holds—maybe 'Vietnam' will not have been another futile war. May God be with you and support you in this truly noble cause."[37] For Urban, the "noble cause" was peace.

The Westphalls' attempt to establish the memorial as a national monument to the Vietnam War was eclipsed by the efforts of the Vietnam Veterans Memorial Fund (VVMF), whose goal was to plant a memorial in the nation's capital. Senator Domenici co-sponsored the legislation that granted the fund a prominent site on the Washington, DC, Mall and introduced an amendment to the Senate version of the bill stipulating that the VVMF would redirect any surplus money to the Angel Fire memorial and that the secretary of the interior, at his discretion, could also provide funds to maintain the chapel.[38] The House of Representatives version, however, contained no provision about the chapel and a House-Senate conference committee adopted the House version.[39] The bill signed into law by President Jimmy Carter deals exclusively with the memorial in the nation's capital.[40] Efforts to have the state of New Mexico support the Angel Fire memorial also failed.[41]

The VVMF's success in Congress is easily explained by the fact that the Vietnam Veterans Memorial would occupy a place at the center of the nation's commemorative landscape, on the Washington Mall, between the Washington Monument and the Lincoln Memorial. Here, the memorial would assume a national significance to which the Angel Fire chapel, in a sparsely populated part of northern New Mexico, could only aspire. The leaders of the VVMF—even when they claimed, self-deprecatingly, to be naïve about the ways of Washington—also proved more adept at pulling the strings of government and its associated bureaucracies than the Westphalls and their supporters were.

Both memorials focus on the troops who served in Vietnam, calling themselves "veterans" memorials, not "war" memorials. Both emphasize the sacrifices of those who died. The Angel Fire memorial turned the singular to the general by beginning with one family's loss but augmenting it by showing a changing array of photographs of casualties other than David, and referring by extension to all the other troops killed in the war; the VVMF comprehended the individual and collective aspects of mourning by requiring that the memorial display the name of every member of the U.S. armed forces who died in Vietnam.

The memorials, however, differed in their qualities and purposes. The Angel Fire memorial's attraction lies in its graceful architecture, its natural setting, and the story of a family's grief for a dead son and brother. The scale of the chapel's interior is intimate, not grand. As one veteran said, "Going into the chapel is a very emotional experience. . . . When you know the story of [Victor] Westphall, it becomes even more emotional."[42] As a grieving father, Westphall became a representative for all the others who had lost their children to the war, and he also became a sort of symbolic father to the many veterans who came to the chapel to find solace. His personal story engaged people's sympathies but it also tended to make the chapel into something other than a memorial of national scope. Although many found his sincerity touching and his single-minded dedication impressive, in his low moments he himself recognized that his mission to preserve the memory of his son could also be dismissed as a crank's obsession.[43] Westphall often quoted passages from David's writings, inscribed near the entrance to the memorial, which assert the dignity of every person and decry the destructive effects of greed, lust, and pride.[44] While Westphall drew a profound significance from David's writings, these texts were hermetic in their meaning and did not broaden the memorial's appeal. Most visitors accepted Westphall's advocacy of peace and were moved by his personal story of loss, but they did not engage with his commentaries on David's writings, or with his messages about destiny and personal responsibility. However often Victor Westphall's homilies were reported by the media, they failed to seize the imagination of the public.

In contrast, the VVMF had a less idiosyncratic and ideologically contentious message bearing on the need for national "healing" and societal acknowledgment of Vietnam veterans. Whereas Victor Westphall had strong moral convictions and was willing to launch jeremiads about the nation's shame, the leaders of the VVMF declared from the organization's inception that they wanted to avoid making any political judgment about the war. Instead, they made a sentimental appeal based on the needs of Vietnam veterans. They claimed that Vietnam veterans had been neglected by their country for too long. According to the memorial fund, the veterans had been unjustly rejected by a society that wished to forget the war, but this rejection redoubled the emotional wounds that veterans suffered as a result of serving in a controversial and ultimately unpopular cause. The VVMF asserted that national recognition of veterans' service and sacrifices would help to give them the welcome home that they did not receive when they returned from Vietnam. American citizens who had taken different positions on the war could come together in bestowing this overdue recognition on the veterans. Thus, Americans divided by the war could reconcile with one another in embracing Vietnam veterans in a "healing" process.

If the VVMF were to achieve their goals of healing and reconciliation, it was important that the fund not become embroiled in leftover conflicts about the rights and wrongs of the war. For this reason the leaders of the fund said that the memorial would make no political statement; it would simply honor those who fought and died. The wish to make the monument apolitical may seem unfeasible—any commemoration is bound to make some sort of statement, whether subtle or explicit. Indeed, the moral and political issues that the war raised might seem to demand some sort of statement. Demonstrating that the political controversies that the VVMF wanted to avoid were, in fact, unavoidable, the neutrality they espoused itself became a matter of debate. Paradoxically, it was the very wish to avoid making political statements that prompted ideologically motivated criticism from those who demanded that the memorial express pride in America's war effort. Right-wing veterans wanted to vindicate those who had served in Vietnam and to justify the U.S. war itself, banishing the guilt and shame that they said wrongly tainted memories of the cause for which Americans fought and died. Ultimately, to overcome these objections, the VVMF had to show the same persistent determination that Victor Westphall demonstrated at Angel Fire.

In August 1980, a month after the legislation authorizing construction of the Vietnam Veterans Memorial was signed into law, presidential candidate Ronald Reagan told an audience of military veterans that the Vietnam War had been a "noble cause" that "should have been won."[45] Reagan said that it was time for the nation to get over the "Vietnam syndrome": the public's fear that an initial commitment of military forces might snare the nation in a conflict from which it could not be easily extricated; and political and military leaders' worry, following the experience in Vietnam, that a military effort might be undermined by a collapse of support on the home front.[46] Five years after the Vietnam War ended with the defeat of America's South Vietnamese ally and the unification of Vietnam under a Communist government, Reagan argued that the "Vietnam syndrome" had made American foreign policy timid, allowing the Soviet Union to expand its influence around the world. The United States had suffered setbacks and its enemies were on the march in Southeast Asia, in the horn of Africa, in Central America, in Southwest Asia, and in southern Africa. Republicans and neo-conservative intellectuals charged that President Jimmy Carter had not defended U.S. interests when he failed to free the U.S. hostages in newly hostile Iran and "gave away" the Panama Canal by signing a treaty restoring it to Panama. Whereas Carter had declared that Americans suffered a debilitating "crisis of confidence," Reagan promised to restore Americans' confidence, pride, and strength.[47]

Implicitly rejecting Westphall's judgment of America's shame and his appeal to the nation's conscience, Reagan said that Americans had been wrong to succumb to feelings of guilt about their nation's actions in Vietnam, as if they had done something "shameful" there; these feelings of guilt and shame restrained American foreign policy, strengthened the United States' enemies, and also dishonored the memory of the American troops who had died. In an echo of the "stab-in-the-back" myth that circulated in Germany after World War I, Reagan suggested that the U.S. government's loss of will and determination had betrayed the war effort. The solution Reagan proposed was for Americans to reassert their patriotism and pride, and for the United States to strengthen its military forces. This would end the years of weakness and vacillation he attributed to the presidency of Jimmy Carter, his opponent in that autumn's presidential ballot.

Reagan's use of the chivalric word *noble* reminded Americans of the days, only a few decades past, when jubilant crowds greeted the U.S. forces that liberated

Europe, whose military actions were crowned with victory and decorated by the badge of honor. His assertion of the nobility of the United States' cause also reminded Americans of the moral certainties in the world that the World War II generation inhabited.[48] Cold war orthodoxies had come apart as the war in Vietnam stirred conflict on the home front. In the 1960s and 1970s, the New Left and antiwar veterans denounced the Vietnam War as imperialism necessitated by the interests of a capitalist system.[49] This radical critique of the war brought revolutionary and socialist ideas closer to the mainstream of American political discourse than they had been since the 1930s. Cold war orthodoxies had also broken down within the narrower spectrum of opinion in which American electoral politics was contested.[50] Liberal opponents of America's war in Vietnam had come to see it as misguided, doomed to defeat and too costly in money and lives. For their part, supporters of the war blamed liberals and radicals, weak-willed politicians and fractious journalists for undermining the will to stay the course in a war that should have been won. Adherents of these contrary perspectives continued to clash about the "lessons" of the Vietnam War for present and future U.S. policy in the postwar period, ready for another ideological fight in some new foreign policy context.

As a partisan of one viewpoint in this post–Vietnam War conflict in American politics, Reagan won the November 1980 election. On assuming office, he won congressional approval for the massive arms buildup that he said was necessary to restore America's strength. To that extent, his call to arms during the campaign was successful and he managed to rally members of both major political parties to support part of his program. Renouncing passivity in the face of America's adversaries, Reagan denounced the Soviet "evil empire" and said that it was high time that the world realized that, "by golly, you don't futz around with Uncle Sam."[51] Once in office, Reagan announced that there was a "spiritual revival" going on and a new pride in the country.[52] Yet, for all his willingness to celebrate America's resurgent pride, Reagan's advisers recognized that his campaign declaration that the war was a "noble cause" was politically problematic and divisive.

Reagan's assertion of a stridently ideological interpretation of the war was one way of trying to overcome division. In trumpeting the rightness of the war and gainsaying those who doubted its morality, Reagan sought to end debate and uncertainty. His definition of the Vietnam War as a noble cause was a heartfelt belief of which he would have liked to convince the public. But it was never likely to become the new orthodoxy among a public who had been bitterly divided and whose convictions had become deeply entrenched during the long years of war. Many saw the U.S. war effort quite differently, as an enterprise of doubtful morality and wisdom, and some were quite certain that the war was wrong.

Reagan's attempt to vindicate the war threatened to reopen the war-era rifts that divided Americans. The *Denver Post* said, "Reagan is right. As individuals and a nation, we generally fought for noble motives in Vietnam." The *Arizona Republic* said that "Reagan deserves high marks" for calling the war a "noble cause." The *Wall Street Journal* praised him for laying the groundwork for a debate about the rights and wrongs of the war: "He has had the nerve to open old wounds in an effort to develop a new philosophical basis and summon the sort of commitment he thinks

America will need for the confrontations ahead."[53] But not every editorial page was as enthusiastic about opening old wounds. For every editorial that applauded Reagan's courage and frankness, another condemned the president for sounding naïve and ignorant. The "noble cause" idea, according to the *Miami Herald*, might have been attractive to some but was "regrettably divisive, simplistic, and wrong." The *Idaho Statesman* also called Reagan's view of history "simplistic." The *Chicago Sun-Times* elaborated, cataloguing a train of U.S. deceptions and crimes in Vietnam: "Who can forget official U.S. duplicity in the Diem coup, the 'secret wars' in Cambodia and Laos, the falsified bombing records, the fragmentation weapons against civilian targets? And the defoliants? 'Hearts and minds'? [The] My Lai [massacre]? The lies to the American Congress and the American people about the scope of the war and the prospects for peace? Noble?"[54]

Public opinion poll results demonstrate how difficult it was to vindicate the war as a "noble cause." In a series of polls taken between 1975 and 1990, between two-thirds and three-quarters of the respondents felt that the war was "a mistake," "wrong," "wrong and immoral," or something similar (see Table 1). In February and June 1985, a poll question with a variant wording asked whether the war was wrong

Table 1. U.S. Public Opinion on the Ethics and Morality of the Vietnam War, 1975–1990

Polling organization	Month/ year	Word or phrase describing American action in the Vietnam War	Percentage agreeing
Roper[1]	6/75	The wrong thing	66
Gallup[2]	11/78	More than a mistake, fundamentally wrong and immoral[3]	72
Research and Forecasts[4]	11/80	Unjustified	66
Gallup	11/82	More than a mistake, fundamentally wrong and immoral	72
Roper	8/84	The wrong thing	65
Gallup	11/86	More than a mistake, fundamentally wrong and immoral	66
Gallup[5]	3/90	A mistake	74
Gallup	3/90	Not a just war	68

Source: Roper Center for Public Opinion Research, University of Connecticut, Storrs (RC).
Note: All the polls were of national adult samples.

1. Roper Organization polls, June 14–21, 1975, and August 11–18, 1984.
2. Gallup Organization polls for the Chicago Council on Foreign Relations, November 17–26, 1978, October 29–November 6, 1982, October 30–November 12, 1986.
3. In the Gallup poll questions with this phrasing, the positive results shown are the aggregate of those who "agreed somewhat" and "agreed strongly" with the proposition.
4. Research and Forecasts poll sponsored by Connecticut Mutual Life Insurance, September 1– November 15, 1980.
5. Gallup Organization poll, March 12–15, 1990.

Table 2. U.S. Public Opinion on "The Vietnam War: A 'Noble Cause'?" 1985–2000

Polling organization[1]	Month/ year	Word or phrase describing American action in the Vietnam War	Percentage agreeing
CBS/NY Times	2/85	Wrong, not immoral	11
		Wrong and immoral	34
		A noble cause	32
CBS/NY Times	6/85	Wrong, not immoral	13
		Wrong and immoral	38
		A noble cause	34
CBS News	5/95	Wrong, not immoral	7
		Wrong and immoral	40
		A noble cause	33
CBS/NY Times	4/00	Wrong, not immoral	8
		Wrong and immoral	35
		A noble cause	37

Source: RC.

1. CBS News/New York Times polls, February 23–27, 1985, May 29–June 2, 1985, April 15–17, 2000; CBS News poll, May 4–6, 1995. The "wrong, not immoral" responses were volunteered, prompted only by the "noble cause" and "wrong and immoral" alternatives.

and immoral but cued respondents to consider an alternative option: some people, the preamble to the question stated, think that the war was a "noble cause." Did the respondents agree? Despite the cue, only one-third of the samples agreed that the war was a noble cause. The number who felt the war was wrong and immoral still constituted a plurality. Ten years later, another poll prompted the public in the same way and drew the same result: a plurality of respondents believed the war was wrong and immoral, and only 33 percent thought it was a noble cause (see Table 2). These results demonstrate how deeply entrenched was the antipathy to the war. Some were susceptible to the "noble cause" cue, but this result throws into relief the number who held fast to the idea that the war was wrong and immoral. In the middle of the 1990s, 72 percent of a sample of the American public still agreed that the Vietnam War was "one of the worst moments in American history."[55] In October 1998, a generation after the first of these polls was gathered, 63 percent of a sample continued to believe that Vietnam was "more than a mistake; it was fundamentally wrong and immoral."[56]

Every American president since the Vietnam War has wished to close the door on the nation's experience of Vietnam in order for the nation to move forward with a new-found unity. All encouraged Americans to "heal" the nation's "wounds" by leaving their differences behind.[57] But when Reagan attempted to rally the public behind his interpretation of the Vietnam War, he was unable to rise above the polemics that had divided the country during the war. Reagan himself was implicated in these divisive arguments as a wartime governor of California who denounced antiwar protesters.[58] It would have been difficult, therefore, for Reagan to assume the role of an impartial arbiter who could win the public—including those who opposed the war—to a new consensus. Although the Reagan administration had an overriding interest in bringing about a reunification of a society and polity divided by the Vietnam War, the president stumbled at this attempt to bring the nation together.

The political problem that the Reagan government faced in the 1980s was an instance of the classic hegemonic task of achieving ideological leadership over a society by winning the consent and overcoming the resistance of its component groups.[59] Reagan had attempted in the August 1980 "noble cause" speech to validate a particular understanding of the nation's involvement in the Vietnam War. In doing so, he was declaring his own ideological stance, appealing to his audience at the Veterans of Foreign Wars convention but also addressing the wider audience beyond those in the auditorium. His line was greeted with massive applause by the veterans in attendance. But although a candidate for national office sometimes makes statements that appeal to a narrow constituency or that shore up his political base, Reagan's handlers were always keen to avoid alienating the remainder of the electorate except when taking positions on matters that they and the candidate thought essential. Reagan's vindication of the Vietnam War appeared, on these grounds, to backfire. Although it rallied those who had supported the war effort, it provoked those who had opposed it. Far from unifying Americans behind his leadership, it appeared to polarize them along the lines of their war-era divisions. This incident indicates his willingness to take a polemical position but also explains why his advisers sometimes persuaded him to rein in his expression of controversial views to avoid offending too many listeners. In these circumstances, continuing to articulate a stridently partisan position in the debate about Vietnam entailed risks: rather than shaping a new consensus about America's role in the world, his advisers feared, Reagan might find himself lodged on one side of a protracted debate, and perhaps not the majority side.

Reagan aroused less controversy when he rehabilitated the war in a less polemical way, by lauding those who fought in it, deftly inserting a revisionist interpretation of the reason for defeat amid words of comfort, while avoiding the provocative "noble cause" assertion. In the second month of his presidency, Reagan said that Vietnam veterans "had fought as bravely and as well as any Americans in our history. They came home without a victory," he said, "not because they'd been defeated, but because they'd been denied permission to win. They were greeted by no parades, no bands, no waving of the flag they had so nobly served. There's been no 'thank you' for their sacrifice. There's been no effort to honor and, thus, give pride to the families of more than 57,000 young men who gave their lives in that faraway war." The speech stressed the nobility of the veterans' service, not of the cause they fought for. Pride, he said, would not wipe out the families' grief, "but it can make that grief easier to bear. The pain will not be quite as sharp if they know their fellow citizens share that pain."[60] While Reagan's attempt to define the war as a "noble cause" ran into trouble, his appeal for the recognition of those who fought it gibed better with the times. By the start of his presidency, the nation was ready to give the veterans their due.

This book aims to demonstrate the political significance of commemorations that attempted to unify a nation divided by the Vietnam War. Because Reagan's effort to win the public over to his interpretation of the Vietnam War was risky and probably futile, the task of "reconciling" a divided public and "healing" the wounds of the war had to be pursued by other means, and it fell largely to others: among them, the VVMF and the planners of state and local memorials who followed them. Although right-wing militarists, including many of Reagan's core supporters, were enthusiastic about his vindication of the Vietnam War as a "noble cause," many editors and members of the public responded more positively to the memorials' call for "healing" and "reconciliation" than to Reagan's more ideologically assertive interpretation of the war. The paradox is that by disavowing politics in the pursuit of "healing," the memorials pursued an irreducibly political objective, the reforging of national unity damaged by the war. The memorials succeeded by appealing to people's sentiments, and the messages they conveyed thus evaded the public's ideological radar. In promoting "healing" and "reconciliation," the planners of Vietnam veterans memorials helped to shape the politics of the 1980s and beyond.

Because the great wave of commemoration and contemplation of the war's "lessons" occurred during the 1980s, conflicts about the meaning of the Vietnam War were entwined with the political debates during the 1981–89 Reagan presidency. Tensions between hard-right "ideologues" and traditional Republican "pragmatists" inside and outside the Reagan administration played out in the debates about the Vietnam Veterans Memorial. Unless the nation bolstered the pride of its Vietnam veterans, the right-wing militarists argued, it could not count on its citizens to fight in other wars. Equivocation about the rightness of America's cause in Vietnam would lead to weakness anywhere its national interests were challenged. But, in the debate about the Vietnam Veterans Memorial, the right-wingers' views did not prevail. The book's middle chapters show how the Reagan administration, and the president himself, began to recognize the appeal of the discourse of "healing" as a way of bringing together a divided nation, and how the administration's agenda converged with that of the VVMF.

Politicians, journalists, and other commentators celebrated the "healing" that memorials encouraged, but this "healing" came at a price: despite the widespread and strong public sense that the war was wrong and immoral—or perhaps *because* of these views—memorials promoted "healing" by evading some of the crucial moral and political questions that Westphall had raised and that troubled Americans in the postwar period. It was not that political statements were barred altogether, only ones that seemed controversial or divisive. As it turned out, politicians were welcome to make speeches at the Vietnam Veterans Memorial that asserted revisionist "lessons," such as the injunction to fight future wars without restraint, as though there were nothing political about this idea.

Critics of the war's morality were, in contrast, marginalized: political criticisms and moral condemnations of the Vietnam War, which had been a part of the mainstream of public discourse in the late 1960s and 1970s, became anathema in speechmaking at the Vietnam Veterans Memorial and the state and local memorials that came after it. Anything that implied a criticism of the way the war was fought was set aside in the name of "welcoming veterans home." And while avoiding making explicit statements about the war, the memorials implicitly valorized military service as worthy of honor, irrespective of the behavior of individual troops, the conduct of particular operations, or the purposes of the fighting. In line with the trend in commemoration in the 1980s, the influence of antiwar activists at the memorial at Angel Fire waned as the memorial was adopted by a national organization, the Disabled American Veterans, in 1983. The VVAW flag ceased to fly there and condemnations of the Vietnam War gave way to anodyne ideas about the desirability of peace.[61]

In the 1980s, conflicting interpretations of the Vietnam War expressed themselves in arguments about American policy in Central America. This would be the principal testing ground for Reagan's great strategic goal, which came to be known as the "Reagan Doctrine": the aim to "roll back" rather than simply contain the forces of Communism, to demonstrate that Communist gains were reversible. The Reagan administration's critics feared that U.S. support of anti-Communist governments and insurgencies in the 1980s might again take America into a Vietnam War–like "quagmire"—and the majority of the public shared that fear. The Rand Corporation advised, "The American public remains shaken and divided by the Vietnam experience, less willing to support the application of power abroad." Ten Gallup and Harris polls spanning Reagan's first term indicate that majorities ranging from 62 to 77 percent agreed that by embroiling itself in the conflicts in Nicaragua and El Salvador, the United States might become involved in "another Vietnam." As Peter Kornbluh argues, the strategists of Reagan's low-intensity war in Central America "understood that the success of the Reagan Doctrine in Central America required purging the 'Vietnam syndrome' from the American psyche."[62]

Ronald Reagan and the planners of Vietnam veterans memorials did not share the same political agenda, but their agendas coincided at one significant point: their wish to draw the sting out of memories of Vietnam and to unify a nation divided by the Vietnam War. Reagan's interpretation of the Vietnam War formed part of a broader-ranging set of political convictions, underpinned by his anti-Communism and his wish for global U.S. military strength and influence. Some planners of Vietnam veterans memorials shared these views; others did not. But by promoting "healing" and "reconciliation," the memorials played a part in the hegemonic politics of Reaganism. When, in 1984, Ronald Reagan visited the Vietnam Veterans Memorial in Washington, DC, his speech-writers took their cues from the discourse of "healing" that surrounded the memorial—but they added their own spin, transforming the VVMF's call for national reconciliation into an appeal for renewed international strength.

The transformation of Reagan's oratory, often shedding the strident "noble cause" rhetoric in favor of a less provocative rhetoric of "healing" (while repeatedly insisting that U.S. troops should never again be prevented from winning a war), encapsulates a broader shift in public discourses about the Vietnam War. As the war receded into the past in the 1980s, it became more difficult to capture the urgency of the political and moral critiques that had surrounded the war as it was fought. In place of discussions of U.S. foreign policy and military strategy, new ways of considering the war and its aftermath emerged. Central to these was the figure of the U.S. military veteran, whose homecoming experience now became the focal point of a new discourse.

During and immediately after the war, Vietnam veterans were among the leading critics of the U.S. war effort. The most publicly visible Vietnam veterans' organization, VVAW, led antiwar demonstrations. In the early 1970s, veterans were in the forefront of denunciations of the war, bearing witness to what they claimed was a pattern of indiscriminate violence and criminal conduct by U.S. forces. Their testimony set out to substantiate the charge that the most well-known atrocity committed by American troops in Vietnam, the My Lai massacre, was not an aberration or an isolated incident but was consistent with and arose from the military's standard operating procedure in Vietnam.[63] Veterans also complained that they were not treated well by the public after returning from the war, that the Veterans Administration system of medical care did not properly diagnose or treat their postservice psychological distress, and that they suffered the ill-effects of exposure to the chemical defoliant Agent Orange used by the United States in Southeast Asia. These veterans' complaints had a political thrust: a critique of American foreign and military policy and a condemnation of the machinations of the nation's power structure. Veterans' plaintive discourse about events in Vietnam and their poor homecoming experience were part and parcel of a critique of the American war machine, which used up and discarded the nation's citizenry as so many worn-out parts.

In the 1980s, literary authors, memoirists, journalists, and medical professionals, as well as the planners of Vietnam memorials, began to articulate a new discourse about Vietnam veterans: a sentimental and personalized discourse in which the key idea was that veterans had been misjudged and misunderstood by the public. In a variety of fields of writing and representation, these commentators demonstrated that civilian society had wronged Vietnam veterans by rejecting and vilifying them because of their association with an unpopular war: the veterans were blamed for all the repugnant wartime acts that their civilian compatriots wished to abjure; or, civilian society forgot about the war altogether and cast aside any thought of its moral legacies. This obliviousness was just as harmful to veterans as vilification was because it also left them, by default, to carry the whole burden of moral responsibility for the war. Veterans were reminders of a war that Americans preferred to forget. Cast into oblivion, they suffered from alienation and isolation. In the terms of this discourse, the war was a "scar" on the nation's psyche; the divisions it engendered were a "wound." Just as the nation was wounded, so civilian society's neglect and mistreatment of the veterans hurt them. The corollary to this discourse of maltreatment and wounding was a logically connected discourse of "healing." As American society came to terms with its experience of Vietnam, it would be able to embrace its veterans. A society at last welcoming its veterans home would lift the stigma of unjust accusation from them and would itself heal; together, society and the veterans would once again become whole.

Once veterans were wrapped in society's healing embrace as objects of public sympathy and acceptance, their role as the bearers of a political critique quietly fell away. When the Vietnam veterans "problem" was redefined in psycho-sociological terms, an ameliorative vocabulary replaced the language of political critique. The discourse of healing surrounding the Vietnam Veterans Memorial was, therefore, consistent with broader trends in the discourses representing Vietnam veterans. In turn, these were part of a decades-long process, sometimes referred to as the "triumph of the therapeutic," in which a quasi-medical language redefined political and social problems as emotional pathologies curable by the ministration of experts and the adjustment of hearts and minds.[64] In addressing the politics of commemoration, this study considers what was gained and what was lost when the therapeutic discourse of wounds and healing began to supersede other ways of remembering the war.

The "triumph of the therapeutic" in commemorations of the Vietnam War met some resistance. Right-wing veterans, spearheaded by a Reagan-founded organization the Vietnam Veterans Leadership Program, were proud of their service in Vietnam and resented being told that they needed to "heal." They asserted that neither they nor the nation had anything to heal from. In their view, their cause had been a worthy one, they had won all their battles, and the United States lost the war only because of a loss of will on the home front. They agreed with Reagan when he said that the war was a noble cause and they feared that, unless their compatriots shrugged off the guilt and self-doubts that the war had provoked, the nation would be weaker as it faced its enemies in the future. The discourse of "healing" was almost as bad, in the right-wingers' opinion, as antiwar veterans' moral condemnation of the war, because it reinforced the view that veterans were guilt-ridden basket cases or self-pitying victims.

The right-wing veterans demanded that a bronze statue be added to the memorial in Washington, believing that this was the monumental form that best connoted "honor." In state and local memorials around the country, other bronze statues adjoined walls of inscribed names, following the precedent of the Vietnam Veterans Memorial's wall and statue. But in the main, these statues did not celebrate martial virtues in the same way as did the prototype that the right-wingers wanted to emulate, the United States Marine Corps War Memorial (the "Iwo Jima Memorial"). Instead, many of them depicted scenes of injured American troops being cared for by their comrades. A significant number of sculptures depicted nurses ministering to wounded men, in sculptures that used the language of gender to enact family dramas animated by care and sentiment. The modal form of statuary was more consistent with the discourse of "wounds" and "healing" than with the "noble cause" rhetoric.

Although the planners of memorials attempted to avoid divisive topics in the interests of national unity, discussions of memorials were haunted by debates about the war's politics and morality. Wartime atrocities were a taboo topic, a determinate silence in discussions about and speeches at Vietnam veterans memorials. Yet they formed the absent center around which discussions circulated: a "black hole" that exerted its effects on everything in its gravitational field. Atrocities were the unspoken antagonist of every conservative veteran's insistence that the war must be remembered as noble. One memorial planner and designer after another set out to counter negative images about the war by proposing that it best be remembered by statues showing American troops helping, not hurting, Vietnamese children—only to see that idea ruled out by veterans for whom images of Vietnamese children set off psychologically disturbing chains of association that ended with pictures of bodies piled up on a rural path in My Lai, in Quang Ngai province in central Vietnam.

The memorials on which this book concentrates are useful objects of study as the focal points of debate about how the war should be remembered and as catalysts of individual and collective mourning and contemplation. In themselves they are inert objects and they become meaningful only as they prompt or provoke human responses. The debates about proposed designs for memorials can be of interest because participants had to explain how they thought the past should be remembered. But while plans for a memorial can excite debate, public responses to a memorial after its creation are equally significant. A memorial must "take" with the public; if a memorial is never visited, sinking unremarked into the background of a landscape or cityscape, studying it would contribute little to our understanding of a society's confrontation with its past. Memorials are useful objects of study not only because of the debates about their design but also because of the degree to which, and the ways in which, they succeed in embracing members of a society and—another way of saying the same thing—the way the public takes the memorial to itself.[65]

To measure the task that Vietnam War memorials took on in trying to win the support of a divided public, we must first understand the divisions that split the country as a result of the Vietnam War; to understand the appeal of the VVMF's doctrine of "healing," we must see how veterans were represented as sympathetic figures in need of healing and deserving of public recognition and acceptance. The first two chapters examine these two contexts for the memorials' work. Chapter 1 investigates the fracturing of the polity as a result of the Vietnam War, and the way that the nation's leaders contended with the legacy of division and self-doubt—the "Vietnam syndrome"—in debating Central America policy in the early 1980s. Chapter 2 looks at the cultural construction of Vietnam veterans, in whose name and on whose behalf the Vietnam Veterans Memorial was created, and the emergence of knowledge about post-traumatic stress disorder, which won institutional validation in 1980, just as the work of the VVMF was beginning. The Reagan administration sought to overcome the "Vietnam syndrome"; but to do so, it had to contend with the discourses of emotional disturbance and moral perturbation that followed the revelations of atrocities in Vietnam and the discovery of the long-lasting psychological harm veterans had suffered as a result of their service there.

Thus, chapters 1 and 2 establish the discursive contexts—political, moral, and psychological—of the work of commemoration, the discussion of which occupies chapters 3 through 11. Politics, morality, and emotions interacted as Americans debated how the war should be remembered: arguments about the lessons of Vietnam were animated by their participants' anger, left over from the war years; a political subtext involving judgments about the war's morality and legality underlay psychiatric institutions' responses to veterans' trauma. The discussion of public commemoration of the Vietnam War builds on the contexts established in the first two chapters by showing how the planners and designers of Vietnam veterans memorials attempted to unify a divided society, couching their appeal for national reconciliation and the recognition of veterans in the language of "healing."

When the VVMF encountered the opposition of right-wing critics, long-nurtured resentments intensified arguments about the design of the memorial that were simultaneously about aesthetics and geopolitics. The VVMF undertook the daunting task of bringing together a divided society and reconciling the nation with its past. They disavowed politics, but by using an armory of powerful sentiment they garnered honor and recognition for those who fought and thereby furthered the hegemonic project of rehabilitating the Vietnam War itself. This book demonstrates the crucial role that Vietnam veterans played in this contest for "hearts and minds" fought in the postwar United States, as instigators of memorial projects and as objects of sympathy around whom the discourse of personal and national "healing" coalesced.

1

"NEVER AGAIN"

The Vietnam Syndrome in American Foreign Policy

★

THE CONFLICT that surrounded the Vietnam Veterans Memorial in Washington, DC, drew its energy from Americans' conflicting views of U.S. actions in Vietnam. Wartime disagreements about foreign policy persisted in the postwar period as Americans debated the proper "lessons" of the war. The arguments about the war were heated and visceral and led Americans to question one another's morality and good faith. The nation grew to mistrust its leaders as a result of governmental deceit and Americans with differing views of the war were distrustful of and hostile to one another. Jack Smith, a psychologist who had served as a marine in Vietnam, said that everyone blamed everyone else for what had gone wrong: "Military men blame policy makers, right-wingers blame the pinkos and media and protesters, the left blame the right."[1]

The Vietnam Veterans Memorial Fund attempted to bring together all Americans, whether they had supported or opposed the war, in a common project to honor those who had fought and those who had died. But the unity of purpose for which they hoped was undermined by the resentments persisting from the war era.[2] Politically conservative Vietnam veterans who blamed the U.S. defeat on their domestic enemies had too many scores to settle to want to reconcile with their antagonists.

Present politics and culture always intertwine with debates about the past and the proper forms of its commemoration; accordingly, this chapter looks for the sources of 1980s arguments about how to commemorate the war in war-era debates about political and military strategy and in postwar attempts to overcome the "Vietnam syndrome." Understanding the depth and intensity of Americans' disagreements and antipathies will help us to grasp the size of the task that the Vietnam Veterans Memorial Fund took on in asking Americans to reconcile with one another. The first part of the chapter examines the wartime debates that polarized public opinion about the nation's actions in Vietnam, concentrating on "hawkish" criticisms of Lyndon Johnson's policies and of Congress's role in the defeat of South Vietnam; the second

part looks at the impact of the "Vietnam syndrome" on foreign policy in the immediate postwar years, and the Reagan administration's attempts to counter fears of
"another Vietnam," which threatened to undermine his policies in Central America.

The Vietnam War "hawks" had wanted U.S. forces to wage all-out war by invading North Vietnam or unleashing an unrestricted conventional bombing campaign.
They resented the restriction of ground forces to South Vietnam, rules of engagement that they thought hampered the prosecution of the war, and the bombing
pauses that punctuated the U.S. air campaign. They had no doubt about the moral
cause for which they were fighting, defending a fledgling democracy against an
oppressive, Communist state.[3] The United States could have won the war, they
believed, except that it had fought with "one hand tied behind its back."[4] Looking
back years after the war, the Vietnam veteran General John Arick still held this belief:
"I think we should have gone in there with overwhelming force. I think we should
have bombed them into the stone ages."[5] Those who mourned the "lost victory" in
Vietnam blamed their fellow citizens—antiwar protesters, the media, or weak-willed,
"dovish" politicians—for betraying the war effort and causing the United States to
abandon its South Vietnamese ally.

For their part, the "doves" in government believed that the "hawks" had betrayed
the United States' most cherished values. Initially almost unanimous in authorizing
the war, members of Congress later questioned whether the war was necessary;
as U.S. troop levels escalated and the casualties on all sides increased, thousands of
antiwar protesters and concerned American citizens expressed their doubts that the
United States had any right to fight in Vietnam at all, or that the dictatorial South
Vietnamese government was worthy of American support. George Ball, the first
administration dissenter from Johnson's war policies, said that "in Vietnam, . . . we
sacrificed a number of our principles and we've been paying for it in a general degradation of the American spirit."[6] Senator George McGovern (D., South Dakota), a
leading congressional "dove," said that U.S. policy in Vietnam distorted "our most
treasured ideals."[7] Antiwar protesters had the same sense that America's values had
been sacrificed on the altar of war. Daniel Berrigan, a prominent Roman Catholic
opponent of the war, said, "I was morally outraged by the escalation in Vietnam. I
was ashamed that we would be doing something like this, because I had believed in
the history books, and I expected better of our country. Here we were, a superpower,
you know, chewing up an agrarian society."[8] Americans' differences were not simply
intellectual; they were deeply heartfelt, grounded in their concepts of what America
was and what it stood for.

The historian George Herring says that the war "polarized the American people
and poisoned the political atmosphere as had no issue since slavery a century before."[9] The war engendered public suspicion of their government: a few years into
the presidencies of both Lyndon Johnson and Richard Nixon, a majority of the public
rightly concluded that they were not being told all that they should know about the
war.[10] The attitudes of the "Vietnam generation"—people who were on average
twenty years old at the time of the Tet Offensive in 1968—show how a strong "flavor
of political betrayal" soured citizens' trust for their leaders. Twenty years after the

end of the war, a forty-nine-year-old New York woman said, "Up until the 1960s, I basically believed everything about history that I was taught in school. I thought our country was always right, but with the Vietnam War I saw that we weren't always right." A forty-five-year-old Illinois contractor was aggrieved by government deception: "The government was a bunch of liars about the whole thing. . . . I just don't have as much faith in my government any more."[11] In 1988, 70 percent of a sample of the public agreed with the statement, "The Vietnam War showed the American people that U.S. officials who are deeply involved in conducting the war cannot be trusted to give reliable information to the public."[12] The mistrust had its foundations in years of disillusioning experience.

President Johnson's secretary of defense, Robert McNamara, deceived Congress and the nation about the background of the Tonkin Gulf incident that led to congressional authorization of U.S. military action.[13] Johnson downplayed the difficulties the government foresaw in Vietnam because of the political costs of doing so during the 1964 election year. He disguised new military initiatives, preferring to conceal them from the public or to describe them as the fulfillment of previous commitments; his administration's public pronouncements about the likelihood of success in Vietnam were wishful thinking, at best, and deception, at worst; and McNamara deliberately misled the public and Congress about the plans for the war.[14]

Johnson's successor, Nixon, deceived the public by secretly bombing the supposedly neutral country of Cambodia, and by bombing Laos when Congress explicitly forbade targeting Cambodia. When the Watergate scandal broke in 1973 and citizens learned not just about the break-in but about Nixon's illegal wiretaps, the White House "enemies list," domestic surveillance plans, and other administration wrongdoing, public trust for the presidency reached its nadir.

While presidential deception, when discovered, fostered public distrust, the administrations' declared policies in Vietnam were also divisive. Neither Johnson nor Nixon had run for the presidency on a clear pro-war platform. Johnson said on the campaign trail in 1964 that he did not intend to send "American boys" to fight in a war that "Asian boys" should be fighting for themselves.[15] Nixon intimated in 1968 that he had a plan to end the war.[16] The electorate did not therefore give a mandate for the eight years of warfare that followed Johnson's election in 1964. Once their patriotism and loyalty to the presidents were invoked, a majority of the public gave both presidents wide latitude to conduct the nation's military policy, but the support for the war diminished as it dragged on, as the caskets returned by the thousands, and as the public came increasingly to doubt the morality of U.S. troops' conduct and the wisdom of U.S. strategy.

The Vietnam War did not divide the nation down the middle into opposed prowar and antiwar groups. Instead, the war divided U.S. society into several factions, each antagonistic to the others. Many were prepared to "stay the course" with the policies of the Johnson and Nixon administrations; a popular antiwar movement organized teach-ins and demonstrations against the war; "doves" in Congress wanted the United States to extricate itself from Vietnam more quickly than the presidents' policies intended, and public support for this position gradually increased; but the "hawks" wanted the United States to use decisive action—a massive bombing campaign or an invasion of North Vietnam—to achieve a swift victory.

Throughout Johnson's presidency, the hawks pressured Johnson to launch an all-out war on North Vietnam. They argued that by "micro-managing" the war from the Oval Office, and by restricting the targets that U.S. aircraft could attack, Johnson was hampering the chances of military success. The Joint Chiefs of Staff told Defense Secretary McNamara in November 1964 that Johnson should take all the measures necessary for a swift victory, or else withdraw American forces. General Curtis LeMay, chief of staff of the U.S. Air Force, proposed an attack on North Vietnam's "vital centers" that would destroy its capacity to fight, and this view had powerful support in the U.S. Senate.[17] Ronald Reagan, then a Republican Party activist considering his first run for electoral office, called for a declaration of war in 1965, saying, "We could pave the whole country and put parking stripes on it and still be home by Christmas."[18] The Joint Chiefs of Staff and the commander in chief of U.S. Pacific Forces, Admiral U. S. G. Sharp, became increasingly frustrated in 1965 and 1966 that air power was being used in a piecemeal way that could not win the war.[19]

Beset by advisers and critics who favored all-out war or the withdrawal of U.S. forces, Johnson pursued a middle course that satisfied few and that merely avoided the other unpalatable alternatives. Reluctant to elevate the political stakes in Vietnam, and afraid of provoking a military response by the USSR or China, Johnson did not rally Congress and the public behind the military effort by asking for a congressional declaration of war. He increased the number of ground forces by stages, doing enough to stave off defeat at each step but no more. The incremental stepping-up of American ground forces and the intensification of the aerial bombing campaign were, according to the Johnson administration's theory, a graduated exertion of military pressure that would ultimately break the enemy's will to fight, without provoking a great-power confrontation.[20] When step-by-step escalation failed to achieve victory, though, Vietnam began to resemble a "quagmire" in which American forces became bogged down, each step sinking the United States more deeply into the conflict.[21]

Impatient with a long-drawn-out war, some of the public who initially supported the administration gave up on Johnson's policies. As the Louis Harris polling organization reported in February 1966, "more and more the American people are becoming split between those who favor an all-out military effort to shorten the war and those who prefer negotiations to the risk of escalation." Until late in his presidency, a majority was willing to stay the course with administration policy, motivated by a wish to preserve the "sunk costs" of lives lost and prestige invested in the military enterprise.[22] In mid-1967, however, those who disapproved of Johnson's handling of the war began consistently to outnumber those who approved of it.[23] After the Tet Offensive, a nationwide attack on Vietnam's towns and cities that the Communist forces launched in January 1968, most Americans concluded that getting involved in Vietnam had been a mistake and they wanted an end to the war and the domestic turmoil it provoked.[24] But while the impact of the Tet Offensive exacerbated the public's lack of confidence in Johnson's policies in Vietnam, we should not make the mistake of thinking that the majority of Americans changed their views because of moral doubts about the U.S. cause or qualms about the use of force. The number of Americans who identified themselves as "hawks" vastly outnumbered the "doves" in a poll taken immediately after the first shock of the Tet Offensive, and hawks and doves in the populace were evenly split for the remainder of the Johnson presidency. What this means is that disgruntled hawks whose opposition to the war grew out of frustration with the Johnson administration's policies formed part of the majority who thought entering the war was a mistake. Other than their opposition to the war, they had little in common with the doves. The complexities and ambivalences in public opinion, marked by the splits among administration supporters, dovish opponents of the war, and hawkish critics of Johnson's leadership, created lasting fissures in the polity, and the resentments of the frustrated hawks set the stage for postwar recriminations that complicated efforts to commemorate the war.[25]

Opponents of Johnson's policies blamed the government for leading the nation into war and refusing to leave when the public turned against it. From a few thousand demonstrators in 1965, antiwar demonstrations began to attract first tens of thousands and then hundreds of thousands of people. Whether because they opposed the war or because they were unwilling to risk their lives in a dubious cause, thousands of men resisted military conscription, deserted from the armed forces, or resisted the military from within. Protesters compared the U.S. government to that of Hitler's Germany and drew parallels between an acquiescent public and the loyal Germans who permitted the Nazi regime's crimes. Carl Oglesby denounced the American corporate system for fighting a criminal "blitzkrieg" in Vietnam. In turn, supporters of the government accused the protesters of being traitors, either deliberately doing the bidding of the nation's Communist enemies or acting as their dupes. This suspicion of treachery was fostered by congressional supporters of the Johnson administration, who organized hearings expecting to uncover evidence of an international Communist conspiracy behind the antiwar teach-ins.[26] Secretary of State Dean Rusk charged opponents of the war with wanting to let down America's defenses, abandoning the field to the nation's adversaries. The *New York Post* accused antiwar protesters of being "anti-American."[27] Partisans on both sides of the argument denied their opponents' good faith and condemned the forces stubbornly prolonging the war or sapping the nation's will to fight.

Richard Nixon won the presidential election in 1968, defeating Johnson's vice president, Hubert Humphrey, having attracted support because of his plan to end the war.[28] The policies the United States pursued under Nixon between 1969 and 1974 intensified the postwar recriminations. Nixon deliberately polarized the domestic debate about the war in order to isolate and marginalize the antiwar movement and congressional doves.[29] He attempted simultaneously to assuage the hawks and the antiwar critics by pursuing "Vietnamization" (turning over the fighting to South Vietnamese troops) while sporadically escalating U.S. tactics. Nixon's policy was undercut, though, by the overall trend: dwindling support for the presence of American forces in Vietnam the longer the war went on. The troop withdrawals undermined the U.S. military position, and hence its capacity for bargaining with the enemy, since the North Vietnamese had only to wait out the United States. The best that Nixon could achieve was therefore a sham "peace with honor" that satisfied neither those who wanted a swift withdrawal nor those who wanted victory.[30]

In September 1969, public approval for Nixon's policies in Vietnam dipped sharply, reflecting impatience with the rate of troop withdrawals.[31] By November 1969, the majority of the public had shifted from "hawks" to "doves."[32] Nixon responded to the nationwide Moratorium Against the War in October 1969 and attempted to counter the adverse trends in public opinion by making a speech in which he appealed to the "silent majority" of Americans against the "vocal minority" who protested against the war. Polls taken immediately after the speech demonstrated that it was effective in winning public support. Seventy-seven percent of those who heard the speech said afterward that they approved Nixon's handling of "the Vietnam situation." Veterans Day rallies in favor of Nixon's policies attracted thousands of supporters in Washington, DC, and New York. In Pittsburgh, a hundred thousand marched behind banners with slogans such as "Support Our Men in Vietnam" and "Do Not Reason with Treason." Tens of thousands of Nixon supporters demonstrated in cities across the nation, an impressive show of support (even though their numbers did not equal those of the antiwar forces). The boost in support for Nixon's policies was only temporary, though.[33]

Even as Nixon attempted to rally the "silent majority," vocal opposition to the war increased. On November 15, 1969, a quarter of a million Americans demonstrated against the war in Washington, DC, in the largest antiwar demonstration to date in the nation's capital. Although the majority of respondents to a Harris poll said that they disagreed with the antiwar movement's methods, the vast majority, 81 percent, believed that the protesters were raising important questions. By a margin of 50 to 37 percent, they also agreed that the war was morally indefensible and that the United States was wrong to have become involved in it.[34]

Despite the growing opposition to the war, a substantial sector of the public continued to favor escalating the violence in Southeast Asia. In a 1970 poll, while almost a third of the public favored an immediate withdrawal of American forces from Vietnam, almost a quarter favored a stronger stand, even if it meant escalating the war by invading North Vietnam. These figures illustrate the fissuring of the polity, with substantial numbers favoring sharply opposed courses of action; only when combined did these groups outnumber those willing to stay the course with the president's policy. Several other polls indicate the same division of opinion, with many respondents wishing to withdraw from Vietnam, more or less quickly, and others, in declining numbers, wishing for a military victory by means of an all-out effort.[35]

On May 1, 1970, Nixon dramatically escalated the war, triggering a further polarization of public opinion. In "Operation Dewey Canyon," tens of thousands of American and South Vietnamese troops launched a brief invasion of Cambodia to attack Communist "sanctuaries" and demonstrate that the U.S. government still had the capacity to fight hard, despite "Vietnamization." Nixon described the invasion as a test of America's "will and character": if the United States did not use its power to stop Communism, Nixon said, it would appear a "pitiful, helpless giant."[36]

The majority of Americans supported the invasion.[37] In St. Louis, twenty thousand residents attended a pro-war march.[38] But a "rush of protest" swept the country, involving not just students but professional people, Congress, government agencies, and even members of the cabinet. A third of universities and colleges around the country shut down as students and professors protested against the invasion. A furious Nixon denounced the students as "bums . . . blowin' up the campuses."[39]

The war's bloodshed spilled over on the home front. After the governor of Ohio sent the National Guard onto the campus of Kent State University, the troops shot and killed four students, and police killed two students at Jackson State University in Mississippi. These events sparked protests at universities around the country. Four million participated in the nationwide shutdown of the higher education system and almost a hundred thousand demonstrators protested at the White House on May 8. As protest roiled the country, 56 percent of the public said that the United States had made a mistake in sending troops to Vietnam.[40] Congress repealed the Gulf of Tonkin Resolution and the Senate passed the Cooper-Church amendment intended to terminate the Cambodian incursion. The administration resolved to take the offensive against its congressional foes by wrapping itself in patriotic symbols and portraying the legislators as traitors. Two veterans' organizations denounced the "stab in the back" by congressional doves who proposed cutting off funds for the U.S. war in Indochina. An embattled White House adopted a "siege mentality," an "us against them" attitude that pitted Nixon against those he defined as his "enemies": the "liberal" media, congressional critics, and students.[41]

The administration was walking a tightrope between the determination of the enemy to continue the war, and the waning patience of Congress and the public.[42] While the public increasingly disapproved of Nixon's handling of the war, a huge majority supported his "Vietnamization" program.[43] Nixon's problem was that the public liked Vietnamization too much: a majority favored the early withdrawal of U.S. forces, before Nixon was ready to bring them home. In January 1971, 61 percent of respondents to a Harris poll said they would favor the withdrawal of U.S. troops from Vietnam by the end of the year, but almost as many, 59 percent, approved the renewed bombing of North Vietnam.[44] The combined results indicate that some respondents wanted both renewed bombing and an early withdrawal from Vietnam.[45] The majority's support for a renewed bombing offensive as late as 1971 demonstrates that, while they wanted an end to casualties among their ground troops, most Americans were not ready to concede defeat. This finding bears out the results of the polls in the final year of the Johnson presidency: although they were unwilling to meet the continued economic and human costs of the war, a large proportion of the U.S. population could still be identified as frustrated hawks. The appeal of bombing was that it could deliver massive force against its target, taking advantage of America's technological superiority, rather than requiring foot soldiers to slog through the mud, mountains, and forests where the enemy seemed to have the advantage and where the majority of U.S. casualties occurred.

Nixon lifted many of the Johnson administration's targeting restrictions during the "Linebacker I" bombing campaign of May 1972, which was regarded as a great technical success by air power advocates, who credited it with halting a North Vietnamese offensive.[46] As the peace agreement with North Vietnam was in the final stages of negotiation in December 1972, Nixon ordered "Linebacker II," another intense bombing campaign of North Vietnamese cities intended to demonstrate American "resolve" and to reassure the South Vietnamese that they were not being abandoned to their fate. For the first time, B-52 bombers, America's strategic bombing fleet, were ordered to attack North Vietnam's capital, Hanoi, and the major port of Haiphong. The main targets, though, were politicians in South Vietnam, who needed reassurance, and American conservatives, who needed to be convinced that the Nixon administration had not "bugged out," that it had won "peace with honor."[47]

Because the bombing shortly preceded the conclusion of the Paris peace talks, airpower advocates promoted the view that the bombing drove the North Vietnamese to the bargaining table and even that it "won" the war.[48] Domestic commentators and international leaders were appalled, though, by the so-called Christmas bombing, seeing it as testimony to the United States' moral delinquency. The columnist Tom Wicker wrote that it represented "shame on earth, an American shame"; his fellow journalist Anthony Lewis called it a "crime against humanity."[49] Over a third of the public agreed with the statement, "The bombings were wrong, because we lost the support and respect of allies and friends around the world."[50] Nixon's public approval rating plummeted.[51]

Critics of the air war also faced a backlash, though. Jane Fonda had visited North Vietnam and asked U.S. pilots to consider the consequences of the bombing. Assistant Attorney General A. William Olson accused her of treason, and Maryland legislators called for her to be executed, or, at least, for her tongue to be cut off.[52] The Vietnam veteran James Webb—whom we encounter again in debates about the Vietnam Veterans Memorial—later said, "Jane Fonda can kiss my ass. I wouldn't cross the street to watch her slit her wrist."[53] The Tennessee veteran Ted A. Burton said, "These draft-dodgers, Jane Fonda, line 'em up against a wall. I'd gladly oblige 'em."[54] For years after the event, some Vietnam veterans expressed a visceral loathing for "Hanoi Jane," charging her with providing "aid and comfort to the enemy" in time of war, in other words, with treason.[55]

The Paris Peace Accords of 1973 that ended the U.S. war in Vietnam did not end the debates about the war. Critics argued that the accords were hardly different from the peace terms the United States could have achieved in 1969, when Nixon took office. This argument made the last four years of the war, a period when over twenty thousand American troops lost their lives, appear pointless.[56] Paul Kattenburg, a foreign service officer, said that after 1968, "it was immoral as well as cynical for the United States to continue waging war for another four years."[57] Nixon and Secretary of State Henry Kissinger were bound to claim that they had achieved some sort of success and hence to broadcast the claim that their bombing campaigns and a more effective use of ground forces had arrested the Communist forces' efforts to conquer South Vietnam. But some saw through the ruse. John Negroponte, one of Kissinger's aides, said, "We bombed the North Vietnamese into accepting our concessions."[58]

Believing that air power had proved its worth in 1972, the hawks claimed that it would have won the war if Johnson had launched an all-out attack in 1965, when support for the war was still high.[59] This was a reprise of the "stab-in-the-back" myth following Germany's defeat in World War I, allowing those who could not abide the fact of defeat to blame military failure on scapegoats.[60] According to the myth, America's forces did not lose; they were prevented from winning. As one veteran, filled with rage, said to the psychiatrist Jonathan Shay, "I won *my* war. It's *you* who fucking lost."[61] This idea that, in contrast to a civilian establishment, the troops won "their" war, took a powerful hold on Americans. In a 1979 poll, 47 percent of the public and 72 percent of Vietnam-era veterans agreed with the statement that the troops in Vietnam "were asked to fight in a war which our political leaders in Washington would not let them win." Oddly, though, only 40 percent of the veterans and 28 percent of the public in the same poll believed that the war could ever have been won.[62] These results demonstrate that at least some of the veteran respondents must have believed two mutually exclusive ideas: that politicians prevented them from winning the war, and that the war could never have been won. Both ideas exonerate veterans from responsibility for the outcome of the war. They pin the blame on the nation's leaders, because entering a war that could not be won and preventing victory having entered are equally failures of leadership.

In June 1973, three months after the withdrawal of the last American troops from South Vietnam, Congress cut off funds for military action in Indochina, effective in mid-August 1973. This action restricted the president's ability to order a resumption of bombing. In November, Congress passed the War Powers Act over Nixon's veto, in an attempt to reassert the legislature's exclusive Constitutional prerogative to declare war.[63] Congress then passed an amendment to the Military Procurement Authorization bill that banned the funding of any further U.S. military action in Indochina.[64] The record of congressional opposition to a renewed use of U.S. forces set the stage for postwar accusations. Nixon said that Congress signed South Vietnam's death warrant because the legislation removed the threat of U.S. military retaliation against a Communist offensive.[65]

Nixon's administration ended in disgrace for the president, and his resignation prevented his living up to the promises of military aid he had made (without congressional sanction) to the South Vietnamese government. Nixon's successor, Gerald Ford, blamed Congress for South Vietnam's defeat, which, coming barely two years after the Paris Peace Accords, made a sham of "peace with honor." Congress refused to allow the resumption of U.S. bombing of North Vietnam and of Communist forces in the south during their spring 1975 final offensive; and it refused to provide the South Vietnamese government with the military aid Ford repeatedly requested.[66] The legislators' decision reflected the wishes of the war-weary American people.[67]

Nixon had once said that only Americans could defeat the United States in Vietnam. He claimed that indeed Americans did so in 1975.[68] Although there are no grounds for believing that additional help at that stage would have done more than stave off defeat for a few days or weeks, Nixon and Ford promulgated a latter-day "stab-in-the-back" accusation that pinned the blame for South Vietnam's defeat on weak-willed politicians in Washington.[69] Ronald Reagan concurred: Congress, he said, had taken from the commander in chief the authority to enforce the terms of the Paris Peace Accords. It then "with unprecedented irresponsibility" refused to authorize the money to allow the United States to keep its pledge to support South Vietnam.[70]

For Vietnam veterans and others with a psychological investment in the war, the collapse of South Vietnam was a wrenching spectacle. If the United States was prepared to allow its ally to sink, without unleashing its full arsenal, then why had it committed its forces in the first place? Why had the veterans and their fallen comrades in arms fought and bled? Either the war had not been worth fighting and winning, or the government had lost its will to fight and abandoned a worthy cause. Some veterans thought that their government had betrayed an ally, abandoned their cause, and rendered the nation's losses worthless. The Vietnam veteran Kevin Maloney, there at the end, said, "I think we turned our backs on those folks [the South Vietnamese]. I don't buy the peace-with-honor stuff. We shagged out of there and left them to the North Vietnamese. . . . I do think about it a lot, still."[71] Opponents of the war felt the same way as those who vainly craved victory. "I feel my son's life was utterly wasted," said William Ransom, a lawyer who campaigned for an unconditional amnesty for war resisters.[72]

America's leaders quickly tried to consign the war to oblivion. Before Saigon, the South Vietnamese capital, fell, President Ford said the war was "finished as far as America is concerned," receiving a standing ovation from an audience of students.[73] On the flight back to Washington after the speech, a senior aide summed up the administration's attitude by raising his glass in a toast: "[Expletive] the war!"[74] In a phrase more consistent with presidential decorum but hardly different in substance, Ford declared on April 29, 1975, that the evacuation of Americans and Vietnamese from South Vietnam to the fleet in the South China Sea "closes a chapter in the American experience."[75] Ten days later, he said, "The war in Vietnam is over. . . . And we should focus on the future. As far as I'm concerned, that is where we will concentrate."[76] Secretary of State Kissinger concurred that America needed "to put Viet-Nam behind us and concentrate on the problems of the future."[77] But this wish to turn away from a painful experience left many veterans feeling abandoned. Myra MacPherson, who interviewed hundreds of Vietnam veterans for her book *Long Time Passing*, wrote that, almost a decade later, they felt "an indescribable rage that they, for so long, seemed to be the only Americans who remembered the war's suffering and pain."[78]

President Ford did not improve the climate of resentment by pardoning Nixon for the crimes the disgraced former president had committed in office. Pardoning Nixon, he said, would set the seal on this closed chapter. Cynics and disgruntled Democrats suspected that he had made a "deal" with Nixon, exchanging the presidency for an eventual pardon. Ford justified the pardon by saying it was necessary for rapid healing: "You can't pull a bandage off slowly." But as he later put the matter, "I began to wonder whether, instead of healing the wounds, my decision [to pardon Nixon] had only rubbed salt in them."[79]

"Healing the wounds" also involved the question of how the government should treat those who resisted the Vietnam War. President Nixon had rejected the notion of "healing the wounds" of the country through an amnesty for war resisters, saying illogically that it "takes two to heal wounds" and that "we all have to pay for our mistakes" (before he accepted Ford's pardon).[80] Some veterans agreed with him, but others argued that those who followed their consciences and resisted the draft had been proven right. "I think there should be an amnesty," said one Vietnam veteran who had been "gung ho and patriotic" when he went into the service but never would have gone if he had known "all the facts."[81] In the waning days of the war, pro-war and antiwar lobbies superimposed arguments about the morality of the war onto the amnesty issue.[82] President Ford extended a "discharge under honorable conditions" to military deserters who were wounded or decorated, in the "spirit of reconciliation," but his "earned clemency" program for draft resisters and other deserters was of little value to its recipients and was taken up by very few, paling in comparison to his treatment of Nixon.[83] One draft resister said he resented being asked to "shuffle and scrape and mumble, 'I'm sorry folks,'" just so Ford could feel better about "letting Nixon off the hook."[84]

The end of the war did not bring about reconciliation between its opponents and supporters. Instead, mutual resentment and recrimination persisted for years. An antiwar protester, thinking of the fellow citizens who used to insult her and threaten to run her family out of town because of her stance, said, "I see absolutely no reason we should forget or forgive those bastards."[85] Supporters of the war did not disappear after it was over, but now they were free to espouse the war's lessons and settle old scores because speaking in favor of the war entailed no further costs in lives or money. Norman Podhoretz said that critics of Nixon's policies in Vietnam should be "ashamed of their naivete" for supporting an enemy that they had a moral duty to oppose. He found them "almost impossible to forgive."[86] Conservatives blamed the media for misreporting the war, and particularly for misrepresenting the January 1968 Tet Offensive as a defeat for the United States, thus undermining public support for the war effort.[87] This criticism fed into the view that defeat in Vietnam had resulted from a failure of will on the part of the government, fomented by disloyal and biased reporters.[88] The hawkish journalist Hanson Baldwin, who had advocated massive bombing and a blockade of North Vietnam, wrote that it was "clear that the blame for the lost war rests, *not* upon the men in uniform, but upon the civilian policy makers in Washington—those who evolved and developed the policies of gradualism, flexible response, off-again-on-again bombing, negotiated victory, and, ultimately, one-arm-behind-the-back restraint and scuttle-and-run" (emphasis in original).[89] This catalogue of resentments and recriminations constituted the legacy of social division that the Vietnam Veterans Memorial Fund eventually set out to "heal."

Jimmy Carter's election as president in 1976 inaugurated a re-examination of the moral grounds on which American foreign policy was constructed. His views of the Vietnam War differed sharply from the "noble cause" idea that would be articulated four years later by Ronald Reagan. Carter criticized the "intellectual and moral poverty" of American policy in Vietnam, pointing to the danger of resorting to military means in distant places where American territory was not threatened. "The Vietnamese war," Carter said, "produced a profound moral crisis, sapping worldwide faith in our own policy and our system of life, a crisis of confidence made even more grave by the covert pessimism of some of our leaders." According to Carter, intervention in Vietnam had been conditioned by the assumption that Soviet expansion was almost inevitable but must be contained, and that the world itself was bi-polar, divided into rival blocs allied with or hostile to the United States. But the world had changed, Carter observed. In the postcolonial era, people's aspirations and their struggles against poverty could not be reduced to the cold war struggle between East and West, the Soviet bloc and the U.S.-led alliance. The United States needed a new foreign policy that reflected this new reality. "We can no longer separate the traditional issues of war and peace," Carter said, "from the new global questions of justice, equity, and human rights."[90]

Carter announced that human rights would be the new lodestar of American foreign policy.[91] "Human rights" was a high-minded cause that might attract a public disillusioned by the application of cold war orthodoxies in Vietnam, but it was also a convenient stick with which to beat the Soviet Union.[92] The focus on human rights did not mean a return to cold war bi-polarity, though, because Carter's policy also distanced the United States from some of the right-wing, repressive regimes that had been its clients. The Carter administration demonstrated that the United States would no longer support a dictatorial government simply because it was a loyal anti-Communist ally.

Carter denigrated manipulation and coercion as means of conducting international relations, and he said that one country should not use military force to impose its system on another.[93] The administration's anti-interventionist approach to conflicts abroad was summed up in Secretary of State Cyrus Vance's statement in May 1979: "Let me state first that the use of military force is not, and should not be a desirable American policy response to the internal politics of other nations."[94] Throughout his presidency, in keeping with the détente policy pursued by his Republican predecessors in the White House, Carter sought to reach arms limitation agreements with the Soviet Union. As late as March 1980, Vance said, "We seek no return of the cold war, of the indiscriminate confrontation of earlier times."[95] By this time, though, the tide of events had turned against Vance's conciliatory approach. Although many Americans were relieved that the U.S. government was reluctant to lead the nation into another war, others chafed against what they perceived as weakness. The cumulative toll of successive international reversals persuaded the administration to change course, a shift underlined by Vance's resignation in April 1980.

The setbacks began during the Ford administration but assumed the dimensions of a worldwide crisis under Carter. Governments in Southeast Asia, Africa, and Southwest Asia aligned themselves with the Soviet Union.[96] In February 1979, Islamic revolutionaries took power in Iran after the shah, an American client, had abandoned his throne, a turn of events that was a "political calamity" for President Carter.[97] Carter said that he would not use military force to determine the political destiny of Iran. "We've tried this once in Vietnam," he said. "It didn't work, as you well know."[98] In July 1979, Sandinista revolutionaries overthrew the government of Nicaragua in America's Central American "backyard," deposing one of the regimes that had long been a U.S. ally but that had lost the military support of the Carter administration as a result of its poor record on human rights.[99] The string of set-backs looked likely to continue in the region. A socialist insurgency in El Salvador attempted to overthrow a repressive government made more vulnerable by the interruption of U.S. military aid. These events seemed to substantiate Nixon's fear that a United States whose international credibility declined would be reduced to a "pitiful, helpless giant."

Carter defined America's problem as a "crisis of confidence" that threatened the nation's future. As he put it, this crisis struck at "the very heart and soul and spirit of our national will." All around, the result of the governmental uncertainty was "paralysis and stagnation and drift." Prominent in the list of causes was the war in Vietnam: "We were taught that our armies were always invincible and our causes were always just, only to suffer the agony of Vietnam."[100] This statement suggested that the cause for which the United States had fought in Vietnam was "unjust," and that the moral failings of America's fight contributed to the nation's postwar decline. One commentator drew the lesson for the Pentagon: Americans could no longer be expected to fight or support a "bad war." Carter's critics, however, said that he was the problem, his presidency characterized by political, economic, and military failures at home and abroad. The Committee for the Present Danger, a group of cold war policy makers and intellectuals, decried the "culture of appeasement" that had allowed the Soviet Union to exert its influence unopposed. Under Carter's leader-ship, Jeane Kirkpatrick argued, U.S. allies had been held to a stringent standard with respect to their human rights policies, whereas the offenses of "totalitarian" Soviet-allied nations had been ignored. To Carter's critics, his approach to foreign policy was not a corrective to the "arrogance of power" but was weakness; his government's abstention from the threat of force licensed Soviet opportunism and gave heart to America's enemies abroad.[101]

On the home front, Carter tried to resolve the conflicts dividing the Vietnam generation by instituting a pardon for those who had resisted the draft. His "blanket pardon" excused all but a handful of draft resisters, but not all veteran offenders (i.e., those who had committed disciplinary infractions while in uniform). He justified his program as part of "healing [the] wounds" of the war, recognizing an obligation "to forget many harsh words and harsh acts."[102] Conservatives were offended that those who had refused their nation's call were allowed to escape punishment. The chair-man of the Republican National Committee said that the pardon program was "a slap in the face of all Americans and families who did their duty." But for advocates of amnesty—especially for the many in-service offenders who were disproportionately black, poor, and with low incomes—the program fell short.[103] Carter subsequently introduced a discharge review program to consider regrading the discharges of those who had "bad paper": anything less than an honorable discharge.[104]

"Clemency" and "pardon" presuppose wrongdoing on the part of the person being excused; "amnesty" would have had no such implication, because the word means forgetting what has been done, without a presumption of rightness or wrongness. Carter's pardon program therefore maintained the notion of the culpability of the draft offenders or the deserters, although some thought them heroes who ought to be applauded, not forgiven, for breaking the law in opposition to the war.[105] (Those who had the courage of their convictions and, in the spirit of Henry David Thoreau, chose jail rather than military service were widely respected. They seemed "the most guilt-free of their generation," neither consumed by misgivings about their service in Vietnam nor ashamed that they had evaded the war and let others serve in their place.)[106] Although the majority of the public preferred Carter's pardon program, the split in public opinion about the rights and wrongs of military service in Vietnam was reflected in the substantial number (almost one-third of the respondents to an opinion poll) who would have preferred an amnesty.[107] Carter's program, though, ran into criticism from veterans' groups and from Republican Party politicians (who apparently saw no significant distinction between pardon and amnesty). A veteran who thought the pardon program too lenient said, "They should shoot them. That's all. Deserters too."[108] Another veteran organized a protest march against the pardon program in Statesville, North Carolina, and nailed a number of military decorations, a Bronze Star, two Purple Hearts, and several campaign ribbons, to the walls of an outhouse. Other veterans did the same and one added an artificial limb. They doused the outhouse in gasoline and burned it down, in graphic testimony to the persistent bitterness among members of the Vietnam generation and to these veterans' view that granting military resisters a pardon demonstrated that Carter devalued military service.[109] Criticism of the pardon program thus connected with the charge that Carter's policies were weakening America's defenses.

Carter never entirely abandoned his hope for peaceful coexistence with the Soviet Union. Nevertheless, a parallel policy track of confrontation in regions of East-West competition came to the fore, and his scruples about human rights violations in U.S. client states began to evaporate. The Carter administration began once again to arm and support anti-Communist governments in Central America.[110] Meanwhile, it vacillated between treating the Sandinistas as a locally inspired movement susceptible to U.S. influence and a Cuban-supported regime who would turn Nicaragua into a Soviet satellite. As relations between the United States and Nicaragua deteriorated, Carter suspended aid shortly before he left office.[111]

In November 1979, the sense of crisis in foreign policy intensified when radical Iranian students took Americans hostage in the U.S. Embassy in Tehran. The Soviet Union invaded Afghanistan in December 1979, compounding the crisis in Washington and damping Carter's hopes for peaceful coexistence.[112] As Secretary of State Vance recalled, the invasion of Afghanistan upset the balance in the administration between hard-line anti-Sovietism and coexistence. "The scales tipped toward those favoring confrontation," Vance said.[113] Zbigniew Brzezinski, Carter's zealously anti-Soviet national security adviser, concluded that the lessons of Vietnam had been "overlearned," particularly by Democrats on the dovish, McGovernite wing of the party.[114] Carter invoked the public's patriotism and called for the support of the American people in facing down the Soviet Union. With more hope than conviction, Carter said that the Soviet Union had underestimated America's "strength and resolve and unity and determination," but none of the actions he took influenced Soviet conduct in Afghanistan, and the words seemed to carry an empty threat.[115]

The Iranian hostage crisis dragged on through the whole of 1980. In April, U.S. Special Forces' attempt to liberate the hostages in Iran ended in a debacle, with the loss of eight American lives.[116] Although the public had rallied around the president in the early period of crisis, Carter's approval ratings collapsed in April.[117] With the hostages still in captivity and the Soviet Union still in Afghanistan, Carter could do nothing but appeal for public patience.[118] By the time of the 1980 presidential election, Richard Thornton comments, virtually every major foreign policy initiative of Carter's presidency "had either failed or was failing, and every important relationship was in disarray."[119] These international setbacks weakened Carter's campaign for re-election that November.[120]

Cold warriors and the religious right bemoaned the setbacks during the Carter presidency. Retired marine general Lewis Walt had warned, "The United States has been brought, by its own civilian leaders, to a position of military inferiority to the Soviet Union." The fundamentalist preacher Jerry Falwell's jeremiad echoed General Walt: "America is in serious trouble today. It has lost its economic and military prominence among the nations of the world."[121] The setbacks in Southwest Asia and Central America seemed to confirm this historic decline in America's position. The United States still possessed a huge military arsenal but unless it was able to influence other nations, it faced the "paradox of impotent power": an inability to translate its armed might into international authority.[122] America's post–Vietnam War malaise thus seemed to threaten the United States' ability to defend its international interests.

Ronald Reagan, the Republican Party challenger in the 1980 presidential election, accused President Carter of making a "shambles" of the nation's defenses. He said that Carter had been oblivious to the Soviet drive for world domination and timid in the face of Soviet advances. "The response from the administration," Reagan said, "has been one of weakness, inconsistency, vacillation, and bluff." The ebbing of U.S. military strength and Carter's faltering leadership had, Reagan said, encouraged America's enemies. In the western hemisphere, "the Caribbean is being made, by way of Cuba, the Soviets' surrogate, into a red lake." Reagan promised to pursue a policy of "peace through strength," restoring a "defense capability that provides a margin of safety for America." Reagan scoffed at the idea that the United States had "had its day in the sun; that our nation has passed its zenith." He believed that America's best days lay ahead. Reagan heaped praise on the armed forces and said that it was time to restore national pride after a time when it had become "shamefully fashionable" to deride and condemn military service.[123]

Speaking to the Veterans of Foreign Wars in August 1980, Reagan blamed the "Vietnam syndrome" for making Americans apologetic about their nation's past and timid in the face of aggression. His revision of the history of the Vietnam War was part of his effort to revive the nation's pride and sense of purpose. Reagan said, "We dishonored the memory of fifty thousand young Americans who died [in Vietnam] when we gave way to feelings of guilt as if we were doing something shameful, and we have been shabby in the treatment of those who returned."[124] Reagan recognized the political force of activated emotion. Since his time as governor of California, he had been adept at putting into words his supporters' inchoate resentments and desires.[125] According to Reagan, by shedding its guilt and shame and remembering its efforts in Vietnam with pride and self-belief, the nation would restore the dead to the place of honor that had been unjustly denied them and would give veterans of the Vietnam War the recognition they deserved.

Reagan said, "For too long, we have lived with the Vietnam syndrome. This is a lesson for all of us in Vietnam. If we are forced to fight, we must have the means and determination to prevail, or we will not have what it takes to secure peace. And . . . we will never again ask young men to fight and possibly die in a war our government is afraid to let them win." The last sentence contains a poetic density of ideas. "Never again" is at once a reading of the past and a pledge about the future. It exonerates the troops (sentimentally rendered as "young men") and wipes out the stain of their defeat, which was not their fault but the government's; it urges determination in any future conflict. Never mind that it was a simplistic and reductive interpretation of the history of American failure in Vietnam. It operated equally at the strategic and emotional levels, expressing Reagan's conception of military preparedness while satisfying in veterans a deep longing for vindication.[126] On hearing this declaration, the assembled delegates to the Veterans of Foreign Wars convention broke into "sustained and boisterous cheers."[127] Reagan had begun rehearsing the idea during his 1966 gubernatorial campaign when, in a challenge to Johnson's war policy, he voiced the "suspicion" that the troops were "being denied the right to try for victory." He discovered during his run for the presidency in 1976 that the admonition that the troops should never again be denied victory was a "rafter-shaking applause line." In a March 1980 campaign speech he repeated the promise never to send the troops to fight in a war their government is afraid to win, adding, "It is time we purged ourselves of the Vietnam syndrome, which has colored our thinking for too long." If this "purge" succeeded, the nation could resume its place on the world stage with its pride ascendant, its veterans rehabilitated, and its strength revived. No wonder, then, that Reagan rallied his conservative supporters and gratified Vietnam veterans hungry for validation of their service by repeatedly making the same pledge in speeches throughout his presidency.[128]

His advisers, though, saw foreign policy as an area of weakness for Reagan in the 1980 election. Although anti-Communists were one component of the electoral bloc that brought Reagan victory in 1980, a large majority of the electorate thought that Carter was the candidate "best able to keep us out of war."[129] Reagan's attempt to portray Carter as weak and indecisive could backfire if the electorate saw Reagan as a warmonger. Consequently, campaign managers persuaded him to tone down his rhetoric and to project amiability and reasonableness, convincing voters that he was not a saber-rattling militarist.[130] After this careful modulation of the candidate's image, the electorate responded to Reagan's promise of a restoration of national strength and esteem, helping him to win the 1980 presidential election by a substantial margin. Once in office, he led the effort to ensure that the United States resumed the mantle of a superpower.[131] Reagan's neo-conservative acolytes had argued that détente—the lowering of tensions between the Soviet Union and the United States—was a deception intended to lower the United States' guard.[132] Reagan showed that it would not last long when, in his first news conference as president, he said that, so far, détente had been a "one-way street" that the Soviet Union had exploited to pursue its own aims.[133] A resurgent America would challenge Soviet expansionism. "I'm happy to tell you," he said to a West Point graduating class early in his presidency, "that the people of America have recovered from what can only be called a temporary aberration. There is a spiritual revival going on in this country, a hunger on the part of the people to once again be proud of America—all that it is and all that it can be."[134]

Reagan's supporters came to Washington determined to reverse Vietnam War–induced disillusionment so that the public, Congress, and military officers would overcome their reluctance to use force abroad.[135] Conservative internationalists believed that because the United States "bugged out" in Vietnam, the Soviet sphere of influence expanded around the globe—in Ethiopia, Angola, Mozambique, Afghanistan, Nicaragua, and elsewhere.[136] John H. Taylor, an assistant to Nixon, said that "between 1975 and 1980 . . . over 100 million people were either lost to the Communists or by the West because of Congress's, the media's, and the Carter and Ford administrations' fear of 'another Vietnam.'"[137] According to this view, President Carter's "giveaway" of the Panama Canal, the Nicaraguan revolution, and the Iranian hostage crisis were all symptoms of American moral weakness, of which its enemies had taken advantage.[138] Jeane Kirkpatrick, appointed as Reagan's ambassador to the United Nations, claimed that Soviet gains were made all the easier by liberals' reflexive tendency to "blame America first no matter what went wrong in the world." As a result, the United States had yielded ground, and the Soviet Union had taken advantage of U.S. hesitancy by intensifying its support of "wars of national liberation" and by building up its nuclear arsenal.[139]

Reagan set out to compensate first with huge expenditures on military equipment. His secretary of defense, Caspar Weinberger, expanded Carter's projected increases in military expenditures, beginning a massive arms build-up. With the backing of the president, the Pentagon restored the B-1 bomber program, proceeded with the deployment of a new generation of missiles, the MX, set out to create a six-hundred-ship navy, and later initiated the "Star Wars" missile defense system and began to develop aircraft with "stealth" technology, all in the name of negotiating with the Soviet Union from a position of strength.[140]

Resurgent military power was crucial to the U.S. capacity to assume global leadership; but as Helga Haftendorn remarks, the renewal of a broad national consensus about America's military posture was imperative for global power projection.[141] Advocates of a more active U.S. foreign policy "wished to rehabilitate the memory of Vietnam as a first step toward the global reassertion of American power in the 1980s." They "realized that the legacy of Vietnam required revision before a revitalized policy of anti-Communist containment could be adopted."[142]

Within weeks of Reagan's inauguration, Kirkpatrick warned of a looming threat in Central America, which would be the first test of whether Reagan could overcome the "Vietnam syndrome" sufficiently to hold the line against Communism. She said that America's position in the Western Hemisphere had deteriorated to the point where "we must now defend ourselves against a ring of Soviet bases being established on and around our borders." The administration began to debate what to do about this threat, contemplating direct military intervention among other policies. In February 1981, U.S. forces conducted naval exercises off the coast of Cuba, the largest maneuvers in the Caribbean up to then.[143] In the first year of the Reagan administration, the United States resumed "lethal" military aid to the Salvadoran government and massively increased other forms of assistance.[144] U.S. advisers began to train Salvadoran military units in rapid reaction tactics using U.S.–supplied helicopters. Beginning with a $2 million covert program of CIA activities, the administration resumed aid to Guatemala's repressive government.[145] But from the early days of its involvement in Central America, the administration downplayed the Vietnam analogy. In March 1981, reassuring a Senate committee that a request for military aid did not foreshadow an escalating involvement, Under Secretary of State Walter Stoessel Jr. said, "We are doing our best to insure that a similar situation does not develop in El Salvador with what happened in Vietnam."[146]

While bolstering anti-Communist allies in the region, the administration set out to undermine Nicaragua's socialist government. It formally terminated economic aid to the Sandinista government in April 1981. The CIA began coordinating its efforts with the head of the national police in Nicaragua's neighbor, Honduras, to provide financial support, bases, and training to former members of the Nicaraguan National Guard. They would form the kernel of a counterrevolutionary force opposed to the Sandinista government—the *contras*.[147] In late 1981, the National Security Council approved a program of political and paramilitary activities against the Nicaraguan government and left-wing insurgencies elsewhere in Central America.[148] But when the covert program of aid to the *contras* was disclosed in the fall of 1982, it provoked "widespread Congressional concern and fear that the United States was becoming involved in another Vietnam."[149]

Reagan's opponents invoked the "Vietnam trauma" whenever he contemplated deploying American forces in a part of the world where there was an armed enemy.[150] By analogy, an initial commitment of troops was dangerous because they could be drawn into a Vietnam-like "quagmire" and, once committed, these forces might not be easily extricated. But Reagan's supporters believed that if the United States was so averse to risks that it would not commit its troops anywhere for fear of "another Vietnam," it was already defeated before a shot was fired and it would steadily lose territory, allies, and influence around the world. The problem for the administration was that there was no clear domestic consensus in favor of a more aggressive foreign policy. In the early 1980s, fewer Americans supported the United States' taking an "active part in world affairs" than at any other time since World War II.[151] Aside from fears of another Vietnam, Democratic Party legislators and much of the public doubted whether repressive governments and counterrevolutionary forces in Central America deserved American aid.[152] And the American people did not see a vital U.S. interest in the question of who governed Nicaragua or El Salvador. A Gallup poll taken early in Reagan's first term did not encourage intervention in the region: in March 1981, only 2 percent of respondents favored sending U.S. troops to El Salvador, and fewer than 20 percent supported military or economic aid.[153]

To win congressional funding for aid to the region, Reagan needed to win the votes of at least some Democrats, because the House of Representatives was controlled by the Democratic Party throughout his presidency. The Democrats did not always vote as a bloc, and the committed pro- and anti-*contra* aid groups in the House of Representatives were evenly matched in numbers. The success or failure of Reagan's requests for *contra* funding therefore rested on a relatively small number of swing votes, mostly those of conservative southern Democrats and moderate Republicans. Reagan's lobbying of reluctant legislators was not always sufficient to win them over, particularly when his popular approval rating among the electorate was low, and when military and CIA activities in Central America made the administration appear too warlike. Public fears of "another Vietnam" and congressional worry that a small-scale intervention in Central America might escalate to Vietnam War–like dimensions led to constant skirmishes between the administration and legislators.[154]

Reagan's White House advisers preoccupied themselves with the calculation of whether it was worth picking a fight with congressional opponents about Central America, and whether and when to appeal over their heads to the public. While Reagan was prepared to fight issues of principle even when they polarized Congress and the public, he was reluctant to squander political capital on issues he did not consider vital. "Simultaneously an ideologue and a pragmatist," he was both a politician who sowed ideological discord and one who sought, frequently with success, to rally the support of the majority.[155]

Reagan was the most successful Republican Party politician of his generation because he managed to draw together its divergent factions, as well as voters who had not previously identified themselves with the party. Reagan's supporters included traditional Republicans—economic conservatives who supported a strong defense, tax cutting, and deregulation of the economy; the "New Right," or "movement conservatives," many of them Roman Catholics and evangelical Protestants who focused on social issues such as abortion and school prayer and opposed gun control and school busing; and military and foreign policy conservatives who favored Reagan's assertive nationalism.[156] Reagan also made inroads into the traditional Democratic Party base: white southerners, union members, blue-collar workers, and white ethnics who were attracted to Reagan's social conservatism and anti-Communism. Reagan's appeal to these varied constituencies resulted in his electoral victories in 1980 and 1984 but this success was also a potential source of weakness: the coalition had to be carefully managed so that its constituent parts did not break into rival factions. Tensions among these constituencies emerged not only in the electorate but also in the White House and Congress.[157]

Foreign policy was one arena in which the Reagan administration was torn between ideological hard-liners and moderate "pragmatists." Committed anti-Communists in the State Department, such as Kirkpatrick, Elliott Abrams, and Secretary of State Alexander Haig, wanted to halt the revolutionaries in Central America.[158] But some of Reagan's closest aides saw no advantage in focusing public attention and consuming Congress's time in debating the contentious issue of the United States' posture in Central America. According to Haig, these advisers were too afraid of "another Vietnam" to engage in an effective anti-Communist policy there.[159]

Haig believed that the United States should reverse its enemies' gains in Central America by mounting a military campaign against the insurgents in El Salvador and, if necessary, by blockading Cuba (which, according to international law, would have constituted an act of war). Haig wanted to make a large commitment to Central America right from the start to avoid the sort of slow build-up of forces that had occurred in Southeast Asia, which he believed had allowed the enemy time to adapt. Better, therefore, to intervene quickly with massive force. As he wrote, only "a determined show of American will and power" could persuade the Soviet Union to rein in Cuba's support of the Salvadoran insurgency. Moreover, only a clear military victory would resolve the psychological blows that the United States had suffered in Vietnam, Angola, Afghanistan, and elsewhere. As Haig recognized, the problem of foreign confidence in the United States originated in American self-confidence, because the U.S. public's fears of "another Vietnam" made friend and foe doubt the nation's capacity to risk military action, undermining that intangible yet crucial component of power projection: "credibility." Haig thus proposed that America undergo a kind of behavioral therapy—a "steady accumulation of prudent and successful actions"—designed to cure the public of its aversion to war.[160]

Haig's thesis was that the Soviet Union's sphere of influence, having expanded, was now vulnerable at its peripheries.[161] The advantages and disadvantages that the United States and the Soviet Union had experienced in Vietnam were reversed in Central America, where the United States had short and the Soviet Union long supply lines, making it far more costly and difficult for the Soviet Union to support its allies in the region. An overt military campaign would be more effective politically than a covert or proxy war, because the symbolic weight of a U.S. victory in Central America would be magnified if the United States proclaimed and executed its strategy in the full glare of public scrutiny. El Salvador would be the place where the United States would restore its reputation for toughness and demonstrate its resolve. Haig assured Reagan, "Mr. President, this is one you can win."[162]

Haig's plan ran into the opposition of fellow cabinet members, the armed forces, and legislators. Secretary of Defense Weinberger opposed sending troops to El Salvador. Weinberger was afraid that another jungle war might reenact, not resolve, the trauma of the Vietnam War. He cautioned that involvement in Central America, once it engaged the United States' energies and prestige, could lead to another Vietnam. Nor did the president's highest-ranked military advisers, the Joint Chiefs of Staff, eagerly seek another arena of limited warfare. Hard-line conservatives dismissed their thinking as a symptom of the Vietnam syndrome. In 1983, some two and a half years into the debate about U.S. policy in Central America, officers who had commanded troops in Vietnam launched a public campaign against the use of U.S. combat troops in Central America.[163] Senator Nancy L. Kassebaum (R., Kansas) said the similarities between the El Salvador conflict and the Vietnam War were becoming increasingly evident. "The comparison to Vietnam has been used many times, and I have never felt comfortable with it," she said. "But the parallels seem to grow more striking as time goes on."[164]

A White House "troika" of key advisers urged caution for pragmatic reasons: they were concerned that the administration should not use up its political capital over Central America. The White House chief of staff James Baker III, deputy chief of staff Michael Deaver, and presidential counselor Edwin Meese III were highly attuned to the public mood, too much so according to Haig. Deaver and Meese had been with Reagan since his days as governor of California and had special positions of influence. Meese had a knack for distilling a lot of information and presenting it to the president in three or four key points. He began as the most powerful of the three, although his influence was not matched by bureaucratic skill. (He was said to have a "bottomless briefcase" into which policy papers would disappear, never to be seen again.) Deaver was the president's closest confidant. Highly attentive to the presentation of policy and its likely impact on public opinion, he had the president's ear and his political instincts usually prevailed in policy conflicts. Baker had campaigned for George Bush, Reagan's rival for the 1980 Republican presidential nomination, and was mistrusted by far-right Republicans, but he made an alliance with Deaver and steadily accumulated influence during Reagan's first term. He had exceptional administrative skills and became the most respected member of the White House staff. Although Meese was said to be the most conservative of the three, in fact they had few ideological differences. Their occasional disagreements tended to concern matters of tactics and priorities—which still left a good deal of room for debate.[165]

Deaver, though, saw the administration as "split right down the middle between the moderates and conservatives." The troika's views conflicted with those who took a harder line with regard to Central America policy. Deaver and the other pragmatists wished to place the emphasis in Reagan's first term in office on achievements in the domestic arena—for example, his tax cuts and deregulation of the economy—and they calculated that an overemphasis on foreign policy in Central America would bring political costs.[166] As Peggy Noonan, a Reagan speechwriter, recalled, "No one wanted the *contras* to lose, no one wanted the Sandinistas to flourish, but there was plenty of disagreement on whether to devote a great deal of time and effort to the issue."[167] Frustrated, Reagan's New Right supporters charged that the pragmatists surrounding Reagan were thwarting his natural ideological inclinations, that his advisers would not "let Reagan be Reagan."[168]

Of all the arenas of international competition, though, the hard-liners had the greatest influence over U.S. policy in Central America, so much so that confrontation usually trumped diplomatic compromise.[169] And what made the contest between pragmatists and hard-liners evenly balanced was that Reagan himself was convinced of the rightness of opposing socialist revolutions in Central America. The use of the morally charged terms "freedom fighters" for the *contras*, "evil empire" for the Soviet Union, and "noble cause" for the Vietnam War signaled that in the renewed global cold war, Reagan was a zealous anti-Communist whose natural sympathies inclined to the Central America hawks.

Haig, another anti-Communist true believer, spoke ruefully of the White House troika's sensitivity to the public mood. "Every day," he complained, they "put their finger to the wind to see what the people wanted."[170] Haig was not exaggerating the White House's sensitivity to public opinion. In his first twenty-nine months in office, Reagan met more than twenty-five times with his longtime pollster Richard Wirthlin. The White House commissioned Wirthlin to conduct opinion polls on topics such as aid to El Salvador and to the *contras*, and Wirthlin gave Reagan a "report card" saying how he could most effectively marshal support for his policies. The polls helped pinpoint which political issues were causing Reagan trouble with various constituencies, and Wirthlin suggested ways to fine-tune the administration's message to minimize those problems; the polls could then test how well the alterations in policy or in its presentation worked. Noonan recalled that in policy discussions, Wirthlin's polls were immensely influential because he was the only one with "hard data" about the popularity of policies: "actual numbers on actual paper." "Everyone else," Noonan writes, "has an opinion; the pollster has a fact." Public opinion polls were discussed in more than half of the meetings of White House senior staff. White House aides received daily summaries of the polls, and the White House Office of Planning and Evaluation analyzed the polls for senior staff in its "Public Opinion Digest."[171]

The results of the public opinion polls showed the Reagan administration's stance on Central America was deeply and consistently unpopular. No wonder Reagan's advisers considered foreign policy "politically treacherous territory" for their boss. Statements such as the "noble cause" assertion had earned Reagan the reputation of a trigger-happy extremist. Between 1980 and 1982, Wirthlin found that a steady 25 percent of American voters thought Reagan was "likely to start an unnecessary war" and throughout the president's first term, Wirthlin and Deaver worried about the electoral costs of this perception.[172] Having persuaded Reagan to tone down his rhetoric during the 1980 campaign, his advisers remained aware of the potential electoral disadvantage of his brand of militant anti-Communism, which might cost Republicans support in the 1982 midterm elections. The major public opinion organizations confirmed the findings of the White House's privately commissioned polls. In early 1982, polls showed public opposition to Reagan's policies in Central America rising sharply, with almost two-thirds of respondents to a Harris poll disapproving of Reagan's handling of El Salvador.[173] In February of that year, a Gallup poll found that 74 percent of a sample of the public who were knowledgeable about the conflict in El Salvador said that it was likely that U.S. involvement there could turn into "a situation like Vietnam—that is, that the United States would become more and more involved as time goes on."[174] In March 1982, polls by CBS/New York Times, the Harris organization, and Time Inc. found that large majorities (60 percent,

71 percent, and 74 percent, respectively) agreed that it was likely that El Salvador would become another Vietnam.[175]

Opponents of Reagan's unpopular Central America policy expressed—and played on—these fears through slogans such as "No Vietnam War in Central America" and "El Salvador is Spanish for Vietnam."[176] Anti-intervention groups centered on churches, trade unions, and community organizations, with the memory of the Vietnam War fresh in their minds and with anti–Vietnam War activists in their ranks, mobilized grass-roots opposition to Reagan's policies. Criticism of figures associated with Reagan's Central America policy, such as Kirkpatrick and Assistant Secretary of State Elliott Abrams, a die-hard anti-Communist, became vitriolic; in turn, Abrams expressed contempt for his critics. Ideological conflicts between the administration and its opponents polarized the debate, with little shared middle ground between advocates of contending Central America programs.[177] The broad-based public opposition to intervention in Central America restricted the Reagan administration to the use of "advisers," military exercises, and overt and covert support of right-wing governments and "freedom fighters." Restraint in the deployment of U.S. combat forces, however, allowed a new version of counterinsurgency, low-intensity conflict, to be tried. Central America became its principal laboratory.[178]

The Reagan administration's policy of covert intervention in Central America grew out of the internal conflicts within the administration, which initially pitted State Department activists against the secretary of defense and set anti-Communist hard-liners against pragmatist White House advisers concerned about public opinion.[179] Into the impasse stepped William Casey, the director of Central Intelligence, who proposed funding and arming anti-Cuban and anti-Soviet forces in Central America, including the Salvadoran government and the Nicaraguan *contras*.[180] Nicaragua would be one of the proving grounds for what eventually became known as the "Reagan Doctrine": the support of indigenous insurgencies against governments the United States regarded as outposts of the Soviet Union.[181] In its role as supporter of "freedom fighters," the United States would not have to risk its wealth and its own troops; it could far more cheaply arm and equip a guerrilla force to bleed its enemies white. As Casey remarked, "It is much easier and less expensive to support an insurgency than it is for us and our friends to resist one. It takes relatively few people and little support to disrupt the internal peace and economic stability of a small country."[182]

Lawmakers who were skeptical about the administration's Central America policy wanted, even so, to avoid being blamed for "losing" Central America to Communism. When couched in terms of national security, the president's requests for military and economic aid to client states and the *contras* were often hard to resist. Early on in Reagan's first term, though, Democratic legislators added conditions to aid to El Salvador. The number of U.S. military advisers in El Salvador would be limited to fifty-five. Congress used the power of the purse to impose another condition on U.S. involvement, stipulating that further aid to El Salvador would be dependent on the administration's periodic certification of the Salvadoran government's human rights record. Here, though, the condition was weak: El Salvador did not have to have a perfect or even a good human rights record, as long as the administration said that it was "improving." Death squads, some with links to the country's security forces, operated largely unhindered in El Salvador, with only half-hearted American attempts to persuade the Salvadorans to curb their activities.[183]

In 1982, the administration significantly stepped up its political and military engagement in Central America. The United States and NATO staged naval exercises in the Caribbean and a joint Honduran–U.S. force staged a war game on the Honduran coast simulating combat against an aggressor force, the Sandinistas. The United States increased its military presence in Honduras, near Nicaragua's border. Early in the year, matters were in a particularly delicate state because Reagan was again considering using presidential emergency powers to give military aid to El Salvador, as he had once before. Congress expanded his powers to make emergency military transfers, and Reagan granted $55 million in this way in February 1982. Public opinion remained hostile to U.S. involvement, with White House and State Department mail running as high as twenty to one against the Salvadoran buildup.[184]

During 1981 and 1982, James Baker insisted that Reagan not invest too much personal attention to the unpopular issue of Central America. But early in 1983, it appeared that without the administration's biggest asset, Reagan himself, its request for a big aid package for El Salvador would be defeated in Congress.[185] Congressional Democrats couched their objections to the aid request in their fears of "another Vietnam." "The similarity to Vietnam is so close it's almost uncanny," Clarence Long (D., Maryland) said. "There is the unwillingness of people to fight, incompetent corrupt leadership, and calling everyone a Communist."[186] Long, the chairman of the Foreign Operations Subcommittee of the House Appropriations Committee, was the only member of Congress who had a son wounded in Vietnam, and he was determined not to let the United States enter "another Vietnam." House speaker Tip O'Neill had voted in 1964 for the Tonkin Gulf resolution, and his conscience never forgave him.[187] In considering Reagan's requests for money for El Salvador, he said, "There's just a strong feeling around here that it's another Vietnam situation."[188]

Reagan believed that public fear of "another Vietnam" eased the pressure on Congress to provide funding for his Central America policies, and he was sure that this "was a result of the post-Vietnam syndrome."[189] He responded by wagering his political capital and leading the campaign for congressional funding of El Salvador and the Nicaraguan *contras*. His goal, as he had announced in his March 1980 speech, was to "purge the 'Vietnam syndrome' from American life" and to win domestic and international support for his Central America policy.[190] He delivered a major address on Central America to the annual conference of the American Legion in February 1983, pointing to the danger to U.S. national security posed by Marxist-Leninist governments tied to Cuba and the Soviet Union.[191] In a speech at the Commonwealth Club in San Francisco ten days later, Reagan offered a version of the "domino theory," saying, "The threat is more to the entire Western Hemisphere and toward the area than it is to one country." If Communists won in El Salvador, following the revolution in Nicaragua, Reagan said, the other countries in the region would soon follow. Nevertheless, Reagan denied that events in El Salvador were a replay of the early stages of the advisory effort in Indochina and insisted that there was "no parallel whatsoever with Vietnam."[192] Speaking to the National Association of Manufacturers a few days later, Reagan said, "The Communist agenda . . . is to exploit human suffering in Central America to strike at the heart of the Western Hemisphere." At stake in the region, he said, was the national security of the United States.[193]

In April 1983, this sequence of speeches culminated in an address to a joint session of Congress. Reagan reminded the legislators of how close Central America was to the United States and said that vital trade routes passed through the Panama Canal and the Caribbean. The conflicts in the region were also a symbolic test of American will. "If we cannot defend ourselves there," Reagan said, "we cannot expect to prevail elsewhere. Our credibility would collapse, our alliances would crumble, and the safety of our homeland would be put in jeopardy."[194] A White House outreach group on Central America opened its offices in May 1983 to take the public campaign forward, and in July the State Department's Office of Public Diplomacy for Latin America and the Caribbean began parallel efforts.[195] Aided by this "public diplomacy" program, and lobbying of legislators by the president, the Reagan administration won support in Congress for large increases in military assistance to the government of El Salvador.[196] In November 1983, Congress for the first time approved military assistance to the *contras*, transforming the program from a covertly funded operation to a publicly funded one.[197]

The problem was that the more the president devoted his rhetorical powers to Central America policy, the more he gave Congress and the public reason for worry; if, as he said, the fate of Central America was crucial to U.S. security, then it seemed all the more likely that the United States might send troops there. The most loudly applauded line in his congressional address was the promise, "Let me say to those who invoke the memory of Vietnam, there is no thought of sending American combat troops to Central America."[198] Reagan's insistence that he had no intention of sending U.S. troops there undermined the message that the area was one of vital interest to the United States. The difficult trick was to mobilize support for military aid to the region without provoking fears that this action might lead to another Vietnam.[199]

In attempting to explain that there was "no comparison whatsoever in this situation [Central America] and Vietnam," Reagan offered a narrative of the beginnings of U.S. involvement in Vietnam. His intended argument was inconclusive, since it did not convincingly refute the comparison between Vietnam and Central America, but his historical account is nevertheless revealing. Reagan stated that the 1954 Geneva Agreement created two new countries, North Vietnam and South Vietnam, and that the United States intervened to support the "duly elected government" of South Vietnam against North Vietnam.[200] In fact, the final declaration of the Geneva Conference stated that the division of Vietnam across a military demarcation line was "purely provisional," and that this boundary "should not in any way be interpreted as constituting a political or territorial boundary."[201] After its temporary division, the country was to reunify with a national election in 1956.

Reagan was never one to let an inconvenient fact interrupt the grand sweep of a historical idea. His close aide Lyn Nofziger, with him since his governorship of California, said: "Truth is not the same thing to him as to you and me. If Ronald Reagan tells a story three times it becomes true, at least to him." Reagan blamed North Vietnam's Communist leader Ho Chi Minh for refusing to hold the 1956 election, but it was in fact South Vietnam, the United States' ally, that balked at the election because of the certainty, recognized at the time by the American government, that Ho Chi Minh would easily win.[202] The United States then embarked on a nation-building operation to try to create a viable anti-Communist South Vietnamese state, but the effort was always undermined by the doubtful legitimacy of the South Vietnamese government from its very inception.[203] The fatal weakness of the South Vietnamese government, which survived because of repression and U.S. support, not because of the freely expressed will of the people, was a problem for which the United States never found a solution, no matter how many dollars, weapons, and troops it poured into the country. A tissue of confabulation, Reagan's account of the creation of South Vietnam was the foundation on which his convictions about Vietnam were planted: this is what one would have to believe in order to consider the war a "noble cause."

The contested meanings of the Vietnam War—a "noble cause" or a quagmire to be avoided—set the political context for understanding the arguments about the Vietnam Veterans Memorial. Americans' grievances against one another had deep roots in the war era. America had begun to come apart during the war years and these fissures still marked the political landscape of the 1980s. Citizens had learned to mistrust their government because of the deceptions of the Johnson and Nixon administrations. Americans blamed each other—for the defeat, or for the loss of esteem the United States had suffered because of the way it had fought. Their divergent views of what had gone wrong in Vietnam were not merely academic disagreements about the past but had real world consequences in the present and future. The ideological descendants of the Vietnam War–era "hawks," led by President Reagan, wanted the nation to recover from the "Vietnam syndrome" so that it could reassure or intimidate others by wielding the credible threat of military force. Those who remembered the United States' war in Vietnam as immoral or unnecessary were disturbed by efforts to rehabilitate the war's memory, to transform it into a "noble cause" and hence to make "another Vietnam" more likely. All three post–Vietnam War presidents wanted to reforge the nation's unity: as President Ford had put it, to "heal" the wounds of the war. The Vietnam Veterans Memorial Fund undertook this task of national reunification as it tried to bring together veterans and others with sharply divided convictions about the war.

— 2 —

"SOMETHING RATHER DARK AND BLOODY"

Atrocities, Post-Traumatic Stress Disorder, and the Pathologization of Vietnam Veterans

★

THE CULTURAL construction of Vietnam veterans played a central role in shaping the remembrance of the war. The veterans were living embodiments of the war and their difficult readjustment to civilian society became a metaphor for the nation's problems in integrating the Vietnam experience into the pattern of national life. In the early 1970s, antiwar veterans, the most publicly visible and organized body of Vietnam veterans, were an anomalous, alienated group challenging received ideas about the moral virtues of the American military.[1] By the end of the decade, though, veterans' image had undergone a sea change. They remained plaintive figures but their complaints were shorn of their foreign-policy content.[2] The major demand that veterans' advocates made was no longer for an end to American imperialism; now the veterans were said merely to crave recognition and acceptance by their fellow Americans. In this guise, they would benefit from the "healing" that the Vietnam Veterans Memorial promised.

The difficulties the troops faced on their return from Southeast Asia to what they called "the World" were not unique, but Vietnam veterans as a group faced a particularly difficult homecoming.[3] Other unpopular wars, such as World War I, had the compensating virtue of victory, but Vietnam veterans could not claim its laurels. Instead, they carried the stains of defeat and disgrace.[4] Revelations about atrocities against Vietnamese civilians tarnished Vietnam veterans' reputation in the eyes of their compatriots as well as undermining the government's claims about the morality of the U.S. war effort in Vietnam. While antiwar veterans claimed in 1971 that violence against Vietnamese civilians was standard operating procedure in Vietnam, veterans who denied this claim resented the stigma that it attached to service in Vietnam. In 1971, they could do little but silently rage when they saw opponents of the war tarring every member of the U.S. forces in Vietnam with the stain of atrocity—rage, and bide their time until they had the chance to set the record straight.

49

The most vocal and publicly visible veterans in the early 1970s were activists in Vietnam Veterans Against the War (VVAW), an organization that came to the fore just as other antiwar groups were dissolving into factional fighting.[5] In April 1971, VVAW organized "Operation Dewey Canyon III," a series of demonstrations in Washington, DC, that brought the antiwar veterans national prominence.[6] Although half a million antiwar protesters demonstrated in Washington and 250,000 rallied in San Francisco, the protests by the 900 veterans of VVAW stood out among the remainder of the week's activities. John Kerry, a navy veteran and VVAW leader, gave an eloquent oration before the Senate Foreign Relations Committee on April 22, 1971 (a month before appearing at the dedication of the Angel Fire memorial). Clean-cut and well-spoken, Kerry denounced U.S. military violations of the Geneva Conventions and condemned many of the "accepted policies" of U.S. forces in Vietnam. He referred the senators to VVAW members' testimony that war crimes in Vietnam were commonplace.[7] The following day, veterans returned their military decorations to Congress, one man calling them "my merit badges for murder."[8]

Its membership never exceeded a few thousand, but VVAW's influence on public discourse about the war did not depend on numbers.[9] "Antiwar warriors," veterans protesting against a war while it still went on, were an unusual, if not unprecedented, phenomenon.[10] Because VVAW consisted of those who had served their nation in Vietnam, they could not be dismissed as hippies and radicals.[11] Nor could they be accused of wishing to avoid service; they had already done their stint in Vietnam and "carried the weight of tested patriotism."[12] The White House's Pat Buchanan observed during Dewey Canyon III that VVAW "are getting tremendous publicity; they have an articulate spokesman; they are being received in a far more sympathetic fashion than other demonstrators."[13] The Vietnam veteran and writer Philip Caputo felt that VVAW were "the only people who have a *right* to say anything against the war" (emphasis in original).[14] Allen Lynch, a Medal of Honor winner, said that anti-war veterans had a right to protest because "they were there, they walked in the jungles. . . . If anybody had a right to make a statement, they did."[15]

By the time VVAW launched Operation Dewey Canyon III, the nation had been exposed to disturbing truths about the war that heightened the veterans' antiwar message. The atrocity that U.S. forces perpetrated at My Lai came to stand for all the wrongs that Americans perpetrated in Vietnam, and it delivered to the world the message that "America is capable, like other nations, of evil in war."[16] The massacre and all it symbolized helps to explain something that Reagan's August 1980 Veterans of Foreign Wars convention speech implicitly addressed but that remained unstated and mysterious: why Americans might feel guilty or ashamed about their nation's actions in Vietnam.

Early in the morning of March 16, 1968, Charlie Company, of the 1st Battalion of the 20th Infantry Brigade, a unit of the Americal Division, entered a group of hamlets marked on U.S. maps as My Lai, in Quang Ngai province.[17] The company had suffered casualties in the preceding weeks, mainly from snipers, mines, and booby traps, but had never had the enemy in their sights. They were told that they would take the enemy by surprise and that they could expect fierce resistance. However, the Viet Cong battalion they had been expecting to find was not in the village. By then they had come to believe that all the Vietnamese people in the area were the enemy, even women and children. Despite receiving no hostile fire, they set out over a period of several hours to gather groups of villagers of all ages, from babies to elderly people, and machine-gunned some five hundred Vietnamese civilians or killed them with grenades. In parts of the village the killings were organized and systematic; elsewhere the soldiers ran wild. They raped women and girls and mutilated corpses. It was a "Nazi kind of thing," participants said afterward.[18]

By this time, murder, rape, and arson had become common among many of the Americal Division's combat units, especially those operating in Quang Ngai province. Charlie Company itself had perpetrated "brutal and inexcusable" killings of Vietnamese civilians before their attack on My Lai. The soldiers held the Vietnamese people in low regard, some of them considering the villagers subhuman, "on the level of dogs."[19] Because officers participated in attacks on civilians and failed to institute disciplinary proceedings against the perpetrators, some troops became convinced that this behavior was acceptable. Like units throughout Vietnam, Charlie Company was encouraged to achieve a high "body count," the Pentagon-sanctioned measure of progress in the war. Officers up to the top echelons of the Americal Division were more interested in sending on favorable reports about their operations than in asking awkward questions about civilian deaths.[20] Divisional and brigade commanders' initial investigation of the My Lai massacre was perfunctory and negligent. They thus became complicit in a cover-up.[21] Impressed by the high body count Charlie Company had racked up, General William Westmoreland, the commander of U.S. forces in South Vietnam from 1964 to 1968, singled them out for praise, congratulating them for an "outstanding action."[22]

The cover-up succeeded until the spring of 1969 when Ronald Ridenhour, a Vietnam veteran, wrote to political leaders and military officers in the United States telling them that, after talking to his fellow soldiers while in Vietnam, he had become convinced that "something rather dark and bloody" had occurred in March 1968 in a village that they referred to as "Pinkville."[23] The army began an investigation. Then photographs of the atrocity came to light and millions saw them when they were published in *Life* magazine and on network television (see fig. 4).[24] Horror-struck, some of the public initially refused to believe the evidence before their eyes, fabricating stories to explain away the fact that American troops had killed hundreds of unarmed civilians.[25] The photographs, though, lent undeniable facticity to VVAW's arguments that the war was immoral and that it brutalized its participants.

A month before VVAW's Operation Dewey Canyon III, a court-martial handed down the sole conviction in the post-massacre trials: Lieutenant William Calley, commander of Charlie Company's 1st Platoon, was found guilty of the premeditated murder of at least 22 civilians, although his platoon may have been responsible for the deaths of 150 to 200.[26] Every other perpetrator got away with his crimes.[27] Anyone looking for clues to why Calley became a mass murderer was hard pressed to find them in his background. Neither he nor his men appeared, at first glance, to be moral monsters; they seemed instead to be unexceptional products of their place

Figure 4. My Lai Massacre, March 16, 1968. Photo by Ronald S. Haeberle, copyright © Time Inc., courtesy of Getty Images.

and time.[28] The massacres therefore delivered disturbing news about what ordinary Americans are capable of doing. And Charlie Company's typicality lent weight to VVAW's claims, confirmed by journalists' reports from the field, that atrocities were widespread.[29]

Reports of the My Lai massacre stirred thousands of other Vietnam veterans' misgivings about the war. Some had participated in or witnessed the wanton killing of civilians; many others returned to the United States with doubts about the rightness of America's military actions. Told that they were saving the country from Communism, they had discovered that the population in large parts of the Vietnamese countryside seemed indifferent, if not hostile, to the Americans' presence; much of the South Vietnamese army seemed to lack martial qualities; and the South Vietnamese government was repressive and corrupt. When they returned home, the veterans resented the fact that their fellow citizens seemed to be carrying on life as usual while Americans fought and died far away; and they were angry that they were now carrying the moral and psychological burden of the war, while civilians could keep it at a safe emotional distance. Many felt a barrier of communication between themselves and their fellow citizens and believed that they could talk about the war only to fellow Vietnam veterans.[30]

Veterans began to work through their experiences in "rap groups" that formed spontaneously when they gathered to talk in VVAW's Manhattan office. The veterans confided in and confronted one another in striving to discover the emotional and political truths of their time in Vietnam.[31] Bobby Muller, a VVAW supporter, said that those involved in the organization enjoyed "camaraderie, brotherhood, and a form of therapy, to just be able to work through all of what we needed to work through, sharing our experiences."[32] By affirming the reality and commonality of their experiences, veterans gained the moral strength to speak out publicly against the war. When they spoke at demonstrations and testified at mock war crimes tribunals, VVAW members set out to demonstrate the criminality of the U.S. war effort and, by undermining the war's moral basis, to hasten the U.S. withdrawal from Vietnam. But the former warriors' assumption of a public voice also had a therapeutic aspect.[33] Their testimony was the outward expression of their inner efforts to make sense of their experience, redeem the waste of war, salvage some self-respect, or atone for what they had done.

In 1970, the psychiatrist Robert Jay Lifton testified before a U.S. Senate subcommittee that events such as the My Lai massacre were endemic in Vietnam and were made more likely by the dehumanization that allowed troops to kill the enemy. He predicted that mild to severe psychological disturbances might emerge after lying dormant in veterans for months or even years. And he linked Vietnam veterans' psychiatric problems to the nation's moral quandaries: "The Vietnam veteran," Lifton said, "serves as a psychological crucible of the entire country's doubts and misgivings about the war. He has been the agent and victim of that confusion." The public and politicians were responsible, he argued, for allowing the war, and therefore the atrocities, to continue.[34] In May 1970, he and the psychiatrist Chaim Shatan spoke at a public meeting against the Kent State killings and the invasion of Cambodia. Members of VVAW attended the meeting, setting the stage for the collaboration between the therapists and the veterans.

In early 1971, Lifton testified at the "Winter Soldier Investigation," a nonjudicial war crimes tribunal that VVAW organized. As he had in his Senate testimony, Lifton said that the Vietnam War was an "atrocity-producing situation."[35] He helped persuade the veterans at the tribunal to focus on U.S. atrocities for a combination of political and therapeutic reasons: to erode public support for the war and to allow the veterans to confront experiences that had left them feeling confused and ashamed. The hearings brought together 150 veterans who described war crimes in which they had participated or that they had witnessed. As they explained, "We intend to show that the policies of [the] Americal Division which inevitably resulted in My Lai were the policies of other Army and Marine divisions as well." The veterans stated that the indiscriminate or deliberate killing of civilians was the U.S. forces' "standard operating procedure." They testified that American units tortured prisoners, raped women, and mutilated corpses. Whenever U.S. troops killed civilians, the witnesses said, the deaths were counted as Viet Cong casualties. The organizers structured the hearings so that participants testified according to their military unit. If veterans who served in geographically dispersed units and members of the same units who served at different times all testified about the same sort of events, their accounts would dispel the notion that the crimes were isolated incidents. The hearings would thus reveal that Americans' abuse of Vietnamese civilians was systematic, and they would demonstrate that war crimes were the inevitable result of American policies.[36]

After the hearings, the New York VVAW chapter invited Lifton, Shatan, and other therapists to join the rap groups. Shatan organized a volunteer panel of more than thirty medical professionals to meet with veterans, individually and in groups. The psychiatrists' position in the groups was unusual: the therapeutic model they used was not based on the "transference" relationship between therapist and patient, as in Freudian psychoanalysis and psychodynamic therapy; nor would the professionals be in a position of authority, which they normally assumed in group therapy. Instead, they were invited to join the groups as co-equals. The common thread they shared with the veterans was their opposition to the war.[37]

In the early 1970s Shatan and Lifton were deluged with inquiries from individuals and organizations around the country interested in setting up their own rap groups. The main reason for these approaches was the absence of effective treatment by the Veterans Administration (VA), the government-administered program of health and other benefits for veterans. By the mid-1970s, hundreds of rap groups had been organized. In Manhattan, several hundred veterans and some twenty therapists participated in the rap groups, individual therapy, or workshops that grew out of the rap sessions.[38]

Lifton said that the psychiatrists who participated in antiwar veterans' rap groups acted from a mix of political and therapeutic motives, just as the veterans did. The therapists, though, felt a tension between these motives. Early on, many practitioners thought that the veterans needed conventional group therapy and that to give them anything else would be to cheat them. Lifton and a minority of other therapists advocated a more unorthodox, politically engaged project. Although they appreciated the importance of therapeutic work, they were committed to the creation of a new political and therapeutic relationship: a dialogue between professionals and veterans based on a common stance of opposition to the war. According to Lifton, the friction between the two models for the rap groups—therapy or political activism—was never resolved, although the more politically motivated therapists tended to stay longer with the project. "Those professionals who conceived the effort in a more narrowly defined therapeutic way, and who I suspect were less politically and ethically committed to an antiwar position, tended to leave."[39] Wilbur Scott comments that "the rap group regulars—veteran and psychiatrist alike—intended to go public with their experiences and conclusions as a means of protesting the war. For many of them, the personal healing and political functions were flip sides of the same coin."[40]

The psychiatrists began to elaborate intellectual models for understanding the veterans' traumas. Shatan wrote that "Post-Vietnam Syndrome confronts us with the unconsummated grief of soldiers—impacted grief, in which an encapsulated, never-ending past deprives the present of meaning. The sorrow is unspent, the grief of their wounds is untold, their guilt is unexpiated." The veterans might seem cynical, Shatan said, but their "numbed apathy" arose from "a surfeit of bereavement and death." Building on Freud's essay "Mourning and Melancholia," Shatan argued that "psychic numbing" prevented the veterans from mourning and thus imprisoned them in a persistent state of resignation. Shatan also drew attention to the delayed onset of post-Vietnam syndrome. The syndrome, he observed, set in some nine to thirty months after veterans returned from Vietnam. As well as psychic numbing, veterans might experience rage, alienation, and the feeling of having been scapegoated. The press noticed Shatan's work and referred to Vietnam veterans suffering from post-Vietnam syndrome as "living wreckage," isolated, suicidal, with ruined relationships, drug problems, and employment difficulties.[41]

Like Shatan, Robert Jay Lifton argued that to avoid painful feelings such as guilt and anger, many veterans unconsciously resorted to psychic numbing, which, although it initially protected the psyche, restricted the veterans' capacity to live their lives fully. Some veterans, in contrast, indulged in excessive, "self-lacerating guilt," a continuous reenactment of retribution against the self. The healthier alternative Lifton proposed was "animating guilt," guilt given form and direction. Veterans could transcend guilt by releasing the energy it engendered.[42] Protesting against the war could, according to Lifton, constitute a "survivor mission" that would channel the veterans' guilt and anger to a productive and purposeful end. A survivor mission, he proposed, could help restore the meaning of which their lives were robbed when their participation in the Vietnam War submerged them in waste and degradation. In this sense, political action helped to fulfill the therapeutic ends of rap-group participation. In his Winter Soldier testimony, Lifton said that civilians who resisted "the truths of American atrocities" that veterans wanted to communicate impaired the veterans' "renewal," their "return." Sharing their truths with the wider society was a part of the veterans' "becoming . . . human" again after their war-induced dehumanization.[43]

The Nixon administration identified the politically engaged psychiatrists as enemies and harassed them in various ways, for example, tampering with Lifton's and Shatan's mail. It was not just that the psychiatrists supported antiwar activity. The notion that Vietnam veterans were psychologically traumatized was itself subversive. Clinicians and researchers took opposed positions depending on their theoretical allegiances and their attitudes toward the war. Psychiatrists who supported the administration's policy in Vietnam pointed out that the American Psychiatric Association's diagnostic and statistical manual did not include a listing for post-combat mental illness and they therefore denied the validity of post-Vietnam syndrome. In contrast, opponents of the war predicted an epidemic of psychological disorders among Vietnam veterans. As the Vietnam veteran and psychologist Charles Figley wrote, "The post-Vietnam syndrome became a frightening buzz word among clinicians and journalists but, in fact, was a thinly veiled position of opposition to the war: stop the war or more young killers will be released to terrorize the population." Traumatized veterans, in this account, were a symptom of the brutalizing horror of combat, and their psychiatric conditions became part of the debate about the rights and wrongs of the war.[44]

Many therapists in the key institution concerned with veterans' health needs, the VA, resisted seeing the roots of psychiatric patients' conditions in their service in Vietnam. At a VA hospital in Boston in September 1969, Sarah Haley, a newly appointed psychiatric social worker, interviewed her first patient. Anxious and agitated, he reported that he had been present at the My Lai massacre. He had not taken part in the killing and was afraid that some of his former comrades would make good on threats to come after him and kill him. The story had face validity: if his former comrades thought that he was a potential witness against them and were unaware of the White House decision that their civilian status gave them legal immunity, they had a plausible motive for hunting him down. Haley's psychiatric colleagues dismissed the story, though, and said that the patient was "obviously delusional, obviously in full-blown psychosis." This was the first of many atrocity stories that Haley encountered. In the next three years, she saw 130 veteran patients, of whom 40 reported that they were responsible for atrocities.[45] Haley wrote up her experiences in a frequently cited article.[46] By this time, other VA psychiatrists treating veterans had also run up against the resistances of the VA and began to treat the veterans in experimental groups that became precursors for traumatized veterans' treatment programs.

Floyd Meshad, a social worker in the Wadsworth VA hospital in Brentwood, California, contributed to an emerging treatment model geared to the needs of Vietnam veterans. Meshad had served in Vietnam as a military psychiatrist and was badly injured when the helicopter he was traveling in was shot down. On his return from service, he began to work for the VA, frequently ranging beyond the precincts of the Wadsworth hospital complex. He walked the shoreline around Venice and encountered hundreds of veterans sleeping in the open in Pacific Ocean Park, on or under the old Venice Pier. With the support of another psychiatrist, Meshad set up a Vietnam-veterans-only clinic at the hospital and persuaded some of the veterans to attend a rap group there. He also set up off-site rap groups, one near the beach, one in the predominantly African American neighborhood of Watts, and another in the barrio in East Los Angeles.[47]

Before practitioners could persuade the VA to address the needs of psychologically traumatized Vietnam veterans, they had to overcome a huge obstacle. The second edition of the psychiatrists' desk manual, the *Diagnostic and Statistical Manual of Mental Disorders (DSM-II)*, current at the time, contained no listing for war neuroses. The manual's first edition, *DSM-I*, published in 1952, included an extensive class of "gross stress reactions" resulting from exposure to "severe physical demands or emotional stress," including combat.[48] *DSM-II*, although published at the height of the Vietnam War, in 1968, omitted the gross stress reactions category, replacing it with "(Transient) Adjustment Reactions of Adult Life," which does not specifically concern exposure to trauma.[49] One example of an adjustment reaction involved fear of combat, but this was regarded as a transient, not a chronic, phenomenon, and there was no mention of delayed onset. As a result, Vietnam veterans with the symptoms of mental illness were rarely diagnosed with a war-related condition. Many psychiatrists failed to take a history of the veteran's service experience and made their diagnosis without knowing whether the patient had seen combat or had been in Vietnam at all. In the absence of a recognized classification for war neurosis, Vietnam veterans were diagnosed instead with personality disorders, depression, or schizophrenia, or with disorders such as alcoholism that ran concurrent with or were the consequences of their war-related conditions. Psychiatrists who worked

with a large number of Vietnam veterans, however, learned to recognize a recurrent pattern in their complaints and worked around the psychiatric nomenclature
by writing in an informal working diagnosis of "traumatic war neurosis" alongside
the official diagnosis couched in the *DSM-II* terminology.[50]

In 1974, the trustees of the American Psychiatric Association (APA) decided to
prepare a third edition of the manual, *DSM-III*, and set up a task force to develop a
new set of diagnostic classifications. The therapists who had worked in the rap groups
saw in *DSM-III* an opportunity to introduce a diagnosis covering the conditions of
traumatized Vietnam veterans. Official recognition of "post-combat syndrome"
would, they thought, allow the veterans to be correctly diagnosed and to obtain appropriate treatment and compensation. Lifton and Shatan approached Roger Spitzer,
the head of the *DSM-III* task force, to propose that post-combat syndrome be included
in *DSM-III*, and he set up the Committee on Reactive Disorders to study the matter.
The committee included three members of the APA's task force and three members
of the Vietnam Veterans Working Group, which Shatan had established.[51]

Lifton's earlier work with atomic bomb and Holocaust survivors provided him
with a model and a language with which to talk about Vietnam veterans' moral
anguish. He found that all three groups suffered from the "death imprint" as well as
"psychic numbing" and that these catastrophic experiences brought forth "universal
psychological tendencies."[52] Shatan was also struck by the similarities among the
experiences of Vietnam veterans, prisoners of war, and concentration camp survivors.[53] The working group came to believe that post-combat syndrome might be
an instance of a larger phenomenon encompassing people other than war veterans.
This view helped to broaden support for the validation of post-combat syndrome
beyond the core group of psychiatrists advocating for Vietnam veterans' needs. The
working group won over Nancy Andreasen, who chaired the APA's Committee on
Reactive Disorders and had observed stress reactions of the sort identified by the
working group among the burn victims she had treated. In 1976, the APA's Task
Force on Nomenclature and Statistics proposed that "Catastrophic Stress Disorders"
be included in *DSM-III*. The Vietnam Veterans Working Group persuaded the task
force to add "Delayed Catastrophic Stress Disorder" to the two categories, "Acute"
and "Chronic," that the task force initially proposed. In 1978, the Committee on
Reactive Disorders recommended that *DSM-III* adopt a diagnosis under the heading
"Post-Traumatic Stress Disorder." This diagnostic label appeared in *DSM-III* when
it was published two years later.[54]

Having shifted from "Post-Vietnam Syndrome" to "Post-Combat Syndrome" and
thence to "Post-Traumatic Stress Disorder" (PTSD), the diagnosis encompasses a
much broader set of conditions than war trauma. *DSM-III* defines PTSD as a condition involving "recurrent painful, intrusive recollections" or "recurrent dreams or
nightmares" of a stress-inducing event; in extreme cases, sufferers experience disso-
ciative states (popularly known as "flashbacks"). Other symptoms include diminished
responsiveness to the external world—or "psychic numbing"—hyperalertness, an
exaggerated startle response, sleep disturbances, and avoidance of activities or situations that might arouse recollections of the traumatic event. The traumatic stressor

is defined as an event outside the range of common experiences that will evoke significant symptoms of distress in most people. The kinds of stressors cited include rape or assault, military combat, natural disasters, accidents, bombing, torture, and death camps.[55]

From the start, critics were skeptical about the validity of the diagnosis—whether PTSD constituted a disorder distinct from other, established clinical diagnoses—and doubts about its clinical validity were increased by the breadth of its characteristic symptoms, spanning cognitive, emotional, and behavioral spheres.[56] These doubts left a lot of room for debate about how many suffered from PTSD. Whereas veterans' advocates and therapists initially proposed that between one-sixth and one-half of all Vietnam veterans might suffer from PTSD (between 500,000 and 1.5 million veterans), later estimates reduced this figure to a much smaller range: between 2 and 15 percent.[57] The description of PTSD in *DSM-III* had another basic problem: the designation of the condition as a single disorder, regardless of the type of stressor that causes the patient to develop symptoms. True, the *DSM-III* definition of PTSD institutes a distinction between natural disasters and stressors caused by human design, stating that the latter's effects can be more severe and longer lasting. It makes no distinction, though, between the trauma of perpetrators and of victims and does not recognize that the guilt that a patient feels might be justified according to an external standard. Instead, "guilt" is glossed as "guilt about surviving when others have not, or about behavior *required for survival*" (emphasis added).[58] *DSM-III* therefore ignores the possibility that someone might feel guilty as a result of having inflicted excessive, gratuitous, or indiscriminate violence on others—that is, not behavior "required for survival"—or of having participated in military operations that involved those kinds of violence. Counterintuitive though this might appear, it is consistent with Shatan's view that "the gap between victimizers and those once destined for the [concentration camp] ovens is narrower than might be expected."[59]

Lifton had insisted on moral clarity about the war, explaining, "To gloss over a veteran's relationship to the atrocity-producing situation and its contributing elements was to leave him with a socially induced psychic wound." Eliding the social and historical facts of the war would, according to Lifton, leave the veteran's recovery incomplete and would deny the veteran and society a "fuller grasp of, and a capacity to move beyond, the dubious place they had both been."[60] But his own views about PTSD failed just as completely. Through excessive historicization—subsuming the atrocities under their social and historical context—Lifton precluded a rigorous consideration of individual responsibility for criminal acts. The only valid ways of achieving the historical accounting that Lifton advocated would have been to identify individual perpetrators of particular crimes and follow the chain of responsibility upward to the commanders who were guilty of ordering or permitting the crimes; alternatively, the precedent of the post–World War II Tokyo and Nuremberg tribunals would have allowed one to start at the top by establishing the guilt of higher officers when units under their command had abused civilians. Lifton appeared uninterested, though, in identifying individual perpetrators because he wished to cast judgment on the war and on the nation as a whole.

Lifton's condemnation of the war was so sweeping that the taint of death immersion touched all its participants, with no significant distinctions of kind or degree. He believed that all Vietnam veterans were likely to have participated in or witnessed the willful destruction of civilian life and property, gratuitous cruelty, mutilation of corpses, or other atrocities; all might be equally inclined to feel guilty for having served in the U.S. forces or for having survived when others did not. As he described the Vietnam veterans' moral burden during his Winter Soldier Investigation testimony, "There's a quality of atrocity in this war that goes beyond that of other wars in that the war itself is fought as a series of atrocities. . . . Now if one carries this sense of atrocity with one, one carries the sense of descent into evil. This is very strong in Vietnam vets." Those who participated in the My Lai massacre were in an advanced state of numbing and brutalization, Lifton said, arising from the "malignant environment we created" in Vietnam, "an environment of murder." But in Lifton's view, not just the perpetrators of particular crimes but American society as a whole had become immersed in evil, so that "we are responsible for one long, criminal act of behavior in our project in Vietnam."[61] One can appreciate the tactical benefits of this position: spreading the responsibility for war crimes over the whole society helped to secure the political cooperation of Vietnam veterans because individuals were not singled out for blame. The problem was, though, that a responsibility shared by all might be claimed by none. Lifton's all-encompassing judgment of the nation and its citizenry was morally flawed on two equally serious grounds: it tainted all Vietnam veterans, including those innocent of any crime; and it allowed perpetrators to hide their personal guilt among the mass. Lifton's view was inconsistent with the laws of war, blurring the important differences between the responsibility of political and military leaders for national policy, the responsibility of particular individuals for specific crimes, and the position of others who had not committed criminal acts.[62]

The public too was reluctant to pin criminal responsibility on particular individuals, as became evident in its reactions to the guilty verdict in Calley's trial and to his life sentence. Many Americans were more exercised about the treatment of one of their own than about the murder of Vietnamese villagers. A Gallup poll found that almost four out of five Americans surveyed thought that the life sentence imposed on Calley was "too harsh."[63] Seventy percent felt that Calley "was being made the scapegoat for the actions of others above him."[64] Eighty-one percent of respondents to a Harris poll said that they were "sure there are many other incidents like My Lai involving American troops that have been hidden."[65] They were right: we now know that other American units participated in atrocities against Vietnamese civilians, but the Department of Defense successfully covered up these crimes for decades.[66] Eighty-eight percent of the public thought that higher-ups should also be tried for the crime of which Calley was convicted.[67] *Newsweek* captioned photographs of Calley and the massacre with the question, "Calley Verdict: Who Else Is Guilty?" *Time* accompanied a drawing of Calley with an almost identical query, "Who Shares the Guilt?"[68] Yet when no trials of higher officers took place, much of the public was content to resolve the "scapegoating" issue by urging leniency for Calley and pushing to the back of their minds the fact that those they believed were ultimately responsible for the atrocity walked free.

The Nixon White House received over three hundred thousand letters and telegrams, running a hundred to one for the release of Calley. "Free Calley" bumper stickers began to appear everywhere. Calley received four marriage proposals and two hundred people asked him to autograph his photograph in *Time* magazine and return it to them. A few days after Calley's conviction, future U.S. president Jimmy Carter, then governor of Georgia (where the court-martial took place), proclaimed a statewide American Fighting Men's Day and exhorted the citizens of the state to "honor the flag as 'Rusty' [Calley] had done." George Wallace, governor of neighboring Alabama, took part in the "Rally for Calley," organized by the American Legion. Governor Evan Whitcomb of Indiana ordered state flags flown at half-staff because of the verdict and asked Richard Nixon to pardon Calley. A record titled "The Battle Hymn of Lieutenant Calley" sold more than two hundred thousand copies within days of its release and was played by radio stations throughout the country.[69]

Both doves and hawks, congressional liberals and conservatives, criticized the supposed scapegoating of Calley. The journalists Rowland Evans and Robert Novak commented, "To doves, Calley's crime was a mirror image of American immorality in Indochina: the lieutenant had become a scapegoat for the sins of Presidents, Secretaries of Defense and four-star generals. To hawks, Calley was raised to heroic stature as the American warrior, tethered and restrained by politicians refusing to permit the military to seek victory."[70] Many VVAW members agreed that Calley was a scapegoat.[71] Peter Mahoney said that it was inconsistent to punish him while aerial bombardment and artillery fire killed countless Vietnamese civilians without anyone's being accused or punished. "How can we isolate and punish instances of criminality in a war that was totally criminal? Where is the logic of sending one man to jail for killing civilians with bullets and making heroes of others for killing civilians with bombs? Of course, that is the way of our society. Those who give the orders are never punished; only those who get caught obeying them are allowed to be crucified."[72]

"Every last Vietnam [veteran] is guilty along with Calley of committing war crimes," the leading VVAW member Jan Barry said, because the standard operating procedures of U.S. forces were violations of the laws of war.[73] John Kerry testified that he himself had participated in indiscriminate fire on civilians in free-fire zones, when "we would destroy every hut along the river bank and sink every sampan in sight," shooting any civilian who ran away, including "grandmothers and grandfathers and children."[74] After the Calley verdict, Kerry read a statement saying, "We are all of us in this country guilty for having allowed the war to go on. We only want this country to realize that it cannot try a Calley for something which generals and Presidents and our way of life encourage him to do. And if you try him, then at the same time you must try all those generals and Presidents and soldiers who have part of the responsibility. You must in fact try this country."[75] This could be considered a principled stance, but it could also be seen as self-serving, generalizing onto the whole of American society the responsibility for crimes such as those that Kerry himself admitted to. Few were willing to do what a group of VVAW members did when they went to the Pentagon, demanding to be arrested for war crimes "along with Lieutenant Calley."[76] Most of the witnesses at the Winter Soldier Investigation refused to cooperate with military investigators by allowing their testimony to be used to prosecute individual perpetrators.[77] As Kerry explained, they were calling for an examination of national policy and did not want to see ordinary servicemen convicted while their commanders walked free.[78]

No less an authority than Telford Taylor, the chief U.S. prosecutor at the Nuremberg tribunal, stated that if General Westmoreland and America's civilian leaders had been tried according to the standards applied in the post–World War II war crimes tribunals, they might well have been convicted.[79] The grounds for Taylor's view are hard to dispute: the legal standard determining a commander's responsibility for a crime is whether he knew, or ought to have known, that it was likely that a crime would be committed and took insufficient steps to prevent it.[80] Westmoreland knew before the My Lai massacre that American forces were abusing civilians in Quang Ngai and that they recognized no distinction between the civilian population and the Viet Cong guerrillas.[81] The practical result was that the civilians ceased to enjoy the immunity from attack to which their noncombatant status ought to have entitled them. This knowledge prompted Westmoreland to go to Quang Ngai to speak to the commander of the Americal Division. The steps that he took were clearly insufficient to prevent the atrocity, and Westmoreland admitted that he did not give instructions forbidding the killing of civilians. He later made statements that made it clear that he did not value Vietnamese people's lives.[82] Had the United States been a defeated and occupied country at the end of the war, rather than a superpower with undiminished control of its own territory and population, Westmoreland and others would probably have ended up in the dock.

In the absence of such an overturning of the institutions of government, it was hardly likely that any U.S. court would prosecute Westmoreland, no matter what tribunal precedents and international law seemed to require. Such a move would have constituted an indictment of the whole U.S. war effort and would have undermined the nation's system of political and military authority. What did seem possible, though, was a process of national self-examination. Frank Reynolds of ABC News said, "My Lai—those women and children are in our consciousness now and they are also *on* our conscience." "The massacre," Jonathan Schell wrote, "calls for self-examination and action." He went on, "If we deny the call and try to go on as before, as though nothing had happened, our knowledge, which can never leave us once we have acquired it, will bring about an unnoticed but crucial alteration in us, numbing our most precious faculties and withering our souls. For if we learn to accept this, there is nothing we will not accept."[83] This was a resounding call for the examination and mending of the nation's moral being. Neither the president nor the public, though, felt that their souls were in jeopardy; they certainly showed no interest in the route to salvation that Schell advocated.

With approval of Nixon's handling of the Vietnam War sinking and public sympathy for Calley at a high level, the White House considered how to handle the Calley verdict.[84] It delegated research on the legal issues to the office of the White House counsel John Dean. A young Vietnam veteran named Thomas Pauken working in the counsel's office advised Dean about how far, and in what ways, the president might intervene after Calley's court-martial delivered its verdict. Pauken made a subtle distinction between a "final review" that in general accepted the findings of the military legal process and a more active intervention—which he discouraged—that would set a precedent in cases of other court-martialed troops and would place the president in a difficult position. "If the President reduces substantially or remits the sentence of Lt. Calley," Pauken argued, "part of American public opinion and much of world opinion would accuse the President of endorsing . . . the commission of atrocities by American soldiers in Vietnam." Leaving a heavy sentence unchanged, though, would have its own drawbacks: if the president did this, Pauken argued, "he would be accused of undermining his own men in the field and permitting Lt. Calley to be sacrificed as a scapegoat." The White House counsel's office therefore advised a cautious approach.[85]

President Nixon, though, saw the matter in political, not legal, terms. Riding the wave of popular sympathy for Calley, Nixon ordered that, pending his appeal against his conviction, Calley should be released from the military stockade and confined to the relative comfort of the bachelor officers' quarters on the Fort Benning military base. Nixon then announced that he would personally review the case after any final sentence was decided, an action that, as Pauken had predicted, military officers saw as undermining the military justice system. The Pentagon was concerned that leniency toward Calley would confirm the widely held view that his actions were the product of the nation's war policy, and that Americans did not consider Asian lives as worthy of respect. The White House's main concern was how to improve Nixon's chance of re-election in 1972.[86] The Nixon administration therefore commissioned opinion polls to test various possible responses to the Calley conviction, allowing it to fine tune its actions to suit the public mood. The polls established that an overwhelming majority of the public supported the president's intervention in the case and a substantial number, about half the public, would have liked him to go further by freeing Calley right away. Nixon's approval ratings jumped by 13 percent as soon as he had announced that he intended to review the verdict and that Calley had been released from the stockade. Nixon concluded that the public gave little consideration to deaths of the inhabitants of My Lai. Blaming the "dirty rotten Jews from New York" for the media coverage of the massacre, he said to Henry Kissinger in language now familiar from his tape recordings, "Most of the people don't give a shit whether he killed them or not." Consistent with the public preference for leniency, Calley's life sentence was reduced, first by the reviewing authority to twenty years, then by the secretary of the army to ten years. In November 1974, after a confinement of three and a half years, Calley was paroled.[87]

Mary McCarthy criticized "the determination of the left not to consider *anybody* a war criminal short of a three-star general" (emphasis in original). As she argued, there was something like a tacit conspiracy, "a great nationwide breathing together of left, right, and much of the middle to frustrate punishment of the guilty."[88] It is hard to see how the left was responsible for the failed prosecution of middle-ranking officers, the consequence of which was that courts-martial of their commanders were likely to fail.[89] McCarthy's criticism of the left's moral complicity does, however, have some force: by using the massacre as a means of criticizing government policy but denying that lower-ranked soldiers should be punished, antiwar activists let all but higher officers off the hook. This stance made them complicit with right-wingers, who wanted no one punished, and with the majority of the public, who wanted no one scapegoated.

There was another basic problem in VVAW's approach. Their strategy of testifying about or confessing to atrocities succeeded to a degree in undermining the moral basis of the war, but the better it worked, the more it backfired. It "stirred the sentiment that many Vietnam veterans themselves were worthy of contempt," as Wilbur Scott remarks. "Even those in sympathy with what VVAW was trying to accomplish," he writes, "sometimes found it difficult to accept and make sense of the stories without despising those who reported them."[90]

Steven Silver, a psychiatrist sympathetic to the predicament of veterans, argued that American civilians blocked off any disturbing feelings about societal responsibility by stigmatizing veterans. "Vietnam veterans became outlaws, pariahs, whose distinctiveness from society was emphasized." Because Vietnam veterans were "symbols of an event [the Vietnam War] which was a severe stressor on the fabric of our country," other Americans found it convenient to turn away from them. Nonveterans could cast off feelings of guilt and failure by projecting them onto veterans, "relieving the psychological burden carried by people within society. Such," Silver ruefully commented, "is the purpose of scapegoats."[91] The veterans suffered a blanket moral stigma that was the logical correlative to the blanket legal exoneration they seemed to enjoy because of the government's evident lack of will to pursue most of the perpetrators of the My Lai massacre, and because the public suspicion that war crimes were widespread was not matched by military investigations and prosecutions of a scale congruent with that suspicion. Some civilians found it convenient to shun Vietnam veterans as repositories of national guilt; veterans anxious about civilians' indifference or hostility protected themselves from negative encounters by keeping their distance, but their doing so heightened the barriers between veterans and nonveterans.

The tense relations between Vietnam veterans and civilians augmented the difficulties of the veterans' readjustment to civilian life and compounded any psychological problems they experienced. The rate of neurospsychiatric casualties among veterans increased not in the period when the war was escalating but in the early 1970s, as the war was winding down.[92] This phenomenon may simply be an artifact of the delayed onset of psychiatric symptoms characteristic of PTSD, but some writers speculated that the rate of psychiatric illness might also have been worsened by changing societal attitudes toward the war, which the troops carried with them into the field and which affected their homecoming. James Reston has written that the combat veteran after 1968 was the first soldier "to be openly deprived of the battlefield mythology of gallantry and victory." After the My Lai massacre, veterans experienced "searing internal debate" that may have contributed to PTSD and other psychological and behavioral problems.[93]

The principal predictors for PTSD were the intensity and duration of exposure to traumatic stress.[94] However, environmental factors such as unit cohesion and morale could mitigate or exacerbate the effects of stress. Once a service member's tour of duty was over, the most salient environmental factor affecting the incidence of PTSD was the social support he or she received. The homecoming experience was therefore seen to play an important part in contributing to or intensifying veterans' postwar distress.[95]

The way veterans returned to the United States worsened the problem. Most troops in Vietnam joined their units as individuals, rather than shipping to the theater of war with a cohesive unit, and each had his own DEROS (date of expected return from overseas). American psychiatrists and recruiters during World War II had come to the realization that everyone has a breaking point and even the bravest soldier will collapse eventually under the strain of continuous combat. This principle became the basis for manpower policy during the Vietnam War. The armed services designated one year (or thirteen months for marines) as the normal tour of duty for troops in Vietnam, with each individual entitled to a rest and recuperation leave partway through the tour.[96]

The fact that everyone had his (or, in the case of nurses and other female personnel, her) own DEROS tended to undermine the military units' esprit de corps and exaggerated the isolation that veterans felt when they returned to the United States. As Shatan writes, they "returned piecemeal—without their units, without their buddies, and with no parades to welcome them."[97] Departure from Vietnam often brought combat veterans ambivalent feelings: joy and relief at having survived but guilt at leaving the field when one's accumulated experience might keep one's buddies alive. When a service member rotated back to the United States, instead of shipping back with a unit that had served together for the duration of the war, as many troops did at the end of World War II, he or she traveled as an individual, often by air. A veteran could be back in the United States within forty-eight hours of being in combat.[98] This rapid transition precluded a period of reflection on the war experience and prevented veterans from "decompressing" by sharing their thoughts and feelings with their peers.

Veterans long afterward complained that the nation's military and political leaders did little to ease the transition—for example, by instituting a debriefing process to allow veterans to come to terms with their memories of combat. Part of the reason for this inattention was that the individualized tour-of-duty policy had seemed at first to work well, because the psychiatric casualty rate was much lower during the Vietnam War than it had been during World War II and the Korean War.[99] This figure was deceptive, though. First, troops in Vietnam who might otherwise have been discharged as psychiatric casualties were treated instead as disciplinary cases or were given administrative "general discharges," thus artificially lowering the psychiatric casualty figures.[100] Second, the prospect of an approaching DEROS encouraged troops suffering from the strain of combat to hang on until the end of their tour, sometimes self-medicating with alcohol or drugs as a way of coping. Initially experiencing relief when they reached the end of their tour of duty, veterans were unprepared for postwar emotional troubles.[101] As clinicians and researchers into post-traumatic stress discovered, the symptoms of delayed stress (by definition) often appeared months or years after exposure to the stressor—for Vietnam veterans, long after their return from the field.

The social divisions in opinion about the war meant that Vietnam veterans received criticism from both sides: opponents of the war sometimes expressed hostility to veterans, and supporters of the war said it was not fought effectively and that servicemen were in part responsible for this failure. The veterans were called "baby-killers" and "losers," drug addicts and suckers.[102] Arthur Egendorf, a rap group coordinator who conducted a government-sponsored study of Vietnam veterans, remarked that the typical homecoming stories were of two kinds: at an American Legion hall or Veterans of Foreign Wars post, World War II veterans asked Vietnam veterans, "We won our war. How come you didn't win yours?" Alternatively, the veteran returning from Vietnam got off the plane in Oakland and some hippie spat on him, calling him "baby killer."[103] Figley offers a typical statement by a veteran that is almost identical to Egendorf's: "The first day home I was called a 'baby killer' by my kid brother and the 'bunch who lost the war' by some drunk down at the VFW [Veterans of Foreign Wars post]."[104] William Broyles, editor-in-chief of *Newsweek* and a marine lieutenant in Vietnam, wrote, "Veterans were spit on and jeered at and turned away from jobs as likely drug addicts or crazies. We had no parades, no speeches. At best we were treated with a tolerant politeness, as if we had just recovered from a disease that was so socially embarrassing it best not be mentioned."[105] As Christian Appy has written, stories about protesters referring to veterans as "baby killers" or returning veterans being spat at by hippies (often female) became parables of social rejection, stories that summed up Vietnam veterans' sense of being mistreated.[106]

The "baby killer" vignette appeared so frequently in veterans' accounts of their relations with civilians that it evolved into a kind of shorthand: a pithy summary of perceived insults, sidelong glances, or embarrassed silences, concentrating the psychological truth of this profusion of encounters and feelings in an economical sketch. Detached from the historical events that motivated the accusation, the parable became a plaintive expression of veterans' resentment at their unfair treatment by society. Veterans who describe such encounters turn the accusation against the accuser and transform themselves from accused perpetrators to injured parties—"look," the veterans implicitly say, "this is what they accuse us of doing; this is what they unjustly call us." Astonishingly, even veterans who admitted that they killed children in Vietnam complained that they were called "baby-killers" when they returned, as though they could safely assume that their listeners would automatically agree that the accusation is always unjustified.[107]

Two large-scale surveys, conducted in 1971 and 1979, asked Vietnam veterans to describe their postwar experiences and asked nonveterans about their attitudes toward the veterans. In 1979, 29 percent of Vietnam veterans believed that what the United States did to the Vietnamese people was "shameful." Only 60 percent of veterans had always been proud to wear their uniforms in public places when they were home on leave. A quarter were happier when people did not know that they had served in Vietnam. Thirty percent, among them 39 percent of "non-whites," agreed with the statement, "Coming home was a big let-down because so few people appreciated the service you had put in."[108]

Although the majority of the public said that they had positive attitudes toward Vietnam veterans, there was still a sizeable minority who did not: 18 percent of the general public and 20 percent of those who thought the United States should have stayed out of Vietnam said they had an unfavorable attitude toward Vietnam-era veterans.[109] The fact that almost one-fifth of the public admitted having unfavorable attitudes toward them might have translated into a large number of negative encounters between Vietnam veterans and others, with cold-shouldering, if not active hostility. As Brende and Parson write, when the veterans talked about their war experiences they often found that "those to whom they were talking seemed bored, scared, repulsed, anxious or even angry." After a few such encounters, "most Vietnam veterans 'shut off' and adopted a personal policy of silence about Vietnam."[110] But the perception that veterans were treated unsympathetically by some bothered others. As the authors of the 1971 survey summed up, "the whole question of the treatment of returning veterans is a serious burden on the conscience of the American public."[111]

For all their sympathy, the public perceived Vietnam veterans as victims; their feelings for the veterans were more pity than respect. In 1971, 61 percent of the public agreed that the Vietnam War was one that the United States could never win. Forty-nine percent thought that Vietnam veterans were "suckers," having risked their lives in the "wrong war in the wrong place at the wrong time."[112] By 1979, this figure had grown: 63 percent of the public and 57 percent of Vietnam era veterans agreed with the statement, "Veterans of the Vietnam War were made suckers, having to risk their lives in the wrong war at the wrong place at the wrong time."[113] Myra MacPherson wrote that these figures indicated a "growing sympathy" with Vietnam veterans.[114] But the rising number who thought that Vietnam veterans were suckers also signifies a measure of condescension, even disparagement, and the solidification of the notion that veterans were victims.

Compounding the stigma they carried, veterans also saw themselves portrayed in the media as psychopaths and criminals. Robert Brewin, a Vietnam veteran, observed in 1975 that the Vietnam veteran was the "bad guy of the moment" in cop shows, which always needed villains.[115] Such representations, a simplistic and negative version of the emerging psychiatric knowledge about Vietnam veterans' psychological difficulties, suggested that veterans were "walking time bombs," "depraved fiends," and "psychopathic killers" plotting evil or ready to respond to provocation with explosions of violence.[116] Lazy script writers who needed to establish the motivation of some deranged criminal found a ready-made "bad guy" in the stereotype of the drug-abusing, psychopathic Vietnam veteran, prone to flashbacks in which he would return to combat mode.[117] For example, in one episode of the *Kojak* detective show, in the investigation of a murder, Kojak (played by Telly Savalas) instructed his staff to round up suspects by obtaining a list of "recently discharged Vietnam veterans."[118] Brewin suggested that presenting veterans as bad guys also allowed American society to deflect lingering guilt arising from the whole Vietnam experience, particularly the My Lai massacre. According to Brewin, after seeing veterans portrayed repeatedly on television as sadists, criminals, and drug addicts, their minds twisted by their wartime experience, employers became wary of hiring veterans and the public shunned them.[119]

In the late 1970s, feature films were replete with images of psychologically disturbed veterans unable to readjust to civilian society.[120] Travis Bickle (played by Robert De Niro), the main protagonist in the film *Taxi Driver*, is a marine Vietnam veteran, and there is little other explanation for his isolation and his murderous campaign to cleanse the city's streets.[121] In *Apocalypse Now*, the assassin Captain Willard (played by Martin Sheen) describes how difficult his homecoming was. At the end of his first tour in Vietnam, he finds himself at home waking up to "nothing." In a voice-over, Willard says, "I hardly said a word to my wife until I said yes to a divorce. When I was here [Vietnam] I wanted to be there. When I was there all I could think of was getting back into the jungle." Willard says about the U.S. command, who ordered him to kill an officer whose methods had become "unsound": "I began to wonder what they really had against Kurtz. It wasn't just insanity and murder—there was enough of that to go around for everybody." From the maverick officer and demigod Colonel Kurtz (Marlon Brando), to the surf-loving martinet Colonel Kilgore (Robert Duvall) and the visionary photographer, Kurtz's disciple Hurley (Dennis Hopper), it is difficult to find any sane character in *Apocalypse Now*, and the war itself is represented as a hallucinatory nightmare.[122]

Two other films of the late 1970s offer an alternative to *Apocalypse Now*'s representation of the evil and madness of the war. The film *Coming Home* is loosely based on the postwar experiences of the antiwar veterans Ron Kovic and Bobby Muller, its script commissioned by Jane Fonda after she saw conditions in a VA hospital.[123] Much of the early part of the film is set in a hospital in 1968 and we see many veteran patients, badly injured mentally and physically. One says, in passing, that he suffered flashbacks about the incident in which he was injured; another troubled young man kills himself. In the opening scene, a veteran explains to a group of fellow patients why some justify the war and say they would fight again: they have to lie to themselves, he says, or else admit that the war had no good purpose, that their buddies' lives were wasted, and that their injuries were for nothing. The film thus teaches its audience about the damage and disillusionment the war brought on Americans who fought.

The drama turns on the contrast between two marines. Luke Martin is a wheelchair-bound veteran (played by Jon Voight) who takes the path to emotional health when, true to Lifton's creed, he turns his anger at the government into antiwar action, chaining himself to the gates of a marine induction depot and lecturing to a group of high school students. Bob Hyde (Bruce Dern) is a troubled but repressed active-service officer who returns from Vietnam with a minor, self-inflicted wound.

Frustrated by superiors who will not let him fight effectively and appalled by subordinates who mutilate the bodies of the enemy, he is a cauldron of rage and confusion. During an R and R leave, his wife, Sally (Jane Fonda), asks him what the war is like. Bob cannot answer her. He says the war is what it is but is not "like" anything. After his return from the war Bob threatens Sally with an assault rifle, calling her a "slope cunt" (a derogatory reference to Vietnamese women) when he finds out that she has been having a relationship with Luke. Ultimately, with his brand of violent masculinity obsolete and his quest for heroic stature unfulfilled, Bob is able to escape his anguish only through suicide. The didactic message condemns misogyny and celebrates a new kind of man, expressive, in touch with his feelings, and able to communicate his determination that other young Americans will not follow in his footsteps by going to war.

In *The Deer Hunter*, a similar repertoire of emotional and physical injury portrays the war's effects. Here, too, a veteran of the war in Vietnam is unable to describe the war to anyone who was not there. A soldier in dress uniform enters the bar where a community celebrates a wedding before three of its number go to Vietnam. All he can say in response to their questions about the war is, "Fuck it." One of the friends, Steven (played by John Savage), returns from Vietnam a triple amputee, temporarily reducing his wife, Angela (Rutanya Alda), to bed-ridden mutism. Michael (Robert De Niro) returns from Vietnam without disabling wounds but finds it difficult to be close to others. "I feel a lot of distance. I feel far away," he says. Nicky (Christopher Walken) loses his mind after being captured by the Communists and is unable to communicate to hospital staff or to call his girlfriend, Linda (Meryl Streep), at home. He goes AWOL in Saigon, spending his time reenacting the psychological torture his Vietnamese captors inflicted on him when they forced him to play Russian roulette. Nicky becomes a star performer in Russian roulette contests, gratifying callous Vietnamese gamblers who bet on which of two competitors will die.[124] Michael tries to rescue Nicky, returning to Saigon when it is about to fall to the Communists. The rescue attempt fails when Nicky shoots himself. Somehow Michael manages to return Nicky's body to the United States, despite the imminent fall of Saigon. The film ends with the community reconstituted, grieving for Nicky and singing "God Bless America."

The Deer Hunter and *Coming Home* presented millions of Americans with a sympathetic image of troubled veterans in need of understanding, no longer a source of inexplicable menace. Figley, as an expert on PTSD, applauded the two films, saying that they heralded "the beginning of the end of the Vietnam nightmare."[125] He also celebrated the fact that some television shows were beginning to exhibit a new "enlightenment" about the psychological predicament of Vietnam veterans, saying that this would have a "healing effect." Meanwhile, Vietnam veterans began to write novels and memoirs about the war and the homecoming experience that helped American readers understand their moral quandaries and psychological difficulties. Books such as Philip Caputo's *A Rumor of War*, Tim O'Brien's *If I Die in a Combat Zone*, and Ron Kovic's *Born on the Fourth of July* asked their readers to see the veterans not as brutish killers but as people who had struggled with the perplexities of fighting against an elusive enemy in Vietnam and who faced more turmoil when they returned to an indifferent America.[126]

By 1979, as the large-scale Harris survey demonstrated, by and large, the public felt sympathetic toward Vietnam veterans. According to the stereotypes and complaints by the veterans' advocates, they were isolated, vilified outcasts and the public and prospective employers were hostile, indifferent, or fearful. The attitude of the survey respondents, though, indicates that negative attitudes toward veterans were not widespread among employers. For example, in 1979 employers rated Vietnam veterans at 9.3, on a "feeling thermometer" scaled from 1 to 10, with 10 the warmest and 1 the coolest. This rating was considerably higher than the one they gave news media, members of Congress, antiwar demonstrators, and draft evaders.[127]

At the end of the 1970s, in another reflection of the growing understanding of and sympathy for veterans' needs, the state finally began to address the war's psychological consequences. Legislation to provide Vietnam veterans with postservice treatment had failed in Congress repeatedly in the 1970s, defeated because of the resistance of the "iron triangle" of traditional veterans' organizations, the VA, and unsympathetic congressional committees. In 1971, Senator Alan Cranston (D., California), chairman of the Senate Subcommittee on Veterans' Affairs, introduced legislation that would have provided substance abuse and readjustment counseling for Vietnam veterans. The American Legion and the Veterans of Foreign Wars, dominated by World War II and Korean War veterans, did not want resources shifted from existing programs. The VA was equally committed to the status quo.[128] Because the bill emphasized alcohol and drug problems, it carried a controversial antiwar implication: it suggested that having fought in the war was somehow turning the veterans into addicts. The notion that they needed to use substances to mask their feelings or make daily life more bearable led, by a train of associations, to all the things about the war that Americans had done their best to forget. As Cranston had said in describing the proposed legislation to the VFW, "Vietnam veterans seem especially likely to suffer from these [substance abuse] problems." This suggestion that the Vietnam War might have been uniquely distressing "pressed a very sore nerve" and was a "reminder of the controversy, of the unrest, of the political turmoil and other images that swirled around our last and longest war."[129]

Cranston's bill was defeated in the House Committee on Veterans' Affairs, whose membership was dominated by World War II veterans who insisted that "a veteran is a veteran is a veteran," and that Vietnam veterans needed the same basic health care programs that had served previous generations. Critics characterized the proponents of treatment programs for Vietnam veterans as "crackpot, screwball, self-serving psychologists and psychiatrists who were probably all against the war anyway and were only looking for a surefire way to get some money out of the Veterans Administration." Worse still from their perspective, opponents of the legislation identified it with members of VVAW, who were "probably all crazy before they got into the service in the first place."[130] The House committee members were generally more hawkish than their Senate counterparts and they subsequently defeated the bill several times after it was approved by the Senate committee.

The APA's acceptance of the PTSD diagnosis was important in overcoming congressional resistance to the provision of special programs for Vietnam veterans. Congress finally passed the legislation in 1979 when the APA was in the process of incorporating post-traumatic stress disorder into *DSM-III*, after the VA had accepted the draft definition of "post-traumatic disorder."[131] The political battle lines had by then been redrawn: members newly elected to Congress after the Watergate scandal, including some Vietnam veterans, were more inclined to question vested interests. Some of them became members of the relevant congressional committees. Jimmy Carter's election to the presidency in 1976 brought Max Cleland, a disabled Vietnam veteran, into position as administrator of the VA. Cleland drew attention to the neglect that Vietnam veterans experienced, saying that they never had a ticker-tape parade and were considered "co-conspirators in some escapade with sinister undertones. . . . No wonder so many of them feel confused, or even guilty."[132] The VA stopped opposing the bill. The Disabled American Veterans organization lent its support to the legislation, the first of the mainstream veterans' associations to do so.

In July 1979, Carter signed into law PL 96-22, establishing the Vietnam Veterans Outreach Program. The law mandated the VA to establish storefront outreach centers (colloquially, "vet centers") staffed by professional counselors, with veterans among their practitioners and support personnel. Cleland dedicated the first such center in November 1979 and by 1981, 137 centers around the country were up and running.[133]

The vet centers reached out to veterans who mistrusted the government and who were reluctant to set foot in VA facilities, whose psychiatric wards had a ghastly reputation.[134] The vet centers' staff profile helped to overcome the doubts of the most hard-to-reach clients: by the end of the second year of the outreach program, 80 percent of vet center employees were Vietnam veterans and 50 percent were minorities.[135] Even after *DSM-III* legitimized PTSD, many VA doctors and clinicians were skeptical about the validity of the diagnosis. Thus, a large part of the burden of treating veterans with PTSD fell by default on the vet centers and there was a huge pent-up demand for their services from veterans who had been unable to obtain treatment elsewhere. In their first year of operation, the vet centers served a quarter of a million clients.

Anger and grief were everyday fare at vet centers and VA medical centers and they often had a political edge. "Hardly a day goes by now that I don't see at least one of the Vietnam veterans who is asking ultimate questions about the morality (or immorality) of the Vietnam conflict," wrote a chaplain whose pastoral experience stretched from a college in 1969 to a medical center in 1982.[136] But assessing the relative weight of individual and collective responsibility for morally questionable actions was made difficult by institutional approaches to therapy. A practitioner in southern California vet centers and VA facilities said that the therapists depoliticized the veteran patients' moral questioning. "A more professional model," he explained, supplanted the earlier use of "peer counseling" and "rap groups." The "professional" approach excised politics from therapy because politics distracted attention from what was seen as the proper locus of treatment and recovery: the individual psyche. "Following early [group therapy] sessions, in which discussions of politics and the VA are tolerated to promote group identification and cohesion, these topics are discouraged; they foster a 'victim' mentality, with its inherent dynamics of externalization, blame, self-pity, and dependency." The picture one gets is of patronizing therapists indulging the veterans in their complaints, but only long enough to get them comfortable with the group; then the "real" business of therapy would begin. Discussions of politics and complaints about the VA detracted from the preferred approach, an "intense commitment to personal responsibility for problems and their solutions, rather than externalization and blame."[137] *Externalization* and *blame* were pejorative terms from the perspective of the "professional" approach because they detracted from personal responsibility. But "externalization" and "blame" are another way of describing historical and moral judgment. As an observer of therapy in a VA psychiatric unit noted, centering the whole burden of responsibility on the individual patient without providing an acceptable route to expiation, reparation, or forgiveness tended to leave patients stuck with persistent guilt.[138]

Illustrating the difficulties VA psychiatrists had in finding a consistent approach to questions of responsibility, other therapists encouraged veterans to eschew responsibility for their actions—to "de-responsibilize" them—by attributing the actions to external causes. If they addressed guilt at all, these therapists concentrated on survivor guilt.[139] Both approaches—rejecting or encouraging externalization—evaded the historical accounting that might have been indispensable to successful therapy because they precluded the patient's efforts to weigh his own responsibility in relation to that of others.

It was not just the VA's bureaucratic rules that prevented the examination of moral questions. Therapists unable to take on an emotionally difficult burden unwittingly preempted the veterans' revelations with a reflex exoneration or sympathy that blocked off emotionally costly avenues of talk.[140] If, as one psychotherapist proposed, the "real pain of PTSD lies in the oscillation between self-condemnation and furiously blaming others," a therapist's arresting the working-through of these feelings was likely to leave the veteran patient at an impasse.[141]

In 1982, the depoliticization of therapy in the vet centers took a further step with the VA's appointment of Arthur Blank as director of the outreach program. Blank's background might have led one to think that he would support a politically engaged approach to therapy. Blank was an in-service psychiatrist in Vietnam who had taken an active antiwar stance after his return to the United States. He was an early member of VVAW and organized its Connecticut chapter. At a demonstration in 1967, he said that Vietnam veterans had a "special duty" to tell the American people "what our country is doing to the people of Viet Nam and to our own soldiers there." In 1975, Blank set up a treatment program for psychologically traumatized Vietnam veterans at a VA medical center while teaching at the Yale University Psychiatric Institute, where Lifton was one of his colleagues. Blank's VVAW credentials were not unusual. In 1982, 10 percent of the vet center program's staff were former members of VVAW.[142]

Under Blank's stewardship, though, the vet centers—under attack by Reagan administration budget cutters, and therefore politically vulnerable—aimed for "professionalization," replacing many of the streetwise peer counselors with university-trained nonveterans. Blank also downplayed his former VVAW membership, at one time even denying that he had been a member. After the Reagan administration announced that it opposed extending the program beyond 1984, Blank ordered that the vet centers stop giving support to causes perceived as left wing. For example, he ordered his regional managers to prevent discussions of the Agent Orange issue, which pitted veterans' advocates against chemical companies. He directed the vet centers to stop their outreach work to veterans in prison. He restricted the amount of time that counselors could spend in a session with a client, aiming to increase the through-put of veterans so that the centers might be seen to deliver value for money. Some likened this "numbers game" to the preoccupation with the body count in Vietnam.[143] But Blank saw the cost-effectiveness of the program, measured by the number of clients seen, as a defense against charges of wastefulness.[144] Congress rewarded Blank's leadership in 1983 by passing PL 98-160, which extended the life of the vet centers program until 1988. By 1985, the number of vet centers had increased to 189 nationwide and Congress authorized continued funding until 1989 at least.[145]

Blank edged away from the original vision of vet centers reaching out to veterans in the neighborhoods where they lived and which they frequented. He set out to relocate the vet centers from their storefront locations to VA hospitals, and nine centers were so moved. He resisted the ambition of counselors like Meshad to reach out more to homeless veterans. He neglected the specific needs of female veterans.[146] In a telling conflict, Blank clashed with Jack McCloskey, the team leader of San Francisco's Waller Street vet center. McCloskey's background was in therapy outside the auspices of the VA. In the 1970s, through the organization "Twice Born Men," he developed an innovative approach to therapy and training of Vietnam veterans, by means of a self-help program.[147]

McCloskey had been a leader of VVAW—variously, the president of the San Francisco chapter, the California state and regional coordinator, and briefly the national president—and he still insisted on wearing his VVAW and War Resisters' League buttons to work. The strength of his commitment to antiwar work arose from the conviction that the war was wrong. This realization imposed an overwhelming moral imperative on him, because, he said, if the war was wrong, "then my buddy died for nothing. . . . The only way we could justify the deaths of our buddies over there was by saying, 'We've got to stop it.'"[148] In 1979, a veterans' organization he helped to found, Swords to Plowshares, won the first lawsuit against the VA, forcing it to pay retroactive compensation to a veteran suffering from delayed stress. He was outspoken and had a good deal of nerve: from the audience, he began an impromptu dialogue with Jimmy Carter at a White House reception, speaking out about Vietnam veterans' unmet needs.[149] McCloskey drove in the vet center car to demonstrations against the Reagan administration's policy in Central America. As he described his "survivor mission": "I had made promises to dead people that this shit wouldn't happen again."[150] Antiwar posters and a dartboard decorated with Reagan's likeness hung in the vet center.[151]

As if his espousal of left-wing causes were not sufficient to incur the displeasure of his superiors in the VA, McCloskey made his own position more vulnerable by allowing alcohol to be drunk at the vet center and, as rumor had it, by imbibing heavily himself. McCloskey refused Blank's order to check the DD-214 discharge papers of new clients before counseling them, with the result that some of the clients his staff saw turned out not to have been Vietnam veterans at all. These misdemeanors provoked the concern of his erstwhile ally Meshad, the manager of the outreach program's western region, who had his own difficulties with Blank, and for whom McCloskey was becoming a liability. Faced with the hostility of both the regional manager, Meshad, and the national director, Blank, McCloskey responded to an ultimatum by resigning from his post at the Waller Street vet center. His fate was symbolic of the purging of other activists from positions in the outreach program, marking a shift away from the politicized rap groups to a more bureaucratic and professional model.[152]

Once Vietnam veterans had secured access to treatment in VA facilities and in the vet centers, therapists and other veterans' advocates began to encourage a broader social "healing" process that would benefit the veterans and society. Veterans' advocates argued that if the public treated veterans with indifference or hostility, the chances that a veteran might develop PTSD correspondingly increased. The corollary was that the nation would benefit veterans by offering them sympathy and understanding. Figley's hope for a "healing effect" was typical of a usage that became ubiquitous in the late 1970s.

The terms *trauma* and *healing* signified all sorts of personal and social afflictions related to the Vietnam War, and their remedies.[153] Writers in military-oriented publications, scholars, journalists, and activists demonstrate how far this language had spread. In an article titled "The Collapse of the Armed Forces," Colonel Robert D. Heinl argued in 1971 that social turmoil and political betrayal had reduced the morale, discipline, and battle-worthiness of U.S. forces to possibly their worst level in history. He suggested that the military's travails "mirror the agonizing divisions and social traumas of American society."[154] Political commentators and scholars used the word *trauma* to describe both the period of American involvement in Vietnam and the war's subsequent after-effects in American society.[155] "Vietnam is the wound in American life that will not heal," *Time* magazine wrote in reporting the conviction of Lieutenant Calley.[156] A VA medical center staff member wrote of the "scars" from Vietnam remaining on the national conscience.[157] Referring to social divisions as a bleeding wound, a poem advocating amnesty for war resisters read, "Let them come, those who fled, / back to our bleeding nation / and let the wound be healed / before it is too late."[158]

Adding to the confusion of terminology was the dual meaning of the word *syndrome*, as applied to the post–Vietnam War context. Whereas post-Vietnam syndrome had been a precursor of post-traumatic stress disorder, referring to a psychiatric condition, "the Vietnam syndrome" was used to refer to U.S. foreign policy. The term became labile. Depending on the context, it might refer to a public aversion to military risk-taking overseas, to a condition suffered by Vietnam veterans, or to a broader "trauma" in American society—and this overlay of meanings suggested an association among all three phenomena. In 1973, Lifton had written, "Some veterans, ambivalent about having the term 'post-Vietnam syndrome' applied to themselves, suggest that it is more genuinely applicable to America at large."[159] The idea caught on. The draft resister and journalist Howard Wolinsky said, "They talk about the post-Vietnam traumatic syndrome as a psychiatric problem in some devastated vets, but I believe the term fits the whole country."[160]

The similarity between "post-Vietnam syndrome" (veterans' psychological condition) and "the Vietnam syndrome" (the weakening of the U.S. international position because of its post-war hesitancy) is telling. The use of *syndrome, trauma,* and *healing* to refer both to veterans' psychological state and to the nation's strength and unity suggested that somehow veterans' health and the nation's interlocked. The metaphorical extension of the health-related terminology treated political problems as medical ones, shifting the discursive terrain from the strategic to the therapeutic arena. The solution to the nation's problems would be found not in the critique of American power but in ameliorative care.

In July 1978, the therapist Jeffrey Jay wrote, "The veteran's conflicts are not his alone, but are bound to the trauma and guilt of the nation. And our failure to deal with our guilt renders the veteran the symptom-carrier for society and increases his moral and emotional burden."[161] The public sensed that they owed the veterans a debt. As the authors of the 1979 Harris survey wrote, "Public attitudes are flavored with more than a tinge of guilt, while for many veterans of the Vietnam era, the reception accorded them by their peers remains a source of resentment and of the feeling that their sacrifices have not been appreciated, particularly by the nonveteran members of their own generation."[162] The recognition that the nation's negative feelings about the war, when projected onto the veterans, compounded their stress, imposed an imperative on the public to treat veterans better.

The benefits would not, however, be restricted to the veterans; they would be reciprocal. Egendorf said that veterans could help their fellow citizens by working through their war experiences and thus assisting the nation to find meaning in the sacrifices of the war years: "American society ultimately gains from their efforts to derive significance from the confusion and pain still associated with that conflict."[163] Or, as another therapist, Harry Wilmer, said, veterans' combat nightmares were "symbolic of our national nightmare." For the veterans and the nation to recover, veterans had to overcome their reluctance to talk about the war so that Americans could "face the nightmare horror—hear it, see it, know it."[164]

In the early 1980s, the idea took hold that veterans' and society's wounds had to be healed together. "The veterans are the human part of this story [of the Vietnam War;] . . . they are among the 'scar tissue' of our society. Because the war itself was the wound, we now must sit down and listen to veterans tell their stories and help them deal with their own consciences. We need to learn what they did, what they were forced to do, and what they were forced to endure since the war."[165] The co-ordinator of a Veterans Administration PTSD program wrote that the "encounter between a returning army and its society is not so much the lancing of an abscess by the physician as it is a vast and dynamic process for a nation." This encounter, he reflected, constituted a "healing dialogue" between the veteran and the nation, and within each of them.[166] The veterans as scar tissue; the war as a wound to be healed or cauterized, an abscess to be lanced; the aftereffects of the war as a national trauma: this language suffused discussions of the legacy of Vietnam as the 1970s turned to the 1980s.[167] It was time for the nation to confront the nightmares of its past in order to heal. Just as public sympathy would be the key to the veterans' well-being, listening to the veterans would be the path to national recovery. Shatan said, "We dare not turn away from [Vietnam veterans] and their unique knowledge."[168]

Vietnam veterans remained figures about whom the public had some ambivalence, though. The inadequacy of the juridical response to the My Lai massacre left no clear path to resolving the question of how high up the responsibility for the killings went, or how widely shared the guilt was. Given the public's suspicion that atrocities were common, and because the identity of most of the perpetrators was unknown, any Vietnam veteran might conceivably have committed or witnessed such crimes. Blameless Vietnam veterans therefore felt unjustly stigmatized whenever nonveterans exhibited discomfort with or hostility toward them. Americans struggling with the moral consequences of the war felt a paradoxical push-and-pull reaction to veterans: listening to veterans might help the veterans and the nation as a whole to confront the nightmares of the past; but turning away from veterans could keep painful ideas and feelings about the war at bay.

The residue of unallocated guilt continues to exert a pernicious effect on the lives of Vietnam veterans. What My Lai reveals about the U.S. conduct of the war ought to have troubled Americans ever since, although the burden of conscience appears to have weighed more heavily on Vietnam veterans than on others.[169] Veterans who played no part in atrocities in Vietnam understandably wished to shed the blame that unjustly adhered to them. Typical of such views is the statement by the late Lewis Puller, a marine officer in Vietnam, who wrote that he was "deeply offended by the notion that the hideous atrocities committed by Calley and his men were commonplace in Vietnam."[170] At a panel discussion on the Vietnam War, three of the five speakers, all Vietnam veterans, denied that any atrocities had taken place in their area of operations in Vietnam.[171] Their denials betray two tendencies: the wish to distance themselves from the disturbing knowledge of the human capacity for evil, and a defensive response to the taint of atrocity that has touched all Vietnam veterans. One of them, Harry Summers, never ceased to repeat that the My Lai massacre was an aberration.[172] Another veteran told a reporter, "*I* never killed a kid in my life. Never killed, never raped any women" (emphasis in original).[173] Thomas Kiley, a Quincy, Massachusetts, veteran said, "I don't have any guilt about Vietnam. I neither witnessed nor took part in any atrocities. Nor did anybody else in my platoon."[174] Despite the intent of these uncoordinated statements to deny that atrocities were widespread across South Vietnam, they draw attention to veterans' persistent anxieties about their perception by the public. No Vietnam veterans that I have met defend Calley's actions, but many offer explanations for his actions and try to balance the My Lai atrocity by bringing up atrocities committed by the Viet Cong, such as the killings at Hué during the Tet Offensive. Their complex responses imply that they believe that it was a concatenation of circumstances that made Calley a killer; that others might have done the same as he did, in his place.[175]

Vietnam veterans continued for years to struggle with the question of moral responsibility left over from the My Lai massacre, a ghost that refuses to be exorcised. In March 1996, one of the contributors to the Vietnam veteran–oriented "vwar-l" talklist raised the issue of American-perpetrated atrocities in the Vietnam War. The query touched off a heated exchange that reveals how painfully sensitive veterans are to the suggestion that all Americans are responsible for atrocities. In the midst of the exchange, one Vietnam veteran contributor strongly contested the charge that "we are *all* responsible [for the atrocities committed in Vietnam by Americans]." He wrote, "Speaking for myself, I was *not* responsible for any atrocities. I never saw one, never knew first hand of one, or had any authority to prevent one. Should I have refused to go to 'Nam? Is that why I am responsible? Because I am an American?" (emphasis in original).[176] Another veteran wrote, "Continuing on in this extremely narrow inquiry keeps alive the despicable notion of Vietnam veterans, as a lump, being monstrous babykillers. I survived that once, and have no intention of seeing the issue raised again. I am not a babykiller, nor mangler of Viet Namese civilians. I killed people who were trying to kill me."[177] Yet the sense of injury that the "baby killer" image provokes is the best evidence that the issue remains alive for Vietnam veterans, no matter how unfair they believe the stigma of atrocities to be. The continuing output of conferences and publications in the decades after the end of the Vietnam War also testifies to the persistence of the My Lai massacre as an unsettled issue.[178]

The journalist Peter Marin interviewed a number of psychologists and psychiatrists, all of whom found it difficult to help Vietnam veterans resolve their guilt about having committed atrocities.[179] Veterans, Marin said, were not helped by being portrayed as victims of the society that had sent them to war who could be compensated by increased acceptance and gratitude at home. The veterans' problems were moral; they had a profound sense of having done wrong.[180] But Marin stated only half the problem. The other half was that many veterans angrily denied having done any wrong whatsoever. Depending on the stance they took, these veterans were divided by a chasm that therapists were unable to traverse and disturbed by moral questions that juridical and psychiatric institutions alike seemed unable to resolve.

The trouble with much of the psychiatric discussion of veterans' mental illnesses was that it muddied the problem and tended, Marin said, "to empty the vets' experience of moral content, to defuse and bowdlerize it." Marin questioned the assumptions underlying the composition of a published table that listed a number of stress-producing events. One of the items in the list was "Death of Buddies and Atrocities," an amalgamation that seemed to Marin to make performing or witnessing atrocities morally or psychologically equivalent to enduring the deaths of one's friends.[181] He also suggested that attributing the feeling of guilt to delayed stress "obfuscates the real nature of the veterans' experience." Marin's analysis leads us to the insight that a narrowly conceived psychiatric approach to veterans' problems—and a popularized, media-friendly advocacy of "healing" for veterans—may be profoundly misconceived if they fail to engage with the historical, political, and ethical sources of veterans' pain and anger. These approaches may leave Vietnam veterans as the symptom carriers for a society that refuses to recognize unpleasant facts about its past. The superficially appealing "healing" that memorials promoted in the 1980s may thus be a willful misconstrual of the nation's needs, irrelevant to veterans' psychological problems, and ultimately ineffective in solving them.

According to Marin, psychological terms such as Shatan's "impacted grief," whose appearance of medical precision mask their vagueness and wooliness, become "systems of denial, a massive, unconscious cover-up" in which veterans and nonveterans "hide from themselves the true nature of the experience the words are supposedly identifying."[182] Eric Dean argues that, as a result of the efforts of the early theorists of the disorder, PTSD cast its net widely over aspects of human behavior that had not previously been classified as indicative of mental illness. PTSD is such a grab-bag of symptoms that it may pathologize the normal grieving process and the normal disturbances that arise as a result of exposure to or participation in violence.[183] We can see this as part of a larger social phenomenon: the fixing under the medical gaze of a continually increasing portion of human thought and behavior. The effects of the initial medicalization of veterans' pain and anger were compounded by the institutional approaches to therapy. With the depoliticization of the modes of treatment that the early activist psychiatrists advocated, Vietnam veterans' moral repugnance at the war was transformed into a psychiatric symptom. Dissidence became pathology.

Once the war ended, the antiwar veterans movement dwindled in size.[184] Veterans' special status in protest movements also diminished. As one antiwar veteran put it, "We are no longer dissidents against the war but just hippies."[185] The antimilitaristic potential of the veterans' witnessing diminished as the 1970s gave way to the 1980s. Veterans remained plaintive figures but the public discourse had now shifted: among therapists, veterans' advocates, and media discussions of veterans' predicament, the complaints were more about how they were mistreated after their return home, not about how they were used as instruments of national policy in Vietnam. The remedy for their moral pain and for the nation's ills would be found not in a transformation of the United States' global posture but in a task closer to home: recognition by their fellow citizens.

When a metaphorically extended medical terminology described the nation's predicament as a larger version of veterans' ills, the psychiatric discipline's blank spots also expanded across this wider discursive field. Psychiatric institutions had demonstrated their unwillingness or inability to address Vietnam veterans' moral pain. When a morally vacuous "healing" emerged as a solution to both veterans' and society's wounds, its promise of a therapeutic solution appealed to Americans who were fed up with the residue of division, uncomfortable silence, and ill-feeling left over from the war but who were unready for the painful work of self-criticism that a proper historical accounting of the nation's wrongdoing in Vietnam would require. As we see in the next chapter, the principal popularizers of this discourse of healing were the creators of the Vietnam Veterans Memorial.

3

THE DISCOURSE OF HEALING AND
THE "BLACK GASH OF SHAME"

The Design of the Vietnam Veterans Memorial

★

ON JULY 1, 1980, within a few months of the American Psychiatric Association's validation of the condition Post-Traumatic Stress Disorder (PTSD), President Jimmy Carter signed the congressional resolution authorizing the creation of a Vietnam Veterans Memorial in the nation's capital.[1] The Vietnam Veterans Memorial Fund (VVMF), the memorial's sponsors, espoused a depoliticized version of the discourse of healing and reconciliation that emerged in discussions of Vietnam veterans and the "post-Vietnam syndrome" in the 1970s. The fund eschewed the antiwar politics that the activist psychiatrists and Vietnam Veterans Against the War promoted as part of the veteran's "survivor mission"; and they refused to say, as Reagan would the following month, that the war was a "noble cause." The VVMF stated that the memorial would be apolitical and would make no statement about the war, because they wanted to appeal to Americans with any shade of opinion. Avoiding politics while creating a war memorial may seem impossible, but it appeared to be a necessity to the VVMF because the war still divided Americans. Proposed monuments in Washington had to negotiate a path through a thicket of red tape and a maze of regulatory bodies; this bureaucratic approval process provided ideologically motivated opponents many opportunities to obstruct memorial projects and the VVMF wanted to avoid the obstacles that had snared some well-known predecessors.[2]

Jan Scruggs, the founder and president of the VVMF, appeared at first glance an unlikely leader of a national commemoration effort. In Vietnam, Scruggs was a junior noncommissioned officer—a corporal—in the 199th Infantry Division. His background was working class—his father was a milkman and his mother a teacher in Bowie, Maryland. His lowly military status and humble origins proved to be virtues, because they seemed to offer implicit guarantees of the project's neutrality. As the public face of the VVMF, Scruggs presented himself as an ordinary American and a representative of the "grunts"—the foot soldiers that America had sent to fight in Vietnam. Scruggs refers to himself in an article about the memorial as "a redneck and all that," and most of the writers who have dealt with the story of the memorial follow Scruggs's self-presentation by emphasizing his lowly origins: Chris Buckley calls him a "redneck" and "grunt"; Elisabeth Bumiller uses the phrase "a determined, scruffy veteran"; Tom Wolfe describes him simply as a "prole."[3] Scruggs was not a politician attempting to exploit the "lessons" of Vietnam for policy purposes; he was not, in any obvious way, an ideologue with an axe to grind. As such, Scruggs was the ideal figurehead for a memorial project that always claimed that it was independent of the government and that campaigned under the banner of political neutrality.

Scruggs's memoir introduces him as a twenty-nine-year-old veteran inexperienced in the ways of Washington, who had never seen a press conference, let alone held one, until he announced the creation of the VVMF on May 28, 1979. He had been inspired by seeing the film *The Deer Hunter* on the tenth anniversary of the day in Vietnam when a mortar round set off an explosion in an ammunition truck, injuring him and killing his buddies.[4] The scenes in *The Deer Hunter* showing young blue-collar men, Vietnam-bound, in industrial western Pennsylvania deeply affected Scruggs. Unable to sleep that night, he experienced a flashback of the day he was wounded. Scruggs saw pieces of bodies and human organs scattered around him. He saw the faces of those who had died but could not recall all their names. The next morning, Scruggs told his wife, "I'm going to build a memorial to all the guys who served in Vietnam. . . . It'll have the name of everyone killed."[5]

Scholars treating the history of the creation of the memorial have taken this account at face value as the originating moment for the memorial.[6] Among the details that are often recounted is Scruggs's naïve statement to reporters at his first press conference that "the only thing we're worried about is raising too much money." After several weeks, as Scruggs ruefully confessed in his memoir, the wire services reported that the VVMF had raised only $144.50, a pittance compared to the $1 million that Scruggs estimated creating the memorial would require. The paltry sum provoked wry smiles and jokes on network television.[7]

In other autobiographical passages, Scruggs writes that about 90 percent of his infantry company were draftees and half of them were killed or wounded during the "year-long nightmare" in Vietnam.[8] The young private who saved his life when Scruggs was wounded became one of the casualties, killed in an ambush.[9] Massive protests against the war during his tour of duty undermined the sagging morale of troops in the field. Scruggs bitterly recalled carrying the lifeless bodies of close friends through the mire, and this bitterness, he said, would probably never subside. Scruggs complained that the media had committed "collective character assassination" by stereotyping Vietnam veterans as "violence-prone, psychological basket cases." This characterization redoubled problems for the returning veteran: "Upon returning from the war, I, like many others, found that being a Vietnam veteran was a dubious distinction. The true tale of the Vietnam amputee being told 'It serves you right' after returning to college illustrates the psychological quagmire that the youngest-ever corps of U.S. veterans endured upon coming home. To many it was, and still is, an embarrassment to admit having served in Vietnam."[10] This description of Scruggs's postwar experiences matches the complaints of other veterans and seems to explain his personal motivation for wanting a memorial that would recognize and honor those who served. His personal accounts do not tell the whole story of the memorial's origins, though, and his self-deprecating narrative about his early naïveté does not do justice to the man.

Scruggs was no ordinary "grunt." After serving in Vietnam, he took a master's degree in counseling psychology at American University and conducted a psychological study of the effects of the war on college veterans. As a graduate student, he was influenced by Robert Jay Lifton's work on the survivor complex, studying the experiences of survivors of the Holocaust and Hiroshima. His work was sufficiently well regarded that he testified before a congressional committee in favor of the vet center program in 1976 and 1977, well before seeing *The Deer Hunter*. Scruggs's research addressed Vietnam veterans' emotional distress, low self-esteem, high divorce rates, and political alienation. He believed that Vietnam veterans suffered because society's conflicts about the war made it turn away from them. In Scruggs's mind, helping veterans to recover from the aftereffects of the war was tied to the twin tasks of fostering national reconciliation and breaching the divide between veterans and nonveterans.[11] While he was researching his master's thesis he formed the idea that a memorial honoring Vietnam veterans could overcome the nation's divisions.[12] He also believed that a memorial could provide veterans with a place to confront and make peace with the ghosts of the past, thus easing the "survivor guilt" from which many of them suffered.[13]

Scruggs's research was published in the journal *Military Medicine* and was footnoted in scholarly work on PTSD.[14] William Greider wrote about Scruggs's work in the *Washington Post*, to which Scruggs contributed an op-ed piece in May 1977.[15] In this column, Scruggs wrote that, for Vietnam veterans, "The victory parades and hero status awarded to previous generations of military returnees were simply not present. . . . There is a major issue here for this country to resolve, for the indifference and lack of compassion that the veterans have received is, to a large degree, a reflection of our lack of national reconciliation after Vietnam." The discussion of the veterans' poor welcome is familiar from the literature on PTSD, and the claim that "national reconciliation" would help has precedents. Scruggs, though, added a new proposal to these established arguments: "No efforts can provide compensation, of course, to the Americans who made the ultimate sacrifice in Vietnam. For them, perhaps, a national monument is in order to remind an ungrateful nation of what it has done to its sons."[16] This proposal for a national memorial appeared almost two years before his *Deer Hunter*–inspired flashback.

This record of research, testimony, and publication demonstrates that, while his account of his reaction to watching *The Deer Hunter* is undoubtedly true, Scruggs's pose as an ordinary "grunt" inspired by a flashback to create the memorial was just that: an artful piece of public relations that made for a compelling *Mr. Smith Goes to Washington* story line, the sort of thing that the press lapped up. If any reporters saw beyond the personal narrative, the media coverage of Scruggs's story in the next few years gives few signs that they thought his lobbying or his academic work would interest their readers.

Scruggs's proposal for a memorial flowed, however, not just from his personal experiences as a veteran but also from the therapeutic discourse about veterans' adjustment problems. Naming the dead was intended, he said, to further "cathartic healing."[17] One of the orthodoxies that Scruggs borrowed from the therapeutic community was that one should separate the warrior from the war, recognizing the service of the warrior without honoring the war itself. In writing about returning veterans' treatment by civilians, the psychologist Charles Figley had said, "I wish this country could have two cognitive notions. One, being ashamed of this war. Two, being proud of its veterans."[18] Elaborating this idea, he wrote, "The tragedy is that many who fought the war, beginning with the Vietnam Veterans Against the War, ended up condemning the warrior as well."[19] Unfortunately, few Americans could or would "separate the warrior from the war."[20]

It was not just Scruggs who heeded this idea. It was also taken up by the president. Carter said in 1978, "Because the war did not have the full backing of the American public, neither did those who fought in Vietnam. Many civilians came to confuse their view of the war with their view of those who were called upon to fight it. They confused the war with the warrior. Yet I know that all Americans join me in stating that the courage and patriotism of those who served in Vietnam have earned them full measure of honor and respect."[21] The VVMF's concept of "separating the warrior from the war" in order to honor those who fought had its roots in the therapeutic discourse about veterans and enjoyed the sanction of the top echelon of government.

Later, Scruggs disclosed that he wanted the names on the Mall as way of "getting even for the people killed in Vietnam. Just getting their names up on a wall in Washington, DC, was an act of revenge, a way of getting even for their deaths."[22] Scruggs did not express his motives in this language while trying to get the memorial built. His resentment superficially contrasts with the more benign language of healing and reconciliation. Actually, the language of revenge gives a complementary undertone to the VVMF's official discourse: catharsis, healing, and revenge are all paths to restitution or resolution, expressing a wish for balance after things have gone out of kilter.

While Scruggs was leading the memorial project, his language tended to focus on his personal motives for its creation (the screening of *The Deer Hunter* and his flashbacks) rather than its academic foundations or its connections to political rhetoric, highlighting his experience as an ordinary foot soldier and veteran rather than his professional training. In its publicity materials, the VVMF embraced the logic of the psychiatric discourse about veterans' adjustment problems but popularized it by using ordinary language, appropriating the powerful metaphor of "healing" to provide a compelling rationale for the memorial. The VVMF emphasized the veterans' difficult homecoming experience rather than what they did in Vietnam; the Liftonesque notion that veterans needed to undertake an antiwar "mission" to heal from the war was long gone. The mission now would be building a memorial, welcoming the veterans home, and uniting a divided society.

In an early statement to one of the bodies with oversight responsibility for monuments in Washington, DC, the VVMF wrote: "The Vietnam Veterans Memorial is conceived as a means to promote the healing and reconciliation of the country after the divisions caused by the war. Through support of this project, Americans of all political persuasions and opinions regarding the rightness of the national policy in Vietnam may express their acknowledgment of the sacrifice of those who served there. The memorial will further the psychological readjustment of the veterans of the war, for whom there were no parades."[23]

The memorial fund demonstrated their own short memory in claiming that there were no parades; there had been some, but they did not gibe with the prevailing idea that veterans had been mistreated on their return home, and so the parades were ignored or forgotten.[24] Be that as it may, the principles set out in its statement were ones that the VVMF adhered to with perfect consistency throughout all the subsequent debates about the shape the memorial should take. Veterans' need for healing became the basis of a sentimental appeal to Americans to put aside their differences. The veterans' emotional needs trumped matters of strategy and politics.[25]

Scruggs first pitched the idea of a memorial at a planning meeting for the Vietnam Veterans Week declared by Congress in May 1979. The other participants in the meeting dismissed the idea, saying that veterans needed practical help and benefits, not a memorial.[26] Scruggs's message was timely, though. Others were beginning to see a link between unifying a nation divided by the war and addressing Vietnam veterans' unmet needs. Congressional leaders in the Vietnam-era Caucus, consisting of those who had served in the military during the war years, recognized that the first step toward the twin goals of national unity and healing for the veterans was to separate those who fought from the historical event. As Representative Wayne Grisham (R., California) said, "We may still have differing opinions about our involvement in the Vietnam War, but we are no longer divided in our attitudes toward those who served in Vietnam."[27]

The president himself drew attention to the way Vietnam veterans' needs had been neglected. "There were no chamber of commerce proclamations," Carter said during Vietnam Veterans Week, "no bands that played martial music to welcome back most of the veterans of that war." He said that those who served in Vietnam had demonstrated an "extra measure of patriotism and sacrifice" because they fought without the support and appreciation of those back home. Many opposed the war, and Carter recognized their right to do so, but the unhappy result was that both during and after the war, Vietnam veterans were treated "as an unfortunate or embarrassing reminder of the divisiveness of the war itself."[28] Scruggs's call for the nation to recognize veterans and distinguish them from the war itself thus chimed with the views of the nation's highest elected official.

Scruggs won his first ally at the Vietnam Veterans Week planning meeting: Robert Doubek, an attorney and former air force intelligence officer.[29] On Doubek's advice, they formed the Vietnam Veterans Memorial Fund, Inc., as a nonprofit corporation.[30] Having joined forces with Scruggs, Doubek adopted the same line of reasoning, that there was a link between recognition of veterans and the imperative of national reconciliation. As Doubek wrote a few months later to the director of the Washington State Department of Veterans Affairs, "Even while a fitting and proper acknowledgment by the American people of the service of Vietnam veterans is long overdue, the memorial may ultimately address an issue of even greater significance— the reconciliation of the divisions in our society due to the war. Through support of the memorial, Americans of all political beliefs and opinions regarding U.S. policy in Vietnam can unite in expressing their acknowledgment of the sacrifice of those who served there."[31] News reports about the VVMF's fundraising problems caught the eye of a Washington insider, Jack Wheeler, a graduate of West Point, Yale Law School, and Harvard Business School, who was assistant general counsel at the Securities and Exchange Commission.[32] He contacted Scruggs and offered his help. Wheeler compared his occasional studies at Virginia Theological Seminary with Jan Scruggs's training at American University, saying that their backgrounds, respectively in theology and psychology, had convinced both of the necessity for a healing process. In fact, Wheeler foreshadowed the memorial fund's themes as early as June 1978, when he advocated healing and reconciliation for veterans. "There is much in [Vietnam veterans'] lives to heal and much to affirm. Learning from Vietnam will proceed, if at all, only when our country can fully acknowledge the integrity of service and the embodiment of cherished values in the soldiers sent to Vietnam; and full reconciliation with our living veterans requires this same acknowledgment, perhaps as much as it needs a just resolution of veteran claims to education, medical and work assistance."[33] Wheeler's message was similar in ethos and language to Scruggs's plea for healing and reconciliation. The three veterans made common cause. Scruggs, Wheeler, and Doubek assumed the key administrative posts in the VVMF, with Scruggs as president, Wheeler the chairman, and Doubek the project director and secretary.

Wheeler was an intense and temperamental character, often charismatic, sometimes overwrought.[34] Wheeler grieved for friends of his who had died in Vietnam, West Point classmates whom he revered and who, unlike Wheeler, had volunteered for combat duty in Vietnam. Not just Scruggs and Wheeler but almost all of the veterans who became involved in the memorial seem to have been laboring under heavy emotional burdens or powerful moral imperatives—a duty to ensure that the dead were remembered, to redeem their loss, and, for some, to vindicate the war effort itself.

Three former West Point classmates of Wheeler's joined the support team: Art Mosley and Richard Radez became officers of the VVMF and proved to be efficient administrators; Tom Carhart had no official title in the VVMF but was a willing office volunteer and lobbied for the VVMF on Capitol Hill. Carhart had gone through his training as a West Point cadet specializing in pranks, the most notable of which was stealing the Naval Academy mascot, a goat, before the Army–Navy football game.[35] In Vietnam, Carhart had commanded infantry platoons and was wounded twice. He briefly led the "Tiger Force," which became notorious after the war when it was revealed that the unit had committed atrocities and "kill[ed] anything that moved" in its area of operations, man, woman, or child.[36] He was the rare veteran who spoke candidly about the rush of combat: he found it "thrilling" and became "elated" in battle. "I killed—and I enjoyed it."[37] His superiors described Carhart as exemplary in qualities such as courage and enthusiasm, but they also felt he was impulsive and sometimes showed poor judgment. Carhart was relieved of two commands in Vietnam, in part because of his tendency to follow his own, sometimes idiosyncratic, sense of duty rather than unquestioningly obeying his superiors. He had disobeyed orders by participating in the Phoenix program, assassinating Viet Cong suspects. He had a tendency to become unglued and once struck an enlisted man—one of the most disgraceful things an American officer can do, according to the creed of the U.S. armed forces. Eventually, his volatility and single-minded pursuit of his own moral convictions would become a problem for the VVMF. Early on in the memorial fund's life, though, he managed to secure a $45,000 bank loan to pay for the mailing of a million fundraising letters, without any collateral apart from his "sacred honor."[38]

Wheeler recruited another mover and shaker, James Webb, a highly decorated marine veteran and a rising star on Capitol Hill.[39] Webb became a member of the VVMF's National Sponsoring Committee. Like Carhart, Webb was a combat veteran who had commanded an infantry platoon in Vietnam, his trademark being "loyalty to his men and insubordination to his superior officers."[40] He had good connections in the Republican Party, having served as the minority counsel for the House of Representatives Committee on Veterans' Affairs. Webb made his political mark by opposing Carter's plan to extend a pardon to some deserters and to upgrade the discharges of veterans who had received less than honorable discharges. In contrast, he pleaded for clemency and an honorable discharge on behalf of a marine veteran convicted of the point-blank shooting of a group of unarmed women and children in Vietnam. Webb argued that they were not "innocent civilians" because of his supposition that they supported the Viet Cong.[41] He had also written a well-received novel, *Fields of Fire*, in which one of the characters muses plaintively that there is no memorial to those who bled and died in Vietnam. The novel points out the inadequacy of domestic "welcome home" parties for returning troops still numb from the fighting.[42] The Vietnam veteran's "anonymity and lack of positive feedback," Webb said, "have intensified all the other difficulties he has faced.... With the exception of a few well-publicized disaster stories, he is invisible."[43] He was proud of his service in Vietnam, telling an audience gathered to see him awarded the Department of Veterans Affairs' first Vietnam Veteran of the Year Award: "To be blunt, we seem to have reached the anomaly where the very institution, and the same newspapers, who only a few years ago called on us to bleed, have now decided we should be ashamed of our scars. Well, ... I'm not ashamed of mine."[44] Webb's strong convictions about the Vietnam War and the treatment of veterans gave him compelling reasons for involving himself in the memorial; but his self-righteous prickliness and the strength of these convictions sharpened conflicts when others disagreed with him. Webb and Carhart, with similar political perspectives, became friends.[45]

Apart from Scruggs, these officers and supporters of the VVMF had been junior officers in Vietnam—lieutenants and captains. Wheeler, Carhart, Radez, Mosley, and Webb were graduates of the elite service academies at West Point and Annapolis. However, they represented a range of views and experiences of the war. Webb remained strongly convinced of the rightness of America's war. Carhart had turned

Figure 5. Southeast Asia Memorial, United States Military Academy, West Point, New York. Created by the West Point Classes of 1960 through 1969, in Memory of Their Classmates Who Fell in Battle in the Vietnam Conflict, dedicated October 1980. Photo by author.

against the war for a time, worked for the antiwar presidential candidate George McGovern's election in 1972, and applied to join Vietnam Veterans Against the War but then resolved in his mind the United States had been right to fight the war. Wheeler, Radez, and Mosley were not so sure. While in uniform Wheeler had questioned the merits of the war and, unusually for a West Point graduate, did not volunteer to serve in one of the combat arms in Vietnam. He was given permission to attend business school after graduating from West Point, and he spent his time in Vietnam operating the computers that kept track of progress in the statistics-driven war effort. Radez and Mosley were opposed to the war and, while in Vietnam, signed a petition supporting the Vietnam moratorium. Their different judgments about the rightness of the war drove a wedge between Webb and Carhart and the others; and the fact that, apart from Scruggs, only Webb and Carhart had been in combat was another dimension that set them apart. Both in Vietnam and after the war, combat troops tended to denigrate those who served in noncombat billets, referring to the latter as REMFs (rear echelon motherfuckers), and this derision appears in Carhart's writing and resonates in interviews.[46]

Wheeler had raised funds for a Southeast Asia memorial (fig. 5) on the grounds of the United States Military Academy at West Point and drew on this experience when he volunteered to help create a Vietnam memorial in Washington, DC.[47] Some of the veterans from whom Wheeler solicited funds resisted donating for a memorial to a historical experience that had been painful and disillusioning for them. Supporters of the memorial had a range of views. Wheeler's classmate Major Wesley Clark (later, the supreme commander of NATO and a presidential candidate) believed the Vietnam War had been a "noble cause"; others believed that the war had been a terrible mistake. What united them was an agreement that a traditional memorial—a realistic statue—would not do.[48] Wheeler settled on the concept of a landscape design and discovered that promoting this concept aided his fundraising efforts. His experience at West Point, he said, "showed that in the current America people are most attracted to landscaped-type memorials," because such memorials are uncontentious and preserve "park-like settings for people to use." Landscape memorials are nonspecific in meaning and are conducive to a healing process—or so he thought.[49]

The West Point Southeast Asia Memorial, funded by the graduating classes of the 1960s, is set along a reservoir and consists of winding pathways, stone benches, and a tree stump, signifying lives cut short. Contrasting with this memorial is a statue, a few steps away physically but a generation and a world away iconographically (fig. 6). Donated by the West Point classes of 1935 and 1936 (who had led troops in World War II), the American Soldiers Monument is dedicated to the American fighting man. The statue, by Felix de Weldon, hails passing traffic from a pedestal and shows an officer in a 1940s-era uniform with his arm stretched in a "follow-me" stance, leading

Figure 6. American Soldiers Monument, United States Military Academy, West Point, New York; Felix de Weldon, sculptor. Presented to the Corps of Cadets by the Classes of 1935 and 1936, dedicated 1980. Photo by author.

two men into battle. The two memorials represent different generations, in subject matter and in style, and so one is surprised to read the inscriptions indicating that both were dedicated in the same year, 1980. The different preferences of the World War II–era veterans and the Vietnam veterans, the first for a traditional-looking sculpture, the second for a landscape memorial, foreshadow some of the aesthetic debates that surrounded the VVMF in the next two years.

The plan to create a memorial in the nation's capital needed political support. Two Republican senators from states bordering the District of Columbia became the memorial fund's most important supporters in Congress: Senators Charles Mathias of Maryland and John Warner of Virginia. Senator Mathias advised the VVMF that the best way to handle the bureaucracy that often delayed efforts to create memorials in Washington was to have Congress pass legislation authorizing a memorial and designating its site. Mathias himself suggested the location: Constitution Gardens, on the Washington Mall, the commemorative core and the symbolic heart of the nation, between the nearby Lincoln Memorial and the Washington Monument. One could not imagine a more prominent or desirable location for a memorial. The VVMF organizers heeded the warning that contention about the memorial design might prevent the allocation of land to a memorial project.[50] The legislative grant of a prominent site before the selection of a design would reduce the risk that the memorial effort would bog down in bureaucratic inertia, its momentum disrupted by aesthetic disagreements. The VVMF enthusiastically pursued Mathias's plan, preferring Constitution Gardens to another proposed site, a more remote location across the Potomac River.[51] As Doubek said, "We thought the most important thing for the memorial was a prominent site because the Vietnam veterans had been shoved aside for so long."[52]

Introducing the legislation authorizing the construction of a memorial in honor and recognition of America's armed forces in Vietnam, Mathias used the memorial fund's language of reconciliation: "For all Americans, this memorial will express the spirit of reconciliation and reunion that preserves us as a nation. The Vietnam War provoked a bitter debate at home and divided families and generations. Today, Vietnam is now far enough in the past that we can look hopefully to the reconciliation of the country after the divisions caused by the war."[53] Mathias said that a location on the Mall was symbolically appropriate because it was once the scene of demonstrations, a battleground of opinion and a locus of dissent regarding America's role in Vietnam. It was also fitting that the memorial be placed near the Lincoln Memorial, because not since the Civil War had the nation suffered "divisions and wounds" as grievous as those caused by the Vietnam War. In the words of Lincoln's second inaugural address, Mathias said it was time to bind up the nation's wounds and he proposed that "the question of the morality of the war must be laid aside. . . . Time has a way of reconciling us to history. Wounds heal. Divisions mend."[54]

Senator Warner, closely associated with military causes and a member of the Senate Armed Services Committee, joined Mathias as a sponsor of the legislation. In December 1979, with the memorial fund desperately short of money, he held a fundraiser for defense contractors that raised $40,000 in donation pledges.[55] One by one, other senators joined them as co-sponsors of the legislation until they achieved unanimity. The Senate passed the bill authorizing the memorial on April 30, 1980, the fifth anniversary of the Communist forces' capture of Saigon.

When Representative John Hammerschmidt (R., Arkansas), a member of the House Veterans' Affairs Committee, introduced the legislation in the House of Representatives, he recited an angry speech written by Webb, in which Webb settled old scores with antiwar protesters. Webb felt the "hurt of an angry decade" before veterans began to gain some recognition, when they were left to "stew in the bitter juices of an effort begun nobly and ending ignominiously."[56] Webb was angry that antiwar activists had claimed the role of spokespersons for their generation. Webb had a point: even the veteran antiwar activist Bobby Muller acknowledged that, although the spokespersons for the Vietnam veterans community up to that time were generally left-wing and antiwar, they did not represent the whole Vietnam veteran population, most of whom had not been heard from.[57] Webb also said he resented the fact that members of Vietnam Veterans Against the War had transformed their antiwar activities into career-enhancing credentials, as World War II veterans had once done with their campaign ribbons.

Defying the VVMF's doctrine of reconciliation and healing, Webb wrote in the speech that the Vietnam Veterans Memorial would reclaim the Mall from those who had protested against the war. He said that it was now the veterans' turn to gather on the Mall (ignoring the fact that one of the most celebrated antiwar protests, the Vietnam Veterans Against the War encampment, had been a gathering of veterans there). The timing of Hammerschmidt's speech in the House of Representatives dismayed Scruggs and Wheeler, who had wanted their patron Senator Mathias to be first to propose the legislation in the Senate. They accused Webb of jumping the gun and glory seeking, perhaps to curry favor with Hammerschmidt. Scruggs and Webb fell out and their working relationship never recovered from this conflict.[58]

At a press conference to mobilize support for the House legislation, Webb persuaded Representative Don Bailey (D., Pennsylvania) to speak about the memorial. Bailey, awarded the Silver Star in Vietnam and the most highly decorated Vietnam veteran in the House of Representatives, also bore a grudge against the antiwar protesters. Contrary to the VVMF's pitch for the memorial, he said that the memorial should not promote reconciliation and that America had lost the war because of the antiwar protesters. The memorial should be a patriotic answer to them. Hammerschmidt's speech and Bailey's press conference showed that the antipathies of the Vietnam War era were very much alive. The fact that both men were associates of Webb's bespoke further trouble to come.[59]

The statements by the dovish Senator Mathias and the hawkish representatives Hammerschmidt and Bailey capture the range of opinion among supporters of the memorial: Mathias wanted an end to political divisions in the name of national healing and thought that it was time to set aside questions of right and wrong; but Hammerschmidt and Bailey seemed to want to carry on the bitter debates of the war years. They preferred to vindicate America's cause in Vietnam and shove the memorial down the throats of antiwar protesters rather than to reconcile with their former antagonists. The problem was not that there was serious legislative opposition to the memorial: it was worse than that. The memorial won the support of people with conflicting agendas, and these crossed purposes would vex the VVMF once the memorial entered the design stage.

Congress approved a bill authorizing the memorial and allocating Constitution Gardens for a memorial "in honor and recognition of the men and women of the Armed Forces of the United States who served in the Vietnam War." The legislation provided that the government would pay none of the memorial's expenses and that, although the memorial would be privately funded, statutory agencies (the Commission of Fine Arts and the National Capital Planning Commission) and the secretary of the interior would all have the power of approval over the memorial's design. At this moment of legislative success for the cause of a memorial, Congress had set the stage for the battles to come.

In July 1980, on signing the bill that authorized the creation of the memorial, President Carter gave a speech that betrayed the tension between reconciliation, on one hand, and vindication of the war effort, on the other. He said that the nation had been divided by the war and that in order to set aside its divisions it had forgotten the veterans, "adding to their pain the additional burden of our Nation's inner conflict." However, he had seen a change in people's attitudes, with a new willingness to acknowledge the nation's debt to the Vietnam veterans, and this bespoke "healing" and "reconciliation."[60]

Carter echoed Figley's ideas about separating the warrior from the war: "In honoring those who answered the call of duty, we do not honor the war." But the rest of his speech did not live up to this creed. Carter said that without honoring the war, "we honor the peace [the U.S. forces] sought, the freedoms that they fought to preserve, and the hope that they held out to a world that's still struggling to learn how to settle differences among people and among nations without resorting to violence." But if the troops fought to preserve certain freedoms, the distinction between honoring their service and honoring the war evaporates. Carter's other proposition—that by fighting in Vietnam the troops sought peace and held out the hope for settling differences without force of arms—is Orwellian and sanctimonious gibberish. Having denied that he would make any political statements about the war, Carter made his polemical claims without any reasoned justification. The avoidance of "political statements" thus translated into the absence of political reasoning, allowing statements about abstractions such as "freedom" to stand undefended.

An emotive climax of the signing ceremony was Carter's reading a passage from Philip Caputo's A Rumor of War that decries the absence of Vietnam War memorials. In the passage, Caputo pays tribute to Walter Levy, who died trying to save a fellow marine. Addressing Levy, Caputo says, "You embodied the best that was in us," and, he continues: "You died for the man you tried to save, and you died *pro patria*. It was not altogether sweet and fitting, your death, but I'm sure you died believing it was *pro patria*. You were faithful. Your country is not."[61] The phrases *"pro patria"* and "sweet and fitting" refer to the poet Horace's exhortation to soldiers: "Dulce et decorum est pro patria mori" (It is sweet and fitting to die for one's country).[62] Caputo's reference is laced with irony because he reads Horace through an intertext: Wilfred Owen's poem "Dulce et Decorum Est" warned, a half-century before Levy's death, that Horace's noble sentiment was an "old Lie" designed to send hapless young men to their deaths in the trenches of the Western Front.[63] Carter's speeches demonstrate a sustained effort to keep this irony at bay. He had recited Caputo's eulogy once before, revising the passage by omitting the key sentences: "It was not altogether sweet and fitting, your death, but I'm sure you died believing it was *pro patria*. You were faithful. Your country is not."[64] When signing the memorial legislation into law the following year, Carter managed to restore most of the missing sentences but did not answer the words "You were faithful" with "Your country is not." Instead he provided a paraphrase and added his own clumsy gloss: "To die for one's country is a sacrifice that should never be forgotten."

Caputo's eulogy bemoans the absence of memorials to the Vietnam War, contrasting Levy's fidelity to his comrade with the fickleness of the nation: "As I write this, eleven years after your death, the country for which you died wishes to forget the war in which you died. Its very name is a curse. There are no monuments to its heroes, no statues in small-town squares and city parks, no plaques, nor public wreaths, nor memorials. For plaques and wreaths and memorials are reminders, and they would make it harder for your country to sink into the amnesia for which it longs." Carter summarized the passage and said, "Now, we'll build a memorial to the Walter Levys who died on the other side of the world, sacrificing themselves for others, sacrificing themselves for us and for our children's children. With this memorial we will say with Caputo: 'We loved you for what you were and what you stood for.' We will prove with this monument that we care, and that we will always remember." The gushing bathos smothers the bitterness in Caputo's text.[65]

Wheeler reports that the passage by Caputo was read not just at these two White House ceremonies but at numerous other such events around the country. The passage served as a kind of manifesto for the creation of a national memorial. As the chairman of the VVMF, Wheeler echoed Caputo in 1984 by addressing Levy with fresh news: "Walter Levy, there is a Memorial." He continued, "Philip Caputo helped us build it."[66] Scruggs echoed this sentiment in his memoir: "Sitting far back in the audience [listening to Carter reading the Caputo passage in the Memorial Day ceremony], Scruggs smiled. 'Just you wait,' he whispered to his wife. 'Levy's name will be on the Mall a couple of blocks from here.'"[67]

The references to Caputo's writings are based not just on an obtuse interpretation of the passage about Levy but also on a selective reading of *A Rumor of War*. They ignore the disturbing passages in which Caputo admits that he was responsible for retaliatory attacks on Vietnamese civilians to exact revenge for his platoon's being the target of sniper bullets and land mines, and that he was court-martialed for covering up a murder. The "explanatory or extenuating circumstance" for his actions, Caputo said—in the same way that Robert Jay Lifton explained the crimes of his compatriots—"was the war. . . . The thing we had done was a result of what the war had done to us." This is a refrain that one hears again and again as veterans try to understand or explain the things they did. As his memoir continues through the end of his time in Vietnam, Caputo reveals that he came to the conclusion that it "was being fought for a bunch of corrupt politicians in Saigon," and that "every American life lost was a life wasted." Caputo joined Vietnam Veterans Against the War on his return from Vietnam and attempted to return his campaign ribbons to President Richard Nixon in 1970. Referring to Levy and Sergeant Sullivan, to whom he dedicates the book, he writes of his feelings on returning from Vietnam: "Something in me cried out against the waste of their lives. The war was lost, or very nearly lost. Those men had died for no reason. They had given their all for nothing."[68] This view was deeply entrenched in American culture. Scruggs himself had said, "I still wonder if anything can be found to bring any purpose to all the suffering and death."[69] Twelve years after the publication of *A Rumor of War*, half of a national opinion poll sample agreed that the soldiers who lost their lives in Vietnam died in vain.[70]

These doubts about the justification for Americans' sacrifices in Vietnam were part of the reason for the memorial effort. Caputo's call for commemorations expressed a desire to make up for the forgetfulness of the country and also to compensate for America's military defeat. The dead required a special form of recognition *because* their deaths had been in vain; the meaning of the deaths was particularly problematic, since it could not be assessed as the necessary cost of victory. Some other meaning had to be adduced. The selective invocations of Caputo's writings captured the pathos of his appeal but not the desperate search for some restorative meaning in a war that appeared to have none. Had Carter read the passages unabridged, listeners might have recognized sooner the scale of the emotional and political tasks that the VVMF had taken on.

Once Carter signed the bill authorizing the construction of a Vietnam veterans memorial, the principal tasks that remained were to choose a design, raise the funds required to construct the memorial, win the approval of the statutory oversight agencies and the secretary of the interior, and take on the personnel or hire the firms required to create the memorial and administer the project. Fundraising proceeded throughout the remainder of 1980, and the VVMF raised $700,000 by the end of the year.[71] With no design, the memorial fund had to base the fundraising campaign on something other than a clearly visualized plan, and they pitched the "five Rs": responsibility to the nation's own; reconciliation of the divisions caused by the war; remembrance of the nation's unrecognized heroes; rehabilitation by healing the wounds of rejection by society; and renewal in national pride.[72] Although the "five Rs" disappeared from VVMF's later publicity materials, the concepts remained alive: remembrance would advance reconciliation and healing and would lead to a renewal of national pride.

The crucial task on which the project hinged was the design, and to proceed, the VVMF needed to settle on the criteria for selecting one. Scruggs contributed the concept that had been with him from the beginning: the names. From Wheeler came the idea of a landscape solution, putting the memorial in a garden setting and making its orientation horizontal rather than vertical so that it would not compete awkwardly with the Lincoln Memorial and Washington Monument.[73] Wheeler's precepts constituted the first of eight design elements that the VVMF reported to one of the statutory review bodies: "An overall landscaped solution, emphasizing horizontal rather than vertical elements." The fund also contemplated that the memorial would include "a sculptural statement, in one or more pieces integrated into the garden design." They assured the committee that "the design concept proposed by the VVMF envisions a memorial which would harmonize with and enhance the existing landscape where it is created."[74]

In advocating a landscape design without "visual disruptions," the memorial fund was heavily influenced by the predilections of the Commission of Fine Arts and the National Capital Planning Commission, both of which would have to approve the eventual design. These bodies were protective of Constitution Gardens and concerned about anything that would interrupt the sight lines or interfere with the landscape of the Mall. J. Carter Brown, the chairman of the Fine Arts Commission, lost no opportunity to tell people that the Mall was hallowed ground. He referred to Constitution Gardens as "one of the great triumphs in Washington or in any other city" and as "sacred soil."[75]

The VVMF announced a national competition to select a design in October 1980. A jury of eight distinguished architects, landscape architects, and sculptors, chaired by a writer and editor, would award $20,000 to the winner and smaller prizes to the runners-up.[76] The jurors were all white men and none had served in Vietnam. Initially, Wheeler had said that the jury must include an African American, a woman, and two representatives of the fund—but he was overruled by his colleagues.[77] The VVMF deliberately excluded Vietnam veterans, afraid that the presence of one or two on the jury would smack of tokenism, or that the other jurors might defer excessively to them.[78] To educate the jury and the competition entrants in the sensibility of Vietnam veterans, the VVMF prepared a reading list for them, with selected titles dealing with the war and the veterans' experience.[79]

The specifications sent to competition entrants were that the memorial should be reflective and contemplative, harmonize with its surroundings, contain the names of all the war's dead and missing, and make no political statement about the war. The competition program states: "The hope is that the creation of the Memorial will begin a healing process, a reconciliation of the grievous divisions wrought by the war. Through the memorial both supporters and opponents of the war may find a common ground for recognizing the sacrifice, heroism, and loyalty which were also part of the Vietnam experience. . . . The memorial should be conciliatory, transcending the tragedy of the war." The memorial would also become "a symbol of national unity, a focal point for remembering the war's dead, the veterans, and the lessons learned through a tragic experience."[80] The problem was that some of these goals were mutually antagonistic, if not contradictory. If the memorial were to be a site for lesson learning, its message and appearance would necessarily attract close political scrutiny. Sympathy for the veterans and for the dead was intended as the common ground for commemoration, but, although this might be a theme on which all could agree, what if the "lessons" that the memorial advanced did not appeal to everyone? Potentially just as damaging, what if the basic concept of the memorial, that it be apolitical, fell short of some people's expectations? How would the theme of reconciliation be realized? "What are you going to do," the journalist Peter Braestrup asked officers of the VVMF, "show a hippie hugging a Marine?"[81]

Even if one accepted that reconciliation would be a good thing, it remained unclear where the responsibility for promoting it lay. In a 1980 symposium initiated by Wheeler, Philip Caputo argued that the "burden of reconciliation" lay more with the antiwar side than with Vietnam veterans. "Because they are the ones who were doing the most criticizing," Caputo said, overlooking the fact that one could be both a veteran and an opponent of the war, as he must have been aware, given his one-time membership of Vietnam Veterans Against the War.[82] For those who agreed with Caputo, reconciliation did not mean evenhandedness. It meant the vindication of the warriors' actions and the abjuration of the protesters' beliefs. As Representative Hammerschmidt's speech revealed, Webb, a memorial-fund sponsor, also thought that the protesters had had their day and that now it was the turn of those who were proud of their service. For veterans like Caputo and Webb, neutrality would not suffice. The VVMF put a different gloss on the concept of "reconciliation" in a November 1980 document, explaining that as well as overcoming domestic tensions left over from the war, reconciliation also means the reduction of hostility between the United States and Vietnam.[83] This goal, which reminds one of Victor Westphall's tentative attempt at rapprochement with Vietnam at Angel Fire, disappeared almost immediately from the VVMF's objectives: It was never mentioned again as the memorial became embroiled in arguments with right-wingers for whom this meaning of "reconciliation" would have been anathema.

Those who had received the design competition program and were preparing their entries sent in various queries about the rules, and, for equity's sake, Paul Spreiregen, the competition's professional adviser, collated all the questions with his answers and sent them to all the potential entrants.[84] Noting that the rules forbade any "political statement," one competition entrant asked what the VVMF meant by this phrase. Spreiregen answered, "any comment on the rightness, wrongness, or motivation of U.S. policy in entering, conducting, or withdrawing from the war." Another entrant asked whether the memorial might "acknowledge those who resisted the Vietnam War?" adding, "Should the memorial include reference to all those who suffered or died because of the war, . . . South Vietnamese, private citizens, etc.?" Spreiregen responded, "We pretend no denial that many people were affected by the Vietnam War and that many died. This memorial is to honor those Americans who served and died in the war. The memorial is not a commemoration of the war or of others who were affected or who died. Designs that deal with other matters other [sic] than the stated purpose and philosophy of the memorial will be disqualified."[85] Let us leave aside the extraordinary claim that the memorial was "not a commemoration of the war" and concentrate on the decision to rule out any references to opposition to the war, indeed any civilians, and the Vietnamese people (on whose behalf, against whom, and on whose territory the war was fought). This mandatory exclusion had important political motivations and effects, despite the VVMF's supposed disavowal of politics. In a reversal of Nixon's "Vietnamization" program, it meant that the war, although an international event, was domesticated, "Americanized," transformed into a U.S. affair and that contemplation of the moral issues the war had raised was ruled out of bounds. The decision to commemorate only those who served in the military deepened the obscurity into which the war's political character and moral meaning were cast. The foot soldier could be remembered but not civilians such as protesters, the secretary of defense, or the president.

The competition's eventual outcome was heavily influenced by the design criteria, the most emphatic of which was that the memorial should harmonize with the site. Spreiregen spelled out this requirement many times in instructions to the design competition entrants, reminding them, for example, that "the memorial must not challenge or adversely detract from existing nearby memorials." He was emphatic on this point, writing, "Do not overwhelm the site. Let the memorial design be an extension of the existing character of Constitution Gardens, not an imposition on it. . . . Our intention is that the memorial be carefully integrated into the existing Constitution Gardens; that it be an intrinsic part of it, sensitively wedded to it. . . . We do not want to alter Constitution Gardens or the Reflecting Pool or the Lincoln Memorial setting."[86] Although the memorial fund announced that it had no preconceived ideas and that landscape, sculpture, or architecture were appropriate design elements, the design criteria seemed to place large-scale sculptural entries to the competition at a disadvantage because they were likely to appear as "impositions" on the landscape. The requirement that the fifty-eight thousand names be listed required a large ground on which the names could appear and the requirements of political neutrality and harmony with the surroundings tended to discourage depictions of the war itself. Nevertheless, the VVMF were still anticipating, consistent with their eight original precepts, that some sort of a sculpture might be a part of the eventual memorial. Their estimate of how much the memorial would cost to build was predicated on the following design concept: "a landscaped garden containing the inscription of the names of those killed in Vietnam along with a work of sculpture."[87]

To encourage the competition entrants not to violate the character of the Mall, the VVMF attempted in the competition program to reinforce the entrants' knowledge of, or—where appropriate—provide some remedial education in the design of the city and Constitution Gardens. The program explained that the design of Constitution Gardens conforms with the principles of the landscape architect Frederick Law Olmsted and that the site's "roots are in English landscape design, which derived in part from an English appreciation of Chinese garden art." The program also stated, however, that the memorial would necessarily assume a place within Pierre L'Enfant's plan of Washington, which features ceremonial avenues meeting at squares and circles, emphasizing key political landmarks and giving onto grand vistas. The memorial would need to accommodate the intimate scale of Olmsted's system and the geometry of L'Enfant's axial plan for the city.[88]

The competition brought forth 1,421 entries, the largest number up to that time in any design competition in Europe or the United States. The "bewildering variety" of submissions to the design competition and the extravagance of some of the entries indicate that many of the entrants had not taken the directives about urban and landscape design to heart.[89] A critic in the journal of the American Institute of

Architects remarked that, along with classical, modern, and postmodern designs, the entries included "a large category best described as naive."[90] The submissions included an enormous peace symbol, a giant pair of combat boots, a massive hand holding a liberty torch, a forty-five-foot sculpture of a mourning figure, three knights on chargers crossing the rolling clouds of Valhalla, and a huge block punctuated by protruding pieces of a helicopter, a jet aircraft, and a ship.[91] The designers of such entries appeared to have scant regard for Olmsted's theories or the principles of English landscape design.

One might conclude from these designs that some of the competition entrants were indifferent to the commemorative landscape of the Mall. However, the approach they took was deliberately assertive rather than simply negligent. The subsequent debate about the winning design demonstrates that some Vietnam veterans did not want an unobtrusive memorial and felt that to accept one would slight the sacrifices of those who fought and fell. Thus, the requirement that the design show sensitivity to its surroundings took on an unexpected political significance since, in the minds of some prospective designers, an obtrusive memorial was more appropriate than one that excessively respected its site.

The contrast between the amateur designs that clashed with their surroundings and those submitted by members of the "design establishment" is best exemplified by three entries from the latter group. The one by Charles Atherton, secretary of the Fine Arts Commission, used a combination of walkways, trees, lampposts, and benches, displaying the names of the dead on a low, angled wall.[92] Atherton intended his design to "enhance the park," but it was so unobtrusive that it diminished the significance of the event it commemorated. Henry Arnold, as co-designer of Constitution Gardens, could be forgiven for submitting a design, with four collaborators, that preserved the site from any aesthetic intrusion. The design, a memorial grove with trees, paths, and canted granite name-posts arranged around a pool filled with water lilies, was so harmonious that it might not be recognized as a memorial at all.[93] W. Kent Cooper's design, submitted with three others, called for aluminum name-posts with engraved names designed to wash off after ten to fifteen years, and a steel sculpture that was intended to erode. The posts could be dismantled after memories of the war faded.[94] Had this design been selected, the names would have disappeared before the end of the twentieth century—after a brief sojourn on the public stage of national memory. Veterans wishing for affirmation of the fracture the war created might well have regarded the decorous and discreet approach these designs took as a violation of their experience.

While the competition jury was deliberating about the design, Webb sent the VVMF a newspaper clipping about the outcome of another design competition, light-heartedly warning that an unfathomable modernist design might emerge from the VVMF's. In 1979, the Military Order of World Wars, a veterans' organization founded in 1919, co-sponsored a competition to select the design for a memorial to the residents of Travis County, Texas, who died in the Vietnam War. Not anticipating any adverse consequences, the veterans enlisted the help of the Austin Contemporary Arts Association and selected Ira Licht, director of the Lowe Museum in Tallahassee,

Florida, and former director of Art in Public Places for the National Endowment for the Arts, to judge the competition. Licht chose *Infinity of Life*, a concrete grid set with ninety-eight concrete egg shapes representing the ninety-eight Travis County residents who died in Vietnam, with two open spaces for foliage to grow through. The local veterans were appalled by this choice, which they denounced as an "egg crate"; in its defense, one of the members of the design community mustered the argument that, while the memorial's meaning was obscure to some people, so was the meaning of the Vietnam War. The veterans rejected Licht's choice and reactively plumped for a runner-up in the competition, a pair of stone shafts separated by a slit that allowed the sun's rays to play on the names of the dead. Ultimately, though, the veterans' organization settled on a more traditional monument, consisting of a granite obelisk topped with a lone star.[95] The culture clash between art professionals and tradition-bound veterans put observers on notice that, in holding a competition to select the design for their monument, the VVMF was taking on a task fraught with risks. Webb added, "We're not going to get an egg carton, are we?"[96]

The VVMF competition jury completed its deliberations and on May 1, 1981, announced the winner, the second- and third-placed designs, and fifteen honorable mentions. The winning design, competition entry 1026, consisted of two black, polished granite walls sunk into the ground, inscribed with the names of all the dead and missing from the Vietnam War (figs. 7 and 8). They met at an oblique angle and tapered to their extremities, forming a chevron shape. The memorial was to be set in Constitution Gardens' grass lawn, the ground gradually sloping down to the face of the stone. The designer turned out to be Maya Ying Lin, a Yale architecture student, who described the memorial as a cut in the earth, "an initial violence that in time would heal" as the grass grew up to the pure, flat surface of the stone.[97] The names were to be inscribed in chronological order, the list beginning at the vertex (meeting point) of the two walls, continuing along the length of the eastern wall, and resuming at the end of the opposite, western wall, to continue until the last name met the first "so that the time line would circle back to itself and close the sequence."[98] The design specified that the walls were over 10 feet high at their vertex and each one was 200 feet long (to accommodate all the names, they would grow to almost 250 feet in length).

The jury had begun from the premise that the successful design must be horizontal, not vertical, and that it had to fit the site. (One juror remarked, "The program says simple and meditative. Therefore that means heavy, and not vertical, horizontal not vertical." Another concurred, saying, "I begin to look for a simple solution of serenity not conflict, one more horizontal.")[99] The winning design admirably fulfilled the competing requirements of the commemorative program. By creating a giant "rift in the earth," the memorial managed to suggest the enormity of the historical experience it commemorated without overwhelming its surroundings. Its huge scale, dark color, symmetry, and dramatic lines were dignified and grand without eclipsing or challenging the nearby Lincoln Memorial. The memorial's walls linked with the Lincoln Memorial and Washington Monument by pointing to them. Because of the glassy sheen of the polished black stone specified in the design, the memorial would reflect the two monuments. And because it depended on them, creating new relationships between them, it could not exist elsewhere. The jury described the design as "superbly harmonious with its site." Moreover, its horizontal orientation would not disrupt the sight lines in the park. The site itself, a juror said, was "the most important part of the memorial."[100]

The memorial would be unique—a dark memorial in a city full of white monuments. Its minimalism seemed to fit the criterion of making no political statement. Even before they discussed entry 1026, one juror advocated a minimalist work of art, because it would be an "empty vessel" into which visitors could pour their own

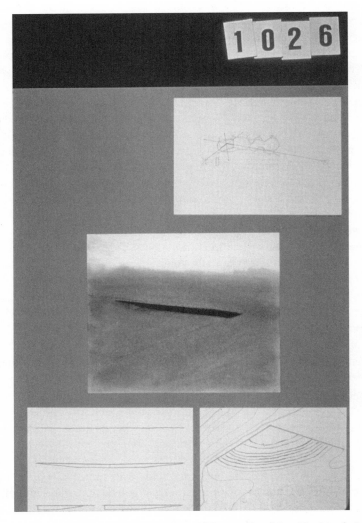

Figure 7. Entry 1026, Vietnam Veterans Memorial Competition; Maya Ying Lin, designer.
Division of Prints and Photographs, Library of Congress.

meanings; referring to Lin's design, another juror said that everyone would see in it what he or she was prepared to see.[101] The jury spoke of the power of gathering the names together—and this was the only design that consisted primarily of the names, with little else. One juror said that the design implied "a sedimentary rock that goes right across the whole country, . . . the exposed fundament that underlies the surface." Another said that it was "as though the ground had subsided and on the rock were the names." But although they had no difficulty in visualizing the completed monument, the jurors were concerned that the design would not be well understood by laypersons; they knew it would need explaining.

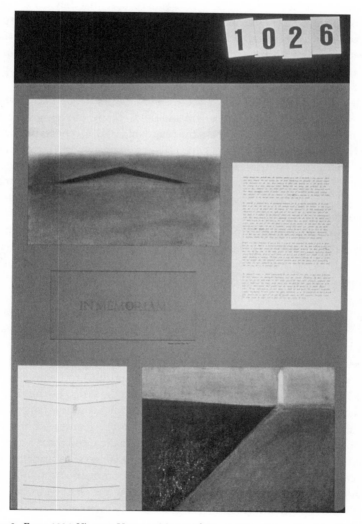

Figure 8. Entry 1026, Vietnam Veterans Memorial Competition; Maya Ying Lin, designer. Division of Prints and Photographs, Library of Congress.

When the winning design was presented to the officers and staff of the VVMF, it was met with an awkward silence of several seconds. Scruggs later said he thought it looked like "a big bat." Doubek was equally skeptical, regarding it as a memorial to the dead that left out the living. Wheeler was the first to speak. He said, "This is a work of genius." The VVMF group applauded, but without fully understanding the design.[102] One problem was the execution of the drawing: it was rather amorphous and the completed monument was not easy to visualize. As one of the jurors had said, "To choose this one would show clearly that the jury was not influenced by the 'presentation.'"[103] Although the VVMF officers voted unanimously to endorse the jury's choice and Scruggs outwardly evinced enthusiasm, he thought, "It's weird and I wish I knew what the hell it is." The VVMF staff realized that they had a large public relations problem, because the memorial required at least five minutes of explanation before it could be understood. When the design was unveiled to the press and public a few days later, the VVMF ensured that a scale model was available, to help viewers visualize the memorial, although they found it did not show up well in photographs. Later, they made a six-by-seven-foot model that photographed better.[104]

The design was well received by professional journals. The two largest veterans' organizations, the American Legion and the Veterans of Foreign Wars, began campaigning for contributions. The American Gold Star Mothers, women whose children had died in military service, gave a statement of support. Tens of thousands of letters, containing contributions large and small, began arriving at the offices of the VVMF.[105] By July 1981, the VVMF had gathered $1.5 million in contributions. Presenting the design to the Fine Arts Commission, the VVMF explained once more that the memorial was to honor the service and sacrifice of those who fought, without making any political statement or saying anything about U.S. policy in the war. Spreiregen, the organizer of the design competition, pointed out that because any symbol, whether representational or abstract, tends to arrest thought rather than arouse and expand it, the lack of symbolism in the wall spoke in its favor.[106] There was one lone naysayer at the meeting of the Fine Arts Commission, a veteran who said that the minimalist design "accomplishe[d] little" and was so "inconspicuous and meaningless" that "no memorial would be a better alternative." He wanted the memorial to honor the dead as heroes, in a nobler manner.[107]

The members of the Fine Arts Commission were impressed with the design, and they agreed unanimously to give conceptual approval to the memorial. Soon after, the National Capital Planning Commission did the same. By this time, Ronald Reagan had assumed the presidency, and his interior secretary, James Watt, also gave the design preliminary approval. But some criticisms emerged: the memorial seemed to concentrate exclusively on those who had died, and there was no inscription to indicate that it commemorated the Vietnam War. One journalist suggested that the casualties of the Vietnam War were to be commemorated by "something resembling an erosion control project."[108] Another wrote that, because the memorial would be sunk into the ground, "it is as if the very memorial itself is intended to bury and banish the whole Viet Nam experience."[109] But the two regulatory bodies had agreed to the design, and so none of these criticisms seemed likely to derail the project. The VVMF set about raising the $7 million they estimated the memorial would cost, in time to begin construction with a view to dedicating it on Veterans Day, November 11, 1982.[110]

The VVMF decided to add inscriptions at the memorial's vertex to bookend the chronological ordering of the names. One inscription would appear at the top of the east wall, before the first name; another would follow the last name, at the bottom of the west wall. The prologue would read: "In honor of the men and women of the Armed Forces of the United States who served in the Vietnam War. The names of those who gave their lives and of those who remain missing are inscribed in the order they were taken from us." The epilogue would read: "Our nation remembers the courage, sacrifice, and devotion to duty and country of its Vietnam veterans. This memorial was built with private donations from the American people."[111]

The chronological ordering of the names was also a matter of frequent complaint. Critics said that this arrangement would make it difficult to locate any particular name and proposed that the names be listed in alphabetical order. But the memorial fund and Lin pointed out that an alphabetical listing would appear bureaucratic and impersonal and make the memorial resemble a telephone directory—there are, for example, thirty-four Robert Smiths on the wall, including five with the same middle name.[112] Listing the dead in the sequence that they fell would, however, emphasize the uniqueness of every individual while also evoking the nation's ethnic diversity in the mixture of names with different national origins. In Lin's words, it would make the chronicle of death resemble an "epic poem."[113]

The relationship between Lin and the veterans in the VVMF was awkward. Lin was a young Asian American student, and her youth and her gender seemed to pose problems for some veterans in the VVMF and among the design's critics. A few of the latter group also found her ethnicity objectionable. Lin did not mix well with some of the veterans and claimed to have little interest in the war. Having not been personally touched by the war—she was only nine years old when the Tet Offensive took place—she treated the memorial as a design problem and did not ask the veterans about their experiences in Vietnam.[114] The veterans, in contrast, had strong emotional responses to the idea of commemoration. Each of them had friends whose names would be on the wall. Lin regarded the memorial as hers, but the veterans regarded it as theirs. The VVMF hired Cooper-Lecky Partnership as architect of record, charged with bringing the memorial to completion. Lin was taken on as a consultant. But she found that neither Cooper-Lecky nor the VVMF would defer to her views, even though she was the memorial's designer. She felt that they patronized her at times and treated her as an apprentice, even, Scruggs later remarked, as a "little girl."[115] In the months that followed, when the VVMF began to consider further modifications of the design, she felt alone in defending the integrity of her original concept.

After a summertime lull, the memorial's critics unleashed a barrage of complaints against the design in the fall and winter of 1981. The VVMF had initially received critical letters from antiwar protesters who said that there should be no memorial to an immoral war. Some unreconstructed hawks also said that the nation should not commemorate a war it had lost. After the design was unveiled, all the criticism came from conservatives, who saw the memorial as a "slap at U.S. policy."[116] The memorial's ambiguity troubled veterans and journalists who had strongly supported the war's morality and political purposes and who wished the memorial to assert the war's worthiness. The right-wing journal *National Review* led the attack, calling the design "Orwellian glop" and demanding that the Americans who gave their lives in Vietnam be memorialized by a "suitable sculpture—as if they had died at Gettysburg or the Ardennes."[117] In the *New Republic*, Charles Krauthammer said that the memorial's purpose was to impress upon the visitor "the sheer human waste, the utter meaninglessness of it all." Listing the names without an explanation of the cause for which they died would, he said, be akin to treating the dead "like the victims of some monstrous traffic accident." Lin's wall was a "disservice to history" and to the memory of those who died.[118] Webb, Carhart, and others who disliked the design began to meet at a restaurant in Arlington, Virginia, and reinforced one another's complaints about the memorial.[119]

Politicians and their aides in the Reagan White House began to monitor the dissension. Morton Blackwell was the liaison to the veterans' community in the White House's public liaison office; he also described himself as "President Reagan's liaison to all the conservative organizations in the United States," although at this stage his identity as a "movement conservative" caused the memorial fund no alarm.[120] Blackwell reported that, despite the *National Review*'s attack, there were no "bad vibes" about the memorial design in the White House. He offered to be the VVMF's "listening post" in the White House and to help them get to key people if any problems came up.[121] Blackwell had previously suggested that, because the major veterans' groups were on the VVMF's side, the White House was unlikely to oppose the memorial. He told the VVMF that, although Secretary of the Interior Watt would have to give permission for construction to begin, the White House would make the decision.[122]

The brewing debate reached boiling point when Carhart denounced Lin's design at a meeting of the Fine Arts Commission as a "scar," a "trench," and a "black gash of shame and sorrow."[123] This attack was significant because it was so angry and because Carhart had been a supporter of the memorial fund. Linking the memorial's design to the conflicts about the lessons of the war, he endorsed President Reagan's statement that the Vietnam War was a noble cause and claimed that virtually all Vietnam veterans held this view. He charged that the memorial's design did not express pride in the noble cause and complained that there was no flag or insignia on the design, only a "random scattering of names."

Carhart questioned the right of non–Vietnam veterans to select the design, claiming (incorrectly) that none of the jury members had served in the armed forces. (Four of the eight jury members were veterans.)[124] He argued that the design jury chose a design that reflected the war at home, "since it is the only one they knew." Furthermore, he said, "one needs no artistic education to see this memorial for what it is, a black scar. Black, the universal color of sorrow and shame and degradation in all races, in all societies worldwide. In a hole, hidden as if out of shame. . . . Perhaps that is an appropriate design for those who would still spit upon us. . . . Can America truly mean that we are to be honored by a black pit?" He suggested that a jury of Vietnam veterans would have chosen a "white, above ground, and low key" design that would not detract from other monuments, explaining, "We seek only to be accepted in our society. We do not want to divide. We are still waiting to be welcomed home."[125]

If anyone were curious about what kind of memorial Carhart would have preferred, he had already provided an answer. He had read a book titled *Anyone Can Sculpt* and submitted an unsuccessful entry to the Vietnam Veterans Memorial Competition—a statue of a soldier holding a casualty in his arms, with a base formed by a large Purple Heart (fig. 9).[126] Crudely executed, the sculpture is sentimental and banal. Yet it expresses Carhart's grief and his perception of the patriotic devotion of the men of his generation. The soldier's pose recalls a moment during his tour

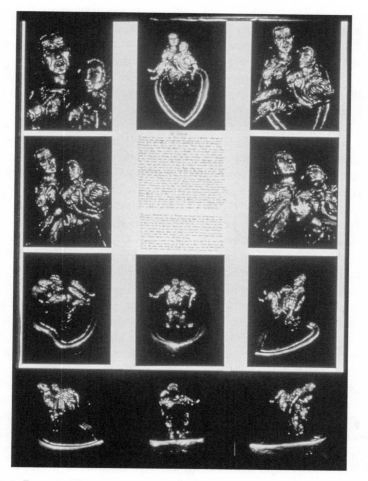

Figure 9. Entry 658, Vietnam Veterans Memorial Competition; Thomas Carhart, designer. Division of Prints and Photographs, Library of Congress.

of duty in Vietnam when Carhart lifted the body of his radio operator onto a heli-copter. He described the symbolism of this gesture: "I am just an American soldier lifting the body of a fallen brother-in-arms up into a helicopter. But at another level I am offering him back to America for all of us here, as evidence of our selfless com-mitment. This is, finally and undeniably, the Offering of those in my generation of Americans serving in Vietnam: our lives offered for our country."[127] Jesse, one of the characters in Larry Heinemann's novel *Paco's Story*, ridicules a memorial design that closely resembles Carhart's submission: "He'll be standing on an effigy of a Purple Heart, with his knees all loosy-goosy, like he's surfing, but holding a corpse of a dead GI heavenward, as if just that minute he clean-and-jerked it. And you got to know that statue will be some dipped-in-shit, John Wayne crapola that any grunt worth his grit and spit is going to take one look at and say, 'Boo-*she-it!* Ah mean *bull*shit.'"[128] Whether or not Carhart's design deserved such derision, the VVMF could easily have described him as a sore loser. He had entered his design into an anonymous competition and the judges had considered it along with all the others. Had his design won, one assumes that Carhart would not have complained about the decision-making process or the composition of the jury.

Carhart claimed that he was spat at on his return from Vietnam, and that the young, the media, the intelligentsia, and liberals treated Vietnam veterans as en-emies. He resented the fact that Vietnam veterans were made to feel like losers. In his mind, he and his fellow veterans did not lose the war: "The only thing we lost over there was the support of our countrymen back here." Carhart talked volubly about shame, externalizing and projecting it onto the memorial's design: "[People in the future] will see this as the memorial established long ago by America to those who served in Vietnam. And they can only see that as some ugly, dirty experience of which we are all ashamed." Carhart's anxiety about contamination is expressed through the connection he made between dirt and shame, reinforced by the poly-valent sexual imagery that colored his language. Using vaginal, anal, and penile imagery, Carhart spoke of the memorial as a black gash, a black ditch, a black shaft thrust into the earth, a black trench, and a black hole. In a television broadcast a year later Carhart described the memorial as a "black sarcophagus," connecting this image of the containment of death with the sexualized images of cutting, penetration, and ap-ertures. Choosing a symmetrically opposed metaphor, the following year James Webb praised the "uplift[ing]" power of the Washington Monument's "white phallus... piercing the air like a bayonet" and agreed with Carhart that the Maya Lin design was a "black slash of earth." Webb's rhetorical offensive called up the father of the country to stand tall and lead the charge, blade drawn, while Lin's memorial became a "slash," a figure of castration and sexual difference, low to the ground like a crouching, feminized insurgent. Webb, a skilled writer, claimed to be fully aware of the significance of his own rhetoric and seemed to delight in flaunting this sexually exhibitionistic language, deploying metaphor itself as a weaponized phallus that he could defiantly thrust in his audience's face. Less in control of his language as he cycled through one sexual metaphor after another, Carhart could only attempt to keep the threat of contamina-tion at bay by insisting, "I am not ashamed. We are not ashamed."[129]

Figure 10. United States Marine Corps War Memorial (the Iwo Jima Memorial); Horace Peasley, designer, Felix de Weldon, sculptor, dedicated November 10, 1954. Photo by author.

Shame is a social emotion, an internalization of the disdain that one perceives in or anticipates from the people around.[130] Carhart insisted on a memorial that offered an unambiguously affirmative representation of the war and those who fought it, allowing no room for doubt or shame. Lin's design was intended to allow the memorial to reflect viewers' images back to them. Carhart saw in the design his reflection in others' eyes, and did not like what he saw. But, as another veteran said, "The shame is in the eye of the beholder. If there's someone who finds shame looking at that monument, then it's within themselves."[131]

Carhart and his allies spoke approvingly of de Weldon's U.S. Marine Corps War Memorial—the statue of a group of marines raising the Stars and Stripes during the World War II victory at Iwo Jima—for its depiction of "heroic figures rising in triumph" from their pedestal (fig. 10).[132] De Weldon was still active and had already created one monument to an anti-Communist counterinsurgency campaign in Southeast Asia: the British campaign in Malaya.[133] Some of the public arrived at similar views independently or formed them after being influenced by press coverage of the controversy. One citizen wrote President Reagan from Elgin, Illinois, saying, "I suggest that a memorial be built that is similar to the Iwo Jima memorial in Washington, D.C., that shows the true heroism that American G.I.'s displayed in Vietnam." Another wrote to Reagan asking whether he would like to be remembered by a "black hole in the ground."[134] Some veterans' organizations added their voices to the memorial fund's critics. The Marine Corps League dissociated itself from the memorial fund, calling the memorial "an insult to those it is intended to memorialize."[135] A Sacramento American Legion post refused requests from the Legion's national headquarters to raise funds for the memorial because it would "dishonor" the dead. The post commander said that they considered the memorial a "tombstone."[136]

Opposition to the Lin design surfaced also among conservatives in the House of Representatives. Six representatives wrote to Secretary of the Interior Watt, pointing out what they saw as a discrepancy between the legislation authorizing the memorial and the VVMF's stated goals: while PL 96–297 authorized the VVMF to create a memorial in honor and recognition of members of the U.S. armed forces who served in Vietnam, the VVMF "twisted things," in the representatives' view, by emphasizing the recognition of "those who served and died." In seeking an explanation of why the VVMF emphasized the dead, the representatives quoted Scruggs's May 1977 *Washington Post* article, in which he referred to Americans who had made the "ultimate sacrifice" and said that for their sake, a memorial was needed "to remind an ungrateful nation of what it has done to its sons."[137] The politicians argued that this negative perspective was out of keeping with Congress's intentions in authorizing the memorial. They complained that the sunken black wall would be a "memorial to the dead," not to living veterans, and that it would be a "grisly reminder of something ugly and shameful in America's past." At this stage, though, the congressional critics were not demanding that Watt reject the design. They had heard that the VVMF had already agreed to some changes in the design (presumably, the addition of an inscription) and they urged Watt to query the VVMF about further changes, advising him not to be rushed into approving the memorial hastily.[138]

Carhart was the first of the memorial fund's supporters to oppose the Lin design publicly. A more formidable opponent was the widely respected Webb. Webb had disapproved of the design ever since he first saw it but had refrained from speaking out against it publicly, at the behest of Wheeler.[139] He considered the Lin design a "mass grave" and "a new version of the [Austin, Texas] egg carton."[140] Assured that some changes in the design would satisfy his concerns, he eventually ran out of patience and began to suspect that Wheeler was stringing him along until the statutory approval process had run its course, at which point it would be too late to make any changes. When Webb finally broke with the memorial fund in November 1981, he was angry, accusing several of its officers of being less than candid in their dealings with him, and of being "vicious" in launching personal attacks on Carhart.[141]

Scruggs was taken aback by the rancor of the argument. "What this all goes to prove is that this country is not recovered from the war," he said. "When people start ganging up on a guy who's just trying to honor Vietnam veterans, I think it's a lot more than aesthetics. It shows we need to do a lot of healing."[142] Indeed, the argument did involve a lot more than aesthetics. The critics of the Lin design resorted to old-fashioned red-baiting. They excavated the fact that, in June 1957, a witness at a hearing of the House Un-American Activities Committee named Garrett Eckbo, a member of the design competition jury, as a Communist; they began spreading rumors that one, perhaps more, of the jury members had Communist affiliations.[143] This tactic came straight out of the Nixon White House's playbook. As Nixon's aide

Charles Colson had said of fundraisers for the Democratic presidential candidate George McGovern, "All we have to do is find one of them a Communist and we can discredit the entire operation."[144] Echoing the complaints that the memorial was a "trench" and "ditch," President Nixon's former speechwriter, the political pundit Pat Buchanan, wrote, "Not a single Vietnam veteran served on the judging panel that selected Maya Lin's design. No Vietnam veteran was *allowed* to serve on a panel which contained several members outspokenly hostile to the national effort to stop North Vietnam's conquest of the South; one member allegedly had a long association with the American Communist Party. . . . The hour is late; but not too late for urgent appeals to Congress and, especially, President Reagan, whose Secretary of the Interior must approve the digging" (emphasis in original).[145] Critics of the memorial fund began to telephone Secretary of the Interior Watt "with allegations that jurors were communists."[146]

The memorial fund spent weeks investigating the validity of the charge that Eckbo, a distinguished landscape architect, was a Communist, obtaining copies of the House Un-American Activities Committee transcripts and of several anti–Vietnam War statements that he signed.[147] Eckbo denied that he was a Communist, referring to the accusations as a smear and "a throwback to the bad old days."[148] The VVMF attempted to spike rumors regarding the political affiliations of the jury chairman, Grady Clay, and quietly tried to establish whether other jury members had participated in antiwar activities.[149] Anticipating media queries whether some of the jurors were antiwar, the VVMF prepared the answer, "We are all antiwar. The allegation that the design selection was influenced by antiwar sentiment smacks badly of McCarthyism and is without merit."[150] The struggle to limit the damage of these rumors, consider responses (the VVMF's notes include the query, "Can we sue?"), and establish the facts to avoid future ambushes, caused some strife. One VVMF staff member wrote that he was "lied to" about Eckbo's anti–Vietnam War activities by Eckbo or his defenders and he referred to the denials that the VVMF issued as a "cover-up."[151]

Webb resigned from the VVMF's National Sponsoring Committee and wrote to others on the committee telling them why.[152] The VVMF heard that he contacted the Veterans of Foreign Wars to persuade that organization to withdraw its support from the memorial fund.[153] James Stockdale, a former prisoner of war in Vietnam and a Medal of Honor winner (and H. Ross Perot's running mate in his 1992 presidential campaign) also left, although William Westmoreland continued to support the memorial. On December 18, 1981, Webb aired his objections in the *Wall Street Journal*. Condemning the idea that the memorial should be neutral, he called Lin's design "a nihilistic statement that does not render honor to those who served" and "a wailing wall for future anti-draft and anti-nuclear protesters."[154] He said he felt "insulted by" the winning design and that the planned memorial would be a place to go and be depressed.

As others had, Webb complained that no Vietnam veteran had been on the jury and that several of its members "had been bitterly opposed to the war." Webb called for a "compromise" between the VVMF and their critics: he asked that the memorial be white, not black, above ground, not sunk into it, and that a flag be placed at the juncture of the two walls. At this stage his demands did not include the addition of a statue, and Webb denied that his confederates wanted to see "a Vietnam era update of the Iwo Jima memorial," despite their praise for de Weldon. Unless the VVMF made the changes he demanded, he called for the public to reject the design by withholding the financial contributions on which construction of the memorial depended.[155]

Webb invoked the interests of the honored dead in support of his arguments. He said that inscribing the names of the dead on the memorial was an invasion of privacy, "and such an act should not be done except in the most *affirmative* sense of 'honor and recognition.' Understatement is not called for" (emphasis in original).[156] Grady Clay responded that subtlety was "not negative, but merely the deeply pervasive presence of an emotional content." He pointed out that the published program of the 1980 design competition did not require the competitors to produce a "proclamation" in the shape of a towering sculpture with wide visibility.[157] The VVMF prepared talking points for the media: they explained that the stone was black because of its reflective qualities when polished, and that the Iwo Jima memorial and the Seabees monument also used black granite; they pointed out that the major veterans' organizations, the American Legion, the Veterans of Foreign Wars, and AMVETS (American Veterans of World War II, Korea, and Vietnam), supported the memorial, as did the American Gold Star Mothers. They said that they had received contributions from 250,000 individuals and that their mail indicated that there was widespread support among Vietnam veterans. These points readied them for the battle that Webb's opposition heralded.[158]

Webb's withdrawal of support was a heavy blow to the VVMF because he was both well known and well connected. Doubek described the publication of his *Wall Street Journal* article as a "big hit."[159] Webb had a distinguished service record, having been decorated eight times during the Vietnam War.[160] He had many contacts among Republican legislators and he played the Washington game with an insider's knowledge. The publication of Webb's article coincided with a staff meeting at the Department of the Interior, and his objections came to the attention of Secretary of the Interior Watt. One of Watt's deputies repeated the canard that the design jury contained no veterans. Asserting that the war was, as Reagan had said, a "noble cause," the staffer repeated the points that the memorial should be white, above ground, illuminated, with a flag, and the names listed alphabetically.[161] Conservative members of Congress also quoted the article in letters to Watt, or clipped and sent it to Watt, asking him to withhold his approval of the memorial design.[162] However, the VVMF heard that Watt saw no reason to take any action on the matter; that he thought it was up to the people spreading rumors about "Communists" on the jury to back them up with proof; and that unless he saw overwhelming evidence that the majority of Americans disliked the memorial he would be satisfied with the process for establishing it.[163]

The VVMF began to lobby the White House to ensure that Secretary Watt did not block construction. The memorial fund had begun to cultivate the Reagan White House even before the design competition concluded, inviting the president to participate in a ceremony at the memorial's future site and asking the vice president to attend the unveiling of the winning design.[164] As a sign of administration approval, the first lady took a place on the memorial's National Sponsoring Committee, sent a message of support to be used in a fundraising radiothon, and agreed to sign thank-you letters to anyone who gave the memorial fund $500 or more.[165] The White House reciprocated the VVMF's invitations by inviting Scruggs to attend a White House briefing with other veterans' representatives, where Scruggs presented Reagan with a plaque.[166]

The debate about the memorial's design, perhaps inevitably, was caught up in the political currents of a resurgent United States shaking off post–Vietnam War inertia, readying itself once more to undertake military action around the world. In an unpublished essay explaining why he thought the memorial's design so important, Carhart expounded a Reaganite interpretation of the cold war. Carhart argued that a memorial that made the Vietnam War appear shameful would undermine the United States' international position by reinforcing antiwar sentiments. He warned that "international Communist forces are gearing up in Central America" while the left "continues to scourge us with 'no more Vietnams.'" Carhart insisted that the country should not be ashamed of the principles it fought to protect in Vietnam. And he asserted that the "slaughter" in Vietnam and Cambodia since the Communist victory proved that the United States had every reason to rid itself of shame, guilt, and penitence. "We are tired of the guilt trip foisted on us by those who didn't serve. It is time for America to recover the courage of her convictions," he wrote, "to come out of the shadows of Vietnam and reassume her rightful place as the true beacon of liberty in the world today." As Carhart saw it, a patriotic memorial would help to inspire in Americans the courage and sacrifice required for world leadership.[167]

J. Carter Brown, the chairman of the Fine Arts Commission, would have none of Carhart's bombast. In response to Carhart's objections at the commission's October 1981 meeting, he said that the memorial's simplicity gave it an extraordinary dignity and nobility and that it did not require "a lot of corny specific references." The design had been selected by professionals who knew their business, Brown said, and he pointed out that the whole trend in memorial design had been away from "bits of whipped cream that are put on fancy pedestals." Symbols are inadequate to express the enormous impact of some national experiences, he explained. Furthermore, another member of the commission pointed out, the Fine Arts Commission had not judged the memorial competition but had been charged with performing its statutory duties to review the design; responsibility for the selection of the memorial's design rested with the VVMF. The jury process, as everyone knew, had already been completed. Accordingly, despite Carhart's and Webb's complaints, the Fine Arts Commission unanimously reaffirmed its decision of July 1981 to approve the memorial.[168] The journalist James Kilpatrick commented that it would become "the most moving war memorial ever erected. . . . Speaking with a poignant, almost unbearable eloquence, the memorial offers only the names of the dead."[169] A few days after the commission's decision, Senators Mathias and Warner invited the president to show his support for the memorial design by appearing with the memorial's plan at a press event. Reagan declined this opportunity to give it his seal of approval but an annotation on the White House's internal correspondence regarding the invitation indicates that he was "supportive of [the] project."[170]

In response to the attempts by Carhart and his allies to alter the memorial's original design, the VVMF and the Fine Arts Commission took up distinct but allied positions. The Fine Arts Commission asserted an essentially apolitical position. If it defended an ideology, it was an aesthetic ideology that held the Mall as a sacred space not to be violated. There was nothing intrinsically political about the commission's position, except insofar as its aesthetic preferences brought it into conflict with the right-wing partisans. Carhart's aesthetic was conservative in its preference for figurative sculpture but radical in its indifference to the memorial's setting. It was as if the right-wing veterans felt, "We were violated by our treatment in Vietnam and after. So why not erect a memorial that will transform the existing character of the Mall?"

Just as the Fine Arts Commission was politically agnostic, the VVMF promoted no particular aesthetic ideology, deferring to the design experts. In contrast to their critics, the VVMF were willing to accept that because the Vietnam War was different from World War II, it needed its own, unique form of commemoration. Moreover, the fund believed that because of the wide diversity of attitudes about the war, the public needed an expansive, if ambiguous, monument and could not be rallied behind a partisan standard. The VVMF disavowed any political statement. They ruled out a memorial that assertively justified the American war, foreseeing that it would provoke the war's opponents. Rejecting Victor Westphall's recognition of Vietnamese casualties of the war, the VVMF and their advisers formulated competition rules that barred any representation of Vietnamese people or the antiwar movement; but they also ruled out any explicit justifications of the war itself. Fearing that the memorial would become the occasion for ideological conflicts—as indeed it did—the VVMF adopted a supposedly apolitical discourse of "healing" and "reconciliation."

Animating the arguments about the memorial's design, in addition to the two sides' opposing commemorative agendas, was each side's unwillingness to concede to the other the right to speak for the dead. The VVMF asserted that those who fought and died should be remembered and that, to achieve this goal, one had to "separate the warrior from the war"; the right-wing critics asserted that the war effort itself should be vindicated so that the dead might be relieved of any taint of dishonor. Whereas the VVMF wanted reconciliation among the opponents and supporters of the war, their critics refused to reconcile with those they believed had betrayed the country.

The stage was set for a conflict that contradicted the fine, but somewhat abstract, rhetoric of "healing." As Webb put it: "Rather than healing, bringing us together, it pulled out of the attic all the old attitudes that had disrupted our country decades before. . . . And we were like scorpions in a jar, with the rest of the country shaking it."[171]

4

A "DANGEROUS POLITICAL ISSUE"

The War about Memory in 1982

★

IN DECEMBER 1981, the Texas billionaire H. Ross Perot, a one-time supporter of the Vietnam Veterans Memorial Fund (VVMF) who had paid the costs of the design competition, forcefully took up Carhart's denunciation of Lin's wall and demanded that the memorial make an affirmative statement of America's honor. Perot was a fiercely conservative businessman who had enjoyed a special relationship with the Richard Nixon White House. He used the massive wealth he accumulated through government contracts to organize private citizens groups to back Nixon's policies in Vietnam. He was an authoritarian and he sometimes exhibited fears of malevolent conspiracies that observers considered paranoid delusions. (For example, at various times he thought that the Vietnamese had hired a Black Panther hit squad to kill him and that a six-member Cuban hit team was after him.) The *Washington Post* said of him, "[He] is an enormously rich and willful man who has used his wealth to intimidate enemies, critics and even employees, who is insulated from his mistakes by oodles of money and fawning aides and has the mentality of a bully."[1] These proved to be unfortunate character traits in one whom the VVMF had invited into their circle of supporters. Throughout 1982, Perot threatened to use every means at his disposal, backed by a small battalion of pollsters, lawyers, and accountants, to pressure the memorial fund to change the memorial's design.

As the ensuing crisis threatened to delay, if not wreck, the memorial project, the Reagan administration was dragged into the controversy. At first, the administration tried to keep out of the arguments about the memorial. Republican members of Congress stood on both sides of the issue, and other conservatives were divided about the merits of the design, so the administration risked offending some supporters however it intervened. Arguments about the design also risked reopening the political fissures that split the nation during the Vietnam War years. The memorial's principal legislative sponsors were Republican Party senators and, while mainstream veterans' organizations sided with the VVMF, no one was certain where the weight of opinion among ordinary veterans fell. The key member of the administration with statutory responsibility to approve the memorial design was the arch-conservative secretary of the interior James Watt. Watt, an "austere zealot," had to issue his approval before groundbreaking could begin on the Constitution Gardens site.[2] Because of the timetable for construction, Watt had to approve the design by the spring of 1982, at the latest, or else the memorial would not be ready for its planned dedication that November. Any delay would upset the whole schedule for constructing the monument. This situation compelled the president's inner circle to become involved, behind the scenes, to prevent Watt's exacerbating a conflict on which the White House had no wish to expend its political capital.

The White House's behind-the-scenes activity is an object lesson in the problem of maintaining a hegemonic coalition—which entails winning broad support for a political program, achieving ideological leadership over society, and managing the divisions within the ruling bloc. As the former Reagan presidential counselor Edwin Meese recalls, the memorial was a significant issue for the White House because Ronald Reagan was trying to revive the spirit of the American people. The Vietnam War was divisive and Reagan wanted to overcome those divisions. The memorial's purpose of fostering national reconciliation was consistent with that goal.[3] Arguments about the memorial posed a problem for Reagan, though, because they pitted some of his core supporters against one another. The discord surrounding the Vietnam Veterans Memorial also tended to revive arguments about the Vietnam War during the crucial period when the public feared that administration policies would create "another Vietnam" in Central America. As we saw in Chapter 1, debates about Central America reached a critical juncture in 1982—just as the argument about the memorial design was coming to a crisis. The Reagan administration therefore had converging motives for its concern about the commemoration of the U.S. war in Southeast Asia. Arguments about the memorial could divide Reagan's domestic supporters, and contentious memories of the Vietnam War undermined support for his foreign policy.

The Reagan administration's role in nudging the project along has not been recognized by scholars. Journalists and historians have instead accepted the memorial fund's claim that it overcame every obstacle to creating the memorial, including the opposition of powerful antagonists and the indifference of the government. While this claim creates an engaging David-and-Goliath story, and while it accords with the picture of societal neglect that was the memorial fund's starting point, it fails to acknowledge the government's involvement with the memorial fund's troubles, not just as a hindrance in the shape of Secretary Watt but as an indispensable ally.

The arguments about the Vietnam Veterans Memorial attracted, at most, the sporadic interest of Reagan's advisers, whereas Central America policy was a consistent preoccupation. But Reagan's advisers judged the costs and benefits of the administration's decisions about Central America policy and its stance regarding the Vietnam Veterans Memorial within the terms of a common political calculus. Reagan could satisfy his conservative supporters (and follow his own lights) by adopting an aggressive stance in Central America but only at the cost of alienating the congressional "moderates" whose support he needed, and of entrenching the positions of his political opponents. Similarly, the Reagan administration could have supported the memorial fund's critics. But doing so would have provoked a public battle with the VVMF and defeated the object of achieving "healing." It would also have offended important constituencies, such as the mainstream veterans' organizations. Presidential advisers James Baker and Michael Deaver, the White House "pragmatists," exercised a moderating influence on zealous administration conservatives regarding the Vietnam Veterans Memorial, just as they did with Central America policy. Throughout 1982, Reagan's advisers picked their way delicately through a political minefield. They did not want to refight the Vietnam War in 1982—not in Central America, not in Congress, and certainly not on the Washington Mall—and they wanted to minimize the pressure on the ideological fault lines of the Vietnam War era. Conservative ideologues outside the administration, though, saw no need for such circumspection.

Perot was one of the first benefactors of the VVMF, donating $10,000 in early 1980 and, later, an additional $160,000 to cover the costs of the design competition, and was one of the first to disavow the design. Like James Webb, Perot initially communicated his antipathy in private conversations with officers of the VVMF. The VVMF tried to win him over to Lin's design and keep his support but their efforts failed.[4] After Carhart's denunciation of the memorial, Perot decided to enter the fray publicly and did so with a vengeance.[5] Perot was a man of action, a maverick with a combative style that ran contrary to the VVMF's ethos of reconciliation. He lacked the "bedside manner" required to minister to a nation of victims in need of "healing." A decade after the memorial controversy, when Perot ran for president of the United States, a journalist described him as the "anti-Freud" whose approach to life and politics ran contrary to the "therapeutic society" described by scholars such as Philip Rieff and Jackson Lears.[6]

Through sheer determination and ruthlessness, Perot caused the VVMF enormous problems in 1982. His campaign resulted in the addition of Frederick Hart's three-person statue to the memorial design. But it also helped to consolidate the VVMF's support, leaving a substantial paper trail of behind-the-scenes activity running through the VVMF archive. As well as winning the goodwill and financial assistance of thousands of contributors from around the country, the VVMF had the support of influential individuals and institutions: retired generals, three of the major veterans' organizations, former presidential cabinet officers, and corporate executives.

Perot's old-fashioned aesthetic tastes ran the gamut from Frederic Remington to Norman Rockwell.[7] (He and Reagan had similar tastes: Reagan loved western art and on taking office, he had several works by Remington moved into the Oval Office. Alongside a collection of art and memorabilia, Perot displayed a framed horseshoe, from his youth when he broke horses, while Reagan displayed a collection of miniature saddles in the Oval Office.) Perot praised Felix de Weldon's Iwo Jima Memorial, saying, "This is an appropriate memorial to the Marines who fought in World War II; and, believe me, they love it. Give us an appropriate memorial for the men who fought in Vietnam."[8] Perot asserted that Lin's design for the Vietnam Veterans Memorial was "a tombstone" and a "trench," and that Vietnam veterans considered it to be "an apology, not a memorial." He said the wall remembered the dead but ignored the living and he objected to the memorial's color, to its being below ground level, and to the chronological ordering of the names.[9]

The critics' denunciation of the memorial indicates a rush to judgment and a misunderstanding of the design. The critics had not grasped one of the memorial's key features—that black granite, when polished, becomes highly reflective—or that inscriptions on white stone would be more difficult to read. They also failed to visualize the completed memorial and overemphasized the fact that it would be sunk into the ground. As is now clear, the gradient of the slope to the wall is too slight to justify the epithets "ditch" and "trench." A ditch or trench, after all, has two steeply angled sides, not one gradual slope. The effect of the slope is to make the wall appear to rise above the visitor, and the memorial is not hidden away but is clearly visible across an expanse of grass. Yet, misunderstandings aside, the critics' exaggerated attention to the supposedly subterranean characteristics of the memorial makes evident what they disliked and what sort of memorial they thought appropriate. They recoiled from the possibility that the Vietnam experience would be hidden from view, as if it were a shameful memory.

Perot did not expect his generosity in funding the design competition to go unrewarded and took a proprietary interest in its result, apparently believing that he had the prerogative to change it. He felt that he spoke for the majority of Vietnam veterans and proposed that a Gallup poll be organized to measure their feelings about the design, agreeing to underwrite its costs.[10] In December 1981, Perot told Jan Scruggs that the memorial design should be scrapped and a new competition held. He said he would fund a new design competition and force the result through the Commission of Fine Arts. As Scruggs recorded the discussion, "He feels that most veterans are against [the Lin design] and in 30 days we will have a big controversy on our hands." Later that day, in response to Perot's pressure, Scruggs agreed to seek a compromise with the critics of the design.[11] The danger was that a well-organized campaign to assert veterans' opposition to the design might prompt Watt to refuse permission for construction to begin. The vocal opposition of former supporters such as Carhart, Webb, and Perot cast a shadow over the project, and the prospect that Perot would seek to mobilize veterans in opposition to the design was intimidating. Scruggs asked, "Who in the world would want to take on H. Ross Perot, much less a little group of veterans?" Scruggs was playing the customary role of underdog—but one that did, at that time, reflect the disparity in resources between the memorial fund and the billionaire.[12]

Reagan's advisers became aware of the design controversy because of VVMF lobbying, media reports, and direct communications with the memorial's supporters and opponents. Frederick Daly, a Vietnam veteran who had recently met Deaver at a diplomatic event, wrote to him in late November 1981, complaining that the memorial was a "black hole of shame." Daly said that it was "another example of liberal 'whiners' who insist on using any symbolism to denigrate the Armed Forces and their role in Vietnam." Deaver began monitoring the debate about the memorial design in an attempt to decide what the administration should do. In turn, the VVMF devised a strategy for mobilizing support by identifying allies in the White House, the Veterans Administration, and the Department of the Interior, as well as friendly senators who could influence the administration.[13] They were learning how to play the Washington game. In the next two months, White House staff members Ken Cribb, Morton Blackwell, Craig Fuller, Bob Giuffra, and Deaver himself debated how to respond to the controversy. Their involvement shows how the memorial controversy claimed the attention of the administration's domestic policy staff from its highest echelons on down.[14] Annotations such as "What is this about?" and requests for further information indicate that this was the first time that some of the staffers had encountered the issue.[15]

Deaver was President Reagan's right-hand man, closer to Reagan than any of his other advisers and able to have a say on any and all issues. He had a reputation in the White House for being a "conciliator, a facilitator, and a bearer of vital messages to the president."[16] For the next two years, he focused on the delicate political negotiations surrounding the Vietnam Veterans Memorial at each moment of crisis, whenever White House involvement was required. On Deaver's orders, Bob Giuffra, a volunteer in the Office of Public Liaison, prepared a memorandum listing the critics of the design and the reasons for their displeasure. The problem, as Giuffra summarized it, was that while the creation of the memorial enjoyed "universal support," the design was "very controversial." Giuffra listed the criticisms: the memorial resembles a "black hole"; the sunken ground will be "an ideal spot for anti-military demonstrations"; black is the "universal material of dishonor and shame"; the flag is not a central part of the design; the names are in chronological, not alphabetical order; the design jury contained no Vietnam veterans. Giuffra noted, however, that architectural critics in major publications endorsed the design. He listed three options for the administration: Watt could prevent construction of the current design, thereby reopening the design process; the White House could push for changes, such as placing the memorial above ground, changing the color to white, or placing the names in alphabetical order, as the memorial's critics demanded; or the administration could do nothing. Deaver, seeking a political compromise but without any strong views about the pros and cons of the design, advocated the second option, pushing for one or another of the changes.[17]

Watt, Giuffra said, did not want to "re-open [a] dangerous political issue" by returning the memorial to the drawing board. At this time, his department's inclination was to do nothing.[18] He wanted to avoid becoming personally involved unless presented with evidence of Communist influence on the design or of overwhelming public antipathy for it. The VVMF sent Watt an eleven-page letter detailing support for the memorial "from all segments of American society." But their opposition was also mobilizing, including members of Congress. In late December 1981, Representative Henry Hyde (R., Illinois) and twenty-seven colleagues sent a letter to all their Republican colleagues in the House asking them to lobby the White House not to allow construction of the memorial to begin. Hyde was an ardent anti-Communist and one of the leading congressional supporters of Reagan's Central America policy. "We feel this design makes a political statement of shame and dishonor," he and his colleagues wrote, "rather than an expression of our national pride."[19] Then Hyde and his supporters—now numbering thirty-one signatories, all but two of them Republicans—wrote another letter to Reagan, enclosing Webb's 1981 *Wall Street Journal* article that called Lin's design a "wailing wall" and asking the president to tell Secretary Watt to deny permission for groundbreaking.[20] Hyde's spokeswoman said that the "black trench" was "gruesome and unedifying."[21] Duncan Hunter (R., California), a Vietnam veteran and one of those who signed the letter, said the V-shaped memorial reminded him of the war-era peace symbol, ignoring the fact that the walls' oblique angle was far too wide for that. The VVMF also enjoyed support in Congress, though; Representative Lawrence DeNardis (D., Connecticut) urged his fellow congressmen not to sign Hyde's letter, saying that there was an "odor of mischief" around the effort to discredit the design-selection process.[22] But the memorial fund's congressional supporters had not yet mobilized as effectively as the opposition had.

In mid-January 1982 the White House noted that Watt was still studying the design but was planning to make a decision "soon." White House domestic policy staff decided to contact the major veterans' groups to obtain their views. Scruggs heard from Morton Blackwell that so long as those groups were on the VVMF's side, the White House "would be unlikely to come out against us." Confirming the high-level White House interest in the controversy, Lyn Nofziger, Elizabeth Dole, and Richard Darman, aides just below the top tier of advisers to the president, were assigned to take follow-up action. The administration became convinced that a compromise between the VVMF and the detractors of the Lin design could be worked out.[23] Watt, though, upset these hopes by telling the VVMF that the memorial was on hold. He wanted reassurances that veterans' groups, business leaders, and unions were positive in their support for the memorial design, not merely acquiescing. Such assurances would shore up his flank against an attack by the right should he displease the critics by approving the memorial. The VVMF accordingly geared up to launch a campaign of letters to Watt from veterans' groups and prominent Americans.[24]

U.S. Representative John Ashbrook (R., Ohio) tried to keep the pressure on the administration by appealing to President Reagan in late January 1982. Asserting that the Vietnam War was a "noble cause" fought to "save a people from the slavery that is communism," he asked that a new design be chosen, one that was "ennobling, bold, and bright." Ashbrook implied that the memorial's failure to express the "noble cause" idea might undermine Reagan's efforts to strengthen the nation's military position. He wrote, "Our position in the world . . . is much improved with your program to rebuild our national defenses. Re-establishing America as the number one military power in the world will check communism and maintain the peace. I respectfully suggest that requesting plans for a new Vietnam Veterans Memorial will help redirect the nation's view of that war and its meaning. It will assist in instilling the belief in our youth that fighting for freedom is indeed a high calling of an American."[25] The representation of the past, as Ashbrook saw it, was intimately connected with contemporary politics. Shaping the meaning of the Vietnam War for a new generation was a key to making America "number one," and a bold affirmation of the "noble cause" in a new memorial design would, he proposed, bolster the nation's fighting strength in its continuing contest against Communism.

The VVMF, though, had influential supporters who rallied to their cause. The position of the major veterans' organizations became clear. The American Legion, the largest membership organization of American veterans, pledged a donation of $1 million. The Veterans of Foreign Wars (VFW), the second largest, contributed $180,000. Apart from Webb and Stockdale, no other members of the National Sponsoring Committee resigned. Its members included two first ladies, Rosalynn Carter and Nancy Reagan, a former president, Gerald Ford, and William Westmoreland, who had promised the VVMF the future royalties of his book *A Soldier Reports*.[26] Large corporate donations began to arrive at the VVMF's office; eventually, they would total $1.5 million. The memorial fund approached its target of raising the $8 million necessary for completion of the memorial. Former ambassador to South Vietnam Ellsworth Bunker and former secretary of the army Stanley Resor (both of whom had been appointed to their posts by President Johnson and continued to serve under Nixon) lobbied Watt to give permission for groundbreaking on March 1. Bunker had been a war hawk until the end, and the fact that the wartime doves Senators Charles Mathias and George McGovern joined him in the lobbying effort demonstrates that support for the project was bipartisan and encompassed a range of political perspectives on the war.

With opponents and supporters of the memorial fund lobbying hard, the White House remained undecided about its stance. Senior White House staff, including Baker and Meese, examined the large-scale model of Lin's design in the White House's Roosevelt Room. As Scruggs wrote, "Some liked it; some did not. No one wanted to kill it. And no one wanted to defend it. They seemed to view the whole issue as a problem that would not go away."[27]

The VFW warned Scruggs that the Reagan administration might cast off the memorial as a sop to the far right. Reagan had failed to satisfy some of his conservative supporters on social issues, such as abortion and school prayer. With mid-term congressional elections less than a year away, the administration might try to appease right-wingers by sacrificing the memorial. The VFW was well-informed. The Reagan administration had asked members of the New Right (also known as "movement conservatives") to be patient during his first term, postponing action on the social issues while the White House concentrated on its economic program and defense buildup.[28] According to Meese, the economic program and defense were prioritized not because the social issues were unimportant but simply as a matter of "timing and strategy."[29] But for movement conservatives, the social issues were just as high a priority, if not more so. Blackwell, the White House veterans' liaison and point man in the administration for the movement conservatives, listed the issues on which there had been little legislative activity after Reagan was elected in 1980: gun control, abortion, school prayer, pornography, the death penalty, tuition tax credits, busing, and so on. Blackwell said, "Virtually every effective conservative group's leaders privately would express to me their disappointment, ranging from dismay to disgust," with the White House's lack of leadership on the social issue agenda.[30] And reinforcing the VFW's warning, one of the leading congressional critics of the VVMF, Representative Hyde, was also a leading abortion opponent.[31] The debate about the memorial was adding to the pressure on this fault line in the Republican Party: would the Reagan administration disappoint the far right regarding the memorial design as it had done on the social issues throughout Reagan's first year in office?

Adding to the pressure on the VVMF, Perot had commissioned a Gallup poll of former prisoners of war (POWs) to seek their views on the memorial's design and threatened to conduct a poll of all Vietnam veterans.[32] According to Scruggs, he promised to call off the second poll if the VVMF agreed "to make some compromises with the opponents of the design."[33] Facing a concatenation of problems—Watt's uncooperativeness, the mobilization of congressional opponents, and pressure from Perot—Scruggs agreed to meet the opponents and asked Perot and Warner to set up the meeting. Watt, admitting that he was under "heavy political pressure," told the memorial fund that he was pleased that the meeting had been scheduled.[34]

Perot used his connections with former POWs to foment opposition to the memorial in the run-up to this meeting. Former POWs, having been held in grim conditions and often mistreated by their Communist captors, were among the most obstreperous and politically conservative of veterans and the most likely to demand retrospective vindication of the war. Perot had a special standing with them, based on his wartime effort to improve their conditions in POW camps. (He tried to fly twenty-six tons of food to the POWs during the war and organized a welcome-home celebration for them in San Francisco when they were released.)[35] He had also gained credibility by succeeding where the 1980 Desert One operation had failed, successfully freeing two employees of his company, Electronic Data Systems (EDS), from captivity in revolutionary Iran.[36] Scruggs said afterward that Perot flew a group of POWs to Washington to lobby other veterans' organizations to oppose the memorial, a claim that Perot denied.[37]

In the meeting on January 27, 1982, the VVMF's opponents outmaneuvered their supporters. Scruggs's account says that forty-eight hours before the meeting, a "key congressional aide" warned the VVMF that Perot had "brought a lot of ex-POW officers," adding, "they're calling the smaller veterans groups. It's going to be stacked in favor of a small minority. You're walking into a trap." At the meeting, the "trap was set to spring," and the VVMF supporters found themselves outnumbered, according to Scruggs, by about four to one. The numbers present in the Senate committee room were unrepresentative: the VFW and the American Legion had a combined membership of 4.5 million veterans, over a million of whom were Vietnam veterans, but they had only five representatives in the room, whereas some individuals in the room opposed to the memorial's design represented far smaller organizations—or no one but themselves.[38] The discussions were heated—a White House observer said there was "quite a screaming match" at the beginning—and the meeting lasted for almost five hours.[39] According to Scruggs, one critic after another voiced the familiar complaints about the memorial's color and its lack of patriotism.[40] Former POWs moved many of the participants to tears talking about their years of captivity in North Vietnam and about why they objected to the original design. "It was a fierce, emotional evening," one participant said. "It was a nasty five hours."[41] Despite the unanimous decision of the competition jury and approval by the oversight commissions, the VVMF officers felt themselves "one compromise away from seeing the entire project completely destroyed."[42]

Retired Brigadier General George Price, an African American officer who was an early supporter of the memorial, objected to the pejorative references to the color black, which temporarily arrested references to the "universal color of shame and dishonor."[43] Recalling the event, he said that he also told the critics to stop speaking in a "bigoted" way about Lin's "heritage."[44] After his intervention, no one proposed changing the color of the memorial to white. The VVMF had already agreed to add inscriptions at the meeting point of the walls. The first line of the memorial's "epilogue" was to read, "Our nation remembers the courage, sacrifice, and devotion to duty and country of its Vietnam veterans." The VVMF agreed at the meeting to change the word *remembers* to *honors*.[45] The VVMF also offered, as they had resolved to do before the meeting, to add a flagpole flying the Stars and Stripes, but these changes were insufficient to satisfy the critics and the meeting remained deadlocked. The impasse continued until the evening, when General Mike Davison, a long-time supporter of the VVMF, proposed a "compromise" that transformed the original design: with the bronze statue of a soldier in a "Follow me" pose in mind (presumably prompted by de Weldon's American Soldier Monument at West Point or perhaps by a famous statue at Fort Benning, Georgia), he proposed that a statue and flag be added to the wall.[46]

Senator John Warner, chairing the meeting, acclaimed the proposal as the basis for a compromise. The VVMF officers agreed. The proposal was put to a vote by those present, and it passed. A deal had been made. The VVMF's opponents agreed to stop their efforts to block the groundbreaking for the memorial. The VVMF agreed to review all the sculptural competition entries in the search for a suitable addition to the memorial. The VVMF and their opponents would meet again in six weeks to consider the options.

Scruggs's recollection that he was outnumbered in an "ambush" is inaccurate. No minutes of the meeting remain but there is an attendance sheet that indicates that if the critics did control a majority of those in the room (which is questionable), their advantage was not overwhelming. There is certainly no evidence that the room was packed with former POWs or that Scruggs was outnumbered, as he felt, by four to one.[47] Perhaps the critics were simply more vocal, insistent, and uncompromising. Scruggs himself burst out in the course of the debate, "We could have brought hundreds of our vet volunteers and Gold Star Mothers."[48] Yet the VVMF did not do this. Anticipating that Perot was intending to pack the meeting, why, we might ask, did they not bring their supporters? The VVMF did not bring all their officers to the meeting, let alone mobilize their supporters. And why, if the numbers in the meeting were unrepresentative, did the VVMF feel bound to reach agreement with those present?

The opponents had crucial advantages in the bargaining that were unrelated to their numbers. First, the VVMF, not the critics, were fighting against the clock. They needed to break ground in March if they were to meet their November 1982 dedication date, so all the time pressure was on them. Second, they believed that if they refused to modify the design, the project might not just be delayed; it might founder.[49] The opponents felt no need to reach an accommodation with the VVMF. They appeared willing to sink the project if it was not to their liking, and the VVMF did not call their bluff. In contrast, the VVMF were committed to "reconciliation" and felt a need to win their opponents' approval. It was not the number of opponents at the meeting that made the difference but their determination to cause trouble and to keep causing trouble until they got what they wanted.

The VVMF took a weak bargaining position in the meeting. They had decided to go ahead with the meeting in Lin's absence, which was hardly a sign of commitment to her design. Scruggs said that the VVMF were afraid that she would refuse to make any accommodation with the opponents.[50] Before the debate had properly begun, the VVMF representatives offered to add a flag, and they had already conceded that the memorial should have an inscription other than the names. As the debate dragged on, the proposal for the "compromise" of an added statue came from one of the VVMF's own supporters, Mike Davison. True, a majority supported the "compromise," but the vote was taken only after another VVMF supporter, John Warner, had spoken in favor of the addition of a statue—a feature that the VVMF had contemplated since before they announced the design competition. The meeting took place on Warner's home turf, and he was in the chair. If the VVMF's leaders walked into an ambush, they did so with their eyes open. General George Price revealed years later that the VVMF officers and supporters had agreed on the proposed compromise before the meeting, planning to have Davison put forward the proposal to add a statue at the decisive moment.[51] Of the VVMF's key officers, only Jack Wheeler felt strongly that the original design should not be changed.[52] Scruggs fostered the myth of being out-numbered in an "ambush" rather than concede his own complicity in compromising Lin's design, whose power he did not yet understand. And if the VVMF thought that by touting the change as a concession to Perot they would quiet him later, they made a serious misjudgment. Perot had learned that he could roll over the VVMF, and this knowledge encouraged him later to persist in the same tactics with equal, if not greater, vigor. The new task of selecting and siting a sculptural addition ensured a protracted period of collaboration between the VVMF and their critics and new occasions for conflict.

Representatives of the VVMF and the critics met Watt to tell him of the agreement, and Representative Hyde told him that it "ameliorate[d his] concerns" about the original design. Watt said that he would now be able to approve the project but wanted to see the revised plans before allowing groundbreaking.[53] Tom Shull attended the January 27 meeting as a White House representative; but because he was a White House fellow, a low-ranking and little-known staffer, his presence did not signal high-level White House involvement. Shull's immediate supervisor, Jim Cicconi, worked closely with fellow Texan James Baker as his special assistant;

through Cicconi, Shull reported to Darman and Baker. During the controversy about the design, Shull became a crucial link in the communications between the VVMF and the White House. Shull set out the terms of the agreement in a memorandum circulated to senior White House staff members, stating, "There is no reason to hold up the plan to break ground by March 1." However, the report concluded, "if there is concern that the VVMF will not aggressively seek to place a statue at the site, dedication of the memorial could be contingent on the completion of both the statuary and the current memorial design."[54] As a precaution, Shull suggested that if Watt approved the design subject to the fulfillment of the compromise, he should first obtain a detailed letter of intent from the memorial fund "just so they don't welsh on the deal later."[55]

The "compromise" was a betrayal of the official decision-making process. The VVMF had announced an open design competition, published the rules, and convened a jury, which had deliberated and chosen a winner. Now, the result was being changed by a bargain struck in a smoke-filled Senate committee room by the VVMF and a group of self-appointed custodians of public memory. No wonder Scruggs wrote, "Some of the vets felt dirtied."[56] This unseemly arm-twisting had succeeded in the same precincts where the Gulf of Tonkin Resolution had once been shepherded past a compliant Congress. No one had thought to consult the memorial's designer, Maya Lin, or to consider the responses of the statutory review bodies that had already approved the design.

If the VVMF had known the direction in which some administration officials were leaning, they might have taken a stronger stand in the meeting. On January 28, the day after the "compromise" meeting, Fred Hummel, of the National Institute for Building Sciences, called the recently appointed national security adviser William Clark. Clark was an old friend and trusted confidant of Reagan's. Like Deaver and Meese, he was part of Reagan's inner circle from his days as governor of California. Clark pretended no expertise in national security matters but could be trusted to ensure that any issues that merited Reagan's attention reached the president's desk. (Clark had been Reagan's chief of staff in California, known for having devised the "mini-memo" that succinctly laid out any issue for Reagan's consideration on a single sheet.)[57] Hummel summarized the facts about the memorial dispute, with seven numbered points, urging them on Clark's and Reagan's attention. Their cumulative logic powerfully supported Lin's design and undermined the critics' position. The first five points established that her design was selected appropriately in an open design competition and that there was no objection when it was originally unveiled; it was "a very appropriate, proper solution" that the National Park Board and the American Institute of Architects endorsed. Points 6 and 7 set out the nub of the problem: "6. If it [the memorial] isn't built, it will be an embarrassment to the President. 7. James Watt objects." Hummel ended the message by saying that he was "very concerned that you [Clark] and the President are aware of this issue."[58] Hummel's message was circulated to Clark's top aides, including Robert McFarlane and John Poindexter (who would both in turn succeed Clark as national security adviser and would become notorious because of their involvement in the arms-for-hostages, "Iran–Contra" scandal). McFarlane requested a status report to be prepared for Clark by the following day.[59] The National Security Council normally restricts itself to foreign and security policy, so its interest in the memorial is striking. As further indication of the perceived implications of the memorial, the key annotation for record-keeping purposes was not just "Vietnam" but also "Defense Policy."

The National Security Council status report confirmed that Watt was willing to do whatever the White House told him to do. It gave a more equivocal summary of the political problem than Hummel's, though, recognizing the risks that the White House's involvement would entail. The report noted that some of the most vocal opposition to the memorial design had come from two former members or advisers of the VVMF. The political difficulty was that opposition and support for the design cut across political lines—that is, the issue divided Reagan's allies and supporters on the right. Thus, the argument about the memorial threatened to open up a rift in the political coalition that Reagan led. "At least thirty-one Republican Congressmen," the report read, "have written in opposition while James J. Kilpatrick, Bob Hope, General Westmoreland, and *National Review* are supportive. In addition substantial contributions have been given by both the American Legion and the VFW who strongly support the project and the current design. No one knows the feelings of veterans collectively, only that they are split." Furthermore, according to the report, if Watt disapproved the design, his decision was quite likely to "kill the project completely" because any new design would provoke just as much vocal opposition as the current one. Disapproval of the design would draw the president into the fight, because it would prompt the VVMF's congressional and public supporters to launch a countercampaign. The report advised, "A role other than that of a 'fair arbiter' by the Executive Branch in the controversy is likely to be a no-win move—inviting attack from either side."[60]

In the days after the "compromise" meeting between the VVMF and their critics, the White House buzzed with communications about the breakthrough, and National Security Council staff participated in the discussions. Veterans' liaison Blackwell reported that there was a "break in the impasse."[61] Meese might have been expected to play a pivotal part in discussions about the memorial, since he supervised the president's domestic policy staff and sat on the National Security Council. Because his role in the "troika" with Baker and Deaver was dealing with federal government agencies and departments, he would logically be the one to give Watt the White House's ruling once the administration was satisfied that a durable compromise had been achieved. Years later, though, Meese could not recall any specific decisions that he made regarding the memorial, either to smooth its path or to hinder it; nor does the documentary record show that he attempted to obstruct the VVMF's cause. This absence of any specific record of his role may be the most important fact about it. The strategy of the VVMF's congressional critics included lobbying Meese (presumably because of his reputation as the most conservative member of the troika) and activating the conservative network to "make a lot of noise." That Meese did not take up the cause of the VVMF's critics deprived them of their most likely ally in the White House's top echelon.[62] Meanwhile, the memorial fund was building a network of supporters inside and outside the administration.

A VFW telegram reached Meese, reminding him that one-quarter of the VFW's 1.9 million members were Vietnam veterans. "We do not want to see any further obstacles," the VFW said, "in the way of completing this worthy project on schedule."[63] While the VFW leadership wholeheartedly backed the memorial fund, there were some dissenting voices among the members: a representative of a VFW post in Pennsylvania wrote to Ronald Reagan asking him to delay the construction of the memorial, because it favored only the dead and "insulted and degraded" all who served in the war.[64] Because the leadership of the organization did not break ranks and the organization's hierarchy behaved in a disciplined fashion, it is impossible to tell how widespread such opinions were among the rank and file. Other voices of dissent reached the White House. Representative Carroll Campbell (R., South Carolina), whose brother had been killed in Vietnam and who was one of the co-signatories of Hyde's letter to Reagan, wrote again to the president, telling him he was affronted by the memorial because it said "nothing about duty, honor, or love of country."[65] (Evidently, he was unaware of the wording of the inscription the VVMF had settled on.) The Coronado [California] Republican Women passed a resolution requesting that construction of the memorial be stopped and that an uplifting monument be commissioned. They asserted that Americans in Vietnam fought for "the noble cause of freedom" and that the "proposed black subterranean monument would not express . . . feelings of respect and gratitude, but on the contrary would stand as confirmation of the negative views of those dissidents who were so destructive of our war effort, and so contemptuous of those who served in it."[66]

The White House also swirled with false reports about what the "compromise" entailed. In a management meeting in early February, Meese understood, correctly, that the memorial would now include a flag but, erroneously, that the stone would be "white marble." Roy Adams, a member of the staff of Senator Jeremiah Denton (R., Alabama), who was a former POW and a "New Right" senator, came away from the January 27 meeting with the understanding that a statue would be placed in front of the black wall. He believed that the wall would provide a "backdrop" for the statue, and that the inscriptions would be reworded to be more patriotic—"something like 'the cause we were fighting for was a just cause.'"[67]

On February 4, 1982, Scruggs met Watt and they worked out the details of the deal. The VVMF would submit a new plan to Watt, who would review it and send it on to the Fine Arts Commission and the National Capital Planning Commission for final approval. White House staff predicted that Watt would "probably approve" the arrangement. The plan could unravel, though. Watt knew that the review bodies would have to reconsider the memorial's design now that it had changed, and that they had been enthusiastic about Lin's wall. He heard that the Fine Arts Commission was inclining against the "compromise"; their opposition could undo the agreement between the VVMF and their critics. In anticipation of the possibility that one or another of the commissions would balk at allowing the modification of the design,

Watt announced he would delay permission to break ground until they agreed in principle to allow the statue and flag to be added to the site; the members of Congress who had objected to the original design would also have to agree. A tense stand-off ensued.[68] March 1, 1982, the day scheduled for groundbreaking, came and went without a permit.

With each passing day adding to the sense of crisis, the VVMF's officers debated their options, wondering whether they should make a fight of it by organizing a behind-the-scenes campaign of pressure on Watt or by publicly denouncing him. They factored into their calculations that Watt, a controversial secretary of the interior, was simultaneously involved in several other public arguments, increasing the political pressure on his department. The VVMF considered suing Watt. They contemplated whether to return Perot's money. Each alternative posed its own problems, because the more active they became in confronting their antagonists, the more they entrenched the conflict.[69] They also faced the possibility that Watt might refuse permission for construction altogether.

The VVMF decided to soft-pedal even though Scruggs, Robert Doubek, and others initially "wanted to declare all-out war on Watt." Wheeler said that if the memorial was to stand for "healing," the VVMF should avoid a battle. They should get the statue approved and show that they would keep their promises. Elliot Richardson, a former cabinet secretary who supported the memorial fund, also urged caution and advised Scruggs to build up a record of reasonableness in dealing with Watt. The VVMF should avoid a fight if they could but remember the principle of "time on target": bring all your fire on your target at once, giving your enemy little time to respond.[70] This lesson would eventually pay off.

Scruggs took the path of reasonableness. He called Morton Blackwell and reassured him that the VVMF believed that Watt was acting in good faith, while expressing embarrassment about the VVMF supporters who were beginning to pepper Blackwell and his boss, Elizabeth Dole, head of the Office of Public Liaison, with complaints. The veiled message was that the VVMF were aware of the pressure being brought to bear on the administration but that they had not yet begun to fight in earnest. In turn, Blackwell assured Scruggs that Watt would urge the National Capital Planning Commission and the Fine Arts Commission to "approve speedily the compromise design." His message was that permission for groundbreaking rested on the commissions' approvals of the "compromise." Blackwell wrote up these mutual assurances in a memorandum to veterans and service-related groups, encouraging them to contact the commissions with their views.[71]

On March 4, the National Capital Planning Commission approved the statue and flag in concept, allowing them to be placed centrally on the memorial site, as long as the location and design of these additions did not compromise or diminish the memorial as originally conceived. This left only the Fine Arts Commission to rule on the matter. At least one commission member was convinced that the memorial's design was complete and that nothing should be added. However, J. Carter Brown, chairman of the commission, was concerned that if the commission refused to compromise, the whole design would be discarded, and they would have no way of knowing what would be proposed in its place. Having won the backing of his colleagues, he wrote to inform Watt that the commission would favor, in principle, the addition of a statue and flag—without, however, making any promises about where the new elements would be located. In fact, his letter broached the idea that they might be grouped near the guide that would help visitors find the location of a specific name, in an area that would be the "entry point" for visitors.[72] His assurance that the statue and flag would be approved appeared to remove the last obstacle to Watt's allowing groundbreaking.

On March 11, the VVMF and their critics held their scheduled meeting to review the slides of competition entries that included sculpture.[73] Perot had done a little more arm-twisting before the meeting. He sent the results of the poll of former POWs to the VVMF.[74] The results were very negative about the design: only one-third of the former POWs who responded liked the design and two-thirds disliked it. Seventy percent thought the memorial should be white, not black. Eighty-two percent thought the memorial should be above ground, not sunk into it. Perot agreed not to release the results if the VVMF again played ball. There was still intense disagreement about the memorial's overall design. Kent Cooper, of Cooper-Lecky Partnership, the architect of record charged with bringing the memorial to completion, argued that the memorial did not need "patriotic claptrap." He said that a flag—which he tactlessly called a "long, stringy object"—was unnecessary. For their part, some of the VVMF's opponents wanted to do away with Lin's design and start from scratch.[75] The VVMF and Perot, however, had come to terms with the fact that the wall would be built and a statue and flag added.

It was still unclear where the statue and flag would be located—how integral to the memorial's design they would be, and how close to the inscribed granite walls. Scruggs records in his memoir that the VVMF "walked into another ambush" and that Perot won a vote to change the meeting agenda to consider not just the selection of the sculpture but also the location of the statue and the flag.[76] However, just as Scruggs had exaggerated the "ambush" aspect of the January meeting, his recollection of the March event is also faulty (perhaps to justify the VVMF's later disavowal of the meeting's decision): consideration of Perot's proposals for the location of the statue and flag was an agenda item from the start.[77] The majority at the meeting voted that the flagpole should be placed at the apex of the two walls, making the flag a focal feature, and the statue positioned somewhere in front of the walls, in line with their intersection, putting it in the foreground with the wall in the background. Perot proposed that those present appoint a sculpture committee to choose the sculptor and decide on the precise location of the statue and flag, and the meeting agreed to this as well. William Lecky, of Cooper-Lecky Partnership, was unhappy with the decision and refused to accept that unless the statue and flag were the central focus, the memorial would be unpatriotic.[78] Some of the VVMF's critics were also dissatisfied and wanted to wait until the National Capital Planning Commission and the Fine Arts Commission agreed to the location of the statue and the flag before asking Watt to allow groundbreaking. But because the memorial fund undertook to recommend the sculpture committee's proposals to the statutory review bodies, the critics believed that they had achieved their ends.

Meanwhile, Secretary Watt was coming under pressure from those who saw the conflict about the memorial's design as a threat to its creation. The two largest national veterans' organizations threw their considerable weight behind the VVMF. The commander of the VFW wrote to Watt urging him to approve the memorial and allow groundbreaking. The American Legion, unimpressed by the critics' claims to speak for the Vietnam veterans' community, mobilized its members to support the memorial fund.[79] The Legion never wavered from its support for the memorial. As far as its leaders were concerned, the memorial fund had conducted the design competition fairly and no one had the right to hijack the result. A flurry of complaints about the delay in groundbreaking began to issue from American Legion departments and auxiliaries to the White House on March 8. Although many of these complaints were superseded by events, they demonstrate the Legion's commitment to the memorial, and its capacity to mobilize its officers. Various elected officials from around the country added their pleas for a groundbreaking permit.[80]

On March 15, soon after the second "compromise" agreement was reached concerning the location of the statue and flag, Tom Shull called the Department of the Interior and transmitted the message, "The White House wants to get it [the memorial] done." Watt was away from Washington, giving a speech in Denver, Colorado, when the message reached him, so he instructed his staff at the Interior Department to sign the groundbreaking permit on his behalf. Prepositioned at the National Park Service headquarters to receive the permit, Doubek soon called the VVMF offices with the eagerly awaited news: at last they had the precious permit in hand.[81]

Nothing at the time was said in public about the White House's role in the groundbreaking decision. Scruggs and Wheeler eventually revealed that Reagan had ordered Watt to allow groundbreaking, but not until after the November 1988 election. A few months before this public disclosure, Wheeler acknowledged privately, "There would be no Vietnam Veterans Memorial on the Mall if the President and First Lady had not helped us." But earlier he had privately said the same about Shull, using almost the same words—which seems appropriate because in March 1982 Shull had been the one who delivered a presidential decision of which Reagan himself might not have had any specific knowledge. (Senior White House staff used to make day-to-day decisions about the details of policy on the basis of Reagan's stated views.)[82] Shull was authorized to deliver the White House's groundbreaking decision to Watt by Jim Cicconi, who was acting on Baker's (and, at least notionally, the president's) wishes, but the White House senior staff did not visibly intervene, perhaps because of their reluctance to offend the memorial fund's conservative critics, or because they did not want to show the White House's hand and have the memorial seen as an administration project. The VVMF's public reticence until Reagan's final year in office seems to confirm their tacit agreement to keep the White House role quiet.

Watt granted permission for groundbreaking on condition that the VVMF add "better and proper language bringing honor" to those who served in Vietnam, as well as a statue and flag. He said that he had been assured that the Fine Arts Commission and the National Capital Planning Commission would approve the additions to the memorial, and he stipulated that the statue and flag must be in place before the memorial was dedicated. Representative Hyde declared his satisfaction with the plan to add a flag at the apex of the walls and a statue of a "heroic fighting man" in front of them. Groundbreaking was scheduled for March 26, and the timetable was closely monitored by White House staff, who sent a representative to attend. At the groundbreaking, Scruggs returned to the conventional script, reciting the complaints that there had been "no monuments, no testaments, no memorials" to Americans who served in Vietnam. He declared, "Let this memorial begin the healing process and forever stand as a symbol" of national unity.[83] It appeared that the commemorative effort was back on track.

The VVMF appointed a four-person sculpture committee, consisting of two of their critics, Webb and Milt Copulos, a political conservative connected with the Heritage Foundation, and two supporters, Art Mosley and Bill Jayne, to choose a sculptor. All were Vietnam veterans. The committee selected Frederick Hart to create the statue, agreeing to pay him $330,000, considerably more than the $20,000 Lin had received as the winner of the design competition. Hart was the obvious choice, as the highest-placed sculptor in the original design competition. (The team of which he was a member had won third place.) He had apprenticed under Felix de Weldon, a credential that appealed to both sides of the debate about the memorial, because the VVMF themselves had once considered commissioning de Weldon to produce the sculpture.[84] Hart had ingratiated himself with the VVMF from their early days and had also been considered as a possible recipient of a commission to create the memorial before the design competition was held.

Scruggs and Senator Warner told reporters that the sculpture would be a "strong, commanding figure symbolizing all those who served in Vietnam."[85] Webb proposed that a sculpture of a single figure would not do, however, because it would not represent America's ethnic diversity, and the sculpture committee instructed Hart to create a grouping of three figures, one of whom would be an African American.[86] Wheeler, considering the prospect of a multifigure statue, feared that the sculpture committee was planning to commission "another Iwo Jima memorial" and tried to restrict the statue to a single figure.[87] Webb overruled this objection by insisting that the sculpture committee had been granted autonomy.

During the spring and summer of 1982 the VVMF went about the enormous task of creating a definitive list of Vietnam War casualties, cutting and polishing the granite, building the memorial's foundations, and engraving the names on the wall. Hart completed a maquette (sculptural model) of three infantry troops, incorporating detailed depictions of the soldiers' arms and accoutrements, based on his long conversations with veterans about life in the field.[88] It was rumored that some of the equipment on which the sculpture was modeled was Webb's.[89] There was some debate about whether the figures should carry weaponry or whether that would be "too provocative"; in the end, they were armed, although they carried their weapons by their sides or on their shoulders, not pointing at an imaginary enemy. The result met the approval of Perot, who, years later, exhibited a maquette of Hart's sculpture in a display room as one of the mementoes of his own career. By June 1982, a Styrofoam mockup of the sculpture was erected at the Constitution Gardens site to provide a preview of the completed memorial. Various locations were tried, but consistent with the vote taken at the March meeting between the VVMF and their critics, all were within the V formed by the two walls. The VVMF invited Meese, Baker, and other White House advisers to see the maquette.[90] The first wall panel was installed at the memorial and unveiled in the presence of four families of the dead. Theresa Turowski, whose son had died in Vietnam twelve years before, said she was pleased with the memorial taking shape. "I think it's a great honor for his name to be up there," she said. "It's about time they did something."[91]

Lin, who had been silent about her dislike for the additions to the memorial for some time, came out publicly in July 1982 with her objections to the March 1982 agreement. "This farce has gone on too long," she told the *Washington Post*. "I have to clear my own conscience." She said that what a visitor saw first when coming to the memorial was crucial. "I don't want it to appear they're going to shoot you when you start walking down toward the walls. The sculpture is going to make one feel watched."[92] What was significant was the position of the statue. Lin said that if the statue were placed in front of the wall, it would treat the wall "as no more than an architectural backdrop."[93] She suggested that the addition of the flagpole at the wall's apex would make the memorial appear like a large golf green. She later described Hart's statue as "trite," a "generalization" and "simplification," like an illustration from a book. For his part, Hart said that the "art mafia" had foisted the original memorial design on the VVMF and that their decision was overruled by a groundswell of popular opinion. Lin's wall was "intentionally not meaningful," he said, elitist in contrast to the statue's populism.[94] The objects of Hart's attack responded in kind. For example, Henry Arnold, the designer of Constitution Gardens, roundly condemned the addition of the sculpture: "The proposed undistinguished, made-to-order statue is a sentimental response to a difference of opinion. The result is more likely to serve as a memorial to pettiness and corruptive endeavor." Vietnam Veterans Against the War weighed in with its opinion: it "categorically" opposed the addition of a statue and flag "because war in any form is not 'noble' but rather catastrophic and beneath the dignity of intelligent life."[95] But the antiwar veterans group was by now a tiny sliver of its former strength and what it thought no longer had much political impact.

Despite the supposed "compromise" about the addition of a statue, Perot remained suspicious of the VVMF and maintained pressure on the memorial fund throughout 1982. According to Perot, Webb and other opponents of the design had told him that the fund was "really grossly misusing money."[96] He therefore demanded an audit of the VVMF's accounts while simultaneously pressing the memorial fund to keep their promise to place the statue in a prominent position. After CBS's Morley Safer interviewed Perot in early May 1982 for a segment to be broadcast on the *60 Minutes* program that fall, the VVMF heard that Perot forcefully said that the statue and flag must be placed at the center of the memorial.[97] The VVMF countered by sending *60 Minutes* the names of supporters, including officers of the American Legion, who they said "led the political fight against the detractors."[98]

The VVMF officers believed that Perot used pressure for an audit as a means of exerting control over their decisions regarding the statue and flag.[99] It is possible that Perot sincerely believed that there had been misuse of money by the VVMF. He and the other critics also mistrusted the VVMF's intention to fulfill the terms of the March 1982 "compromise." A VVMF document states, "Ross is driven by a desire to get a wedge on the VVMF to have some control over November 11 activities/Flag/Statue[,] etc."[100] Perot's representatives, however, denied the link between the audit and the design. Scruggs also speculated that Perot was jealous of the VVMF's success because he had not received enough personal recognition for his contributions. Perot had told fund officers that he had tried to have a Vietnam War memorial built in Washington—its inscription, visible from the White House, would have read, "First commit the nation, then commit the troops"—and they believed that he resented the fact that they had succeeded where he had failed.[101] While pressing for an audit, Perot attempted to insert a representative into the VVMF's office to work on the modifications to the memorial's design; Scruggs thought that this effort was "dangerous" and that they should not let Perot "run VVMF."[102]

Perot's strategy was effective. Scruggs was afraid that if Perot demanded an audit insistently, people would believe that something was amiss; and he discussed the steps the VVMF might take to "appease" Perot and his confederates regarding the inscription, statue, and flag. The VVMF tried a combination of means to repel Perot's attacks: they appealed to his comradeship as a veteran dedicated to commemorating those who fought in Vietnam; they tried from the start to satisfy his wish for favorable publicity—for example, by attempting unsuccessfully to have President Jimmy Carter mention Perot when signing the memorial's authorizing legislation—and they frequently anticipated or responded to Perot's perceived touchiness about receiving credit for the memorial.[103] VVMF documents from May 1982 describe Perot as "strictly a publicity seeker" who likely sees the memorial as "a wonderful P.R. freight train that is moving toward its destination and has left him behind."[104] When all else failed, they stonewalled him. The VVMF were in a double bind because to respond to Perot by conducting an audit would appear to validate his complaint that one was required but to refuse to do so would make it seem that the VVMF had something to hide.[105]

This was a tricky situation and one of the low points in the ugly behind-the-scenes fights about the memorial. Years later, Wheeler recalled how fierce the conflict with Perot became. "He pushed me and pushed me to give up the wall," Wheeler said. "He said, 'I'll wipe you out.' It was like being sliced with a knife. The next thing I knew, I was getting threatening phone calls." The VVMF hired the Washington law firm of Williams and Connolly, which they knew to have successfully crossed swords with Perot's lawyers in the past, to represent their interests. Their principal advocate at the firm was Terry O'Donnell, an Air Force Academy graduate who had worked in the Nixon White House and had been President Gerald Ford's appointments secretary. The appointment of O'Donnell as the VVMF's counsel was a canny political move, because O'Donnell had developed a good working relationship with senior Reagan White House staff members James Baker and Richard Darman when all three were members of the Ford administration.[106]

Perot demanded that until the statue and flag were in place, the VVMF must not hold a dedication ceremony for the memorial. The VVMF, however, planned to call the November 1982 event a salute to Vietnam Veterans, rather than a dedication, even though it would coincide with the completion of the granite wall and would constitute a dedication in all but name.[107] They also assured Perot (falsely, as it turned out) that a "replica" of the statue could be in place by the time of the ceremony. The major veterans' and military organizations were participating in what would be the "largest public relations event ever for Vietnam veterans," Scruggs pointed out, with the American Legion playing a leading role.[108] Scruggs hoped, therefore, that Perot could be cajoled into participating, rather than stand on the sidelines caviling. Nothing availed, though, to quiet the cantankerous Texan. He was dissatisfied with the audit of the VVMF's accounts performed by Peat, Marwick, Mitchell and demanded another audit by one of the "big eight" accounting firms. Between May and July 1982, Perot repeatedly demanded full access to the VVMF's records, finally insisting on a yes or no response to his request and threatening to sue unless his demand was met, in which case the results of the investigation would become a matter of public record.[109] This pressure for an audit fitted a pattern of past conduct: Perot had previously made donations to charities and then asked that his representatives be allowed to conduct a detailed review, at Perot's expense, of their financial records. He was an inveterate snoop, who used private investigators to collect information on business rivals and even his own executives. Richard Shlakman, a vice president of EDS and the firm's in-house lawyer, later recalled that it was Perot's "genetic disposition" to "find the dirt."[110] Perot extended an offer to fund a review of the VVMF's records, which they declined. Instead, they agreed to have Peat, Marwick, Mitchell perform a special audit of their disbursements. The VVMF tried to conciliate Perot and even invited him to fund an "open house" for Gold Star Mothers during the National Salute to Vietnam Veterans, but they drew the line at giving him access to their records.[111]

To satisfy Perot's complaints without allowing him to trawl their files, the VVMF set up an independent audit committee of prominent businessmen to oversee all VVMF accounting activities and act as a "buffer" against Perot's demands for his own audit.[112] The VVMF also mobilized their own heavyweights. Acting as an intermediary, General Davison, a former West Point commandant and U.S. Army commander in Europe, reassured Perot that the fund's activities were above board.[113] Demonstrating their growing aptitude for inside-the-Beltway politics, the memorial fund deployed Elliot Richardson and Cyrus Vance, both former White House cabinet secretaries, to beat off Perot's attacks.[114] Richardson was an extraordinarily experienced politician with a reputation for personal integrity who had been advising VVMF about their dealings with Watt.

Like O'Donnell, Richardson had worked with Darman and Baker in the administration of Gerald Ford. His connection with Darman had even deeper roots. From

1970 to 1977, Darman had been part of Richardson's inner circle, following him as his assistant as Richardson took up various posts in the Nixon and Ford administrations. Darman resigned along with Richardson during the "Saturday Night Massacre," when Richardson refused Nixon's order to fire the Watergate special prosecutor, Archibald Cox. (Their principled stand, which some Nixon loyalists saw as betrayal, compounded Republican right-wingers' suspicion of the "pragmatist" Darman.) In the Reagan administration, Darman formed the same sort of association with Baker that he had had with Richardson: he served as Baker's deputy during Reagan's first term and left the White House with him when Baker became secretary of the treasury. While in the White House, Darman chaired the important Legislative Strategy Group. (Along with the "troika" and Craig Fuller, he was considered part of a "big five" that ran the White House.) Darman also had a close personal connection to Tom Shull, whom he had taught at Harvard between his stints in government. While the relationships among O'Donnell, Richardson, Darman, and Baker gave the VVMF high-level connections in the White House, during the controversy about the memorial, Shull formed a close bond with fellow West Point graduate Jack Wheeler. Shull conceived an enduring respect for Wheeler, thus establishing a cooperative relationship at a lower level in the White House hierarchy and reinforcing the VVMF's lines of influence with the administration "pragmatists."[115] The identity of the members of the VVMF's support network highlights the memorial's role in the uneasy relationship between the contending wings of the Republican Party: if one had wanted to diagram the relationship between the far-right ideologues and the moderate "pragmatists," a checklist of the latter group would have included all the memorial fund's White House supporters.

The VVMF discovered that Richardson had confidential knowledge about the tangled skein of relations between Perot and the government during the years when Nixon was president, and they even imagined that Perot became nervous at the sound of Richardson's name. They decided to play Perot at his own game: if Perot was trying to get some dirt on the VVMF in order to intimidate them, they would try to shut him up the same way.[116]

During the Nixon presidency, Perot and the government enjoyed a mutually beneficial relationship, leading a Nixon aide to describe Perot as "the ultimate insider [who] knows his way around the corridors of power almost better than anybody I know."[117] Perot's company, EDS, lent Nixon a plane and seven employees for his campaign's use during Nixon's 1968 run for the presidency, and after Nixon took office the Internal Revenue Service allowed a tax deduction for the EDS employees' salaries. Perot was Nixon's most substantial financial backer in the 1968 election. Perot and the White House coordinated a campaign focusing on U.S. POWs in North Vietnam to rally public support for the administration and to mount a propaganda offensive against the North Vietnamese government, providing Nixon with a rationale for stalemating the peace negotiations in Paris. In 1969 and 1970, White House staff pursued Perot as a benefactor who might fund "private" groups the administration was fostering to rally support for the Vietnam War: a pro-war group to counter antiwar rallies, a right-wing think tank, and a pro-war scholars group.

Perot formed the "United We Stand" organization to demonstrate that the American people stood behind their government and spent about $1 million in this campaign, paying for newspaper ads, television airtime, and thirty million postcards to publicize the plight of the prisoners and call for support of the government's Vietnam policies. Perot also spent millions of dollars to shore up a Wall Street brokerage firm at the White House's request. During the 1970 mid-term elections, Perot became the largest individual contributor to congressional candidates' campaigns. Twelve recipients of Perot's donations later voted for a $15 million tax break designed to benefit his corporations.[118]

The rewards Perot gained from his dealings with the government were substantial. White House intervention and "sweetheart contracts" allowed EDS to obtain 90 percent of the computer work on Medicare contracts, and the profits the company generated led *Ramparts* magazine to dub Perot "America's first welfare billionaire."[119] While Richardson was secretary of health, education, and welfare, a General Accounting Office investigation and congressional hearings considered allegations of excessive EDS profits, a conflict of interest in the awarding of a Texas Medicare contract to EDS, and noncompliance with government regulations in the awarding of it.[120] Perot asked Richardson's department to help settle the contract disagreements between EDS and state governments and Richardson came under White House pressure to comply.[121] The government investigation cleared EDS of profiteering and Scruggs learned that despite EDS's supposed "sloppy accounting procedures" Richardson had "saved Perot's ass."[122] How he did so is not recorded, but in any case, the VVMF's attempt at playing hardball was unavailing. The obvious flaw in their strategy for facing down Perot was that if Richardson's department had shown undue leniency toward Perot's company it would reflect at least as badly on Richardson as on Perot. Whatever Richardson knew about Perot's past business dealings, his influence did not shut Perot up, and he cautioned the VVMF to keep Perot at arm's length, warning them not to allow him to go "'fishing' through VVMF's records." He said that it was unlikely that Perot would "exert any influence at the White House, where he was regarded as an "eccentric." Vance also advised the fund not to indulge Perot's demands and to sever relations with him.[123]

The section-by-section construction of the wall went on in August and September 1982 and the revised design underwent a renewed approval process. After some debate between the sculpture committee and Cooper-Lecky Partnership about how close together the statue and wall should be, the VVMF sent a proposal for the placement of the statue and flag to the Department of the Interior, and Watt sent the proposal on to the National Capital Planning Commission and the Fine Arts Commission. Watt was enthusiastic about the addition of a "heroic" statue and flag to the site, saying that the changes would mean that the memorial honored surviving veterans as well as those who died serving their country. "Design aesthetics," he said, "are a secondary consideration." Scruggs met Watt at the memorial site, where Watt told him, off the record, that the memorial was "beautiful." Watt was still threatening, however, to forbid the dedication ceremony from taking place unless the Fine Arts Commission and the National Capital Planning Commission approved the central location for the statue and flag agreed to in March. The American Legion and the VFW forcefully told Watt, though, that they were determined to go ahead with the National Salute to Vietnam Veterans.[124]

As construction of the wall proceeded, there was a tentative rapprochement between the VVMF and Carhart and Webb. Webb had, after all, been serving on the sculpture panel; Hart had been commissioned to design a statue and his work had gone ahead. Webb suggested that the VVMF invite Carhart and Copulos to tour the memorial site.[125] Carhart proposed that Perot be invited to an unveiling of a section of the memorial planned for September.[126] He said that while he disliked certain aspects of the memorial design, he would "no longer fight them" and added, "That's what compromise means."[127] However, a few days later, Carhart renewed his attack, saying that Congress had never demanded a listing of all America's dead, and that the names on the wall added "a funereal tone to the whole affair." He suggested that the veterans on the wall should be given a "decent burial": that the slope in front of the memorial should be filled in, a flower garden planted, and the statue and flag installed on top.[128]

The imminent October meeting of the Fine Arts Commission, which would review the Hart sculpture, concentrated people's minds. White House staff carefully monitored developments, recognizing that the dedication planned for November 13 hinged on the Fine Arts Commission's approval.[129] Lin's position regarding the siting of the statue was bolstered by the American Institute of Architects, which submitted a proposal for a distant location for both statue and flag but did not succeed in mustering support beyond its own membership.[130] Perot finally released the results of the February 1982 poll he commissioned in which former POWs registered their antipathy to the original memorial design.[131] The poll's publication on the eve of the Fine Arts Commission meeting was evidently designed to maximize the poll's impact on the commission's decision. When *60 Minutes* aired its report on the memorial shortly before the meeting, it showed Perot threatening that he would "spend whatever time, money and energy" were necessary to oppose any "double-dealing" regarding the placement of the statue and flag. "And I'm going to have a lot of powerful allies," he warned. The broadcast showed Perot as a rather menacing figure; Lin, in contrast, came across as quite reasonable and sympathetic. Morley Safer, the interviewer, suggested that the Hart statue was superfluous to a memorial as simple as Lin's wall and questioned why the memorial fund's critics refused to accept the result of a design competition that was conducted fairly, according to the rules. Wherever Safer's sympathies lay, though—and the broadcast seemed to cast favorable light on Lin—the outcome appeared final: Secretary Watt declared on screen that unless the Fine Arts Commission approved the agreed changes, "there will be no Vietnam memorial here in Washington, DC."[132]

At its October 1982 meeting, the Fine Arts Commission considered the memorial fund's formal recommendation that the statue be placed facing the wall, some 150 feet from it, slightly off center from a line bisecting the angle of the walls. The flagpole, 50 feet tall, would be at the apex of the walls.[133] Carhart, Webb, Perot, and their congressional ally, Don Bailey (D., Pennsylvania), endorsed the sculpture panel's plan.[134] Undersecretary of the Interior Donald Hodel testified that his department would allow a permit for the November unveiling ceremony only if the new plan were approved. The Fine Arts Commission, however, voted down this recommendation. The sculpture, Brown said, should not be placed in front of the memorial, where it would "shiver naked out there in the field." To minimize the intrusion of the statue and flag on Lin's design, he suggested that they might be placed together near a path leading from the Lincoln Memorial to the wall, along with an alphabetical directory to help visitors locate a particular name on the wall. Hart supported this proposal, although he was unable to persuade Webb and Carhart of its merits.[135] Having voted down the VVMF's submission, the commission gave conditional approval to the statue and flag and agreed to reconsider their precise location once the VVMF were ready to submit a new plan. Explaining the commission's decision, the magisterial Brown was casual to the point of dismissiveness in his reference to the official discourse of "healing." He said that the commission was responsible for approving a design that pleased all Americans, not just a group of veterans, "although we recognized the need for healing and recognition and all of that. But it was up to us to take the long view."[136] The phrase "and all of that" perfectly captures Brown's lofty detachment from the memorial fund's language.

Having fulfilled their promise by submitting a plan in keeping with the provisions of the March 1982 "compromise," the memorial fund were able in good conscience to switch their allegiance to Brown's alternative proposal. They began to strategize with Brown, agreeing that it would be best not to overreact to criticism but instead to "isolate the extremists" by getting the majority to shut them up. This maneuvering appears to justify all Perot's suspicions about the untrustworthiness of the VVMF as negotiating partners; but one can hardly blame them for using the statutory review process as a check on the strong-arm tactics of the critics, who wanted to override the jury's and the commission's prior decisions. Because the commission had approved the addition of the new elements in principle, it would be difficult for Watt to justify canceling the November unveiling of the wall. To try to put the debate about the design to rest, Senators Mathias and Warner invited the president to attend a press event where he could review plans for the memorial, but the president ducked the invitation.[137]

Soon after the Fine Arts Commission hearing, Perot, Scruggs, and Lin appeared on the ABC News *Nightline* broadcast. Lin again came across sympathetically, speaking clearly and without rancor about her design and the reasons for the controversy. Perot cited his poll results, although the host, Ted Koppel, said that a poll of 324 POWs was hardly representative of the millions who served in Vietnam. Scruggs said the methodology of the poll was flawed and that it was not worth the paper it was printed on. He said the questions were loaded and that it was difficult for respondents to give their impressions of a memorial that they had not yet seen. All three interviewees anticipated the National Salute, when veterans and others would see the memorial for themselves. Perot said that if the veterans liked it, he would be satisfied; if not, they should "come out of the closet" and make their views known.[138]

The *Richmond Times-Dispatch* editorialized against the Fine Arts Commission's decision. It called Lin's wall a "big black boomerang" and complained that the wishes of veterans had been ignored when the commission voted against a central position for the statue. The newspaper argued that the congressional resolution mandating the memorial had required that it "honor" those who served in Vietnam, whereas the wall lent itself to contemplation, not honor. Comparing the wall to a minimalist artwork by the sculptor Carl Andre, the *Times-Dispatch* suggested that tourists would prefer Hart's statue. It said the wall would appeal to the antiwar crowd. "Most Vietnam veterans," it claimed, "evidently think that it's horrible." In contrast, the *Dayton Journal Herald* pointed to the superfluity of the Hart statue—and the risk that others might want to add their own embellishments—by printing an editorial cartoon showing the ground in front of the wall cluttered with kitsch garden furniture alongside Hart's statue: pink flamingos, a bird bath, Christmas reindeer, and a Civil War cannon for good measure.[139]

The critics reacted to the Fine Arts Commission decision by crying "foul." Representative Bailey, Senator Steve Symms (R., Idaho), and six other Republican members of Congress wrote to Watt asking him to forbid the dedication unless the central positions for the flag and statue were approved.[140] Supported by Webb, Carhart, and Copulos, Bailey said that, without the flag and statue as an integral part of the design, the memorial would be exactly what was originally intended: "a monument designed specifically to avoid carrying any political message." If the memorial did not conform to the March 1982 agreement, Bailey undertook to propose legislation that would achieve this goal. If all else failed, he and his fellows would acquire a piece of land and create a Vietnam veterans memorial as a totally private venture.[141] Despite the legislators' objections, the momentum for the National Salute to Vietnam Veterans was unstoppable. The Department of the Interior took no steps to block the event. The wall would be dedicated.

One art critic has likened the antagonism between wall and statue to a conflict between Jane Fonda and John Wayne, and therefore a political argument pitting antiwar against pro-war forces.[142] The effective spectrum of debate was considerably narrower, though. On one side were supporters of the memorial fund led by moderate Republicans; on the other were ideologically motivated cold warriors and militarists in the right wing of the Republican Party and on its fringes. The remnants of the movement against the Vietnam War were simply absent from the debate. Unlike the right-wingers who, after the design of Lin's wall was unveiled, demanded a bronze statue, a flag, and an inscription bringing honor to those who served, the left did not make equivalent demands for a graphic depiction of the wrongful acts the U.S. forces had committed in Southeast Asia with an inscription reading "Never Again." The left did not try to turn the memorial into a symbol that would stay Reagan's hand in Central America, as some of the memorial fund's critics wished to make it into a symbol that would strengthen the United States in its fight against Communism. To believe that a roster of the dead is an antiwar statement is to forget that the opposition to the war was not based simply on an aversion to American casualties but was expressed in far broader moral and political terms.[143]

The critic's "John Wayne versus Jane Fonda" interpretation also oversimplifies the complex relationship between aesthetics and politics in the Vietnam Veterans Memorial. The argument over the memorial design in Austin, Texas, and the distinction between the two West Point memorials help to illuminate the conflict in Washington, DC, by reinforcing the fact that it was also a conflict between tradition and novelty. Honor and respect had come to be associated, in some minds, with traditional forms, such as obelisks and realistic statuary, presumably because of the Washington Monument, the Iwo Jima Memorial, and a hundred other memorials. The fact that the Austin veterans' organization favored an obelisk should notify us that the issue was not simply about abstraction versus realism—an obelisk is, after all, a geometrical form, but it was nevertheless acceptable to the veterans because it is a familiar one, with unambiguously positive connotations in the nation's roll of honor.

"Too bad it wasn't a simple war," Scruggs observed. "Then we could put up a heroic statue of a couple of Marines and leave it at that."[144] Webb, Carhart, and the other critics' preference for a realistic statue did not arise from an indiscriminate commitment to realism at any price. One has only to imagine their reaction to a realistic statue of Ho Chi Minh on the Mall to see this point. Their commitment to a statue and flag demonstrates only their wish for the laurels they believed that they had been unjustly denied. Here was the paradox: *because* the Vietnam War was different from other wars—doubtful in its morality, and a disillusioning defeat—the memorial fund's critics insisted that they be given a memorial just like one that might have commemorated previous wars. Only this could remove the stigma of defeat and dishonor.

Hart had stated that Lin's wall was opaque in meaning, a "blank canvas" whose indifference to the public bespoke the elitism and arrogance of modernism, whereas his own work was accessible and "populist."[145] The critic Tom Wolfe had already elaborated this idea, seeing the arguments about the Vietnam memorial as one battle in a long war between modernist aesthetes and the rest of the world, which, unaccountably, the aesthetes were winning. In an article about the conflict between advocates and detractors of the wall, he referred to numerous instances in which the "mullahs of modernism" foisted their doctrine on a hapless public. Wolfe suggested that the Vietnam memorial was the product of this East Coast–dominated artistic orthodoxy contemptuous of public tastes and that Lin's wall would be obscure to the public.[146] Following Wolfe, William Stensland, a friend and ally of Webb's, said that the memorial pitted the "art world" against the "common man."[147] Ordinary veterans did, indeed, prove susceptible to the worrying criticisms of the memorial that they heard—at least until the memorial was dedicated so that they could make up their own minds. Had the critics succeeded in destroying the memorial before it was built, their views would have become self-fulfilling: the "common people" would never have seen the memorial and the critics could have said whatever they liked about the people's tastes, having created a fact on the ground to suit their ideological visions.

A veteran named J. E. Nelson, a former sergeant in the air force and a Republican, after reading a reprint of Wolfe's criticism of the memorial in his local newspaper, the *Sacramento Bee*, wrote to President Reagan to complain about the creation of a "tribute to Jane Fonda." Reagan replied, "You have every right to be angry and, believe me, I join you." But what was Reagan agreeing with? Surely not with Wolfe's critique of the memorial design, since the Department of the Interior was allowing the wall's unveiling to go ahead. The rest of Nelson's message chimed with Reagan's views, though. Nelson said that Lyndon Johnson had erred by not declaring war. He said that the war was "a job that was needed but was totally . . . inadequately executed from beginning to end." Reagan, while not quite engaging with Nelson's train of thought, added his own: "Those of you who fought in Vietnam fought as bravely and as well as any American fighting man has ever fought. To those who insist that conflict was immoral, let me say the only immorality was in a government asking men to fight and die for a cause that government was unwilling to let them win. . . . I see that Memorial in Washington as a final recognition of a sacrifice made in a noble cause—the defense of freedom for people who could not defend it themselves."[148]

What might be unclear, without the paper trail establishing the behind-the-scenes maneuvers, is why the Reagan administration gave so little support to the VVMF's critics, who seemed to be demanding for Vietnam veterans the respect and honor that Reagan, too, insisted that they receive. Yet the administration decided not to back the critics, even though they espoused an essentially Reaganite vision of a resurgent America and insisted on a patriotic assertion of pride in America's role in Vietnam, just as Reagan did. Among the reasons for this decision was that the administration was mindful of the broad support for the VVMF. No one near the top of the White House hierarchy was particularly convinced of the arguments against Lin's wall. It was more important to the White House and Senator Warner to cobble together a "compromise" that would allow the memorial to be constructed than to insist on either the aesthetic vision of the original memorial design or the ideological purism of the critics. The important thing was to get the memorial built, and neither Ross Perot's wealth, Carhart and Webb's rhetoric, nor the right-wing congressmen's lobbying had sufficient clout to make the project worth derailing, no matter how often they recited Reagan's "noble cause" line. As for the details of where the statue should be located: those were not important enough to undo the White House's support for the memorial.[149]

John Bodnar, inverting Wolfe's class analysis, argues that the Vietnam Veterans Memorial was initiated by "ordinary people," such as Scruggs and other Washington-area veterans, and won the support not just of political leaders but of "ordinary citizens" around the country. Lin's design was "skewed toward the personal interests of ordinary people." Although Scruggs was satisfied with the design, others turned against it. The "powerful and dominant interests of patriots and nationalists" opposed the design. Carhart changed his mind about supporting the memorial fund and, Bodnar reminds us, both he and Webb, another prominent opponent, were graduates of elite service academies, where they had been "fully exposed to the ideologies of national service and glory." Bodnar also names Perot as an opponent and draws attention to his wealth. In contrast, Scruggs had served as a grunt, Bodnar says, and reflected a warrior-centered opposition antagonistic to those in authority.[150] Thus, while Wolfe places a university-trained elite on the side of Lin's wall, because of their aesthetic preferences, Bodnar places a military-trained elite in opposition to the wall, because of their ideology.

The two analyses could be squared if they were modulated so that two sectoral elites—one cultural, the other military-political—clashed, but both Wolfe and Bodnar tend to see their elites as embodiments of social classes. Their analyses are therefore mutually antagonistic; they cannot both be right. In fact, neither is entirely correct. Wolfe's notion that the public would fail to understand Lin's wall was proved wrong by the overwhelmingly positive response to the memorial, which readily evoked and accommodated the emotions of visitors. Bodnar's analysis has considerably more subtlety in trying to account for the multiple constituencies that the memorial had to assuage or satisfy. However, the attempt to render the argument about the memorial as a conflict pitting one social class against another fails. There were graduates of elite service academies on both sides of the debate: balancing the Annapolis graduate Webb and the West Pointer Carhart among the critics were Wheeler and Mosley, both supporters of the VVMF and both service academy graduates. (If affiliation with service academies had any bearing on the conflict it was in its Annapolis versus West Point subtext, because many of the memorial fund's supporters had West Point connections, whereas several of the leading critics, joined by the maverick West Pointer Carhart, were graduates of the naval academy.)[151] There were members of Congress on both sides of the debate. While Perot disliked the wall, other wealthy businessmen supported the VVMF without making a fuss about the design. What was at stake in the argument about the memorial's design cannot be boiled down into class terms; nor was the argument solely an aesthetic question. The conflict was about politics—but it was about geopolitics in the 1980s as well as the debates concerning the U.S. role in Vietnam. The VVMF's critics were concerned about the effects of the "Vietnam syndrome" on American foreign policy. They believed that because too many people regarded America's war in Vietnam as immoral and shameful, the public had become hesitant about military action and the government was less able to defend the nation's interests beyond its borders. The critics resented the antiwar movement, particularly antiwar veterans, for focusing attention on American forces' crimes. Claiming to be proud of their service, and even to have "won" their war, they demanded an assertive statement of pride and honor. The goal of ideological neutrality offended these critics. A memorial on the Washington Mall would sum up the nation's idea of the Vietnam War, and they saw an assertion of the nobility of America's cause as a vital precondition for the restoration of the United States' international strength and leadership.

The preferences of the memorial fund and their critics became politicized not because of the inherent meaning of one kind of design or another but because of the political and moral meanings with which realistic statuary had been invested, the ambiguity of Lin's design, the initial absence of an inscription and a flag, and the negative connotations that some attached to the wall's color and to the fact that it was sunk in the ground. This last feature was exaggerated by the memorial's detractors, who found all kinds of significance in the "burial" of the memory of the war.

This "burial" notion was based, however, on a misunderstanding or misrepresentation of the memorial's design, whose true shape would become evident only when people saw the wall for themselves. Its ambiguity made Lin's design agreeable to the VVMF, because they wanted to avoid making a statement about the war; but this ambiguity also made her memorial susceptible to the projections, no matter how wild, of the critics.

Despite the arguments and attacks, the VVMF were successful in raising the funds required to complete the memorial, and the installation of the memorial's granite panels proceeded rapidly as the date of the National Salute approached. By the time they completed the construction, the memorial fund had raised over $7 million. About $3 million came in the form of large donations (gifts of over $5,000), mainly from corporations, veterans' organizations, and foundations; but there were almost half a million donations in all, many coming in small amounts from ordinary citizens.[152] Some family members sent the $20 it would cost to inscribe a single name on the wall. The AFL-CIO raised over $50,000, and the International Brotherhood of Boiler Makers, Iron Ship Builders, Blacksmiths, Forgers and Helpers raised almost $11,000. Radiothons around the country raised hundreds of thousands of dollars.[153] The number of donors demonstrates the high level of public support that the memorial had won, and the notes and letters accompanying the donations show that people gave out of a range of motives—wishing the loved ones they mourned to be remembered, wanting recognition for Vietnam veterans, and wanting to ensure that the war itself was not forgotten. Donors included some who said that they had supported the war and others who said they had opposed it. Some donors of small amounts demanded refunds because they objected to the design; they included those who disliked Lin's wall and those who were offended by the modifications to her design. For example, Jack A. Kelley, a former air force captain, asked for a refund of his twenty-five dollars because the wall's "grossly negative" appearance made it "an extension, for all time, of the antiwar activists' view of the G.I." Joan Gooding, however, asked for a refund of her twenty-dollar contribution because the Frederick Hart statue marred the simple wall like a "contagious wart."[154]

For some donors, the design of the memorial was simply not an issue. John Shelton, a veteran who had flown over Hanoi during the war and now ran a crop-dusting business in California, donated what he said was some of his combat pay to the memorial fund. He anticipated coming to the National Salute and wrote, "I won't be representing anyone but a handful of ghosts whose blurry names and strangely boyish faces need badly to be part of the national conscience; who need badly to be welcomed home. Then I can come home and grow old with my kids and forget that stinking place. Personally, I don't care if you erect a giant bronzed jungle boot. All I want is their names up somewhere."[155] Three days after Shelton wrote his letter, on October 29, 1982, construction of the wall of names was completed. It remained only to dedicate the memorial for the "healing" to begin.

5

"HOME TO AMERICA'S HEART"

The National Salute to Vietnam Veterans

✯

JACK WHEELER said that the unveiling of the Vietnam Veterans Memorial would "mark the end of a phase during which it was more comfortable for Americans to pretend we have no Vietnam veterans among us." More than mere acceptance, he said, the dedication would show that "America affirms the integrity of her fighting forces without apology or stain." The National Salute to Vietnam Veterans, he explained, would expose, and thereby end, "the denial that has characterized the country's reaction to the war." He called the November 1982 national salute "probably the single most important step in the process of healing and redemption."[1]

In the week leading up to the salute, veterans and the families of the dead began coming to Washington from around the country. Veterans hired buses and organized fundraisers to buy air tickets for the long journeys from the West Coast and Texas. They filled their gas tanks and drove in caravans of vehicles from Boston, Cleveland, and Denver. Five veterans drove for twenty hours straight from Green Bay, Wisconsin. Jesse Acosta, a member of the Coast Guard serving in Alaska, saved for months to make the trip.[2] Another veteran walked three thousand miles to Washington in fatigues and carrying a full combat pack, as he had marched twelve years earlier in Vietnam. "It was as if they were all drawn by the same ghostly bugle," a Beaumont, Texas, newspaper observed.[3]

Once in Washington, thousands of these out-of-towners visited the Vietnam Veterans Memorial wall for the first time. Having heard of the controversy from afar, they could now make up their own minds. A Gold Star Mother said, "I'm more impressed now that I'm here. I was quite concerned. The Vietnam War was a wrangle and now the monument. It's very pretty. It's going to stand forever." A few days before the dedication, a singing group from Skidmore, Missouri, quieted the crowd lingering at the wall when they began to sing "America the Beautiful."[4] Another night, squabbling veterans became still when a group wearing black berets harmonized "Amazing Grace," then followed with the repeated strains of, "Find the cost of freedom, buried in the ground. / Mother Earth will swallow you, lay your body down."[5] Some of the visitors stayed late into the night, keeping vigil over the names. They drank toasts to each other and friends whose names were on the wall, traded stories about their time in "the Nam," and patrolled with flashlights around the newly completed wall. One night, marine veterans purloined an American flag from a hotel and held it up at the meeting point of the two walls. Others illuminated the flag with matches and flashlights.[6]

The Vietnam Veterans Memorial Fund (VVMF) saw the national salute as an announcement of the Vietnam veterans' presence in society, as the welcome-home parade they missed when they returned from the war, and as a celebration of the common citizen soldier. "It was not a week of generals, admirals, politicians or defense analysts," one newspaper reported, "but one of ordinary American men and women who once went to fight a war. [Jan] Scruggs, an enlisted man severely wounded in combat, conceived the memorial and salute."[7] Many commented on the way ordinary veterans had taken the lead in commemoration, lending the story of the memorial an appealing "everyman" quality—the underdog overcoming the odds to achieve success. But it also expressed a simmering resentment. As a Chicago newspaper said, "Many veterans are angry that the country took so long to honor those who served in Vietnam and that it was the veterans themselves—through the sponsoring VVMF—who had to set the wheels in motion for the memorial.[8] Tersely resentful, a navy veteran said, "It's about time we were recognized." A New Mexico man who served as an army sergeant in Vietnam said of the dedication parade, "They should have had this when we first came back."[9]

These sentiments were consistent with the VVMF's message: the country had been indifferent to the veterans and the government had ignored them. The journalist Hodding Carter said that the dedication was a "homecoming [the veterans] had to organize for themselves because nobody else would do it for them."[10] In the feature film telling the story of the memorial, To Heal a Nation, Scruggs (played by Eric Roberts) says, "Instead of the veterans building a memorial to give to the government, I think maybe the government should have built a memorial to give to the Vietnam veterans."[11] The columnist Mary McGrory said the same: "Naturally they had to organize [the parade] themselves, just as they had to raise the money for their wall, just as they had to counsel each other in their rap centers, just as they had to raise the cry about Agent Orange."[12] The New York Times wrote that "long after it became apparent that no one else was going to give them homecoming, the veterans are doing it for themselves."[13] Newsweek also complained that the veterans had raised the money for the memorial and staged the parade "almost by themselves."[14] All of these complaints ignored the government's role in granting the memorial its site and running interference for the VVMF.

Newspapers around the country wrote that the dedication gave Vietnam veterans their due after years of neglect. Many touched on the familiar theme that their fellow citizens had unjustly stigmatized the veterans for fighting in Vietnam and that it was time to undo this wrong. The Minneapolis Star and Tribune wrote, "Vietnam veterans have suffered the burden of fighting for their country in an unpopular war.

After nearly a decade of silence, this Veterans Day is a time, finally, to recognize the contributions of Vietnam veterans." The *Chattanooga Times* said, "It is a good time for the nation to turn back to Vietnam, if only long enough to say we realize those who fought there were not responsible for the war and ought not to have suffered the extra burden of reproach. It is a good time to say thank you."[15]

Among the tributes to the veterans there were still subtle differences of opinion. While all agreed that the veterans had been mistreated, some patronizingly saw them as victims of the war, while others wrote defiantly that they had been warriors in a noble cause. The *Post-Tribune*, published in Gary, Indiana, wrote, "For years, the revulsion against the Vietnam war had rubbed off on the men who fought there. Of course, it is time to unite and to view the Vietnam veterans as victims, not the provocateurs [sic]." In *USA Today* the former antiwar protester Samuel Berger (once a speechwriter for George McGovern and later the national security adviser for President Bill Clinton) endorsed the idea of the veterans' victim status: the war, he said, should be separated from the "victimized" people who had fought it, and "it's time to right that wrong." The editors of the *Dallas Morning News* agreed that Vietnam veterans had been mistreated. But, citing Norman Podhoretz's defense of the morality of the U.S. war effort, they affirmed the cause for which the troops fought. Southeast Asia would be better off if the United States had won the war. The soldiers fought bravely and "nobly," the newspaper said. "The shame of the war is not theirs. It is their country's, for changing its mind" and beating a "hasty retreat" from Vietnam.[16]

The president's attendance would have counted for a lot, for veterans who craved the country's recognition. The VVMF invited Ronald Reagan to speak at the dedication of the wall on November 13 or, with Nancy Reagan, to be guest of honor at an entertainers' salute on November 10, where they could rub shoulders with old friends from Hollywood. The fund also asked the president and first lady to serve as honorary chairmen of the National Salute to Vietnam Veterans.[17] In the summer of 1982, Scruggs lobbied members of Congress to endorse this invitation, updating them on the progress of the memorial's construction and predicting that two hundred thousand people would take part in the salute.[18] Nine representatives and twenty-five senators, seventeen Democrats and the same number of Republicans, wrote to the president asking that he and the first lady be honorary chairmen. Elizabeth Dole, who headed the White House's Office of Public Liaison, also recommended that the Reagans accept the invitation. Senator Orrin Hatch (R., Utah) encouraged the first lady to participate in the national salute by lighting the first candle at the beginning of the planned candle-lit vigil of November 10.[19]

Most of the letters of support contained fairly routine borrowings from VVMF boilerplate. Senator George Mitchell (D., Maine) wrote that the Vietnam War was a "divisive period" in the nation's history and that "we are only now beginning to heal the wounds caused by that conflict." It would be appropriate, Mitchell said, for the commander in chief to chair the ceremonies. Other letters went beyond the VVMF's rhetoric in drawing out the political significance of the salute. Senator Paula Hawkins (R., Florida), a New Right politician, said that the controversy surrounding the unpopular war in Vietnam obscured the dedication of those who served in America's armed forces. Making essentially the same argument as Representative Ashbrook had a few months earlier, she said that the renewal of respect for those who fought in Vietnam was crucial for the revival of the nation's military strength: "We cannot expect men and women to effectively defend our great nation without pride in their serving. I can think of nothing that will do more to restore the dignity and respect of our fighting forces than this Salute to Vietnam Veterans." Hawkins said that the president's participation in the national salute would remove the stigma from service in Vietnam and restore needed pride. "Your involvement would be a . . . signal to the world that we stand with pride behind our fighting men and women."[20]

Reagan's aides debated the extent to which the president should participate. The National Security Council staff discussed the matter on November 5 and the following day, with the weekend approaching, the White House had still not decided.[21] On November 9, the press quizzed Reagan on whether he would visit the memorial, and he replied, "I can't tell until somebody tells me. . . . I never know where I'm going"—at once an indication that he wanted to duck the question and a telling indication of the degree of influence his aides had on the presidential schedule.[22] One concern was the possibility that Vietnam Veterans Against the War and other demonstrators might be present. Reagan's closest advisers, cautious as ever, wanted him to maintain a discreet distance.[23] The main reason for worry was the design controversy. Secretary of the Interior James Watt had allowed groundbreaking on condition that the memorial not be dedicated before the addition of the statue and flag. The VVMF therefore scrupulously avoided using the term *dedication* in official statements, although in practice everyone involved was now using it. James Webb suggested that at least one panel of the wall of names not be installed so that the memorial could be seen as unfinished. However, with the prospect of thousands of veterans and family members arriving in Washington for the National Salute to Vietnam Veterans, Watt did not want to block completion of the wall and risk disappointing relatives when they found that the names of their loved ones had been left out. All the panels were installed. With the statue and flag not yet added, Michael Deaver persuaded President Reagan to duck the dedication. For all his talk of the nobility of the Vietnam War, the president could not muster the goodwill required to brave any right-wing criticism and show his appreciation of those who fought it. Dole was upset that her plan for the president to participate in the salute was turned down. The president and first lady did, however, accept the title of co-chairmen of the National Salute to Vietnam Veterans and co-signed a message for the souvenir booklet with the program of events, but otherwise they assumed no ceremonial role.[24]

The memorial fund and their critics continued to clash during the days of the salute. True to the discourse of "healing," the Episcopal Church decided, on the initiative of its communicant Jack Wheeler, to hold a service remembering those who served in Southeast Asia, those who died and were listed as missing in action, and "those who actively sought a change in the policy regarding U.S. involvement in Indochina, and those who chose to resist military service."[25] The idea of remembering those who had opposed and resisted the war was more expansive than the memorial fund's commemorative program, as we can recall from the "Questions and Answers" to the competition entrants. The church's gesture to the antiwar groups was too much for Milt Copulos, the conservative critic who had served on the sculpture committee. He objected to putting the missing and fallen on a plane with the war's opponents and resisters, because it insulted those who served and died in Vietnam. Copulos wrote that the memorial was important because "it will stand forever, and the message it carries will influence the way succeeding generations view the American serviceman's role in the war." The left, Copulos said, wanted their service to be viewed "with shame."[26]

Copulos conducted a poll of veterans at the salute, asking them where they would prefer to see the statue and flag located. Meanwhile, the accusations of financial impropriety fueled by H. Ross Perot brought a new blow: in the midst of the VVMF's work organizing the salute, an Internal Revenue Service agent served them with a summons. The VVMF cooperated and the IRS conducted an investigation of their records and found no irregularities. However, the VVMF laid in store more trouble for the future by omitting Perot's name from the list of donors in the national salute's souvenir booklet—and by failing to mention his sponsorship of the design competition. This may have been tactful, because of Perot's antipathy for the memorial, but it could also have been conceived as a slight. Maya Lin, too, received little recognition. She stood on the reviewing stand during the parade, holding a small American flag and occasionally smiling as the marchers passed by. She was not recognized in the official program of events.[27]

As an alternative to taking part in the salute, a National Security Council staffer proposed that the president make a strong statement honoring Vietnam veterans at a wreath-laying ceremony at Arlington National Cemetery, followed by a short, pithy speech. This proposal was turned down.[28] Another alternative was for Reagan to devote his regular weekly radio address on November 13, the day of the memorial's dedication, to the national salute. The Department of Defense drafted a speech for the broadcast, with input from national security adviser William Clark and his deputy, Robert McFarlane. Reagan did not deliver this address, either, but seeing the draft allows us to look over the shoulders of the Defense Department and the National Security Council as they considered the dedication.

The speech linked the plight of America's Vietnam veterans with the neglect of America's defenses, both resulting from the "national trauma" of Vietnam. Making the same case Representative Ashbrook and Senator Hawkins had, the speech warned that a nation that forgets sacrifices such as those its troops made in Vietnam "risks its very existence." However, the speech continued, in 1980 (the fortunate year that Reagan was elected) America "began to awaken from a decade of pain" by rebuilding its defenses and remembering the Vietnam veteran. Dedicating the memorial demonstrated to the world that America remembers its veterans, and the speech proposed, recalling the words of Abraham Lincoln about an earlier divisive war, that it was time to "bind up the nation's wounds."[29] The speech's reference to the Vietnam War as a "just cause" (a rhetorical notch down from "noble" but still a strong endorsement) and the notion that remembrance is the key to future strength shows that the Reagan administration saw the connection between commemoration and the nation's military preparedness. Here, the administration's ideas resembled those of the memorial fund's critics, as well as Ashbrook's and Hawkins's; the affinity between their views may help to explain the administration's caution about associating too closely with the memorial. But the administration was also taking a wait-and-see approach, because how the nation and its veterans responded to the memorial would become much clearer during and after the dedication.

The national salute began on November 10, 1982, with a round-the-clock vigil and reading of the names of dead, in alphabetical order, at the National Cathedral. As visitors entered, they passed under the tympanum (the ornamental space set in the triangular pediment above the doorway) carved by Frederick Hart, one of the credentials that helped win him the sculpture commission. Volunteers from around the country read the names from behind a wooden altar set with candles, white chrysanthemums, and bamboo. A Marine Corps veteran who had served as a sergeant in Vietnam began with the A's: "Gerald Aadland, James Downing Aalund, Daniel Lawrence Aamold." The recitation went on day and night at the rate of about a thousand names an hour, with only a short break each morning. A veteran of the 1st Air Cavalry Division came from his farm in Pittsville, Wisconsin, and read his quota of 276 names while wearing the uniform of a captain in the army reserve. Occasionally, the ceremony faltered as the readers were overcome with emotion. An army reserve officer attending the reading was moved to tears. "I never had the opportunity to attend the funerals of my friends," he said. "This is it." The reading, punctuated by prayers, went on until November 12. Of all the events during the national salute, the editors of the *Sacramento Bee* wrote, "it is those names, like a drumroll, that will command the attention. . . . They are not symbolic, they are the reality—the tragedy of war and the dedication of American soldiers—that Veterans Day has always memorialized."[30]

The volunteers, who read the names in half-hour shifts, had practiced pronouncing them correctly, with a Polish priest, a Spanish teacher, and a rabbi providing expert advice.[31] Names like Jose Maldonado, Kazuto Moriwaki, and Michael Patrick Murphy reflected the ethnic diversity of the American population.

> [Among them were] rhythmic Spanish names. Tongue-twisting Polish names, guttural German, exotic African, homely Anglo-Saxon names. Chinese, Polynesian, Indian, and Russian names. They are names which run deep into the heart of America, each testimony to a family's decision, sometime in the past, to wrench itself from home and culture to test our country's promise of new opportunities and a better life. They are names drawn from the farthest corners of the world and then, in this generation, sent to another distant corner in a war America has done its best to forget. But to hear the names being read . . . is to remember. The war was about names, each name a special human being who never came home.[32]

The author of this commentary, *Newsweek* editor-in chief William Broyles, a Vietnam veteran, found no irony in the fact that many came from afar seeking a better life only to see their offspring sent to fight and die far from America's shores. For him, the willingness of ethnically diverse Americans to give their lives in service to the nation underlines their devotion to it. Their sacrifice affirms the ideal image of the nation that made it a beacon of hope to millions.

Ronald Reagan saw a television news segment criticizing him for not attending the dedication, saying that Vietnam veterans deserved better. Responding to his aides' concern that this was bad publicity, the president and first lady quickly decided to make an unannounced visit to the National Cathedral. They lit a candle as the names were read out and stayed for twenty minutes—from Burd to Burris.[33] "The names that are being read are of men who died for freedom just as surely as any men who ever fought for this country," Reagan told reporters in a "choked voice." Vietnam veterans had as much right to be proud of their service, the president said, as those who had fought in any of the nation's wars. But even at this solemn moment he was unready to put aside polemics about the rights and wrongs of the war: "The tragedy," he added, "was that they were asked to fight and die for a cause that their country was unwilling to win." Asked how he thought the dead would be remembered, he said, "We're beginning to appreciate that they were fighting for a just cause."[34]

It required a gloss such as Reagan's to make the names politically meaningful. In themselves, they licensed no judgment, positive or negative, of the war. A list of names of the dead could be a roll of honor; but it could also be a litany of protest; or, as the critics of the memorial feared, it could be a meaningless recitation, like reading the telephone directory. The socially sanctioned meanings would be shaped by the ceremonies surrounding the dedication. Although the next day's papers reported Reagan's visit to the cathedral, his distance from the center of the dedication events meant that it would largely be left to others to endow the deaths with meaning.

During the Vietnam War, local newspapers listed the names of citizens from their areas killed in Vietnam and ran with them messages of grief, honoring the dead and resolving to carry on the fight in which they fell. But the names of the dead had also been recited in protests against the war: they were read out in Washington as part of the 1969 "March Against Death" and Operation Dewey Canyon III in 1971, reminding listeners of the war's costs and implicitly accusing the war's architects of responsibility for the deaths.[35] A 1969 *Life* magazine article paired images with the names of the 242 Americans who died in Vietnam between May 28 and June 3, 1969. The display of photographs of mainly youthful faces resembled a high-school yearbook; the accompanying story referred to the deaths as a "tragedy."[36] In the context of a mounting tide of antiwar sentiment this article marked *Life* magazine's shift in editorial policy from unquestioning support of the war to skepticism. Whether the names of the dead were redolent with meaning or mute signifiers of nothing at all depended on the context and the predispositions of the reader or listener. When the names were read for the National Salute to Vietnam Veterans, the National Cathedral resonated with respect and honor. One of those who attended wrote in a diary about the dignity of the event: "All very quiet, all very subdued. No fanfare."[37]

The listing of the names on the wall was democratic. The dead were not inscribed in order of rank, as often occurred in American Civil War memorials and sometimes in memorials to World War I, where officers and other ranks were listed separately.[38] All the names were given equal weight. A veteran from New Mexico said that this made the memorial perfect: "Our memorial doesn't have just the generals' names on it. There is no prejudice as to rank. The privates are allotted the same amount of space as the majors. I have nothing negative to say about it."[39] The memorial lists the first and last names, and a middle name or middle initial, along with suffixes such as "Jr." or "III." It perfectly balances the individual and collective aspects of mourning and commemoration. Each person is named individually, but all are treated as one whole corpus. They are not organized by service (U.S. Air Force, Army, Coast Guard, Marines, Navy), branch (e.g., artillery, engineers), unit (e.g., 173rd Airborne, 5th Marines), home state, or any other grouping. They are, simply, those who served in the American forces and who died while in service in Southeast Asia or were deemed to be missing in action. The "unit" to which they all belonged is the highest aggregation: the nation's armed forces—and by implication, the nation itself.

Most U.S. personnel served one-year tours of duty in Vietnam (marines served thirteen months). The chronological listing of the names means that all those who died during a veteran's tour of duty are grouped within a sequence of consecutive panels. Veterans therefore formed particularly strong associations with certain sections and panels of the memorial. A sequence of names in alphabetical order indicates that those troops fell on the same day, sometimes in the same battle, allowing veterans to find clusters of names that have particular meaning for them—such as several friends they may have lost in a single firefight. Stand in front of the memorial and, by finding alphabetized sequences of many names, you can still see where, in the chronicle of death, major battles occurred.

Despite its demographic comprehensiveness, the list of names on the wall reflects decisions about whom to include and exclude. Listed are all those who served in the U.S. military forces and who died as a direct result of their presence in the Southeast Asian theater of combat, or who were classified as missing. Each name is separated from its neighbors by a symbol. The decision to place a diamond next to the names of those identified as KIA (killed in action) left open the question of what to do about the approximately 1,350 classified as missing in action, almost all of whom had been subject to a Defense Department presumptive finding of death. Initially, the National League of Families of American Prisoners and Missing in Southeast Asia had not wanted the missing to be listed on the wall at all.[40] The VVMF finally decided that those still officially designated MIA (missing in action) would be listed chronologically at the date they went missing, and their names accompanied by a cross matching the size of the diamond, which could be changed to a diamond if the government reclassified the individual as KIA or surrounded by a circle if he returned alive. This decision took care of the awkward problem of whether, and how, to include the names of those whom the National League and others believed to be alive. Over the years, the remains of several hundred of the MIAs have been recovered and the crosses changed to diamonds. No MIAs have turned up alive since the dedication of the memorial and consequently none of the crosses has been enclosed by a circle.[41] In this and in other cases, because of the difficulty of deciding whether a particular person's name should be on the wall, the VVMF deferred to the Department of Defense.[42]

Although the dates that bookend the sequence of names are 1959 and 1975, it became clear after the dedication that these did not correspond to the first and last deaths. A year after the memorial was unveiled the name of Captain Harry G. Cramer, who died in 1957, was added to panel 1-E, the first panel of the east wall. The date inscribed at the top of that panel could not be changed and remains 1959. Then, after a years-long campaign by his family, the name of Sergeant Richard B. Fitzgibbon Jr., who died in 1956, was added. Fitzgibbon was not killed by enemy action but was murdered by a fellow air force sergeant. His is the first recorded death on the wall, but because there was no space on panel 1-E, his name is inscribed elsewhere. Fitzgibbon has another distinction: six months after the marines landed in South Vietnam, his son, Lance Corporal Richard B. Fitzgibbon III, was killed in action. His name is inscribed on panel 2-E, adjacent to the panel where his father's name, by dint of date, should have been. Theirs is the only father-and-son pair of names on the wall.[43]

The terminal date of 1975 for the last death overlooked the continuing toll of postwar deaths. Military personnel who died in Vietnam from noncombat causes— illness, accident, murder, or suicide—were included in the initial listing, which ended with the marines killed recapturing the *Mayaguez* off the coast of Cambodia in May 1975. But people wounded in action in Vietnam whose deaths after returning home could not be exclusively attributed to their wounds were not.[44] This judgment must have seemed arbitrary, particularly to the families of those whose deaths years after the war appeared to have resulted from injuries that had required nursing throughout that time.[45] But independently adjudging the claims made on behalf of such postwar casualties would have put the VVMF in the difficult position of deciding whether or not a death was the direct result of the Vietnam War. It would also have raised the question whether postwar deaths attributed to exposure to the chemical defoliant Agent Orange should be recorded on the wall, and this was one controversy the VVMF managed to avoid.

Some Americans who died in Vietnam were civilians—government employees, including members of the CIA and the State Department, and members of aid organizations. Some of these civilians were an integral part of the American war effort. Others, who worked for the Civil Operations and Revolutionary Development Support program (CORDS), were involved in the "other war," the battle for the hearts and minds of the South Vietnamese. Their names, too, were left off the wall. John Paul Vann, a celebrated and highly decorated army officer, died in a helicopter crash in Vietnam's Central Highlands in 1972, but his name was not recorded on the wall because he was at that time a civilian adviser in the pacification program, not a soldier.[46] What about the journalists killed in the theater of war? What about the USO and Red Cross workers, affectionately and patronizingly termed "donut dollies," who tried to distract the troops from the hardships of military service? A Vietnam veteran from South Dakota came to the dedication wondering whether the names of four Red Cross women who died in a plane crash with a friend of his would be on the wall.[47] They were not. Only members of the U.S. armed services were listed. Eight women's names do appear on the wall—those of the eight military nurses who died in Vietnam. Names have been added to the wall since its unveiling. Some are the names of veterans who died outside Vietnam and whose death the Department of Defense attributed directly to wounds received in theater; the names of others who had died in Vietnam but whose records were lost in military bureaucracy were also added.[48]

The names of foreign citizens who died while serving in the U.S. armed forces appear on the wall, but the names of America's allies—Australian, New Zealander, Filipino, South Korean, Thai, and South Vietnamese forces—do not. Neither do the names of the North Vietnamese soldiers and Viet Cong guerrillas who died in the war, or of the civilians in North and South Vietnam who were killed by both sides. Years after the dedication of the memorial, the artist Chris Burden created "The Other Vietnam Memorial," consisting of twelve copper panels, each seven feet by twelve feet, mounted on a central pole and hinged so they can turn, like pages in a book. The panels carry three million Vietnamese names, representing the number of Vietnamese people killed during the years of American involvement in the Second Indochina War—an implicit criticism of the wall's silence about these deaths.[49]

The inclusions and exclusions signify that the commemoration refers exclusively to members of the U.S. military service, implying that the nation is imagined in its purest form through the names and bodies of those who served and died in uniform. While this may seem a common-sense approach to commemorating a war, it is not the only way to think about the war. Warfare is one of the very few collective actions in which a nation acts *as* a nation. Fighting a war involves decisions in Washington—in the White House and Congress, for example—as well as events in the theater of combat. It also involves arguments around the kitchen table and protests in the streets. But the monument is the Vietnam *Veterans* Memorial, not the Vietnam *War* Memorial. By centering on those who fought and died, the wall emphasizes the foot soldier and field commander, not the president or Congress. Political and strategic factors would be implicated in a war memorial but are sidelined in a veterans memorial that carries a roster of the dead.

The gathering together of the names ignores the extent to which the war both divided the public and brought the armed forces into disarray.[50] Some of those named on the wall were "fragged" (assassinated) by their own comrades, and it is also likely that named nearby are some of those who did the fragging or otherwise rebelled against their commanders' authority.[51] Yet the memorial's symmetry and formal unity belie any recollection of incidents of in-service resistance to the war, or of the certain fact that some of those named died while fighting in a war in which they did not believe. The relationship the memorial creates between the nation and its honored dead tidies both into imaginary unity.

An estimated 150,000 people watched the veterans' parade and attended the dedication. This large turn-out marked a high degree of public recognition—although a twenty-seven-year-old spectator said "there should be millions here," not simply a crowd comparable to that at a pro football game. The VVMF gave the parade the slogan, "Marching along together again." It was more than a reenactment of wartime marches, though; it also compensated the veterans for what they missed when they first came home. The parade coordinator, Colonel K. H. Hunter, said, "The National Salute to Vietnam Veterans Parade is a glorious and long overdue event—the parade they never got." Like other hometown newspapers, the *Bismarck Tribune* agreed: "At long last, our Vietnam vets seem to be getting their parade." Colin Campbell, a spectator, said, "It's an historic event. It's an overdue welcome home for the Vietnam veterans, ten or eleven years too late." As the parade passed by, Washington residents held up signs large and small saying, "Welcome home!" Veterans in the parade were gratified, although there was something double-edged about a welcome home years after the event, an implied criticism of the poor reception that the veterans initially received. But this shortcoming could now be made good. The memorial fund's vaunted reconciliation would be achieved by the public's embracing the veterans as they might have done long ago—and by the veterans' returning the embrace. Mark Bloom, a helicopter pilot in Vietnam said, "It's been a long time coming home. It's the first time in 12 years I haven't felt like an alien." A veteran in the Pennsylvania section of the march clasped his hands above his head and shouted back to the crowd, "We're home, right here! We're home!"[52]

As the fifteen thousand veterans marched past, Eddie Martinez, a government employee said, "We owe 'em a great deal. They had this coming to them for a long time. This is our way of saying thank you." Older veterans from World War II and Korea gave the veterans the thumbs up. Two children in the crowd watching the parade held hand-lettered signs saying, "I'm proud my Daddy is a Vietnam vet." The crowd included people who had once opposed the war (a reminder that many in the antiwar movement had claimed that they were supporting the troops and felt no hostility to its veterans). A woman who had protested the war in the 1960s, said, "It's time for everyone to get together and say thank you." Another woman, who wore an antiwar button and who was in her teens when the war ended, said, "They're finally acknowledging the veterans. It's about time." Jim Peebles, a twenty-six-year-old graduate student, was one of those who had not appreciated the Vietnam veterans at first. He admitted, "I'm sure I contributed to the national disavowal. My being here is a way of saying, 'I'm sorry for the way America was.'" A woman in the crowd said, "A grateful nation is finally coming together." Another woman along the parade route held up a sign that said simply "Thanks!" Reciprocating, a marching veteran shouted back at the crowd, "Thank you, people." Grace Barolet O'Brien, an evacuation hospital nurse in Vietnam, said that linking arms and marching down Constitution Avenue with other Maryland veterans was "one of the highlights of my life." Seeing the crowd greeting the marchers and saying, "Thanks" and "Welcome home" made her want to cry. "I felt so appreciated for what I had done and felt proud to have served my country in Vietnam."[53]

The behavior of marchers and onlookers and the placards they carried testify, though, to the persistence of the nation's sharp wartime divisions. Alongside affirmations of pride were expressions of bitterness and cynicism, such as, "Next time, let us win it." A couple of marine veterans wore buttons saying, "I'd do it again—Vote for Reagan." One placard said: "I am a Vietnam veteran. I like the memorial. And if it makes it difficult to send people into battle again . . . I'll like it even more." James Mahoney, a navy veteran in the audience holding a placard that read, "No more wars, No more lies, No more stone memorials" had the sign wrenched from his hands and smashed by a passing member of the New Jersey contingent. Chanting, "Hell, no, I won't go," Vietnam Veterans Against the War (VVAW), carried signs reading, "No More Vietnams," and "We won't be fooled again." Other VVAW signs read, "Honor the Dead. Fight for the Living"; "We Want Jobs"; and "Test Treat Compensate for Agent Orange."[54]

The presence of opponents and die-hard supporters of the war at a march honoring those who served in Vietnam demonstrated that the first condition for the fulfillment of the VVMF's goal of "reconciliation" was being met. Rather than participating in opposed demonstrations and counterdemonstrations for and against the war, as they might have done during wartime, they were at least participating in the same event. Though outright conflict, such as the clash between Mahoney and the New Jersey veteran, was rare, the expression of a plurality of points of view on a common stage did not mean harmony—it could also mean competition to define the meaning of the event (as if the demonstrators and counterdemonstrators were forcibly mingled, jostling rather than happily rubbing along together). Perhaps the veterans with protest signs were not really at odds with the others, though, but were simply adding an extra ingredient to the general demand for attention and redress, while displaying (aside from the occasional clash) the marchers' diversity and mutual tolerance—a vivid enactment of the doctrine of reconciliation.

The meaning of some of the messages was diffuse. An Indiana veteran carried a sign that read, "57,000 killed in vain. Shame, horror, deceit, treachery." He said his message was "for 20 guys in my unit, blown away in one day."[55] But what were his historical and moral judgments of the war? If the United States had won the war, would the deaths still have been in vain? Who was betrayed, and by whom? The message conveys outrage at the deaths, without clarifying whether the problem was that the United States sent troops to fight in Vietnam or that, having sent them, it lost the war. Peter Poccia of New York City, who had served as a navy corpsman (the marine equivalent of an army medic), joined other antiwar groups at the end of the line of march. He carried a hand-lettered sign that read, "We killed, we bled, we died for worse than nothing."[56] The message conveys indignation; but was "for worse than nothing" a protest against the goals of the fighting, or its result?

The march was headed by a small group of veterans in camouflage uniforms carrying flags, including a Veterans of Foreign Wars flag and a POW/MIA (prisoner of war/missing in action) flag, flanked by other marchers bearing rifles at the slope. After them came the color guard in dress uniforms carrying the flags of all fifty states. They led the marchers under a huge Stars and Stripes held above the street by metal piers. Then came the fifteen thousand veterans, who marched in state contingents arranged in alphabetical order, starting with Alabama, along Constitution Avenue to the memorial. From Alabama's point to Wyoming's rearguard, the parade took two and a half hours to process down Constitution Avenue. Onlookers in their thousands shouted out the names of the states as the contingents marched by, saying, "Thank you, Indiana, thank you," or "Yeah, Iowa," or "God bless you."

Don Lassen, the editor of a paratroopers' publication, would have preferred the marchers to be organized around military units, each one led by its own color guard. Such an arrangement would have emphasized the marchers' wartime affiliation to particular divisions and branches of service rather than their postwar civilian identities as citizens of states. Lassen's criticism of the marching order correlated with his antipathy for the memorial itself, which echoed Carhart's. He said, "The same guys that insisted on fighting a no-win war have conspired to produce a no-theme memorial. The only thing that makes sense in the memorial are the figures and the flagpole—and that is what the original designer objects to." He recommended that at the dedication, his readers fill in the memorial with a bulldozer to conceal the walls. Contrary to Lassen's wishes, the parade organizers' mustering the marchers in state formations implicitly conveyed the federal creed of diversity and unity, E Pluribus Unum (Out of many, one). The marching order allowed the veterans to re-enact the forging of a unified nation from its constituent parts, making material the theme of national "healing."[57]

The color guard that led the parade was smartly turned out and marched in military step. Many of the marchers who followed wore military fatigues, saved from their wartime service or purchased from military surplus stores. American Indians from California and North and South Dakota wore traditional feathered headdresses with their combat uniforms. One carried a staff with the colors of American Gold Star Mothers, decorated with two feathers to symbolize the two worlds the veterans were in, America and Vietnam. Other participants mixed military and civilian clothes. One marcher wore a fatigue jacket and jeans; another camouflage pants and a plain undershirt; a third marked his involvement with military events by wearing a camouflage soft-brimmed "boonie hat" and a bandolier of bullets. Some were clean cut but others had long, unkempt hair and scraggly beards. They carried banners and signs. Although some uniformed marchers wore polished combat boots, others wore sneakers. The rag-tag style of participants gave them the appearance of a Third World army or irregular troops, not a U.S. military force. Colonel Max Sullivan, who spoke at the dedication ceremony, said of them: "Worst looking bunch I ever saw," but then he added, "and I loved every one of them."[58]

The South Boston contingent set themselves apart by wearing suits and, at their own request, marched separately from the rest of the Massachusetts contingent. "Southie," a clannish working-class Irish American neighborhood, had suffered triple the national Vietnam casualty rate. They had already created their own Vietnam veterans memorial and carried a printed picture of it on their banner. Southies had always fought in the nation's wars. "If our country calls, we're there," said a Southie marine who lost a leg in Vietnam. Their leader, Tommy Lyons, saw Vietnam as a war like any other. He thought the nation was beginning to see it that way, too. It was his idea that the Southie contingent wear coats and ties, with red carnations on their lapels. As an "island of spiffiness" in a scruffy sea, Lyons thought that they could show the world that "we are in the mainstream."[59]

As the parade proceeded, the marchers spontaneously assumed a disciplined marching order. Initially, some veterans deliberately walked in ragged lines in order not to reenact the regimentation of military life. As Scruggs recalled: "No more military bullshit. . . . But then they found themselves unconsciously getting in step out of respect for dead comrades. Up and down the ranks, GI's started counting cadence."[60] The former warriors began to sing "The Battle Hymn of the Republic." Then, despite themselves, they fell in with the regularity of seasoned marchers, their limbs remembering the accustomed rhythms learned in boot camp a decade or two before. At noon, army and navy F-4 jets roared overhead, reminding marchers and audience alike of America's awesome military power, and the familiar throb of rotor blades echoed the sound of helicopters ferrying the troops into combat and retrieving the dead and wounded from the battlefield.[61]

If the varied slogans on signs and buttons show that several causes competed to lay claim to the march, chief among them was patriotic loyalty to the symbols of the state. Many marchers wore their campaign ribbons, decorations, and divisional shoulder-patches; but in a gesture of nonconformity, buttons and badges were dotted about their uniforms away from the regulation position above the jacket's top pocket. Some buttons and badges festooned the marchers' motley collection of headgear—berets, boonie hats, military "soft covers," wide-brimmed cavalry hats, and visored civilian caps. Many of those in uniform wore U.S.-flag shoulder patches, and those in and out of uniform carried small Stars and Stripes. Veterans from Palo Alto made an elaborate float decked out in red, white, and blue and topped by a resplendent eagle. The flag was the consistent motif that repeated throughout the multitude, and the variety of modes of dress made it stand out as one of the few common elements drawing them together.

Another recurrent theme was the POW/MIA issue. A float carried a "tiger cage" with a prisoner inside, reminding onlookers of the Americans still considered as MIA whose names were on the wall. A pair of marchers carried a banner with the now-famous POW/MIA symbol: a picture in a white circle on a black ground of a prison camp captive, drawing attention to the belief that POW/MIAs remained in Southeast Asia. Others carried a banner reading, "MIA POWs Are *Left to Rot* in S.E. Asia. Why?"[62]

Veterans in wheelchairs led most state delegations. Some walked with the assistance of crutches. Some had prosthetic arms. Their visible injuries and disabilities demonstrated that they had paid a high price for membership in that group. But there was also a political price to pay for participation in the parade. General William Westmoreland, the commander of U.S. forces in Vietnam from 1964 to 1968, was in the reviewing stand. As the marchers were about to pass by, he left the stand to lead the parade, carrying two small American flags and wearing a button that said, "I'm proud to be a Vietnam veteran" (fig. 11).[63] Westmoreland was a controversial figure, the architect of the failed attrition strategy in Vietnam who at the time was involved in a lawsuit against CBS Television regarding over-optimistic U.S. estimates of Viet Cong troop strength in 1967.[64] The Smithsonian Institution's Edward Ezell says that Westmoreland's leaving the reviewing stand during the national salute was

Figure 11. Retired General William Westmoreland leads the veterans down Constitution Avenue in the dedication parade. Photo by Richard Hofmeister, Smithsonian Institution, Washington, DC.

a spontaneous decision, and that the general decided to join the march "moments before the parade began."[65] But Westmoreland had confided his plans to the veterans gathered in Washington hotels well before the event. It is therefore plausible that his seemingly spontaneous gesture was stage-managed to prevent anyone from organizing a protest against his presence. Westmoreland marched well ahead of the Alabama contingent, diminishing the risk of any spontaneous acts of protest. His position in the line of march also meant that Westmoreland effectively headed the parade. (A few years later, Westmoreland again climbed "spontaneously" from the reviewing stand to join the ticker-tape parade coinciding with the dedication of the New York City Vietnam veterans memorial.)[66]

Whether they wanted to or not, the veterans in Washington had to march behind General William Westmoreland, conscripted into a re-creation of the military authority structure in Vietnam. "Nobody," Mary McGrory wrote, "even those who grumbled about 'lying generals,' seemed to mind."[67] Many accounts say that Vietnam veterans greeted Westmoreland enthusiastically whenever he turned up to tell them that they had nothing to apologize for and that they had won every engagement they fought.[68] Such accounts seem to overlook the degree to which Westmoreland's military leadership was derided, even by supporters of the war effort. The last thing that members of VVAW wanted to do was to march behind Westmoreland. Nobody asked Jim Everett, for example, the Orlando, Florida, veteran who threw his medals onto the White House lawn on May Day 1971, how he felt about Westmoreland's heading the march.[69]

The only evident protest, apart from VVAW (who were not protesting the memorial), came from a group called Black Veterans for Social Justice, whose members held their own parade and a counterdemonstration on a nearby hill. About a dozen members of the group planted a red, black, and green flag in the grass—colors associated with black nationalism—and greeted the crowd and the speakers with loud boos. Their spokesperson, Brother Jay Jones, criticized the absence of African American veterans from the ceremonial events. (This criticism overlooked the presence of General George Price among the dedication ceremony speakers.) "We want to bring the black perspective on this march," he said. "More black and Third World people fought on the front line in Vietnam than in any other war. But the sons of rich white people hauled ass to Canada and now they've been pardoned, and that shows me I was a fool."[70] Ernest E. Washington Jr., an African American veteran who marched with the Boston contingent, said of the dedication: "I couldn't stand it. Couldn't stand the fact that the president couldn't make it. Couldn't stand Westmoreland being in the parade waving a flag. We might as well have had [former secretary of defense Robert] McNamara and the whole crew march and wave flags."[71]

For veterans who objected to the aims or conduct of the war, the choice was stark: march in the parade and fall in step behind the general or remain outside, on the fringes. Some chose to stay out. Reginald "Malik" Edwards, a marine veteran who joined the Black Panthers after the war, had this to say: "I was in Washington during the National Vietnam Veterans Memorial in 1982. But I didn't participate. I saw all these veterans runnin' around there with all these jungle boots on, all these uniforms. I didn't want to do that. It just gave me a bad feeling."[72] Where, Edwards asked, were the memorials to the Vietnamese civilians killed at My Lai and Cam Ne (where a member of his platoon launched a grenade into a schoolroom full of children)? For those undisturbed by such questions, the parade's appeal to veterans was compelling, insidious, and seductive: be welcomed home, hold your head up proudly, and honor your lost comrades. If a degree of flag-waving goes with the parade, so much the better. The event brought together pride in self, in comradeship, in military order, and in the nation. The process was anything but subtle, yet because it involved the use of symbols such as the flag and military marching order not associated with a specific political party, it did not clearly violate the VVMF's commitment to being "apolitical."

Edwards's sharp political critique prevented the memorial dedication from submerging his opposition to the war; but it must have been difficult for most veterans, even those ambivalent about the war, to feel more than a vague disquiet. They were, after all, winning the recognition and praise they had craved. It required an unusual strength of mind for an antiwar veteran to distance himself from the national embrace into which the dedication invited him, and to resist the ideological contents of the emotionally satisfying package. Here we see the effectiveness of the memorial's avowedly "apolitical" approach to commemoration. By eschewing any partisan political statement, the memorial could achieve the larger political goals of cementing identification with the nation and reconstituting pride in military service.

John Bodnar has written that the parade expressed "sentiments of loyalty to a community or brotherhood of soldiers rather than to a nation of patriotic citizens."[73] But this statement oversimplifies the matter. The parade allowed some participants to affirm their loyalty to a nation that had neglected them; it allowed others to thumb their noses at those who had criticized the war. For those concerned about unemployment and veterans' health, it brought attention to veterans' continuing needs. To those not bothered about ideologies and causes, it was more about comradeship. The symbolic importance of the event was that it blurred the lines between the veterans' solidarity with one another and their sense of belonging to the nation.

As the crowd gathered at the memorial after the parade, Scruggs addressed them from a podium atop the walls, flanked by the Stars and Stripes and the flags of the five armed services. A military honor guard in dress uniforms stood atop the wall facing the audience, displaying the flags of every U.S. state and territory (fig. 12). The assembled audience stood with state placards held aloft—resembling one of the quadrennial political conventions, suggesting that the whole nation was represented in the audience (fig 13).[74] Scruggs spoke of the poor reception Vietnam veterans received on their return to the United States and said, "All of us can now say that we are proud to be Vietnam veterans and that we are proud to have helped our country during a time of crisis and I know that our country appreciates our service." He spoke of his dream of creating a Vietnam veterans memorial and said, "Today we see this dream is a reality. . . . Let it begin the healing process and forever stand as a symbol of our national unity." Chaplain Owen Hendry of the U.S. Air Force found an apt saying from the prophet Isaiah: "I have called you by name. You are mine." A bugler played "Taps."[75]

Defense Secretary Caspar Weinberger had sent a letter to the VVMF, which Scruggs read out to the crowd, saying to the veterans, "When your country called, you came. When your country refused you honor, you remained silent. With time, our nation's wounds have healed. We have finally come to appreciate your sacrifices and to pay you your tribute you so richly deserve."[76] This official governmental response to the dedication reinforced the VVMF's narrative of societal neglect of veterans giving way to "healing." But during a Veterans Day ceremony at Arlington National Cemetery, Weinberger made a more militant point. He said that the "terrible lesson" of the Vietnam War was that "we should never again ask our men and women to serve in a war that we do not intend to win." The line was greeted with massive applause.[77]

Senator John Warner's dedication ceremony speech made the same point, challenging the concept of an "apolitical memorial" that the VVMF had espoused. In words identical to Weinberger's, and that therefore clearly represented the official government line, Warner declaimed, "We should never again ask our men and women to serve in a war that we do not intend to win." He listed other "sober lessons of history" that Americans learned in Vietnam that they must "never forget": "We learned that we should not enter a war unless it is necessary for our national survival. We learned that, if we do enter such a war, we must support our men and women to the fullest extent possible."[78] As if to underline the costs of defeat, representatives of the war's losing side gathered behind the speaker's stage. About

Figure 12. The formal military honor guard of serving troops stands on top of the Vietnam Veterans Memorial wall, while an informal honor guard consisting of Vietnam veterans stands below. Photo by Jeffrey Ploskonka, Smithsonian Institution.

Figure 13. Still carrying their state signs from the parade, veterans gather in front of the wall.
Photo by Dane A. Penland, Smithsonian Institution.

two dozen Vietnamese people unfurled South Vietnamese flags, yellow with three red stripes (the same colors as those of U.S. veterans' Vietnam service ribbons). Their group, the National Front for the Liberation of Vietnam, promoted the overthrow of the Communist Vietnamese government. One member wore a sign on his back that read, "Freedom and Justice Are What Vietnam Veterans Fought For."[79]

Warner's speech reflected the emerging consensus in the Republican Party about the "lessons of Vietnam." Reagan's "noble cause" idea had provoked negative comments and, while he never repudiated the idea, he did at times moderate his rhetoric, avoiding the adjective *noble*. The judgment that Vietnam veterans had been prevented from winning the war was a crowd-pleaser that tended to excite less criticism. As we have seen, it was ever-present in the speeches by Republican leaders such as Caspar Weinberger, John Warner, and Reagan himself. It implied that the outcome of the war was not the veterans' responsibility; it removed the stigma of defeat from them and, by extension, from the nation: we could have won, if our politicians had had the will to fight to victory. For right-wingers still frustrated by America's defeat, the lesson of the past could be applied in the future: in any future war, the United States must use all the force necessary to achieve victory. The "lost victory" idea was replete with meaning, assuaging those who needed comfort and inspiring those who wanted to gird up for the next fight.

Warner's rhetoric gained momentum by riding the popular sympathy with Vietnam veterans, inflecting this sentiment by demanding that service personnel be supported not just after a war but fully during wars too. His speech clearly disobeyed the memorial fund's creed of making "no political statements." Setting out the conditions under which the nation should go to war and insisting on the public's obligation to support its troops in the field is clearly a political statement; and arguing that the nation prevented its troops from winning in Vietnam is a controversial political and historical judgment. Yet these statements escaped any reproof from VVMF officers or anyone else, perhaps because what counts as a "political statement" depends on who is judging the statement and by what criteria. Because Warner's judgments reflected a ruling ideology attempting to define a new common sense, and because they came from a national leader rather than a speaker from some marginal group, the VVMF did not perceive them as political. Scruggs quotes Warner's speech in his memoir of the VVMF's work, without criticism or comment.[80]

As with the parade, the mere act of listening without protest made accomplices of the listeners in the discourse of national reunification—and in the revision of history. When veterans applauded the line about allowing the troops to win, they sealed a bargain: by endorsing Warner's questionable political judgment about the war, they were rewarded and comforted by the banishment of defeat. The veterans and those whose lives and deaths the wall recalled did not lose; they were prevented from winning. The idea was infectious. A Mexican American veteran at the dedication of the wall said, "I don't think we lost a war. We did our part." Another veteran said, "The politicians didn't want us to win." A pair of veterans at a reunion at one of Washington's hotels discussed the tradition of victory from which they had felt excluded. One said to the other, "We won the war." The other replied, "Politicians lost it." Later, a voice in the crowd said, "We didn't lose. Spread the word."[81] Vindicated, the warriors were as good, as noble, as honorable as any military force their nation fielded. The diary entry of a Gold Star widow read, "There was a sense of patriotism and a sense of righting a wrong, . . . of making the fact that those men served in Vietnam not something to apologize for anymore."[82] The bargain was not a quid pro quo but a "win-win" proposition: all at once, feel better about yourselves, win the nation's plaudits, and sense the rising of the nation's strength. The only cost to veterans: silencing any small, inner voice that questioned Warner's judgment and entertained doubts about the nation's purposes and conduct in Vietnam—or about their own actions.

After the speeches, the barriers around the memorial were removed, and the audience crowded around the wall (fig. 14). Then, as one witness, Sal Lopes, described the scene: "All hell broke loose, and everyone went to the Wall and all the emotion just poured out. . . . People were touching it, guys were crying very openly."[83] People began to do what Scruggs had observed visitors doing when they saw the first panels: they touched the memorial with their hands. They ran their fingers over the inscriptions and searched for names, sometimes fearing that they would find the name of a buddy they had lost track of. One veteran said, "I ran into some old names. They were guys I knew. [I was] hoping they made it back. It was kind of a bummer."[84] Two veterans searched for each other's name. Both had been seriously wounded and each believed that his friend had died. Unable to find the name they sought in the directory, they went to the section of the memorial where they thought it would be. There, instead, they saw each other.[85]

Figure 14. A woman and children react after finding a name on the wall during the 1982 dedication. Photo by Dane A. Penland, Smithsonian Institution.

Members of the crowd wept. Visitors who had not seen the memorial before were amazed by its power. They saw what the design jury had spoken about many months before: looking along the wall, one could see the Washington Monument reflected in its black surface. The visitors' own reflections were mirrored in the stone's shiny surface, and the names seemed to mingle with the reflections. The multitude mirrored in the black granite became an amorphous mass, a ghostly crowd seemingly gathered on the other side of the wall. Visitors for the first time experienced the uncanny feeling that they were in the presence of the dead, separated by a membrane, insubstantial yet impenetrable. They hugged and comforted one another.

Eleanor Wimbish left the first of many letters at the memorial addressed to her son, Billy Stocks, who had died in a helicopter crash in February 1969. Although she said she was a private person, the letters were reported in the media and the stories made Wimbish's grief an emblem of the emotion at the wall.[86] Visitors left hundreds of offerings there during the weekend. Each one encapsulated a story of human loss and grief. Reports of these first reactions to the memorial drew others. A woman from Columbia, Maryland, wrote of her first love, whom she had known as a teenager in 1957. "We were very young (and, no doubt, very naïve), but we were very happy." She moved away and they lost touch. Years later she learned that he had been killed in Vietnam. "In spite of all of the rhetoric about America forgetting, from that day on I never have. . . . I will go to Washington and try to find his name on the memorial. I hope I'll be able to touch it, but mostly I want to remember and say goodbye. And Donny, . . . you were my first love and I will never, ever forget."[87]

On the eve of the dedication, a member of VVAW in San Antonio, Texas, said, "The memorial is fine, but I think it's a cosmetic attempt at appeasement of the Vietnam veteran. . . . And the four-day celebration sponsored by the government is just so much confetti. It's not dealing with issues facing the Vietnam veteran, such as training and education." "We need jobs," another veteran said. For a minority of veterans, the wall offered no comfort or reconciliation. A Buffalo, New York, veteran who was a counselor of other veterans at the dedication said, "This is the government's attempt to close the chapter on Vietnam. The memorial doesn't do anything for me." "I look at those names," one visitor said, "and think, 'What a waste.' I don't see the Wall as a tribute; I see it as a magnification of all the waste the war caused. That's why I don't like the Wall."[88]

An unemployed veteran from Janesville, Wisconsin, Jerry Hardy, said that, although he was glad to see the names on the memorial, "they still put us in a hole."[89] Will Howe, a 25th Infantry Division veteran, said, "It's black because we lost." He had brought his wife and two children from California to see whether the memorial was "as bad as everyone says it is." He found himself agreeing that it was.[90] But some of those who had opposed the design because it was black, below ground, and designed by a nonveteran changed their minds when they saw the memorial. John Devitt, who flew to the dedication from San Jose, California, said: "While I was there, I felt myself change. My attitude became more positive."[91] John Behan, a Vietnam veteran, had been one of the wall's opponents who held that it was a "black gash of shame." All it took was one visit to the memorial and, he said, the "impact turned me around completely."[92]

Others were confused. They had heard the criticisms of the memorial but found it powerful and moving when they saw it for themselves. Interviewed on November 16, after his return from the dedication, Allen Lynch, a Medal of Honor winner, said, "I really haven't made up my mind about the design—such as the idea that it is black and it's below ground. To be very honest with you, I don't want to get into the trap of not liking it because nobody else likes it. . . . But I think the memorial has a lot of positives. It takes the names of all the people who died in Vietnam and it lists them forever."[93] A Montana veteran's participation in the salute won him over to the memorial: "I didn't like it at first, but when I saw the memorial's dedication parade with all those so-called 'baby killers' walking, crutching and rolling to the memorial, laughing and crying all the way, I figured it couldn't be all that bad."[94]

Anticipating intense reactions to the memorial among emotionally troubled visitors, the Veterans Administration stationed thirty counselors at three downtown hotels that were being used as veterans' reunion sites and set up a mobile unit at the memorial. Other counselors mingled with the crowds. And indeed the expectations of strong reactions, both positive and negative, were borne out. Lily Adams, a nurse in Vietnam, said, "I went to [the National Salute to Vietnam Veterans], dealt with my grief at the Wall, and left a hundred pounds lighter." A veteran of the First Infantry Division said of the parade, "It washes it out, closes a chapter." Frances Rauschkolb, who lost her son, Jan, in Vietnam in May 1969, remembered that afterward, she and her husband bottled up their feelings. They were "encased in a cocoon for fourteen years. . . . We shut out the world." But, she said, the dedication of the Vietnam Veterans Memorial "opened up so many things for us. It showed us that there is so much love, so much compassion." The Vietnam veteran Mike Kentes was at the dedication. It used to take him two hours to get to sleep every night—no nightmares, but he used to re-enact a battle he had fought before falling asleep. After the dedication of the wall, he found that he was able to fall asleep right away. Visits to the memorial became part of the therapy of veterans who suffered from post-traumatic stress disorder. For some, though, the emotional weight of the war prevented them from approaching the wall. Pat Johnson, a nurse in Vietnam with painful memories that she rarely spoke about, signed up as part of a group to attend the dedication. When the time came, though, she could not go. "I didn't feel that I could emotionally take it." Years after the war, some nurses had still not begun to grieve and would not come to the memorial. As the 1980s wore on, the phenomenon of "tree vets" emerged: veterans who lingered at the perimeter, unable to face the wall.[95]

The VVMF's rhetoric of healing and reconciliation became irresistible to the media. Whether because their observations of public behavior at the site led them to the terms *healing* and *reconciliation* or whether they repeated what a dozen stories and press releases had already said, journalists seized on the words. The *Chattanooga Times* editorialized that the memorial "holds a special promise. The promise of healing old wounds." The *Deseret News*, of Salt Lake City, wrote, "The wounds in the national psyche caused by the Vietnam War have lessened if not entirely disappeared. Certainly it's time for a reconciliation of sorts." The newspaper quoted Scruggs's call for "national catharsis" and "healing [for] some of the wounds of the war." The *Washington Post* editorialized that in the memorial, "the intended theme of reconciliation is beautifully served." Other publications sounded the same themes at the dedication and for years afterward.[96]

The press were early adopters of the VVMF's terminology of healing and reconciliation, yet the "vox pop" interviews by journalists and filmmakers who covered the national salute suggest that few veterans or members of the public spoke this language at the time. They continued to express their responses in terms of pride, gratitude, and the enjoyment of a belated welcome home. A rare exception was Robert Hunter, who mobilized veterans and family members from his home state of Oregon for a trip to the dedication in Washington to "assist the natural healing process necessary to finally put the Vietnam experience into perspective."[97] Looking back, Hunter said, "I feel I regained a part of my past that I had lost in Vietnam, in those five days. It was five days of personal and national healing."[98] He was one of five Oregon veterans who, after the national salute, began to organize the effort to create a Vietnam veterans memorial in his home state, and the VVMF's language made the journey with them from Washington to Portland. Other veterans also used the term *healing* to describe their experience at the national salute: but it is notable that they did so in interviews that took place later, after the drip-feed of media reports using the memorial fund's language had begun to permeate their thoughts. For example, in an oral history published in 1985, Grace Barolet O'Brien, the evacuation nurse who had felt proud marching down Constitution Avenue with the other vets, said that the national salute was "a healing time for many of us." By then, she had begun working as a volunteer at the Vietnam Veterans Memorial in Washington, DC, and so had naturally become habituated to the VVMF's discourse.[99]

The spread of this language and the sentiments expressed in these statements record the VVMF's success in two senses: first, the memorial was doing its work of allowing veterans to affirm their pride and release their grief, and to find some comfort in expressing their emotions; second, ordinary Americans, not just editorial writers, had adopted the fund's language of healing. The memorial did not dictate their words, but neither did their expressions of emotion arise entirely independently. As the subsequent ubiquity of the language of healing would demonstrate, when Americans contemplated the Vietnam War, the words with which many expressed themselves seemed to flow along currents that the VVMF had set in motion, along courses that the VVMF had prepared. The waters of private mourning and public commemoration mingled in that confluence.

Mary McGrory wrote, "Nobody except the press seemed to notice that the current Commander-in-Chief, who calls Vietnam 'a noble cause' but won't visit the memorial, didn't show." McGrory was wrong. People noticed and complained. Ronald Reagan received letters and telegrams from citizens criticizing him for not attending the memorial's dedication. Margaret Hamilton, of Wallingford, Connecticut, said that his absence had cost him her vote. Lynne Burgess, of Stamford, Connecticut, scolded Reagan: "You could have taken a clear, strong step toward healing the wounds of Viet Nam. . . . You refused to lend the dignity of the Presidency to the dedication ceremonies. America deserved better." Keith Hazen, of Malone, New York, said that Vietnam veterans had not received the respect they were owed, and that they might stop being treated as second-class citizens if the president had been able to pay his respects to those who died.[100] Reagan received no thanks, of course, for the undisclosed White House role in ensuring that the memorial was dedicated on time.

The only place where a public acknowledgment of the White House's role is there for the sharp-eyed to see is in the thank you's on the last page of the dedication souvenir program. Along with the names of Elliot Richardson, J. Carter Brown, and General Price—with Watt, Copulos, Webb, and another 270 journalists, politicians, and veterans' leaders—one finds three names that obliquely signal the White House's role: those of Edwin Meese, whose responsibility for dealing with federal government departments and agencies made him the member of the White House "troika" nominally charged with handling relations with Watt; Thomas Shull, who, irrespective of this formal division of responsibility, personally conveyed to Watt the White House's order to allow groundbreaking; and Morton Blackwell, the White House's liaison with the veterans community.[101] Indecipherable to anyone unfamiliar with the whole story, the names outline the history of the memorial fund's struggles—a "join-the-dots" diagram with none of the dots connected.

Scruggs later reflected that the memorial had become a "symbol of reconciliation, symbol of unity."[102] Its dedication promoted the goal that the Reagan administration, no less than the VVMF, wanted to achieve: reunifying the nation around a common sympathy for Vietnam veterans. Or, at least, people began to chorus the message in public—and that was half the battle won. At the Entertainers Salute at the Daughters of the American Revolution's Constitution Hall, the actor Jimmy Stewart, as master of ceremonies, spoke eloquently about the "long hard road" that had brought the veterans there, about the controversy and disappointment that they had met along the way. "Here, tonight, we're going to put that behind us," he said.[103] A week after the dedication, the *Washington Post* received a letter from Meg Maguire: "As one who marched down Constitution Avenue years ago protesting that terrible Vietnam conflict, I have continued to experience an unsettling rejection of those who had anything to do with it—including our soldiers. Last week, through the faces, the stories, the words of dedication and the sleek, silent granite softened by the etched names, I, too, was healed. May we always remember."[104] Always remember, as Maguire enjoined; put the past behind us, as Stewart wished. These seemingly contrary responses to the past expressed a shared wish to quiet disturbing memories, to remember in a composed and certain way so that the past could be left behind. To remember in order to forget.

In a statement recognizing the memorial during a Veterans Day ceremony, Ronald Reagan said, "For too long, America closed its heart to those who served us with valor. It's time that Vietnam veterans take their rightful place in our history along with other American heroes who put their lives on the line for their country." This statement of recognition was something with which virtually everyone, including the supporters and opponents of the VVMF, could agree. Reagan added an ideological note while remaining true to the spirit of valediction. He said that the reality of Vietnam today, with torture and repression forcing hundreds of thousands of boat people (refugees) to flee from the country, "suggests that the cause for which our Vietnam veterans fought was an honorable one." Not noble (as in the Veterans of Foreign Wars speech) or just (as in his visit to the National Cathedral) but honorable: this choice of words marked a subtle modulation of Reagan's rhetoric. The speech also harmonized with the memorial fund's appeal for healing when Reagan quoted Lincoln's words about the need to "bind up the nation's wounds," and talked of "putting the divisiveness of Vietnam behind us."[105]

As ideological constructs, Vietnam veterans served the rhetorical needs of Reagan's speechwriters. As Harry Haines has written, they had been an "inexplicable anomaly" in the nation's midst, separated from their compatriots and hence dramatizing society's divisions.[106] Their assimilation into the body politic could symbolize with commensurate force the reconstitution of the nation's imaginary unity. The veterans served as a signifier in political speech all the more powerful for summoning up earnest sentiment. A week after the salute, Reagan thanked Vietnam veterans "from the bottom of my heart" and said that, with the dedication of the memorial, the "Vietnam veterans finally came home once and for all to America's heart."[107]

When Senator Alfonse D'Amato (R., New York) encouraged Ronald Reagan to attend the dedication, he made a succinct link between the memorial and America's international position: "The National Salute to Vietnam Veterans is an essential part of the domestic healing process which must be completed to fully restore our national will and sense of purpose in the world."[108] William Broyles, reflecting on the dedication a week later, expressed the same idea, couching it in the language of healing. For Broyles, the healing had still not happened: "Vietnam divided us and troubles us still, not only in the hearts and minds of veterans and their families, but in our crippled self-confidence. It is a specter we have yet to put to rest, a wound in need of healing."[109] The link between personal and national healing that the memorial fund had promoted was beginning to catch on; it had clearly taken hold in Broyles's imagination. The dedication of the wall had resulted in a public outpouring of affection for Vietnam veterans, but anyone hoping that this would mend the spirits of veterans suffering from post-traumatic stress disorder was seeking magical solutions for deeply entrenched problems. What remained unclear was how the memorial could contribute, beyond the individual lives it touched, to the restoration of the nation's "will" and "sense of purpose in the world."

6

"IN UNITY AND WITH RESOLVE"

The Statue, the Flag, and Political Speech at the Memorial

⭐

THE DEDICATION of the Vietnam Veterans Memorial did not bring an end to the conflicts between the Vietnam Veterans Memorial Fund (VVMF) and their right-wing antagonists. During the whole of 1983, the memorial fund's detractors kept up a campaign of obstruction and harassment, first in Congress and through the office of the secretary of the interior, then through a McCarthyite lawyer, and finally through a zealous investigative reporter's television broadcasts. The attacks failed, partly because of the goodwill the memorial fund had garnered during the National Salute to Vietnam Veterans and partly because the Reagan administration tended to favor the VVMF throughout the arguments. Beset by opposition to its policies in Central America, the Reagan administration used two commemoration events in 1984—the Memorial Day interment of an unknown soldier of the Vietnam era and the Veterans Day dedication of the Frederick Hart statue—as opportunities to bolster national unity. In 1988, near the end of his administration, Ronald Reagan returned to the memorial and said that the process of "healing" he had announced in 1984 was now complete.

Both the VVMF and the White House downplayed their cooperation. When Jan Scruggs described the VVMF's relationship to the Reagan administration, he said that it was often antagonistic. There was some factual support for this description. After all, James Watt, the secretary of the interior, was sympathetic to the memorial fund's critics, with whose ideological perspectives he agreed. President Reagan did not attend the memorial's dedication in 1982, and the White House did not help with the planning for the National Salute to Vietnam Veterans. The story that Scruggs bases on these facts is one of administration hostility or indifference, a theme captured by the repeated statement that the national salute was a homecoming that the veterans had to organize for themselves.[1] No one from the Reagan administration contradicted this account. But it is only part of the story, and the parts that are omitted are also important—not only because the full story is richer than the partial account but also because the omission itself is significant. Ordinarily, politicians are all too happy to take credit for their achievements. Why, in this case, did the White House allow the VVMF to take all the credit?

The whole purpose of the memorial, to foster unity by appealing to the heart, not to political convictions, would be undermined if the administration publicly adopted the memorial as a White House cause. A close identification between the memorial and the White House would also undercut the VVMF's claim that the memorial was an apolitical project led by nonpartisan veterans. And it might cost the White House the favor of anyone offended by the design. The VVMF and the Reagan White House therefore shared a common purpose in keeping quiet about their alliance. Thus, a myth grew up that the memorial fund succeeded against the odds and despite the opposition of the powerful—not that the odds were loaded in its favor by occasional, deft White House interventions.

In December 1982, the VVMF submitted a new site plan to Watt based on the "entrance experience" proposal—essentially, J. Carter Brown's plan that placed the Hart statue near a path approaching the west end of the wall, with directories of names and the flagpole nearby. However, Watt failed to forward the proposal to the Fine Arts Commission for consideration at its mid-December meeting, giving rise to disquiet among the VVMF's supporters and a stern rebuke of Watt by AMVETS (American Veterans of World War II, Korea, and Vietnam).[2] Watt's delaying tactic gave the VVMF's opponents in Congress the opportunity to trump the Fine Arts Commission by passing a law specifying where the statue and flag must stand. Representative Don Bailey, as he had threatened, drafted legislation stipulating that the flag would be placed at the memorial's apex and the statue in line with the meeting point of the walls—as H. Ross Perot, Tom Carhart, and the other critics wanted. The VVMF, joined by the American Legion and the Veterans of Foreign Wars (VFW), opposed this move. After Bailey lobbied his House colleagues by telling them of the March 1982 "compromise," the lame duck House of Representatives passed the legislation in the waning hours of the 97th Congress. The vigilant Senator Charles Mathias, however, blocked the legislation in the Senate. Bailey himself was a lame duck (he had lost his seat in the November 1982 congressional election) but the legislation's co-sponsor, Representative Duncan Hunter (R., California), was re-elected and would be able to reintroduce the legislation in the next session.[3]

When the VVMF brought an architect's model of the "entrance plaza" for the statue and flag to Watt's office, they found him in a meeting with Perot, Bailey, and a delegation of the VVMF's opponents.[4] Now that the House had passed a law mandating a central location for the flag and statue, the VVMF feared that Watt might temporize until the Senate held hearings to consider a similar bill.[5] It looked as though the White House would be drawn into the conflict if it dragged on. A White House memo said, "One group pushing a specific plan [presumably the VVMF] has threatened to go directly to James Baker III requesting [that] Watt be ordered to act according to their desires. [Senator John] Warner has stalled this effort, trying to keep this no-win issue out of the White House."[6]

The next morning's newspapers brought ill tidings for a White House trying to stay out of the quarrel. Philip Geyelin wrote in the *Washington Post* that the "outpouring of warmth and long overdue thanksgiving" during the National Salute to Vietnam Veterans had, for a time, appeared to overcome the rift between the VVMF and their critics. However, Geyelin wrote (accurately or not), Watt's determination to set himself up as arbiter of the conflict and to dictate the position of the statue and flag threatened to widen the rift "in a way that can only rub raw the deeper Vietnam wounds."[7] A White House aide commented, "We are risking some political embarrassment over a very minor matter."[8] The VVMF's supporters tried to pressure Watt directly and indirectly, through the White House, to send the VVMF's new site plan to the Fine Arts Commission. Senators Mathias and Warner wrote to Watt admonishing him that it would be in the best interest of all parties, "including the [Reagan] administration" to lay the conflict to rest and Mathias also encouraged Michael Deaver to intercede with Watt.[9] Scruggs complained to Jim Munro, the president of Time, Inc., and a friend of James Baker's, that Watt was acting "as if he answers to H. Ross Perot rather than acting in the best interests of the Reagan Administration," and he encouraged Munro to tell Baker about the problem. Munro responded by saying to Baker, "It appears that Secretary Watt's lack of . . . action regarding the placement options he has received may lead once again to divisiveness over the memorial that only a short while ago served to unify our country. That would be a shame."[10] As January wore on, it became increasingly difficult for the administration to stay out of the argument.[11]

In an attempt to break the impasse, the VVMF sent Watt a letter with the two other proposals for the placement of the statue and flag (the central location that Perot and Carhart favored, and the proposal by the American Institute of Architects for a more distant location), so that Watt could forward all three to the Fine Arts Commission (fig. 15). The VVMF decided to give Watt a week to ponder the matter without pressing their case by speaking to the media. Still, no word issued from Watt. The VVMF heard that Watt was preoccupied with other issues and that he felt "no pressure" on this one.[12] As Scruggs saw it, Watt was stalling because he knew that the Fine Arts Commission would not approve the Perot/Carhart proposal: this was a reasonable supposition because Brown, the commission chairman, had recommended the "entrance plaza" at the commission's October meeting, so the commission was bound to prefer that option. The VVMF's opponents wanted to fight the flag and statue issue in Congress, a battle that Scruggs thought the VVMF would win but "one that we would like to avoid."[13]

The continuing dispute about the memorial took place in the context of heightening concern about the political costs of Reagan's Central America policy, which his advisers believed might hurt his electoral prospects in the November 1984 presidential election. Although Congress never invoked the War Powers Act, it did try to exert some control over Central America policy through its authority over the public purse. Congress funded aid to the Nicaraguan counterrevolutionaries, the *contras*, on condition that it was used to interfere with arms shipments from Nicaragua to the FMLN (the Salvadoran revolutionaries) and not to overthrow Nicaragua's socialist

Sandinista government. Legislators continued to require periodic certification of progress on human rights in El Salvador as a condition of aid to its government.[14] Despite these restrictions, U.S. military assistance to right-wing Central American governments and the *contras* massively increased between 1981 and 1985.[15] The *New York Times* editorialized against Reagan's cavalier approach to certification, saying that he was indifferent to the Salvadoran government's disdain for human rights and life. El Salvador was not Vietnam, the newspaper conceded; but as the United States had learned in Vietnam, "democracies will not long support ruthless wars that betray their ideals."[16] And Democrats in Congress complained about Reagan's circumventing the normal budgetary process by reprogramming funds or using presidential emergency powers to send aid to El Salvador. This maneuver reminded them of the way presidents had financed the Vietnam War.[17]

In December 1982, the House of Representatives passed the Boland Amendment, banning covert aid to assist the overthrow of the Sandinista government in Nicaragua or to provoke warfare between Nicaragua and Honduras.[18] In the debate leading to its adoption, Representative George Miller (D., California) said, "Some of us came

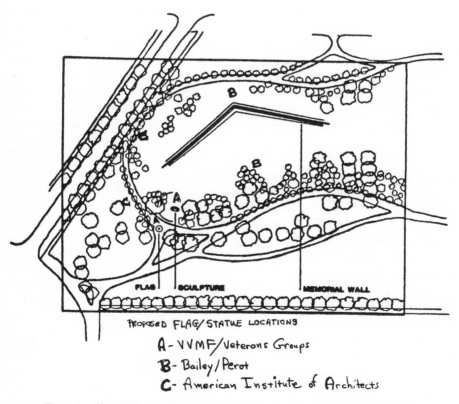

Figure 15. Plan of Vietnam Veterans Memorial site, with proposed locations for the Frederick Hart statue and flagstaff, sent by the Vietnam Veterans Memorial Fund to Secretary of the Interior James Watt, January 14, 1983, VVMF-MD.

here to stop [the] Vietnam [War]. . . . And here is a chance to stop the new one."[19] The leftist rebels in El Salvador launched offensives in the autumn of 1982 and renewed them in January 1983, encouraged by political turmoil in the Salvadoran government and security forces. The former senior editor of the *New York Times* called El Salvador a "no-win situation, reminiscent of Vietnam."[20] In the face of rebel military successes, an administration official pointed to the fragility of the Salvadoran government and warned that any sign of weakened resolve on the part of the United States government might set off a panic: "If the sense spreads that the U.S. will desert them, I don't know what they'll do. It's Vietnam all over again."[21]

Just as these echoes of the Vietnam War were resonating in the debates about Central America policy, Secretary of the Interior Watt finally spoke about the statue and flag's placement. What he said threatened to set off a new round of conflict about the Vietnam Veterans Memorial at a time when the Reagan administration would have preferred to avoid one. The intensifying political crisis in Washington and Central America made the White House want to curtail an unnecessary debate about the aesthetics and symbolism of the Vietnam Veterans Memorial. The memorial's dedication the previous November had begun, it seemed, to draw some of the poison from the "Vietnam wound." Now, Watt's stubbornness looked as though it might extend the arguments about the memorial design, drawing out the quarrels about how noble the war effort had been, how the returning veterans had been treated, and all the other vexed questions about the Vietnam War. The White House consequently took steps to ensure that it would not have to fight a simultaneous two-front war of words about Vietnam on Capitol Hill and on the Mall.

Watt announced that he intended not to send any of the three proposals for the position of the statue and flag to the Fine Arts Commission, which meant that the decision about their location might be delayed indefinitely. It was January 28, a Friday, and Watt said that it might take a year or more for an agreement to be reached.[22] Watt was stalling; he favored the central position for the statue that the Fine Arts Commission had rejected and he appeared willing to engage in a protracted battle of wills to decide whose plan should prevail. But within a few days he changed his mind and, in a humiliating reversal, he told the Fine Arts Commission on February 1 that he would go along with any of the three proposals he was forwarding to the commission—although he preferred the central location for the statue and flag.[23] This change of heart has never been adequately explained.

Publicly, the Department of the Interior explained Watt's reversal by saying that Senators Mathias and Warner had persuaded him. It was also a matter of record that the leadership of the major veterans' organizations, the American Legion, the VFW, and AMVETS, had greeted Watt's Friday decision with impatience and dismay.[24] Behind the scenes, the veterans' organizations were mobilizing to lobby the White House in favor of the memorial fund. AMVETS wrote to Edwin Meese and Deaver complaining about Watt's "delaying tactics" and stating, "The position of the nation's major veterans groups on this matter is clear: We want the Vietnam Veterans Memorial completed."[25] After Bob Doubek briefed the VFW, they wrote to Watt asking him to forward all three proposals for the placement of the statue and flag to the Fine Arts Commission and sent a copy of the letter to Vice President George Bush to keep White House pressure on Watt.[26] Watt was simultaneously under political attack for numerous decisions he had made as secretary of the interior, including ones about conservation, Native American affairs, and oil drilling on public land. He had announced that his objective as secretary of the interior was to ensure that the country "will mine more, drill more, cut more timber to use our resources rather than keep them locked up."[27] These policies, and his outspokenness about them, brought him into conflict with conservationists and others. Calls for his resignation were mounting just as the argument about the flag and statue was reaching its crisis.[28]

Jack Wheeler thought that these attacks made Watt "vulnerable" and he recommended that the VVMF seize the moment and "pull out all the stops" in lobbying the White House.[29] Scruggs immediately sent off a flurry of letters to Reagan's advisers. He warned Meese and Bush that "without action the situation could become potentially harmful for the Reagan Administration and the veterans community."[30] Wheeler, Scruggs, and Doubek invited the president and first lady to an escorted visit of the memorial, but the couple declined the invitation.[31] Scruggs tried to arrange a meeting with Bush, claiming, "Failure to complete the memorial at this time could fester into a major embarrassment for all concerned—VVMF, the veterans community, and the Reagan Administration."[32] The VFW's Cooper Holt wrote to Bush the following day, "If the placement of the agreed upon statue and flag is not settled immediately we will once again be in the unfortunate position of fighting the Vietnam War all over again—not only in the halls of Congress, but also in the news media. Mr. Vice President, you know as well as I do that we do not need this at this particular time, nor do I think we can afford it."[33] The entreaties paid off: Bush's military liaison responded by inviting Scruggs and Doubek to a meeting at the Old Executive Office Building to discuss the statue and flag on January 28. Bush had visited the memorial and was moved by the visit, leaving with tears in his eyes after walking the length of the wall. He reportedly "got mad" at the "right wing" among the White House staff that was opposed to the VVMF's proposal for the statue and flag.[34]

Although unreported at the time and unnoticed by subsequent scholarship, the White House played a pivotal role in Watt's change of mind. VVMF contacts inside the White House informed Wheeler and Scruggs that shortly before Watt's reversal Reagan's closest aides, Meese, Baker, and Deaver, had decided to tell Watt to take all three options to the Fine Arts Commission.[35] Terry O'Donnell, the VVMF's legal counsel, gave Scruggs a confidential report that the VVMF's determined lobbying of the White House "turned the tide." As O'Donnell explained the behind-the-scenes machinations, Watt's peremptory announcement of a deadlock confounded the White House's efforts to settle the matter. "At that point, the White House got offended and the matter went directly to Reagan. Watt was told to sign off ASAP [as soon as possible]! [The] White House position is that it is helpful to have it resolved now." Thus, it was the White House that decided that Watt should reverse himself, giving the green light for what became the final configuration of wall, statue, and flag.[36] (The decision-making processes of the White House suggest, however, that "going directly to Reagan" means the decision was made by the top tier of Reagan's aides.)[37]

This episode was one of the defining moments in the White House's relations with the memorial fund and it also provides telling evidence of the balance of political forces within the administration. The fund learned that the right-wing resistance to their plans was led in the White House by Morton Blackwell. This was news: their only previous warning of his opposition was that Milt Copulos had, evidently regarding Blackwell as an ally, sent him a copy of the October 1982 *60 Minutes* broadcast to complain about its supposed bias. The identification of Blackwell as a conservative point of resistance to the VVMF's memorial plan is plausible, though. Blackwell and other far-right staff members in the Office of Public Liaison tended to view it, according to Mark Peterson, as "the focal point for the advancement of right-wing issues and the accommodation of conservative organizations." It later became clear that Blackwell had a grievance against the White House "pragmatists," voicing his frustration at what he saw as the thwarting of the far-right agenda in Reagan's first term. From the point of view of the memorial fund's critics, this was the nub of the problem: Blackwell appears to have been their highest-ranking White House ally but he was a second-tier staff member in an office that had relatively little influence on policy. He could therefore have done little more than encourage Watt to hang tough in the matter of the statue and flag, and when matters came to a head he and Watt had to defer to the irresistible force of the troika, joined by the vice president.[38]

The White House, which had tried to avoid becoming involved in the conflict because the argument was a "no-win" issue, was consistent in its wish to keep its role quiet. Scruggs annotated O'Donnell's confidential report with the "follow-up action": "Do not tell anyone of White House role."[39] The VVMF complied. Scruggs could not conceal his glee, though, when confiding to Elliot Richardson, "We used some pretty effective tactics to outflank our opponents in the White House."[40]

Kirk Savage reminds us that public monuments do not appear automatically or by happenstance: "they are built by people with sufficient power to marshal (or impose) public consent for their erection."[41] This was no less true of the Vietnam Veterans Memorial than of any other national monument. The extraordinary thing is that the VVMF were able to convince anyone at all that theirs was an insurgent effort in which ordinary veterans overcame the resistance of the powerful. They did more than this: they managed to get almost every commentator to overlook that Congress authorized the memorial, allotting it the most sought-after real estate in the nation's capital, that one president signed the authorizing legislation, and that key advisers in his successor's administration overruled the memorial's opponents. So the myth of the little guy triumphing over the odds—a compelling story, and one of the core narratives in American culture—became attached to the Vietnam Veterans Memorial, occluding the fact that this was a memorial supported and sanctioned from first to last by the nation's most politically powerful individuals and institutions.

On February 8, 1983, the Fine Arts Commission approved positions for the statue and flag according to the "entrance experience" solution. Together they formed what Carter Brown called "the front door, the overture" to the memorial. The plan enjoyed the support of Frederick Hart and representatives of AMVETS, the VFW, and Vietnam Veterans of America. The statue would be located 120 feet from the west wall in what the landscape architect Joe Brown called a "soft, ushering outdoor room" framed by a copse of trees. The flag would be placed at a new intersection of pathways leading to the memorial, at the west end of the site, in the direction of the Lincoln Memorial, some 35 feet from the statue.[42]

The decision to place the statue and flag to the side of the memorial was more easily defensible because, by this time, the memorial's design was better understood. An estimated one million Americans had visited the memorial and it had received massive press coverage, most of which referred approvingly to the memorial's power.[43] A volunteer guide for the National Park Service reported that the overwhelming majority of visitors to the memorial left with a favorable impression. He described Secretary Watt's "meddling" with the design as a politicization of the memorial.[44] As the critic Benjamin Forgey wrote, "Experiencing that place simply obliterates the shrill oversimplifications of the debate concerning the esthetics of the memorial. . . . It takes ideological blinders to ignore the basic fact that it works."[45]

At the Fine Arts Commission hearing, a Veterans Administration therapist, Steven Silver, testified about the memorial's therapeutic effect. Silver said that he and his staff regularly brought veteran patients to the memorial to help them work out their buried feelings. In his view, the memorial's openness to interpretation was an advantage because it did not "impose a concept" on the visitor. Using a variety of metaphors, Silver said that the memorial was like a Rorschach inkblot test; it was an empty vessel into which viewers could pour anything they carried; it served as an emotional lightning rod. Imposing a statue in front of or on top of the memorial would restrict the viewer's emotional responses. And Silver was one of the first to point out a problem: not all Vietnam veterans were infantrymen, as represented in Hart's statue, and so some might not identify with the figures.[46]

Still, the memorial fund's critics were unhappy. James Webb was convinced that, unless they were placed centrally, the sculpture and flag would be "a mere sideshow, off in the woods."[47] Milt Copulos testified that the poll of veterans at the memorial's unveiling indicated that a vast majority wanted the flagpole in a more prominent position. The VVMF were forearmed with a professional analysis of the poll's methodology, and Scruggs argued that the poll was unrepresentative and flawed.[48] The ever-present Carhart said that he had bled for his country and "a lot of my brothers died there" for principles that the flag embodied. "If we could hear from those men and women who died, where would they want that flag?" he asked. He answered for the dead: "Right on top! Not hidden off in the trees somewhere." Carhart blustered that the flag and statue might be moved "by popular acclaim some time in the future." Representative Hunter said that veterans would feel "betrayed" because the positions of the flag and statue had been determined by the March 1982 meeting and accepted by all parties. Brown replied that the Fine Arts Commission had never given its assent to this arrangement and he reminded Hunter that Congress had mandated that the design be reviewed by the Commission of Fine Arts and the National Capital Planning Commission. Hunter brought out a copy of a press release by Scruggs and Senator Warner that announced the March 1982 agreement. "Well," the patrician Brown sniffed, "we can all be grateful that the United States of America is governed by laws and not by press releases."[49]

Congressional critics kept harping on their old themes. Representative Larry McDonald (D., Georgia) referred to the wall as the "black hole of Calcutta." He told the House of Representatives that the memorial's designer "did not want it to be a manifestation of glory and pride—but of shame." He brought up Garrett Eckbo's name, saying that Eckbo "actively supported the pro Viet Cong movement from his Berkeley, California, sanctuary." As if Berkeley were not a sufficient synonym for leftism, the word *sanctuary* evoked the territory in Cambodia, adjacent to Vietnam, where the Communists located bases during the Vietnam War. McDonald complained that placing Old Glory and the statue away from the "immediate vicinity" of the memorial would amount to a "total insult" to veterans. It was too late to argue this point, though. The White House and the VVMF had come to an understanding and Reagan now began to refer to "healing" as well as to the "noble cause" idea in his speeches about Vietnam. The administration set about mending fences with the veterans' organizations that Watt had offended. Deaver replied to the AMVETS complaints by reporting that Secretary Watt had taken all three proposals for the placement of the statue and flag to the commission, which had made its decision. Deaver also wrote a conciliatory letter to Scruggs and appears to have drafted similar letters to Senators Mathias and Warner.[50]

The resolution of the argument about the placement of the statue and flag allowed the president to invoke the memorial as a symbol of national unity. In a speech to the Conservative Political Action Conference in February 1983 following the Fine Arts Commission's decision, Reagan said that America needed to strengthen its armed forces, and then he invoked the Vietnam Veterans Memorial as a "reminder of how our nation has learned and grown and transcended the tragedies of the past."[51] Had there still been institutional deadlock over the placement of the statue and flag, such references to the memorial would have been quite risky: the president would have left hostages to fortune, because a new flare-up over the design might demonstrate the persistent discord that the "tragedies of the past" still provoked. Being able to talk about "transcending" the divisive legacy of Vietnam was one of the premiums that the administration gained from the completion of the memorial's plan.

The president's speechwriter had asked the VVMF to contribute some relevant facts and ideas associated with the memorial. Reagan's speech quoted Scruggs's statement that "a lot of healing" went on during the National Salute to Vietnam Veterans. Scruggs commented that the speech was "nice, standard stuff about how the [Vietnam Veterans Memorial] has helped recognize Viet vets and heal the nation's wounds, etc."[52] The rhetoric of "healing" had become routine fare available to the memorial fund, journalists, and politicians—even the president.

Reagan described an incident during the national salute when a group of students met a group of former marines in a restaurant and cheered the veterans when they left. The fact that the appreciative nonveterans were students was a telling detail, because students were once associated with the anti–Vietnam War movement.

The friendliness of a new generation of students to the veterans therefore marked a historical shift. Reagan drew the lesson: "We Americans have learned again to listen to each other, to trust each other. . . . And we've learned—and I pray this time for good—that we must never again send our young men to fight and die in conflicts that our leaders are not prepared to win."[53]

It could hardly be that this lesson was newly learned, because, as we recall, Reagan had used that line in his 1980 speech to the VFW and had been reciting it in speeches ever since his attempt at the presidency in 1976.[54] The idea that those who fought in Vietnam were denied victory by their own government was gaining increasing currency. It became the premise of a set of "revenge" movies—*Uncommon Valor*, *Missing in Action*, and *Rambo*—in which Vietnam veterans return to Vietnam and rescue American prisoners still held in captivity there. In rescuing the prisoners, the veterans vindicate themselves and exact revenge against their own government, as well as against their Vietnamese enemies.[55] Reagan's speech employed memorial-inspired reconciliation to conjure up a national consensus in favor of the revisionist view that politicians betrayed the troops in Vietnam and prevented them from winning the war. Reagan's assimilation of the memorial's rhetoric of healing sought to rally the public behind his established views. In a sign of his growing confidence, Scruggs pretended nonchalance, greeting the speech as a "nice plug" but "nothing worth getting too excited about."[56] In fact, the VVMF regarded the speech as a significant gesture of the president's favor and immediately responded by inviting the president, Meese, and others at the White House to a briefing.[57]

The VVMF sought any opportunity to inveigle presidential involvement with the memorial. But as long as the potential for conflict about the memorial persisted, the administration exercised fine judgments in calibrating the closeness of its association with the memorial. When, in July, the VVMF invited the first lady to accept an award in recognition of her efforts on their behalf, the White House staff debated whether she should accept the award privately or with the media present. One staff member proposed to Deaver that it "might not be a bad idea to accept this award publicly." In the end, though, the first lady declined the award. The White House and the VVMF were involved in an intricate dance. The VVMF were eager for the endorsement that the first family could give them; the White House measured how much political advantage it could glean from an endorsement, and whether any advantage outweighed the disadvantages of involving themselves in a memorial that still had residues of controversy attached to it and was considered incomplete without the statue.[58] In January 1983 National Security Adviser William Clark proposed that Reagan make an unannounced visit to the memorial and Deaver approved the plan. Three months later Meese visited the memorial for what seems to have been a scouting mission before the president's own low-key, nonceremonial visit to the memorial on May 1, 1983, during which Reagan left flowers at the wall.[59] "It's quite a place," Reagan confided to his diary, and the visit was "a very impressive & moving experience."[60] Everyone temporarily enjoyed some moments of relief.

On July 1, 1983, a fifty-five-foot flagpole flying the Stars and Stripes was installed. By now, with the memorial wall created, the memorial fund no longer felt an overwhelming imperative to avoid any "political statement." For the inscription on the flagpole's baseplate, they first considered a piece of graffiti from the Khe Sanh combat base: "For those who have fought for it, freedom has a flavor the protected will never know." This militant statement was rejected, though, perhaps because of the division it instituted between the fighters and "the protected," which was too far removed from the rhetoric of national healing. Instead, the memorial fund chose an inscription that reads, "This flag represents the service rendered to our country by the veterans of the Vietnam War. The flag affirms the principles of freedom for which they fought and their pride in having served under difficult circumstances." The words echo the remarks about serving under "difficult circumstances" made by the former prisoner of war Jeremiah Denton, now a U.S. senator (whose support both the memorial fund and their critics had tried to cultivate), when he returned from captivity in Vietnam. They also recall a valedictory by Richard Nixon's defense secretary James Schlesinger to troops returning from Vietnam: "Under circumstances more difficult than ever before faced by our military services, you accomplished the mission assigned to you by higher authority. In combat you were victorious and you left the field with honor." The new inscription did not quite match Schlesinger's victory plaudits, but in comparison with the prologue and epilogue inscribed on the wall, it marked a ratcheting upward of the rhetoric of patriotism in its reference to the veterans' "pride" in their service and in the statement that the troops fought for "freedom."[61]

The wall had been completed and dedicated on schedule; the argument about the placement of the statue and flag had been settled; the statue was being fabricated, and although it would not be ready by the date originally planned for its dedication, November 11, 1983, there appeared to be no further impediment to its installation. The VVMF sent a report to Congress in September 1983, outlining their progress to date and saying that the memorial had "fostered reconciliation of the divisions caused by the Vietnam War." The report said that the memorial drew fifteen thousand visitors a day and was one of the most visited attractions in Washington, behind only the National Air and Space Museum and the Lincoln Memorial. Over two and a half million people had visited. Just as the country recovered after the Civil War, the VVMF said, the "need to restore our national unity after the divisions of Vietnam is just as great and the Vietnam Veterans Memorial has helped America to begin the long overdue healing process."[62] But old grudges continued to be expressed, demonstrating that a lot of "healing" remained to be done.

In February 1983, the specter of McCarthyism materialized on stage when Roy Cohn, a reactionary, unethical lawyer who had acted as Senator Joseph McCarthy's counsel in the anti-Communist "witch hunts" of the 1950s, pressed for the audit that Perot demanded. It was as though an exorcism had gone terribly wrong and the memorial fund, hoping to lay the ghost of the Vietnam War to rest, had instead awakened the malevolent spirits of America's anti-Communist repression. What next? One might have half-expected "tail-gunner Joe" himself to rise from the grave, glowering darkly and searching for treason. Cohn's entrance on the scene worried Scruggs, who told Richardson, "[Perot] has a mean streak and . . . wants to get even with me or the VVMF." In response, Richardson, who had known Cohn since 1947, described Perot as "a mean man [who] has hired a mean lawyer." Richardson said he would be glad to make Cohn feel embarrassed about taking on Perot's cause.[63] Cyrus Vance, who had held high office in the Pentagon and State Department under three presidents, also interceded with Cohn on the VVMF's behalf.

Cohn was quite open about the fact that he was acting for Perot. His nominal clients, though, were William Stensland and John Baines, two Texas Vietnam veterans and leaders of the Vietnam Veterans Leadership Program (VVLP) in San Antonio, who had learned of the alleged irregularities in the VVMF's finances from Webb and Perot.[64] Neither Perot nor Webb wished to be publicly associated with the hiring of the lawyer and having Baines and Stensland hire Cohn was a subterfuge that succeeded at least in keeping Webb's name out of the case. However, noting that Stensland and Baines were acquaintances of Webb's, Scruggs rightly saw Webb's fingerprints on the "Roy Cohn affair."[65]

Baines, a Seabees veteran who knew Webb through the VVLP, was angry when he first came back from Vietnam, complaining that the troops "fought a war they weren't allowed to win." He said, "I've carried this thing around on my chest for ten years. . . . I was so damned mad when I came back from Vietnam, it took me a couple of years to even start getting my head straight." Stensland, who had taught Webb at Annapolis and was said to be the model for a crusty Naval Academy instructor in one of Webb's novels, said that he felt more comfortable in the jungle than among antiwar protesters at home. He repeated the story that Scruggs had told in a 1979 article, of protesters' telling maimed veterans "you deserve it." Stensland said that the memorial design was chosen by "intellectuals" who did not fight the war; most veterans did not understand Maya Lin's "surrealistic" wall, he said, but they could understand Frederick Hart's "simple and realistic" statue.[66]

Having read articles criticizing the memorial's design in the fall of 1981, Stensland took on board all the standard criticisms. He suggested that the 2.7 million Vietnam veterans should have selected the memorial's design, and, ignoring the fact that the critics were the ones who made a "fuss" about the design, he asked, "Why didn't we just find a creative Vietnam [veteran] artist and produce something without all this fuss?" Cohn initially expressed great eagerness to take the case when Baines and Stensland met him in New York and told him of what they had learned about the VVMF's finances. Within a few weeks, though, Cohn reported to Baines that there was nothing in the accusations against the VVMF. He was quite abrupt with Baines, who had the impression that Cohn had been warned off: a sign that perhaps Richardson and Vance's intercession had succeeded. Cohn told Vance that he thought Perot was "angry at the VVMF more than he is concerned about our audits." He assured Vance that he would try to persuade Perot to discontinue his efforts against the VVMF, at least regarding the audit.[67]

In the autumn of 1983, a series of television broadcasts by an investigative reporter, Carlton Sherwood, a marine veteran of the Vietnam War, repeated the charges about VVMF financial impropriety. The reports were scheduled to run on Washington's CBS affiliate WDVM on consecutive nights coinciding with the anniversary of the memorial's dedication. Sherwood charged that the memorial fund had raised over $9 million but had spent only $3 million on construction. Just as Scruggs rightly suspected that Webb was somehow involved in the Cohn affair, he also thought that Webb had put Sherwood up to investigating the VVMF.[68] Sherwood's third segment featured Perot and Carhart complaining that the VVMF would not open their financial records to scrutiny, with Carhart asking again, "If they've done nothing wrong, why not show the books? . . . I don't know what they're hiding. . . . If it comes out that they . . . misused money given by widows and orphans and people who were hard up, and they used it in ways other than they were legally allowed to use it, then I will feel that they have been slimy, treacherous, dishonorable, dirty people, and I won't rest until I see that things have been righted."[69]

In the search for ammunition with which to attack the VVMF, Sherwood found out about the long-standing grievance between the Angel Fire memorial in New Mexico and the VVMF. He learned that the Westphalls were aggrieved because the memorial fund had failed to deliver the money that the fund's early publicity materials said that they would raise for the memorial at Angel Fire.[70] Douglas Westphall, David's brother, had vented his impatience with the memorial fund in 1980, when he said they had exploited the chapel as a means of launching their own "belated memorial effort." In the interview by Sherwood, Victor Westphall confirmed that the fund failed to give the chapel the $100,000 that he felt they owed.[71] Scruggs admitted to Sherwood that the VVMF had said that they would raise funds for the Angel Fire chapel, and that they had not done so. But, he pointed out, building the Vietnam Veterans Memorial in Washington was a priority and Westphall should wait until it was completed. Nonetheless, Sherwood reported the VVMF's failure to live up to this pledge as an example of their untrustworthiness.[72]

Sherwood also interviewed a Vietnam veteran who said that the VVMF had turned down a donation of $1 million from the Disabled American Veterans (DAV), a 750,000-strong veterans' organization, rather than open their books to it. The DAV may have had an ulterior motive in making the offer, though. Beginning in 1977, the DAV quietly began to fund the Angel Fire memorial, and as it assumed increasing financial responsibility for the chapel, it inherited the grievance against the VVMF from the Westphall family. Although it did not actively participate in the attacks against the VVMF, the DAV was noticeably cooler toward the memorial fund than the other major veterans' organizations were. Pointedly, in the autumn of 1982, just before the National Salute to Vietnam Veterans, it decided formally to adopt the Angel Fire memorial, rededicating it as the DAV Vietnam Veterans National Memorial in May 1983. The DAV's million-dollar offer was contingent on the VVMF's actually needing the money. Some of the VVMF's contacts suspected that this meant that the DAV wanted to examine the VVMF's accounts to establish whether the VVMF had surplus funds that could be used to fund the Angel Fire memorial. Sherwood's report did not go into the intricacies of these supposed obligations and the fact that the VVMF had turned down the DAV's offer of financial support was given no explanation other than the VVMF's reluctance to open their books to scrutiny. In conjunction with Perot's accusations, the VVMF's unwillingness to fulfill this apparently reasonable condition appeared therefore to warrant suspicion.[73]

According to the highly decorated Vietnam veteran David Christian, a supporter of the VVMF, Sherwood questioned how anyone could want a memorial designed by a "fucking gook" (a derogatory term the U.S. troops used to refer to Asian people).[74] Sherwood also pursued other, novel lines of attack. He had discovered that Wheeler, the VVMF's chairman, had received an Article 15 administrative punishment for unauthorized use of a jeep in Vietnam. WDVM broadcast this information in the second segment, where Sherwood also cast aspersions on Wheeler's courage and patriotism, saying that Wheeler had not served in combat in Vietnam and had re-signed his commission from the army when the war was at its height. This was a wounding charge against the VVMF, whose officers had brought Carhart and Webb into their inner circle precisely because, apart from Scruggs, there were few combat veterans in the leadership.[75]

At this stage, though, the critics' carping drew little public sympathy. There was a certain irony in charging the memorial fund with excessive expenditures, since the attacks on the VVMF had led to their having to add a statue, hire lawyers, and expend administrative time on defending themselves, all of which cost money. Bobby Muller, executive director of Vietnam Veterans of America, said that he was "outraged" by the "smear attack" on the VVMF.[76] The media were overwhelmingly favorable to the memorial. *U.S. News and World Report* said in a headline that the wall had "healed our wounds." Attributing both wisdom and prescience to Maya Lin, it said that she was the one person unsurprised by the strong emotions the memorial evoked. She explained, "It's not meant to be cheerful or happy, but to bring out in people the realization of loss and a cathartic healing process. A lot of emotion is let go when you visit the memorial. A lot of people were really afraid of that emotion; it was something we had glossed over. From what I've read, the wall is working." The article reported on the mythology growing up around the memorial: people had begun to feel that the names had voices, that the wall was inhabited by the spirits of the dead, and that, when raindrops beaded and ran down the granite, the wall wept.[77]

The presidential administration was by now also clearly in the VVMF's camp, not in that of the critics. On November 7, 1983, the day of the first broadcast in the WDVM series, Reagan issued a statement celebrating the first anniversary of the Vietnam Veterans Memorial. He praised the memorial as a "peaceful but eloquent" monument to those who had served their country in an "honorable endeavor." He singled out Scruggs, Doubek, and Wheeler for praise, saying that Wheeler "worked not only to raise the money needed to build the memorial but, also, to help this na-tion heal the wounds of the Vietnam War." Reagan added, "Congratulations on a job well done."[78] Elliot Richardson read the message praising the memorial fund's officers at a Veterans Day ceremony at the memorial.[79] No mention of faulty ac-counting; and Reagan's use of the term *healing* demonstrated his assimilation of the VVMF's discourse.

With the White House on board, the VVMF rebutted Sherwood's charges in detail, pointing out that Sherwood had failed to identify the critics of the memorial fund's accounting as outspoken opponents of the memorial's design.[80] A month before the rebuttal, a half dozen members of the House of Representatives, including the long-standing VVMF critics Duncan Hunter and Tom Ridge (R., Pennsylvania), both Vietnam veterans, wrote to the U.S. General Accounting Office (GAO), the investigative arm of Congress, asking it to conduct an audit. Senators Mathias and Warner and the VVMF joined in this request.[81] The VVMF hoped this audit would put an end to the sniping at their financial probity. The VVMF's allies in Congress confirmed that the GAO's involvement would preempt any hostile congressional action and assured Scruggs that if Representative Hunter "trie[d] anything" they would "get him in line."[82] In another defensive maneuver to establish whether the VVMF were vulnerable to further attacks, their lawyers obtained copies of VVMF officers' and directors' military records and ascertained who else had requested them. The Pentagon agreed to protect these records.[83]

The GAO audit report cleared the VVMF of any wrongdoing.[84] Released in May 1984, the report found that, although the VVMF had initially offered to support the memorial at Angel Fire, they had not broken any laws when they changed their minds. In line with the memorial fund's rebuttal document, the report said, "The [Vietnam Veterans Memorial] Fund has never donated the [promised] $100,000 to the Chapel and has cited several reasons for its action. The primary reason was that public statements made by the Chapel founder in May 1980, that his Chapel honored all the dead of the Vietnam conflict, including North Vietnamese and Viet Cong, concerned Fund officials. . . . The Fund informed us that a donation to the Chapel has not been finally rejected since the DAV has assumed operation of the Chapel. Now that the DAV is involved, Fund officials are satisfied that there is no longer any thought that the Chapel will honor enemy veterans."[85] (The continued reference to the Vietnamese as "enemy veterans" ten years after the conclusion of hostilities between the two countries is telling.) Thus, the VVMF opportunistically used Westphall's offer to commemorate the dead on both sides as an ideologically iron-clad excuse for reneging on their promise of support to the chapel; principled or not, their explanation underlined the philosophical differences between the two memorials. Scruggs wrote to Perot in June 1984, saying that the GAO report had given the VVMF a "clean bill of health."[86] Sherwood quit his job at WDVM when the station backtracked from his story, and the New York Times reported that his career was in "ruins."[87] A year after Sherwood's broadcast and on the eve of the memorial's conveyance to the United States (when ownership of the memorial was officially transferred to the federal government), WDVM broadcast an apology to Wheeler and the other VVMF officers, accepting that its suspicions had been unfounded, and it donated $50,000 to the memorial's maintenance fund.[88]

Representative Ridge, one of those who had asked for the GAO audit, was still unhappy. He claimed that there were inconsistencies and inaccuracies in the GAO report.[89] Two years later, when the Senate voted to award the Congressional Gold Medal, Congress's highest civilian honor, to Scruggs, Wheeler, and Doubek, Ridge proposed that Webb, Copulos, and Carhart also receive the Gold Medals. This proposal was voted down in the House of Representatives. Ridge then led efforts to deny the medals to Scruggs, Wheeler, and Doubek, arguing that it was inappropriate to honor those who built the memorial—a point that contradicted his earlier efforts to award the medal to their opponents. The House of Representatives voted in favor of the award but did not achieve the necessary two-thirds majority and the bill failed. Wheeler commented, "There's no question we are still wrestling with the demons of Vietnam." Scruggs was magnanimous in the face of Ridge's vindictiveness. "For me," he said, "it was just a great satisfaction to build the memorial and to take part in an effort that's done so much for our country. My only goal was to get the 58,000 Americans on the memorial, and that's been accomplished."[90]

With the memorial on the way to completion, the Reagan administration set about organizing another commemoration of those who fought the Vietnam War: the interment of an unknown serviceman. For the administration, this was an opportunity for the nation to set aside past divisions in celebration of the honor and patriotism of those who served in Vietnam—and because there was already a site in Arlington National Cemetery dedicated to this tradition, the administration hoped that this time, the commemoration would not be encumbered with controversy. The project tied in with the large political purpose of uniting the nation but also to the narrower goal of helping Ronald Reagan win the Vietnam veterans vote in the November 1984 election.

The tradition of honoring an unknown soldier had arisen in World War I, when thousands of unidentified bodies were buried in mass graves and others were vaporized by explosions or lost in the mud of the Western Front.[91] The grave of a representative unknown gave the nation and the families of the dead a place to mourn. Because the body could not be identified, it could be that of anyone with no known grave. In that sense, the tradition of honoring the unknowns had the same inclusive motive as naming all the dead on the Vietnam Veterans Memorial: to mark a place where all were remembered. But this tradition met its historical limit in the Vietnam War.

Defense Secretary Caspar Weinberger wrote in March 1984 that members of Congress, veterans' organizations, and the National League of Families of American Prisoners of War and Missing in Southeast Asia all supported the interment of a Vietnam unknown at Arlington National Cemetery. This would represent "the highest honor our Nation can give to the Vietnam veterans."[92] As early as Reagan's first year in office, a "skirmish" was fought over whether the Pentagon could provide the remains of an unknown, a spokesman for the army adjutant general referring, in an odd turn of phrase, to the "lack of viable candidates."[93] The families of the four potentially identifiable dead persuaded the Reagan administration in 1982 to postpone the designation of one of them as an "unknown" because the remains might later be identified. Under pressure from veterans' organizations, the administration determined to inter an "unknown Vietnam soldier," despite the difficulty in the age of DNA tests in finding remains that could accurately be called unidentifiable. The Central Identification Laboratory decided in 1984 that a set of skeletal remains was unidentifiable, and the ID documents and scraps of a flight suit discovered alongside them mysteriously disappeared. There was an embarrassing denouement to the story when it was discovered some years later that the remains were identifiable after all; Michael Blassie's remains were returned to his family for burial. Indeed, forensic scientists had thought since before the interment at Arlington National Cemetery that the remains probably belonged to Blassie, but the administration had strongly encouraged the Pentagon to discover an "unknown."[94]

The remains of the unknown left Hawaii in an elaborate military ceremony involving a twenty-one-gun salute, a flyover by four jet fighters, and an honor guard of over 180 members of all the armed services. After a sea journey to California, the flag-draped coffin was flown to Washington, where it lay in state in the Capitol Rotunda. From there, it was placed on a military caisson and brought for burial with full military honors in Arlington on Memorial Day, May 28, 1984. Playing on the belief that Americans were still held captive in Southeast Asia, Reagan said that the interment ceremony would not write the last chapter of the history of the Vietnam War; that there would be "no last chapters" and no closed books until the last American missing in action had been accounted for.[95] Reagan revisited the points he had made the previous year to the Conservative Political Action Conference. He repeated Scruggs's statement that "a lot of healing went on" at the November 1982 dedication of the memorial. He recited the line about transcending the tragedies of the past, offered the warmed-over anecdote about the veterans and the students, and trotted out the familiar sentiment about the absence of a parade, flags, and gratitude. He even repeated the line that the war was a noble cause. His voice choking with emotion, Reagan asked rhetorical questions reinforcing the unknown's "everyman" status: "As a child, did he play on some street in a great American city? Did he work beside his father on a farm in America's heartland? Did he marry? Did he have children?" The questions poetically invoked and encompassed the whole nation—although the prosaic answers to the questions turned out to be, yes, no, no, and no, once Blassie was identified.[96] Reagan drew the points together by saying that, during the parade down Constitution Avenue, "there was a feeling that this nation, as a nation, we were coming together at last and that we had, at long last, welcomed the boys home."[97] Reagan's participation in the ceremony apparently had the desired effect: the national coordinator of the National Vietnam Veterans Coalition, an umbrella organization for fifteen groups, including the VVMF, the Military Order of the Purple Heart, and Agent Orange Victims International, wrote to tell Reagan that the ceremony "will be historically noted as a positive turning point in how Vietnam veterans are perceived by the American public." The president's "wonderful remarks" would bring about "a lot of healing."[98]

Reagan's eagerness to sponsor the Arlington ceremony contrasted with his continued hesitancy about making an official visit to the Vietnam Veterans Memorial. Reagan declined an invitation to visit the memorial on the day he honored the Vietnam unknown serviceman.[99] Representative David Bonior (D., Michigan), a Vietnam-era veteran who was a consistent opponent of Reagan's foreign policy, had long supported the VVMF and veterans' programs. He urged the president to visit the memorial, saying, "The Memorial which has done so very much to honor the veterans and to heal the nation's wounds after a bitterly divisive era should not be neglected by the President on this upcoming Memorial Day."[100] In considering the invitation, a White House staffer asked, "Any problem? You may recall the controversy involving Jim Watt."[101] A presidential appointments scheduler recommended a visit while the remains of the unknown serviceman were lying in state at the Capitol Rotunda, or just after the interment ceremony at Arlington National Cemetery, saying, "Recognizing the Memorial during the week of interment of a Vietnam Unknown would be viewed as a healing act."[102] Yet the president still avoided visiting the memorial on a ceremonial occasion, despite the growing bipartisan accord that the memorial was healing America's divisions.

This emerging consensus was welcome because, in the interval between the dedication of the wall and the addition of the Hart statue and flag, there was a good deal of public and congressional discord about Reagan's foreign policy. During the contentious 98th Congress, bookmarked by the mid-term election of 1982 and the presidential election of 1984, legislators asserted Congress's Constitutional prerogatives in foreign policy making: to give the president their "advice and consent" and to provide the resources only for policies of which they approved. They clashed with the president over appropriations for military and intelligence activities and warned the administration about the possible illegality of CIA efforts to overthrow the government of Nicaragua. A majority of the public, in response to questions from pollsters for CBS News, Louis Harris and Associates, ABC News, and the Gallup Organization, disagreed with Reagan's Nicaragua policy.[103] In early 1983, Reagan suffered another defense policy set-back when Congress rebelled against the MX missile program and legislators from both parties, in both houses of Congress, denounced his defense budget for including "exotic and farfetched weapons."[104]

In his memoirs, Reagan admitted that one of his greatest frustrations was his "inability to communicate to the American people and to Congress the seriousness of the threat we faced in Central America." Time and again, he said, he spoke about Central America on television, addressed Congress, or spoke at meetings, hoping there would be an outpouring of support for his policies that would apply "the same kind of heat" to Congress that helped pass his economic program. The public was unenthusiastic about his policies and failed to put pressure on legislators.[105] And when he attempted to unite Americans in a new consensus supporting his military build-up, his strident rhetoric was often divisive. Surveys by Richard Wirthlin, Reagan's pollster, found that the 1983 speech in which Reagan referred to the Soviet Union as an "evil empire," his statement countenancing limited nuclear war, and an off-the-cuff remark about beginning bombing the Soviet Union in five minutes had "put some Americans' teeth on edge."[106]

In October 1983, the consequences of real warfare came home to Americans. U.S. forces invaded the Caribbean island of Grenada and deposed the socialist government there after a week of fighting, at a cost of 18 American servicemen dead and 116 wounded.[107] In Lebanon, a terrorist bomb struck a U.S. barracks in Beirut, killing 241 marines.[108] Even before the Beirut bombing, a New York Times opinion survey found that, by a 2-to-1 margin, the public saw parallels between involvement in Lebanon and the way American involvement began in Vietnam.[109] But an administration official saw signs of hope in congressional approval of the troop deployment in Beirut: "When we came into office, one of our primary missions was to get Americans out of the 'Vietnam syndrome' and get them accustomed again to the idea that projecting power overseas can help the cause of peace. . . . Well, it's worked. There's a consensus on Capitol Hill in favor of keeping American troops in a battle zone."[110] The Beirut bombing changed all that, precipitating a withdrawal of the marines to ships safely offshore. This reaction to the Lebanon bombing demonstrated how, for all of Reagan's tough talk, and despite the massive arms build-up over which he presided, the United States was still extremely reluctant to commit its forces where they might suffer casualties. In contrast, the success of the Grenada action heartened conservatives. The columnist George Will said that it had "large symbolic value" and that "U.S. soldiers' boot prints" on Grenadan soil had made U.S. power seem "credible."[111] Taken together, the Lebanon and Grenada experiences demonstrated the administration's application of the "lesson" it had taken from Vietnam: "Win quickly or get out quickly."[112]

Defense Secretary Caspar Weinberger had been appalled by the antimilitary backlash after the Vietnam War. He said, "You can't fight Congress and public opinion and an enemy at the same time. . . . That's why Vietnam was the crime of the century." He condemned the piecemeal, gradualist deployment of military forces and the use of troops for diplomatic rather than military objectives; he opposed the commitment of U.S. combat troops to Central America.[113] In the aftermath of the Lebanon bombing, Weinberger devised six tests governing the use of military power that codified the "lessons" of Vietnam by stating that U.S. forces should be used only in pursuit of a vital interest, as a last resort, with the full backing of the people and Congress, and that all the forces necessary for victory should be committed. The references to using force wholeheartedly in pursuit of victory may give the tests, which became known as the Weinberger Doctrine, an air of assertive militarism. In fact, Weinberger's was an extremely cautious statement, imposing strict limits on the circumstances in which the United States would use its armed forces.[114] As Lou Cannon sums up Weinberger's approach, "He supported only those military actions that offered a reasonable prospect of immediate success in behalf of a strictly limited objective."[115] Secretary of State George Shultz, who had replaced Alexander Haig in June 1982, used to ask what the forces were for if the United States committed them only to combat where the odds were vastly disproportionate, as in Grenada. He once asked Weinberger, "Cap, why are you buying all this military equipment if you never want to use it?" This, he said, was "the Vietnam syndrome in spades."[116]

Each of the six tests reflected a negative counterpart in Vietnam, and Weinberger said that by adhering to them, the United States would avoid being drawn into a "quagmire" in Central America.[117] If the U.S. effort in Vietnam was confounded by a lack of clear objectives, the incremental expansion of force, and an absence of public support, future U.S. military efforts would avoid these failings by setting clear objectives and using sufficient force to achieve these aims before public support waned. The six tests, though, connected public opinion with military events in a way that underlined the risks of any military deployment. It is rarely possible for a military power, even one as preponderant as the United States, to guarantee the swift and successful outcome of a conflict; and even if an initial consensus for military action existed, there could be no guarantee that it would persist in the face of setbacks, moral qualms, or slow progress. Thus, the Weinberger Doctrine betrayed unease about the possibility that another military intervention might turn sour.

Despite the secretary of defense's caution about the commitment of forces, hardliners in the administration wanted to depose the socialist government of Nicaragua, and here the administration's actions were belligerent and its talk shrill.[118] In the summer of 1983, Reagan approved a memorandum by National Security Adviser William Clark, one of the Central America hardliners, saying that the United States should pursue a policy of destabilizing the government of Nicaragua. Reagan stepped up the rhetoric against the Sandinista government, calling it a "dictatorship of counterfeit revolutionaries."[119] The Defense Department organized the "Big Pine II" military exercises near Nicaragua to intimidate the Sandinista government by demonstrating America's military might. One of the central purposes of the exercises was to set off a fear of invasion among Nicaragua's people and leaders. The United States garrisoned Nicaragua's neighbor, Honduras, constructing military bases, training camps, storage depots, and airports there and building it into a logistics, intelligence, and radar hub for the *contras*. U.S. and Honduran forces conducted joint military exercises, and two U.S. aircraft carrier task forces performed maneuvers off Nicaragua's coasts and in the air. The scale of this "unparalleled military display" had never been seen before in the hemisphere, even during the build-up to the 1961 Bay of Pigs invasion. The facilities constructed were large enough to maintain a large-scale U.S. presence in Honduras, or to allow Honduras to be used as a staging area for an attack on Nicaragua.[120] An administration official said that the aim was to persuade the "bad guys" in Nicaragua "that we are positioned to blockade, invade, interdict, if they cross a particular threshold."[121] The United States also tried to destabilize Nicaragua economically by cutting its sugar export quota and sabotaging its efforts to obtain loans and credit from international institutions.[122]

While the military exercises were going on, CIA-backed *contra* forces operating out of Honduras and Costa Rica attacked targets inside Nicaragua. The aim of these raids was four-fold: to cause material economic damage, to force the Sandinistas into taking repressive measures fomenting popular discontent, to cause them to divert resources from economic development to defense, and to provoke a Nicaraguan cross-border response that would give its neighbors and the United States a *casus belli*. The *contras* specialized in attacking rural health-care facilities, agricultural cooperatives, and schools, killing nurses, doctors, teachers, and agronomists. They intended these attacks to disrupt the Sandinista program of improving the lives of people in the countryside. Damaging though they were to the Sandinistas' revolutionary experiment, these actions also meant that the *contras* remained politically unpopular in Nicaragua. The Reagan administration's policy of support for the *contras* was unpopular in the United States, too. Throughout 1983, a series of public opinion polls showed public opposition to Reagan's policy of support for the *contras* as running between 60 and 80 percent, and Wirthlin's private polls for the White House showed about the same.[123] In the midst of Big Pine II, a Harris poll found that 67 percent of the public thought that U.S. involvement in El Salvador and Nicaragua "looks too much as though it could turn out to be another Vietnam for this country."[124] At a presidential news conference, the reporter Helen Thomas referred Reagan to polls demonstrating public opposition to the military exercises and fears that they might lead to war. She asked him whether he was concerned about this opposition, in view of the lessons of Vietnam. He replied, "There is no comparison with Vietnam and there's not going to be anything of that kind in this."[125]

Secretary of State Shultz wanted to use aid to the *contras* as part of a twin-track policy of military pressure and diplomacy to win concessions from the Sandinistas during negotiations. The U.S. government was, however, full of hard-liners—particularly in the National Security Council, but also in his own department—who were suspicious of any negotiations. They frequently undermined Shultz's efforts and were strong enough to bring about the removal of State Department officials involved in negotiating with Nicaragua.[126] The result was incoherence in U.S. policy, with the State Department and the National Security Council rival centers of policy making, and the secretaries of state and defense conducting their own private battles for influence with the president. Shultz was not given advance notice of the Big Pine II exercises, which he described in scathing terms: as he saw it, a Pentagon reluctant to commit American military forces in combat took every opportunity to show them off in maneuvers; but this show of force simply conjured up the "specter of another Vietnam" in Congress. The news of Big Pine II caused "the worst legislative defeat of the Reagan administration to that date."[127] In July 1983 the House of Representatives defeated Reagan's request for aid to the *contras*, amid references on both sides of the debate to the parallels between Central America and Vietnam.[128]

The administration had already embarked on a public diplomacy campaign in an attempt to build support for its policies. In addition to the spring 1983 series of presidential speeches (discussed in Chapter 1), Reagan appointed the National Bipartisan Commission on Central America, headed by Henry Kissinger, which began its work in mid-1983 and delivered a report in January 1984 recommending a $90 billion package of military, economic, and humanitarian aid to the region. Its bipartisan composition barely papered over its ideological biases, though, and its staff refused to allow liberal witnesses to appear at its hearings. Ultimately, the commission was unable to build the "national consensus" that it aimed at and its report had little influence on policy.[129] A week after the report was issued, a Harris poll found that a majority of Americans rejected every one of its recommendations. In an election year, though, both the administration and its opponents in the legislature had to step carefully. The Democratic Party was afraid of being accused of "losing" El Salvador.[130] After Reagan gave a televised prime-time speech, the House of Representatives narrowly approved military aid to El Salvador, but congressional support for Reagan's policy rested on a knife edge and was jeopardized by frequent administration gaffes.

Planning for the president's re-election had begun soon after his inauguration, with Deaver and Baker, aided by Wirthlin's polls, involved from the start in gauging the electoral costs and benefits of administration policies. In the run-up to the

November 1984 presidential election, foreign policy was one area in which Reagan appeared vulnerable.[131] The State Department's Lawrence Eagleburger explained the public's lack of enthusiasm for the administration's Central America policy by saying, "There is a lot left of the Vietnam syndrome, the concern that we will become directly involved militarily and that it's a bottomless pit."[132] As Secretary of State Shultz saw it, the machinations of the hard-liners in Central America made Reagan look like a "warmonger." Deaver, Baker, and Nancy Reagan wanted the president to be seen, instead, as a "man of peace."[133]

Reagan's closest confidants had reason for concern. It was not just the risk of deepening U.S. involvement that worried the public; the things their government was caught doing also troubled people. The public and Congress were disturbed when it came to light in April 1984 that the CIA had aided the *contras* in mining the approaches to Nicaragua's harbors. A CBS/New York Times poll found that 67 percent of the public disapproved of the U.S. role in the mining, and only 20 percent approved. When the government of Nicaragua complained about the mining at the World Court, the United States handed the Sandinistas a huge propaganda victory. When the court accepted the case, despite a U.S. plea that it fell outside the court's jurisdiction, the United States refused to accept its judgments over Central American matters for the next two years, in contravention of international law and its own treaty obligations. International and domestic opinion was dismayed at this show of international lawlessness. In April 1984, the Republican-controlled Senate voted, with a large, bipartisan majority, to condemn the mining, and in June, the upper chamber for the first time rejected one of Reagan's requests for aid to the *contras*.[134]

In July 1984, Louis Harris and Associates asked a sample of Americans whether, with military exercises in Honduras and off the coasts of Central America, "there is a danger that we could get involved militarily in another Vietnam." Sixty-three percent said yes.[135] In October, there were new revelations about a CIA manual for the *contras* that advised them on assassinating Sandinista officials (the *Washington Post* dubbed it a "murder manual") contrary to presidential directives forbidding assassinations. In the same pre-election month, Congress again tried to rein in the administration, suspending aid to the Nicaraguan counterrevolutionaries by passing the second Boland amendment ("Boland II"). This time, Congress seemed to have definitively cut off all further military aid to the *contras*, by comprehensively listing the activities the law prohibited. Representative Henry Hyde, a particularly vehement supporter of *contra* aid, who had mobilized his colleagues to sign letters hostile to the VVMF, called the prohibition of further funding "dangerous and tragic," saying that the United States had built up the *contra* forces only to abandon them with barely a prayer. One of the co-signatories of Hyde's January 1982 letter against the VVMF compared Democrats who wanted to cut funding of the *contras* to Neville Chamberlain appeasing Hitler at Munich. He accused them of "making the world safe for Communism."[136] At stake was not just the fate of the *contras* but the Reagan Doctrine itself—the ability of the administration to fund and arm anti-Communist insurgencies. Nicaragua was its first test and had now become a symbol: "it represented the ground on which the Reagan ideologues had chosen to make their stand against the Vietnam syndrome."[137] Reagan told Robert McFarlane, who had succeeded William Clark as national security adviser, to help the *contras* "hold body and soul together" until funding was restored; the instructions, when relayed to Oliver North, a zealous National Security Council staffer, led to the whole illegal enterprise of selling arms to Iran and using the funds to pay for arms for the *contras*. But the administration's National Security Planning Group had already decided, in June, to begin the search for alternate, third-country sources of funding for the *contras* (which Baker considered an "impeachable offense")—an enterprise that eventually ballooned into the Iran–Contra scandal.[138]

In disturbing news for Reagan's re-election campaign, Wirthlin reported that a plurality of Americans considered the world less safe than it had been four years before, and by a twenty-eight-point margin, they believed that Reagan was more likely to start an unnecessary war than his Democratic Party rival for the presidency, Walter Mondale. Wirthlin's data showed that Central America policy was a "sore point" with the electorate.[139] In the months before the election, the Pentagon consequently lowered the profile of the U.S. military presence in Honduras, sharply reducing troop numbers and keeping military exercises off the front pages of newspapers. This stratagem helped to prevent an electoral backlash. Exit polls revealed that those who thought Central America was a major issue in the presidential election voted by a 2:1 ratio in favor of Reagan's opponent, Walter Mondale; this heavily skewed margin was not decisive, though, because the tactic of lowering military tensions reduced the number who considered Central America a major issue to only 4 percent of voters. As soon as Reagan was safely reelected, though—the day after the election—three new military exercises began in Honduras, and the administration announced that another four would start within a few weeks.[140]

In response to public and congressional anxieties about Reagan's foreign policy, the administration sought opportunities for the president to appear statesmanlike, not strident, and to project the image of a leader who carefully weighed the costs of war. The VVMF's second National Salute to Vietnam Veterans, or Salute II, provided just such an occasion. Anticipating that some three hundred thousand veterans from all wars would be present for the dedication of Hart's statue *Three Infantrymen* (fig. 16), the president's schedulers strongly recommended that he attend.[141] On Veterans Day, November 11, 1984, five days after his re-election, Reagan gave the keynote speech at the dedication. He spoke of the representativeness of the three figures and remarked on the youthfulness of their faces on which we see "expressions of loneliness and profound love and a fierce determination never to forget."[142] Later, Reagan said that the statue of the three servicemen moved him because "their eyes reflected their strong sense of duty and their determination to accept their responsibilities."[143] His speech said that those who died in Vietnam did so uncomplainingly, asking only to be remembered. He praised the survivors for keeping faith with the dead and for having fought steadfastly, "deaf to the voices of those who didn't comprehend."

The speech's major theme was reconciliation between veterans and American society. This theme crowned the success of the VVMF's discourse of healing, but Reagan's speechwriters cleverly turned the concept in a direction that accorded with

Figure 16. *Three Infantrymen*, Vietnam Veterans Memorial, Washington, DC; Frederick Hart, sculptor, dedicated November 11, 1984. Photo by author.

the administration's geopolitical policy. Inducting Vietnam veterans into the ranks of the nation's "true patriots," Reagan thanked them for their patience in awaiting recognition by a public that was unable to recognize their "stainless patriotism" because of its distaste for the war. As Reagan put it, a "rethinking" on all sides allowed Americans to leave behind the divisions that once threatened to tear American society apart. "We can forgive ourselves," he pronounced, "for those things that may have been wrong" in the war's conduct. "And it's time we moved on, in unity and with resolve, with the resolve to always stand for freedom, as those who fought did, and to always try to protect and preserve the peace." The plea for unity connoted both overcoming the divisions about the Vietnam War and uniting in the face of present and future international challenges. The commitment "always" to stand for freedom clearly had no temporal limit, but it also lacked any geographical predicates. It applied around the globe, for all time—which is as much as to say that it applied at the present moment in El Salvador and Nicaragua.

For Reagan, "healing" meant renewed strength: "It's been said that these memorials reflect a hunger for healing. . . . Sometimes when a bone is broken, if it's knit together well, it will in the end be stronger than if it had not been broken."[144] The speech marked the marriage of the VVMF's recuperative discourse and the administration's foreign policy aims. Reagan and the VVMF had different agendas. The VVMF simply wanted a memorial that would honor those who fought and died, and they tried to avoid the pitfalls of political conflict in getting it built; the Reagan administration wanted to unite a country divided by the war so that it could pursue an active foreign policy without constantly wondering when a new fissure would open up along the fault lines in the polity. They found common cause in the completion of the memorial, and their rhetoric converged on the term *healing*. In the context of Reagan's foreign policy, the appeal for healing and "unity . . . with resolve" assimilated the theme of reconciliation into a call for a united America's resumption of world leadership, backed, if necessary, by military force.

Reagan ended the speech by signing the memorandum conveying the memorial, now considered complete after the addition of the statue, to the United States, although this transfer of ownership was complicated by backstage wrangling. William Clark had left the office of national security adviser to replace Watt as secretary of the interior, following Watt's resignation in October 1983 (after he made a remark that managed in the space of a single sentence to be offensive about race, gender, and disabilities). The VVMF asked that Clark and Reagan sign the Memorandum of Conveyance at the site. Even this simple act proved problematic. The White House balked at allowing the president to be the official signatory of the memorandum on behalf of the United States and said that he would sign merely in witness to the secretary of the interior's official signing. The White House counsel's office believed that the president's signature would increase the chances of his being named as a party to any dispute that might develop "over what has already been a fairly controversial memorial."[145] This little wrangle sheds light on the complexity of the White House's position. Reagan had been too cautious to make an official visit to the memorial in 1983, even when he spoke publicly of "healing" and "transcending the tragedies of the past." Now that the memorial was complete, Reagan talked of national unity but was still chary of contention. In fact, in his speech, the image of the broken bone knitting together stronger "in the end" betrayed the continuing division. "I hope that before my days as Commander in Chief are ended the process will be completed," he said, and that day was still four years away.[146]

For members of the 82nd Airborne Division, a reunion coinciding with the dedication of the Hart statue marked a new comradeship. For the first time, the retired generals who had commanded the division in Vietnam attended one of the reunions. For years after the end of the war, the enlisted men thought that their generals regarded them as undisciplined, insubordinate "losers." Now, one general told them that they were the best he had ever served with; another told them that they could be proud and that their recognition was "long overdue."[147] But not everyone celebrated at the statue's dedication. An antiwar veteran listening to Reagan's speech wore a tee-shirt with the words "No more Vietnams" and was one of the few willing to talk politics to a *Washington Post* reporter. "Revolutions don't have to be snuffed off with the military," he said. "I'm afraid we're going to make the same mistake down south [in Central America]."[148] Few African American veterans attended Salute II. Vietnam Veterans of America said that they had gone out of their way to invite blacks to the Veterans Day weekend events but admitted that these efforts had been largely unsuccessful. Robert Holcomb, a black veteran, commented that African Americans had trouble identifying with veterans' organizations the majority of whose membership was white. "They're in a void and don't know where to go," he said. Black veterans also felt left out of the positive reappraisal of veterans and the war itself. "We don't feel a part of the whole hoopla, the resurrection, . . . the effort to reverse the 1970s view of the war," said Bill Edward, an Urban League program coordinator who worked with black veterans.[149] Tom Carhart also felt out of sorts. He was present at the unveiling of a statue that might never have been added without his complaints, but he hung back, a lonely figure at the edge of the crowd.[150] He still believed that the wall was an "open urinal."[151]

Framed by a copse of trees, Hart's three-figure sculpture stands on a low pedestal behind chains and stanchions that prevent an audience from coming right up to it (fig. 17). Hart claimed that, while the wall was "a metaphor for the war itself," its focus on the dead worked "at the expense of the veteran."[152] At the unveiling, a marine veteran of Vietnam saw it the same way: looking at the wall, he said, "I feel that's for the boys we lost down there." Turning to the statue, he said, "And I feel that's for us that came back."[153] The three figures' sight lines point across an expanse of grass to the meeting point of the walls and the statue therefore directs the viewer's attention to the names. (The relationship between the statue and the wall would be quite different if the statue faced in the opposite direction, as some of the memorial fund's critics proposed—the wall would then provide a backdrop for the statue.) The figures' relationship with the trees, lawn, and wall makes it appear that the soldiers have emerged from a forest into a clearing where they are suddenly arrested by the sight of the wall facing them. One touches another's back, as if to stop him in his tracks. The sculpture shows the three figures not in heroic or athletic poses but carrying their weapons in a relaxed posture, halting after their walk.[154]

The realistic depiction of troops in the field lends itself to narrative, rather than symbolic, interpretations. The use of a polychrome patina on the cast bronze accentuates the sculpture's hyper-realism: the figures' flesh contrasts in color with their uniforms and weapons. The juxtaposition of statue and wall is eerie because these two components of the memorial are so incongruous yet the figures' attitude suggests a relationship between them. To make sense of this relationship, we have to imagine that the figures have been transported across time and space from the Vietnamese jungle to the Washington Mall, or that the names of the dead materialized on a granite wall before troops patrolling in Vietnam. "One senses the figures as passing by the treeline," Hart said, "and caught in the presence of the wall, turning to gaze upon it almost as a vision."[155] Because there are insufficient contextual elements to secure either scenario, the juxtaposition is ultimately jarring and the dissonance tends to shut down any attempt to comprehend the sculpture and wall within a common narrative frame. Nevertheless, visitors try to combine them into a coherent concept. One marine veteran remarked that the statue "is a fire team walking point for the wall," but this interpretation ignores the fact that the figures face the wall, not away from it as they would if "walking point."[156]

Eventually, the folklore of the memorial resolved that the three soldiers were "coming out of the bush and upon seeing the Wall are frozen in time and space. Their eyes, set deep, revealing the toll that war extracts from innocence, are searching the black granite wall to see if *their* names have been etched."[157] This idea has an eerie

Figure 17. The Frederick Hart statue and the flag, forming the memorial's "entrance experience." In the background of the photograph at the far right, visitors cluster around one of the name locators that specify the panel and line number of each name. Photo by author.

appeal, as if a visitor stumbled into a graveyard and imagined that he might find his own grave. Another veteran, returning to the memorial to see the dedication of the statue, remarked: "The first time I couldn't understand why they just put up a wall. It wasn't until I came back and saw the *rest of us* up there, looking over it all, that I understood. That's *us* coming out of the bush up there. We're gonna watch them. We're there for them forever."[158] The expressions on the three figures' faces help to secure this interpretation: without signs of physical wounds, the three figures in the statue seem exhausted and perplexed as they gaze upon the inscribed mural naming their fallen comrades. Yet this cue to the audience is redundant; visitors to the wall do not need the sculpture to tell them how to respond to the names or how soldiers feel about their lost friends. If visitors do need such sentimental instruction, the message would likely be lost on them. None of the narrative connections between the two elements works very convincingly, although the effort to produce them bears testimony to a rage for coherence: the compulsion to transform any juxtaposed objects into a story. The statue and wall are simply and irremediably there, near each other, the artifacts of a compromise that succeeded politically, not aesthetically.

The controversy about the placement of the flag rumbled on for years. Right-wing members of Congress intermittently tried to legislate that it should fly at the memorial's apex, above and behind the meeting point of the walls.[159] Representative Robert Dornan (R., California) repeatedly introduced legislation mandating a central position for the Stars and Stripes (while continuing to describe the war as a "noble cause") and never recovered from his sense of grievance at the betrayal of the deal the memorial fund struck with its critics. He reminded anyone who would listen that, at the "compromise" meeting, "the gentleman from California [Hunter] himself took the flag on a miniature [pole] into one of the conference rooms in this building and put it at the apex of the memorial where all agreed the flag was supposed to be. At that time they all agreed that the flag would be there. They even voted on it."[160] But the chorus of critics refighting the battle for the memorial had dwindled to one or two lonely voices such as his.

Having compromised with their critics in adding the statue, flag, and inscriptions, the VVMF strove to keep the memorial free from unauthorized encroachments. Every Memorial Day and Veterans Day, the VVMF hold official ceremonial events at the memorial.[161] Other, smaller-scale events take place, such as Father's Day ceremonies in which children of the dead participate. But early in their custodianship of the memorial, the VVMF and the National Park Service decided that it should not be used for political demonstrations or for commercial activities. This decision has protected the wall from exploitation by those who would enlist the dead in some political cause. Even before the wall was dedicated, the VVMF learned of plans by Vietnam Veterans Against the War (VVAW) (by now a tiny organization much reduced by sectarian splits among its leaders) to hold "Dewey Canyon IV," stopping at the memorial after a demonstration.[162] Scruggs warned the "off the wall" group that it would be "100 percent inappropriate to misuse our site for VVAW's PR purposes."[163]

Other groups have sought to promote their causes at the memorial from its early days. The VVMF and the National Park Service made successive decisions and requested legislation in Congress to keep at bay the advocates of causes such as the POW/MIA (prisoner of war/missing in action) issue, hucksters who wanted to sell memorabilia, and political demonstrators who wanted to use the wall to heighten whatever message they were promoting. In December 1982, Vietnam veterans from Ohio held a vigil to call attention to the twenty-five hundred Americans still listed as MIA. They asked veterans from other states to participate in the vigil by standing guard at the memorial for a week at a time, and by September 1983, veterans from fifteen other states had done so.[164] The VVMF insisted, though, that these groups remain outside a boundary line fifty feet from the memorial site.[165] The motives of some of the participants in the vigil groups were questionable. One group, Veterans' Vigil-POWs/MIAs, took $1,000 in donations in their first three days of operation in July 1985; they quickly folded their tent and furled their flags when the National Park Service informed them that no organization is allowed to solicit money on federal parkland. In 1986, a Vietnam veteran and the daughter of an air force pilot still listed as missing fasted and lived in a bamboo cage near the memorial to symbolize the fate of the MIAs. "The Last Firebase," a stall that sells memorabilia and draws attention to the POW/MIA issue, was set up to support the cage's two occupants. This and other POW/MIA-oriented stalls have continued beyond the perimeter for years. Their relationship with the memorial fund has been antagonistic. The Last Firebase, for example, sold tee-shirts and other paraphernalia making unauthorized use of the image of the *Three Infantrymen* statue, over which the VVMF and Hart held copyright. Scruggs complained that the hucksters near the memorial changed the memorial's sacred ground into a sort of flea market: he said, "The money changers have to be chased from the temple." As well as protecting the memorial's sanctity, his concern was to exclude others from commercially exploiting the statue's image, which earned the memorial fund and Hart tens of thousands of dollars from the sale of authorized memorabilia. Hart and the VVMF sued the tee-shirt seller for profiting from the image of *Three Infantrymen*. In 1995 the National Park Service outlawed tee-shirt sales on Washington's federal park land.[166]

Just as commercial activities were eventually banned, so too were political demonstrations. In July 1983 the Ad Hoc Committee for July 2 Emergency Mobilization decided to hold a march that would rally in front of the Vietnam Veterans Memorial, drawing attention to the danger of "another Vietnam" in Central America.[167] An organizer for the demonstration drew parallels between the early years of American involvement in South Vietnam and the sending of economic and military aid, including military advisers, to El Salvador.[168] AMVETS complained that the demonstrators were planning to use the memorial as a "staging area." Characterizing the demonstrators as "Communist," AMVETS complained that these opponents of U.S. intervention were advancing the interests of "Marxist tyranny in Central America." They urged the VVMF to prevent this "desecration."[169] The planned demonstration caused consternation. Scruggs commented wryly that, with the antiwar veterans and politicians speaking at a rally protesting against Reagan's foreign policy, the memorial would become the "wailing wall" Webb once feared it would become.[170] Scruggs considered trying to persuade the National Park Service not to give the demonstrators a permit to stop at the memorial, but he suspected that the request for an injunction would fail in court.

The Park Service advised against the VVMF's mobilizing a "vigilante group" to protect the memorial from the unwanted intrusion, and Scruggs accepted that any "fracas" leading to arrests would make matters worse. The demonstrators agreed to sustain the reverential character of the site by rallying two hundred yards away from the wall. Ron Kovic, the antiwar Vietnam veteran slated to be a keynote speaker at the rally against the Reagan administration's foreign policy, agreed to praise the memorial and ensure that everyone respected it.[171] In his speech, he invoked the memories of the dead and had the temerity to speak for them: "We will never let them do to us what they did to us in Vietnam," he declared. "Never, never again. If the dead could speak off that wall over there, if their voices could be heard, they would tell you that you are right in what you are doing today."[172]

Not everyone agreed with Kovic's views of what the dead would say. The VFW called the demonstration "a mass obscenity" that desecrated the memorial and dishonored the dead. A dozen men claiming to be Green Beret veterans gathered to "guard the wall."[173] A group that favored Reagan's Central America policy, the Captive Nations Vigil Committee, decided to mount a counterdemonstration against Communism. Milt Copulos, who had been on the VVMF's sculpture committee, spoke at their rally. He said he was overwhelmed with "intense anger . . . that these people were trading on the names of the men who died in combat." He accused the critics of U.S. foreign policy of sympathy with the Marxist revolutionaries in Central America and with the Communist government of Vietnam.[174]

Duncan Hunter, the Republican congressman from California who had been one of Copulos's allies during the arguments about the placement of the statue and flag, said that despite the best efforts of veterans, the VVMF, the National Park Service, and Congress, "the memorial has become politicized." He reminded his congressional colleagues that the memorial "was designed to honor those who served, and not to become a focal point for partisan demonstrations."[175] Meanwhile, tensions were also growing between the VVMF and "vigil groups," such as those highlighting the POW/MIA issue, who requested large numbers of the memorial fund's brochures. A Park Service official refused this request in a move that distanced the vigil groups from the memorial's official custodians. Using the July 2 demonstration as the rationale for clearing the environs of the memorial from all such groups, Scruggs asked the Park Service to expand the memorial's "buffer zone" to include the system of walkways approaching the wall. The Park Service introduced regulations forbidding demonstrations within the boundaries Scruggs proposed. Scruggs said that the buffer zone would prevent the memorial's being "politicized" by "any political views pro or con." In 1985, "No Greater Love," an organization of children of Americans who lost their lives in Vietnam, held a Father's Day ceremony at the memorial focusing on those still listed as MIA; the National Park Service asked them to move away from the area in front of the wall because their "organized activity" was not permitted by the regulations. Even a group of Marine Corps veterans who wanted to perform a wreath-laying ceremony were asked to move on. The regulations did not, of course, prohibit official Memorial Day and Veterans Day ceremonies, and after a time Father's Day ceremonies involving children of the dead were allowed to resume.[176]

John Kerry televised an advertisement in his 1984 campaign for the Senate that showed him standing before the Vietnam Veterans Memorial. In each of his campaigns for public office, Kerry stressed his military service and (except in his 2004 presidential campaign) his work in the antiwar movement. A veteran supporter of Kerry's campaign, Lawrence Chartienitz, asked, "Who but another Vietnam veteran could stand before the memorial and say I want to go to the Senate to work for peace?" But Kerry's critics were less indulgent. Richard Dacy, a former officer in the National Order of the Purple Heart, said that the ad "makes it seem as though 57,000 names on that wall are endorsing him. They aren't here to protest it." Al Hallenbrook, the director of Veterans Services in Brookline, Massachusetts, echoed Dacy: "[Kerry] is using the bodies of 56,000 dead soldiers to score political points." Both sought to defend their dead compatriots from being drafted into the service of a cause they did not endorse—particularly in the light of Kerry's antiwar credentials.[177]

The question remained: What constituted "political views" that would be an inappropriate use of the Vietnam Veterans Memorial? Despite the stated imperative for the memorial to be a place of apolitical "healing," speakers at ceremonies there have often made politically partisan and ideologically loaded points, often in support of military strength and resolution on the home front. Not all the voices at the memorial have belonged to Vietnam War "hawks," though. On Veterans Day 1986, Kerry, now a senator, was invited to speak at a ceremony at the wall. "For a long time," he said, echoing the VVMF's slogan, "Americans did not distinguish the war from the warrior." But, he said, the country had changed its attitude to Vietnam veterans. "This wall reminds us of a special responsibility that we have to avoid any glorification of war," he admonished, as close to an antiwar statement as any officially sanctioned speech at the memorial has come.[178] Generally, though, Democrats speaking at ceremonies at the wall have tended to avoid explaining their opposition to the war and have specialized in calls for bipartisanship and reconciliation. Former Senator George McGovern, the wartime dove who ran against Richard Nixon in the 1972 presidential election, spoke at the 1992 Memorial Day ceremony. McGovern, whose presence at the memorial at the invitation of the memorial fund was the most important political fact about the occasion, made no mention of his antiwar position, stressing instead his unremitting support for veterans and recalling his own service in wartime. The speech was enthusiastically welcomed by the audience, including many who appeared to be Vietnam veterans.[179]

At times, antiwar politicians were treated as dissidents whose message was out of keeping with the reverential atmosphere of the site. Early in 1991 Democrat Paul Wellstone of Minnesota, the newest member of the Senate, irked veterans by giving a press conference at the memorial opposing the first Gulf War. With tears in his eyes, he left a bouquet of roses near the name of a Marine Corps captain from

Northfield, Minnesota, his own hometown, and took a rubbing of the name. "This is not the time to rush to war," he said. The context was the George H. W. Bush administration's proposal to use force to expel the Iraqi army from Kuwait. The use of the memorial as a site for the press conference played on public fears of "another Vietnam": a month before Wellstone's appearance at the memorial, 40 percent of the public thought it likely that fighting in Iraq could become "another prolonged situation like the Vietnam conflict."[180] Two weeks after Wellstone's statement, amid the congressional debate about the use of force, a poll found that 54 percent of Americans were worried that war with Iraq would become "another drawn-out war like Vietnam."[181] Veterans in his home state saw Wellstone's use of the memorial as the site for his press conference as inappropriate and pressured him to apologize, a demand to which he acquiesced.[182] No one had regarded Senator Warner's 1982 appeal for unity in support of foreign military interventions as partisan and ideological; yet critics of Wellstone considered that he was exploiting the memorial for political purposes.

Similarly, Representative Dornan, a long-time critic of the memorial fund, was criticized for allowing politics to intrude on the memorial. Dornan held a press conference near the memorial, although outside the buffer zone. His aim was denouncing Senators John McCain (R. Arizona) and Kerry for forging an "unholy alliance" to settle the vexed POW/MIA issue and bring about a normalization of relations between the United States and Vietnam. Wayne Smith, a Vietnam veteran, quietly approached Dornan and respectfully told him that the Vietnam Veterans Memorial, some five hundred feet away, was not the place for a "political" press conference. "We have to move on," Smith said.[183]

Since the 1983 Ad Hoc Committee demonstration, no rallies for or against American foreign policy have taken place at the memorial. Yet there have been no obstacles to prevent pro-veteran statements at ceremonies from slipping over into appeals to support American troops whenever they are in the field. In 1986, Fred W. Smith, a Vietnam veteran who was chairman of Federal Express Corporation, said that when the "inevitable test" came again and the nation's young were asked to risk their lives, they would enjoy the nation's committed support, "or we will not let them fight at all." He continued, "Some say the cause for which we fought was not worthy of your lives." Addressing the dead, he made this commitment: "We pledge to you we will not let those who disparaged our efforts and your sacrifice escape this fateful truth: freedom has a terrible price. Millions now live in tyranny, many in the lands where we fought. We leave it to each conscience as to who was right and who was wrong." The conclusion that Smith's listeners were clearly expected to reach was that those who served and those who died were vindicated, their cause just, the proof lying in the fact that the Communist victory had brought "tyranny" to Vietnam. Those who opposed the war ("disparaged our efforts") were consequently wrong. The lesson was the need for continued vigilance and readiness to fight: "our reason and our riches will not save mankind from a darker fate if we people are not ready to defend the principles on which democracy exists."[184] Far from being condemned as an imposition of politics into a site whose neutrality must be preserved, this statement was the precursor of numerous such speeches at the memorial over the years.

President Reagan had no qualms about enlisting the memory of the "boys of Vietnam" in the continuing cause of national defense. "They were quite a group," he said at Arlington Cemetery on Memorial Day 1986, "the boys of Vietnam—boys who fought a terrible and vicious war without enough support from home. . . . They learned not to rely on us; they learned to rely on each other. . . . They chose to be faithful. They chose to reject the fashionable skepticism of their time. They chose to believe and answer the call of duty. They had the wild, wild courage of youth. They seized certainty from the heart of an ambivalent age; they stood for something." Americans must recover their courage and their dedication to a cause, he said. "And we owe them something, those boys. . . . We owe them a promise to look at the world with a steady gaze and, perhaps, a resigned toughness, knowing that we have adversaries in the world and challenges and the only way to meet them and maintain the peace is by staying strong." He attributed the quality of "resigned toughness" as well as "tenderness" and a "wounded" quality to the figures in the Hart statue. This was a brilliant speech, accommodating the public's lack of enthusiasm for foreign military adventures but asserting the need for armed readiness nevertheless. America would be tough, but with a "resigned" toughness, accepting its obligations without rancor but with a steady gaze. If America were to do this, it must overcome its horror for war and the risk-aversion born of the conflict in Vietnam. How better to disarm Vietnam War–inspired opposition than to invoke the example of those who believed when others did not, who fought in Vietnam when others debated the "efficacy of the battle." All this rhetorical effort marks the seriousness of the problem that Reagan and his speechwriters knew they were confronting: the continued public fears that a military intervention overseas would become "another Vietnam."[185]

In November 1988, his last Veterans Day as commander in chief, Reagan again spoke at the Vietnam Veterans Memorial, on only his second official visit. He and Nancy Reagan walked along the wall hand in hand and left a note addressed to their "young friends." Paying tribute to the war dead, he said, "In our hearts you will always be young." He said, "I am not speaking provocatively," but he could afford to be controversial now. His presidency was nearing its end; he had endured the skirmishes about Central America policy and survived the calls for impeachment following the Iran–Contra scandal that dogged the waning years of his presidency.[186] In honoring those who died and those who were willing to give their lives in service to their nation, Reagan unashamedly referred to the Vietnam War again as a "noble cause." He asserted the rightness of America's military purposes in Vietnam, asking, "Who can doubt that the cause for which our men fought was just?" After all, "however imperfectly pursued," it was the cause of freedom. "Vietnam service is once more universally recognized as a badge of courage and pride." The shame and guilt that he had mentioned in his 1980 VFW speech had been dispelled. Nobody took issue with him.

Reagan recited the mantra, "Young people must never be sent to fight and die unless we are prepared to let them win." Again, this refrain: that if only the country had dropped more napalm and white phosphorus, had expended more bullets and high explosives, had used more chemical defoliants, had destroyed more targets, the war could have been won. But he modulated the overtly ideological content of the speech with less strident sentiments. Reagan spoke of the nation's love for its veterans after long years of neglect. "For too long a time, they stood in a chill wind, as if on a winter night's watch. And in that night, their deeds spoke to us, but we knew them not. And their voices called to us, but we heard them not." The unmistakable biblical resonances of the passage transformed the veterans into Christ-like figures, enduring the agony of trial and vilification while faithless America, like Peter after the night in the Garden of Gethsemane, "knew them not." But, this being Reagan on the subject of his nation, redemption would inevitably follow: "Yet in this land that God has blessed, the dawn always at last follows the dark, and now morning has come. The night is over. We see these men and know them once again—and know how much we owe them, how much they have given us, and how much we can never fully repay. And not just as individuals but as a nation, we say we love you." Four years earlier, he had hoped that by the end of his second term of office, the nation would have healed. His final appearance at the memorial marked the completion of that process. "It appears to me," he said, "that we have healed. And what can I say to our Vietnam veterans but: Welcome home." These emotive messages at once reinforced and softened the passages in which honoring the warriors tied in with assertions of the rightness of the war.[187]

At the same ceremony, Virginia senator-elect Charles Robb, a Democrat, said, "We all come here in a spirit of reconciliation." Just as it had after the Vietnam War, the country, he said, needed a period of reconciliation and healing after the recent national election that had chosen George H. W. Bush as Reagan's successor. Unity was particularly necessary, Robb said, in the field of foreign policy. Echoing the same words from Abraham Lincoln's second inaugural address that appear in the undelivered speech drafted for Reagan in 1982, Robb continued, "We come here to bind up the wounds . . . that caused the nation so much pain." Robb was a marine veteran of the Vietnam War and a specialist in foreign and military policy: in the Senate, he would serve simultaneously on the Armed Services, Intelligence, and Foreign Relations committees. He also happened to have been Lyndon Johnson's son-in-law. (In one of the most famous photographs of the Johnson presidency, we see Johnson at a table, head bowed, his face hidden, his forehead touching his hand, listening to a tape recording Robb sent him from Vietnam.)[188] Robb pleaded for unity so that American foreign policy could "energetically engage" with the tasks of defending America's ideals and interests abroad. The message was similar to Reagan's: America must conduct a policy characterized by "vigorous opposition to tyranny"; anything less would be a failure to acknowledge America's debt to those named on the memorial. America's policy should be "tempered but not paralyzed" by its experience in Vietnam.[189]

The consensus between Reagan and Robb marked a bipartisan spirit. Their agreement papered over the clear foreign policy differences that bedeviled relations between the Republican and Democratic parties, particularly when the government was embroiled in the scandal about the illegal funding of the *contras*. But, although their consensus was true to the VVMF's goal of reconciliation, were their speeches "apolitical"? Both were strident calls for a vigorous national defense, invoking those remembered on the wall in the name of that cause. While expressions of militant nationalism may seem standard fare for any politician, one can hardly imagine a more overtly political task than girding the nation to maintain international vigilance, with a willingness to fight energetically and a determination to win. And while Scruggs generally avoided speaking on foreign policy matters in keeping with the VVMF's "apolitical" approach, he once expressed views that fitted squarely with the Reagan-Robb consensus. Speaking of opponents of the United States' use of military force, Scruggs said, "Some of those attitudes may be dangerous to the country and the free world. A lot have a real bad attitude toward the military—that we should never interfere anywhere. If we lived in a perfect world, that would be fine, but we don't."[190]

The journalist Colman McCarthy pointed out that the bipartisan consensus did not encompass all that might be said about the war. Where, he asked, were the names of the Vietnamese people killed during the war? He suggested that a memorial to them, and to those who resisted military service, would be appropriate. He cited the views of a Vietnam veteran who had supported the war but now believed that the antiwar protesters were right. "I thought the war was right at the time. I now believe it was a massive crime against humanity and against the environment." McCarthy claimed that such views, although largely silenced, debunked the myth that a new consensus had been achieved. "There wasn't a consensus during the Vietnam War and there isn't one now." Underlining this point, McCarthy quoted another unnamed Vietnam veteran:

> They want to call us heroes for serving the country. They offer us recognition and honor, even a national monument. Heroes for serving a country that burned down villages and shot anything that moved. Recognition for being the agents of and pawns of a ruthless death machine that systematically tortured and butchered civilians, that rained flaming jelly gasoline and poison gas on old men, women and children. Receiving a past due debt of honor for using the most advanced, blood-curdling and flesh-tearing weapons of terror the world has ever known. A monument for being the tools of a modern imperialist army that vainly attempted for over 10 years to crush, grind and pulverize the people and land of Vietnam.

McCarthy pointed out what usually went without saying: no such views were on offer in politicians' Veterans Day speeches. Voices of dissent such as those of the veterans he quoted rarely appeared any more in the media, even though the veterans' antiwar movement had once, briefly, commanded national attention. This silencing pointed to a danger: when the last vestiges of dissent have been papered over, new wars become more likely. "Sanitizing the last cause as 'just' is a way of cleaning up preparations for the next one."[191]

The historian George Mosse argues that the memory of World War I was reshaped to render the war as a sacred experience, to transform war graves into shrines, and to emphasize the meaningfulness of sacrifice in order to encourage allegiance to the nation in future conflicts.[192] America's political leaders undertook an equivalent project of national reunification after the Vietnam War, the memory of which threatened to divide Americans into hostile camps and to undermine Americans' willingness to stomach future wars. Memorial Day and Veterans Day audiences at the memorial have applauded pro-military rallying cries demanding that Americans support their troops in the field come what may. No one in the audiences at the numerous ceremonies I have witnessed in the past twenty years and more has questioned or shown any discomfort at such statements of pro-militarism; whether or not they have been glad of the chance to assert their pride in the nation and its veterans, they have not heckled or spoken back.[193] The memorial has fulfilled its supposedly "apolitical" program of "healing," enabling a resurgent America to honor its fallen soldiers. Unorthodox views and unsanctioned speakers have been literally marginalized, kept outside a buffer zone and criticized if they encroached on the memorial's hallowed ground. Only some voices were permitted to partake of the sacred atmosphere of the memorial, and their role was sacerdotal: their words gained weight from the borrowed sanctity of the wall, and they undertook the priestly task of giving meaning to the lives and deaths its inscriptions recalled. The speakers inevitably found the meaning that they sought in the truisms of ideology. When they spoke of "healing," they defined it as national strength and unity, and when they praised the fallen warriors, they demanded full support for other, imagined, legions marching in the future. No one protested, least of all the dead.

7

"NO SHAME OR STIGMA"

The Vietnam Veterans Leadership Program

✦

RONALD REAGAN'S wish to neutralize the "problem" of the Vietnam veteran as outsider is evident in his speeches praising Vietnam veterans' faithfulness, applauding other Americans for welcoming them home, and observing that America had consequently transcended "the tragedies of the past" and come together "in unity and with resolve." The Reagan administration's wish to do away with negative stereotypes of Vietnam veterans is also evident in the activities of a little-remarked federal organization, the Vietnam Veterans Leadership Program (VVLP).[1] In this chapter, we see how the Reagan administration would have liked ideally to construct the image of the Vietnam veteran. Downplaying (if not entirely ignoring) the growing literature about post-traumatic stress disorder (PTSD), the VVLP asserted that Vietnam veterans were proud of their service in Vietnam and felt no residual guilt or shame about their participation in the war. If this assertion about Vietnam veterans' pride persuaded the public, it would do away at a stroke with all the moral soul-searching about what Americans had done in Vietnam and would nullify the negative stereotype of Vietnam veterans as traumatized victims. This was a huge undertaking, but in Thomas Weir Pauken, the former aide in the Nixon White House who founded the VVLP, the Reagan administration had found someone with ideological motivation, energy, and force of will that might be equal to the task.

Defined as a social problem by the federal vet center program and by media reports of PTSD, Vietnam veterans reminded other Americans of all that had gone wrong in the Vietnam War. A congressionally mandated large-scale study of Vietnam veterans found that, while a minority suffered from PTSD, "many more, about half of all Vietnam veterans, were still suffering from less acute forms of distress—almost two million men struggling to avoid unsettling emotions, blaming their pain on others, or diminishing themselves through self-punishment and self-pity."[2] Their psychological distress set off a chain of associations that led back to criticisms of U.S. government policies during and after the war. Veterans' "unsettling emotions" suggested that they might have seen or done disturbing, perhaps shameful, things in Vietnam; their alienation might easily be linked with their poor treatment by the government and the poor welcome they had received from their fellow Americans; reports (accurate or not) of their violent anger reminded the nation of the deep political divisions that still beset American society. All the linked problems from which veterans were said to suffer—unemployment, marital difficulties, high rates of incarceration, and homelessness—could be taken as evidence of the terrible psychological wound that the war had inflicted on the veterans, and they reinforced Americans' aversion to the trauma of "another Vietnam War." The VVLP attacked this train of interconnected ideas at its source: by disseminating positive stories about proud and happy Vietnam veterans.

The VVLP countered the stereotype of the traumatized Vietnam veteran with positive role models and statistics showing that Vietnam veterans were, on the whole, well educated, employed, and emotionally healthy. Its employment program assisted a very small number of veterans, but even a single job placement could generate a positive media story that contributed to the optimistic PR campaign. Staffed by Republican Party stalwarts, the VVLP challenged films and television documentaries that portrayed Vietnam veterans in a negative light or that questioned the rightness of America's cause in Vietnam. In these ways, the VVLP advanced the Reagan administration's attempts to rehabilitate the reputation both of Vietnam veterans and of the Vietnam War.

The VVLP's founder, Pauken, had definite views about the war and its veterans that aligned him with the critics of the Vietnam Veterans Memorial Fund. His ideological combativeness ran counter to the memorial fund's promotion of reconciliation between Vietnam War–era antagonists.[3] His views lined up with those of Tom Carhart, who questioned the memorial fund's orthodox language of "healing" and "reconciliation." As Carhart said to the 60 Minutes reporter Morley Safer, "The license of Congress is not to heal the wounds of Vietnam. The license of Congress is to honor and recognize those who served in Vietnam, not those who went to Canada, not Jane Fonda and her friends."[4] Pauken concurred, approvingly quoting another veteran's observation that the memorial's inscription honored Vietnam veterans but said "not a word about 'healing.'" He visited Frederick Hart's studio as the sculptor was fashioning the Three Infantrymen statue and took the side of the Vietnam Veterans Memorial Fund's critics in the argument about the statue.[5] Pauken saw the Vietnam Veterans Memorial as "the monument to our generation's great fault line . . . between those who went and those who didn't; between those who served and those who chickened out." To Pauken, the inscription on the memorial honoring the warriors' courage, sacrifice, and devotion to duty and country demonstrated that Vietnam veterans "won't accept the inevitability of a leftist victory here at home. We have not forgotten those issues that permanently divided members of our sixties generation into warring factions."[6]

Pauken wanted to reclaim the legacy of service in Vietnam from antiwar veterans who, in his view, had wrongly made the country feel ashamed of its fight against Communism in Southeast Asia. He denied that Vietnam veterans had anything of which to be ashamed or from which they needed to heal. Pauken argued that Vietnam veterans suffered less from the lasting psychological effects of the war than from the negative image of veterans as victims. His views were rooted in decades of political action. An "outsider conservative," he was ready to take on the mantle of national leadership when the "bankrupt leadership class" of the 1960s—liberals and technocratic pseudo-conservatives—at last surrendered its power. He titled his memoir *The Thirty Years War*, referring to the long campaign by him and other conservative activists to reclaim America from the "corporate liberal" and leftist tides that dominated the 1960s. Decades after his return from military service in Vietnam, Pauken was still "in there fighting" this ideological civil war.[7]

Although the VVLP fostered the construction of Vietnam veterans memorials around the country as part of its program of "recognition events," we concentrate in this chapter on the organization's other activities. The VVLP's achievements do not match the scale of those of the Vietnam Veterans Memorial, with its millions of visitors, but its work does allow us to register the Reagan administration's multifaceted approach to recuperating the legacy of Vietnam. Pauken is a compelling figure in his own right, popping up as an opinionated anti-Zelig wherever the political battles of the Vietnam generation were at their thickest: on college campuses in the 1960s, in the counterinsurgency warfare of Vietnam's Mekong Delta, in the domestic surveillance activities of the Nixon White House, and finally in the Reagan administration's effort to redeem the reputation of the Vietnam War. The generational conflicts of the Vietnam War era are written across Pauken's personal history, and his career forms a counterpoint to the course of the Vietnam Veterans Memorial Fund's relationship with the Reagan White House.

As the memorial fund's agenda converged with the Reagan administration's between 1982 and 1984, Pauken's relationship with the White House grew strained. Eventually he became disaffected with the Reagan administration because of what he saw as corporate liberals' excessive influence in it. Pauken complained about the ascendancy of the same White House "moderates" or "pragmatists" who had sided with the memorial fund in the battle with the right-wingers. (He said that they had gained control of the personnel selection process early in Reagan's presidency and confined "movement conservatives" to lower-level and subcabinet jobs.)[8] By 1984, when Reagan spoke of healing in his speech at the Vietnam Veterans Memorial, Pauken had fallen out of step with the White House and as Reagan began his second term of office in 1985, Pauken headed back to Texas; his departure marks a shift in the administration's line, from Reagan's 1980 statement that the Vietnam War was a "noble cause" to the more complex and sentimentally inflected references to the war that Reagan's speechwriters later conceived.

Pauken cut his teeth as a cold warrior and conservative man of action during the rough and tumble of campus battles with the New Left in the 1960s. In the fall of 1965, a student at Georgetown University, Pauken was the national chairman of the College Republicans, which claimed eight hundred chapters on college campuses and 110,000 members. (Morton Blackwell, the movement conservatives' chief advocate in the White House during Reagan's first term, served under Pauken as executive director of the College Republican National Committee.) Seeing New Left groups such as Students for a Democratic Society gaining support on campuses and organizing teach-ins against the war, Pauken mounted a counteroffensive. He organized the bipartisan National Student Committee for the Defense of Vietnam and gathered signatures on a petition intended to prove that the New Left's views were unrepresentative of student opinion. He debated opponents of the war in teach-ins and organized demonstrations in support of the United States' fight against Communism in Southeast Asia. As the 1960s wore on, though, he found that the New Left displaced College Republicans as the most numerous and influential political force on U.S. campuses.[9]

In 1967, Pauken enlisted in the army as a private and was commissioned in the military intelligence branch the following year. He arrived in Vietnam on New Year's Day 1969, just as the "accelerated pacification program" in the Vietnamese countryside was at its height. As a province intelligence officer working under civilian cover as a Defense Department analyst, he ran a network of Vietnamese agents. In a period of intense conflict for political allegiances in the Vietnamese countryside, Pauken operated near the Cambodian border and in the Mekong River Delta, South Vietnam's most populous region and a hotbed of Communist organization. The 1968 Tet Offensive had brought many Viet Cong guerrillas out of their hiding places and civilian disguises to fight, and be killed, in the open. The loss of many of their most experienced and skilled fighters depleted the Communist ranks and many hamlets that had once been regarded as secure bases of Communist support were now designated as "contested." The United States and its South Vietnamese allies tried to maximize this advantage by identifying and capturing or killing the Communist cadres (political organizers of the Communist "infrastructure") in the countryside, the backbone of the insurgency. The Communists fought back fiercely, attempting to recruit new forces and using threats and assassinations to keep South Vietnamese government officials out of the villages. During Pauken's time in Vietnam, the U.S. and South Vietnamese forces intensified the Phoenix Program, instituted by the Central Intelligence Agency (CIA), which involved capturing or assassinating suspected Communists. Pauken's duties as a province intelligence officer involved using Vietnamese informants to finger Communist political and military "targets." According to one of his superiors, such duties would typically involve maintaining regular contact with the CIA agent in the area and passing on intelligence to the local representative of the Phoenix Program.[10]

Despite the opportunity to put his anti-Communist ideals into practice, Pauken was frustrated with the conduct of the war and in his frustration revealed the maverick streak that sometimes hampered his later career. His critical views, confided to a reporter, found their way into an article in *U.S. News and World Report* that said that unless the United States changed its policy in Vietnam, it was likely to lose the war. The article, attributed to an unnamed intelligence officer (in reality, Pauken), charged that South Vietnam's leadership was corrupt, riven by factions, and motivated by personal ambition; in contrast, the Communist cadres were dedicated, highly motivated, and more organized than any other political force in South Vietnam.

Without a transformation in the relative strengths of these two forces, the article stated, American attempts to win the war by technological means were "doomed to failure from the beginning."[11] As a researcher and analyst in the Joint Intelligence Command, Pauken wrote a paper on the Indochinese Communist Party's chief ideologist, Truong Chinh, and he came to respect Truong as someone who knew what winning the war required. Some of his military intelligence colleagues began to rib him by calling Pauken "Truong Chinh." Like the Viet Cong cadres whose dedication he respected, Pauken was a true believer.[12] To him, the role of the U.S. armed forces was simply to defeat Communists, but he saw that the effectiveness of career military officers was diminished by the same self-interest that infected South Vietnamese leaders: they were sometimes too concerned with getting their "tickets punched" by fulfilling a series of assignments to help them win promotion. Officers had six-month assignments so that they could all have "command time," which improved their personnel records but meant that they were transferred just as they were getting the hang of their job. After a one-year tour of duty, they went home. "That," Pauken remarked, "was not a good way to run a war."[13]

On his return to the United States, Pauken braved protesters at San Francisco airport carrying signs rooting for Ho Chi Minh and the Viet Cong, and he began fighting on a new front: the Nixon White House.[14] Later, the New York Times described Pauken as the Nixon administration's spokesman for college campuses, but this title does not do him justice.[15] Although his name appears in few histories of the Nixon presidency, Pauken was one of those charged with planning and managing a new domestic security regime to counter political dissent. The White House's campaign against its domestic enemies had many operatives and relied on loyal spear-carriers such as Pauken as much as on better-known hatchet men such as Charles Colson.[16] Pauken was a diehard anti-Communist whose main complaint against the Nixon White House was that it was full of technocrats and pragmatists rather than people with an ideological commitment to the conservative philosophy. Pauken was involved in discussions of some of the murkier aspects of Nixon's campaign against domestic opposition. He joined the White House Fellowship Program as deputy director and worked part-time in the White House counsel's office giving general advice on the home front in the Vietnam War: how to bolster public support for the war and counter antiwar activities. It was in this capacity that he advised John Dean on how to handle the Calley case (as discussed in Chapter 2).

Pauken's experience as an intelligence officer and as a student activist won him an assignment keeping tabs on domestic disorders and the antiwar movement.[17] In the same period that, with White House collusion, H. Ross Perot was funding "moderate, responsible" student leaders to join pro-Nixon rallies, Pauken received reports about the activities of groups organizing such events, including the "March for Victory in Vietnam," intended to counter a demonstration by Vietnam Veterans Against the War. Pauken also handled the other end of the administration campaign. He received reports from informers at meetings planning antiwar demonstrations, learning which groups were represented at the meetings, and what they planned to do. This job of sifting and compiling reports on subversives was similar to the tasks he performed as an intelligence officer, and Pauken griped in Washington, as in Vietnam, about the precision and organization of the material he received. Just as police forces around the country were trying to infiltrate antiwar groups, Pauken monitored antiwar demonstrations in Washington.[18] He recommended that the government adopt a game plan to respond to protests because large-scale demonstrations "might lead to serious consequences in terms of our domestic order and credibility as a world leader."[19] Pauken also participated in discussions of how to revive an anti-Communist body created in the McCarthy era, the Subversive Activities Control Board, after the Supreme Court invalidated its surveillance activities on First Amendment grounds.[20]

As a Vietnam veteran who believed in the war, Pauken was incensed that the media treated Vietnam Veterans Against the War as an organization representing the views of Vietnam veterans at large. He complained later, "The guys who acknowledged their 'guilt' for having served in Vietnam and 'begged forgiveness' from the Left were held in high esteem by the mainstream press." In Pauken's view, the news media were also responsible for portraying the typical American soldier as a murderer of women and children, leading the public to hurl the epithet "baby killer" at veterans.[21] After the war, Pauken remained upset by negative portrayals of Vietnam veterans: "I have been distressed since the time I returned from Vietnam, to see the image of the Vietnam veterans portrayed as losers, fools, or dope addicts. Now, there is an additional new mythology—it is Vietnam veterans as guilt-ridden victims, ashamed of their service."[22] The myth was "so wrong that it was almost unfathomable," Pauken said, "but people believed it."[23] He took particular offense at John Kerry, who regularly appeared on the television screen and at cocktail parties in Washington's Georgetown neighborhood denouncing the U.S. war effort: "As far as I was concerned, Kerry was purely and simply an opportunist, parlaying his involvement in the antiwar movement into a budding political career."[24] (Pauken might have been amused to learn that some of Kerry's colleagues in Vietnam Veterans Against the War thought much the same thing.)[25] Pauken describes in his memoir his eagerness to correct the impression that John Kerry and the antiwar-veterans' group were legitimate representatives of Vietnam veterans, saying he was frustrated that "there wasn't much support then for such an initiative." "It would take another decade," he points out, "before Vietnam veterans would finally band together to correct the record."[26]

Pauken advised Dean on a new blueprint for domestic surveillance: the "Huston Plan." On Nixon's orders, a young lawyer, Tom Charles Huston, devised a plan to centralize all the government's intelligence-gathering activities in the White House and put the intelligence agencies to work spying on domestic groups that the administration regarded as threats. Huston had been president of Young Americans for Freedom, a radical right-wing youth group, in the same period that Pauken had led the College Republicans. According to the plan, Huston, like Pauken a former army intelligence officer, would head an interagency committee that would give indirect presidential authorization for the conduct of illegal wiretaps, buggings, mail intercepts, and break-ins.[27] A Senate investigating committee later described the Huston Plan as "a virtual charter for the use of intrusive and illegal techniques against American dissidents as well as foreign agents."[28]

Despite its illegality, Richard Nixon approved the plan in July 1970 but revoked his approval after a few days because of objections by the Federal Bureau of Investigation (FBI). (The directors of the CIA, the National Security Agency, and the Defense Intelligence Agency evidently had no objections to the illegal activities for which the plan called.) The FBI took offense because the Huston Plan challenged its exclusive prerogatives in domestic intelligence gathering, and because its director, J. Edgar Hoover, feared that the plan would be exposed. It was not therefore constitutional scruples but institutional turf battles and caution that put the plan on hold.[29] Pauken too advised Dean that the Huston Plan would create more problems than it would solve and that there were better ways of beefing up the surveillance of "subversive groups."[30] When several of Nixon's aides urged implementation of some aspects of the plan, Pauken's boss, Dean, took on Huston's responsibilities for internal security and domestic intelligence. Pauken himself was charged with helping to set up an interagency intelligence advisory committee, which Dean called a "toothless" version of the Huston Plan.[31]

The activities that the Huston Plan countenanced did take place, although not on Pauken's watch. The government's repressive measures included the FBI's tapping the telephones of journalists and officials of the National Security Council to identify the source of news leaks; the FBI's gathering of information that could smear people on Nixon's "enemies list"; the use of the Internal Revenue Service to target those on the list; the White House "plumbers" burglary of the offices of Daniel Ellsberg's psychiatrist, to discredit Ellsberg after he leaked the "Pentagon Papers," the multivolume study of the decisions leading to the American war in Vietnam; and the infamous Watergate burglary and cover-up, involving obstruction of justice by numerous members of the White House, from the president on down. But by this time, Pauken had fortuitously left the White House. He departed under something of a cloud, after writing an unauthorized article (again, in *U.S. News and World Report*), leading his program director to call his actions "disloyal, selfish and immature." On the advice of Dean's deputy, Fred Fielding, he began studying for a law degree.[32]

After he left the White House, Pauken spent the remainder of the 1970s, as he puts it, "in political exile": a law student, an attorney in private practice, and an unsuccessful candidate for elective office.[33] With the election of Ronald Reagan in 1980, though, Pauken's moment arrived. He became a member of the presidential transition team, working with his friend Fielding, Dean's deputy in the Nixon White House who stepped into Dean's shoes as White House counsel under Reagan. Reagan appointed Pauken as director of ACTION, the federal voluntary service agency with oversight of the Peace Corps, VISTA (Volunteers in Service to America, the "domestic Peace Corps"), and other volunteer organizations.[34] Pauken took great satisfaction in replacing the Jimmy Carter appointee Sam Brown as the head of ACTION. Brown had been an antiwar activist and an organizer of the October 1969 Moratorium when Pauken was nearing the end of his tour in Vietnam.[35] (Brown suspected that, when he was director of ACTION, the far right saw him as a "radical who was subverting the federal government from within.")[36] Pauken believed, according to his memoir, that his experience of "battling the New Left crowd over the years" would help him undo the "damage" Brown had done at ACTION, which he believed Brown had turned into "a playpen for New Left activists during the Carter years."[37] Looking back, a journalist observed that Pauken was appointed to head ACTION "in order to 'de-radicalize' the place."[38]

Pauken's "reputation for right-wing zealotry" raised the hackles of liberals in Washington. Democrats were appalled that this Nixon henchman would assume responsibility for the Peace Corps, one of the embodiments of Kennedy's inaugural call to "ask what you can do for your country." This was not the main obstacle to Pauken's confirmation in the Senate, though: the confirmation hearings provoked a fight, with "ugly charges" being made about Pauken's service in Vietnam. The *Washington Post* suggested that, because of Pauken's intelligence activities in Vietnam, the Peace Corps would be tainted by suspicions that it was engaged in espionage. This was a sore point because the CIA was rumored to have used the Peace Corps as cover for its agents during the Vietnam War years, even though doing so was prohibited.[39] The outgoing director of the Peace Corps warned that using the agency for intelligence purposes would "undermine its mission and endanger its volunteers in the field." Perhaps Pauken's awareness of this issue explains why he testified at his confirmation hearing that "his principal work in the Delta was involved as an analyst." In fact, that was his "cover" in Vietnam; to his embarrassment, the truth about his job in Vietnam and his attempt to conceal it came out, redoubling the concerns about his record as an intelligence officer. Senate Democrats subjected Pauken to an "inquisition" because of his army intelligence role. After a grueling examination by Senator Alan Cranston (D., California), Pauken was confirmed by the full Senate in May 1981—but he was not allowed to take charge of the Peace Corps. Its supporters made sure that it once again became an independent agency, as it had been before Richard Nixon moved it under the umbrella of ACTION.[40]

VISTA remained under ACTION's authority and suffered as a result. Pauken and the Reagan administration attempted to persuade Congress to abolish it; they succeeded in cutting VISTA's budget from $33 million to $11.8 million.[41] Pauken made a point of ending VISTA's funding for "leftist" local projects, such as Ralph Nader's Public Interest Research Group, the Midwest Academy, and the Laurel Springs Institute.[42] Yet many VISTA volunteers were relatively conservative, middle-class people with a missionary instinct who provided uncontroversial bread-and-butter services for the poor, did not mind working within a bureaucracy, and were not the banner-waving radicals Pauken assumed them to be. A former chief of field operations for VISTA said that decisions to support or cut VISTA programs were often made after "political screening" by local Republicans. Pauken fired or transferred a large number of career civil servants and allegedly hired many Republican Party loyalists under an employment program intended to bring people with unique skills into the civil service.[43] His first rule was "personnel make policy," and he made a point of filling ACTION posts with "a band of tough-minded and able conservatives."[44] Congressional critics were angry at Pauken for cutting poverty-oriented programs, and he was hauled before several congressional subcommittees to explain his actions.[45]

Before his appointment as director of ACTION, Pauken had conceived the idea of an organization in which successful Vietnam veterans mentored others. He had been inspired at a Dallas Vietnam Veterans Day reception when he encountered a number of men he knew as business and community leaders but had not guessed they were Vietnam veterans. Pauken decided to bring together successful veterans—whom he believed to be the majority—to help those with problems, and, once installed as ACTION's director, he resolved to found an organization that would fit with the agency's voluntarist ethos.[46] The idea of a federally supported veterans' self-help project had been bubbling up for some time but had so far been attempted only on a small scale, in three cities.[47]

While his nomination as administrator of ACTION was being considered, Pauken pulled together a group of Vietnam veterans, including Jack Wheeler and James Webb (before the two had a falling out) to plan the creation of a new organization to uplift Vietnam veterans and improve their image. The VVLP emerged from their discussions. The organization would be national in scope, with local VVLPs headed by Vietnam veterans in several dozen places. ACTION would fund the first three years of office costs, and the VVLP would also draw funds and services from other federal agencies. Because the VVLP was funded indirectly by these other federal agencies, Congress never appropriated money for the organization, and some congressional opponents therefore questioned the legality of the program. The lack of direct funding, however, was one of its appeals to the Reagan administration: it was a way of doing something about the Vietnam veterans "problem" without creating a long-term charge on the federal budget.[48] The VVLP's aim was to coalesce a group of Vietnam veteran professionals—lawyers, doctors, and businessmen—in cities across the country (the original goal was fifty cities, later scaled down to forty-one), where these local volunteers would establish branches as charitable corporations. Each local VVLP would be headed by a volunteer chairman, with a salaried program director running the office, organizing volunteers, soliciting in-kind contributions from businesses, and identifying potential employers. A pool of successful local leaders would provide guidance for Vietnam veterans with lingering problems.[49]

Many of the VVLP's leaders and supporters had Republican Party credentials—to such an extent that one of its founders referred to it as a "national Republican Vietnam veterans club." James Webb, a national adviser to the VVLP, explained with disarming candor, "I've heard [the VVLP] called a Republican country club. . . . Well, it's a Republican administration." Despite his changing political affiliation, Webb was a Republican throughout his time as a VVLP adviser. Edward Timperlake, who succeeded Wheeler as national director of the VVLP, and Ronald Ray, who chaired the Kentucky VVLP, were Reagan appointees and Republican Party organizers.[50] The Los Angeles VVLP chairman Leo Thorsness was reprimanded by the U.S. Air Force for making "politically tinged statements" against George McGovern and later ran against McGovern as the Republican candidate for senator from South Dakota. This pattern was sustained around the nation: Sam Bartholomew, who chaired the VVLP in Tennessee, was a legislative assistant and campaign manager for the Republican senator Howard Baker. John McCain, the chairman of the Arizona VVLP, was a Republican representative (and later senator) from that state. Charles Hagel, part of the VVLP leadership, later became a Republican senator from Nebraska. Jerry Wamser, the program director of the VVLP in St. Louis, ran unsuccessfully as the Republican candidate for mayor of that city. John Baines, the chairman of the San Antonio VVLP, was finance director for Representative Tom Loeffler, a Republican. Max Cruz, the chairman of Florida's VVLP, was a "politically-connected Republican." Of the VVLP's national advisers, Jock Nash worked for Nevada's Republican senator Paul Laxalt; and Roy Adams was special assistant to the former prisoner of war (POW) and Republican senator from Alabama Jeremiah Denton.[51]

Ronald Reagan gave the VVLP his personal authorization in July 1981 and officially launched it at a ceremony in the White House Rose Garden on November 10, 1981. He demonstrated his commitment to the organization by meeting its leaders several times in subsequent years and encouraging others to support it. The organization enjoyed special privileges, such as a presidential message supporting a VVLP fundraiser, a departure from the president's "long-standing policy" of providing a single annual message for all veterans rather than one for each veterans' group that asked.[52] At the inauguration ceremony, Reagan echoed the psychiatrists, social workers, and other veterans' advocates who had drawn attention to veterans' need for recognition. Reagan said that Vietnam veterans "never received the thanks they deserved"; they "fought as bravely as any American fighting men have ever fought"; their recognition was "long overdue."[53]

Reagan also addressed veterans' negative public image. He explained that "contrary to an unjust stereotype," not just the majority but the "vast majority" of Vietnam veterans "readjusted quickly after returning from Southeast Asia." According to Baines, the San Antonio VVLP chairman, Reagan called on VVLP leaders at a private meeting to "turn the image of the Vietnam veteran around, once and for all." Baines, a real-estate developer, contrasted the VVLP's approach to that of the vet centers: "We'll have a nice office with nice furniture. It won't be a 'store-front mission.'"[54] Emphasizing veterans' achievements rather than focusing on their problems, Reagan said in his speech that many Vietnam veterans "succeeded and excelled in their post-war endeavors."

Reagan's Rose Garden speech went beyond the homilies about the need to recognize Vietnam veterans and again presented the revisionist argument about the reason for defeat in Vietnam, stating that American forces "were not allowed to win" the war. The corollary was that the American people should show more unity and martial determination so that they would never again betray their troops in the field. Reagan spelled out this conclusion at the national VVLP training conference in January 1983, when he uttered the perennial crowd-pleaser to conservative Vietnam veteran audiences: "As long as I can help it, no one will ever again be asked to fight for their country unless it's for a cause that our country is determined to win."[55] Helping veterans was intimately tied to Reagan's geopolitical goals. The VVLP would "not only benefit the individual Vietnam veteran but also foster patriotism and restore public pride in military service during wartime."[56] As the president said in his Rose Garden address, "Recognition and appreciation for all [Vietnam veterans] went through is long overdue. We should always remember that in a hostile world a nation's future is only as certain as the devotion of its defenders, and the nation must be as loyal to them as they are to the nation."

Reagan's statement demonstrates the clear political subtext beneath the VVLP's veteran-centered purposes. Giving a Vietnam veteran a job or a pat on the back would not just help the veteran but would strengthen the nation's military preparedness. Complaints about veterans' high unemployment, their poor reception by other Americans, their psychological distress and high suicide rates all tended to reinforce the idea that the war had blighted their lives and must never be repeated. Doing away with this negative impression would make the nation more capable of projecting its power abroad because it would diminish the public's reflex aversion to the risk of war. According to a review of the VVLP's activities, "The VVLP's commitment to service, and its positive, forward-looking behavior, will affect national defense in perhaps a modest, but direct way. By affirming the integrity of military service during the Vietnam War, the network helps to restore a national perception that military service is an honorable calling, a basic form of service to be highly regarded."[57] Other Republican politicians confirmed the theme that Reagan asserted: honoring veterans was a key task in improving the national defenses. Senator Paula Hawkins's 1982 letter said that men and women could not be expected to defend the nation without pride in their service; and Defense Secretary Caspar Weinberger said dramatically in 1984, "A nation which forgets the sacrifices of its heroes risks its very existence."[58]

Creating the VVLP and hiring its staff put Pauken in a key position to shape the organization. Local VVLPs had to apply to ACTION for grants to meet their expenses and pay the salary of the local program director, so Pauken enjoyed substantial influence over the organization's branches. Because the VVLP's national director reported to Pauken, and because there was a turnover of three national directors over the VVLP's federally funded lifetime while Pauken was a fixture, his personal influence over the VVLP was all the greater. Pauken's fiscal conservatism fitted the Reagan administration's budget priorities. (He took pride in cutting ACTION's staff in half and reducing its budget by 25 percent during his four years at its helm). Congressional and media critics challenged Pauken for neglecting to measure the cost-effectiveness of the VVLP's programs, while VISTA programs were being cut. But, whether or not it delivered value for money, the VVLP's reliance on self-help and volunteerism meant that it required relatively little federal funding. Its cost to the federal government was about $2 million a year for three years, a small sum in comparison with the funding for other departments with responsibility for veterans (for example, the $300 million in federal funds appropriated for two years under the Emergency Veterans' Job Training Act of 1983), and tiny in relation to the needs of the nation's 2.7 million Vietnam veterans. Federal participation in the program would be phased out by September 1984, after which the local VVLPs were encouraged to operate with other sources of funding.[59]

For Vietnam veterans who needed help, the VVLP was supposed to provide employment counseling and direct assistance, but most VVLP offices achieved remarkably little in the way of jobs for veterans. By March 1983, after eighteen months of operation, the VVLP claimed to have placed only 1,010 veterans in jobs in the whole country and to have referred a similar number to employment services or placed them in jobs indirectly—at the cost of over sixty-six thousand hours of volunteer time in the forty-one offices throughout the country.[60] Critics charged that even that achievement was exaggerated. Yet, a month after the release of these figures, Webb said that the organization had done more for less money than the jobs programs of previous administrations. If true, this fact merely underlined how long the government had neglected Vietnam veterans' employment needs. By the end of the three years of federal funding, the program had placed almost 3,000 veterans in jobs—at a cost of over $5.5 million in ACTION grants and the equivalent of over $5 million in the cost of volunteer time and material donations.[61]

With its small budget and limited life, the VVLP could not hope to meet all the employment and counseling needs of Vietnam veterans. It was described as a "catalyst" rather than a service provider, intended to complement, not duplicate, other federal programs.[62] Eugene Gitelson, chairman of the New York VVLP, said that it practiced a form of "triage," ignoring the veterans with severe emotional and physical problems who were the most difficult to help, as well as those who were likely to succeed on their own. "We are looking to help the 15 percent who are in the middle group," he said, "between the very successful and the ones who have failed to adjust."[63] VVLP leaders said that the organization's "primary thrust" was the creation of a "favorable climate" for Vietnam veterans seeking jobs, rather than the placement of veterans in specific positions. Thus, improving the public's perception of veterans in order to make them more employable became a significant aspect of the VVLP's jobs program. In turn, the VVLP's employment programs made for media-friendly, upbeat human interest stories: local press coverage often focused on a handful of veterans who had found jobs through the VVLP. As the VVLP's final report states, "Success stories make great feature articles, the more about veterans helping each other and their communities the better."[64]

Skeptics who noticed that the VVLP did not deliver much help for unemployed veterans dismissed its efforts as "window dressing"—parades, sporting events, and Vietnam veteran salutes. The employment director of the Disabled American Veterans described the VVLP as merely a "public relations effort."[65] Yet this criticism of the organization's employment programs is a backhanded compliment to what in effect became its primary mission—recasting Vietnam veterans' image. The VVLP's ultimate goal was to have Vietnam veterans perceived as "the primary source of leadership and stability in the community." A more realistic interim goal, however, was to ensure that employers were not deterred from hiring someone simply because he was a Vietnam veteran.[66] The rationale of "image enhancement" was to make veterans more attractive to employers, but the ideological effects of improving the image of Vietnam veterans diffused into areas having nothing to do with getting them jobs. Whether or not the vast majority of Vietnam veterans actually *did* better because of the VVLP's efforts, a successful public relations campaign would make them *look* better and they would thus cease to be embodiments and reminders of a national trauma.

The VVLP's employment programs and symbolic support programs also advanced the Reagan administration's preference for nongovernmental solutions to social problems. Reagan said that "every citizen" should keep in mind that in times of economic hardship "showing our gratitude to the Vietnam veteran will take more than leaving it up to the Federal Government to provide money and programs."[67] In other words, unemployed veterans should seek private-sector jobs and not hope for assistance from the federal government. As the chairman of the VVLP in Wilmington, Delaware, said, "The Leadership Program is in line with the President's attitude of moving the country forward and away from government control and toward the individual's involvement and responsibility. We don't have to keep turning to the government—individually we can take responsibility."[68] According to this theory, positive role models and a chance to prove themselves could boost the life chances of struggling veterans better than a handout and coddling, which would only encourage veterans to feel sorry for themselves. The *Wall Street Journal's* editorial page praised the VVLP because "instead of organizing alienated veterans to demand bigger entitlements [it] is trying to attract veterans who are in good shape and can give other vets advice on how to be likewise."[69]

The preference for individual rather than governmental solutions led some VVLP officers to disregard genuine problems for which institutional redress might be appropriate. Rick Fromme, of the North Carolina VVLP, brushed off the illnesses believed to result from exposure to chemical defoliants in Vietnam. Issues such as Agent Orange "are interesting, but they're history," Fromme said. This was an odd viewpoint, since the class-action lawsuit against the chemical companies that produced the chemicals was about to go to trial. A month after Fromme's dismissive remark, the case was settled out of court with a $180 million settlement paid by the defendants into a fund to benefit Vietnam veterans and their families.[70] After serving in areas sprayed with Agent Orange, Tom Carhart, the program director for the Connecticut VVLP, had suffered a malignant cancer in 1970. His wife gave birth to a stillborn child the following year. Some veterans believed that cancers and miscarriages were caused by veterans' exposure to Agent Orange. But despite these events Carhart concluded that he had not been harmed by the chemical and renounced any part of the settlement of the veterans' class-action suit against chemical companies that had manufactured Agent Orange. "I am proud of my service to my country and I will not shake the money tree of corporations whose supplies of materials to the government resulted in no damage to my health," Carhart said a few days after the announcement of the Agent Orange settlement.[71]

The VVLP's approach to veterans' problems demonstrated a macho denial of war-induced psychological injury. Pauken said that in the 1970s, the popular image of Vietnam veterans ranged from "psychos to societal victims, something akin to 'sick puppies' deserving sympathy." The media had treated veterans in a sensationalistic way for a decade after the last combat troops left Vietnam, treating them as a "group of ticking time bombs."[72] In Pauken's view, though, the "overwhelming majority" of Vietnam veterans resented the image of "guilt-ridden victims of an unjust war." They were, he said, proud of their service. "We want it known that there is no shame or stigma to being a veteran of the Vietnam War," he declared.[73] Until the VVLP came along, most federal programs had, in Pauken's view, encouraged troubled veterans to remain preoccupied with what had happened in Vietnam. This barely veiled attack on the vet center program implied that that it was irrelevant to Vietnam veterans' true needs. Pauken said that the "so-called 'Post-Vietnam syndrome'" was the product of veterans' having come home to face "a barrage of hostility."[74] "All the counseling in the world won't help you if you can't get a job," Thorsness of the Los Angeles VVLP chipped in.[75] But as they faced the realities of dealing with struggling veterans, some VVLP staff and volunteers began to find it difficult to draw the line between encouraging veterans to help themselves and providing emotional advice and support. There was sometimes overlap in personnel between local VVLPs' and vet centers' staff, and in some places a degree of convergence between their programs.

The Indiana VVLP negotiated with a nearby vet center to bring its services to the VVLP office in Merrillville, Indiana. There, the VVLP program director acknowledged that he helped veterans with emotional problems.[76] The VVLP program director in Portland, Maine, was also a community outreach specialist at the local vet center, and he saw the VVLP as an extension of the vet center's goal of raising Vietnam veterans' self-esteem "by using veterans who have been able to overcome their situation in Vietnam."[77] The director of the Louisville, Kentucky, vet center also acted as a volunteer for the VVLP of Kentucky and recognized that veterans suffered from a continuum of problems that could not be easily isolated from one another, ranging from employment to PTSD and the "psychological trauma" caused by the public's perception that the war was "a waste."[78] The St. Louis VVLP also established close links with local vet centers.[79] From these examples it becomes clear that not all VVLP staffers maintained a sharp demarcation between the upbeat, practical-solution-oriented approach the VVLP generally favored and the vet centers' orientation to emotional and behavioral problems.

These local initiatives were, however, exceptions to the organization's governing ethos, which the *Washington Times* summed up as, "The VVLP tells Vietnam vets there is really nothing wrong with them or America."[80] If only America could be convinced of this truth, perhaps finally the nation could put the Vietnam War behind it. But however much Reagan and the VVLP might have wanted this outcome, traumatized veterans who suffered from PTSD, unemployment, alcoholism, and other ills continued to be reminders of a national nightmare that could not simply be wished away. How many "good news" anecdotes would it take to make people forget the "hard luck" stories that reinforced memories of the Vietnam War as horrific, atrocious, and immoral? The slow drip of public relations might take eons to erode the war's negative associations, sedimented by year after year of painful experience.

If anecdotes alone could not do the job, perhaps some statistics would help. Richard Kolb, chairman of the Houston VVLP, compiled data demonstrating that, contrary to the popular image, Vietnam veterans were not poorly educated victims dragged unwillingly into military service by the draft and then tossed onto the scrap heap of unemployment once released from military service. Kolb had wanted to counter this negative view for years but did not collate the data until he became active in the VVLP. In 1982 he produced three thousand leaflets containing facts and figures about those who served in Vietnam, sending copies to VVLP branches around the country.[81]

Kolb's research showed that the majority of in-country troops were not draftees. (The fact that the army was disproportionately made up of draftees suggests, however, that some servicemen volunteered for the navy and air force, rather than waiting to be drafted, out of a wish to avoid frontline service as a rifleman in the army.) Among the other "myths" that Kolb's research challenged was that those who fought in Vietnam were overwhelmingly made up of the poor and minorities and were poorly educated. Point for point, the Houston VVLP countered these assumptions with carefully selected facts: the troops sent to Vietnam were the best educated army America had ever fielded; blacks suffered a lower casualty rate than the proportion of blacks of military age in the U.S. population; three-quarters of all troops were from families above the poverty line. Kolb raised doubts about the extent to which atrocities occurred in Vietnam and stated that the majority of the public thought Calley's trial was unfair. He referred to "atrocity stories" and "atrocity mongering" as a "favorite ploy" of opponents of all America's wars, as if revulsion at the murder of civilians were simply an underhand tactic of the antiwar movement.[82]

Reinforcing the fact sheet was a "true/false" checklist inviting respondents to check their own beliefs against the facts. Anyone who agreed that most servicemen who went to Vietnam were poor and uneducated, that atrocities were commonplace, and that blacks served and died in disproportionate numbers—or thirty-two other commonly held beliefs—would find that these beliefs were false. Each of Kolb's facts is debatable—the spinning of the conventional wisdom about those who fought prompted Wallace Terry, the author of a best-selling oral history by African American veterans of the Vietnam War, to wonder whether blacks would one day be told they had not been in Vietnam at all.[83] But the point was that at least now a debate was possible and those who decried the "poverty draft" would no longer dominate the field if the VVLP could marshal its own carefully footnoted arguments.[84]

Kolb's data went from Houston to all points, by way of the leaders of other VVLP branches. When an errant magazine or newspaper published one of the "myths" about Vietnam veterans, a prompt letter to the editor would set the publication straight. For example, Jackson Andrews of the Kentucky VVLP's advisory board wrote a letter to the *Louisville Courier-Journal*, correcting information that the newspaper had published on Vietnam veterans' rate of incarceration and suicide statistics—which he described as "specious nonsense."[85] Kolb himself wrote similar letters to national publications, and Webb wrote an article puncturing the myth of the high suicide rate among Vietnam veterans and other stereotypes.[86] Myths about the supposedly high rate of suicide among Vietnam veterans were particularly hardy, taking on a life of their own and resisting factual refutation: once a false statistic was reported in a news story as fact, it was picked up by other media and then circulated uncontrolled, each subsequent report seeming to validate the original false one.[87] In 1989 Kolb became the publisher and editor-in-chief of *VFW* magazine, the official publication of Veterans of Foreign Wars. This publication provided a further means of getting the word out into the veterans community. In 1993, *VFW* magazine prominently published a summary of Kolb's findings, reiterating the points about the ethnic, class, and educational status of those who served in Vietnam and stressing that the troops served honorably and felt pride in their service.[88]

Representative Richard Hammerschmidt (R., Arkansas) entered the VVLP's facts and figures into the *Congressional Record* in 1982, elaborating Kolb's data by denying that Vietnam veterans were prone to criminal acts and that PTSD was a "mental disease." (Instead, he termed it an "emotional disorder.") Nevertheless, while being generally upbeat about veterans' well-being, Hammerschmidt reprised the well-worn phrases about veterans' need for "healing." As he put it, PTSD "stems primarily from the war's aftermath—public indifference, peer hostility, intellectual contempt and official effrontery. The societal tissue needed to heal the spiritual scar carried by many Vietvets will be found when U.S. society as a whole purges itself of the post-Vietnam syndrome."[89] Hammerschmidt proposed that Americans should appreciate the patriotism that compelled the veterans to serve their country. Public pride in Vietnam veterans' service would provide them with the "emotional support" they needed. Hammerschmidt, following the VVLP, advocated "healing," but not in the sense of the psychiatric care of Vietnam veterans. Instead, it was American society whose attitudes needed to be reformed and rehabilitated. Then the nation and its veterans would become whole.

As part of its "national media and image campaign" geared to "image enhancement and symbolic support," the VVLP promoted parades, public ceremonies, Vietnam veterans recognition days, and memorials.[90] A marcher at the VVLP-led parade in Hobart, Indiana, said, "This is the ticker tape parade we didn't get 15 years ago." At a VVLP-organized ceremony in St. Louis, Indiana, buglers played "Taps" for the American troops who were killed in Vietnam, and their names and dates of death were read out. "We licked the hell out of the Viet Cong," William Westmoreland declared at a VVLP-sponsored Vietnam Veterans recognition dinner in Arizona. "You fellows who fought in Vietnam did not lose. . . . I don't think any troops could have done better than you did." To recapture the goodwill of the National Salute to Vietnam Veterans, the Minnesota VVLP planned a Minnesota salute to Vietnam Veterans in the fall of 1983. Its executive director said, "I think the public began to get a different perception of Vietnam veterans then, and I think Vietnam veterans began to get a different perception of themselves. They're proud of themselves now." Donald Grigg, program director of the VVLP in Pine Bluff, Arkansas, chimed in by saying that he was supporting a state memorial to the Vietnam War to "remind us to never do this again unless we're allowed to win." An editorial in his local paper said that it was essential to keep Grigg's statement in mind as Central America "heats up."[91]

In their "image enhancement" campaign, the VVLP's public affairs staff vetted film scripts to determine whether they were worthy of Pentagon cooperation. Such assistance could be extremely helpful to filmmakers who needed access to military hardware.[92] Marcia Landau, the VVLP's media director who reviewed many scripts, remembers that the organization evaluated the first "Rambo" film, *First Blood*.[93] In the film, Rambo (Sylvester Stallone), a Vietnam veteran, falls foul of the police in a small town in the Pacific Northwest. When mistreated by them, he experiences flashbacks of being tortured by Vietnamese captors during the war. Using the skills he learned in the Special Forces, Rambo takes revenge on the town, destroying large parts of it in a calculated rampage. In 1982, the mentally disturbed Rambo character helped reinforce the public perception of Vietnam veterans as psychological wrecks with hair-trigger tempers, according to George Skypeck, a VVLP national adviser. "It was a horrible stereotype," he said, "but it took hold."[94] Because the film portrayed its hero as a "psycho," the VVLP turned down *First Blood* as a vehicle worthy of government support. Pauken criticized another film, *Coming Home*, for portraying veterans as guilt-ridden and ashamed of their service. He said that its producer, Bruce Gilbert, was "rooting for the other side to win the war."[95] "I've had enough of what I call the Vietnam veterans as victims gang," Pauken said. "The time has come to call into question the phony posturing of aging antiwar activists of the Vietnam era who during that war had nothing but contempt for American soldiers in Vietnam."[96] Pauken also criticized the documentary *Frank: A Portrait of a Vietnam Veteran*, broadcast by PBS, which presents the story of a drug-ridden Vietnam veteran wracked by guilt over an atrocity in which he participated and fearful that one day he will snap and murder his children.[97] It did veterans no good, Pauken said, to encourage them to "wallow in self-pity."[98]

Local VVLP leaders joined in the chorus of voices demanding that the media portray Vietnam veterans in a less negative way. Stan Horton, of the Houston VVLP, said at the dedication of the Vietnam Veterans Memorial that the change was occurring in steps. More and more, the public was "seeing vets not as baby killers but, at worst, as dupes—and, at best, as people who did their patriotic duty."[99] But the image of the veteran as dupe was hardly a desirable one, even if it represented an improvement over the "baby killer" slur. Mark Treanor of the Baltimore VVLP said that the image of the Vietnam veteran had become "kind of a loser, a sucker. . . . It's a harder image to fight than the drug addict–baby killer stuff."[100] Grigg of the Arkansas VVLP complained that many television shows and newspaper stories portrayed Vietnam veterans as "drug-crazed, anti-authoritarian and violence prone." Why, he asked, did newspaper headlines say something like, "Vietnam vet charged with murder"? How many times did headlines say, "World War II vet charged with murder" or "Korean War vet charged with murder"?[101]

After interviewing Pauken, journalists in local newspapers disseminated the critique of media stereotypes. The *Madison Messenger*, a Tennessee newspaper, wrote, "All Vietnam veterans don't go to sleep with their M16s [automatic weapons] hidden under the mattress and wake up screaming in the middle of the night as depicted many times in movies and television."[102] An Iowa columnist wrote, "If a Vietnam veteran commits a violent crime, the fact that he's a Vietnam veteran invariably will be mentioned in the headline or high in the story—as if the crime and the war were connected. But if a Vietnam veteran bowls a 300 game, the story about his achievement surely won't mention his service in Vietnam. The fact that the person served in Vietnam is considered irrelevant to a story about normal behavior."[103] Lou Filardo, a copy editor with the *New Orleans Times-Picayune/States-Item*, said, "Vietnam vets are the only minority group in the country still being identified as members of a minority group in crime stories. The wire services are notorious for it."[104] Whether the VVLP's complaints had any effect on the portrayal of Vietnam veterans is difficult to measure, but one commentator credited the organization with at least some success. Despite his organization's reference to the VVLP's programs as window dressing, the national commander of the Disabled American Veterans wrote that the VVLP had helped to restore the pride, dignity, and integrity of those who had served in the Vietnam War. The "VVLP's focus on the positive has done much to dispel the tendency of too many to view the men and women who served in Southeast Asia as the victims—or worse yet the villains—of the Vietnam War."[105]

The VVLP's campaign to counter stereotypes and misrepresentations one story at a time was effective practice for its response to the most important media event during its period of federal funding: the broadcast of the thirteen-part PBS series *Vietnam: A Television History*.[106] Apart from the creation and dedication of the Vietnam Veterans Memorial, with which the documentary's production period closely coincided, this series vaulted the Vietnam War into public awareness as no other postwar event had. While the project was a milestone in bringing the war into discussion, it hit some raw nerves, and the controversies it generated drew a barrage of criticism from the VVLP and its allies.

The documentary series originated with a proposal in 1977, but much of the production took place in 1981–82, and the series finally aired in the fall of 1983, when the public had been primed by the unveiling of the Vietnam Veterans Memorial in Washington, and 2.5 million had visited it.[107] The public's receptiveness to discussion of the Vietnam War had increased in the interim. As the documentary's executive producer, Richard Ellison, recalled, the conventional wisdom when WGBH, the Boston affiliate of PBS, launched the project was that the war was a "closed chapter." However, the climate had "completely changed" by the time the series aired, with plays, books, and films about the Vietnam War being steadily produced and Vietnam veterans, "silent so long," being heard.[108]

The underlying purposes of the series chimed with those of the Vietnam Veterans Memorial Fund. Ellison said that millions of Vietnam veterans complained that "they have been ignored or short-changed by an ungrateful government, and that the American people have buried all remembrance of the war." The series would help the American public to "face up to the unfinished emotional and social business of the war." In doing this, though, it would adopt an even-handed approach, neither indicting nor defending the conduct of the war. In this respect, the series' ethos was identical with the memorial fund's. It would treat the "individual experience" of combat troops "with sympathy" and give the veterans some of the attention they were asking for.[109] Ellison was also aware of the war's continuing impact on politics and international affairs, as the experience of Vietnam conditioned American responses to other arenas of conflict. "Discussion of every tension point on the globe from El Salvador to the Persian Gulf to Namibia," he said, "is laced with Vietnam metaphors."[110]

The depth of feeling that still surrounded the Vietnam War became increasingly clear to the producers as their work proceeded. Elizabeth Deane, a writer and producer for the series, observed that the producers thought that by the time the series aired, enough time would have passed for Americans to have let go of some of the "high feelings and anger" generated by the Vietnam War, and they would be able to look at the war dispassionately. "I no longer believe that," she wrote later. Few Americans had let go of their "war-era views," she observed. "They may look like normal people, going about their daily lives in 1982. But at the mention of Vietnam, they fall reflexively into their warlike poses of 1968, angry and braced for a fight."[111] Ellison speculated that the controversies surrounding the war made it difficult to find corporate underwriters for the series, and queries by possible funders indicated that they were concerned about the way that topics such as the My Lai massacre, Agent Orange, and the Christmas bombings would be covered.[112]

Aiming for historical accuracy, the producers recruited fifty scholars to advise them, and production coincided with a month-long series of seminars in the fall of 1980. The historians had different perspectives on the war, as did the producers of various episodes. These differences generated a great deal of argument about the documentary's content, ranging from arcane details to major interpretive points. One adviser objected that the "LBJ Goes to War" episode was too "positive" in its portrayal of President Lyndon Johnson, while another thought that "Peace Is at Hand" was too "negative" about the Nixon administration.[113] The advisers and producers struggled to achieve balance in controversies about the Phoenix Program (an assassination program or not?) and about the political philosophy of America's enemies (Communist or nationalist?). The difficulty in settling such issues led to "temperamental and ideological strain." Partway through the process, Ellison described the production team as "battle-fatigued, and the war is far from over."[114] In an "eyes only" commentary on various controversial topics, a member of the production team wrote to Ellison and the chief correspondent, Stanley Karnow, "I pray for you both incessantly."[115] The controversy continued after the series aired.

The VVLP's Kolb offered a stinging three-page rebuttal to the PBS series, saying that it denigrated the U.S. troops while lauding the enemy. Instead of veterans proud of their service, "we got the guilt-ridden vet ready to repent for the camera—the type most highly prized by the antiwar movement." Members of Vietnam Veterans Against the War were taken as spokesmen for all Vietnam veterans, he complained. Ho Chi Minh was portrayed, Kolb wrote, "as the reincarnation of George Washington." Ignoring the variety of views the producers considered in creating the series, Kolb criticized them for consulting "the leftist literary and 'think tank' establishment," pointing out the "pro-Hanoi" sympathies of several. In a move similar to the attack on the memorial fund juror Garrett Eckbo, Kolb said that Karnow had written for a "far-left" publication in 1950 and had "impeccable" credentials as a war-era dove. Kolb said that the series' National Endowment for the Humanities grant was "approved by the same Carter Administration that saw America as a criminal and amoral imperial power in Vietnam."[116]

Bill Jayne, then national director of the VVLP, and Grigg of the VVLP in Arkansas also wrote critical reviews of the series' pro-Communist bias. Jayne said that the episode on Tet 1968 was inaccurate because it was equivocal about whether Communist atrocities in the imperial capital of Hué were part of a deliberate campaign of murder, and because the episode suggested that the United States used excessive force in recapturing the city. Grigg wrote that the series was "devoid of any sign of the savagery" of Viet Cong activities. He was also perturbed by the "well-meaning" Veterans Administration spots at the beginning and end of each episode, encouraging Vietnam veterans to visit vet centers. "I wonder," Grigg said, "if anyone else knows that 90 percent of Vietnam veterans have not experienced any service-connected problems?" He accepted that the vet centers had a purpose, but, he added, "they have a tendency to package all Vietnam veterans in the same mold." Shamus Maloney, program director of the VVLP of Western Pennsylvania, said that the PBS series was "the last of a long line of fairy tales" that "slander" the Americans who fought in Vietnam.[117] Pauken sent his VVLP chairmen and program directors a copy of a critical review that said the series favored the antiwar protesters and presented the North Vietnamese point of view.[118] From there, the word spread—a VVLP supporter in western Kentucky received copies of the critical review from two people, which suggests that the original recipients copied them and sent them on.[119]

Various right-wing groups joined the VVLP in countering the "biases" in the PBS series by producing documentaries of their own. An ultraconservative group called Accuracy in Media (AiM) produced a documentary titled *Television's Vietnam: The Real Story*, intended to correct the series' perceived inaccuracies, and its head, Reed Irvine, tried to persuade local PBS affiliates to broadcast it. The documentary begins with Charlton Heston addressing the audience and showing images of the Vietnam Veterans Memorial. He asks whether those whose names were inscribed on the wall died "on a fool's errand with no purpose." Worse, did they die in an effort to block the Vietnamese people's "legitimate aspirations for national unity"? "Or were they engaged in a noble cause," he asks, "an effort to halt the spread of Communist tyranny?" He remarks that "many experts" are convinced that *Vietnam: A Television History* presents a "distorted and inaccurate view" of the war. The criticisms involved some of the same topics that the series' historical advisers had struggled over: for example, whether the Vietnamese revolutionaries were Communists or nationalists, whether Ho Chi Minh was romanticized, and how independent of North Vietnam was the National Liberation Front (the revolutionary movement in South Vietnam whose armed forces were referred to as the "Viet Cong"). Following Heston, the historian Douglas Pike accuses the documentary of "misus[ing] history" and of violating its promise to "develop a kind of pride in America, [and] help end the trauma of the Vietnam experience."[120]

Former Ambassador to South Vietnam Elbridge Durbrow had initially welcomed *Vietnam: A Television History*. He told Ellison that he hoped the documentary would correct "half-truths" that had led to the Vietnam syndrome: "the continuing national phobia against any U.S. involvement abroad no matter how much it may be in our interest, all hidden behind the completely misleading and wrong catch phrase 'No more Vietnams.'"[121] After the documentary was broadcast, he added his voice to those of the other critics in AIM's documentary.[122]

The critics interviewed in *Television's Vietnam* include politicians who thought that the PBS series undermined America's readiness to counter the Communist threat. In his on-film interview, Representative McCain, one of those who had asked the General Accounting Office to audit the Vietnam Veterans Memorial Fund, takes stock of the series' political effects. He says that he sees the legacy of the Vietnam War in the U.S. Congress, in Central America, and in the "reluctance of the United States to understand that we have vital national security interests throughout the world and we have an obligation" to protect freedom and maintain America's interests. Senator Steven Symms (R., Idaho), who had opposed the 1982 dedication of the Vietnam Veterans Memorial, warns in the film against allowing misinformation to deflect the United States from its anti-Communist fight in El Salvador. Heston stresses the importance of distilling the right lessons from history, that it was right to resist Communist aggression. Media disinformation, he says, was crucial to the United States' defeat in Vietnam. Likewise, the distortions in *Vietnam: A Television History* might undermine America's will to continue the fight against Communism in Central America.[123]

The VVLP joined AIM's effort to counter the PBS series. Bill Jayne appears in *Television's Vietnam* to correct the alleged falsehoods in the PBS documentary. Heston introduces him by stating that Jayne's personal contact with veterans refutes the claim in the "Legacies" episode that up to 30 percent of Vietnam veterans are "haunted" by their war experiences. Jayne criticizes the series for presenting the "stereotype" of the veteran "as a loser, a victim."[124] Ronald Ray, chairman of the Kentucky VVLP, referred approvingly to the AIM documentary, saying that it was going to "set the record straight."[125] The Arkansas VVLP filmed thirty-second spots telling of veterans' accomplishments and demonstrating the inaccuracy of the Vietnam veterans stereotype.[126] Local VVLP members were interviewed for an hour-long special, *Vietnam Vets: A St. Louis Profile*, a follow-up to *Vietnam: A Television History*. Combining the rhetoric of the Vietnam Veterans Memorial Fund and the VVLP, the producer said, "We're going to show a different picture of the Vietnam vet than has been presented in the past decade. . . . We want to help people separate 'the war from the warrior' and see vets as they really are."[127]

Countering the supposed misrepresentations in *Vietnam: A Television History* came under the rubric of VVLP's campaign to improve veterans' image, but it blended with the politically motivated criticisms of the series as a handicap in the continuing war against Communism. The VVLP produced its own half-hour documentary, consisting largely of "talking head" narration by VVLP leaders and supporters, to put across a positive image of service in Vietnam. *When Their Country Called*, with Pauken as presenter and interviewer, emphasizes Vietnam veterans' success in attaining positions of respect in society. In the interviews, the veterans complain about their treatment when they first came home but say that they are proud of their service and that if they had to go back in time and make the decision once more, they would choose to fight again in Vietnam. James Webb says that participating in the war is probably the most important thing he will ever do in his life, and that, in the clash of political philosophies in Vietnam, Americans fought on the right side in defending the freedom of forty million Vietnamese.[128] Another VVLP-produced documentary titled simply *Vietnam* claims that it will set right the myths and misinformation surrounding "the most misunderstood conflict in America's history," arguing that the Tet Offensive was a major victory for the United States but was misreported by the media. Senator Symms speaks in this documentary as well as AIM's. He says that the war was lost not in Vietnam but in the Senate and the House of Representatives. Leo Thorsness, of the Los Angeles VVLP, says that his years as a POW were worthwhile because the war saved Thailand, the Philippines, Malaysia, Singapore, Indonesia, and Taiwan from Communism. "We made a major difference. It was not a waste."[129]

Webb's role as a spokesperson for the VVLP and Pauken's sympathy with the views of the Vietnam Veterans Memorial Fund's critics might make one suppose that the two organizations were natural antagonists. They certainly had distinct overall messages: whereas the memorial fund spoke of "healing" veterans' and the nation's ills, the VVLP denied that there was much wrong with America or its former warriors except unjust stereotypes or unwarranted feelings. Actually, though, the VVLP and the Vietnam Veterans Memorial Fund had a complex relationship. They shared personnel and, although the unabashedly political goals of the VVLP contrasted with the memorial fund's supposedly "apolitical" program, they had some common purposes. The VVLP's "symbolic support" program encouraged the creation of Vietnam veterans memorials. Jack Wheeler, the chairman of the Vietnam Veterans Memorial Fund, was the first national director of the VVLP. Jayne, the director of public relations for the memorial fund and a member of the fund's sculpture panel, was an assistant director of the VVLP from the start and its director just before its "sunset."[130] A year before the creation of the VVLP, Jayne wrote a press release for the memorial fund that anticipated the VVLP's program of correcting negative stereotyping of Vietnam veterans and that even referred to their leadership potential: "Popular movies and television shows most often portray the Vietnam veteran as a hopeless loser with a proclivity toward pointless violence. . . . The majority of Vietnam veterans, however, flatly contradict the popular stereotype peddled by Hollywood. Many, in fact, believe that the Vietnam veteran . . . will provide the nation with its best source of leadership in the trying times ahead."[131] After the formation of the VVLP, Jan Scruggs married the discourse of healing with positive assertions of pride in service and veterans' leadership. Although Scruggs was not a VVLP officer, he praised the organization and commended its goals. In a speech to Vietnam veterans in New Mexico, he said: "The bitter divisiveness of V[iet] N[am] has eased in the way that a wound heals with time. Viet vets are no longer afraid to express pride in serving their country. The American people are coming around and realizing that V[ietnam] vets deserve the respect. Finally a positive image is taking hold and of course we are lucky to have Mr. Pauken of ACTION with us. Because he is carrying out a brilliant idea. The Vietnam Veterans

L[eadership] P[rogram]. Showing the nation that V[ietnam] vets are not losers, but rather leaders."[132]

The lines of sympathy and influence between the VVLP and Vietnam Veterans Memorial Fund ran in both directions. Nine VVLPs led state delegations to the National Salute to Vietnam Veterans, and Kolb, in his role as chairman of the Houston VVLP, was invited to speak at the dedication of the memorial in November 1982. He said that he had no objection to the original memorial design, although he thought it was vital to add the statue and flag. He lamented the divisions in American society that resulted from the war and said, "Public indifference, peer hostility, intellectual contempt and official effrontery have left a spiritual scar on most Vietnam veterans. Only American society can provide the tissue needed to heal the scar. The Vietnam Veterans Memorial—as society's symbolic offering—is part of that tissue."[133]

Despite Pauken's antipathy to the notions of healing and reconciliation, local VVLP leaders echoed the Vietnam Veterans Memorial Fund's language when they spoke of America's need to heal and asked Americans to "separate the warriors from the war." Mark Treanor, the chairman of the Baltimore VVLP, said it had taken too long for the country to separate the warriors from the concept of the war, and he described a ceremony honoring Baltimore's Vietnam veterans as "making no political statement."[134] Edward Timperlake, while deputy director of the national VVLP, said, "Although I personally refuse to concede the moral high ground to those that opposed the war, I feel separating respect for the warrior from the issue of the war would greatly aid in destroying a stereotype [that Vietnam veterans are losers and suckers]."[135] Philip Vampatella, the program director of the Maine VVLP, said, "It's time to separate the warrior from the war."[136] Discussing the Vietnam Veterans Memorial being constructed in Sharon, Vermont, and Maya Lin's wall in Washington, DC, the program director of the Vermont VVLP wrote, "I like to think that there was a certain amount of healing for all of us in taking care of this piece of unfinished business left over from Vietnam."[137] A year after the dedication of the Vietnam Veterans Memorial a journalist in California even said that the VVLP was formed in order to "remove the warrior from the war," conflating its program with that of the Vietnam Veterans Memorial Fund.[138] The VVLP's final report said that, over the past three years, one of the important lessons the organization learned was, "Separate the warrior from the war, and the VVLP from partisan politics."[139] Thus, we can see that there was no across-the-board antipathy between the memorial fund's ideas and those associated with VVLP and, indeed, that those ideas at times seemed to converge.

There were also tensions, however, between the two organizations. Although the VVLP counted among its leaders and advisers officers of the Vietnam Veterans Memorial Fund, its leaders and advisers also included some of the fund's leading critics, such as Webb, Carhart, and Tom Ridge, who denied the memorial fund officers congressional honors. Don Bailey, who had proposed the legislation mandating a central position for the memorial's flag, became chairman of the VVLP in Pittsburgh after losing his seat in Congress. William Stensland, who, along with Baines made common cause with Perot in hiring Roy Cohn, was the program director of the San

Antonio VVLP Baines chaired. Although Pauken appointed Wheeler as national director of the VVLP, Wheeler lasted in the job for barely a year, resigning in June 1982, as Perot was demanding access to the Vietnam Veterans Memorial Fund's records. Pauken's special assistant at ACTION joined those who questioned the memorial fund's financial probity and the memorial fund suspected that Pauken was behind his attacks.[140] While the precise roots of the conflict are murky, it is clear that Pauken's stance demanding vindication for America's war effort in Vietnam was closer to Carhart's and Webb's views than it was to Wheeler's call for national "healing." Pauken also had a personal allegiance with Webb, who had come to his aid when Pauken's nomination to head ACTION ran into difficulties.[141]

John Fales, Pauken's special assistant, was one of those who alleged financial shenanigans at the Vietnam Veterans Memorial Fund. (Fales, a veteran blinded in the Vietnam War, was known in high places: he once had the distinction of representing Ronald Reagan at a commemorative ceremony.) He had been a participant in the January and March 1982 "compromise" meetings of the memorial fund and their critics as a representative of the Blinded Veterans Association and he was firmly in the camp of the memorial fund's antagonists. He had also been interviewed by Carlton Sherwood in the WDVM series investigating the memorial fund's finances, and it was he who told Sherwood that the Disabled American Veterans had offered to donate $1 million to the fund contingent on the fund's agreement to open their books to them and that the fund refused.[142]

Once the General Accounting Office (GAO) released its report about the Vietnam Veterans Memorial Fund's finances, Sherwood's attacks ended; but Fales continued the assault on the memorial fund through his column, published under the nom de plume "Sergeant Shaft," in *Stars and Stripes*, a publication oriented to the armed forces and veterans. The GAO's report, a response to the tag-team attacks first by Perot and Cohn, then by Sherwood and Fales, finally opened the memorial fund's books to public scrutiny and allowed critics to cherry pick facts and put a damaging slant on them. In December 1983, Fales attacked the integrity of Scruggs, Wheeler, and "the gang at the Vietnam Veterans Memorial Fund" for failing to support the chapel at Angel Fire and for wasting funds on a "prestigious and ultra-expensive law firm."[143] From May to August 1984, Sergeant Shaft regularly attacked the memorial fund and their finances, publishing details of the fund's expenditures, such as fund-raising costs and salaries.[144]

Scruggs was given an opportunity to reply to Sergeant Shaft in the August 1984 *Stars and Stripes*, but in the same issue, Sergeant Shaft printed a letter purportedly written by a reader named Jerry Kronski linking Scruggs with fellow "traitors" Jane Fonda and the antiwar veteran Bobby Muller, the founder of Vietnam Veterans of America. "Kronski" wrote, "All your info about the Memorial Fund's fat salaries makes me want to chisel my brother's name off that wall just like Scruggs chiseled and cheated us."[145] However, it turned out that no one with the family name Kronski was listed on the memorial. Scruggs complained to *Stars and Stripes*, suggesting that Fales had fabricated the letter. He demanded an apology and retraction, threatening legal action. He charged that Fales had libeled the Vietnam Veterans Memorial Fund by accusing them of abusing the public trust and sent *Stars and Stripes* a copy of the GAO report exonerating the memorial fund.[146] Scruggs then learned that Fales was leaving *Stars and Stripes*. The "Sergeant Shaft" column would continue, however, in another publication, the *National Vietnam Veterans Review*, which had already published Sergeant Shaft's charges about the memorial fund's failure to support the Angel Fire memorial, as well as Scruggs's response. Scruggs wrote to the *Review*, warning that the memorial fund would not put up with Fales's "libelous" attacks.[147]

Fales's campaign against the memorial can hardly have escaped the attention of his boss, Pauken, and the Vietnam Veterans Memorial Fund thought that the two were in cahoots. This dragging out of the conflict between the memorial fund and their critics was inconsistent with the prevailing discourse of reconciliation that by 1984 united the White House and the memorial fund. Pauken's appointment as the head of ACTION had coincided with the first flush of the Reagan presidency, when Pauken came to Washington eager for ideological battle with Democrats and corporate liberals. But Pauken felt that the Reagan White House had betrayed the creed of true conservatism. By 1984, when Pauken broke with the "moderate" or "pragmatic" wing of the administration, the conflict between Fales and Wheeler had become a matter of concern for both the memorial fund and the White House. In one of his *Stars and Stripes* columns Fales had expounded on a letter to Wheeler by Pauken's friend the White House counsel Fred Fielding. The memorial fund guessed that Pauken had got his hands on the letter and passed it on to Fales, in order to stir up trouble for Wheeler. The memorial fund's counsel asked Fielding to rein Pauken in, reminding him that Pauken had already been warned that "carrying on this vendetta in public was not helpful to the Administration."[148] After the White House had brought Interior Secretary James Watt into line, the presiding message was unity and the continued sniping against the memorial by Pauken's friends was a political liability.

The conflicts that pitted Wheeler, Scruggs, and the Vietnam Veterans Memorial Fund, on one side, against Pauken, Fales, Baines, Stensland, Carhart, and Webb, on the other, marked the rift between moderate conservatives, who wanted to reunify a nation riven by the Vietnam War, and uncompromising ideologues, who insisted on the rightness of their cause in Vietnam. A similar division also, in Pauken's view, cut across the Reagan White House team and set him against the administration's moderates. Pauken described a "man of principle" as one who was willing to fight for what he believed in even when that view was unpopular, and he contrasted such a man with the "corporate liberal" crowd, who are primarily concerned with being on the winning side. Blocked from further appointments in the second Reagan term because of his falling out with what he termed the "George Bush–Jim Baker wing of the Republican party," he quit as head of ACTION and returned to Texas.[149] He left the Reagan team proudly holding the banner of true conservatism aloft, ready to do battle again with his principles intact. The VVLP's period of funding by the federal government came to an end and the national organization expired, although some local VVLPs soldiered on for years (and are still in existence at the time of writing).

Vietnam veterans' public image did improve in the mid-1980s, although the VVLP's efforts were only part of the reason. The National Salute to Vietnam Veterans in 1982 and the 1984 dedication of the Hart statue played a large part in presenting Vietnam veterans to the public in a sympathetic way. *Vietnam: A Television History* and writings by and about Vietnam veterans helped to satisfy a public craving for understanding of the war. Television series such as *The A Team* and *Magnum P.I.* provided positive representations of Vietnam veterans—now they could be heroes working for justice, rather than ready-made villains for cop shows.[150] And for all the VVLP's caviling about the "sick puppy" image that it promoted, the spreading knowledge about PTSD made veterans' psychological troubles and adjustment difficulties more understandable and helped diminish the stigma of Vietnam veteran status.

In the middle of the decade, two major parades helped draw public attention to veterans' need for public recognition, and nonveterans came out in large numbers to applaud the former troops as they marched by. In New York City, in 1985, some twenty-five thousand Vietnam veterans staged a march down Broadway to accompany the dedication of the Vietnam Veterans Memorial in downtown Manhattan, a few blocks from Wall Street. The commemoration was promoted with the slogan, "It's time," and a flyer advertising the dedication parade was headlined, "In case you missed the parade when you came home, there's one in New York on May 7." The press duly reported the march as "the ticker-tape parade they finally got": tens of thousands of New Yorkers lined the route and office workers in adjoining buildings showered the marchers with 468 tons of ticker tape.[151] Commentators were remarkably uncynical. Troops in Vietnam had said that they fought for the benefit of munitions manufacturers or others with economic or political interests in Southeast Asia.[152] After the war, some veterans continued to harbor the suspicion that the war was fostered by capitalist interests.[153] Yet although the memorial was located a few blocks from Wall Street, sandwiched between corporate office blocks, there were no pointed references in the coverage of the parade to the charge that the war was fought to enrich the corporations headquartered in New York's financial district.[154]

The following year, a march in Chicago saw another huge outpouring of affection toward Vietnam veterans. A crowd of some 350,000 watched the veterans march through the streets of downtown Chicago. They held hand-lettered signs saying, "Welcome Home Vietnam Vets and Thank You," "We Thank You, We Love You, Welcome Home, You're the Best," and "We're Still Proud of You." In a mark of the growing recognition of Vietnam veterans, the number of marchers, estimated at 200,000, surpassed those that marked V.E. Day and V.J. Day at the end of World War II. Ronald Reagan said that the Chicago parade was a sign that America was "leaving the Vietnam syndrome behind."[155]

A pair of films released in mid-decade also ensured that the Vietnam War remained in the public's consciousness. *Rambo: First Blood Part II* and *Platoon* had quite different messages, though.[156] In the 1985 sequel to *First Blood*, John Rambo (Sylvester Stallone) is freed from jail and sent on a mission for which his skills in jungle warfare make him uniquely equipped: to rescue American captives still in Vietnam. Echoing Reagan's views about politicians' preventing the U.S. forces from winning, he asks, on the eve of the mission, "Do we get to win this time?" And this time, Rambo overcomes the treachery of the American "spooks" who try to sabotage his mission, single-handedly fighting off the Vietnamese army and its Soviet advisers in order to return triumphally with the rescued prisoners whose existence malign forces in the American government had attempted to cover up. With a blend of determination, guerrilla skills, exploding arrowheads, and a genetic mix of Native American and German blood, Rambo is the ultimate soldier, and his success demonstrates that the war was lost not because of any shortcoming in the American warriors but because of betrayal by other Americans. Reagan expressed a strong affinity with the Rambo character, whose revanchism accorded with the "Reagan doctrine's" aspiration to "roll back" Soviet gains around the world. Considering terrorist threats against American citizens, Reagan said, "Boy, I'm glad I saw *Rambo* last night; now I know what to do next time." After ordering the bombing of Colonel Muammar Qaddafi's headquarters in Libya in 1986, Reagan began to sign his letters "Ronbo."[157] For all its triumphalism, though, *Rambo* retained some of the same plaintive quality as its predecessor, *First Blood*. The film ends with Rambo saying that he and other Vietnam veterans want only to be loved by their country as much as they love it. The self-pitying resentment expressed in the film's opening and conclusion bears out that a sense of grievance is the predominant feeling tone of Vietnam veteran–related discourse across the whole political spectrum, uniting the right-wing *Rambo* with VVAW's criticism of the government for its neglect of veterans and the Vietnam Veterans Memorial Fund's complaints about their long-postponed welcome home. And for all that Pauken and the VVLP wanted to replace the image of "whiner veterans" with a more positive one, their grumbling about the media's representation of Vietnam veterans simply added another voice to the chorus of lamentation.

In 1986, the year of the Chicago parade, the film *Platoon* was released, bringing fresh attention to Vietnam veterans' wartime experiences while occasioning a new outbreak of complaints about media misrepresentation. Along with the memorials, parades, the PBS television series, and *Rambo*, the release of *Platoon* was the last of the major events that shaped public consciousness in the 1980s of the Vietnam War and those who fought it. Many veterans said that it was the most accurate depiction of the war they could imagine seeing in the cinema—a far cry from *Rambo*, which was a cartoonish fantasy with little pretense of verisimilitude. A former marine said, "As far as everything they used—equipment and scenery and scenarios—the only way you could have gotten closer to the war was to go through it yourself."[158] Yet others criticized the film for its heavy-handed moralizing, "spell-it-out narration," and emphasis on atrocities.[159] The film touched on a gamut of controversies about service in Vietnam: as well as atrocities and "fragging," it showed examples of cowardice, indiscipline, and drug-taking.[160] The neoconservative Norman Podhoretz said that the platoon's behavior "blacken[ed] the name of every man and woman who served the United States in the Vietnam War."[161] Bob Duncan, who served in the 1st Infantry Division at the same time that *Platoon*'s scenarist and director, Oliver Stone, was in the 25th, said that the film "managed to take every cliché—the 'baby killer' and 'dope addict'—that we've lived with for the past 20 years and stick them in the movie about Viet Nam."[162] Some African American veterans complained that it showed blacks as lazy, lacking leadership ability, and having to be pushed into combat.[163] B. G. Burkett, who criticized the negative stereotyping of veterans in the same way that the VVLP did, said, "I just think the story was totally exaggerated. . . . What they [the filmmakers] have done is take every stereotype that exists and put it on that one platoon and imply that one platoon was out in that for 365 days a year, and that just didn't happen." Burkett, a stockbroker, was an economically successful Vietnam veteran who resented the fact that scruffy men in camouflage fatigues had come to epitomize the "Vietnam veteran" identity, so that the public now associated veterans with "derelicts and bums." "The public has in its mind that we're a bunch of losers," he said. "This movie is not going to make them think we're a bunch of good guys. It's only going to explain *why* we're a bunch of bad guys."[164]

Burkett and other critics of the film objected to one of its central episodes, an atrocity in which members of the platoon kill two Vietnamese civilians and burn a village to the ground in retaliation for the killing of one of their comrades. One of the soldiers, Bunny, brutally beats a one-legged Vietnamese man to death, and Sergeant Barnes, the senior noncommissioned officer, shoots a Vietnamese woman and threatens to kill her daughter in order to extract information from the woman's husband. Barnes is in a white-hot rage and the interrogation appears to be as much a pretext for violence as an attempt to obtain useful intelligence about the enemy. Other members of the platoon egg on Barnes, saying, "Let's do the whole fucking village." The platoon teeters on the edge of committing a My Lai–type atrocity before Elias, a sergeant with a conscience, arrives and puts an end to the attack. The central character, Chris, has come to his senses after almost joining in the frenzy of violence, and he is appalled by Bunny's and Barnes's actions. He stops several soldiers raping a Vietnamese girl and remonstrates with them. Elias, a skilled fighter who refuses to have anything to do with the killing of civilians, reports Barnes's actions to his superiors and provides a moral counterpoint to Barnes's brutality. Thus, the film shows that Americans were responsible for committing atrocities but it also demonstrates that not all the Americans who fought lost their moral compass in Vietnam.

The moral pivot of the drama is the conflict between Elias and Barnes. Consequently, like many other representations of the war in the 1980s, the film is overwhelmingly America-centered: the Vietnamese people are minor characters who do not figure significantly except as victims of atrocities, nameless assailants, or targets to be shot. In a frank confession of this self-involved, narcissistic viewpoint, Chris says at the end, "We did not fight the enemy, we fought ourselves." This is true both symbolically (Elias and Barnes are Chris's "two fathers" who fight for "possession" of his "soul") and literally (Barnes shoots Elias and Chris shoots Barnes).[165] Involuted as it may be, this depiction of fratricidal violence carries a reminder of the death of the war's first recorded American casualty, killed, as shown in Chapter 5, by a fellow sergeant. The high drama of the conflict between Barnes (whom Stone compares to Captain Ahab and Achilles), and Elias (read "Hector"), and the intense psychological conflicts the film portrays, lends service in Vietnam a certain mystique and grandeur. The film also privileges the grunt's experience, because most of the action is shown from the foot soldier's point of view, and the emotional journey from arrival in country to departure for "the world" centers on Chris's visceral experiences and moral growth. *Platoon*'s release reinforced "Viet chic," a vogue for Vietnam veteran status, and "Viet guilt," the regret expressed by some men that they had missed out on a defining experience of their generation and had not had the chance to test their manhood in combat but had seen others serve in their stead.[166] For better or for worse *Platoon* helped to define Vietnam veterans' identity in the late 1980s—perpetuating all the negative images that the VVLP wanted to play down, yet also bringing sympathetic attention to veterans for the physical and moral ordeal that they had undergone in Southeast Asia.[167]

The VVLP's influence on the image of Vietnam veterans was likely outweighed by the impact of the Vietnam Veterans Memorial and films like *Platoon*, which not only reached millions of visitors and audience members but, more important, touched their emotions. While it is certainly true that the image of Vietnam veterans shifted from the "psycho" stereotype of the mid-1970s to the more complex and sympathetic portrayals of the mid-1980s, it is difficult to measure the degree of influence of any single factor, such as the VVLP's work: did the VVLP change anyone's minds, or was the organization simply swimming with the current? To the extent that its message reached readers, viewers, journalists, and editors, it at least helped to define the current's direction, and its views certainly reached many. For example, several million readers received its criticism of pejorative stereotypes when Kolb's findings were published in *VFW* magazine, giving statistical ammunition to those who preferred to see service in Vietnam positively, and Kolb's facts continued thereafter to flow through the veterans' community and beyond.[168]

In addition to the indeterminate number of people its "image enhancement" efforts influenced, the VVLP's historical significance rests on the fact that it was founded by the government, staffed by members of the president's political party, and answerable to a political appointee: it therefore provides the clearest picture of how the state would have liked people to see Vietnam veterans. The VVLP engaged in ideological warfare about how the Vietnam War should be remembered and questioned received ideas concerning the condition of its veterans. VVLP leaders asserted American pride in the face of critics who, they said, falsely claimed that the war was something of which to be ashamed. Following from this, they denied that those who served in Vietnam were anguished by their service and said that the only reason that Vietnam veterans had problems was because of the way that other Americans treated them. Commemorations, VVLP leaders believed, should stress pride in service and the belated recognition that veterans deserved. In the next chapter, we see how these core ideas spread in a wave of memorial building following the creation of the Vietnam Veterans Memorial and stirred debates about how Vietnam veterans should be regarded: as citizens proud of their service to the nation; as hapless, often deranged, victims; or as troubled but sympathetic figures, in need of recognition, whom the memorials could help to "heal."

8

"A CONFRONTATION BETWEEN FAITHS"

The Kentucky Vietnam Veterans Memorial

⭐

IN THE DECADE between the completion of the Vietnam Veterans Memorial wall in 1982 and its tenth anniversary, scores of Vietnam veterans memorials were constructed around the country.[1] Studying them can provide useful confirmation and amplification of the debates surrounding the creation of the Vietnam Veterans Memorial in the nation's capital, distinguishing idiosyncratic, accidental matters from recurrent themes. This chapter focuses on the Kentucky Vietnam Veterans Memorial, whose leading advocate, the chairman of the Vietnam Veterans Leadership Program (VVLP) in Louisville, wanted the memorial to make a clear political statement justifying the war. The Vietnam War, he believed, was a confrontation between faiths, in which the God-fearing and freedom-loving democracies opposed Communist oppression, and that was how he demanded it should be remembered. Because he insisted that the Kentucky memorial make, rather than avoid making, a political statement, the debate about the Kentucky memorial's design provides a counterpoint to the arguments about the memorial in Washington. A survey of the other memorial efforts initiated after the 1982 dedication of the national Vietnam Veterans Memorial establishes that planning for the Kentucky memorial was initially quite distinctive in challenging the prevalent discourse of "healing" and the ethos of "separating the warrior from the war." Ultimately, though, it fell into a measure of conformity with these predominant approaches to commemorating the Vietnam War.

Although state and local memorials did not undergo as much public scrutiny as the national Vietnam Veterans Memorial did and did not bear the burden of having to create a durable statement about the war for the nation as a whole, they nevertheless faced some of the same pressures: every time a group planned a memorial they had to consider how best to memorialize the war and those who fought in it; they anticipated responses from a public with diverse views of the war; and, even if they wished to express an ideological message, they had to consider and perhaps even embrace a diversity of opinion. These conditions were the same as those faced by the Vietnam Veterans Memorial Fund (VVMF).

In one important sense, though, the people who planned state and local memorials after 1982 operated in a completely different world, one that had been transformed by the creation of the Vietnam Veterans Memorial itself. The controversy attached to the national memorial alerted them to the likelihood of intense ideological and aesthetic debates, so that they were forewarned to a degree that the officers of the VVMF were not. The national memorial's successful reception by the public and commentators after its unveiling also gave local groups an aesthetic model to follow. It would no longer be possible to dismiss ordinary Americans' receptivity to abstract or modern designs after they responded positively to Maya Lin's wall—indeed, the public were more responsive to the wall than they had been to any other public monument in living memory. The "compromise" that added a bronze statue to the wall also proved to be influential on later commemorative plans—but in state and local memorials, planners tried to integrate figurative and abstract or architectural components from the start, rather than trying to insert statues into existing designs, as in Washington, DC.

The memorial in the nation's capital also provided examples of what to avoid: having seen the design jury castigated for not including Vietnam veterans in its number, the planners of memorials around the country sought to insulate their juries (and therefore the commemorative efforts) from this sort of criticism. Vietnam veterans chose the design for the Vietnam Veterans Memorial in Cincinnati and, as their leader said, it "wasn't chosen by a high-powered group of art people; it was chosen by the veterans themselves."[2] Stan Horton, the Houston VVLP program director, said that the committee selecting the winning designs for Vietnam veterans memorials in Harris County, Texas, would include members of area veterans' groups and Gold Star Mothers.[3] The Minnesota Vietnam Veterans Memorial organization included two Vietnam veterans (one of them the sculptor Rodger Brodin) on a ten-person design jury chaired by a landscape architect.[4] In Arkansas, the office of the secretary of state and a committee of Vietnam veterans oversaw the selection of a design for a local memorial, and the designs considered for the Kansas City [Missouri] Vietnam Veterans Memorial were all produced by Vietnam veterans.[5] Veterans in the New York Vietnam Veterans Memorial Commission took careful note of the controversy surrounding the selection of Lin's design. As a result, they devised a two-tier jury process. A committee that included art and architecture experts and two Vietnam veterans made an initial selection of six finalists in an open design competition; these finalists went to city agencies for the necessary approvals, pre-empting any postcompetition wrangling; a second design committee, on which Vietnam veterans enjoyed a majority, selected the winner.[6]

In contrast, a memorial effort that began about a decade after the one in Washington but that ignored the lessons of the design controversy there encountered the same pitfalls the VVMF did. The first Hawaii Korean–Vietnam Veterans Memorial design, selected by a jury headed by a prominent local architect, featured tall, transparent prisms that some said would be out of keeping with the location, a lawn near the state capitol. It echoed the memorial in Washington by including two black granite V-shaped walls. What disturbed the critics were the crystals, the tallest of which would be forty-four feet high (although one reporter said that they would tower seventy feet over the capitol's lawn). Local veterans' groups complained that they had been "frozen out" of the selection process: a commission consisting of veterans headed the project but they were not responsible for selecting the design. By now, the Lin design and Hart statue had become so familiar that some of the veterans who objected said that they preferred a wall and statue similar to the memorial in the nation's capital. Legislators criticized the memorial design and established a review board to oversee the work of the commission, causing a majority of its members to quit. A new design competition was held. The result was a less dramatic design featuring walkways and inscribed tablets, and the memorial was finally dedicated in 1994.[7] The conflict demonstrated the wisdom of the memorial projects elsewhere that involved veterans in the design selection to avoid giving their critics ammunition if their juries selected a challenging abstract or modernist design.

The VVMF had adapted a rhetoric of "healing" and reconciliation devised by psychiatric practitioners and veterans' advocates. By popularizing this terminology, the fund provided a ready-made discourse for memorials elsewhere. The planning statements of state and local memorials in the decade after the Washington memorial was built echo its founding principles: that memorials should promote healing, separate the warrior from the war, and eschew political statements.

The idea of separating the warrior from the war, promoted by the psychologist Charles Figley, endorsed by President Jimmy Carter, and popularized by the VVMF, had caught on in much of the country as early as 1982. That year, in New York City, a mayoral task force recommended that the city establish a memorial to honor "the service of Vietnam veterans, as distinguished from the war itself." The design committee agreed that it "should not suggest either approval or disapproval of the Vietnam conflict but should acknowledge the service and sacrifice of all veterans."[8] The following year, one of the Vietnam veterans leading the drive to create a memorial in Oak Grove, Kentucky, explained its philosophy: "The soldiers have taken the blame, when they had nothing to do with making the policy that took the United States into the war. That created the emotional scars."[9] In 1982, the first fundraising letter for the North Carolina Vietnam Veterans Memorial in Raleigh said, "The memorial will not honor the war, but those who served and sacrificed there."[10] Steve Acai, the director of public relations for the memorial, said that it would not be "an expression of approval or disapproval of the war, but a means by which all North Carolinians, regardless of differing opinions on the war, can unite in acknowledging the services of those who served."[11]

The term "healing" appeared just as frequently. The memorial in Raleigh was said to be a "symbol of healing and reconciliation." The memorial in Oak Grove would also be "a symbol of the healing process." The inscription describing the symbolism of the interlocking pools of the Kansas City Vietnam Veterans Memorial says that water, like time, can "cleanse and heal," and that the memorial stands as a "symbol of the healing." A steering committee member said the most important thing to come out of the dedication of the Kansas City memorial was "the opportunity to understand, forgive and to heal." Similarly, the inscription on the Vietnam veterans memorial in Brown County, South Dakota, says that it is "devoid of any political ramifications" and seeks to further "a healing process." Veterans saw the Vietnam veterans memorial planned in West Virginia as "a tool for healing."[12]

Separate the warrior from the war; commemorate the war and promote healing without making a political statement: the words spilled freely from almost anyone involved in creating a Vietnam veterans memorial after the one in the nation's capital. It is notable, though, that this language appeared equally adaptable to memorial designs in which representational, landscape, or architectural components predominated. The dedication co-chairmen of the Montana State Vietnam Veterans Memorial, dedicated in 1988, wrote, "The memorial makes no political statement regarding the war or its conduct. It will transcend those issues. The hope is that the creation of this memorial will begin a healing process between all factions in Montana during that period."[13] An almost identical combination of ideas described the purposes of the Minnesota Vietnam Veterans Memorial. Its design competition announcement stated that the design should "evoke a reflective mood rather than make a political statement about war itself." The dedication brochure affirmed that "from the sacrifices made in Vietnam can come the miracles of reconciliation and healing."[14] The physical forms of the two memorials could hardly be more different, though: the Montana memorial is a representational sculpture, whereas the Minnesota memorial is an elaborate landscape design of pools, paths, paving, and structures resembling the state's geography in microcosm. Different from both these memorials in its physical form, the Philadelphia Vietnam Veterans Memorial, an arrangement of inscribed walls and engraved wartime scenes dedicated in 1987, was intended to convey the same message: it carries an inscription saying that it "separat[es] the warrior from the war." The veterans who created it elaborated: "The memorial is part of the healing process."[15]

The recurrent use of the concepts of "separating the warrior from the war" and "healing" in different parts of the country can be interpreted in very different ways: the repetition signifies either that these were meaningful concepts that guided the whole nation's commemorative work; or that they were innocuous, meaningless formulae to which local veterans simply paid lip service. Paradoxical though it may seem, both interpretations are correct: the recurrent concepts had become such standard fare that they could be regurgitated in reflex fashion but their unexamined use is also what best demonstrates their importance in shaping commemoration, even if—or perhaps especially if—those who used the terms were heedless of their significance.

One has only to imagine other organizing principles around which commemoration might (at least hypothetically) have been geared—repentance, for example, or revanchism—to recognize the importance of "healing's" ubiquity: the term occupied the space that other concepts might otherwise have taken up, and if it was bland and meaningless to some users, it nevertheless exerted an unseen force in blocking other ways of thinking about commemoration. Those who mindfully used concepts such as "healing" and "separating the warrior from the war" helped define the "common sense" about American commemoration of the Vietnam War, but the ones who unthinkingly uttered platitudes also played their part. The power of the commemorative discourse is most effective at the moment of spontaneity, when individuals do not speak but ideology speaks through them.

When statements such as these were reported by the local media, they helped to disseminate concepts such as "healing" and "separating the warrior from the war" around the nation. In turn, the public picked up the infectious terminology: for example, a Pittsburgh resident who made a donation to the Vietnam veterans memorial there said, "It's time to heal the wounds and this monument will surely help."[16] The spread of these ideas demonstrates the overwhelming success of the VVMF's ameliorative discourse of "healing" over more overtly political judgments, whether critical or supportive of the American war in Southeast Asia. Across the country, as in Washington, the political goal of national reunification would be advanced by indirection, through the avoidance of overtly partisan statements.

Somewhat at odds with the avowals of "healing" as their stated rationale, however, many veterans' groups welcomed the participation of William Westmoreland in commemoration events. Westmoreland, who had headed the dedication parade of the Vietnam Veterans Memorial, remained a much derided figure in the 1980s, not least by officers (some of whom had served under him) who published criticisms of his strategy and leadership in Vietnam.[17] Throughout the decade, though, Westmoreland accepted every invitation to talk about the Vietnam War, to "be the champion" of those who fought in it, and to preside over commemorations.[18] He led the dedication parade of the South Carolina Vietnam Veterans Memorial in Columbia and spoke at dedication ceremonies of the Vietnam Veterans Memorials in Duluth, Minnesota; Mercer County, Pennsylvania; and Fayette County, Kentucky. Anyone, around the country, who wanted his square-jawed, stubbornly unrepentant presence at the dedication of a Vietnam veterans memorial could count on him. The endorsement given through his participation in these commemoration events was mutual: just as he lent his name to the memorial efforts, so the veterans validated him as a public figure whose support was worth having. But although his involvement in the commemorations might seem to signal their leaders' defiant pride in their service, one could not predict their approach to commemoration from his presence alone. He spoke at the dedication of the Vietnam Veterans Memorial in San Antonio, which was created as a result of the efforts of John Baines, the VVMF's critic; he also spoke at the dedication of the Minnesota Vietnam Veterans Memorial in St. Paul, which faithfully adhered to the discourse popularized by the VVMF. In Minnesota, "healing" perhaps expanded to encompass Westmoreland's rehabilitation as a public persona if not as a military leader.[19]

Significantly, following the lead of the Vietnam Veterans Memorial, local groups around the country called their memorials *veterans* memorials, not war memorials. One rationale for this was that, lacking a congressional declaration of war, the conflict in Southeast Asia could not be officially accorded the title of "war." (Thus, the official designation in the Library of Congress subject catalogue is Vietnam Conflict, not

Figure 18. Kansas City Vietnam Veterans Memorial wall; David Baker, designer, dedicated September 6, 1986. The memorial also features an interconnecting set of pools of water. Photo by author.

Vietnam War.) This problem need not have disturbed those outside Washington, since their memorials, unlike the Vietnam Veterans Memorial, had no need for a congressional mandate (and even the national memorial refers in its inscribed prologue to the "Vietnam War"). Local groups followed the precedent of the national memorial's name because centering on veterans allowed them to avoid making historical and political statements. Instead, their purpose, like that of the national memorial, would be recognition of and sympathy for those who fought and died.

If this was to be their objective, the memorials had to find a means of balancing the individual and collective aspects of commemoration. How could one honor each individual who had fought and died, while also acknowledging the collective aspects of commemoration? Although Vietnam veterans memorials around the country are not uniform in design, in the main they echo the principal component of the national memorial: a wall of names. In Kansas City, Missouri (fig. 18); Dallas; Portland, Oregon (fig. 19); Olympia, Washington (fig. 20); Philadelphia (fig. 21); Sacramento, California; Baltimore (fig. 22), and countless other sites the names of state or local casualties are inscribed on stone walls. Because the inscriptions are confined to the dead and the missing, all these memorials bear the solemn weight of mourning. While this focus on the dead and missing could unite the public whose collective grief the memorials invoke, it imposed a heavy charge on the memorial planners to get the designs right. The memorials had to be worthy of the dead whose names they recorded for posterity, and above all, they must not dishonor their memory. In several instances (Nashville, Sacramento, Des Moines, and Watertown, South Dakota), the memorials use black granite from the same quarry in India from

Figure 19. One of the five inscribed alcoves, Oregon Vietnam Veterans Memorial, Portland; Doug Macy of Walker Macy landscape architects, designer, dedicated November 11, 1987. Photo by author.

Figure 20. Washington Vietnam Veterans Memorial, Olympia; Kris Snider of EDAW, Inc., designer, dedicated May 25, 1987. The inscribed wall is divided by an outline of the map of Vietnam, signifying the domestic divisions in the United States because of the Vietnam War. Photo by author.

Figure 21. Philadelphia Vietnam Veterans Memorial; Perry Morgan, designer, dedicated October 26, 1987. Photo by author.

Figure 22. Maryland Vietnam Veterans Memorial, Baltimore; Paul Spreiregen, designer, dedicated May 28, 1989. Photo by author.

which the stone for the national memorial came. (Very few quarries supply black granite as fine-grained as the stone that Lin's design required. Bangalore, India, was selected because the other two possibilities were ruled out on political grounds, Sweden because of its association with draft evaders, and South Africa because of apartheid.) Sixteen other memorials use black granite from unspecified sources.

Another similarity between the Vietnam Veterans Memorial and several of the state and local memorials, unnoticed by scholars until now, is the involvement of the VVLP. Just as the national VVLP office holders Jack Wheeler and Bill Jayne were involved in creating the Vietnam Veterans Memorial (Wheeler as chairman of the memorial fund and Jayne as director of public relations and a member of the sculpture committee), so local VVLPs around the country led efforts to create Vietnam veterans memorials in their areas. The creation of the memorials was the cornerstone of the VVLP's "symbolic support" initiative. As the program's final report states, "Probably the most evident manifestation" of the symbolic support objectives was "the ongoing campaigning and fundraising for the construction of Vietnam veterans memorials throughout the country."[20]

Many local VVLPs sent delegations to the National Salute to Vietnam Veterans in Washington in November 1982. Because veterans marched in state formations at the salute and they and family members of the dead clustered in state groups during the dedication ceremony, they met others from their home states. Some veterans, inspired by their experience of the memorial in Washington, were moved to create memorials in their own states and localities when they returned home. Robert Hunter, one of the group of five veterans from Oregon whose visit to the national salute, mentioned in Chapter 5, inspired them to create a memorial in Portland, said that the local effort would allow veterans who were unable to come to Washington also to "regain their past."[21] Don Grigg "came away [from his visit to the memorial] inspired and wanting to [do] the same thing in Arkansas."[22] Herman Woods, a double amputee, returned to California and persuaded a state assembly member to sponsor legislation authorizing a state memorial there.[23] Veterans from Alabama, Wisconsin, and Tennessee who visited the dedication of the national Vietnam Veterans Memorial were also inspired to create memorials at home.[24] It is quite likely that local veterans would have created memorials at some point, with or without the VVLP, but the national VVLP considered the creation of memorials around the country a priority. Where local efforts did not occur spontaneously, VVLPs started them. It is notable that a substantial number of state and local memorial projects began between 1982 and 1985, soon after the dedication of the national Vietnam Veterans Memorial and when VVLPs around the country were most active. True to the model of the Vietnam Veterans Memorial, most of these memorials were funded by private donations, though state memorials required a legislative stamp of approval. However, state and local governments frequently made a crucial contribution by providing land for the memorials, for which legislative approval was normally sought. Away from the prized real estate of the Washington, DC, Mall, though, there were usually fewer regulatory hurdles to overcome than the ones the national memorial faced.

In 1983 the Louisiana VVLP sponsored the state Vietnam Veterans Memorial in New Orleans (Westmoreland unveiling the winner of its design competition) and that same year the Tennessee VVLP began raising funds for the memorial in Nashville.[25] The New Mexico VVLP helped to organize the rededication of the memorial in Angel Fire as the Disabled American Veterans Vietnam Veterans National Memorial in the same year.[26] Apart from the Angel Fire memorial, which was already constructed well before the local VVLP gave its blessing, VVLP-sponsored monuments were marked by a signature style. They generally consisted of inscribed stone walls or pedestals accompanying bronze statues—combining the principal elements of the Vietnam Veterans Memorial in the nation's capital. These elements are found in the Louisiana and Tennessee memorials, and in the VVLP-sponsored memorials in Sacramento, California; Little Rock, Arkansas; and Raleigh, North Carolina. Of these, all except the Arkansas statue consist of multifigure groups. In the VVLP-led Western New York Vietnam Veterans Memorial in Buffalo, an inscribed wall is accompanied by an engraving, not a sculpture, of a soldier, sustaining the combination of realistic representation and inscribed masonry found in the others.[27]

Demonstrating the appeal of the language of the VVMF, despite Thomas Pauken's skepticism, VVLP-led memorial projects also tended to borrow the fund's rhetoric to describe their purposes. A veterans' publication said that the VVLP-sponsored Vietnam Veterans Memorial in New Orleans, "makes no political statements about the Vietnam War." Instead, the sculpture by the Louisiana artist Milton Pounds "provides a symbol of state and local unity and will further the reconciliation of our country after the divisions caused by the war. Through support of the Memorial, Louisianans of diverse political beliefs and opinions regarding U.S. policy in Vietnam can unite in expressing their acknowledgment of the sacrifice of those who served there."[28] A member of the Maine VVLP said of the Maine Vietnam Veterans Memorial, "Now is the time to accelerate the healing and to put a positive tone to Vietnam veterans."[29] The assistant project coordinator of the Maryland Vietnam Veterans Memorial, Jack Burk, said the memorial would have "a healing effect on the animosity that existed in the '60s."[30]

Some VVLP leaders, though, wanted their memorials to make a political statement. They were generally unable, however, to come up with an effective way of translating their ideas into visual or material form. Their militant statements usually remained confined to inscriptions or declarations of intent. In Arkansas, Don Grigg, the project director of the VVLP in Pine Bluff, said that the state Vietnam Veterans Memorial would "remind us to never do this again unless we're allowed to win."[31] It is unclear how the memorial, a black granite wall with a statue of an infantryman, fulfills this ambition (fig. 23).[32] The names of Arkansas's dead are reminders of the costs of war but the "allow us to win" interpretation depends on the ideological predisposition of the viewer. The memorial at least achieves what Tom Carhart, James Webb, and others wanted in Washington: the infantryman, an archetype of a "grunt," faces out, toward visitors, with the inscribed wall as a backdrop. The statue is titled *Going Home*, suggesting that the young man has come to the end of his tour of duty. His full pack, belt, webbing, and helmet straps are encumbered with all sorts of equipment, depicted with a meticulous eye for detail.[33] The figure's pose combines with the soldier's load to evoke the wearying infantry slogs through the South Vietnamese countryside, or as the foot soldiers put it: "humping the boonies."[34] With his time in Vietnam at an end, he looks tired but determined, holding his weapon and helmet at his side.

The Tennessee Vietnam Veterans Memorial statue, a three-figure bronze statue by Alan LeQuire dedicated on Veterans Day 1985, stands in a small plaza in front of the Tennessee State Museum's Military Branch in Nashville (fig. 24). In close proximity is a wall inscribed with the names, ranks, and branches of service of residents killed in Vietnam (fig. 25). The use of a three-figure bronze accompanying a

Figure 23. *Going Home*, Arkansas Vietnam Veterans Memorial, Little Rock; Steve Gartman, designer, John Deering, sculptor, dedicated March 7, 1987 (wall), November 11, 1987 (statue). Photo courtesy of Donald Grigg..

Figure 24. Tennessee Vietnam Veterans Memorial, Nashville, Alan LeQuire, sculptor, dedicated May 26, 1986. Photo by author.

Figure 25. Tennessee Vietnam Veterans Memorial wall, dedicated November 10, 1985. The inscribed wall and tablets are offset to the side of the sculpture in a physically constrained site. Photo by author.

black-granite inscribed wall suggests that this memorial is meant to imitate the one in Washington. Because of the distinct settings and difference in scale of the two memorials, however, the one in Nashville is bound to suffer in any such comparison.

An inscription on the memorial in Nashville states: "[Tennesseans served in Vietnam] with distinction and valor, but often without recognition. We, who cherish freedom, dedicate this memorial to their unselfish sacrifice." The reference to the troops' valor is reinforced by the poses of the three figures. The memorial committee went to nearby Fort Campbell and had soldiers adopt stances that they suggested. The sculptor worked from the resulting photographs. "It was basically a design by committee," he said.[35] The three men, positioned in a triangle, are on the alert, their weapons at the ready. To the left, a half-kneeling man in a boonie hat with an M-16 rifle in hand communicates on a radio-telephone while looking up, perhaps scanning the sky for a helicopter. To the right, his RTO (radio-telephone operator), bedecked with the radio equipment, crouches, his finger on the trigger of an M-16. Behind them, a standing soldier keeps watch, his grenade launcher angled ready to fire. The figures represent different ethnic groups and are also said to represent the three grand divisions of the state, East, Middle, and West.

A comparison of the processes that produced the statues in Washington and Nashville is instructive because from different starting points they arrived at somewhat similar results. In Tennessee, the veterans assumed a "hands-on" role in determining the design from the start and found a sculptor who was willing to accede to their preferences. In Washington complaints about the result of the design competition resulted in the formation of a sculpture committee consisting of Vietnam veterans, and they exerted some indirect responsibility for the sculpture's design, first by selecting Frederick Hart as the sculptor and then by discussing the sculpture with him. The VVMF sculpture committee's authority over the design was therefore less complete than the Tennessee veterans' control of theirs, limited by Hart's relative autonomy and by the authority of the statutory commissions who had to approve Hart's design. That these distinct processes both resulted in three-figure bronze statues reflects the influence that the Hart sculpture had over the ones that followed.

Veterans in both settings were preoccupied with painstaking accuracy in the figures, keen to show the sculptors examples of their equipment. Veterans around the country showed the same interest in having their equipment displayed in commemorative statuary. The president of the Vietnam Veterans of America's Cincinnati Local No. 10 said of the memorial planned for Cincinnati's Eden Park: "We didn't want something abstract. That's what brought it down to the memorial of soldiers—the boonie hats, the jungle fatigues, the flak jackets—just the whole attire of the Vietnam vet."[36] In Tennessee, as in Arkansas, Cincinnati, and Washington, the concern with authentic detail is evident in the resulting statues. It was as if the veterans imagined that fidelity to the minutiae of their equipment would insure the statuary's faithfulness to the lived reality of their experience, each lovingly reproduced trigger guard or piece of webbing representing so many days on patrol, so many boring periods of inaction, or so many moments of terror. As LeQuire recalled, the committee members were "very specific about the equipment and what went where." Fred

Tucker, program director of the Tennessee VVLP, suggested that Vietnam veterans would recognize themselves in figures that carried weapons unique to the Vietnam War as well as a bottle of "bug juice" (insect repellent) widely used in Vietnam.[37]

The veterans in Nashville seem to have got just what they wanted. The figures look doughty and resolute, although out of place a few feet away from an ordinary city street. They look as though they are protecting the military museum from a terrorist attack, rather than evoking a scene in Vietnam. The mania for detail without an eye for the statue's physical context expresses the limitations in the veterans' understanding of the language of public commemoration: a public sculpture needs to address itself to a public, not to the narrow expertise of the military history buff. Detailed verisimilitude is not sufficient to this purpose. The presence of a bottle of "bug juice" may speak to the community of Vietnam veterans but it is unlikely to communicate to an audience unversed in military lore; likewise, the notion that the Tennessee statue represents the grand geographical divisions of the state is hermetic, failing to bridge the gap between the artist's intention and the viewer's perception. Ultimately, the memorial's clearest message arises from the sheer fact of the bronze statuary, which the memorial's creators considered the commemorative form best suited to ennobling the troops who served in Vietnam, and from the accompanying inscription, which makes explicit the veterans' intention to honor the troops' "valor" in the cause of "freedom." It is doubtful though, that the statue *instills* a feeling of admiration or respect in many viewers, as opposed to *telling* the audience that this was its intention.

A memorial in South Carolina exemplifies a similar failing: the local VVLP leaders, too, insisted that the memorial convey an ideologically crafted message, but they did not know how to embed that message in a monument. In 1984, the native South Carolinian William Westmoreland announced the intention to create a Vietnam veterans memorial in North Charleston and the South Carolina VVLP assumed responsibility for selecting a design. Its statement of purpose echoed the VVMF's rhetoric: the memorial would symbolize the state and nation's gratitude, and "the healing of psychological wounds over a decade old." South Carolina VVLP project director F. Lee Hunnicutt also explained that he hoped the memorial would "establish a feeling of pride in the service and sacrifice made by the people of South Carolina" to counteract the stigma of shame that many felt. But that message would hardly have been clear in the life-sized bronze sculpture of three figures, *The Three Faces of War*: one figure represented the soldier answering the call to war; another, releasing a dove, represented the peace-seeker; and a third represented death. This is a perfectly reasonable, if banal, set of symbols associated with war but it said nothing in particular about the specific war it was intended to commemorate. The ideological intentions of the memorial planners, described in words, seem inconsistent with the generalizations conveyed by their graphic realization. The memorial did not clearly convey any message, except that the local VVLP leaders, following the Frederick Hart statue, seemed to have an abiding commitment to three-figure bronze statues.[38]

The story of the Kentucky Vietnam Veterans Memorial in Frankfort begins with the same premise—a local VVLP leader's insistence that a memorial communicate a specific ideological message through a three-person bronze statue. There, however, the plot was complicated by an unfortunate combination of traits in the leader, Ronald Ray: an inability to translate his ideas into visual form in a way that was comprehensible and appealing to others, and an unshakeable conviction that he was right. Ray favored a design that would help to mobilize the public in Ronald Reagan's cold war confrontation with America's Communist enemy. But the give-and-take of debate led to the selection of an entirely different design. The result is a striking monument that differs interestingly from the standard statue/wall formula of VVLP-initiated memorials and dramatizes the triumph of sentimental, veteran- and casualty-centered commemoration over frank, ideologically strident messages. The original concept survives in the inscription at the memorial's entrance, but the unifying language of "healing"—no less political than the overt vindication of the war that the VVLP leader initially sought—predominates.

On May 27, 1968, Captain Ray was one of the two Marine Corps officers who delivered the message to Victor Westphall that his son David had been killed in Vietnam. He stayed in touch with Westphall and followed the progress of his project to create a memorial to his son and to others who died in Vietnam. Despite the two men's different ideas about the war, Ray took a friendly interest in Westphall.[39] Ray (who had gone through Officer Candidate School with Philip Caputo) ended his military career as a highly decorated colonel—he was awarded two Silver Stars and a Purple Heart—and went on to have a successful career as a lawyer in Louisville, Kentucky.

Because of his multiple roles as a Defense Department appointee, a VVLP leader, and a memorial planner, Ray personifies the multifront Reaganite campaign to cast America's involvement in the Vietnam War in a positive light. An unreconstructed cold warrior and supporter of the war effort in Vietnam, he disavowed the idea of "separating the warrior from the war," of honoring those who fought it without making a statement about the war itself. For Ray, the Vietnam War was, and remained, a "noble cause." Ray was the VVLP's volunteer chairman in Louisville and, like other VVLP leaders around the country, he presided at meetings of economically successful bankers, investment brokers, and lawyers. Like Pauken, Ray believed that the absence of homecoming parades and the lack of appreciation by society caused the veterans more psychological injury than the war itself.[40] Ray's press interviews were filled with VVLP axioms: he said he worked for the organization "to dispel the ugly stereotype of the Vietnam veteran as loser" who was portrayed on television as "a violent criminal, a drug addict or pusher, or a psycho."[41] But Ray did more than just engage in the post–Vietnam War battle of ideas: he participated in the new cold war in Central America as an official in the Pentagon.

In May 1984, during his time as the Kentucky VVLP chairman, Ray accepted an appointment as deputy assistant secretary of defense for reserve affairs, with responsibility for readiness and training. He would work with James Webb, his fellow marine Vietnam veteran, who had been appointed to the newly created post of assistant secretary of defense for reserve affairs.[42] It was an important assignment: the 1.8 million members of the National Guard and Reserves represented about half the combat capability of the U.S. Army. All the army's infantry scout troops and heavy helicopter companies, and nearly 75 percent of its infantry battalions were in National Guard units. According to the Pentagon's planning, they would be mobilized in the event of a major war (unlike during the Korean and Vietnam Wars, when few active-duty reserve units were mobilized because it would have been politically unpopular to do so). They were also the cutting edge of counterinsurgency warfare: the army had 98 percent of its Civil Affairs and 61 percent of its psychological operations personnel in reserve components. In line with Reagan's "Total Force" concept, the armed forces placed increasing reliance on the reserves as Congress slowed the rises in military spending projected by the Reagan administration. More particularly, while Ray had responsibility for the combat readiness, training, and mobilization of the National Guard and Reserves, those forces were involved in one of the new cold war's hot spots, Central America: they participated in successive military exercises that led the Nicaraguan government to think that its nation was under the constant threat of invasion. The result was that the Sandinistas placed the Nicaraguan economy and society on a continuous war footing. In the spring and summer of 1984, American officials began to talk openly about the possibility of an invasion of Nicaragua. Rather than referring to accidental clashes that might trigger a conflict, American diplomats and military officials talked of "pretexts" for war. Debating how far the Vietnam analogy would hold, some argued that the Sandinistas would retreat to the hills to mount a protracted, Viet Cong–like guerrilla war; others thought that a successful invasion would be relatively easy and brief.[43]

The threat of an invasion shaped the Sandinistas' political and military response, which U.S. strategists used as a tool against them. The U.S. goal was to force the Sandinista army to build itself into a conventional force equipped with heavy weaponry, less adept at fighting a counterinsurgency campaign against the *contras* than small, popularly based units would be. The social and economic costs of the military build-up created hardships for Nicaragua's people, which the *contras* exploited through propaganda condemning the "totalitarian Marxist draft" and complaining that the government spent money on bullets, not food.[44] Whether there as part of an invasion force in training or as a strategic feint to force the Sandinistas into a difficult position, the National Guard and Reserves were instruments of this cynical U.S. strategy.

Because the U.S. Southern Command was the smallest of all U.S. military regional commands, with only ninety-six hundred troops, preparations for any possible military action in Central America required that additional forces be readied for rapid deployment there.[45] As part of the U.S. military build-up and muscle-flexing, between 1983 and 1987 reserve and National Guard units rotated in and out of the region, participating in an "almost continuous" set of military exercises in Honduras. The exercises allowed the reserve units, along with their counterparts in the regular forces, to be deployed in an invasion scenario and to acclimate themselves to the terrain and to tropical conditions during simulated combat. The exercises provided "invaluable" opportunities to observe how personnel and equipment operated in the Central American environment, according to the architect of the U.S. build-up, General Paul Gorman.[46]

On May 1, 1985, further heightening tensions between the United States and Nicaragua, President Ronald Reagan issued an executive order, which declared a "national emergency" and contained a finding that "the policies and actions of the Government of Nicaragua constitute an unusual and extraordinary threat to the national security and foreign policy of the United States." The executive order declared a total trade embargo on Nicaragua.[47] This economic warfare, designed to strangle Nicaraguan trade, added to the costs that the military exercises were imposing on Nicaragua in diverting the country's scarce resources to national defense.[48]

One of the purposes of the military exercises was to "demonstrate to friend and foe alike the capability and willingness of the United States to deploy rapidly in a crisis situation."[49] Although the principal goal was said to be training, an "indirect effect" of the presence of U.S. forces was "countering Cuban/Soviet expansion in the region."[50] The exercises were also a convenient means of assisting the *contras* without having to ask for congressional appropriations. According to Defense Department regulations, the military facilities constructed for training purposes and funded by the Pentagon's operations and maintenance budget were supposed to be "temporary." A General Accounting Office investigation found out, however, that the Pentagon had violated these regulations: the majority of the air strips, barracks, and dining facilities constructed or improved during the training exercises turned out to be to fit for continued use. Most of the military installations were constructed close to the Nicaraguan border and facilities and equipment were left behind for use by the Hondurans and the *contras*. For example, U.S. forces modernized the air base at El Aguacate during the exercises, and it became the command and control and logistics center for the *contra* war, acknowledged by the *contras* as one of their supply bases. Members of Vietnam Veterans Against the War in Pennsylvania complained about the back-door aid, saying that the National Guard had been leaving behind supplies for the *contras*—a charge that Defense Department and National Guard officials denied. The sleight of hand was both consistent with and ultimately overshadowed by the Iran–Contra plot that sent millions of dollars' worth of arms to the Nicaraguan counterrevolutionaries between October 1984 and October 1986, in contravention of U.S. law.[51]

In April 1985, Operation Big Pine III, involving forty-five hundred American ground and air troops and several thousand Honduran forces, supported by tanks, was conducted just three miles from the Nicaraguan border. In the same month, Universal Trek '85, involving sixty-five hundred American troops and thirty-nine U.S. warships, staged a mock amphibious landing on the northern coast of Honduras, supposedly simulating a defense against an invasion by Nicaragua—although the troops performing the landing could equally well have been practicing an invasion. National Guard forces took part in exercises involving infantry, armor, artillery, and medical units. By mid-1985, when Ray left the Pentagon and returned to Kentucky, the U.S. forces had built or improved eight airstrips, two training centers, two radar stations, four base camps, and a twelve-mile "tank trap" near the Nicaraguan border. The largest airstrip at Palmerola was made capable of handling the United States' largest aircraft, the C-5 and C-141 transports, and the most advanced fighters and bombers.[52]

James Webb remained in his post and bore the brunt of opposition to the exercises. In 1986, with public opinion running strongly against aiding the *contras*, a number of state governors complained about the purpose to which the National Guard units were being put and refused to allow units from their states to be deployed to Honduras.[53] As Bruce Babbitt, the Democratic governor of Arizona, put it, "Of course, the Pentagon insists that the Honduras deployments are for training, not operations. But the Pentagon always calls it training when the Guard goes overseas. This is a bureaucratic word game. . . . The truth is that there is no bright line between training and operations in military affairs. War is undoubtedly good training for soldiers, and training can serve operational purposes. . . . It is their operational element—as part and parcel of the president's war policy in Central America—that makes the Honduras deployments controversial, even though useful training is undoubtedly going on." Babbitt quoted the commander of Joint Task Force Bravo at Palmerola air base, who said that the purpose of the exercises was to "intimidate and harass" the Sandinistas. "In the guise of 'exercises,'" Babbitt complained, "the Pentagon has kept thousands of troops rotating continuously through Central America since 1982. In the guise of 'temporary facilities,' it has paved Honduras from coast to coast with air fields and military radars."[54]

The White House considered passing legislation overriding the governors' authority over the National Guard in peacetime but decided against it.[55] In the face of the governors' refusal to allow the National Guard to serve in Honduras, Webb wrote of the guard's vital role: "In the event of a full mobilization, 18 of the 28 Army divisions would be provided wholly or in part by the Army National Guard. The Air National Guard's more than 1,700 aircraft provide 73 percent of our air defense forces, 52 percent of our tactical air-reconnaissance capability, 34 percent of tactical airlift and 25 percent of our tactical fighters."[56] The National Guard and reserve forces that Webb and Ray oversaw were thus a vital part of the nation's war-fighting capacity, but Webb suggested that relying on them might turn out to be a "gamble" if governors like Babbitt hampered the guardsmen's training.

The governors' opposition to the National Guard deployment in Honduras reflected the public's long-standing dislike of the administration's Central America policy. As Allan Nairn reports, from 1981 to 1986, public opinion polls showed that there was a rough 2-to-1 consensus against military involvement in Central America. The April 1986 CBS/New York Times poll reveals just how much fears of "another Vietnam" in Central America correlated with popular opposition to the administration's policy. Those respondents who feared that "the United States will get involved in Nicaragua the way it did in Vietnam" rejected *contra* aid by the enormous margin of 73 percent to 17 percent. Those who did not share the fear of "another Vietnam" split down the middle, with only 44 opposed to *contra* aid and 43 percent in favor.[57] In March 1985 Reagan recorded in his diary the "bad news" that Wirthlin's privately commissioned polls also delivered: "Our communications on Nicaragua have been a failure, 90% of the people know it is a communist country but almost as many don't want us to give the Contras $14 mil. for weapons. I have to believe it is the old Vietnam syndrome."[58]

While Webb's Pentagon deputy and as chairman of the Kentucky VVLP, Ray had a dual role related to both aspects of the problem of "another Vietnam": attempting to shape public memories of the Vietnam War through the Kentucky memorial while simultaneously carrying the fight to America's Communist enemies in Central America. The two campaigns were part of the same enduring fight against totalitarianism. In a letter to the Russian dissident Alexander Solzhenitsyn, Ray said that the VVLP of Kentucky sought "long-overdue and proper recognition" of Vietnam veterans who served not just the United States and South Vietnam but "all of mankind" by "resisting the totalitarianism that was eventually imposed on South Vietnam." According to Ray, the VVLP undertook the responsibility of "insuring that this country understands the *real* lessons of America's failure of will in Vietnam."[59] Learning the correct lessons of the Vietnam War was indivisible from fighting totalitarianism in the Soviet Union or Central America—they were all aspects of the same world-historical struggle.

Ray was not alone in the belief that America behaved unselfishly in Vietnam. In a presentation to university students titled "Vietnam as a Noble Cause," Ray quoted the historian Ernest R. May, who said that the Vietnam War may have been "the most moral or at least the most selfless war in all of American history. For the impulse guiding it was not to defeat an enemy or even to serve a national interest; it was simply not to abandon friends."[60] The sentiment recalled Richard Nixon's statement that "never in history have men fought for less selfish motives."[61] Ray said that America had embarked on warfare in Vietnam for the sake of an ideal: resisting the "horrors of Communism" as exhibited in the Soviet gulags and the Chinese Cultural Revolution. Ray believed that the United States never developed a strategy for victory in Vietnam and that the people eventually tired of the war, but that did not change the fact that it was fought for decent and democratic motives.[62] Ray's ideas tapped into a broadly felt sentiment that Vietnam veterans had not been given their due appreciation when they returned from Southeast Asia;[63] his proposition that the war itself had been unjustly regarded took this one step further.

In his statement of the purposes of the Kentucky memorial, Ray repeated that the Vietnam War was "the most selfless war in our Nation's history," fought not for economic interests but for values—intangibles like freedom and honor. "We cannot overlook the continuing struggle over values which still exists in the world" between the "free" nations and the "Soviet bloc" with its "slave system." He anticipated future struggles: "Does anyone doubt seriously," he asked, "that other young men are going to have to defend our institutions, our values, our way of life[?]"[64] Recognizing the nobility of the cause for which Americans fought in Vietnam would confirm the values for which Americans must be willing to fight and die. In a fundraising letter for the memorial, Ray referred to the fashion in 1984 for talking of "peace and negotiations" (perhaps with Reagan's political opponents in mind, or perhaps thinking of State Department diplomats), but he asserted that lives and liberties must, when threatened, be defended. The Kentucky Vietnam Veterans Memorial would, he said, be a celebration of the willingness to serve and sacrifice in a higher cause than self.[65]

Ray wanted the memorial that he envisioned to reflect his pride in his service in Vietnam and his active role as a fighter in the cold war. The most distinctive feature of the Kentucky memorial, as Ray saw it, was that it would not, like other memorials around the country, avoid a political statement about the war. It would instead reflect the determined sense of service that he felt in answering the call in Vietnam. At the dedication of a flagpole and memorial plaque commemorating service in Vietnam on November 19, 1983, Ray said:

> The emphasis in the last 10 to 15 years has been on "doing one's own thing. . . ." Many well-meaning citizens fear that dedication to a higher cause of God or country has fallen into disrepute, especially among some of the more visible and vocal segments of our society. However, nothing could be further from the truth. Our society and indeed civilization could hardly go on if the only motivating force was an individual's dedication to his own selfish ends. Service has been the watchword that has made this country great. . . . We who served in Vietnam answered a call to life-risking service, but received little, if any, praise or thanks for our service from the society that called us to serve. . . . I think I speak for all Vietnam veterans when I say that I am proud to have answered that call and I am proud that I did the very best I could under those difficult circumstances. We who went to Vietnam were wise because we saw the next thing that had to be done and we did it with a whole heart.[66]

The reference to service "under difficult circumstances," like the inscription on the baseplate of the VVMF flagpole dedicated a few months earlier, echoes the statement by the returning prisoner of war Jeremiah Denton. Ray had also said between the dedications of the two flagpoles that the one in Kentucky would honor Vietnam veterans who had served "under difficult and trying conditions." Ray's reference to Denton's words hints at the importance to him of the prisoner of war (POW) issue, which loomed large in his eventual proposal for the Kentucky memorial.[67]

The Kentucky VVLP followed the organizational model of the memorial in Washington and founded the Kentucky Vietnam Veterans Memorial Fund, Inc., as an independent entity (with William Westmoreland as its honorary chairman). The Kentucky VVMF began considering the memorial design in the summer of 1984, while Ray was in Washington. It remained a VVLP-led project, though: the memorial fund and the VVLP overlapped in membership and shared the same address; the first meeting of the memorial fund's design committee took place at a VVLP picnic; and active members of the VVLP were invited onto the memorial fund's advisory board.[68] Thus, in many respects, membership and decision-making authority appeared to be shared by the two organizations, even though they were administratively separate and kept distinct accounts. The overlap between the two organizations led to some confusion about who was in overall control of the project, even for some of the members.[69] This uncertainty became significant when Ray fell out with the other members of the memorial fund over the design. Then, the Kentucky VVLP asserted its ultimate control over crucial decisions about the memorial.

Initially, the project sailed along smoothly. The memorial was endorsed by the governor of Kentucky, Martha Layne Collins, and in March 1984 won the support of the Kentucky General Assembly.[70] Eventually, the state became a major benefactor, donating $100,000 and the land on which the memorial stands.[71] The memorial fund's advisory board established a design committee, stipulating that it would be best if the memorial's designer were a Vietnam veteran. As part of the fundraising effort, Jim Lundgard, program director of the Kentucky VVLP, toured the official architectural model of the Vietnam Veterans Memorial around the state—the first time it had been displayed outside Washington.[72]

Ray had strong feelings about the memorial in Washington, though. "I don't like the national memorial," he said, in the period before the statue had been added. "I feel bad when I pass it." "It's black, it's in the ground, I don't like the symbols." If you "separate the warrior from the war," he suggested, the warrior's death becomes just like any other—like fifty-eight thousand deaths on the nation's highways. Neither he nor Webb was happy with that idea, Ray recalled. Because Ray had seen the national VVLP borrowing from the VVMF the idea of separating the warrior from the war and because some local VVLPs applied the idea to the memorials they sponsored, he had hesitated before accepting the chairmanship of the Kentucky memorial fund. Separating the warrior from the war had been expedient, he thought, in the 1960s and 1970s, "when we were blamed for the war." But things were different in the Reagan years, because the president and others had declared the Vietnam War a "noble cause." Ray respected the president for expressing this view, and for speaking from conviction, not heeding an opinion poll. Mentioning the "deep" conversations he had had with Webb, Ray said, "In this memorial, we will not be able to avoid making a statement. We should be trying to say that there are some things worth enduring a war for." A design committee colleague concurred: "We're tired of people expecting us to apologize for our service. We want to say something positive, we want to reflect positively on the Vietnam experience."[73]

Even though the design committee was vested with "sole and exclusive responsibility to determine the final design" Ray first preempted its decisions and then tried to countermand them when they did not match his preferences.[74] Whether because they were ideologues with definite convictions or former marine officers with a strong belief in their command prerogatives, people like Ray and Webb found it hard to respect others' contrary views or play within the established rules when the outcomes went against them. Ray took the lead in the design-selection process and, just as Webb had insisted on a sculpture on the Washington Mall, Ray wanted a sculpture in Kentucky's state capital. While in Washington, Ray visited Hart's studio and was struck by the power of the statue he was fashioning, with the sun streaming in through a skylight to illuminate the bronze figures.[75] Jim Lundgard evidently agreed with Ray's tastes, saying in April 1984 that "a sculptor" would be selected soon.[76] Before any members had been appointed to the design committee, Ray started discussing the memorial with a sculptor, Jack Chase, who agreed to submit a preliminary design. Chase was a West Point graduate and highly decorated Vietnam veteran who had entered the national Vietnam Veterans Memorial competition, winning meritorious recognition for his entry.[77]

Chase's views harmonized well with Ray's. The two of them agreed that the Kentucky memorial should validate the American war effort in Vietnam. Ray said that 98 percent of what Americans had heard about the Vietnam War was negative and therefore, "We need to be bold with our statement."[78] When considering why the United States was fighting in Vietnam, both Ray and Chase recalled the brutality of their North Vietnamese enemy. In "Vietnam as a Noble Cause," Ray deflected attention from U.S. troops' crimes in Vietnam by focusing on Communist atrocities. He described the killings by the Viet Cong when they occupied Hué following the Tet Offensive in 1968. Ray was serving as a battalion adviser to the South Vietnamese Marine Corps when they retook the city with the support of the U.S. Marines, uncovering the corpses of the Communists' victims.[79]

"It was in many ways similar," Ray said, "to the present conduct of the K.G.B. in the Soviet Union, or storm troopers in Nazi Germany or during the Cultural Revolution in China when after a knock at the door, people are forcibly dragged from their beds never to be heard from again. We uncovered mass graves and the total dead was nearly 5,000."[80] Chase felt just as strongly about the Communist atrocities in Hué and insisted that the memorial should make a statement about the cause for which the war was fought: "Now, I don't agree with the simplistic thinking so fashionable in current circles which says that we were in Viet Nam without a cause. We saw the cause in the bound bodies in the mass grave in Hué, or in the tears of gratitude on an old woman's face as the ARVN [the Army of the Republic of Vietnam, i.e., South Vietnam], her ARVN started regaining the city. Call it love of freedom, call it self-defense, call it anything, but call it something. It's there. We've seen it. I reject any argument to the contrary." Chase insisted that many Americans felt this need to "call it something," to name the cause for which the war was fought. Hundreds of others, he noticed, were "seeing more clearly than ever before, a need for a memorial that isn't an apology. A memorial that doesn't gloss over the realities, but one which also conveys a sense of resolve and purpose."[81]

Soon after his conversations with Chase, Ray conceived a sculptural memorial consisting, like the Hart statue, of three figures: a prisoner, figuratively representing POWs and, more broadly, symbolizing the opposition between freedom and slavery; a soldier, representing strength, reason, and resolve, symbolizing the willingness to die for a cause and preparedness "to continue the struggle"; and "the universal woman," a grieving wife or mother in the United States, representing the costs of war.[82] The female figure coincided with Chase's approach to commemorating the war: his submission to the national Vietnam Veterans Memorial competition was a sculpture of a female figure titled *Grief*.[83] The image of a prisoner also matched Chase's ideas. He had produced a sculpture of a POW, titled *Bondage*, showing a prisoner clutching at a strand of barbed wire.[84] The inclusion of a prisoner in the proposed design conveyed a dense layering of ideas: it was a reference to the suffering of the American POWs in North Vietnam, a hint at the lingering and politically charged claim that American prisoners were still being held in Southeast Asia, and a representation of the menace of the Soviet gulag. Chase said that commemorating Vietnam should not just be about the past but should affirm America's continuing "resolve and purpose."[85] Ray concurred, saying that the figure of the prisoner "symbolizes the threat of slavery if our resolve is not firm." Ray and Chase agreed, though, that a "positive sculptural message" should be used to "counterbalance any grimmer statement" the memorial might make. The three-figure sculpture thus graphically represented the themes that were important to Ray, as to other Reaganites. Soon after their conversation, Ray informed the design committee's chairman that Chase would be "giving us some sketches for the Kentucky Vietnam memorial."[86]

Had Ray and Chase been allowed to get on with creating the memorial together, no doubt the project would have proceeded harmoniously. But Ray had to obtain the consent of his colleagues on the memorial fund's design committee, and they did not approve the plans that he had conceived. Ray had recruited a fellow marine veteran, Bill Black, to the Kentucky VVLP and they shared the same political perspectives and views of the war.[87] Black told a reporter, "We're proud to have served. There was a time when that was out of fashion, but it would tickle me to death for Jane Fonda . . . to know we're getting together."[88] Black and Ray were in complete accord in their anti-Communist commitments and pride in their service, but this did not guarantee their agreement about the design of the memorial.

By appointing Black as chairman of the design committee, Ray hoped that his proposal would have an easy passage to the committee's approval. However, Ray discovered that Black was no pushover. Black had ideas of his own, and he resented the pressure that Ray put on him to toe the line. He also complained that Ray had gone ahead in his discussions with Chase without first consulting his design committee colleagues. Recalling their dealings regarding the memorial design, Black later described Ray as a "true believer" and "fanatic." When Ray was appointed to his Defense Department post and left Kentucky in May 1984, he lost control of the design process. The design committee did not like Chase's presentation and insisted on its prerogative to decide what form the memorial should take.[89]

Black decided that a carillon (a set of tuned bells) in a campanile (a bell tower) would make an appropriate memorial and he was just as devoted to that idea as Ray was to a sculpture. With Ray in Washington, Black campaigned to win over his design committee colleagues, organizing a road trip to see carillons in Cincinnati and preparing detailed costings. Black conceived the idea that the carillon's bells would be engraved with the names of Kentucky's dead (although it is doubtful that the inscriptions would be visible from ground level). The design committee felt that the theme of captivity proposed in the Chase design could be "too easily misinterpreted in a negative way"; that enough "negative" statements had already been made about U.S. involvement in Vietnam; and that it placed too much emphasis on the issue of POWs. They had not perceived that the prisoner symbolized the contrast between freedom and slavery and saw instead only "a defeated soldier." They also believed that emphasizing mourning, through the female figure, would be inappropriate for a bereaved family who wanted a memorial that would honor their loved one, not mirror their grief back to them.[90] Black, however, had misunderstood the realities of decision-making power and he faced a fearsome adversary in Ray.

Ray pulled out all the stops to win Black over to his ideas, haranguing him late into the evening after a meal. A devout Christian, Ray quoted Whittaker Chambers on the necessity for "freedom-loving people" to stand firm against Communism, the "other faith" casting the shadow of totalitarianism and slavery all over the world.[91] Ray said, "Despite Vietnam, we Americans are still thrust into the maelstrom of a confrontation between two faiths." Chambers was one of Ronald Reagan's heroes. A year before the conflict about the Kentucky memorial, in the speech in which he called the Soviet Union an "evil empire" and "the focus of evil in the modern world," Reagan had quoted Chambers and expressed views identical to Ray's about the conflict between freedom-loving Americans, with their faith in God, and totalitarian Communism, with its faith in man.[92] This was a continuing fight and one in which Ray believed the memorial design was implicated. Ray said, "I feel strongly that we have nothing to apologize for about our involvement in Vietnam. We must be willing to make an honest statement about war and about the Vietnam War in particular." Ray did not understand why Black seemed to oppose creating a memorial that would make a clear statement. Ray was insistent that the three-figure statue would convey the message that he thought was necessary: "Unless free men resolve to stand and fight, the forces of repression and collectivism will prevail and force totalitarianism . . . on more and more people." Ray seemed to hold out the possibility of compromise, saying, "I am not trying to dictate the final form of the memorial." There was, however, little room for meaningful debate because Ray was simply allowing discussion of the "actual form of the figures or their arrangement." He brooked no disagreement about the basic proposal for a three-figure statue.[93]

When the design committee gathered to resolve the differences about the memorial, Ray read them passages from an article arguing that war memorials should evoke the reality and horror of war and that those that fail to do so are at best innocuous but at worst offensive in their blandness.[94] He said that prematurely settling on a carillon was putting the memorial's "message" in the backseat and he questioned whether a bell tower "said" anything. Ray explained his idea of having a grieving woman in a sculpture, saying that his experience as a casualty assistance officer (making calls on bereaved families such as Victor Westphall's) had shown him that "War is grief." He also defended the idea of representing a POW, citing the endurance that the Medal of Honor winner James Stockdale showed in a North Vietnamese POW camp when his captors tried to strip him of his dignity and honor. He read the committee a passage from Solzhenitsyn's *Gulag Archipelago* reflecting on freedom, explaining that the prisoner's captivity symbolizes the threat posed by an evil force. Responding to a suggestion that sculptures could be added to the bell tower's walls, Ray argued, "I am committed to making a statement on what's going on in the country [and the] world today. We can't just put up a bell tower then figure out how to hang something on the side. These men [and] women went to Vietnam when their country called. . . . We owe them a positive statement."[95]

When Ray had finished his extended remarks (which took up over two pages of single-spaced minutes, excluding the textual readings), a fellow committee member deadpanned, "So you don't like the bell tower?"[96] Another committee member asked, "Why does the monument have to make a statement? What we decide to say is not what the families of those who died would say. The statement is in the eye of the beholder." This skeptic added, "By making a political statement, we're straying from our purpose 'to remember.'" And, more damningly, he added, "You're wishing to impose your statement on the dead."[97]

Leaving interpretation to the eye of the beholder was precisely what Ray, Webb, Carhart, and other right-wingers wanted to prevent. Ray's wish for a clear statement had several sources. First, he disbelieved that all truth is relative—it is the historian's task, in his view, to approach the truth as closely as possible and, by extension, those producing memorials would be negligent if they took an "anything goes" or neutral approach allowing all to think whatever they might. Second, Ray doubted the conventional wisdom among military sociologists that foot soldiers fight for the buddies alongside them, not for ideals, nations, or causes. In Ray's view, soldiers must have a cause they believe in. Together, these two convictions, epistemological and ethical, dictated that the cause for which America fought in Vietnam had to be clearly articulated. But contemporary geopolitics made this absolutely imperative. Because the United States was still involved in a long struggle against tyranny, it was vital that the nation display a proper respect for those it sent into battle. Shaming or neglecting those who had already served risked undermining others' willingness to take up arms in the same fight, as Reagan pointed out in his 1981 Rose Garden speech and as Caspar Weinberger warned in 1984. Conversely, remembering the ideals for which Americans fought and died in Vietnam would exemplify and inspire service to a cause larger than oneself: duty, honor, and country.[98]

Ray, Webb, and Carhart had endured the years when people wanted them to feel ashamed of the war. They wanted to fight back, and with a vengeance. They wanted memorials that would plant their convictions into the minds of viewers, with no ambiguity, no chance of escape. The problem with this approach, though, was, first, that its authoritarianism was bound to alienate many in a country with democratic traditions, full of pluralists, skeptics, and individualists; and, second, that the "true believer" memorial planners generally lacked an understanding of how in practical terms they could convert their ideas into material form. When Ray attempted to explain his ideas, they were filled with abstractions that meant little to his colleagues. When he tried to translate them into sculpture, his colleagues disliked the results.[99]

Ray and other ideologically committed VVLP leaders wanted to save their war and their dead from any possibility of dishonor. But the clumsiness of Ray's and Carhart's attempts to fashion a monument compounded the irreducible problem that every viewer sees things in his or her own way: Ray and Carhart could not make others see what they saw in their designs.[100] Where Carhart saw dedication and sacrifice in his proposal for the Vietnam Veterans Memorial, others saw self-pity and mawkishness; where Ray saw grief and the struggle between freedom and slavery, others on the design committee saw defeat and despair.

Mindful of Ray's demand for a clear message conveyed by a sculpture, the design committee agreed to add a sculpture to the carillon and invited proposals from a list of sculptors including Chase, Hart, and others known for their work with bell towers. Discussions were haunted by the fear that the memorial fund would not be able to raise sufficient money to build the carillon—so much so that Black dismissed the possibility of hiring Vietnam veterans to construct the memorial, saying that this would increase the construction costs (even though putting veterans to work was part of the VVLP's reason for being).[101] This anxiety combined with Ray's opposition led the design committee to consider ideas other than, or in addition to, a carillon.

The committee's vacillation did not resolve either the design or the budget problems. Appeasing Ray by incorporating a sculpture into the carillon plan encouraged other design committee members to make their own proposals; in a masterwork of design by committee, none was refused. When a member of the design committee observed that a helicopter symbolized the special nature of the Vietnam War, the committee added a full-sized helicopter to the design. Others thought that water would symbolize life and a representation of a Vietnamese child would symbolize hope for the future, so those elements were also added. By the time the committee had satisfied all these suggestions, artists were asked to consider, in addition to a sixty-foot bell tower containing a "world-class" carillon, some or all of the following: a wall of names, pools of water in which a South Vietnamese civilian rendered in sculptural form was planting rice, a Vietnamese child, and a helicopter. The budget ballooned to over half a million dollars. The design committee proposed adding the memorial to the state capitol's grounds—although one member justifiably worried that the design might overshadow its setting.[102]

According to Black's recollections, Ray threatened to walk off the project—the documentary record reveals only that the design committee acknowledged its differences with Ray's idea and hoped that it would be able to continue to work with him. Showing that there were no differences in the ideological premises of the rival memorial plans, the design committee approved a statement saying that "*honor should be the predominant message*" of the memorial, and that it should "project a positive image of the Vietnam veteran and a sense of his *Continuing Service* to his community" (emphasis in original).[103] Referring to the design committee statement, Ray wrote, "I would encourage a more direct effort to deal with America's reasons for becoming involved in Vietnam in the first place. Vietnam was clearly a 'noble cause.' President Reagan made no bones about his view of America's effort and reasons for going to Vietnam, and we can do no less."[104] Showing steadfastness of which his hero Stonewall Jackson would have been proud, Ray was insurmountably opposed to the bell tower idea and uncompromising in his insistence on the three-figure sculpture he had conceived. Although five members of the design committee had decided to pursue the carillon idea, and although the design statements they submitted in October 1984 indicated that a majority continued to support that idea, in the matter of the carillon Ray's was ultimately the only vote that counted.[105]

Reasserting its control over the project, the Kentucky VVLP reorganized its board and amended its by-laws to empower a four-member executive committee (including Ray) to act for the board of directors. The VVLP met in March 1985 and agreed to inform Black that the design committee must consider designs other than a carillon.[106] The next month, the design committee, whose composition had changed with the addition of new members, bowed to Ray's pressure by agreeing to develop new design parameters.[107] Ray returned from Washington to Louisville in May 1985, having given up his Pentagon post.[108] The VVLP produced a new organization and operating plan, which called for a new jury to be established. A member of the previous design committee complained to Ray about the "insult" to members who were excluded from the new jury and suggested that Ray himself step down as spokesman regarding the memorial's philosophy, since his design concept had differed so greatly from that of others. Black resigned from chairmanship of the design committee, along with two other members.[109] Ray later said to Black that he was glad that "none of our differences have ever degenerated into the acrimony and controversy which arose over and around the national effort."[110] While this demonstrated magnanimity in victory, it was also an unrealistic assessment of what had occurred. When a long-standing member, Wick Gregory, resigned from the VVLP, he condemned Ray's excessive "zeal" and "arrogance" and told him, "Your belief that you alone have seen the light has run off hundreds of talented and resourceful men, who would have gladly served at your side but not under your thumb."[111] The conflict about the Kentucky memorial's design was just as bitter as the one in the nation's capital, just not so public.

Having solicited the advice of Grady Clay, the Louisville writer and editor who had chaired the design jury of the Vietnam Veterans Memorial, the memorial fund began anew and held a competition to choose a design, stating that it "should evoke an emotional remembrance while being aesthetically authentic as a work of art." The criteria stipulated merely that the memorial should display the names of all Kentuckians who died in the Vietnam Conflict or were still unaccounted for and did not attempt to predetermine the form the memorial should take.[112] Eventually, therefore, the Kentucky memorial's design criteria began to converge with those of the Vietnam Veterans Memorial in Washington—despite Ray's earlier insistence on a definite message that would differentiate the Kentucky memorial from others. The memorial's fundraising pitch sounded quite similar, too. A letter soliciting support for the memorial said that during the Vietnam War, Americans "often blamed their differences . . . on the warriors" and that "this state-wide Memorial effort will go a long way towards reconciliation and healing of some of those old wounds."[113]

The proposal that broke the deadlock, unanimously selected by the design committee and approved by a group including state officials, architects, and civic leaders in 1987, differed from both the statue and the bell tower proposals. The proposal was doubly fortuitous. Although striking and original, it was neither a carillon nor a sculpture. It was also well adapted to the site that the memorial fund had been granted the month before, on high ground adjacent to the state Libraries and Archives. Designed by Helm Roberts, the memorial is a giant sundial whose shadow falls on the names of Kentucky's Vietnam War dead on the anniversary of their deaths (fig. 26).[114] A groundbreaking ceremony took place in November 1987, when the gnomon (the sundial's pointer) was dedicated. The memorial itself, with the inscribed paving completed, was dedicated a year later.

Roberts had been proposing a giant sundial to mark historical events in various locations since he came up with the idea in 1974.[115] The twenty-four-foot gnomon is made of stainless steel, and its shadow falls on a plaza made of sand-blasted gray granite quarried in Georgia (fig. 27). Because of the tilt in the earth's axis, each day the shadow of the sun follows a slightly different course, shortening as the calendar approaches the summer solstice and lengthening as it approaches the winter solstice. The names of Kentucky's dead are inscribed on the memorial's paved floor, which serves as its dial, across which the shadow of the gnomon describes a daily arc. The hour radials of the sundial represent the years 1962 to 1975. Curved lines corresponding to the lengthening and shortening shadow represent the months of the year. The name of each person who died in the war is engraved in the space representing the date on which he died, "thus creating a graphic pattern of the conflict."[116] An engraved rectangle symbolizes the twenty-three Kentuckians still listed as missing in action in Southeast Asia. The rectangle is placed behind the gnomon so that the shadow never touches this spot. For all its differences, the Kentucky memorial shares some of the qualities of the memorial in Washington. Although a sundial is a traditional, even an old-fashioned, form, the scale of the memorial makes it stunningly original and the design is strikingly modern: the steel gnomon is shiny and high-tech; the whole arrangement relies on computer-aided design. Both memorials are impressive in scale; both arrange the chronicle of death in a way that encompasses the individual and the collective aspects of war's losses.

The calendric arrangement of the Kentucky memorial signifies the uniqueness of each name and each death but also the rhythmic passage of the seasons and the hours. The time encompassed by the memorial is cyclic, not historical. The sundial and the configuration of names are intended to evoke the duration of the Vietnam War, although the relationship between the hours of the day and the years is taxing for some visitors to grasp. The names are few in number at the extremities—Kentucky's first two deaths occurred in 1962, and one Kentuckian was killed during the American evacuation in 1975. The names cluster most densely at the noon segment and in the hours at either side, which represent the years 1967 to 1969. In gathering individual names into a formal configuration, the memorial somewhat recalls the Vietnam Veterans Memorial in Washington. Because the names are inscribed on the plaza floor, though, one has the disconcerting experience of stepping on, or around them. This feature did not, however, cause the sort of controversy that might have been expected, after the complaints that in Lin's design the memorial was "hidden" low to the ground. Evidently, the success of the Vietnam Veterans Memorial had made those selecting the memorial more adventurous and less tetchy and doctrinaire, at least after the initial confrontation between the statue and carillon; or perhaps the design committee was relieved to find a design with a high visual impact on which they could all agree. The cumulative force of the names is not as powerful in

Figure 26. Kentucky Vietnam Veterans Memorial, Frankfort, Helm Roberts, designer, dedicated November 12, 1988. Photo by author.

Figure 27. Kentucky Vietnam Veterans Memorial, detail, showing the shadow of the gnomon between the areas designating July 1968 and June 1969, with floral tributes left by visitors. Photo by author.

the Kentucky memorial as it is in Lin's inscribed walls and not just because of the smaller number of names—1,069 from Kentucky, compared with over 58,000 on the Vietnam Veterans Memorial. Even 58,000 would have a lesser impact if they were inscribed flush with the ground.

Radiating around the base of the gnomon are the verses from Ecclesiastes 3:1–8, including the lines, "For everything there is a season . . . a time to kill, a time to heal, . . . a time to cast away stones, a time to gather stones together, a time for war, and a time for peace." On Veterans Day, the shadow passes over an inscription from the Gospel of John: "Greater love has no man than this, that a man lay down his life for a friend." Although the biblical quotations must have pleased Ray, they were not added for his benefit but were part of Roberts's design from the start. Indeed, Roberts did not meet Ray until the day of the dedication in 1988.[117] The Ecclesiastes verses refer to war and peace, and to the process of commemoration through their reference to "gathering stones together" (a Jewish commemorative practice). And though unbeknownst to Roberts, the verses also glance at the counterculture: the pop group the Byrds used them in their hit recording of the Pete Seeger song "Turn, Turn, Turn." The war-era song, however, does not blandly accept that there is a time for everything, including war, but "swear[s]" that it is "not too late" for peace making.

The memorial diverges from the initial conceptions of both Ray and of his opponents on the design committee. Striking and ingenious though the design is, the sundial motif says nothing about war in Southeast Asia, though Ray, in his dedication speech, wrung every possible meaning from the passage of time and the contrast between light and darkness in Vietnam: for example, the way that troops counted down the days of their remaining time in country and the terror of firefights at night.[118] The need for this commentary underlines the deficiency of the memorial design in conveying the message Ray had demanded. The sundial design's openness to interpretation places an added burden of signification on the biblical inscriptions and the other words, spoken and written, that surround the memorial.

At the November 1988 dedication ceremony, the names of the 1,069 Kentuckians lost during the war were read at the site, just as the names were read at the Vietnam Veterans Memorial in Washington during the national salute.[119] Visitors knelt to touch the names of their loved ones and others they recognized.[120] In the first Memorial Day ceremony after the dedication, the names were read at sunset, and one by one, 1,046 candles were extinguished, leaving only 23 candles burning, representing those still listed as missing in action. The Reverend Dean Shiflett, minister of Eastland Christian Church, spoke of the importance of Memorial Day: American citizenship, he said, is more than standing for the national anthem and paying taxes. "We must also," he said, "restore an abiding trust . . . and faith in the greatness of America."[121]

When recited, the names of the dead never speak for themselves but are always glossed by some added meaning. At the dedication, Kentucky governor Wallace Wilkinson said that the shadow touching each name represents "God, touching each of his children in turn."[122] When Ronald Ray spoke at the dedication, he said,

"The question of the meaning of the Vietnam experience will continue to unfold for another generation, but it is important to try to give that experience some meaning today."[123] But Ray had already ensured that his interpretation of the war's meaning would be there for all to see, literally bolted to the entrance to the memorial. In the area through which visitors must pass before climbing some steps up to the memorial, there are several inscribed tablets. The inscriptions, titled "American Involvement, 1954–1975" and co-written by Ray, include these words: "America's Vietnam Veterans, upon returning home from Vietnam, often bore much of the brunt of public frustration and anger. President Ronald Reagan took steps to honor Vietnam Veterans for their service with dedications of the National Vietnam Veterans Memorial in 1983 [sic] and 1984 as a crucial step toward national healing and reconciliation and reminded the Nation that America's participation in the Vietnam War was a 'noble cause.'" In Ray's mind, the inscription ensured that the memorial did not, as others did, "separate the warrior from the war."[124] The "noble cause" idea was cast in durable metal for posterity in at least this one place. Yet even Ray could not resist the overwhelming gush of the "healing" discourse, in the inscription and in other statements. A year after the split that divided the Kentucky memorial fund, he had begun to appreciate the conventional terminology of "healing" and "reconciliation," adopting it as an alternative to the more polemical explanations of the memorial he had previously voiced. At the dedication, Ray said, "This memorial is not about Rambo. This is a reconciliation, a 'coming home.'"[125] Earlier, he had predicted that the Kentucky memorial "will go a long way toward reconciling the divisions and differences over the war, and will heal a lot of old wounds of that war."[126] A year after the dedication, he stated, "Regardless of the debate in this country about Vietnam, it was wrong for the country to have treated its veterans the way they did. This is a way for us to heal."[127] Ray's was, however, a Reaganite version of "healing," signaled by his statement, "President Reagan has been a leader in the effort to honor [Vietnam veterans] in their service as a crucial step toward national healing and reconciliation." For Ray "healing" was not the product of a sentimental and depoliticized sympathy for veterans but resulted from the recognition that those who fought in Vietnam undertook "public service of the highest order."[128]

By the time the memorial was dedicated, much had changed in Washington politics. In October 1986, the administration finally managed to restore aid to the *contras*, with Congress's passage of a $100 million aid package. Nevertheless, the Reagan administration did not have things all its own way in Central America policy. William LeoGrande has described Reagan's two-year campaign to win support for the *contras* after passage of the second Boland amendment, Boland II, as "the most visible and controversial manifestation of the Reagan Doctrine" and an effort to return to the pre–Vietnam War era of congressional-executive relations, when Congress acted as a rubber stamp on the president's foreign policy. He adds, "Reagan was still intent upon exorcising the Vietnam syndrome from the national psyche."[129] But despite the restoration of *contra* aid, Reagan's congressional opponents had not acquiesced, and they were still ready for battle. Although Reagan had been re-elected by a landslide in 1984, the Democrats took control of the Senate in the November 1986 mid-term elections. Now, for the first time during Reagan's presidency, they controlled both houses of Congress.

Soon after the mid-terms, news broke about the illegal *contra* aid operation run by Oliver North of the National Security Council's staff in the period when Congress had banned such assistance. Within a few weeks, Reagan appointed a special review board to examine the illegal arms dealing; the Justice Department appointed a special prosecutor to investigate a possible criminal case. In January 1987, the House and Senate created a committee to conduct their own investigation. The committee's final report found that Reagan's foreign policy apparatus was guilty of "secrecy, deception, and disdain for the rule of law." Reagan himself had created or tolerated an environment in which National Security Council staff believed that they were fulfilling his wishes when they diverted funds to the *contras* in defiance of Boland II. In failing to cultivate in his staff respect for the Constitution and the law, he had failed to discharge his oath of office. Later, even worse came to light: Reagan had ordered military support to the *contras* despite Boland II, had promised the president of Honduras military and economic aid in return for permission for the *contras* to remain in that country, and had participated in private fundraising for the *contras*—so he himself was guilty of illegal acts, not simply tolerant of the actions of his subordinates.[130] But the findings of the Iran–Contra committee were just as damaging, because they made it appear that Reagan was, at best, out of touch with what his aides were doing, and his government out of control.

When the Kentucky memorial was dedicated, the wide world outside Washington was also changing, and Ray's commitment to fighting the Soviet "slave system" might have begun to seem less urgent. In March 1988, a peace agreement among the Central American countries was concluded after negotiations that had dragged on for years. The *contras* won a general amnesty and an agreement that they could incorporate themselves into the political life of Nicaragua. In February 1990, with the world transformed by the fall of the Berlin Wall, the Sandinistas peacefully gave up power when Violeta Chamorro was elected president of Nicaragua. In July 1991, the Soviet Union–led military alliance, the Warsaw Pact, broke up. In December 1991, the heads of three of the Soviet Union's constituent republics, led by Russia's Boris Yeltsin, met in a secluded hunting lodge in the Belovezh forest near Minsk and signed documents that dissolved the Soviet Union.[131] The United States' superpower enemy was no more, the cold war ending in the victory that Reagan's policy of "roll-back" had augured.

By then, the public's historical knowledge of the Vietnam War was also beginning to fade. Only two-thirds of a March 1990 national poll sample recalled that the United States was fighting on the side of South Vietnam. Irrespective of the shakiness of the public's knowledge of this basic fact, the Vietnam syndrome appeared to be alive and well in the public's inflated sense of the costs of Vietnam compared with other American wars: a plurality believed that more Americans lost their lives in Vietnam than in any other war.[132] This overestimation of the casualty figures reveals that much of the public still had an amorphous view that the Vietnam War was terrible in its destructiveness.

Powerful voices attempted to fill any void in recollection with their own ideo-logically laden interpretations of the war. Shortly before the collapse of the Soviet Union, Reagan said, "Those Americans who went to Vietnam fought for freedom, a truly noble cause. . . . Vietnam was not so much a war as it was one long battle in an ongoing war—the war in defense of freedom, which is still under assault." What this proposition meant was that the outcome of the fight was still undecided: Vietnam veterans might ultimately partake of victory in a larger war in which theirs, as Reagan said, was just one battle. Some old soldiers, though, were impatient, want-ing to declare victory—or at least deny defeat—despite the disagreeable and as yet intractable facts of history. At the dedication ceremony of the California Vietnam Veterans Memorial on December 10, 1988, General George Price said, "Read my lips. We did not lose a war in Vietnam. . . . We did precisely what the American people asked us to do and that's to represent them on the far shores away from our homes carrying the American flag and we brought it back untainted. . . . We did not lose that war."[133]

The world-historical victory of capitalism gave a geopolitical justification for such thinking, which until then had appeared wishful thinking or outright delusion. In the May 1992 pre–Memorial Day commemoration at the Kentucky memorial, one of the speakers argued that those who fought in the Vietnam War were not defeated but were part of an eventually victorious campaign, the cold war. Thus, they contributed to the fall of the Berlin Wall and the collapse of the Soviet Union.[134] The speech gratified Vietnam veterans in the audience by identifying them as "winners," while the memorial hallowed the speaker's words with the memory of those who fell. "Healing" from the war might now come from feel-good invocations of victory—without any requirement to "reconcile" with lonely hold-outs who still thought the Vietnam War a waste and the cold war propaganda that justified it lies.

The collapse of the Berlin Wall ushered in a period of cold war triumphalism at the Vietnam Veterans Memorial in Washington, too. On November 11, 1989, at the Veterans Day ceremony at the memorial, Senator John Warner linked the concept of healing with victory. The memorial, he said, "conveys the message that victory is ours—not the traditional military victory, but a nation approaching victory with itself . . . a nation healing." Warner did not confine himself, though, to considering America's triumph over its internal demons. This spiritual "victory" had an extra fillip because it correlated with the United States' success in the half-century struggle against the Soviet Union. Just two days earlier, the border between East and West Germany was effectively opened. Along with the democratic changes that had swept through the Soviet Union's Warsaw Pact allies that year, this event heralded the collapse of Communism in eastern Europe. Speaking in front of Maya Lin's wall, Warner remarked, "There is another wall," the Berlin Wall. "And that wall, as we speak, is crumbling down." By extension, Warner referred to the "iron curtain" that Winston Churchill described forty years earlier. "It falls," he said, "because its foundation of communist suppression is being exposed to truth and democracy."[135]

Speaking on the same day at the dedication of the Texas Vietnam Veterans Memorial in Dallas, President George H. W. Bush welcomed the opportunity to voice the same sort of triumphalism. "Look to the very heart of Europe," he said, "to Berlin, and you will see a great truth shining brighter with each passing day: The quest for freedom is stronger than steel, more permanent than concrete." Because of those who had made the ultimate sacrifice in Vietnam as in the United States' other wars, "the peaceful ideals of America are now the ideals of the world." Bush pointed out that half of the visitors to America's Vietnam memorials were children of twelve years and younger, and he responded to the questions that those children might have: Who fought in Vietnam? (His answer: black and white, red and brown Americans, native born, foreign born, the privileged and the poor.) What did they value? (Freedom, dignity and a love of country.) How do we salute them? (By remembering that true peace means the triumph of freedom, and by building memorials that remind us of the troops' selflessness and sacrifice.) America's "brave boys who went to Vietnam had to endure two wars," Bush said, one in the swamps and jungles abroad, and the second for respect and recognition at home. "And with the passage of time, they have won the battle for the hearts of their countrymen—and in my view, it's about time."[136]

In his 1992 State of the Union Address, President Bush inducted Vietnam veterans into the nation's "roll call of honor." "By the grace of God," he said, "America won the cold war. . . . And I think of those who won it, in places like Korea and Vietnam. And some of them didn't come back. Back then they were heroes, but this year they were victors."[137] Winning the cold war changed everything; now the defeat in Vietnam sublated into ultimate victory. Following Bush, at the 1992 Veterans Day ceremony at the Vietnam Veterans Memorial in Washington, Major General Edward Baca of the New Mexico National Guard explained Vietnam's wider significance in the light of the fall of the Berlin Wall and the collapse of the Soviet Union. He too vindicated the war and those who fought it: Vietnam, he said, should no longer be considered a defeat, but as one battle in the United States' ultimate victory in the cold war. America's unblemished record of victories could thus be reconstituted, and Vietnam veterans allowed to take their place proudly alongside the veterans of other wars. The audience applauded, proud to snatch victory at last from the jaws of history.[138] Rather than protesting that this revisionist history was an improper intrusion on the memorial's "apolitical" character, Jan Scruggs published an almost identical argument by Harry Summers in a book of reflections on the memorial: "At the grand strategic level Vietnam was part of the larger struggle between communism and democracy. When Saigon fell, it was seen as a plus for communism and a loss for democracy and the United States. But Vietnam was just a battle in a much larger war, and the final victory of that war is now at hand."[139]

The outcome of the cold war thus provided a powerful interpretive frame in which to produce a positive gloss on the outcome of the Vietnam War; a far greater challenge was to make people feel good about the Vietnam War in itself. In Kentucky, a journalist wrote an article featuring the relatives of several of Kentucky's dead, who had all been killed on the article's publication date, May 28. Sergeant George Nelson Walker went to Vietnam willingly—he did not have to go because a medical exemption could have kept him out of the war. "If I've got to fight communists," he reasoned, "I'd rather fight them there than here." He was killed in Vietnam's Central Highlands on May 28, 1968, shot through the head by a sniper. The day after his wife learned of his death, his last two letters home arrived together. She kept these last two emblems of his life, burning all the others he had sent. In the letters, he was counting down the days until he could come home. "If I had to do it over again," he wrote, "I don't believe I'd be so quick to go." His daughter was eight years old when he went to Vietnam. In 1989, she told the journalist, "Really and truly, I think that it was a good life wasted. I think he went for a good and just reason, but I don't think we gained anything in Vietnam." A friend of Bobby Berning's, another Kentuckian who died in Vietnam on the same day of the month, two years later, said, "I feel that he died in vain. I really do. I can't see where we came out ahead in that war."[140]

The sister-in-law of Charles Ward, another Kentuckian, killed by a landmine, said, "He died for nothing." Her husband, Joe, Charles Ward's brother, said that the government lied in its propaganda that Americans needed to fight Communists over there so as not to fight them on their own doorstep. The American public, he said, is gullible. Lest we imagine that this sentiment was inspired by pacifism, Joe Ward Jr. went on to say that the United States could have won the war had it invaded Cambodia, Laos, or North Vietnam. "But they put a collar on us."[141] As described in Chapter 1, disenchantment with the war arose as often from frustration at the restraints on the conduct of the war as from the notion that the war was fundamentally mistaken in its aims. Yet, whatever its sources and implications, all such thinking that the war was wrong, the U.S. losses a waste of life, had to be overcome if the nation was to "heal."

In a four-day period in May 1992, I observed and interviewed visitors to the Kentucky memorial. Except during the Saturday ceremony coinciding with a local gathering of veterans, visitation was spotty—there were rarely more than one or two groups of visitors at the same time, and for long stretches of time the memorial was deserted. Five of the fourteen with whom I conducted a face-to-face questionnaire survey knew someone whose name was inscribed on the paving. All but one were first-time visitors and only one had come to Frankfort specifically to visit the memorial. Although the low visitation rate suggests that the memorial has a limited appeal to the public, almost all of those who visited said they believed it is an effective memorial to the Vietnam War and several explained this by saying that the arrangement of names treats the dead as unique individuals.[142]

The visitors said they thought that American servicemen were less responsible for defeat in Vietnam than other groups were, such as political and military leaders. Their positive view of Vietnam veterans was consistent with national poll data, which showed that the public viewed Vietnam veterans more favorably than any other group or individual closely associated with the Vietnam War.[143] The lessons that several of the visitors drew from the war included the idea that, if one enters a war, one should fight to win. One, a thirty-six-year-old man, said, "If we're going

to ask our people to die for a cause, the armed forces need total and complete support." All were concerned, though, about the costs of war and some were loath to
trust America's leaders. A forty-six-year-old dentist said that the main lesson of the
war is that the executive branch of the American government "should be more
forthcoming and honest with the American people." He disagreed strongly with the
statement that the Vietnam War was a noble cause that should have been won. He
thought that the war was wrong and immoral. A fifty-three-year-old woman said
that "it was a mistake to go over there for a twenty-year war . . . . Something was
wrong with our leadership." A twenty-one-year-old man employed as a school bus
driver said that the main lesson of the Vietnam War is: "Try to avoid war if [we]
can." The majority of my interviewees—ten of the fourteen—agreed with Ray that
the Vietnam War was a "noble cause." But the variability of their other thoughts
demonstrates that people's beliefs, arising from a complex of attitudes, ideas, and
emotions, cannot be extrapolated from a political slogan, no matter how often they
hear it or how strongly they believe it.[144]

Ray's clear ideological agenda, his institutionally empowered positions in politics
and veterans' organizations, and his leadership of the effort to create a Kentucky
Vietnam Veterans Memorial seem at first to consist with the view that the powerful
shape commemoration, imposing their visions of the past onto ordinary people. But
Ray's limited success in dictating the monument's form demonstrates some of the
things that mitigate the control of the powerful over interpretations of the past. In
Kentucky, institutional processes introduced checks and balances on Ray's power
of decision. Ray did succeed in vetoing a design concept of which he disapproved
and in ensuring that a militant inscription greets visitors to the memorial. But the
variability of visitors' responses demonstrates another check on the agendas of the
powerful. People bring their own meanings to memorials. The one in Kentucky
reinforces a reverential attitude to the dead; but it does not impose a single meaning on their deaths. Some come away from the memorial refreshed and ready to
fight totalitarianism or America's latest enemy; but other visitors come away with
their doubts about entering new wars reinforced. The experience of visiting the
memorial can shade, reinforce, or inflect the visitor's existing ideas, but it does not
control them.

The Kentucky memorial exemplifies the complex process through which a hegemonic view of the past is constructed and resisted. The design process of the
Kentucky memorial inverts the narrative of the memorial in Washington; and yet the
language surrounding the two commemorative efforts converged. In Washington,
the wish to have the memorial embrace all sectors of a divided public led the VVMF
to declare that they would achieve political neutrality by "separating the warrior
from the war." But ideologically committed veterans demanded a statement of
pride and nobility instead, and although they did not get quite what they wanted,
they managed at least to add a three-person bronze statue. In Kentucky, the same
journey was taken, but in reverse. Ray, an ally and colleague of the VVMF's critic
Webb, started off demanding an ideologically assertive memorial in the shape of a

three-figure statue. In the end, he got something rather different, and in the process of transformation, the VVMF's discourse of "healing" increasingly insinuated itself into discussions of the memorial's purposes. The Kentucky memorial thus confirms the importance of "healing" as the core concept of post–Vietnam War commemoration, concentrating within itself meanings such as emotional recovery, national comity, and, with a Reaganite spin, the restoration of military strength.

9

"TODAY, WE ARE ONE PEOPLE"

The Family Drama of Race and Gender in Commemorative
Statuary of the Vietnam War

✦

HEALING, as advanced by the VVMF and other memorial planners in the 1980s, was an all-embracing response to a multifaceted phenomenon: the Vietnam "wound," "trauma," and "syndrome" that encompassed individual veterans' psychological experiences and national divisions and uncertainty. These twin concepts of wounds and healing materialized in a striking number of sculptural memorials to the Vietnam War. Although the most obvious figurative representations of a war might seem to be combat scenes, statues of Americans pointing their weapons do not predominate in Vietnam War memorials. True, some memorials show infantry troops in action. For example, the statue in Nashville, Tennessee, discussed in the preceding chapter, depicts a trio of veterans, one of whom is using a radio-telephone, map and weapon in hand, while the other two, holding an M-16 rifle and a grenade launcher, stand guard. This type of sculpture, however, is not the most common. Combat or post-combat scenes usually show the results of the fighting in the form of American casualties. Some statues show Americans holding up the limp bodies of dead comrades—variants of the pose that Tom Carhart suggested for the Vietnam Veterans Memorial in Washington, DC.[1] Others show Americans in uniform ministering to their comrades' wounds—wounds that motivate the love and care of fellow soldiers and nurses. In these depictions, Americans are not the agents of violence but its victims. The war is rendered in the passive voice. The Vietnam War is not something we did; it is something that happened to us and that did things to us. Vietnam made us bleed and suffer.[2]

The multifigure groups in these commemorative statues attempt demographic inclusiveness. One way of seeing them is as responses to the norms of a multicultural society, in which the condensation of the nation into a single white, male figure would not do. Although this consideration certainly played a part in decisions leading to the adoption of multifigure statuary groups, the results have a broader symbolism. Gender and race become vehicles for depictions of social solidarity. These statuary groups do not celebrate pluralism but rather imagine the nation as a united family in which racial and gender differences heighten the transcendent fidelity of citizens for one another. By showing how the fellow feeling of uniformed personnel transcends these markers of social distinction, the memorial sculptures provide a template for societal reconciliation and healing. The reconciliation they dramatize is, however, deceptive because it does not address the most intractable postwar "wound," the nation's persistent political divisions.

The vast majority of these sculptural works have been ignored by scholarship or have attracted only passing attention.[3] Commemorative statuary of the Vietnam War sustains the approaches to commemoration already evident in the Vietnam Veterans Memorial—a politically interested evasion of politics and strategy, a sentimental concentration on the travails of veterans, a focus on American casualties, and an emphasis on the concept of healing. Two of these approaches—a concentration on veterans and attention to the dead—although apparently at odds, were both adapted to secure public sympathy for those who fought and, by doing this, to disarm political critiques of the war.

Frederick Hart tried to make as lifelike a depiction of American troops in the field as he could in his addition to the Vietnam Veterans Memorial, to the extent that he interviewed veterans to find out how they used and wore their equipment. This effort resulted in telling details, such as the towel loosely draped around the neck of the African American figure, the dog tag strung through the laces of one man's boots, and the bottle of insect repellent stuck in another man's hat band. These features lend the statue the ring of truth for those who served in Vietnam.[4] As described in Chapter 4, Hart also copied items of clothing that veterans had brought back with them from the field, adding to the statue's verisimilitude. Hart's close attention to the specifics of the soldiers' faces, uniforms, and equipment, however, had an unfortunate and unintended result: it brought home the absence of the many groups who are not represented in the statue.

The three subjects of Hart's statue are male infantry troops, not nurses, tank crews, gunners, engineers, supply troops, military police, airmen, or naval personnel. Members of the non-infantry branches—all of which had lost people in Vietnam, whose names are recorded on Maya Lin's wall—consequently complained that they were left out of the statue.[5] One veteran maintained an unrelenting campaign for the creation of a memorial to the canine corps in Vietnam, lobbying for the addition of a dog sculpture to the national memorial. "Ideally," he said, "there will one day be a full-scale dog, out in front of the three soldiers, alerting toward the wall."[6]

In Hart's first maquette, or sculptural model, the central figure in the trio was black, but Hart soon changed the design by shifting the African American figure to the right to avoid giving the appearance that he was the group's leader. Instead Hart placed a white man with a side arm, signifying officer status (or the role of medic), at the center of the group.[7] This unreported change was the silent overture to a sustained period of wrangling about the ethnic roles the statue depicted. Latino veterans who saw the new maquette of the Hart design complained that the memorial contained one African American and two white troops but that none looked Hispanic (fig. 28). One veterans' group made a formal protest about this absence and threatened litigation.[8] Steve Padilla, the editor of *Hispanic Link*, a Washington, DC, weekly, pointed out that about 20 percent of the casualties in Vietnam were Hispanic, a disproportionate share compared to the nation's Hispanic population. Ralph Villa, executive director of the Mexican-American Veterans Association, said that although Hispanics received more Medals of Honor and other combat decorations than any other identifiable ethnic group, the statue "clearly ignore[d] Hispanic interests."[9] In response to such complaints, the memorial fund decided that the figure on the left, holding an M-60 machine-gun, should be changed to depict a Latino. But what did a typical Latino look like? The memorial fund solicited suggestions from those who had complained, and some correspondents obligingly sent in drawings and photographs. Hart modified the facial features of the figure on the left to portray a Latino.[10] The model for the original figure had been Hart's assistant, a broad-faced young man of northern European heritage (but who some thought looked Irish). Hart based the new face on that of a twenty-four-year-old Maryland man "of Hispanic descent" chosen for "the youth in his face" (fig. 29).[11]

This change merely set off more complaints. Now Native Americans and Asian Americans argued that they, too, should have been included in the statue.[12] An Indian union activist from Saginaw, Michigan, demanded, "Change that statue or else!"[13] Jan Scruggs responded by declaring that the Latino figure would henceforth be considered a representative of all minorities other than African Americans.[14] He could be "Jewish, Lebanese, Indian," Hart said.[15] The Department of the Interior chimed in that Hart "used Black, Caucasian, and Hispanic models to suggest the diversity of the combatants. It was, of course, not possible to represent each and every origin or race in the three piece sculptural grouping."[16] This response merely restated the problem the minorities and others complained of; it did not, however, resolve it. Minorities continued to demand specific references to their service—Native Americans, for example, demanded a plaque to recognize their heroics and sacrifices in Vietnam. In 1995, in response to Native American veterans' demands for recognition, the National Native American Vietnam Veterans Memorial, a statue showing a figure holding a rifle in one hand and an eagle-feather staff in the other, was added to *The Highground*, the Wisconsin Vietnam Veterans Memorial. Inscribed around the base are the names of all the Native Americans who died in military service in Vietnam.[17]

Apart from the Native American memorial in Wisconsin, ten single-figure sculptural memorials representing American men who served in the Vietnam War exist in the United States and all but two of these depict whites. The two exceptions illustrate the discomfort that some felt about ignoring the ethnic diversity of the American forces in Vietnam. One of them is the Arkansas Vietnam Veterans Memorial, the sole statue sponsored by the Vietnam Veterans Leadership Program (VVLP) that features a single figure (see fig. 23). A legislator who sponsored the monument said, "Who is this young man? . . . Let me tell you what we know about him. He is black. He is Hispanic. He is an Indian. He is white. He is an Arkansan." The single-figure memorial thus tries to be an "Everyman" that represents all ethnicities. The

Figure 28. Frederick Hart, maquette for *Three Infantrymen*, Vietnam Veterans Memorial, Washington, DC. The facial features of the figure on the left were changed in the final version of the maquette and statue. Photo by Darrell Acree.

Figure 29. *Three Infantrymen*, Vietnam Veterans Memorial, Washington, DC. The facial features of the figure on the left were "Hispanicized" after complaints that the statue ignored Latinos; the facial expression of the African American figure was softened to make him appear less "angry." Photo by author.

only other statue that attempts this feat is the Berkshire County Vietnam Veterans Memorial in Reading, Pennsylvania. Here the sculptor, Tony Giuffreda, made the statue's facial features indistinct and obscured the rank and service insignia on the uniform so that the figure could represent a serviceman of any ethnicity, from any military service—even, Giuffreda suggested, a nurse, although the statue appears to be male.[18] The unconvincing awkwardness of such attempts to condense the diversity of U.S. service personnel into a single figure dictated that most sculptural memorials are instead multifigure groups.

Most statuary designs chosen in the aftermath of the debates about the Hart statue include an obligatory African American in a group of two to four figures, although a Vietnam Veterans Memorial planned for Texas's state capitol includes five figures "to reflect the racial diversity of Texas' culture."[19] The vast majority of the figures in these statues are infantry troops. Memorials that feature several engraved scenes rather than a single statuary group captured in a plausible wartime moment are able to expand the range of representation: in the Philadelphia Vietnam Veterans Memorial pictures of eight war scenes are inscribed on a memorial wall, depicting blacks and whites, men and women, and members of several branches of service; similarly, in the South Carolina Vietnam Veterans Memorial several scenes are inscribed on the faces of a square column depicting personnel from different service branches.

The modal subtype of the sculptures—preponderant in the sense that they outnumber any other identifiable type—shows GIs caring for wounded soldiers or grieving for dead comrades in arms. In San Antonio, Texas, a radio operator tries vainly to save a mortally wounded man. In Phoenix, Arizona, foot soldiers protect an injured squad member. In New Orleans and Raleigh, North Carolina, infantry troops carry a casualty to safety. In rural Moshannon, Pennsylvania, among the bas-reliefs of several marines is a team of stretcher bearers carrying a wounded comrade.[20] In Auburn, California, and New Castle County, Delaware, soldiers hold up the limp bodies of dead GIs. In Glens Falls, New York, a soldier engraved in black granite prays over a field of headstones of fallen friends. In Missoula, Montana, a winged angel bears a dead soldier aloft.[21]

Such scenes, which direct the attention of viewers to the casualties Americans suffered, constitute the majority of the multi-figure memorials in states and localities. But they do not exhaust the proposals for similar statues. The sculptor Michael Chavez suggested that a sculptural Vietnam memorial be erected in the National Cemetery, Santa Fe, showing four men carrying a wounded comrade from the battlefield. Jim Lykins asked veterans to consider adopting *Sky Pilot*, his sculpture showing a soldier comforting his dying friend while a chaplain reads the last rites, as the Vietnam Veterans Memorial in West Virginia. A memorial design proposed for the University of Kansas showed two soldiers supporting a wounded buddy by the arms. One of the finalists in the design competition for the Maine Vietnam Veterans Memorial was a sculpture depicting a soldier kneeling over a wounded man while a standing figure gestures to the sky, presumably calling in a medevac helicopter. Of the 1,421 entries submitted to the design competition for the national Vietnam

Veterans Memorial, 39 depict dead and wounded Americans, far outnumbering the competition entries in which American troops are shown in combat poses.[22] The number of imagined scenes of death and injury is all the more striking because the guidelines issued to entrants to the national design competition did nothing to prompt designs of this sort. (The requirement that the memorial name all the dead does not, after all, dictate that it show a casualty.) Nor was there any such cue in the design parameters of memorials elsewhere. Such vivid representations of death and injury have a symbolic significance extending beyond their literal depiction of battle casualties. They transform death and grief, wounds and care, into moral categories animating the drama of the soldiers' sacrifices and the veterans' suffering.

Statues of hurt GIs being cared for by their comrades sustain in material form the discourse of the healing of a nation divided by war.[23] The memorials undertake this task directly, through their representation of care and comradeship, and indirectly, through what they conceal. The most obvious conflicts—the war itself and the polemics about the war—are not represented directly. Most of the sculptures do not show Americans actively fighting even an implied, off-stage enemy. Apart from rare exceptions, such as the VVLP-supported state memorials in Tennessee and Kentucky, we do not see assertions of the rightness of the war that would signal an ideological difference of views between the war's supporters and opponents. Instead of a rhetoric of conflict, these memorials use a subtler armory: the language of sentiment, articulating themes of recovery and reconciliation.

Take, for example, the Vietnam Veterans Memorial in Phoenix, Arizona (fig. 30). In this sculpture by Jasper d'Ambrosi, a soldier slumps wounded, perhaps dying. A kneeling soldier supports the casualty's head, while a third man tries to pull the caregiver away. The urgency of the standing figure's effort indicates that danger remains present, but the kneeling man is oblivious to it or feels compelled to stay with his wounded friend, whatever the risk to his own life. As Hart did in Washington, d'Ambrosi uses a polychrome patina, so that the figures' flesh tones contrast with their weapons and uniforms. Their arms and equipment are rendered with scrupulous detail, showing that all three are armed with grenades. The two active figures hold M-16 rifles, although they are unprepared for combat—each holds his weapon by its hand guard, his hands far from the pistol grip and trigger. Black granite slabs inscribed with the names of Arizona's dead surround the sculpture, so that the battle scene reinforces the memorial's emphasis on the fallen. The violence that Americans meted out is obliterated by the exclusive attention to the suffering they endured and the anguish of those who tried, perhaps vainly, to save their friends.

The casualty in d'Ambrosi's sculpture has no visible injury. Fragmentation grenades, mines, artillery, and bullets caused horrific wounds. Bullets from automatic rifles tumbled when they hit their targets, to carve up tender bodies, and sometimes fragmented, leaving gaping exit wounds. Some antipersonnel mines had mechanisms that made them spring in the air to disembowel their victims. Flying shrapnel from shells and rockets could scythe a man in half. Yet most of the wounded GIs in Vietnam War statuary are oddly whole—they suffer and die decorously, without so much as a tiny bullet hole. The commemorative statuary of the Vietnam War does

Figure 30. Arizona Vietnam Veterans Memorial, Phoenix; Jasper D'Ambrosi, sculptor, dedicated November 9, 1985. Photo by Ted Engelmann.

not shock the viewer by showing a casualty with his guts exposed. The viewer's attention is less on the ghastly physicality of death in war than on the emotions of the troops. The drama derives from the proximity of their faces, the attitudes of hands and arms, the love with which a man cradles a dying friend.

The statues showing serious injuries—the ones in Sacramento and Marin County, California, that represent amputees—depict wounded, not dead or dying men. They draw attention to the dreadful injuries with which some men returned from Vietnam. Speedy evacuation from the battlefield and the high survival rate of those who reached evacuation hospitals meant that casualties lived with the sort of grievous wounds from which most would have bled to death in previous wars. The few statues that graphically depict severe wounds do not contemplate the injured men's mortality but highlight the suffering of those who survived.

Sculptors do not have to depict physical wounds, though, to convey a sense of injury. In the Cincinnati, Ohio, Vietnam Veterans Memorial (fig. 31), two soldiers, one black, one white, stand in a desultory pose, one with his rifle slung over his shoulder, the other steadying his weapon, its stock grounded, with a hand on its barrel. In this sculpture, the troops are hesitant, not ready for combat. One touches the other on the shoulder in a consoling gesture, implying a state of emotional distress. The sculptor's concept was that one soldier was comforting another for the death of an unseen friend over whom they kept vigil. An implied casualty's absent presence is also felt in the Utah and South Dakota Vietnam Veterans Memorials. In Salt Lake City, a larger-than-life figure slogs through a paddy field carrying his own weapon in his right hand, but with another rifle slung over his shoulder, suggestive of a fallen comrade. In the most recently dedicated state memorial, in Pierre, South Dakota, a single helmeted figure—laden with equipment, and with a towel and a bandolier of bullets around his neck—holds an M-16 rifle in one hand and the dog tags of a fallen comrade in the other.[24]

Rodger Brodin's *Monument to the Living* was dedicated in 1982, before the Hart statue had made multifigure groups the norm. It is a solitary, twelve-foot-high uniformed figure weighed down by a bandolier of bullets and festooned with grenades. The soldier, stationed near the Veterans Service Building in St. Paul, Minnesota, stares at visitors, his arms by his sides and his hands turned outward toward the viewer, in a gesture that conveys bafflement. Like the Cincinnati sculpture, this one focuses on the emotions of the survivor, rather than on the ones who died. The artist describes the figure: "He is young, so very young . . . but feeling older every day. Returning from a war he did not understand, he finds there are no answers, only questions. Where is the hero's welcome? Why do people look past me, as though they don't want to be reminded of this war I can't forget? Why have they forgotten us?" In the sculptor's words, this is a memorial dedicated to those who fought and returned, which "reminds us that not all heroes worth remembering are dead."[25]

Even when a statue shows a dead soldier, the scene's emotional drama often centers on the living. If one member of a sculptural grouping is dead or unconscious, the locus of psychological interest shifts to the attendant in the scene, who stands in for and cues the audience's responses. If we imagine that the injured man succumbed to his wounds, the survivor carries the emotional burden of this death into the present—the moment that a visitor views the statue. While viewers are prompted to grieve for the dead, they are also drawn into emotional sympathy with the survivor. The image of a dead soldier, a despairing friend at his side, or a wounded man being treated by a buddy does not have a single determined meaning. It might prompt pride in the courage and determination of those who fell, or questions about whether the casualties were necessary.

Figure 31. Greater Cincinnati Vietnam Veterans Memorial; Ken Bradford, designer, Eleftherios Karkadoulias, sculptor, dedicated April 8, 1984. Photo by author.

The statuary depicting wounded Americans refers to the over three hundred thousand Americans who were wounded in Vietnam but also conveys a sense of emotional injury: the lost innocence of those who went to Vietnam believing that they were defending another nation against aggression; the betrayed hopes of those who expected appreciation from their fellow citizens. Statues of dead or injured troops are also a commentary on the outcome of the war. Just as a depiction of a moment of victory—the raising of the U.S. flag on Iwo Jima's Mount Suribachi, for example—captures the pride and triumph of a war in which the United States was on the winning side, so a scene of death or injury might seem an apt depiction of defeat. Portrayals of GIs helping one another also declare the loyalty of servicemen to one another in the face of their common dangers and shared hurts. This offers the one saving grace of the war to many who fought it, and the one idea—other than the strained "cold war victory" narrative—that can plausibly, in retrospect, redeem their service; but depictions of comradeship and mutual loyalty throw into relief the nation's lack of care for its returning troops. As much as Brodin's *Monument to the Living*, the scenes of wounding take up the veterans' plaintive demand for compassion.

Scenes of death and injury reverberate with a tradition, both plaintive and reverential, in Western visual arts. Many of the memorials showing dead or wounded Americans conform to the design of the Pietà, the genre of religious art showing the Virgin Mary mourning over the body of the dead Christ, or the Lamentation, where mourners grieve over his mortal remains. The Vietnam veterans memorial in New Castle County, Delaware, shows a limp figure borne up by a standing soldier (fig. 32).[26] The standing figure holds himself with dignity, his feet sturdily planted, his head cast down toward the viewer, his face softened by grief. He does not thrust the dead man toward the viewer in a gesture of resentment and defiance but cradles him against his own body. The dead man's bodily comportment recalls the figure of the dead Christ in European Renaissance art.

The casualty is stripped to the waist. This semi-nudity is "dramatized . . . as an active withdrawal of garments," the soldier's finely modeled ribs further announcing his kinship with the Christ of Renaissance sculptors and painters.[27] Other modern military-related sculptures strip the clothing from casualties. In the 1959 Red Cross Memorial sculpture in Washington, DC, created by Felix de Weldon, the casualty being lifted by two men and a woman—in a latter-day Deposition or removal from the Cross—has bare feet and part of his tunic is torn off, emphasizing the vulnerability of the human form and the kinship of the wounded man to Christ (fig. 33). In the Albany (New York) Vietnam Veterans Memorial, too, a dead or dying soldier, naked to the waist, droops away from a soldier dressed in a flak jacket holding him by the hips (fig. 34). In the New Castle County memorial, the casualty's lolling head and loosely hanging arm demonstrate the artist's mastery of anatomy as well as his knowledge of an artistic tradition. The dead man is not so much an American individual as an intermediary *type*, drawing together the patriotic lore of the twentieth century and the religious iconography of an earlier age.

This soldier's death might be hallowed as a sacrifice. In the Renaissance Pietà, death on the cross brings Christ's mortal life to its end but does not end his immortal divinity; his sacrifice wins the promise of redemption for humankind. In military

Figure 32. New Castle County Vietnam Veterans Memorial, Wilmington, Delaware; Charles Parks, sculptor, dedicated November 11, 1983. Photo by author.

monuments' secular version of the Lamentation or the Pietà, the eternal values that transcend the death of individuals are those of nationhood and devotion to service and to a cause.[28] If a memorial succeeds in evoking pride as well as grief, the patriotic narrative and the sacrificial loss dignify each other. The dead soldier's vitality is not lost but flows into the lifeblood of the nation, sustaining, strengthening, and renewing it. Born of violent revolution, the United States re-enacts this painful birth with the wartime sacrifice of each of its children. As Thomas Jefferson once imagined, the nation is conceived anew at each generation, washed in the blood of patriots and tyrants.

Wartime deaths are intolerable if, however, they lack a commensurate meaning and purpose. Works that refer to the Pietà and Lamentation in an ironic way, or whose viewers are not moved to feel that the sacrifice had some purpose, might provoke despair. An ironic reference to the Pietà would point to the *absence* of a transcendent purpose on which the notion of sacrifice is premised. If young men's bodies are simply consumed by a war that is not deemed vital to the nation, the cycle of renewal is interrupted and the bond between the nation and its citizens is betrayed. Memorials that borrow from the Pietà genre but refuse or withhold compensation for the war's losses convey only the desperate finality of death. If the destruction of a life served no patriotic purpose, it cannot be thought a *sacrifice* and instead remains simply the waste of a unique and irrecoverable individual. Pietà-like memorials to the Vietnam War that try to glorify the death of America's children risk tipping from straightforward to ironic evocations of that genre.

Figure 33. Red Cross Memorial, Washington, DC; Felix de Weldon, sculptor, dedicated 1959. Photo by author.

Figure 34. Albany, New York, Vietnam Veterans Memorial; Merlin Szasz, sculptor, dedicated May 27, 1991. Photo by author.

To understand the importance of contextual elements in Pietà-like statues, we have only to compare the New Castle County memorial with the statue in Auburn, California, discussed in the introduction (see fig. 3). Despite the similarities in the poses of the two figures in both statues, the two memorials could hardly be more different in their contextual elements. The New Castle County memorial towers above the viewer on a broad, elevated brick mound decorated with the insignia of America's military services. This pedestal is inscribed with the names of 166 Delaware residents who died in Vietnam and partly encircled with the legend, "New Castle County Honors the Delawareans Who Served in Vietnam." Before the memorial an inscribed plinth carries the speech made by Senator Joseph Biden (D., Delaware) during the memorial's 1983 dedication. The words were read into the *Congressional Record* and then engraved, with the typeface and format of the publication preserved, onto a plaque. The Stars and Stripes, the state flag, and the POW/MIA (prisoner of war/missing in action) flag fly at the edge of the paved circle that contains the memorial. With signifiers of the nation, the state, the armed services, institutions of government, and ideologically inflected causes fluttering nearby and beckoning the audience, the memorial is surrounded by elements that endow the death with patriotic meaning.

In contrast, the Auburn memorial's inscription, the single word "Why," threatens the designation of the death as patriotic sacrifice. The fact that some saw the inscription as subversive, whatever the disclaimers of the sculptor, is evident in the controversy about the Auburn memorial that resurfaced in 1991, in the context of the 1990–91 Gulf War. A local woman suggested that the now extinguished "eternal" flame be relighted in honor of the troops fighting in the Persian Gulf. The proposal ignited the arguments left over from 1970. Although the proposed lighting of the flame was intended to honor the troops, the fact that the memorial had long been associated with antiwar sentiments might, some county supervisors feared, give residents the wrong impression. They were afraid that local people might think the supervisors were endorsing an antiwar statement. Once again, there were proposals to remove the monument to Auburn Memorial Hall, but the veterans who ran the hall did not want to take it.[29] One supervisor said he feared that removing the memorial could lead to demonstrations. Finally, as a way of defusing the controversy and disarming any hint of protest, the supervisors decided not only to relight the flame but to provide an answer to the provocative word *Why*. In the context of the first Gulf War, a supervisor proposed adding an inscribed answer: "For Freedom."[30] An advocate for this proposal said, "Everybody's looking at it as a patriotic gesture to support our troops."[31] But the inscription was not changed, and it was left to the California VVLP supporter B. T. Collins to provide an oratorical response to the question Why? "I will tell you why," he said at a ceremony marking the rekindling of the eternal flame. Wars are fought, he explained, to guarantee the freedoms won by our ancestors. "It is part of a generation[al] debt that we owe."[32]

The comparison of the New Castle County and Auburn memorials demonstrates that, even though the right-wing advocates of commemorative statuary insisted that this type of monument is transparent in meaning, the interpretation of a sculptural memorial does not reside solely in the comportment of the figures. The expectations and predispositions of audience members are crucial, as they react to cues in and around the monument. Because the New Castle County memorial is replete with statist and patriotic signifiers, it tends to occlude any suggestion that the memorial is a protest against the Vietnam War. Granted, the memorial remains susceptible to a heavily ironic reading, in which all the patriotic signifiers are seen as the cant of war leading to useless deaths—but the contextual elements make this interpretation rather hard work. In contrast, the Auburn memorial literally questions the war in a way that the New Castle County does not, and the plaque reading "Why" calls up the criticisms of the war by the antiwar movement. Although they are similar in their poses, the Delaware and Auburn statues seem to mean different things. Neither the depiction of a dead soldier nor the naming of the dead signifies on its own; what they signify depends in part on the political and material context and on what is in the viewer's mind.

The arguments surrounding memorial designs are significant not because the chosen designs dictate the responses of visitors to the completed monuments but because the debates reveal what the memorial planners thought an appropriate monument, and why. Veterans and others debated whether memorials in Tennessee, Kentucky, and Maine—all three were VVLP-sponsored memorial projects—should depict scenes of battle or wounding. The veterans responsible for selecting the Tennessee Vietnam Veterans Memorial asked the Nashville artist Alan LeQuire to create a sculpture. But when he submitted a design that was, in his words, "like a traditional Pietà," consisting of a wounded soldier held by two others, the Tennessee veterans found it too "defeatist" and directed him to show three soldiers in action.[33] Thus, although the Pietà image matched the themes of wounds and healing that had become the general currency in discussions of Vietnam Veterans Memorials, it did not fit the more traditionally martial image of honor and courage that the Tennessee VVLP wished to project.

Urged by Ronald Ray to consider a statue, members of the Kentucky Vietnam Veterans Memorial Fund agreed that they wanted a "positive" portrayal of the American soldier, although not a combat scene or anything like a figure "charging up the hill with fixed bayonet." Even though the memorial fund did not ultimately select a sculpture as their state memorial, in keeping with the VVLP's emphasis on military readiness, they determined that the soldier should be represented in "protective" or "peacekeeping" mode: in a word, "vigilant."[34] Thus, the figures in the proposed statue would have conveyed the same posture of watchfulness as the statuary in Nashville does. The preference for designs conveying the theme of vigilance, rather than those featuring injury or active combat, reflects the world-historical situation perceived by these local VVLP supporters, and their understanding that commemorating the past laid the groundwork for facing down continuing threats in the present and future.

In Maine, the deliberations took a similar course but the result was a bit different. The designs submitted to a VVLP-sponsored competition in 1984 were displayed in a mall in South Portland. Passersby were attracted to a bronze maquette of three soldiers, one seriously injured with a medic looking after him, and another signaling for a helicopter. Some objected to the depicted scene: "We've had enough of this kind of thing," the wife of a navy veteran said; someone else said, "It's too graphic. I don't think people want to see that."[35] Just as local veterans objected to the Pietà-like scene in Tennessee, too-vivid depictions of injury were unacceptable in Maine. The result was ingenious: the memorial does show a wounded man being supported by a comrade at either side—but it reduces these figures to an outline cut out of a large, triangular corten steel plate. As sunlight shines through the cut-out, it casts an image of the figures on a second, light-colored triangular plate that serves as a projection screen. In the evening, though, when direct sunlight no longer shines through the cut-out, it becomes a silhouette.[36] The flattening out of the image into a two-dimensional cut-out does away with graphic detail while also eliminating a problem that preoccupied all those who created representational sculptures commemorating the Vietnam War: the vexed question of race.

Apart from local exceptions, such as a memorial built in Chattanooga, Tennessee, in the 1970s and a memorial in Boston to an African American, William W. Davis Jr., who died in the war, black veterans did not initiate the creation of Vietnam memorials.[37] In my research at ten sites at which Vietnam veterans memorials were planned or constructed, I met dozens of people associated with the construction of memorials, and almost all were white.[38] African Americans' minimal input into memorial designs demonstrates that the problem of how to represent race in memorials was left to the deliberations of the white people who designed, planned, and organized them. As James Webb said, with defiant pride, of the Hart sculpture, "This is the bottom line: . . . I put a black man on the Mall and they can kiss my ass."[39] This statement accurately reflects the reality of decision-making about Vietnam Veterans memorials, for which the decision-makers were white men like Webb, his sculpture committee cohorts, and Hart. Hart's decision to shift the African American figure from the center to the side of the group exemplifies the way those responsible for memorial designs weighed how to use race to convey carefully calculated meanings.

The decisions to create bi-racial memorials reflected both the received norms of a multi-ethnic society in the 1980s and the realities of the Vietnam War era, the first wartime period when the U.S. armed forces were racially integrated.[40] In some instances, there is evidence of when and how the decision was taken. In the Tennessee Vietnam Veterans Memorial, for example, the sculptor's original design, showing three figures who are all white, was altered so that in the sculpture's finished form the standing figure represents an African American.[41] Even where the decision cannot be so clearly documented, implicit in the designs is the tacit recognition of a requirement accurately to represent of the demography of the armed forces. But wherever a multifigure and bi-racial statue includes a dead or wounded man, a decision had to be made: should the casualty be black or white?

In the majority of cases, the dead or wounded man is white, and at least one of the helpers is black. For example, in the New Castle County memorial, the grief-stricken standing soldier is African American and the corpse he holds up is the inert body of a white. This pattern is sustained in the Louisiana Vietnam Veterans Memorial (figs. 35 and 36), which shows three infantrymen, one of whom is African American, carrying a fourth, a white, to safety; in the Albany memorial, in which the helper is an African American and the wounded man a white; and in the memorial in Marin County, California, which depicts a black infantryman helping a white who has lost his leg in battle. In the Phoenix memorial (see fig. 30), the "fallen warrior" is a Native American who is helped by a white and a black.[42]

The steps leading to the completion of the Rensselaer County, New York, Vietnam Veterans Memorial (fig. 37) illustrate memorial planners' preference for scenes in which African Americans help wounded whites. In this memorial, a three-figure sculpture by Eileen Barry, after a design by Lori Rysedorph, a soldier cares for an injured comrade while another soldier stands guard. Vietnam veterans selected the original design in a competition but instructed Barry to make some changes when they commissioned her to complete the sculpture. In the original maquette, the casualty was an African American. The memorial committee directed that in the completed sculpture, the racial roles of helper and victim be reversed.[43] Now, an African American helps a wounded white soldier. In this way the planners avoided the uncomfortable connotations the original design might have set off—complaints that ethnic minorities and the poor were used as cannon fodder in the Vietnam War and suffered disproportionate casualty rates.

Two memorials run counter to the rule exemplified by the Rensselaer County memorial. The first, the San Antonio, Texas, memorial (fig. 38), was dedicated in November 1986. The chairman of the local VVLP John Baines (Roy Cohn's nominal client in the matter of the Vietnam Veterans Memorial Fund audit) led the effort to create the memorial. The result, though, does not glorify war or even provide a graphic representation of noble sacrifice. And despite the insistence of the memorial fund's critics that a black wall is too bleak and that bronze statuary should honor those who fought, this statue demonstrates only the tragedy of a life destroyed. As such, it hardly meets the militant purpose of strengthening the nation's resolve that the memorial fund's critics said that they hoped for. Indeed, seeing one bronze sculpture after another, one is struck by the mismatch between the rhetoric of the militant anti-Communists and the poses of the sculptural monuments they demanded.

The San Antonio memorial is titled *Hill 881 South* (a battleground near Khe Sanh) and is said to depict a moment in the battle on April 30, 1967, when U.S. Marines took heavy casualties. The sculptor, Austin Deuel, was a marine artist in Vietnam.[44] The prototype for the sculpture was a small-scale work titled *For What* that Deuel exhibited in 1980 in The Vietnam Experience, an art show in St. Paul, Minnesota.[45] In the sculpture, a radioman scans the sky, "looking for air support that never comes," while pressing his fingers to the neck of a wounded marine to feel for a pulse.[46] Deuel said that he witnessed this moment of the battle, and the former chaplain of the marines at Khe Sanh, in his detailed account of the Khe Sanh hill battles, writes that the sculpture depicts the radioman Donald Hossack assisting his mortally wounded lieutenant, Joseph Mitchell.[47] The memorial is striking both because of the urgent drama of the scene and because the figures appear on a steeply angled pedestal that falls off precipitously at its edge, heightening the extremity of the situation.[48] The sculpture has the immediacy of a combat photograph.

Baines saw a version of the small-scale sculpture and was so taken with it that he bought it and asked the sculptor to produce a larger-than-life-sized version for the San Antonio Vietnam Veterans Memorial.[49] Baines warned Deuel that veterans would be highly attentive to the details of the equipment they used, and so, just as Hart had, Deuel obtained and copied all the relevant items of uniform and equipment to ensure that their depiction was authentic. The memorial underwent one significant

Figure 35. Louisiana Vietnam Veterans Memorial, New Orleans; Milton Pounds, designer, William Ludwig, sculptor, dedicated November 11, 1984. The figure on the left represents an African American. Photo by Wayne Ferrara.

Figure 36. Louisiana Vietnam Veterans Memorial, details. Photos by author.

Figure 37. Rensselaer County Vietnam Veterans Memorial, Troy, New York; Eileen Barry, sculptor, dedicated May 27, 1991. Photo by author.

Figure 38. San Antonio Vietnam Veterans Memorial; Austin Deuel, sculptor, dedicated November 9, 1986. Photo by Gil Dominguez.

change, though. In the smaller original that Baines purchased, the two marines are white. But Baines and Deuel, influenced by Hart's depiction of a multi-ethnic group, decided that it would be better if one of the figures was African American. Thus, in the large-scale version, the mortally wounded man is an African American.[50]

The fact that the memorial was based on an event that the artist had witnessed circulated widely in the community of Khe Sanh veterans. Curious pieces of folklore formed around the memorial as veterans tried to match the notion that this was a real moment in the battle with the sculpture's depiction of a bi-racial scene. Some veterans have even identified a particular man as the one depicted as the casualty, because he happens to have been an African American who was killed in action on the same day as Mitchell. It remains unclear, in any event, why Baines and Deuel decided that the survivor should be a white marine and the casualty an African American. The fact that the helper was a radioman had lodged strongly in Deuel's mind, and to assure veterans of the accuracy of the scene, he was careful to depict the authentic details of the man's radio. It may have seemed, then, beyond the bounds of artistic license to change the surviving radioman's race; but evidently, for the purposes of commemoration, the white man whom the radioman vainly tried to save was regarded as expendable, and, in his place, a black body was pressed into the service of the obligatory representation of interracial brotherhood among the U.S. forces in Vietnam.

The only other exception to the "white casualty, black helper" rule is the VVLP-sponsored North Carolina Vietnam Veterans Memorial dedicated in May 1987, a three-figure grouping alongside the state capitol in Raleigh (figs. 39 and 40). Created by the local sculptor Abbe Godwin, *After the Firefight* shows two soldiers carrying a wounded comrade to a landing zone to await a helicopter evacuation. Like Hart and Deuel, Godwin devoted a good deal of research to making the work authentic in its details. She spent several months interviewing Vietnam veterans and reading about the war before she produced the maquette, and her efforts are reflected in their clothing and equipment.[51]

A leaflet distributed at the capitol boasts that the memorial is the first in the monument-rich capitol gardens to feature an African American: the injured man, who is carried by two whites.[52] In another fact sheet, the memorial committee explains: "The composition shows the intense caring that can be the result of the kind of situation the men face in war. One's race, religion, social class, education, and other superficial things that sometimes separate, become totally irrelevant."[53] Fired by enthusiasm for depicting interracial comradeship, the creators of the monument failed to consider that the depiction of two white men transporting a wounded African American from the Southeast Asian battlefield might not, as they naïvely believed, demonstrate the irrelevance of race but might instead carry a disturbing implication about who was dragged off bleeding from the fight, and who did the dragging. Although the memorial committee tried to use race to demonstrate social solidarity, its decision raised all the old questions about the casualty rates suffered by blacks and whites in Vietnam. More than a century after North Carolinans fought to preserve the enslavement of African Americans, the North Carolina Vietnam

Figure 39. North Carolina Vietnam Veterans Memorial, Raleigh; Abbe Godwin, sculptor, dedicated May 23, 1987. Photo by author.

Figure 40. North Carolina Vietnam Veterans Memorial, detail. Photo by author.

Veterans Memorial unwittingly implicated the whole history of racial oppression in the United States.

One has only to reverse the situation in the New Castle County memorial and imagine a white soldier holding up the inert body of a black, or consider the implications of the three-figure statue in Raleigh, to ascertain some politically uncomfortable ideas. Vietnam was said to be a rich man's war but a poor man's fight; critics pointed out that the front-line troops and the casualties in the early years of the war came disproportionately from poor backgrounds and racial and ethnic minorities. As one black veteran said, "Hey, the blacks were the ones that had to do all the fighting. Out of all the guys in the jungle, more than half was black."[54] Over the course of the war, a greater proportion of blacks than whites saw heavy combat.[55] Having a white figure holding up the inert body of a black would signify the laying of a human offering on the altar of the white god of war. If such an image is unappealing, how much more comforting to center the scene on the self-sacrifice of the white, with the black in faithful attendance, in the position of a care giver.

In a discussion of the New Castle County memorial, a journalist identifies a "commitment to civil rights" as "a recurrent theme of the new memorials."[56] In a similar vein, David Glassberg has suggested that the Vietnam memorials showing black servicemen helping white comrades are disguised Civil Rights memorials, constructed in a period when nonmilitary representations of interracial brotherhood might have been controversial.[57] Images of mutual care on the battlefield, according to this interpretation, reflect the growth of interracial understanding in the war years and prefigure an implied postwar solidarity of veterans. The Marin County memorial showing a black soldier helping a white soldier who has lost his leg in battle is titled *The Brothers*.[58] Post-combat scenes allow artists to depict men touching and holding each other while straddling the border between life and death. It is as if love between men can be expressed only *in extremis*, at the instant when one man reaches out to another with a comradeship so powerful as to defy death—dragging a friend back from the brink, or willing him to return from beyond an impassable boundary. Outside the sports arena and "buddy" movies, such eroticized but nonsexual scenes of physical contact have few outlets on the public stage, and in the Vietnam War memorials we are considering, the bonds of brotherhood between men are all the stronger for overcoming the dividing line of race.

The experience of race by service personnel in the field was far more complex, though. Some African Americans experienced racism and discrimination in Vietnam; but in the field, others found that the common dangers troops faced and the mutual obligations they accrued allowed them to transcend racial differences.[59] In some striking accounts of soldierly brotherhood, blacks and southern rednecks learned to love one another and became inseparable except by death; in other veterans' stories, black soldiers found themselves confronted on military bases by Confederate flags and Ku Klux Klan symbols.[60] The difficulties of service in Vietnam were multiplied for African American GIs, who were disappointed that military service did not win them the societal respect African Americans had sought through participation in all their nation's wars. Blacks, indeed, faced criticism at home for fighting a "white man's war"; and they fought against people of color in Vietnam, in a war effort that was itself fueled, in part, by racism.[61] Unsurprisingly, African Americans experienced higher levels of combat stress than whites. Simply having served in Vietnam was stressful for black veterans, irrespective of the intensity of combat they experienced, and their stress persisted longer than that of other veterans.[62]

The multiracial statues do not articulate the double-edged quality of race in Vietnam. In a show of wishful thinking, they demonstrate that the troops' comradeship in the field resulted in solidarity transcending both racial differences and the class differences that consigned many working-class men to front-line units. The memorials' false resolution of real social conflicts in the United States papers over the fraught issue of racism by its indication that black, white, Native American, and Latino veterans served side by side and took care of one another. Moreover, racial conflict and political divisions over the rightness of the war, far from compounding each other, dissolve together in the statue groups. Racial difference acts as a cipher for all the social conflicts that the memorials ignore, and racial reconciliation in the sculptures brings about a symbolic social and political re-unification. By wishing away the most entrenched and enduring problem addressed by the Civil Rights movement—that of racism—the premature celebration of racial equality in the Vietnam veterans memorials highlights the movement's failures as much as its achievements. The memorials rely on the magical resolution of racism in a show of national solidarity in which brotherhood, care, and grief cut across social discord and thus ameliorate the political wounds caused by the Vietnam War.[63]

The theme of reconciliation and healing relies for its expression on masculine, soldierly comradeship in the sculptures considered in this chapter up to now, but it reaches its highest pitch in memorials depicting women in America's uniformed services. These monuments use gender as a marker of difference, enacting the bonding of the nation as a coming together of an American family, centering on a female figure both maternal and chaste. Idealized scenes of women nurturing injured servicemen wrap bonds of sentimental devotion around the nation's military experience in Vietnam. Women's retrospective depiction in memorials is accordingly laden with powerful symbolism. Sculptures showing women grieving over American men echo scenes in which the Virgin Mary accepted the body of the dead Christ, while those that show women caring for the wounded embody the healing and reconciliation that are the near-constant theme running through the commemoration of the war.

The nurses who cared for America's injured boys in Vietnam now minister not only to the veterans' wounds but also, symbolically, to those of a society confused and emotionally injured by the war. Thus, although the addition of a women's memorial to the national Vietnam Veterans Memorial in Washington, DC, has been seen, with some accuracy, as a triumph for military women in the face of their marginalization, statues of American women caring for wounded GIs can also be regarded as the densest and most fully realized expressions of the commemorative tendencies outlined in this chapter. They show those who served in Vietnam in the sympathetic guise of nurturers and the plaintive role of victims; they show the care Americans felt toward each other; and they deploy a powerful, gendered language to show Americans, in Lincoln's words, coming together to "bind up the nation's wounds."

The growing recognition in the 1980s of women's contributions to their nation's armed forces was marked by the success of efforts to create memorials to women in military service in all wars, such as the Women in Military Service Memorial at Arlington National Cemetery (dedicated in 1997, although planning began in 1985). The drive to represent women in Vietnam veterans memorials was thus part of a broader set of social tendencies not exclusively related to the Vietnam War. But the "equal representation" argument is not sufficient on its own to explain the success of the Vietnam Women's Memorial, because there is no obvious reason that the women's demand for representation was more worthy than that of airmen, for example. Advocates of a women's memorial claimed that they were not just a minority or an interest group but represented half the U.S. population; while this claim is accurate, it would not necessarily resolve the issue, because women who served in Vietnam were not the most numerous group among the Vietnam veterans who demanded representation.[64]

In the 1960s and 1970s, as the country was split by the Vietnam War, it was tempting for women veterans not to admit they had been in Vietnam, and easy for them to disappear into the mainstream of society since they did not fit the stereotype of military veterans.[65] As a member of the board of Vietnam Veterans of America put it, "If we men have been in 'the woodwork,' then our sisters have been beneath the basement floor."[66] Isolated from one another and unable to cross the gulf of incomprehension dividing veterans from civilians, many women who had served in Vietnam did not talk about their wartime experiences and did not recognize that the psychological symptoms that they suffered might be related to their war experiences.[67]

Kathy Cordova, a nurse in an evacuation hospital, remembers "the one": the special young man who somehow got through her psychological defenses and made an indelible mark on her. Her recollections resemble those of other nurses in Vietnam who describe a similar experience with their special soldier, with whom they shared the most intimate moment, his last instant of life: "He wasn't out of high school but a year or so," Cordova said. "He talked about high school and sports, his girlfriend, his parents, his life. He was conscious the whole time." Unbeknownst to him, he had suffered a fatal wound—a bullet had severed his spine. Cordova went on: "To this day I'm trying to figure out why he died. Maybe I just didn't want him to. Maybe he was the one. If you're nursing for thirty years, you'll always remember one patient that struck you, and you'll remember forever and ever and you try to think why. . . . They just hit something in you. For me, he will be the one." After facing death and injury day in and day out, she built a protective shell around herself. She stopped crying. When she returned to the United States, she felt anger and guilt, and confused, ambivalent feelings about the war. She began to shy away from human contact.[68]

Lily Adams too tried to protect herself from becoming overly attached to dying patients, by shifting from an intensive care unit to a post as a triage nurse—but she found that she became even closer to the dying in the triage situation. She never allowed a patient to die alone. She came home "angry and hostile," suffered depression, and talked for hours late into the night about the men she had taken care of. Kathy Splinter, an army nurse in Vietnam, recalled the agony of seeing young men of eighteen or nineteen die. She came home and suffered an array of symptoms of post-traumatic stress disorder (PTSD): intrusive thoughts, flashbacks, and disturbed sleep. If she tried to bring up Vietnam in conversation, no one knew how to respond to her.[69]

Diane Carlson Evans, who worked in two evacuation hospitals in Vietnam and then in a postoperative surgical unit where the wounds were more severe, remembered working days as long as sixteen hours. She wasn't afraid of dying, even though the surgical unit came under rocket and mortar attack. Her great fear was of losing a patient because of a mistake induced by tiredness; another danger was of "becoming cold." "You have to shut down in a situation like that; you can't let yourself feel." If she had fallen apart every time she saw a badly wounded patient, she would not have been able to do her job. She tried to be caring and compassionate but found that if she cared too much, she could not sleep for worrying about the patients when they left her unit. So she tried to internalize her feelings and just do her job.

When she wrote to one of her former patients, a fellow Minnesotan with whom she formed a special bond, the letter returned unopened and she found out he had been killed. She wrote to his mother and told her how he was a wonderful kid who never thought of himself but was always helping others. His mother wrote an appreciative reply but when she read it, "I just broke down and cried and cried. I just didn't want to cry anymore. I never wrote to another parent." Back home, she thought of visiting the family of a Minnesotan boy who had died in Vietnam but when she drove to their house she could not get out of the car. "I was afraid they were going to blame me . . . afraid they would say, 'Why couldn't you do more.' What could they say to me? And what could I say to them?"[70]

Lynda Van Devanter, who served as an evacuation nurse in Vietnam, described the grueling experience of endless casualties, her psychological distress at the deaths of the young men she cared for, and her sense that with each death she lost a part of herself. She learned soon after her return that people in the United States did not want to hear about her war. "I had learned my lesson quickly. Vietnam would never be socially acceptable." When she tried to join a demonstration by Vietnam Veterans Against the War, she was told that she could not because she was "not a vet."[71] Other former nurses felt equally unwelcome when they tried to join veterans' organizations: they did not fit the military veteran's masculine stereotype.[72] Female veterans often stopped talking about the war; their accomplishments "became buried through the complicity of silence."[73] And when the women joined therapy groups to deal with their own PTSD, they often fell into a stereotypical "caretaker" role, discounting their own feelings and trying to "heal" the men. Female veterans thus underwent an extreme version of the male veterans' experience of nonrecognition: "if [Vietnam-era] soldiers were the forgotten veterans, women were the closet veterans. Many didn't even know they had a war story to tell. And if they did tell it, who would listen?"[74]

Women's service, and the experience of women veterans, was thus significant out of all proportion to their numbers in the armed services. The issue of recognition and representation was particularly intense for women, who did not feel that their experience was acknowledged by the public or by veterans' organizations: they were the "invisible veterans."[75] The achievement of recognition by female veterans, measured against their prior social invisibility, crowned and exceeded the successes of their brother veterans, making society's acknowledgment of Vietnam veterans seem all the more complete.

Although women served in many capacities in Vietnam—as communications personnel and clerks and in nonmilitary roles with organizations such as the Red Cross and USO—they are commemorated as nurses. The depiction of nurses in commemorative sculptures implicitly refers to the men that they treated, some of whose lives the women helped to save, and some of whom have their names inscribed on memorial walls. As B. T. Collins, the founder of the California Vietnam Veterans Memorial Commission, said, remembering the months that he spent in military hospitals after losing an arm and a leg in Vietnam, "I just want you to know one thing. Our lives were irrevocably changed by the presence of those military nurses. You did something that no one else could do. And I swear to you that we will never ever forget you."[76] The creation of memorials to the women who served in Vietnam would be a sign that the nation respected them and that the men with whom they served kept faith with them. Women's experiences also focused attention on grief at the loss of male soldiers. Jill Ann Mishkel, who served in the same evacuation hospital where Cordova served three years earlier, recalled, "When I did talk, all I can remember talking about is all the people that died. I think that probably sticks with me more than anything else in the whole war—that I saw over a hundred men die in that year. And they were all young, healthy guys. I went to that rap group [a vet center in Connecticut], and I must have cried every week for four months. For a long time, all I could get out was 'They just kept on dying. They just kept on dying.'"[77] Other nurses' feelings also centered on their sense of loss at being unable to save the injured men who came to them.

Women were the quintessential unrecognized veterans; women's service was associated with the death and injury of war; women were symbols of physical and psychological trauma—and, because they were nurses, they also embodied the idea of the treatment of injury. Their gender had made them important figures for the men in Vietnam: they represented the comforts of home, a mother's caring hand, a girlfriend's allure.[78] When the soldier's life was cut short, they symbolized all that he had lost, and they carried all that loss and pain with them when they returned home. This intense sadness concentrated in the nurses' professional, gendered identities, and it was the symbolic importance of gender roles, as much as the growing recognition of women's military contributions, that explains the substantial number of Vietnam memorials that now include representations of female service personnel.

The first statue of an American nurse in Vietnam was dedicated on May 29, 1973. It depicts Sharon Lane, the only nurse killed as result of hostile enemy action in Vietnam, and stands in front of her alma mater, Aultman Hospital in Canton, Ohio.

Figure 41. Westchester County, New York, Vietnam Veterans Memorial; Julia Cohen, sculptor, dedicated October 1987. Photo by author.

(She was killed in a rocket attack while on duty at an evacuation hospital in Chu Lai.)[79] No more statues of American nurses in Vietnam appeared until the wave of memorial construction in the 1980s, amid the growing demands for the representation of women who served. The first result was the dedication in October 1987 of a multifigure group including a nurse, the Westchester County, New York, Vietnam Veterans Memorial (fig. 41).[80] The nurse is shown in urgent action, rather than what would become the more common depiction of nurses in later memorials: touching, nurturing, and soothing. Visitors reach the memorial in Lasdon Park, Westchester County, by following a "trail of honor," dotted with busts of troops from all the services through the whole sweep of American military history.[81] A polished black stone tablet records the names of county residents who died in Vietnam, the Stars and Stripes flying from an adjacent flagpole. A small stone marker headed "Nurses of Vietnam" lists the eight American military nurses who died in the war. Nearby, a powerful, muscular, helmeted figure moves forward carrying a wounded man, stripped to the waist, his body arched backward, his hand flung across his forehead in an exaggerated stage swoon. The soldier carrying the casualty has a craggy face with a powerful, jutting jaw that, along with his angular body, makes him resemble a sculpture from the school of heroic Soviet realism. Separated from them by several feet is a female figure in military fatigues who is running to them to offer some sort of help or treatment. The angle of her body suggests she is sprinting. She holds something at shoulder height—something that must carefully be held upright. It might be medical equipment; one observer's poetic interpretation is that she is holding her heart.[82] Though the scene is puzzling, if nothing else it testifies to the presence of nurses in Vietnam and to the wish to have their service publicly recognized. Subsequent memorials emphasizing the tactile were more successful in mining the rich vein of gendered feeling associated with the Vietnam War.

In the depiction of nurses in the Georgia, New Jersey, and California Vietnam Veterans Memorials, the consistent motif is proximity and contact. All three memorials depict women as healers, touching or bandaging male personnel, perhaps symbolizing the solace that planners hoped the memorials would effect for veterans and the nation. In the Atlanta memorial, dedicated in November 1988, we see a nurse bandaging a wounded man's arm while another man stands by and operates a radio-telephone (fig. 42). The nurse and the wounded man are white, and the radio-telephone operator is African American. The rather stiff, static poses in the Atlanta sculpture contrast with those in the memorial in Holmdel, New Jersey, dedicated in May 1995. The racial and gender make-up of the two statues, though, is remarkably similar: in New Jersey, a three-figure statue shows a standing African American soldier reaching out to a pair of figures, as if to offer help (fig. 43). A woman in nurse's scrubs kneels with her back to him and, with the finger tips of her right hand, she lightly presses a bandage onto the chest wound of a soldier slumped on his back before her. In both statuary groups, the touch that bonds the male and female figures does not cross the racial divide, as though the notion of physical contact between a white nurse and an African American soldier were considered risqué. This configuration sustains the pattern that in a bi-racial group, the wounded man is white.

In the New Jersey statue, the casualty's tunic is spread open, emphasizing his vulnerability and echoing the semi-nudity in the Pietà. He weakly holds up one hand, the fingers slightly curled. The nurse supports the weight of his arm with her left hand, but she does not take his hand in hers because doing so would interrupt the arc of energy between the hands of the two soldiers who reach for but do not touch each other. The reaching hands remind one of Michelangelo's God and Adam in the Sistine Chapel ceiling—and of Larry Burrows's celebrated photograph of a soldier stumbling toward his wounded officer during Operation Prairie.[83] Because the two men are unable to close the distance separating them, the female figure is the one who supplies the touch for which they yearn.

This looks, at first glance, to be a battlefield scene. The standing figure has a rifle, which he steadies with a hand on its barrel, and he is dressed in helmet and flak jacket; the injured man has a grenade clipped to his belt, and the nurse seems to be treating him where he fell. But this is not a realistic representation of a battlefield, because nurses did not go into combat: a wounded soldier would not have encountered a nurse until he was helicoptered to an evacuation hospital, by which time he would have been stripped of his weapon and placed on a litter or gurney, not on the ground. The scene, implausible as a real event, precisely captures the emotional tenor of buddies' separation by death and injury, and the care of nurses who performed triage, administered emergency treatment, held out hope to frightened men, and, sometimes, held a soldier's hand and stayed with him until he died. Sentimental as it may be, this is a beautifully conceived sculpture, the more so because it occupies

Figure 42. Georgia Vietnam Veterans Memorial, Atlanta; Jo Fassnacht, sculptor, dedicated November 11, 1988 (statue) and October 30, 1997 (wall). Photo by author.

Figure 43. New Jersey Vietnam Veterans Memorial, Holmdel; Hien Nguyen, designer, Thomas Jay Warren, sculptor, dedicated May 7, 1995. Photo by author.

Figure 44. California Vietnam Veterans Memorial, Sacramento; Michael Larson and Thomas Chytrowski, designers, Rolf Kriken, sculptor, dedicated December 10, 1988. Photo by author.

a paved area, rather than standing on a socle, and hence invites the audience into its emotional ambience.

The California Vietnam Veterans Memorial in Sacramento's Capitol Gardens (fig. 44), designed in the aftermath of the controversy over the inclusions and exclusions of Lin's wall and Hart's statue, is truly a monument to equal opportunities. Four curved walls describe a broken circle and enclose a small courtyard. On their convex, outward faces, the walls are clad with black granite inscribed with the names of California's dead. On their concave interior side four cast bronze sculptures project from a background into the courtyard. Each sculpture is flanked by six bronze bas-reliefs.[84] The memorial designers were at pains to represent a range of demographic and military groups. The statuary therefore includes three blacks among its eight large-scale figures (although there are no apparent markers of Hispanic, Native American, and Asian American soldiers); it includes representations of the U.S. Navy and Air Force as well as foot soldiers; it shows a POW in the "Hanoi Hilton"; it shows a nurse. One member of the memorial commission was proud to claim (inaccurately) that this was the first memorial in the country to depict women's role in the war (it was dedicated in December 1988, after the Westchester County memorial and well after the statue of Sharon Lane).

A solitary shaven-headed white man in shorts and sandals, seated on a bench with a bowl at his side, represents American POWs (most of whom were pilots and air crew shot down over North Vietnam). The panels alongside him show naval vessels and aircraft of sufficient variety that no one need feel excluded. Another sculpture, representing combat troops, shows two African American marines, one throwing a grenade (fig. 45). This large sculpture is flanked by engravings of the Declaration of Independence and the Bill of Rights, and several bas-reliefs of troops in action.[85] A third sculpture shows an African American and a white marine at rest.[86] The fourth sculpture projecting from the inner side shows a nurse treating a wounded man whose arm has been amputated (fig. 46). Turning her face to the viewer, she reaches out a hand to the soldier's body. Because his face is bandaged (as is the casualty's in the Louisiana Vietnam Veterans Memorial) he becomes Everyman. Alongside this sculpture are bas-reliefs echoing the theme of injury, death, and grief. One, based on a photograph by John Olson, shows marine casualties at the Battle of Hué being evacuated on an armored personnel carrier;[87] others are based on Larry Burrows's moving photographs of a helicopter crew member crying over the death of a comrade after a mission and of a soldier reaching for his wounded officer (the same image that the New Jersey memorial sculpture recalls).[88]

The strongest statement of maternal care is found in the sculpture at the center of the memorial's courtyard (fig. 47). A soldier sits, helmetless, his rifle resting between his legs. He stares into the distance, lost in thought, holding a letter from home, the last page of which, signed "Mom," we can read. The letter, in fact composed for the memorial by Linda McLenahan, who chaired the California Vietnam Veterans Memorial Commission, reminds the young man of his coming twentieth birthday.[89] This calls to mind the often-quoted statistic that the average age of service personnel in Vietnam was nineteen. (The statistic has become an article of faith among those who point to the hardships that U.S. service personnel faced in Vietnam. Veterans who downplay the distinctiveness of the Vietnam War in comparison with other U.S. wars have, however, recently disputed this statistic.)[90] The letter closes with the words, "Please take care of yourself and don't be a hero. We don't need a Medal of Honor. We need a son."[91] Surrounded by walls tallying the number of Californians who died in Vietnam, the letter implies that this young man did not return and instead became a casualty, one of the dead whose names the surrounding black tablets record. The audience is drawn into a before-and-after narrative of maternal love, anxiety, and loss. The various figures in the memorial encompass the nation and the military as a diverse family, while at the circle's center is the implied mother-child dyad.

The Pittsburgh-Allegheny County Vietnam Veterans Monument (fig. 48) uses the symbolism of family and a mixture of racial and maternal imagery to express the theme of homecoming. Set on a bank of the Allegheny River, the memorial consists of a steel frame enclosing a group of sculptural figures. The physical structure and the sculpture's narrative content combine to resolve the distance between Vietnam and the United States and the gap between warriors and civilians. The metal frame typifies Pittsburgh's urban environment, with its steel surface evoking Pittsburgh's famed heavy industries. Yet the memorial's curvilinear outline is quite delicate; it represents the shape of a hibiscus pod, an Asian symbol for rebirth and regeneration. This reference to Southeast Asia is reinforced by the inscription on the ground beneath the pod's canopy, a Vietnamese prayer, with an English translation: "Grant Us

Figure 45. California Vietnam Veterans Memorial, North Wall, *Action Panel*; Rolf Kriken, sculptor. The design was based on a photograph taken south of Con Thien by combat photographer Donnie L. Shearer, United States Marine Corps. Photo by author.

Figure 46. California Vietnam Veterans Memorial, West Wall, *The Nurse*; Rolf Kriken, sculptor. The arrangement of figures was composed by Rolf Kriken and Vietnam War nurses Cheryl Nicol, Rose Sandecki, and Pam White. Some items of the nurses' equipment brought back from Vietnam, such as Nicol's stethoscope, were used to create the sculpture mould. Photo by author.

Peace." The memorial's physical form thus attempts to synthesize Southeast Asian and local elements; and it manages to combine them without any glaring incongruity.

Inside the memorial, two homecoming scenes are played out (fig. 49). An African American woman greets her son. A Caucasian mother and child welcome their husband and father. (Perhaps unwittingly, the composition of the two groups reinforces the stereotype of the absent father in African American families.)[92] Together, the scenes elevate to a public dimension the private moments of homecoming that some veterans may have enjoyed; and they compensate the veterans for the public celebrations they missed when they returned. Local media reports emphasized the idea of homecoming. One article announced, "Pittsburgh finally says 'welcome home' to the men and women involved in the Vietnam War." And T. J. McGarvey, the president of the Pittsburgh-Allegheny County Vietnam Veterans Monument Fund, said the memorial is a "quiet, dignified statement to all that the people of Pittsburgh and Allegheny County do remember and do care."[93]

Figure 47. A visitor leans over the central seated figure in the California Vietnam Veterans Memorial to read the letter from "Mom" he is holding. Photo by author.

Figure 48. Pittsburgh-Allegheny County Vietnam Veterans Memorial; John Middleton and Ed Dumont, designers, George Danhires, sculptor, dedicated November 10–11, 1987. Photo by author.

While memorial planners and designers in various locations were making a point of including women in sculptures commemorating the Vietnam War, a more difficult campaign was proceeding in Washington and throughout the nation to rally support for the addition of the sculpture of a nurse at the national Vietnam Veterans Memorial. Women's names were present on the wall in proportion to the number in military service who died in Vietnam, eight in all.[94] Female veterans explained that they saw no reason to complain until the decision was made to create a statue in which no women were represented. The campaign to add the statue of a nurse to the memorial began in earnest with the addition of the Hart statue.[95] Diane Carlson Evans, the Minnesotan nurse who had been afraid of "getting cold" when she shut down her feelings to do her job, attended the dedication of the Vietnam Veterans Memorial in November 1982 and strained to remember the names on the dog tags of the men who had died during her tour of duty in 1968 and 1969. She wore the hat with a nurse's pin that she had worn in Vietnam and found men coming to hug her, crying and thanking her and all the nurses who had helped save their lives. For the first time since she returned from Vietnam, she cried and afterward spent a year in therapy, memories of her service trickling back. As far as Evans was concerned, the memorial was complete then: "If it had stood alone, it would have been fine. But the three bronze men changed things."[96]

Evans wrote to Jan Scruggs in the summer of 1984, before the Hart statue was dedicated, saying that the addition of the *Three Infantrymen* statue demanded that a memorial to women also be added: "It is time to bring the nurses home, to welcome them home, to give them the honor they deserve," she wrote.[97] She founded the Vietnam Women's Memorial Project and, with admirable determination, began to lobby the Vietnam Veterans Memorial Fund to add a statue of a nurse to the memorial. Evans asked her fellow Minnesota resident Rodger Brodin, a marine veteran and the creator of *Monument to the Living*, to make a statue titled *The Nurse*, based on her recollections of the nurses' experiences in Vietnam.[98] The women's memorial project campaigned to have the statue added to the Vietnam Veterans Memorial. It shows a standing female figure wearing a stethoscope and equipped with surgical scissors,

Figure 49. Pittsburgh-Allegheny County Vietnam Veterans Memorial, detail of homecoming scene. Photo by author.

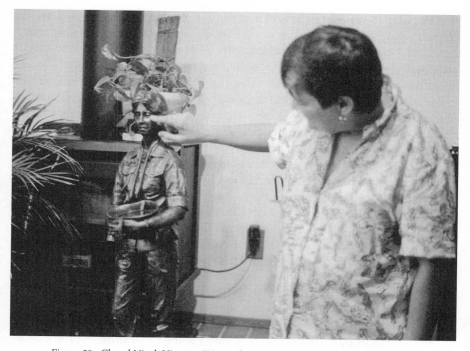

Figure 50. Cheryl Nicol, Vietnam Women's Memorial Project Northwest regional coordinator, with a scale model of Rodger Brodin's *The Nurse*, the first design chosen for the Vietnam Women's Memorial. Photo by author.

holding a GI's helmet, signifying her grief over the soldier who had once worn it. Four small-scale replicas of *The Nurse* toured the country, exhibited to garner local support in a national campaign in favor of the statue (fig. 50).

The Vietnam Women's Memorial Project couched its appeal in the language used by other memorial planners: "A national healing process began in the early 1980s with the establishment of the Vietnam Veterans Memorial. This process is incomplete, however, as is the honoring and recognition of Vietnam veterans who are women."[99] Memorials that bring together male and female figures would, according to this proposition, signify completion, a precondition for psychological closure. But the proposal ran into enormous resistance. The Fine Arts Commission, which had been obliged to accept the addition of the Hart statue as a result of the Reagan administration's endorsement of the Vietnam Veterans Memorial Fund's "compromise" with its critics, balked at any further additions lest the memorial become "a sculpture garden on the Mall."

The subsequent arguments about the Vietnam Women's Memorial recapitulated virtually every point of contention surrounding the Hart statue and Lin's wall. To begin with, the addition of a women's memorial was opposed by Lin, the Vietnam Veterans Memorial Fund, Hart, who saw no need for any statue but his own, and J. Carter Brown, chairman of the Fine Arts Commission, who wondered where it was all going to end.[100] Benjamin Forgey of the *Washington Post* pointed out the obvious irony: the forced addition of the Hart infantrymen statue motivated others to demand representation and created a precedent that made it difficult to make a principled argument against further additions. "If we begin to single out veterans by gender," he asked, "why not select them by ethnic group? Why not an American Indian soldier, an Italian American? Or, if we begin to pay tribute to specialties such as medicine, why not others: why not engineers, or Seabees, or pilots, or supply sergeants." Forgey said that the "separate-but-equal" women's memorial was a bad idea. The wall and the three bronze infantrymen would have to serve for everyone.[101]

After their initial opposition, in May 1986 the Vietnam Veterans Memorial Fund endorsed the addition of a women's memorial to the site. Interior Secretary Donald Hodel also approved the women's memorial. The Fine Arts Commission remained opposed, though. On October 22, 1987, the commission considered and rejected the addition of the Brodin statue of the nurse to the memorial.[102] Brown said that the addition of the women's memorial would appear to be "an afterthought, sort of a putdown, almost a ghettoization." He earned the unending hostility of some female veterans when he compared the campaign for a women's memorial to the efforts to add a memorial to the canine corps.[103] Some women felt that he was comparing them to dogs. The *Washington Post*, agreeing with the commission's decision, asked, "Why honor nurses . . . and not American Indians or certain heroic units of the individual services?"[104] *The Nation* reported that navy seamen, air force pilots, and American Indians had already "begun clamoring for their own statues."[105] The Vietnam veteran and author John Ketwig said that it was all very well to argue that American women had been in Vietnam but there had been plenty of water buffalo there, too, and no one had suggested that they should be commemorated.[106] Lin said that the wall honored all who served equally, whatever their race, sex, or rank. No statue could satisfy all of those who wanted to be represented. Brown said that the addition of the Hart statue had produced envy on the part of all others not represented in bronze by the three infantrymen. Adding the nurse's statue would create a "slippery slope." Brown missed the point, though, of the symbolic resonances of women's service, particularly as nurses, in Vietnam.[107]

The Vietnam Women's Memorial Project reminded their antagonists that women were the ones who nursed soldiers back to health and sometimes watched over them while they died. The organization won the support of five major veterans' organizations: the American Legion, Veterans of Foreign Wars, Disabled American Veterans, Paralyzed Veterans of America, and Vietnam Veterans of America, with a combined membership of six million.[108] Finally, the Fine Arts Commission's opposition was trumped by a congressional resolution when the women's memorial project persuaded legislators to pass a law requiring the addition of a women's memorial to the Vietnam Veterans Memorial.[109] The Senate bill initially said that it would be the final addition to the memorial, although this provision was stricken from the final version passed by the House and Senate and signed into law by Ronald Reagan.[110]

The congressional law was vague about where exactly on the Vietnam Veterans Memorial site the women's memorial should be located—it said merely that it should be placed within the 2.2 acre site of the Vietnam Veterans Memorial.[111] It also remained to be decided what kind of memorial ought to represent the women who served in Vietnam, and here the conflict took a familiar form. The Vietnam Women's Memorial Project wanted no less than what the men had been given: a realistic, bronze statue.[112] They made their preference explicit in the following statement: "The proposed design [by Rodger Brodin] which we are using to represent the contribution of women during the Vietnam War was very carefully chosen to be a composite of the ideals for which all women served. The design also has to balance and complement the statue of the three men. They are bronze, so she will be bronze."[113] The Fine Arts Commission was opposed to any additional sculptures, though, and had rejected Brodin's statue, *The Nurse*. The women's memorial project was advised that it should hold an open design competition because, despite the affection that women veterans had for Brodin's statue, a memorial on such a prominent national site as the Mall ought not to be casually commissioned.[114] The Fine Arts Commission instructed the women's memorial's advocates that the competition guidelines should not specify any particular type of memorial and should certainly not require a statue. The project complied with this direction and held an open design competition, superseding the earlier commitment to the statue of a single nurse.[115] The women's memorial project's leaders never, however, abandoned their goal of having a bronze statue.

The competition jury split in its opinion. The five art and design professionals on the jury chose a nonrepresentational design. The proposed memorial was not sunk beneath ground level but it was flush with the ground (and hence was unobtrusive, preserving the precious sightlines in the Mall that design professionals were so concerned to protect). It consisted of a paved, white grid, conceived by competition entrant Robert Lee Desmond, with 144 mist jets representing the months of America's involvement in the Vietnam War. This choice marks the nadir of the antipathy between design professionals and veterans. A grid: the same kind of geometric and impersonal structure that veterans had overwhelmingly rejected when a professional juror had recommended it in Austin. A memorial flush with the ground: the same kind of low-level design that some veterans had found objectionable when Lin's wall was chosen. Combining these two characteristics, the jurors might have won applause for their perfect success in a perverse assignment to choose the design most finely calculated to offend the hopes of the women veterans—until, that is, one added the inspired fillip of the mist jets. Critics of the design seized on this feature, comparing it to the steam vents that homeless people in Washington sleep on in cold weather.[116]

Unmoved by the persuasive powers of the design experts, the four veterans on the jury favored a realistic, single-figure sculpture, proposed by the sculptor Eileen Barry, quite similar to the original statue of a solitary nurse.[117] The jury, split into irreconcilable factions, announced that both designs were "finalists." After considering combining them, the women's memorial project selected instead one of the honorable mentions in the competition: a multi-figure bronze sculpture by Glenna Goodacre, depicting a wounded soldier, his body stretched in collapse on a pile

of sandbags and his head cradled in the arm of a white female care-giver (fig. 51).
It was one of several competition entries that depicted a woman ministering to a
wounded soldier. In Goodacre's design, the man's face is bandaged, like the one
in New Orleans, so that he can represent Everyman (although his features are sufficiently visible to make him a Caucasian Everyman). The faces of the figures are
smooth and finely detailed, but elsewhere the sculpture has a rougher texture, more
expressive and sensual than the Hart statue, with its crystalline hyper-realism. The
comportment of the casualty's upper body, especially the right arm, unmistakably
recalls that of Christ in Michelangelo's Rome Pietà, and the relationship between the
two figures is similar in the two works, although Goodacre's female figure is more
active in her attention than is Michelangelo's Virgin, whose pose in the Rome work
is of resigned serenity. The uniformed woman, her expression one of concentration
and infinite care, wraps one arm around the man's shoulders, and her other presses
against his chest. Two additional female figures complete the group (fig. 52): one,
whose ethnicity is ambiguous, kneels, gazing sadly at the helmet in her hand; the
other, an African American, looks skyward, some believe in a despairing appeal to
the heavens, others in anticipation of a helicopter to evacuate the wounded man.[118]

By the fall of 1991, all the statutory regulatory agencies had approved the statue
in principle.[119] The agencies also reviewed the plans for its siting. Since the sculpture
was intended to be seen in the round, not frontally, like the Hart statue, the decision
was made to situate it in a small, paved plaza in a copse of trees, a site that, the Fine
Arts Commission approvingly commented, "would offer views of the Wall through
the trees, a new way to experience it, but at the same time, the trees would screen
the women's memorial so that it would not intrude on either the Wall or the Hart
statue."[120] The setting resembles a clearing and reinforces the "medical evacuation"
interpretation (even though, as in the New Jersey memorial, this "medical evacuation" narrative is implausible) so that the standing figure, like Hart's statue, derives
some of her meaning from her relationship to the surrounding trees. And though in
the women's memorial none of the figures' gazes is locked on the wall, the relationship between the injured man and the names of the dead is subtly reinforced by the
alignment of his body perpendicular to a line bisecting the angle of the two walls.[121]

The unshakable wish of the women's memorial project for a figurative sculpture
honoring women was realized at the dedication of the sculpture on November 11,
1993. Evans's statement in the commemorative booklet used gender and family
imagery to indicate that, with the addition of the women's memorial, the Vietnam
Veterans Memorial was complete, men and women were conjoined, and the
American community was therefore made whole. In this statement, as in her dedication speech, Evans referred to the extended American family involved in the memorial project: the "sister veterans" with whom she served, the "brother veterans"
who supported the memorial financially, the parents who wanted recognition for
their lost children, and the sons and daughters who wanted to understand what their
parents' generation had been through. She sustained the national-family metaphor
by addressing her sister veterans as "daughters of America." Evans invoked her
own children, who lent moral support to her work but who reminded her that she
still needed to shop and keep them in clean clothing. The memorial would mark a

Figure 51. Vietnam Women's Memorial, located at the Vietnam Veterans Memorial, Washington, DC; Glenna Goodacre, sculptor, dedicated November 11, 1993. Copyright © 1993, Vietnam Women's Memorial Foundation, Inc., Glenna Goodacre. Photo by author.

Figure 52. Vietnam Women's Memorial. Copyright © 1993, Vietnam Women's Memorial Foundation, Inc., Glenna Goodacre. Photo by author.

coming together of this extended family.[122] Evans had a word for the ones at home as well as those who went to Southeast Asia: "Let us not forget the wives and mothers, daughters and sisters, fathers and brothers, loved ones left at home during war time—praying, worrying, while awaiting our arrival home. This Memorial is also for you—for your 'place' to come together to reflect and cry healing tears of sorrow or joy or laughter."[123] The "welcome home" was being completed at last. America's family, too long divided against itself, was together again. "Today we are one people. United we stand, strong and proud."[124] Evans's dedication ceremony speech created a family drama of separation and parental anxiety, reminiscent of the California Vietnam Veterans Memorial, which the marriage of male and female sculptural figures, sons and daughters of America, resolved by making the community anew. But the racial and gendered inclusiveness of the statuary in Sacramento and Washington, DC, by implication drew a line around the national family. Outside that boundary, a haunting figure's presence was yet marked as a determinate absence.

10

"OUR OFFSPRING"

Children in Vietnam Veterans Memorials

★

AN UNEXPECTED idea kept coming into the imaginations of Americans considering how to commemorate the Vietnam War: scenes involving American troops helping or saving Vietnamese children. The people who proposed some of these monuments said that they intended them to counter the well-known images of U.S.–perpetrated atrocities, which motivated the "baby killer" accusation. Far from superseding those disturbing images, however, the designs betray the extent to which Americans were haunted by images of dead and injured Vietnamese children. Both the defenders of U.S. policy in Vietnam and its critics had used U.S. forces' relations with Vietnamese children as the measure of the justice of the American cause. Pro-war propaganda showed Americans helping Vietnamese children; antiwar propaganda played on the injuries that U.S. forces caused them. These competing ideas survived in the memories of Vietnam veterans, and contradictory images of Vietnamese children remained a part of a political and psychological battleground in the landscape of commemoration. The proposed memorials with sculptures of Vietnamese children reflected a desire to reassert the worthiness of the U.S. cause in Vietnam by showing Americans in a beneficent role; but these designs unintentionally reminded Americans of the vexed moral questions surrounding the U.S. military conduct of the war for which the bodies of dead and injured children had become symbols.

Representations of Americans helping Vietnamese children countered images of America's child victims, but they also butted up against a third image of Vietnamese children, as armed enemies. Veterans recalled that Vietnamese children were sometimes among the guerrilla forces ranged against them, stealing grenades from American troops or acting as lookouts and messengers for the Viet Cong. Sometimes they were deadly dangers, planting bombs or, horrifyingly, being wired with explosives. The three opposed images—Americans helping Vietnamese children, Americans harming Vietnamese children, and Americans being threatened by Vietnamese children—circulated around one another and made the memorial designs featuring the children fraught with emotional conflict. For this reason, while such designs were debated by the selectors of some of the most well-known memorials in the nation, they survived unmodified only in a handful of little-known local sites.

The idea of a memorial featuring a Vietnamese child surfaced early in the discussions of the Vietnam Veterans Memorial in the nation's capital. In March 1981, a Michigan woman wrote to the organizer of the Vietnam Veterans Memorial Fund (VVMF) design competition describing her concept for the memorial. She proposed a life-sized sculpture of an American soldier and a Vietnamese child, with "one hand reaching out, tentatively, not touching, toward the soldier's drooping fingers." Her letter encapsulates the ideological and emotional significance of the relationship between the adult and child: "In this little child's sweet, innocent face I see all we tried to do in Vietnam, stark contrast to what really happened, what we expended through those long hard years, these two human beings a bridge between our hopes and dreams, and cold reality. This tender little child, hoping for help, for protection, in total trust."[1] The child is the symbol of innocent hope, but it is not the child alone who is innocent: in the child's face is "all we tried to do in Vietnam." The child symbolizes *America's* innocence when it entered the Vietnam War, not knowing how much the reality of the war would confound its good intentions.

This woman was one of many around the country who independently came up with similar ideas. The state adjutant of the American Legion in Maine sent a letter to the VVMF in March 1982, with a proposal for the statue that by then the fund had agreed to add: "May I voice the hope that the Vietnam combat [troop] featured be shown as holding a baby or child from that nation in one arm. The feature of such a child would tell the story of so many Vietnam vets who have done much in contributing to the needy children of Vietnam and would dispel the ugly stories depicted in the press and media concerning Vietnam combat vets and children." He explained that this statue would not just emphasize the positive role that the troops played but would counter negative stories about American atrocities: "Many of our Vietnam vets have spoken to me of their concerns over the unfortunate depiction of our Vietnam vets in the news media as 'baby-burners' and 'child killers.' We need to turn *that* story around and we need to *tell* the story of the courage and kindness of the veterans of our nation."[2] A memorial featuring a Vietnamese child would thus correct the negative stereotypes that arose from the My Lai atrocity and photographs of children injured by napalm.

Among the 1,421 entries to the Vietnam Veterans Memorial competition, a dozen submissions featured Vietnamese figures, almost all of them children. Entry number 627 shows an American soldier with his weapon at shoulder arms, holding the hand of a tiny Vietnamese child symbolizing the war's "innocent victims." Entry number 721 shows an armed soldier, kneeling on one knee with his rifle at the ready, its bayonet fixed and pointing forward, protecting two Vietnamese children who shelter behind him. The designer's statement says that the Vietnam conflict was "an event of people suffering, especially children" and that the sculpture would show "the resolve of all to protect the suffering . . . children." Entry number 906 shows a helmeted American soldier with a Vietnamese child held in one arm and another by his side.[3] These designs portray the American armed forces' role in Vietnam as the gallant protectors of the vulnerable, but at the symbolic level the roles of protector and protected reverse: although the American troops physically guard the children, they are the ones who are vulnerable to charges that they fought an atrocity-ridden war in Vietnam; the protected children function as the guarantors of the worthiness of the American cause.

Only two of the proposed designs featuring Vietnamese figures represent them as adults. In entry number 1283, a Vietnamese adult is squatting on the ground holding a child. A standing American soldier reaches out to take the Vietnamese figure's extended hand. One design alone, number 805, shows a solitary Vietnamese adult being helped by an American, but this Vietnamese figure is submerged in a pool of water and is therefore visible only as the tip of a conical peasant hat and an outstretched hand.[4] In the imaginations of the Americans who submitted designs to the Vietnam Veterans Memorial competition, this pair of features, this hat and this hand, represents the sum of independent Vietnamese adulthood—that is, of Vietnamese adults unaccompanied by children. In the sculptural figuration of the Vietnam War, Americans remembered the Vietnamese people to an overwhelming degree as children. Evidently, veterans and others who entered the design competition considered the image of an American soldier helping a small child a powerful encapsulation of the American forces' role in Vietnam.

The consistent attention to Vietnamese children is striking. The entrants to the Vietnam Veterans Memorial design competition were unknown to one another and could not compare notes. The eleven competition entries featuring Vietnamese children were therefore not the result of a concerted effort. Furthermore, a juror recalled that several of the over two hundred designs submitted to the Minnesota Vietnam Veterans Memorial design competition featured Vietnamese children.[5] The unprompted issuing of this concept from the entrants to the two competitions cannot be explained in the same way the scenes of wounding considered in the preceding chapter can, because statuary depicting casualties did begin to constitute a known genre in the 1980s.[6] Because few memorials featuring Vietnamese children were brought to completion, such designs were not the products of imitation and generic example; some other explanation must be sought.

The presence of Vietnamese children in American memorials to the Vietnam War begins to make sense when we remember the use to which such children were put in propaganda justifying U.S. political and military support of South Vietnam. In a 1956 speech to the American Friends of Vietnam, Senator John F. Kennedy characterized the American-Vietnamese relationship as that of an adult and child. Kennedy pledged U.S. support for the fledgling nation of South Vietnam, explaining, "If we are not the parents of little Vietnam, then surely we are the godparents. We presided at its birth, we gave assistance to its life, we have helped to shape its future. . . . This is our offspring—we cannot abandon it, we cannot ignore its needs."[7] Once America sent combat troops to Vietnam, propaganda efforts redoubled and made use of this adult-child image to justify the U.S. role. The 1965 propaganda film *Why Vietnam?*—its voice-over narrated by President Lyndon Johnson—uses images of

Americans saving and caring for Vietnamese children to contrast U.S. nurturance with Communist cruelty.[8] *The Green Berets*, the only Hollywood feature film made during the conflict in support of America's war aims, ends with Colonel Kirby (John Wayne) pledging to look after a small Vietnamese boy whom his unit has adopted as a sort of mascot. Kirby says to him, "You're what it's all about."[9] The U.S. commander in Vietnam, General William Westmoreland, justified the American military effort in Southeast Asia by saying that Vietnam reminded him of a child—it had to crawl before it could walk and walk before it could run.[10] Thus, pro-war propaganda overlaid two images: the South Vietnamese state as a child, a newly founded "nation" in need of tutelage and support; and South Vietnamese children as representative inhabitants of the country. The two child images converged in their ideological meanings, because by protecting the children, the United States forces helped the young nation, and vice versa.

This sort of paternalism in political speech and propaganda had its counterparts in the wartime combat photography and combat art (pictures made by specialists in the U.S. military services) that showed American medical personnel helping Vietnamese civilians (figs. 53, 54, and 55). Images by combat photographers and paintings by combat artists show American medics treating young Vietnamese patients. Others show Americans feeding Vietnamese children, and young Vietnamese smiling after receiving Americans' gifts.[11]

From the time the U.S. forces and their allies liberated German-occupied Europe in World War II, Americans had associated their nation's military efforts with images of their troops helping grateful civilians.[12] Accordingly, the South Vietnam portrayed in 1967 by the *Reader's Digest*, which was strongly supportive of the U.S. war effort, was a "non-stop procession of school reconstructions and orphanage visits" by GIs. A typical story involved "the beloved mess cook who caught a VC [Viet Cong] grenade while planning a Christmas feast for the local children." As Richard Slotkin has argued, such propaganda portrayed the Vietnamese as "orphaned children who have luckily fallen to the paternal care of strong American men." In keeping with this image of beneficence, in 1968 a Vietnam veterans' periodical published an article about American civic actions headlined, "Does He Care? You Bet He Does." The accompanying text, illustrated by photographs, explains, "He cares enough to build for those in need, to help the young, the old, the apprehensive. He will stop a moment and play with the children, or play for them." A photo caption in the same issue contrasts Communist cruelty with American benevolence: "Savage VC terror attacks kill and maim innocent Vietnamese civilians. Here, an Army sergeant helps a child badly wounded in a Saigon attack."[13]

The children's propaganda value placed them on the front line of the Americans' war for "hearts and minds" in Southeast Asia, as U.S. civilian and military organizations tried to demonstrate that the United States was well-meaning and could offer more to the Vietnamese rural population than the Communists could. Pictures of Americans handing out gifts or delivering medical care to Asian children were also used in the campaign to justify the war to the troops and the American people: the war for "hearts and minds" was part of the "war at home."

Figure 53. Sgt. First Class Joe B. Corbin, 57th Medical Detachment, 1st Logistical Command, makes friends with children of former Viet Cong now living in a resettlement village sponsored by the South Vietnamese government, 1967. Photographer unknown. National Archives and Records Administration, Washington, DC.

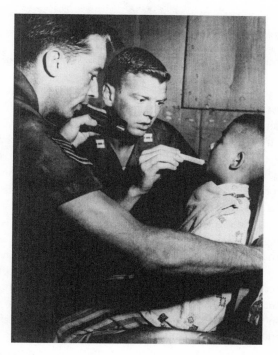

Figure 54. Sgt. John Gordon and Capt. Joe Hill of the 3rd Tactical Dispensary at Bien Hoa Air Base dispense dental treatment to a Vietnamese boy, June 22, 1966. Photographer unknown. U.S. Air Force photograph, National Archives and Records Administration.

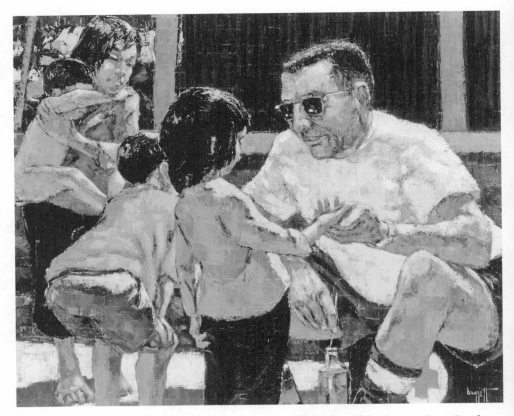

Figure 55. Noel Daggett, *This Won't Hurt a Bit*, oil, 1967. "Doc" Donald R. Watson, a Coast Guard boatswain's mate, applies mercurochrome to a child's infected finger during operations in Vietnam. Courtesy of United States Coast Guard Art Program, Washington, DC.

Although cynics might believe that hard-bitten infantrymen would scoff at such images, seeing through them as propaganda, some soldiers described the same scenes with touching sincerity. In a letter to a friend, a member of the 101st Airborne Division wrote from Vietnam: "There are so few things here that can keep you sane. Everything seems out of whack. . . . To maintain some sense of humanity, I've been going out on Med Caps [Medical Civic Action Patrols]—the medical service taken out to remote villages. I went along as security and got to help treat some of the children. We played games with them, went out for a walk to the beach, took pictures, in general just loved them up."[14] Who knows whether this soldier had seen congruent propaganda images. What seems clear, though, from his letter is that he had his own, emotional reasons for wanting to treat the children and "love them up": as he put it, to keep himself sane in a world that seemed "out of whack." In oral histories recorded after the war, other Americans fondly recall providing medical services for Vietnamese children or helping them in other ways. Jim Noonan said, "In my experience in Vietnam, I never saw anybody shoot a kid indiscriminately, or any of that kind of stuff. If anything, quite the opposite. We'd go out to the orphanages all the time. Because the kids were a source of sanity."[15] Whether or not they were inspired by wartime propaganda, recollections of events such as this reinforced its message about the relationship between the troops and the children. The narratives of Vietnam veterans teem with remembered Vietnamese children, crowding around, receiving candy and cigarettes, and grinning endearingly under the caring eyes of Americans amused by their antics.[16]

Bestowing favors on the people was emotionally satisfying for the troops, whose best instincts were sincerely beneficent. In retrospect, some veterans clung tenaciously to any shred of evidence that they were doing good, not harm, to Vietnam's people. These memories no doubt concerned real events but they converged with the purposes of pro-war indoctrination. Personal recollections, infused with official ideology, persisted as psychologically comforting vignettes signifying all the good Americans wished that they had done. However we explain these recollections, in political or psychological terms, as propaganda or emotion, they belong to the family of recollections that bore fruit in the commemorative designs that showed Vietnamese children being helped by Americans.

When Ronald Reagan narrated stories of Americans helping Vietnamese children, and when the Vietnam Veterans Leadership Program (VVLP) followed him by distributing similar stories, one may be sure that they had the dual purpose of rehabilitating the war effort and making veterans feel better about their service. Soon after assuming the presidency, Reagan gave a speech replete with stories of troops helping children. He told of an artillery man stacking sandbags to protect children in an orphanage from mortar attacks; he recounted the stories of an army engineer distributing gifts to orphans his unit had adopted; and of soldiers and marines building schools, a children's hospital, and an orphanage. (The majority of Reagan's stories in this speech involved orphans, who carried a strong sentimental appeal.) "A 27-year-old chaplain from Springfield, Missouri, came upon an orphanage," Reagan said, "where 60 children were sleeping on the floor of a school and subsisting on one or two bowls of rice a day. He told some men of the [Americal] Division's Fifth Battalion, 46th Infantry, about what he'd seen. A veteran sergeant said, 'Don't worry, Chaplain. Those kids have just got themselves some new parents.' And they had." Story after story of Americans' beneficence followed: as Reagan explained, a senior officer had said that his biggest problem was keeping track of "the incredible humanitarianism of our troops."[17] Just as Kennedy's America had presided at South Vietnam's birth, the American forces that Reagan remembered sustained the parental tradition by "adopting" South Vietnam's orphaned children.

In a clipping distributed by the VVLP, Allen Lynch, who was awarded the Medal of Honor for valor in Vietnam, recalled, "I liked the Vietnamese people—I guess it's kind of like the knight on the shining horse. I guess I could put it this way. We used to put in sick calls in the villages, and you would see people there who were diseased, who were wounded, and we would . . . take care of them. Especially young children. There was a feeling that we had a purpose there."[18] Roy Martin, a counselor with the Mississippi Department of Rehabilitation Services and a supporter of the Mississippi VVLP, said, "I was able to see the Americans through the eyes of the Vietnamese, and they did not see the Americans as the aggressor. . . .

Whenever you saw a GI you saw a bunch of kids. They were fascinated by the GI. Those are the fond memories I have."[19] Distributed in VVLP clippings packets, these stories cease to be merely personal anecdotes and assume a political significance. They justify the American presence in Vietnam by demonstrating that the children trusted the Americans and the Americans were good to the children. Uncorrupted by subversive propaganda, the children could see Americans' goodness—seen through innocent eyes, the Americans themselves became blameless. By remembering the war through scenes like these, the veterans felt heartened: those were their "fond memories"; "we had a purpose there."

In turn, in some Americans' accounts of the war, the children helped the U.S. forces. Children could be talismans of safety, their mere presence a guarantee that local guerrillas would not strike the American forces, or guardians of Americans that they liked. Vito Lava recalled, "Alpha 3 was really a scary place. At Gio Linh and Cam Lo we would see civilians, . . . young kids moving their water buffalo along and harvesting rice and that kind of thing. Even though you realized that some of those civilians might be Viet Cong, it kind of relieved the tension when you'd hear the kids playing or screaming and . . . going about their routine business."[20] John Paul Vann, a counterinsurgency officer, "made friends with a lot of the [Vietnamese] children. Their bright and eager faces moved him. . . . He learned quickly that the children could protect him. They wanted the American who handed out the candy and gum to return, and they would sometimes warn him when there were guerrillas in a hamlet or farther down a road."[21] In the film *Good Morning, Vietnam*, Adrian Kronauer (played by Robin Williams) is warned by a child he befriends that a bomb is about to go off.[22]

The reference to children as a justification of America's presence in Vietnam could be more ambiguous, though. Private First Class George Williams, writing home, mused, "There are a few kids who hang around, some with no parents. I feel so sorry for them. I do things to make them laugh. And they call me 'dinky dow' (crazy). But it makes me feel good. I hope that's one reason why we're here, to secure a future for them. It seems to be the only justification I can think of for all the things that I have done!"[23] The letter was published in full in the book *Dear America*, a by-product of the New York Vietnam Veterans Memorial, a structure made from glass blocks inscribed with letters home from service personnel in Vietnam. When the letter was re-edited for the film version of *Dear America*, the disturbing line about "all the things I have done" was omitted.[24] The reference to the children as justifications of the war effort remained; the mention of hard-to-justify actions, all the more worrying because Williams could have meant anything by "all the things I have done," was evidently too disturbing for inclusion.

An air force pilot who had served two tours in Vietnam said that his comrades in arms volunteered in orphanages to work off their guilt: "For those troubled by the war, who feel bad about the bombing, well, I've seen them try to get close to the people, work in orphanages, dole out food and money, *anything* to atone, *anything* to compensate."[25] Only occasionally did U.S. service personnel ask the obvious question: How did the children populating orphanages come to be orphans? Dan

Bailey, a soldier who suffered from post-traumatic stress disorder (PTSD) after the war, wrote home from Vietnam: "I went down to this orphanage the other day, and these little kids are pitiful. They sleep on plain floors and don't get hardly anything to eat. The reason I want you to tell everyone to help them is because I feel I may have killed some of their parents and it makes me sick to know they have to go on with nothing."[26] The soldier ends the letter giving the address of the orphanage to which his parents' fellow churchgoers might send clothing.

Usually, though, the servicemen were content simply to make a fuss about the children and say, "You're what it's all about." Sandra Collingwood, who worked in South Vietnam for International Voluntary Services and Catholic Relief Services, observed that some Americans who helped in orphanages clung fiercely to their warm memories as a way of feeling better about their wartime service. Collingwood could not bring herself to deny a veteran the comfort that such recollections provided, any more than others could challenge the whole discourse of healing that was shaping public recollections of the war. She said, "I decided on the spot not to challenge him, and I let him talk that through. He had been there. He had seen some of the destruction. And this was the one part of his life while he was there that he felt he was doing some good. I could not deny him that. If that was what was helping to hold him together, I could not deny him that."[27] Thus, stories of troops helping children or taking gifts to orphans could help justify the American war effort—but only with a degree of censorship or self-censorship: the editor's blue pencil striking out Williams's worries about "the things that I have done"; Collingwood's refusal to challenge the veteran's story, although she could see that it was self-serving; other veterans' failure when fondly recalling their work in orphanages to ask the question that Bailey was anxious about: how did eight hundred thousand children lose their parents and therefore come to depend on Americans' handouts?[28]

The juxtaposition of guilt and beneficence was never clearer than in the scenes after the killings at My Lai. According to one of the Americans present, after the massacre there were still a few small children left alive, and the same men who had done the killing "were giving the kids food—you know, just like nothing ever happened."[29] After massacring the civilians in My Lai, William Calley himself became his battalion's S-5 (civil affairs) officer, performing good works in the fields of education, construction, and economic development. Calley, who had tired of killing the Vietnamese civilians, believed in his work: "I had a beautiful thing with the Vietnamese people."[30]

The symbolic weight carried by children can be measured by taking as an extreme example the reaction of some troops encountering a quintessential symbol of "home," a Caucasian child. Their response can be compared to the awe that soldiers felt toward "round-eye" women after some time "in country." A marine officer remembers: "There was a French planter there and a small—very small, I would say three to four years old—blond child, which obviously was Caucasian and belonged to the planter's family. Well, my Marines went absolutely nuts with this little girl standing there waving as we went by. They would unload everything they had of any value to a child. All the candy from C-rations, everything. That little child was buried in everything we could give her. I have to say in all candor that there were some tears and bitter feelings seeing her standing there and relating our own memories to our own children and sisters, etc., who were at home. It was very poignant passing that little child each time."[31] This narrative shows the pent-up wish to give, to do good, to have something or someone on whom servicemen far from home could exercise an unambiguous and unconditional beneficence. In the absence of Caucasian children, Vietnamese children became the recipients of this symbolically loaded generosity and goodwill. The advantage Vietnamese children offered, even if they did not command the extreme response shown to the plantation girl, was that, as natives of Vietnam, their status as American beneficiaries merged with the purposes for which Americans were told they were in Southeast Asia: to defend South Vietnam against "outside aggression." Acts of kindness to the civilians must have seemed as much a part of this picture as giving gifts to the liberated French citizens seen in World War II newsreel films greeting the Americans with garlands and flowers.

Memorials constructed at the end of the Vietnam War show that images of American troops caring for children were part of the conventional repertoire of military commemoration. They often hark back to World War II. Dedicated in 1974, in the period between the departure of the last U.S. combat troops and the fall of Saigon, the Seabees (Construction Battalions) memorial shows an American serviceman, heavily muscled and stripped to the waist, allowing a boy to take his hand (fig. 56). They stand near Arlington Memorial Bridge, connecting Washington with Virginia, with an inscription that reads, "With compassion we fight for others. We build—We fight for peace with freedom." In the background and to the sides are bas-reliefs that show the Seabees pouring concrete, rigging communication wires, pulling sentry duty, and crewing a weapons emplacement. The attractive message and the depiction of the adult-child relationship are just the sort of thing that some Vietnam veterans wanted to believe about themselves and to show the public about their efforts. The sculpture is by Felix de Weldon, beloved of veterans involved in the debate about the Vietnam Veterans Memorial who wanted a noble, bronze monument. But the weapon slung over the Seabee's shoulder is an M1 rifle of World War II vintage, dissociating the sculpture from the Vietnam War era and Vietnam veterans from the good works it portrays.

A Johnstown, Pennsylvania, statue dedicated in the same year, 1974, portrays a standing soldier who cradles a tiny girl in his arms. This memorial straddles two eras. Two Gold Star Mothers asked the sculptor to depict the soldier holding a child, not a weapon, to remind viewers of "the kindness shown by so many soldiers to the children of war."[32] Although this monument was said to honor all American veterans, not just those of the Vietnam War, its dedication in the year after the Paris Peace Accords, and the fact that the figure wears Vietnam War-era fatigues, associates the man with service in Vietnam. The girl, though, is Caucasian.[33] The figures' pose is consistent with pro–Vietnam War propaganda but conflates it with images of U.S. beneficence in World War II Europe.

Figure 56. Seabee Memorial, Arlington, Virginia, Felix de Weldon, sculptor, Anthony Harrer, architect, dedicated May 27, 1974. Photo by author.

The Korea–Vietnam Peace Memorial in Omaha, Nebraska (fig. 57), was dedicated in 1976, soon after the end of the Vietnam War (which explains why it was called a "peace" memorial). The sculpture shows an American serviceman with an Asian child, perhaps eight years old, sitting on his knee and looking trustingly into his face.[34] The man has given the girl water from his canteen; he points into the far distance, behind her. The sculptor, James C. Keith, a World War II veteran, explained that his inspiration came from "the traditional concept that American servicemen were always there to help the children of war-torn lands." "My idea of picturing a service man and child came from wanting to avoid as much controversy as possible during the awkward political climate of those years. The theme of American service men handing out candy bars and caring for children during WWII was at least a pleasant myth. I felt that this same theme could demonstrate the peaceful part Americans played in Viet Nam." The memorial, though, was "at the center of a great deal of controversy reflecting the anti-military mood of the country." Its creators feared that local peace groups would take issue with its symbolism by objecting that the Vietnam War had nothing to do with helping children.[35] They therefore offered the disclaimer that the memorial "has nothing to do with the wars, but with the men

Figure 57.   Korea–Vietnam Peace Memorial, Omaha, Nebraska; James C. Keith, sculptor, dedicated May 30, 1976. Photo by Bill Henry.

and women who served."[36] To avoid appearing too belligerent, the adult figure, although uniformed, has set his rifle and helmet to the side, and the rifle's magazine is missing. Anticipating the orthodox accounts of the national Vietnam Veterans Memorial's ethos four years later, the local newspaper editorialized that the memorial was not there to honor or justify war. "The honor is for those who served and most especially those who died."[37]

That this formulation precedes the Washington memorial's near-identical statement of purpose is interesting not because the VVMF copied the Omaha memorial's language—there is no suggestion that Jan Scruggs and his fellows had even heard of the Omaha memorial—but because it demonstrates that the political context of its times enjoined honoring the warrior, not the war, as a tactical means of avoiding controversies. Reinforced by all the talk surrounding the commemorations that followed, the concept was firmly inscribed in the minds of local veterans twenty years after the Omaha memorial's dedication, when the local leader of Vietnam Veterans of America said that the memorial was "not to honor war but to honor the American soldier for helping peace and for helping the children."[38] In fact, the inscription at the base of the memorial is not so diffident: it describes the bravery and dedication of the U.S. soldiers in the fight against "aggression" in Korea and Vietnam. The image of Americans helping young Asians was a sentimentalized way of promoting this ideological viewpoint. As the sculptor said, "We hope it will someday show that we were in Vietnam and Korea to make a better world for all the children."[39] The child, then, is the harbinger of the world to come, and the soldier points forward, his arm outstretched, as the child gazes at his face. It is as if he is pointing to the still distant future when that better world will have been achieved—or at least to the time when the audience will have come to believe that this was the reason for his fight.

In the 1980s, others who proposed designs for state and local memorials continued to contemplate depicting Vietnamese children with American helpers. In most instances, the sculptures did not materialize but, even so, the surrounding discussions provide revealing statements of what veterans thought would make an appropriate memorial. Their motivations for including the children in the designs are generally faithful to the wartime propaganda and veterans' narratives in which the children are the recipients of American help.

Before the Kentucky Vietnam Veterans Memorial Fund had properly begun to consider designs for its memorial, Bob Manning, a supporter, said: "When I show people pictures I took in Vietnam, they notice the helmet, *the little kids*, the packs. I never felt a lot of grief about being over there. It all comes back to the kids— they were always so hungry" (emphasis in original).[40] Once Ronald Ray persuaded them to consider a sculpture, several members of the memorial's design committee proposed depicting Vietnamese children, echoing the Maine American Legion adjutant in the hope that this would portray American soldiers "help[ing] children," as "protectors, not aggressors."[41] A Kentucky design committee member said, "A child is a symbol of many things—our hope for the future, as well as the presence of actual, real children [in South Vietnam]." Concurring, a colleague said that using a child in a memorial would be a "counterstatement" to all that had been said in antiwar propaganda that showed images of dead and wounded children. Depictions of women and children, he thought, would enable a soldier to appear in a sculpture in the guise of a "protector" and "helper." Children would also symbolize those at home for whom Americans fought and died—their own children.[42]

Kentucky committee members elaborated their thoughts about the memorial in design statements. One said, "My lasting impression is of the American serviceman helping the sick, injured, and particularly small children. I would suggest a statue of an American serviceman walking with a rifle over his shoulder being grasped by the muzzle. He would be holding the hand of a small child with his free hand."[43] Another statement, written by a draftee proud of his service in Vietnam, said, "It's my feeling that we were there to help a people who couldn't help themselves. . . . I was there to help the children. . . . I feel that the figure of a G.I. with his arm around a Vietnamese child would be most appealing, representative, and appropriate."[44]

The proposed use of children in these memorials thus expressed complex themes: the children would represent "what we tried to do" in helping a weaker nation; scenes of Americans helping Asian children would counter the ugly stories of atrocities; and children represented "hope." The problem was that, no matter how clearly a memorial showed a soldier helping a child, it might not dispel stories of veterans as baby killers. One might see hundreds of benign representations of GIs with children and still remember the My Lai photographs. Nor did the concept of "hope" dispel negative memories about Vietnam, because veterans' recollections of their hopeful idealism when they went to Vietnam are often nostalgic or ironic. For example,

Vietnam veterans frequently use references to John F. Kennedy's inaugural address, his call to "ask not what your country can do for you, ask what you can do for your country" as a way of capturing their own idealistic beliefs in the early 1960s.[45] But veterans like Philip Caputo and Bobby Muller quote the inaugural address ironically, as a measure of their subsequent disappointment because of their experiences in Vietnam. The inaugural address symbolizes what they believed before the war stripped them of their illusions.[46] The image of Vietnamese children might have a similar double-edged quality for those who recalled not just hope but also disillusionment. The image of an American helping a Vietnamese child summed up simultaneously the good that the pro-war propaganda said Americans set out to do in Vietnam, and the way those good intentions were shattered by the realities of the war. Although these ambiguities suggest why Americans had second thoughts about the inclusion of Vietnamese children in memorials to the Vietnam War, they did not stop this idea from bubbling up into people's imaginations.

The Roswell, Georgia, Vietnam War Memorial (fig. 58), dedicated twenty years after the fall of Saigon, demonstrates the multi-layered significance of child imagery because, rather than condensing concepts of nurturance, protection, and hope in a single adult-child pair, it contains more than one child. The most prominent child-figure is an American, and the memorial committee's published material indicates that she is the memorial's thematic heart, a symbol of rebirth and regeneration. It is notable that in both the Omaha memorial and the one in Roswell, the child is a prepubescent girl, and the memorial in Georgia derives some of its significance from her gender. As the memorial's dedication program states, "The little girl represents innocence and the future. It is her womb that will bear the future generations and her innocence that will help erase the tragedies of the past as we move forward."[47] The peculiar conceit is therefore of a child as a figure representing fertility and motherhood. Her future is pregnant with the nation's destiny, while the memorial preserves her childishness as an unchanging sign of innocence.

In a bas-relief, the memorial shows multiple scenes of American soldiers and Vietnamese civilians, including a well-known image of an American nurse tenderly holding an emaciated Vietnamese child (figs. 59 and 60). Here, motherhood and childish innocence, which supposedly converged in the figure of the young girl, bifurcate in a conventional image of quasi-maternal nurturance. Originally published in *Life* magazine, the photograph on which this scene is based became the most well-known image of a nurse in Vietnam when it appeared on the cover of the paperback editions of two mass-marketed oral histories, *A Piece of My Heart* and *In the Combat Zone*. The tenderness with which the woman holds the sleeping infant, the proximity of their faces, and the comportment of their bodies make this a latter-day Madonna and Child. But there are some incongruous elements. The child is seriously emaciated. While one of the woman's hands supports his diapered bottom, her other arm envelops his body so that her well-toned flesh contrasts shockingly with his bony arm and protruding ribs. His head lies on her shoulder, cushioned by a towel. This image is notable because it expresses a well of emotions: care, tenderness, and anxiety, encompassed in the woman's nurturant role. By extension, the relationship between the two populations and the two nations is represented as one based on the ministration of the "adult" Americans to their junior Vietnamese dependants, who are in desperate need of help.

The assertion of America's quasi-parental role was overturned when journalists, dissident troops, and veterans began to report in the late 1960s that, far from protecting their Vietnamese wards, America's air forces and ground troops were killing and maiming them. If America was a parent, it was a murderous one, not only sending

Figure 58. *The Faces of War*, Roswell Vietnam War Memorial, Georgia; Teena Watson-Stern and Don Haugen, sculptors, Zachary Henderson, architect, dedicated May 19, 1995. Photo by author.

its own sons to die by the thousands far from home but also killing an uncounted multitude of Kennedy's "godchildren," the very ones it claimed it wanted to protect. In January 1967, *Ramparts* magazine published a report titled "The Children of Vietnam" that "did much to set off national discussion of how U.S. tactics in the war were causing unnecessary civilian casualties."[48] As the war became increasingly unpopular, this sort of challenge undermined the moral basis for America's military support for South Vietnam. The killing of children shattered the official rhetoric about America's parental responsibilities. The repeated refrain that caring

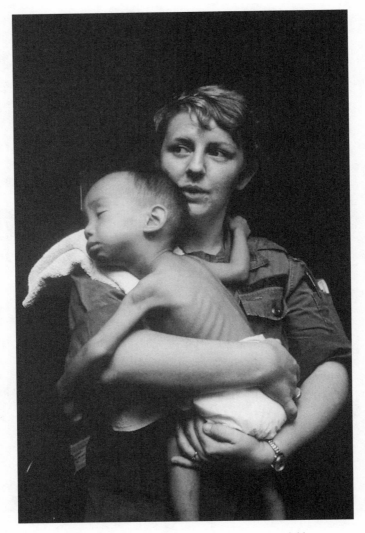

Figure 59. Nurse Donna Hamilton holds a Vietnamese child, 1968;
photo by John Olson. © Life Magazine.

for the children helped to keep the troops sane allows us to understand just why the pictures of the My Lai massacre were so psychologically catastrophic for America's citizens. If helping children was the one redeeming act that could justify the war and maintain the troops' sanity, to see that U.S soldiers massacred women and children undid the picture of the world they wanted to preserve. Suddenly, "you're what it's all about" took on a darker meaning. Americans were catapulted from a world in which they could believe in their own kindness into another, crazy world in which Americans were exposed as monsters. Disturbing images of America's child victims

Figure 60. Roswell Vietnam War Memorial, detail.
Photo by author.

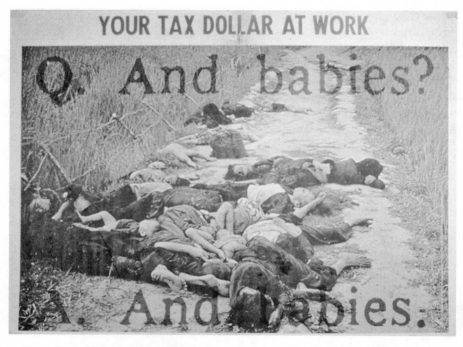

Figure 61. *And Babies?* antiwar poster by Frazer Dougherty, Jon Hendricks, and Irving Petlin, Artists Poster Committee, Art Workers Coalition, 1970. This copy of the poster was mounted on card with the legend "Your tax dollar at work" and carried at an antiwar demonstration in Washington, DC. Collection of the Division of Politics and Reform, National Museum of American History, Smithsonian Institution.

challenged the affirmative representations of Vietnamese children as symbols of U.S. beneficence and hope.

Participants in the antiwar movement seized on photojournalism depicting dead and injured children and turned out antiwar posters with graphic depictions of America's victims. A 1970 poster by the Art Workers Coalition displays one of Ron Haeberle's photographs of the My Lai massacre, showing some seventeen women's and children's bodies strewn where they had been shot on a dirt path (fig. 61). The words: "Q: And Babies? A: And babies" reproduce a question and answer from the CBS correspondent Mike Wallace's interview with the My Lai veteran Paul Meadlo, in which Meadlo admitted to having killed children. A later version of the poster, using the same photograph, identically framed, substitutes for the question and answer the repeated question, "Four More Years?" referring to a slogan in President Nixon's successful 1972 presidential re-election campaign.[49] The lettering in each version is the same dark red, evoking the blood that was spilled.

Numerous other antiwar posters used photographs of dead and injured Vietnamese children. One shows two disfigured children, both burned and one covered with bandages, with a quotation from one of Martin Luther King Jr.'s speeches: "If America's soul becomes totally poisoned, part of the autopsy must read Vietnam" (fig. 62). A quarter of a million leaflets showing the horribly burned corpses of a Vietnamese woman and an infant were dropped from aircraft over California in protest against American forces' use of napalm, an incendiary weapon made of jellied gasoline.[50] Another poster shows an image of a Vietnamese infant injured by napalm, accompanied by the familiar advertising logo, *Johnson's Baby Powder / Made in USA* (fig. 63).[51] As Judith Butler has argued, "In the Vietnam War, it was the pictures of children burning and dying from napalm that brought the U.S. public to a sense of shock, outrage, remorse, and grief. These were precisely pictures we were not supposed to see, and they disrupted the visual field and the entire sense of public identity that was built upon that field."[52] Several antiwar posters imply that the injuries to children were not accidents but part of a deliberate campaign to attack Vietnamese civilians. For example, a poster captioned "This is the enemy" depicts a distressed Vietnamese woman holding an injured child (fig. 64). Other posters protest against the use of napalm, showing Vietnamese women holding burned children in a hideous re-imaging of Madonna-and-Child pictures, showing U.S. military might destroying innocent life and targeting the cherished foundations of civilization itself (fig. 65). One uses the word *napalm* spelled out in blood-red, flame-like lettering.[53]

Injury to children has long been part of the repertoire of war propaganda. Unlike World War I tales of German savagery against Belgian babies, however, the use of such imagery in anti–Vietnam War posters was an unusual instance in which a nation's citizens accused their own armed forces of victimizing the innocent.[54] Thus,

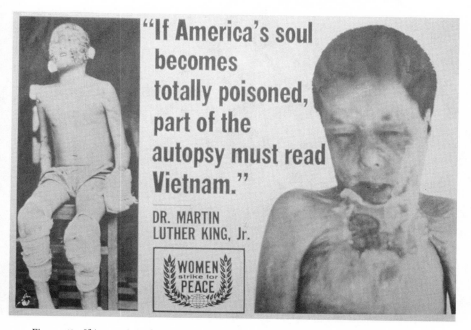

Figure 62. *If America's Soul Becomes Totally Poisoned, Part of the Autopsy Must Read Vietnam,* Women Strike for Peace poster. Collection of the Division of Politics and Reform, National Museum of American History.

the pro-war propaganda did not monopolize representations of Vietnamese children during wartime. It contended with highly publicized photojournalism and antiwar propaganda that had a powerful shock effect. Images of Vietnamese children were drafted into an ideological battleground during the war, and contrasting recollections of the children continued to contend in the postwar years.

Recalling the war-era testimony of Vietnam Veterans Against the War, many veterans interviewed by oral historians spoke out in the 1980s about instances of children being killed or brutalized.[55] In their stories, the veterans recall the transformation in the American attitude, from friendliness to wariness and thence to hostility, once they realized that their hopes of being treated like the saviors of liberated

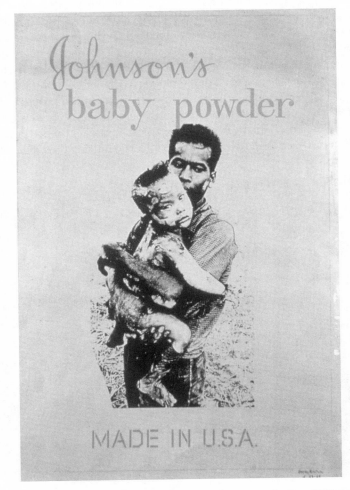

Figure 63. *Johnson's Baby Powder/Made in USA*, 1968, antiwar poster by Gary H. Brown, using a photograph by Felix Green (Associated Press/Wide World), silkscreen on paper. Archival poster provided by the Center for the Study of Political Graphics, Los Angeles, California.

Europe would not be satisfied. Experience could sour the idealistic expectations about grateful Vietnamese children greeting generous troops. "Harold O.," a conscientious objector who served in Vietnam, describes this scene: "I had that World War II image of GI Joe with the little kid in his hand, and the kid's got the helmet on, eating a Hersey [*sic*] bar, right? So, I'd give the kids all my food, sometimes I wouldn't have anything to eat. Well, all along the road there'd be kids yelling, 'Fuck you, GI. Fuck you!' Then, I'd see guys ridin' on a truck take, like, beans and mother-fuckers—[canned] lima beans and ham, stuff that you wouldn't eat—and hit the kids in the head with the cans. Three to six months later, after all the shit came down, there'd be guys shootin' kids. Some kid would come up and say, 'Fuck you, GI.'

Figure 64. *This Is the Enemy*. Archival poster provided by the Center for the Study of Political Graphics, Los Angeles.

Pow! They'd blow his shit away. Blowin' old ladies away. Crazy sons-of-bitches."[56] The perpetrators of the My Lai massacre, the GIs in Charlie Company, 1st Battalion, 20th Infantry, played with Vietnamese children when they first arrived in country. In a documentary about the massacre, Fred Widmer recounts, "You'd play with the kids in between pulling guard duty. . . . You'd always take them stuff, candy, pop, take pictures with them, GIs with the kids." (In the documentary, the camera cuts away to a still picture of a GI with six smiling children.)[57] Not long afterward, the soldiers began to feel bitter toward the Vietnamese, whom they held responsible for American casualties. One My Lai veteran spoke of the anger that developed as a

Figure 65. *What Does Our Flag Stand for in Vietnam? Napalm,* antiwar poster by National Coordinating Committee to End the War in Vietnam. Archival poster provided by the AOUON Archive, Berkeley, California.

result of what he took to be the Vietnamese ingratitude for the Americans' friendly gestures: "We give them medical supplies and they come and kick our ass."[58] The troops began to see the children as hostile, perhaps participants in guerrilla activities as messengers or lookouts, and certainly as Viet Cong in the making. Sa Thi Qui, a My Lai survivor, describes the sequence of events from the villagers' point of view, in a mirror image of Harold O's and Fred Widmer's stories: the first time the Americans came, the children followed them and the Americans gave them candy; the second time, the Americans said nothing, and the villagers gave them water; the third time, the Americans killed everyone.[59]

A veteran chronicles some of the paradoxes and problems of service in Vietnam: the servicemen were not there to win but to survive; the war had no frontlines. "The enemy was 12 years old and cleaned our quarters during the day. At night the rockets came. The Vietnamese whom we were sent to help stole our jeeps, traded them to the VC and refused to fight during afternoon naps. . . . We gave presents to the little kids and we were told of My Lai."[60] The last sentence is the most striking, displacing the American troops' agency through the use of the passive voice—we *did* something when giving presents, but we were merely *told of* something when the My Lai massacre occurred. Who, then, killed the children there? Presumably, the act was performed by some unnamed "they," but "they" and "we" were identified by common membership of the U.S. forces, disallowing the attempt to create a distance between "them" and "us." This difficulty confronts any veteran wanting to disavow the violence that Vietnamese civilians suffered at the hands of the forces of the United States.

Stories about U.S. violence against Vietnamese children, true or apocryphal, were universally known throughout the veterans' community but usually remained the unmentionable, hidden a mile deep or inches beneath the surface of any conversation among veterans or between veterans and others. These were the stories that the "positive" images of the troops recommended by the VVLP were supposed to bury forever. The picture that turned out to be worth a million veterans' stories and that kept violence against children alive in Americans' recollections of the war was the transfixing photograph of Kim Phuc, a young Vietnamese girl, running naked down a country road after being struck by a napalm attack.

On June 8, 1972, a South Vietnamese aircraft dropped napalm on the village of Trang Bang. The bombs missed the guerrillas that were the intended target and hit civilian houses, flames gushing orange from the point of impact. International journalists witnessed the whole scene, having come to see the South Vietnamese military perform a combined air and ground assault, using weapons and tactics that the departing Americans had bequeathed to them. At first there were a few distant shouts and screams and then, as the journalists looked on, civilians came running and stumbling toward them from the scene of the bombing, some horribly injured. An old woman came toward the news cameras carrying a badly burned infant, his charred skin hanging limp from his limbs like ragged clothing. Then a nine-year-old girl came running toward the cameras, crying *"nong qua, nong qua"* (Too hot, too hot). She was naked, having torn off her burning clothes after the bomb hit. Her left

Figure 66. *Nine-Year-Old Kim Phuc Running Down Route 1 Near Trang Bang after a South Vietnamese Napalm Attack*, June 8, 1972. Photo by Nick Ut. Copyright © AP Photo/Nick Ut.

side, neck, and back had been struck by the burning napalm, which also stuck to the palm of her right hand when she tried to brush it off.[61] The photographer Nick Ut brought his camera down to her eye-level and clicked the shutter.

The photograph (fig. 66) was front-page news around the world the next day. By 1972, the public was well aware of the damage being done to Vietnamese civilians by the fighting and knew of atrocities committed by the United States and its allies. The picture of Kim running naked toward the camera seemed not just to prove that war is terrible and that accidents are inevitable but to confirm the allegations that the allied forces were using indiscriminate violence in the name of killing Communists. Kim became a poster child for antiwar activists and a cause célèbre in the Socialist world. As she grew up, after the unification of Vietnam under a Communist government, she became the subject of a propaganda film and went to Cuba for medical training.[62] She had been dreadfully injured, though, and her scars caused her severe pain. She had wanted to train as a doctor but her injuries and ill health prevented her from doing so.

The photograph of Kim running toward the camera, like the My Lai photographs, became part of the repertoire of visual protest against war and one of the best-known images of the twentieth century. It was reproduced by countless documentary filmmakers who wished to encapsulate the horrors of the Vietnam War and by visual artists who wished to reflect on the embodiment of those horrors in the imagery of the war. "Those pictures made a difference," the photographer Michael Carlebach writes, referring to the most well-known images of the war, including the photograph of Kim. "Millions of people would hold the same image in their minds at the same time. Those things, for millions of Americans, *became* the war. And if there was anything that turned America against the war, it was those images, because symbols are powerful things. Symbols can affect reality."[63] The art critic and curator Lucy Lippard has said that those images, along with Eddie Adams's 1968 photograph of General Loan shooting an unarmed Viet Cong prisoner at point-blank range, became "icons of the war, embedded in our consciousness of Vietnam." The photographs and criticisms of the war acted reciprocally on each other. Some people may have decided, as Carlebach proposes, that the war was wrong because they saw the photographs; but the reverse relationship between the photographs' effects and viewers' opinions of the war is just as possible. The images provided visual corroboration of a "pre-existing story line": critical views of the war to which some people already subscribed. Whether the photos brought about or reinforced critical opinions about the war, the important thing from the point of view of commemoration is that the images, as Lippard suggests, provided enduring mental anchor points for these views.[64]

In the documentary *Hearts and Minds*, the filmmaker Peter Davis shows the Trang Bang bombing in a sequence that includes interviews with American pilots and the filmed denunciation of American bombing by a North Vietnamese father whose daughter U.S. bombs had killed. The footage of Kim is intercut with an interview with the former marine pilot Randy Floyd.[65] We see jets flying, the explosion of napalm on a road, a shot of Floyd talking to the camera, Kim running down the road, Kim drinking water and having water poured on her by two uniformed Americans, then Floyd again. All of this footage is accompanied by Floyd's voice-over describing bombing as a technical "game" for the pilots, lethal for the targets that they hardly ever see up close. Floyd's voice-over says, "We Americans have never experienced that. We've never experienced any kind of devastation. When I was there, I never saw a child that had gotten burned by napalm." The documentary cuts away to a shot of a mother with a napalmed baby in her arms. A close-up shows the scraps of skin flapping from the baby's foot. Sitting on a porch in Oklahoma, Floyd describes the devastating effects of cluster bombs and imagines his outrage if someone injured his child the way that he had injured children in Vietnam: "People would suffer [because of the effects of the pellets in the cluster bombs he dropped]. They would live but they would suffer, you know. Then often they would die afterwards. This would cause people to have to take care of them, you know. But I look at my children now. And I don't know what would happen if, what I would think about if someone napalmed them." Other veterans describe the same sort of revelation, when they imagined their own children being harmed as Vietnamese children were.[66] The capacity to see one's own in the place of the other and to imagine the positions of self and other reversed is empathy; these instances of empathy were the starting point for an ethical response to the violence which U.S. forces and their allies inflicted on Vietnamese civilians.

Kim Phuc's image's first appearance in a protest poster was in a photomontage advertising Hiroshima Day in 1972 and connecting the bombing of Vietnam with the atomic bombing of Japan. Kim's image is cut out from the background of Ut's photograph and superimposed on a mushroom cloud. An early 1980s poster conjoins a photograph of children in El Salvador with that of Kim, calling for an end to the arms buildup and a demonstration for "No More Vietnam Wars" in Central America and the Caribbean. The ubiquity of the photograph in magazine articles and documentaries about the war, as well as fine arts and vernacular forms, demonstrates the deep embeddedness of her image in American culture.[67]

Ronald Ray fought hard for a sculpture to commemorate the Vietnam War because he wanted to replace the ubiquitous picture of Kim with a positive figurative image. Ray said that all the most well-known pictures of the Vietnam War were negative ones. Just as the most memorable image of World War II was Joe Rosenthal's photograph of the marines raising the Stars and Stripes on Mount Suribachi (the picture transformed into the Iwo Jima Memorial), the most vivid images of the Vietnam War, Ray said, were General Loan shooting a Viet Cong suspect and "the little girl running down the road burning from napalm." Noting that the "people that control symbols control the outcome," Ray complained that "the power mongers decided that these two pictures would be the symbols."[68] His frustration at the "power mongers" was all the greater because they were hard to pin down. He seemed to see a Masonic conspiracy of photo editors determining just which images would be chosen again and again to ensure that they stick in people's minds. His interpretation implied that those images could be displaced if another "power monger" ruled that a more attractive picture would prevail. The problem, though, was that the power of the images was more profuse and more subversive, located not in some cabal but diffused through a widely distributed network including not only photo editors and filmmakers but also the filigree of neurons and synapses that form the war's photographic archive in the memories of the American people.

Kim was in the mind of the Vietnam veteran who led the effort to build a local memorial in Michigan. Dedicated in 1991, in Oakland County, the memorial demonstrates that depictions of American personnel ministering to children are dense with moral meanings. On the three-sided granite stone are three war scenes: soldiers helping a wounded serviceman onto a helicopter; two prisoners in a Vietnamese prisoner of war camp; and an American soldier holding a Vietnamese baby (fig. 67).[69] Fred Sepelak, the Vietnam veteran who led the effort to create the memorial and who devised the design concept, explained that he was motivated by guilt about the fifty-eight thousand Americans who died needlessly in the Vietnam War. When asked why he wanted a child in the memorial, though, he explained that he wanted a representation of the U.S. military's effect on the villages and hamlets of Vietnam. The image in the memorial shows an American soldier carrying a wounded baby. But what signifies the psychologically complex interplay of child images is that the picture originally in Sepelak's mind was of Kim.[70] Thus, survivor guilt mingled with

Figure 67. Oakland Hills Vietnam Veterans Memorial, Oakland Hills Memorial Gardens, Novi, Michigan; Frederick P. Sepelak and Michael W. Nolan, designers, Steven Pikor, images, dedicated September 20, 1991. Photograph courtesy of Dennis Kushner, Vietnam veteran.

remorse over the violence done to a Vietnamese child, yet when an image took shape, it was not that of the naked, wounded girl. Somehow it had transformed itself into, or been covered over by, a picture that was easier to portray, of an American in an act of rescue.

Representations of Americans caring for injured Vietnamese children can convey the same ideas as other images of American adults helping the children but ratcheted up a notch. If Americans are portrayed as nurturers when they cradle Vietnamese children, then that idea of nurturance becomes more intense when the children have suffered wounds. But a sculpture or an engraving of an American with a dead or wounded Vietnamese child raises troubling questions about the source of that injury. When dead and wounded children are portrayed in antiwar polemics and posters, two contradictory messages collide: the familiar justifications of the war that showed Americans helping Vietnamese children, and condemnations of the war that showed the effects of the war on those children's stricken bodies. Images of Americans helping Vietnamese children connoted positive values such as hope and innocence while the image of an American holding a dead child gave material form to the disillusionment that American veterans felt, having ceased to believe in the purpose for which they were sent to fight and discovering on returning home that their service brought them no esteem.

Michael Page's *Pietà* (fig. 68), a twenty-eight-inch-high sculpture that has been exhibited as part of the Vietnam Veterans Arts Group's "Reflexes and Reflections" show since the 1980s (and since 1996 has been displayed in the collection's permanent museum home in Chicago), is dense with layers of contradictory meanings that run through it, like the grain of the wood from which it is carved. The sculpture does not show a lifeless adult figure, as the title would suggest, but an adult figure wearing a helmet and poncho (resembling the Virgin's cowl) holding a dead or badly wounded infant. The peculiar twisting cant of the infant's arm references that of the dead Christ in Michelangelo's Florence Pietà, making it clear that Page was well schooled in the tradition to which he referred.[71] Page began carving the sculpture as a tribute to the men he served with in Vietnam but the more he worked on the adult's face the more it changed meaning. The Madonna figure started off as male—based on a photograph of an exhausted marine at Khe Sanh with the "thousand-yard-stare" typical of those who had seen too much combat.[72] This, Page says, is a look common to exhausted

Figure 68. Michael Page, *Pietà*, walnut, 1980. Photograph courtesy of the artist.

young men in war. As he worked on the sculpture, the face became more androgynous. The sculpture means to him the fathers and mothers of all soldiers at war, and the children of war, young or old—a symbol of lost innocence and senseless death.[73]

The overdetermined complexity of the losses that Americans felt—lost innocence, a lost sense of national unity and purpose, and the lives lost on both sides of the war—is matched by the conflation of several generic references. Because the dead body in Page's *Pietà* is that of an infant, the sculpture conflates the genres of Madonna and Child and Pietà. The infant has died before its time; it is as if Christ had succumbed to the Slaughter of the Innocents rather than surviving to adulthood. The redemption that his death promised humanity might thus be foreclosed. Did the soldier kill the child, fail to rescue it, or come upon it in some other way? Should we consider the child as a representative of the child victims of war, or of the adult figure's childish innocence, now gone? The indeterminacy of these possible interpretations provides us with evidence of the turbidity of memory in the mind of a veteran unsure of whom or what to mourn—all the war's dead, his own buddies, or children as innocents and innocence lost.

Along with images in veterans' minds of Vietnamese children as Americans' beneficiaries and of children as their victims were images of Vietnamese children as a military threat. Veterans' narratives are peppered with stories of Vietnamese babies being booby-trapped by explosives, of children leading the Americans into ambushes, and of children coming up to unsuspecting American troops and unleashing lethal attacks with grenades and bombs. These stories are likely founded in fact, but they possess a wider significance in relation to the stories of America's child victims. The knowledge that Vietnamese children sometimes behaved as a threat to U.S. forces might mitigate the guilt of American troops who killed or injured children. This proposition tended to recalibrate the scales of judgment, shifting the weight of moral responsibility from the Americans to the Vietnamese Communists. The Communists' use of children as auxiliary military forces demonstrated their ruthlessness and made them, not the Americans, responsible for the children's injuries. The booby-trapping of babies was a particularly heinous act that proved the Communists' depravity. That Americans died and were injured by the booby traps because of their naïve belief that babies would not be used as instruments of war proved the Americans' essential decency. The possibility that children might be armed and dangerous also increased the psychological travails the Americans underwent, making them objects of sympathy. U.S. forces faced the dreadful dilemma of deciding in an instant whether to treat the children they encountered as noncombatants or as sources of potential danger, knowing that, if their judgment happened to be wrong, they might die, or be condemned to eternal moral damnation.

A veteran recording an oral history says, "You can't tell who's your enemy. You got to shoot kids, you got to shoot women. You don't want to. You may be sorry that you did. But you might be sorrier if you didn't. That's the damn truth."[74] Several veterans stress that children sometimes threw hand grenades, or they might be strapped with explosives that would be triggered when they approached American soldiers.[75] Here is one typical story: "We had a little boy taking us sodas everywhere we went.

That little kid always seemed to be around. One time he caught us off guard, too. He paddled his little boat down a narrow canal until he reached us on the side of the bank. He would carry bags full of sodas, and we would trade him the sodas for our C-rations. One time he left one of those bags there. He said we could have it and nobody paid any attention to it. It was a command detonated mine is what it was. Command detonated mine means that this kid left it and it was detonated from a distance. It killed two soldiers. Bam! Just like that."[76] James Webb, the memorial fund critic, said in a television documentary, "With the civilians, in many areas of the An Hoa basin, they actively operated against us and the worst incident that I had, that my platoon went through, began when an approximately seven-year-old girl lured one of my teams into an ambush, into a North Vietnamese ambush."[77] As he spoke, the picture on the television screen switched from his "talking head" to a pan across a still picture of two women, one young and one elderly, and four children—implying that any such group of women and children might be innocuous or a deadly threat, and placing the contemporary viewer in the same uncertainty as that of the wartime GI, for whom the "threat level" of such a group would be unreadable. In an episode of the television series *Tour of Duty*, Lieutenant Goldman (Stephen Caffrey), one of the central characters, says to a female reporter, Alex Devlin (Kim Delaney), that the Viet Cong "would put a grenade in a baby's blanket with the baby still in it if they thought it would kill Americans." This follows an incident where Goldman and Devlin have a lucky escape when a nine-year-old Vietnamese shoeshine boy explodes a bomb in a café they have just left.[78]

In the documentary *Interviews with My Lai Veterans*, Varnado Simpson, one of the perpetrators of the My Lai massacre, explains his killing children by saying that they should not be allowed to grow up to become Viet Cong.[79] A decade later, when Simpson was interviewed again for the documentary *Remember My Lai*, he was consumed by guilt because of the children he killed at My Lai. This time, rather than matter-of-factly justifying killing the children, he lays out an impossible situation for troops unable to identify a proper target: "Who was the enemy? You'd have little kids that would shoot you or stab [you] in the back when you walk away. You know, who was the enemy? How can you distinguish between the enemy, the good or the bad? . . . They all look alike, North or South." He shows a ring binder containing Haeberle's pictures in *Life* magazine. "This is my life," he repeats, indicating a picture of two young boys he had shot.

Chaim Shatan heard Vietnam veterans describe the shift between their prewar selves and the new selves who had lost their sensitivities in Vietnam and learned to hate. An indication that they had passed over a boundary was their perception of children as dangerous: "Occasionally, soldiers felt reassured by the warmth and tenderness that Vietnamese children awakened in them—but this last shred of humanity could be shattered when they saw comrades blown to pieces by a little girl with grenades around her waist under her dress."[80] Other therapists heard veterans express the same sort of fears: "A crying child could be a deadly, explosive trap."[81] The war was "catastrophically stressful" for American troops because they could never know for certain who supported the South Vietnamese government or the

Viet Cong, nor could they "know for certain that the women, children, and elderly *were not* Viet Cong (emphasis in original)."[82]

Truong Mealy, a Southeast Asian who was a Viet Cong agent but then switched sides, claims that children were deliberately trained by the Communists to attack Americans, so that Americans would be "forced to shoot them." Truong gratified his American interviewer, an unreconstructed Vietnam hawk, by saying, "Children were trained by the Communists to throw grenades, not only for the terror factor, but so the government or American soldiers would have to shoot them. Then the Americans feel very ashamed. And they blame themselves and call their soldiers 'war criminals.'" Truong continued that the tactic created a paranoid attitude in soldiers, because once they had seen a child throw a grenade and kill their friends, the Americans did not know which children were friendly. They started hating everyone. "This is where the Communists are so smart and very successful. Their most powerful weapon is psychological warfare."[83] This highly charged interpretation shows the use to which the image of the dangerous child could be put in defusing the accusation of criminality directed at American child-killers: the Americans are now seen as victims of cunning Communist psychological and propaganda tactics. Truong's words have been used exactly as he intended them: after quoting his account of Communist methods and purposes, Gary Solis invokes the "countless instances" when children ambushed American troops and women used "deadly ruses" in setting booby traps to explain the actions of U.S. marines who massacred unarmed Vietnamese women and children at Son Thang (the "Marine Corps's My Lai").[84]

The instability of any such rationalization of women and children's deaths was illustrated by a conversation I had with a counselor for a Veterans Administration PTSD program. He told me that Vietnam was a very difficult war because it was the first one in which American forces were confronted by women with firearms and children with grenades, in which servicemen were therefore forced to break the taboo against violence toward women and children. I suggested that what might be most difficult for the veterans he treated was not that the women and children they attacked were armed but that some of them were not. The counselor agreed and said that he could "never forgive" the American servicemen who killed unarmed women or children.[85] The drastic switch in his responses to the idea of women's and children's deaths—from a defensive rationalization to an equally defensive affective distancing—registers Americans' difficulty in facing up to the fact that it was not some unknown alien *they* who committed the atrocities; it was *our* forces, people just like us. If a trained psychiatric counselor found it difficult to compose a measured response to unacceptable but real violence, first explaining it away and then thrusting it away, how much more difficult was it for members of the public, without any training in coping with the legacy of an atrocity-filled war, knowing that unindicted murderers still walked among them?

The three opposed images of Vietnamese children shifted uncontrollably in discourses about the war. Children's ghostly bodies were superimposed on one another in a palimpsest that allows the outlines of each representation to show through the others. Each of the three incarnations of children's bodies was complex in itself, and they became still more confusing when they interacted or were overlaid on each other. Portrayals of Vietnamese civilians as the beneficiaries of American care were used to justify the war effort. In retrospect, though, the beneficiary role might also animate anger and guilt because the United States abandoned its ally when it withdrew from Vietnam in 1973. Here, the guilt-saturated corollary to Kennedy's "godparent" image is that of South Vietnamese fathers and mothers desperately trying to thrust their children over closed embassy gates or onto departing American helicopters when South Vietnam collapsed.[86] The treacherous beneficiary role might, alternatively, be a nagging counterpoint to the well-known images of Americans' victims, when beneficence gave way to aggression. Images of U.S. forces rescuing injured children bring the portrait of the American as protector to its highest emotional pitch, but they also resonate uncontrollably with photographs of the victims of American massacres, raising disturbing questions about the source of the rescued children's injuries. The stories of booby-trapped and grenade-throwing children were a rationalization of American violence against civilians. And yet these stories also signified universal Vietnamese opposition to America's presence in Vietnam. According to this logic, if even children picked up arms against Americans, and if Vietnamese adults, who treasure their children's lives, were prepared to sacrifice them in these ways, surely the United States had no right to resist their national will. As the Red Cross worker Jeanne Christie remarked about her conclusion on seeing a grenade-throwing child: "I saw very quickly from the kid who had the grenade in Nha Trang that we were not necessarily right for being there. After all, it was his homeland and territory he was defending, and I was the intruder."[87]

The uncontainable complexity concentrated in the image of a Vietnamese child brought about the transformation of two memorials discussed earlier, Glenna Goodacre's design of the Vietnam Women's Memorial in Washington, DC, and the California Vietnam Veterans Memorial in Sacramento. At an early stage in their design processes, the designers of these memorials intended them to include one or more Vietnamese children. Goodacre was one of several entrants to the Vietnam Women's Memorial Competition who submitted a sculptural design showing an American woman helping a Vietnamese child.[88] In Sacramento the original criteria sent to competition entrants specified that Vietnamese children must be part of the memorial, and a large sculpture of Vietnamese children accordingly dominated one of the quadrants in the first version of the winning entry. These children did not survive veterans' reactions to the psychological dangers they posed.

Originally, the kneeling figure in the Vietnam Women's Memorial was to have been standing, tenderly holding a tiny Vietnamese child (figs. 69 and 70). Goodacre had intended this adult-child pair to represent the nurturing comfort that American nurses brought to the innocents they treated. The maternal embrace would also have provided a Madonna-and-Child image to resonate with the Pietà-like image of the wounded soldier and care giver, so that the memorial would have symbolically encompassed the origin and terminus of Christ's earthly life. The harmonies and counterpoints within the ensemble would have transformed the war scene into a vision of beatified sacrifice.

Figure 69. Entry 181, Vietnam Women's Memorial Competition; Glenna Goodacre, designer.

This sort of Madonna-and-Child sculpture can be found in Washington, DC, in the stylized form of a statue honoring the American Red Cross in the grounds of the organization's headquarters (fig. 71). Such a statue was entirely acceptable to commemorate an organization with an unsullied reputation for beneficence, but in a national memorial to those who served in Vietnam, the tiny Vietnamese infant simply could not bear the massive weight of contending memories that bore upon its figure. Rumors circulated in the veterans' community that the child was wounded. Supporters of the memorial project resisted including the child in the memorial, whether wounded or whole. As Diane Carlson Evans, the memorial project's founder, explained, the memorial "is not about the Vietnamese."[89] The memorial project found a further reason for excluding the figure, in the legislation authorizing the women's memorial, which mandated a memorial to U.S. military personnel and no one else.[90] The leaders of the project therefore instructed Goodacre to remove the child as a condition of their selection of the design.[91] Goodacre complied with the request.

A comparison of the competition submission with the realized design helps to identify the change that was made from a standing to a kneeling figure, the infant in the nurse's arms replaced by a helmet. The helmet must have belonged to a U.S. serviceman, perhaps wounded or dead—empty helmets are conventional symbols of the death of American servicemen. In the original submission, the figure wearing a cap was holding the helmet, but because she was scanning the sky her attention was elsewhere; in the revision, the kneeling woman concentrates her downcast gaze on the helmet. Goodacre said at the dedication ceremony of the memorial that the transformed kneeling figure is the "heart and soul" of the memorial. By centering on a woman grieving for a dead American man, the modified design redoubles the idea of America's sacrifices and diverts our attention from Vietnamese victims of the war. The excision of the Vietnamese child from the design was effected deftly, creating few ripples within the veterans' community. In an irony therefore lost on the majority of the audience at the dedication of the Vietnam Women's Memorial, Admiral William Crowe told a story in his address that recalled the devotion of an army nurse at a hospital at Binh Tuy. In Crowe's story, the nurse came forward

Figure 70. Maquette of original design for Vietnam Women's Memorial; Glenna Goodacre, sculptor. Photo by author.

Figure 71. *Motherland*, Red Cross Memorial Garden, Washington, DC; Frederic Sogoyan, sculptor, dedicated 1991. Photo by author.

and took charge of six injured Vietnamese children that Crowe and some other American men rescued after a Viet Cong attack. Crowe described the nurse as "an angel of the Lord at work."[92] So, the scene of Americans saving Vietnamese children surfaced again in a veteran's memory during the dedication of a memorial in which the representation of one such child had been prohibited.

The same sort of censorship changed the California Vietnam Veterans Memorial. At an early meeting of the California Vietnam Veterans Memorial Commission, members stated why they were involved in the project and what kind of memorial they would like to see. One veteran said he wished to see a monument that would capture a feeling of poignancy, "and perhaps, a child who was caught up in it would capture that. I opt for a feeling of awe and peace and at the same time the poignancy and the horror that is contained in that . . . and a child caught up in it captures that as well as anything." Leo Thorsness, the Los Angeles VVLP chairman and a member of the memorial commission, responded positively to the reference to the Vietnamese child and proposed that the memorial show GIs helping Vietnamese children in an orphanage or nursery. As shown earlier, these ways of thinking about Vietnamese children were entirely consistent with the repertoire of storytelling by veterans who wanted to look back fondly on some aspect of their service, or who still believed the war-era propaganda that justified the U.S. war effort. Consequently, the memorial fund produced design criteria suggesting that the memorial reflect the following elements: "The overwhelming majority of those who were killed in Vietnam; the

19-year-old infantry soldiers, their youth, comradery [*sic*], and their fatigue of war; the American women who served; and also the ever-present Vietnamese children."[93]

This last suggestion about the "ever-present" children did not anticipate the negative connotations that sprang from the figure of the Vietnamese child—as an instigator of the "baby killer" charge, as a weapon of psychological warfare, and as a link in a chain of significance that led to guilt, shame, rage, and frustration. The image of a child was innocuous to those who experienced no such feelings; veterans who justified U.S. actions in Vietnam preserved their own moral innocence by consciously or unconsciously ignoring all the dangerous meanings attached to it. Thorsness was therefore unprepared for the storm that the memorial's design criterion set off among local veterans. The executive director of the Veterans Assistance Center in Berkeley, California, said he thought that the idea of including a Vietnamese child in the memorial connoted "guilt." He wrote: "We *all* understand that in a war there is much suffering. Most of the suffering was endured by those who fought and the civilian population who did not fight, especially the children. However, we strongly believe that the Memorial is not the appropriate vehicle to recognize or honor the VietNamese children. The Memorial *should* honor, in its entirety, those who served. Do not dilute this tribute! Do not let guilt dictate this Memorial! This Memorial is a positive step to honor those who served and those who sacrificed" (emphasis in original).[94] The Sacramento Vet Center Coalition was opposed to the inclusion of a child in the memorial, its chairman saying, "It is a memorial to the Vietnamese [*sic*] vet, not the children." A senior staff member at the Viet Vet House in Sacramento was more inflammatory. He said the image of a child could be beautiful; yet he recalled children between the ages of two and twelve being used as couriers of weapons, and as sometimes wired with explosives in order to attack American soldiers. "I was hit by the flying debris of one six-year-old girl," he said. Vietnam veterans' groups throughout Northern California were reported to have opposed representing a child on the grounds that "the Vietnamese children were often as deadly as the adults during the war."[95]

In response to the resistance of the California veterans, Thorsness tried to reinstate the benign image of Americans helping orphanages, using the language of "winning hearts and minds." He told two members of the state legislature who were also fellow members of the memorial commission: "In talking to troops about their service in South Vietnam, the subject of Vietnamese kids comes up often. And the vast majority still break out with a smile and a good story about them. There are no statistics but it seems a significant percentage of the troops who served in Southeast Asia supported, or worked with, an orphanage or school. Certainly one of the strategies was to win the hearts and minds of the South Vietnamese. In many cases, that was accomplished—at least with the Vietnamese children. The essence of what many veterans have told me is those kids became one of the few things that gave them a sense of stability; a sense of reason while they were in SEA [Southeast Asia] in what otherwise became an evermore frustrating effort."[96] But this restatement of the ideological basis for U.S. intervention, expressed in terms of winning the hearts and minds of children, did not win over the opponents. The memorial commission retreated from the idea of including Vietnamese children.[97] In their October 1984 meeting, the commission voted to send out an addendum with the competition announcement, explaining that competition entrants should not be bound by the initial design criteria.[98]

By this time, though, the entrants had already begun to work on their submissions, and some heeded the original criteria. A competition finalist depicts a sculpture of four American troops, two with weapons at the ready and one, apparently a female figure, holding an unconscious Vietnamese child in her lap.[99] The photograph of the nurse and child that inspired one of the images in the Roswell, Georgia, memorial formed part of the competition's third-placed entry.[100] The winning design included a representation of Vietnamese children. One of its four quadrants would have included a sculpture of three Vietnamese boys dressed in shorts and loose-fitting shirts standing behind several horizontal strands and concertina coils of barbed wire (fig. 72). This sculpture was eliminated from the subsequent version of the design. Instead, the quadrant devoted to the theme of healing the sick and injured introduced as its largest and most prominent sculptural element a navy corpsman (the marine equivalent of an army medic) rescuing an infant. As successive versions of the design were discussed with the memorial commission, the planned quadrants were modified with the addition of small bas-relief panels alongside the large sculptures. The figure of the corpsman was ultimately reduced in size in the final design and placed in one of these panels, while the main sculpture in that quadrant became the *The Nurse* (see fig. 46).[101]

In the end, a Vietnamese child does appear in the memorial but not perhaps in the way the commission originally proposed—not one of the "ever-present Vietnamese children" who crowded around GIs, eager for candy, learning GI slang, stealing from them, and sometimes heralding sudden death or injury. Such ambiguous representations are reduced to the image of the Vietnamese infant being carried to safety (fig. 73). It appears to be a picture of a rescue; what is not self-evident is how the child was injured. The bas-relief turns out to have been based on a photograph of a corpsman clutching a child wounded by a U.S. jet that had made a strafing run preparing the ground for a marine landing on the Cape of Batangan.[102] The secret known to all but discussed by none in the debate about the presence of Vietnamese children in the California memorial, the fact that Vietnamese children were the victims, not just the beneficiaries or killers, of Americans, is revealed only to those who research the bas-relief's photographic provenance. The veterans' refusal to allow the image of a Vietnamese child to intrude on their recollections, and the mental work required to forget why this image was so disturbing, heated and pressurized the rhetoric in the argument about the design.

The idea of representing the Vietnamese child was part of an attempt to sentimentalize the experience of Vietnam veterans by depicting a nurturant relationship between Americans and Vietnamese. This attempt at symbolic incorporation blew up in the commission's face, as psychologically dangerous as the Vietnamese children were reputed to have been physically perilous. The image of a child proved uncontainable. The representation of any Vietnamese child beyond the age of independent

Figure 72. Drawing of the preliminary design of the *Vietnamese Children* sculpture for the West Wall quadrant, California Vietnam Veterans Memorial. Courtesy of Michael Larson and Thomas Chytrowski.

mobility was ruled out on the grounds that this child could be a threat. When reduced to the inert prop necessary for staging the paternalistic scene in which many Americans liked to portray themselves, the injured infant nevertheless carried into the corpsman's arms a covert truth about the source of its injury, a truth that few involved in commemorations wished to own.

Those responsible for the design and selection of Vietnam veterans memorials have determined the ideologically acceptable contents of the field of commemoration. In this multicultural age, a statue of a general on a horse or of a single rifleman or doughboy in a town square will no longer suffice to represent the national past.

Figure 73. Bas-relief in lower right panel of West Wall, adjoining *The Nurse*, California Vietnam Veterans Memorial. The bas-relief is based on a photograph of "Operation Piranha" taken by Phil Schutzer for *Life* magazine, November 1965. Photo by author.

Americans have insisted on—or felt an obligation to create—memorials that represent the demographic range of the nation's population.[103] The memorials have attempted to achieve a comprehensive demographic representativeness, but this accords with the desire to symbolize unity rather than to celebrate diversity. The broadening of the scope of representation to include women and minorities underlines the effectiveness of the barrier against representing those outside the symbolic defensive perimeter. The American "family" was completed in the sculptures discussed in Chapter 9, but this entailed the repudiation of those who did not properly belong in the nation's heart. American monuments disowned Kennedy's "offspring," which became abandoned orphans and unmentioned burials in the family's past, guilty secrets that everyone knows. The bodies of America's Vietnamese victims were thus subjected to a symbolic suppression that denied, and hence reenacted in the commemorative arena, the violence they suffered in Vietnam.

— 11 —

"THE WALL IS FOR ALL OF US"

Patterns of Public Response to the
Vietnam Veterans Memorial

⭐

MEMORIALS ARE not simply the products of their designers' imaginations and their planners' motives. Once a memorial is constructed it ceases to be the "property" of those who created it. As visitors enrich the site with their own thoughts and feelings, a memorial becomes a public possession. In this chapter, we obtain some measure of the Vietnam Veterans Memorial's reception in American society by looking at public interaction with the wall and at the way the memorial's image disseminated through American society—in photographic books, children's storybooks, and the various incarnations of the "moving wall," the half-scale replicas that tour the country.

As the media reported public responses to the memorial in Washington and others elsewhere, they influenced the way readers and viewers saw the commemoration of the war. The most frequently enacted—and hence reported—behaviors tended to inspire imitations, some inflected by small mutations that in turn fed into the cycle of report, observation, and imitation. Speech and activity surrounding the memorials thus tended to conform to a conventional but evolving cultural script. Although some anomalies stood outside the self-regenerative cycle of dissemination, reproduction, and elaboration, the reported activities coalesced into a pattern whose course over time can be termed a tradition of commemoration.

A memorial can be changed by major design revisions or incrementally shaped by a succession of small modifications. "Top-down" decisions made for political or technical reasons shaped the physical appearance of the Vietnam Veterans Memorial. This chapter begins by describing some of the significant modifications that, in addition to the statues and flag, transformed Maya Lin's original conception; but just as important as these decisions have been behaviors by the mass of visitors that have become customary rituals. The "top-down" decisions and popular transformations of the memorial have shaped a tradition of commemoration that is multicentric and that has not been controlled solely by the memorial's designers, planners, and custodians.

A clear example of the way the memorial experience differs from its original conception involves the segmentation of the granite wall. In Maya Lin's original design and in early drawings showing the Vietnam Veterans Memorial Fund's conception of the memorial, the black granite appears to be one continuous sheet of rock (figs. 74 and 75).[1] As Lin later described her concept, "I had an impulse to cut open the earth . . . an initial violence that in time would heal. The grass would grow back, but the cut would remain, a pure, flat surface, like a geode when you cut into it and polish the edge. . . . It was as if the black-brown earth were polished and made into an interface between the sunny world and the quiet, darker world beyond, that we can't enter."[2] The practicalities of cutting, polishing, and moving the stone meant that it had to be divided into panels, a series of tablets mounted side by side rather than a seamless ("pure, flat") surface. The construction team found that the maximum practicable width of the slabs was forty inches.[3] As a result, each arm of the wall, east and west, has seventy side-by-side sections, the highest just over ten feet and the lowest eight inches from top to bottom. The names are justified on the right or left margin of the panels (depending on whether they are on the eastern or western arm), which are numbered, 1 to 70E and 1 to 70W, reinforcing their pagelike composition.[4] Name locators at stations on the approaches to the memorial (bound volumes that contain the names in alphabetical order) use the numbering to identify the location of each name. Family members, friends, and comrades in arms of the dead can thus visit the name of a particular individual. Sometimes groups of veterans hold reunions to visit panels associated with their time in country.

This most basic of the secular rituals enacted daily at the memorial was not a part of the designer's concept; her design statement envisions visitors' seeing the names en masse, conveying "the sense of overwhelming numbers." As she explained, "This memorial is meant not as a monument to the individual, but rather as a memorial to the men and women who died during the war, as a whole." She did not anticipate, and therefore did not think through, the issue of how a visitor might search for a name.[5] The refinement of the name locator was added in response to critics' complaints that it would be impossible to find an individual name from among the multitude.[6] The division of the wall into numbered sections facilitated the practice of finding and touching a name that has become a central component of the memorial experience, exemplifying the way that technical considerations and popular practices combined in altering the designer's vision.

Equally significant has been the transformation of the memorial's structure by the addition of the paved paths required by the number of pedestrians. It has often been remarked that soon after its dedication the Vietnam Veterans Memorial became the most visited monument in the nation's capital, something Jan Scruggs had never expected.[7] A year after the wall's dedication, Scruggs said, "I thought everyone would go see it in the first few months, and after that it would be a place like the rest of the Mall where people go to play frisbee."[8] He underestimated the public's interest. In its first winter and spring, the Vietnam Veterans Memorial Fund (VVMF) stated that a million people visited it.[9] In February 1996, 23 percent of a poll sample of American adults said that they had visited the Vietnam Veterans Memorial at some time and

Figure 74. Artist's impression of the proposed appearance of the Vietnam Veterans Memorial as designed by Maya Lin. VVMF-MD.

Figure 75. Artist's impression of the proposed appearance of the Vietnam Veterans Memorial. VVMF-MD.

by November 2000, this figure had crept up to 26 percent. Averaged across the years, this translates into annual visitation by around three million American adults.[10]

Lin's design statement describes a memorial that the public would approach not from its ends, as they do today, but frontally, across an expanse of grass. The designer's statement begins, "Walking through this park—the memorial appears as a rift in the earth—a long, polished black stone, emerging from and receding into the earth. Approaching the memorial, the ground slopes gently downward and the low walls emerging on either side, growing out of the earth, extend and converge at a point below and ahead. Walking into the grassy site contained by the walls of the memorial we can barely make out the carved names in the memorial walls." Early artist's impressions of the memorial accordingly show visitors dotted over an unbroken lawn leading right up to the wall's edge (see figs. 74 and 75).[11] The popularity of the memorial changed all that. The architect Walter Netsch, a member of the Fine Arts Commission, said that it would be a mistake to add walkways to the memorial to accommodate large visitor numbers because that would "destroy the experience." "I think when you finally get there," he explained, "you have to be by yourself with the wall. We do not want to make an army."[12] But this observation was out of touch with the reality of visitation at the wall. The volume of foot traffic combined with drainage problems made it impossible to allow the public to approach the memorial across an expanse of lawn growing up to the edge of the wall.

The National Park Service and the VVMF were concerned that the memorial, sunk considerably below street level and the level of the surrounding parkland, would become waterlogged. Foot traffic along the wall might then churn the ground into a muddy mess the public would have to slosh through. To resolve the problem, when the memorial was constructed, the Park Service and the VVMF arranged for plastic reinforcement to be installed under the grass to protect it from pedestrian damage. For the same reason, the planners decided to install a paved walkway parallel to the wall and separated from it by a twenty-one-inch strip of grass (fig. 76).[13] The paving stopped before it reached the ends of the walls at left and right. In an early architectural model of the memorial showing the paving, most of the human figures are ranged along it, suggesting that it was intended only to provide a solid floor on which visitors would stand and pass in front of the wall, not a route into and out of the memorial site. The memorial fund still imagined that visitors would approach across a lawn.[14]

When the memorial was unveiled to the public in November 1982, the architects had ensured that it remained as true to Lin's concept as could be managed. Part of the appeal of the design, after all, lay in the contrast between the strength of the wall and the softness of the lawn.[15] Grass grew up to the edge of the wall, separating the memorial from the paving (fig. 77).[16] However, this attempt to show the wall rising cleanly out of the cut earth was unconvincing. The Park Service, which was to maintain the memorial, demanded that a gutter be installed along the base of the wall, because power mowers cannot cut grass against a vertical surface. Purists complained that this modification detracted from the designer's concept. One critic noted, "The gutter is modest but clearly damages the design: this is one wall you want to see rise straight up out of the earth like a natural cliff."[17]

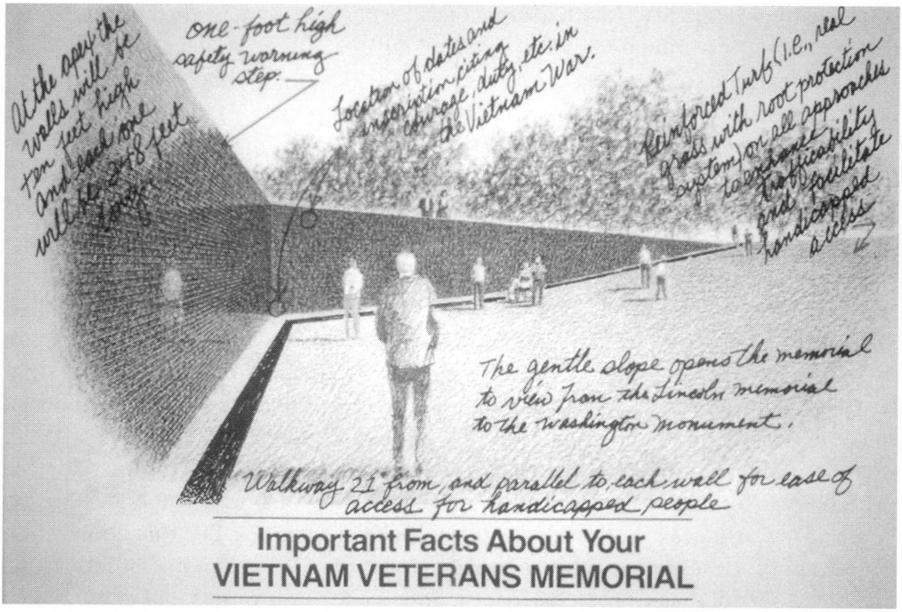

The handwritten annotations on the figure read:

At the apex the walls will be ten feet high and toward one will be 2½ feet long

one-foot high safety warning step:

Location of dates and inscription citing courage, duty etc. in the Vietnam War.

Reinforced Turf (i.e., real grass with root protection system) on all approaches to practicability and facilitate handicapped access

The gentle slope opens the memorial to view from the Lincoln memorial to the washington monument.

Walkway 2½' from, and parallel to, each wall for ease of access for handicapped people

Important Facts About Your
VIETNAM VETERANS MEMORIAL

Figure 76. Artist's impression of the proposed appearance of the Vietnam Veterans Memorial, with walkway added. VVMF-MD.

Within a few months of the dedication, while considering the ideologically loaded issue of where to place the statue and the flag, the Fine Arts Commission also pondered the prosaic problem of drainage. Visitation was so heavy that the plastic reinforcement had proven inadequate to protect the well-trodden grass. In the first year, the sod had to be relaid three times. A month after the dedication, people were again talking about a "quagmire" in relation to Vietnam, but in the form of the "squishy sod and oozing mud" surrounding the memorial. The plastic mesh appeared to be part of the problem: it made it more difficult for surface water to drain. The Park Service resorted to wooden duckboards to channel visitors to the paved walkway because the visitors were reluctant to step on the soggy mulch laid on top of the new sod. They waited in line rather than circulating around the lawn, as the project's landscape architect originally had in mind. The memorial fund and the Park Service acknowledged that some additional paving was needed to link the walkway with the system of paths around the memorial.[18]

Another problem was that the walkway was too narrow to allow groups of people to pass each other. While some visitors gazed at or touched the stone or stood in somber conversation, others who wished to keep moving but avoid passing between them and the wall would step on and off the grass verge, which became flattened into mud.[19] The walkway therefore had to be widened as well as extended. Intent on protecting Constitution Gardens from novel impositions and on defending the original design from intrusions, J. Carter Brown, the chairman of the Commission of Fine Arts, resisted adding paving that was too "architectural" and that would become a part of the memorial itself. He asked instead for flagstones with creeping thyme

Figure 77. The Vietnam Veterans Memorial at the 1982 dedication, showing the turf separating the wall from the paved walkway. Photo by Jeff Tinsley, Smithsonian Institution.

Figure 78. In this 1984 photograph of the Vietnam Veterans Memorial, one can see the cobbles and wedge-shaped lighting fixtures added to the walkway, leaving only a narrow grass strip dividing the wall from the paving. Photo by Jeff Tinsley, Smithsonian Institution.

and grass or moss, with that "wonderful quality that you get in English gardens, where the paths become part of nature."[20] But because of the amount of foot traffic and the poor drainage, this compromise, a flagged path accented with vegetation, was determined not to be a practical solution. By the time of the dedication of the Frederick Hart statue in November 1984, the walkway had been enlarged by the addition of cobblestones at both its forward edge, toward the wall, and the rear edge, adjacent to the lawn, with lighting set among the cobbles. The grass bordering the wall had been reduced to a tiny sliver, in an unavailing effort to preserve a semblance of the original design concept (fig. 78). Finally, this strip of grass too was paved over.[21] With the forward edge of the walkway now abutting the wall, the rear edge was separated from the lawn by chains and stanchions.

Although constructed for entirely pragmatic purposes, the paths have transformed the memorial experience from that envisioned by its designer. Lin had imagined that visitors would cross the sloping lawn to the memorial, where they would be embraced by the walls extending to right and left. This concept explains the logic of beginning and ending the chronicle of names at the vertex of the memorial. At the moment the visitors arrived at the wall, as Lin imagined, they would complete a "circle" at the meeting of the first and last names. "The passage itself," she wrote, "is gradual,"

> the descent to the origin slow, but it is at the origin that the meaning of this memorial is to be fully understood. At the intersection of these walls, on the right side, at the wall's top, is carved the date of the first death. It is followed by the names of those who have died in the war, in chronological order. These names continue on this wall, appearing to recede into the earth at the wall's end. The names resume on the left wall, as the wall emerges from the earth, back to the origin, where the date of the last death is carved, at the bottom of this wall. Thus the war's beginning and end meet; the war is "complete," coming full circle, yet broken by the earth that bounds the angle's open side, and contained within the earth itself.[22]

After taking in the sweep of names and seeing that the walls stretched toward the Washington Monument and the Lincoln Memorial, visitors, Lin imagined, would turn and retreat across the grass.

The "circle" that Lin conceived can best be imagined if you face the memorial's vertex, gazing at its two extremities. If you imagine the tapered points of the walls as penetrating the circumference of the earth, you might imagine the walls forming a subterranean girdle around the world. This implied effect is diminished today because of the paved paths (fig. 79). The walls do not "cut the earth" or appear to be the polished rock face of its subterranean structure; instead, they grow out of solidly architectural foundations (fig. 80). Nowadays, only when a fresh snowfall obliterates the walkways can one see the site as Lin imagined it: a uniform slope unmarked by paths leading to a right angle where ground and wall join. Even then, chains and stanchions running the length of the path interrupt the terrain.[23]

The chains and stanchions protect the margins of the lawn, prevent visitors from tracking dirt onto the paving, and channel them from one end of the memorial to the other. The public therefore enters the memorial area at its extremities, where

Figure 79. Aerial view of the Vietnam Veterans Memorial in 1986. The path from the Women's Memorial to the east wall had not yet been added. Photo by Richard Hofmeister, Smithsonian Institution.

Figure 80. Vietnam Veterans Memorial, May 1994. Photo by author.

Figure 81. The Vietnam Veterans Memorial, west wall, toward the Lincoln Memorial, December 1993. Chains and stanchions encourage the public to keep to the walkway running the length of the memorial. Footprints in the snow provide an index of where the heaviest footfall occurs and contrast with the untouched snow beyond the stanchions. Photo by author.

the deaths that occurred in May 1968 are recorded (fig. 81).[24] The visitors descend the inclined path toward the vertex of the walls, which gradually increase in height until they rise above the visitors. The descent is accompanied by an intensification of the memorial's physical and emotional impact. "It's like walking into the war," one veteran said. "You can feel us getting deeper and deeper into it, more and more death."[25] When they leave, visitors experience a gradual re-entry into the sights and sounds of the city as the wall recedes.[26]

Because of this physical rise and fall, some visitors misunderstand the chronological sequence of the names. The history of the United States' military involvement in Vietnam involved the gradual escalation of its troop numbers from a few advisers to a peak of over half a million personnel in 1969, followed by successive withdrawals. The intensity of the casualty toll roughly coincided with the number of troops in Vietnam, the heaviest casualties occurring in May 1968, when the troop numbers were nearing their height.[27] It is therefore easy for those filing along the memorial walls to see them as representing a time line whose rise and fall matches the cadences of America's escalating involvement and of U.S. casualty figures.

Indeed, in the class at Yale where she drafted her design, Lin had intended the sequence of names to begin at the tip of the west wall and continue to the tip of the east wall, running continuously left to right along the memorial's length. Her teacher objected that this arrangement left the vertex with little meaning, and Lin therefore revised the proposal to begin and end the chronological sequence at the walls' meeting point before she submitted the design to the Vietnam Veterans Memorial competition. Two members of the competition jury nevertheless seem to have believed that the wall formed a time line that rose and fell with U.S. involvement in the war. If experts were confused in this way (and a subsequent scholarly work repeats the error), it is hardly surprising that some members of the public share the same misunderstanding of the memorial's basic concept. But through this misunderstanding they perceive Lin's original idea, still expressed in the wall's tapering profile. Arthur Danto sees the terminal panels as the most important in the memorial and, moreover, disagrees that a closing circle has the right "moral geometry" for the memorial. For him, as for the two jury members, the shape of the wall resembles the shape of the war, with the vertex representing the late 1960s: the war's high point and its turning point. He suggests that, if the chronicle of names began and ended at the wall's extremities, then leaving the memorial after traversing it from left to right would follow the direction of time "and, perhaps, hope." The memorial's physical composition therefore invites two alternate readings: the "circle" motif is secured by the starting and end points of the sequence of names and the inscriptions at the vertex; but the original "timeline" idea remains evident and is reinforced by something that neither Lin nor her teacher had foreseen: that the public enters and leaves the memorial site at either end of the wall.[28]

When the Vietnam Women's Memorial was added, the custodians of the site had to find a way to incorporate new landscaping and architectural elements without compromising the integrity of the original memorial and the surrounding park. The initial plan was for the sculpture to be accessible by one of the existing paths, which runs from the Women's Memorial, steers past the Hart statue, and thence leads to the memorial wall at its western end, toward the Lincoln Memorial. This arrangement would have kept the Women's Memorial somewhat separate, because there would have been a single, indirect route to the wall from the plaza in which it stood. The Fine Arts Commission hoped that this plan would prevent visitors from walking in a trapezoidal route along the memorial wall, to each statue in turn, and then back to their starting point. The arrangement of the paths would ensure that the wall remained central to the commemorative experience—and that no further unsightly paving would alter the original site.[29]

The public, however, had other ideas. They literally beat a direct path from the Goodacre statue to the memorial wall, wearing the grass down to bare earth along their track. After the public had thus voted with their feet, the Park Service acquiesced by paving the route from the Women's Memorial to the eastern end of the wall, thus completing the current arrangement of paths at the memorial site. The principle that the public's footsteps would cross paving, not grass, was so well established, though, that no one argued that the original design concept should now be honored by allowing the public to roam freely across the grass or by removing the chains and stanchions that run the length of the paths abutting the wall.[30]

The physical structure of the memorial has thus been changed by "democratic" modes of activity in which the movements of the multitude combined with the physical characteristics of the site to demand the current architecture of pathways.

What the powerful decide does matter but it is not all that matters. In public commemoration, the public to a significant degree get what they "vote" for—if not with their feet, then with their presence, their observance, and their attention. The custodians of the site reacted to the public's behavior, as well as attempting to direct their movements, and the story of the paths therefore constitutes a perfect physical analogue to the larger pattern of popular interaction with the memorial that has shaped the work of commemoration: those in positions of authority have had to contend with and not simply to control or constrain patterns of popular response.

According to her design statement, Lin imagined that the public's relationship to the memorial would be essentially passive and contemplative. She and the VVMF expected that people would view their own reflections in the black granite, which had been chosen for its reflective qualities. But when the first panels went up, they found that the public responded dynamically to the memorial, approaching the stone and touching it.[31] Visitors felt that touching the name allowed them contact with the person. A mother describes her first visit to the memorial: "When I got close to Panel 42E, there were several young men there in fatigues. I told them I was Dan Lee Neely's mom and they hugged me and told me how sorry they were. When we found Dan's name and I touched it, I just couldn't control the tears. I felt like Dan was there with me."[32] Photographs showing people's hands touching the wall became the typical images used in news articles and books to illustrate visitors' emotional responses to the wall and hence to convey the war's impact on the nation.[33] The wall's reflective qualities also gave rise to eerie ideas of contact with a netherworld behind the wall. "It was like the wall was alive," said David Burton, a 25th Infantry Division veteran. "I could touch it and it was warm and I saw my reflection in it. I was among them, looking out."[34] The wall's surface seemed to some a thin, impenetrable screen separating this world from another, where the troops lived on, still young. By touching the wall, one could brush one's fingertips against theirs.

The importance of touching the wall is graphically expressed in a popular artwork, Lee Teter's *Reflections*, marketed as a poster and sold as a postcard at the stalls on the approaches to the memorial.[35] A middle-aged man, his head bent in grief, reaches out and places his hand on the wall. He has set his briefcase on the ground, his suit jacket draped over it. From the "other side," where one would expect to see his reflection, the mirror image is a younger man, helmeted and in military fatigues, flanked by four other troops. Palm against reflected palm, the visitor is touching his younger self, flanked by his buddies; or perhaps he is encountering five comrades lost in the war. The scene suggests that time and space collapse at the encounter across the wall, as if the scroll of time were punctured and two points separated by years pinned together.

Teter's artwork dramatically evokes experiences like that of Dan Doyle at the memorial. Doyle, who ran a vet center in Richmond, Virginia, made visits to the wall a part of his therapeutic work, as well as his personal journey of recovery. He was a platoon commander in Vietnam, and his life broke apart when he lost two men in combat against a fortified enemy position. He felt that he died on that day and the rest of his life was lived on borrowed time. Speaking of his visits to the wall, Doyle said, "That's where I go to find my men and the pieces of me that are still tied to them."[36] His visits integrated his own past and present, his pre-war and postwar selves.

In another commercially marketed print, Wes Kendall's *A Touching Moment*, we see a gray-haired man, arm-in-arm with an elderly woman, reaching out to the wall, pointing his index finger at a name. From beyond the wall's surface comes the faint image of three soldiers in fatigues. The one in the center, supported by the man at either side, has a bandaged head wound. His pointing index finger almost touches the elderly man's.[37] Unlike those in Teter's *Reflections*, Kendall's figures are not mirror images of each other. The reflected soldiers are set off to the side and both men reach out with their left hands. Their index fingers come toward each other but do not quite connect.

In the discourse surrounding the memorial, touch became a signifier not just for physical contact but, by extension, for emotional contact—an expression of care for others. Friends of the Vietnam Veterans Memorial, a support organization for family, friends, and comrades of those lost in Vietnam, began a program they called "In Touch." John Holman, the group's executive director, explained, "There are a lot of sons and daughters who never knew their fathers. Sometimes veterans want to deliver photographs or mementos to families. Sometimes parents want to talk to men who served with their sons." The program's publicity materials emphasized contact with the wall—illustrated by fingertips touching a name and a grief-stricken man in camouflage fatigues leaning his forehead into the wall, his hand spread against the stone.[38]

Visitors tried to make the moment of contact endure. They took photographs of the memorial and some made rubbings of the names. The rubbings, made by holding paper up to the wall and running a pencil or crayon over the inscriptions (fig. 82), create the visual image of the name and provide a durable trace of physical contact with the wall. They have become treasured artifacts of contact for those who could not travel to visit the memorial.[39] The Park Service makes specially designed pieces of paper, cut to the dimensions of an inscribed name, available at a nearby kiosk. Friends of the Vietnam Veterans Memorial started a service sending rubbings to those who requested them.[40]

On several occasions when veterans dedicated a memorial elsewhere, they first took rubbings from the one in Washington. Philadelphia veterans marched on a "last patrol" from the nation's capital carrying rubbings of the names of Philadelphia's dead in an ammunition case. They placed it at the center of the Philadelphia memorial and ceremonially guarded it until the dedication the following day. New Jersey veterans did the same before the dedication of the New Jersey Vietnam Veterans Memorial (fig. 83).[41] Reading, Pennsylvania, veterans took rubbings of the names of Berkshire County's sixty-four dead and then placed each rubbing, together with a dog tag and an American flag, in a three-inch-long stainless steel coffin. After marching the 150 miles from Washington to Reading, they placed the miniature coffins in a vault at the base of the Berkshire County Vietnam Veterans Memorial, as though they contained holy relics that drew their sacred power from Lin's wall.[42]

Since before the memorial was completed, visitors have made it a site of secular rituals by leaving offerings. The first one occurred when the foundations were being

Figure 82. A visitor makes a rubbing of a name. Photo by author.

laid. A navy pilot had brought along his brother's Purple Heart and asked that it be put into the concrete foundations when they were poured.[43] The Purple Heart is the nation's oldest military decoration, established by George Washington during the Revolutionary War; it still carries his profile at the center of its heart shape. The medal is awarded to anyone killed or wounded as a result of enemy action and so touches on the memorial's persistent theme of the war's wounds. The placing of the medal in the memorial's foundations had multiple resonances: it linked the nation's newest memorial to its most venerable military traditions and to the father of the country (to whose monument the memorial's east wall points). But while evoking history on an epic scale, the story also functioned at the personal, familial scale, telling of a man's devotion to his brother. This story of the Purple Heart, first told by Jan Scruggs, has been compelling to those who heard it, and has been transmitted again and again by those writing about the things left at the memorial.[44] By 1994, a touching detail was added to the story: Scruggs now recalled that after the pilot dropped the medal into the concrete, he saluted and said, "Now the memorial has a heart."[45] The poetic elaboration of the story shows how innovation and repetition combine to create a commemorative tradition, each mutation adding to its evolving genetic code.

In the years following the interment of the Purple Heart, people have left crosses, teddy bears, wreaths, flags, medals, a pair of cowboy boots, and thousands of photographs at the memorial. Visitors have also left messages there—messages to the dead, messages to other Americans, signs that some were holding fast to grief and anger, and others were beginning to let go. At first, the notes appeared to be spontaneous, or nearly so. They were written on scraps of paper bags from vendors' stalls on the nearby Constitution Avenue, on ragged-edged paper torn from notebooks, or on stationery from Washington hotels.[46] Most of the notes and letters were addressed to loved ones whose names were inscribed on the walls. Some notes, in the form of public valedictories or commentaries about the war and its veterans, speak to a wider audience, others to a particular group—for example, the members of a unit who were in combat together on a certain date.

Before the Vietnam Veterans of America's *VVA Veteran* magazine introduced its "locator" section, and before Internet sites allowed war buddies to find one another, the memorial served as a crude bulletin board for veterans. A young man was once seen holding up a sign reading, "Anyone know George J. Parker, USMC [United States Marine Corps]?" with Parker's rank and the month of his death. In 1984, someone taped a picture to the wall, with the message, "This is my father. I never knew him. If anyone who knows him, please write me." Bill Coursey left six snapshots of guys whom he had known in Vietnam, along with his military decorations and a note: "I got medals. You should have got them." He also left a message asking members of his battalion who served in 1969 to contact him. Someone did, just in time: Coursey had been having flashbacks and had started taking his .38 pistol into a dark closet and sitting there, thinking about the war. His fellow veteran suggested various veterans' groups that could help him, and Coursey signed up for counseling.[47]

All the messages at the memorial were left in the awareness that they would be seen by others. They have amplified the memorial's work, by offering public

Figure 83. An ammunition box containing rubbings from the Vietnam Veterans Memorial of the names of New Jersey's dead, with the boots worn by members of the "last patrol," an arrangement of helmet, inverted rifle and boots, and a folded Stars and Stripes, ceremonially displayed at the center of the New Jersey Vietnam Veterans Memorial at its May 1995 dedication. Photo by author.

testimony to the war's losses, making evident enduring grief and testifying to the importance of the individual about or to whom the note was written. (Very few letters are left in sealed envelopes.)[48] They drew sympathetic visitors into a community of feeling and brought survivors out of their isolation. Visitors have left tens of thousands of writings at the wall—poems, letters, prayers, political tracts, mementoes of the dead, copies of letters from Vietnam, and news clippings from the war era—a chronicle of Americans' responses to the war and its aftermath. For some, reading and seeing the letters and gifts seemed "to open the floodgate of emotion that marked the divisive war." Visitors read a letter written to a Massachusetts man whose sweetheart married another man and had two children. "Your dying has forever changed our lives," it said, and many who stooped or knelt to read it were crying by the time they finished. Many of the letters left in the early years of the memorial's existence seemed intended to achieve closure and purge the nation's grief, stressing the heroism and sacrifice of those who died, or decrying the waste of their lives so that the nation would avoid unnecessary wars in the future.[49]

Offerings sustained personal relationships with the dead. A note left with a can of Colt 45 says, "Hey Bro, Here's the beer I owe you—24 yrs. late."[50] Five playing cards making up a royal flush, ace of spades high, were left along with a pack of cigarettes and a letter to an air force casualty that reads, "You seemed to always get burned playing poker, well Pete! Here's a hand for you to get even with on that last deal! and pack of Kools to get you through that last hand!"[51] A mother left a small, tattered teddy bear, one of his first toys, for her son, along with a picture of the souped-up Chevy he drove when he grew older.[52] Veterans left battered combat boots, perhaps a sign that their marching days were over—but also reminiscent of wartime ceremonies in the field where empty pairs of combat boots were mustered in formation to represent those who had died in battle (fig. 84).[53] Two Navaho women left three small, sealed bags, containing sand, piñons, and sage from their Arizona home in honor of Jones Lee Yazzie, a member of the Navaho nation who had died in Vietnam.[54] A photo was left with a note: "Hi, Dad. I'm grown up now."[55] In the late 1980s, more and more notes were left by the children of the men who died.[56]

The media have understandably been fascinated by the offerings at the memorial wall.[57] Here was an unusual phenomenon that seemed to tap into a deep reservoir of feeling and that gave what might otherwise seem ineffable—people's emotions at the wall—a textual and material form. Journalists were particularly keen to find emotion-drenched subjects and they selected for their stories the offerings that came attached to the "juiciest," most "heart-rending" stories.[58] Photojournalists' cameras were drawn to the objects people left at the foot of the wall, the granite provided a magnificently photogenic backdrop, and television multiplied the impact of the offerings by broadcasting their images to millions.[59] The polished black stone allowed any light-colored object to stand out strikingly, and the junction of wall and paving provided an inviting receptacle for the offerings. Objects above a few inches in height were framed among the inscribed names. Some visitors even used the slot between the panels to grip messages adjacent to a name (fig. 85). Seeing the offerings became a part of the experience of visiting the memorial, especially for those who had no

Figure 84. A pair of battered combat boots left at the Vietnam Veterans Memorial. Photo by author.

Figure 85. A visitor inserts a note between two of the granite panels of the Vietnam Veterans Memorial. Photo by author.

personal connection with someone who died in Vietnam and were merely curious or wanted vicariously to partake of the emotions of the bereaved (fig. 86). As the phenomenon of the offerings became well known through media reports, the early, spontaneous notes and messages gave way to ones that showed greater planning. Handwritten messages were preserved from the elements in jiffy bags. People began to leave messages protected under glass in frames that must have been prepared in advance. Media reports about the offerings encouraged imitative behavior and fed into the cultural script of response to the memorial. As Daphne Berdahl has written,

Figure 86. For some visitors, seeing the offerings has become part of the experience of the Vietnam Veterans Memorial. Photo by author.

"This multiplication and amplification of voices has generated an echo that tends to script performances at the Wall. What began as spontaneous expressions of grief has been transformed into ritualized and routinized cultural practices."[60] The formation of a tradition of commemoration involved elaboration, though, as well as imitation. Offerings increased in size and complexity: among the largest are a "tiger cage" intended to publicize the POW/MIA [prisoner of war/missing in action] cause and a Harley Davidson motorcycle, left by bikers who have made the "Rolling Thunder" ride to the memorial every Memorial Day since the early 1990s.

President Ronald Reagan demonstrated that giving offerings was an imitative phenomenon when he explained his leaving a note at the wall on Veterans Day in 1988. He confided to his diary, "It's a tradition that has grown of people leaving letters, gifts, etc. at the memorial."[61] There can be no better illustration of the reciprocal influence of the powerful and ordinary citizens in forming the nation's commemoration of the Vietnam War. While Reagan's administration had authority over the decision to allow groundbreaking and influenced the choice of where to place the Hart statue and flag, in this instance he became the follower of a popular tradition. His note was singled out for inclusion in the Smithsonian exhibition of offerings at the wall. But Reagan's leaving a personal, handwritten note trumpeted the democratic traditions of the republic, with the president as First Citizen, faithfully observing the customs of the country.

Family members brought Christmas and birthday cards. Sometimes Christmas trees would appear in front of the wall. Offerings marked life events of the children whose fathers never saw them grow up, or never saw them at all: mementos of the christening of a child; high school graduation and wedding photos; symbols of the birth of grandchildren. At the unveiling of the memorial on November 11, 1982, No Greater Love, an organization of children of Vietnam veterans, placed a wreath at the vertex of the memorial. Then, children laid a single red rose in front of each of the 140 black granite panels. Similar ceremonies continue up to the present. Beginning in June 1992, children of the dead have regularly held Fathers Day ceremonies at the memorial. These activities created poignant human interest stories that the press eagerly covered.[62]

Some stories have a darker side. One journalist referred to the memorial's "morbid allure" for veterans.[63] Veterans treated it as a funerary site and as a place to die. Before his death, a veteran had asked that his ashes be scattered there during the November 1982 dedication, and over the years others have made the same request—although the Park Service does not officially countenance this practice.[64] A regular at the memorial, Jeffrey Davis, had seen almost his entire company of 160 men wiped out in a single night of fighting in Vietnam. The Washington police officer became increasingly preoccupied with that night, unable to eat or sleep. He became the first Vietnam veteran to kill himself at the memorial in September 1984.[65] Four months later, Randolph Taylor, who had lost his job as a police officer in San Francisco, visited the memorial and touched the names of about a dozen friends on the wall. He thought about the rise of the "new patriotism" taking U.S. troops to places like Lebanon to "win one for the Gipper" (a movie-derived nickname and campaign slogan for Reagan). The following day at the memorial he shot himself in the chest but survived. "I wanted to die with my men," he said.[66] The notion that the memorial created a special place for communion between the dead and the living was thus a complex, many-faceted idea: one could leave gifts and messages for the dead, see their ghosts in the wall's reflections, or cross an earthly boundary to join them.

For the first two years that people left offerings at the memorial, no systematic effort was made to preserve them. Park Service personnel did save some of the objects in a tool shed, though without recording when and where they were left.[67] At the end of 1984, recognizing that the offerings collectively represented a phenomenon of national significance, the Park Service began to gather and preserve them more systematically. Since then, Park Service rangers have collected notes, letters, and objects regularly, noting where and when each item was picked up (fig. 87). Park Service staff transport the offerings to a storage facility in the Washington suburbs (fig. 88).[68] There curators have undertaken the painstaking work of cataloguing and classifying the materials, but the task is Sisyphean and the curating has never kept up with the volume of newly arriving materials. Indeed, it is not even certain how large the collection is.

Between November 1984 and April 1986, more than two thousand objects and letters were gathered at the memorial. The next year, the collection doubled in size, and a year later, it appeared to be growing geometrically: four thousand objects were added. Publicity surrounding an exhibition at the Smithsonian Institution that coincided with the tenth anniversary of the memorial spread the news about the offerings and encouraged still faster growth. (For example, those who left the motorcycle at the wall contacted the exhibition curator to ask when it would be displayed in the Smithsonian.) Between the end of 1992, when the exhibition opened, and 1994, the collection grew from twenty-five thousand to forty-five thousand artifacts. By the end of 2006, the number had reached one hundred thousand. These figures indicate that the rate of growth of the collection is not slacking off but is accelerating.[69]

On ceremonial occasions such as Veterans Day and Memorial Day, when a large number of individuals and organizations leave things at the memorial, the offerings are left in situ for several days to allow visitors a period in which to see the mass of materials on display. Normally, though, the objects are collected daily, and so one finds a constantly changing, constantly renewed exhibition of letters and objects at the memorial.

The curatorial principle of the Vietnam Veterans Memorial Collection in the Park Service archive is unusual in that everything, other than perishable materials, is saved: the people who leave offerings at the memorial are the collective "curator" of the archive (in the sense that they are the ones who choose what is preserved). Museum exhibitions that display the offerings, in contrast, have necessarily operated a selective principle, their curators carefully choosing from among the thousands of objects. In a museum vitrine, a small sample of objects that had only an ephemeral presence at the memorial are lifted from the warehouse where they are usually hidden and made available for enduring public scrutiny.

In October 1992, the first sample of five hundred of these offerings was put on display at the Smithsonian Institution's National Museum of American History in Washington, DC, followed by exhibitions at the Museum of Our National Heritage in Lexington, Massachusetts, the Gerald R. Ford Museum in Ann Arbor, Michigan, and a number of other sites.[70] Interpretation in the exhibitions was hampered by the absence of information about most of the donors and the self-imposed restraints of the exhibition curators and designers, who have been cautious about overinterpreting the materials—attributing to them meanings that were not intended by those

Figure 87. National Park Service rangers periodically bag the materials, noting the date and location where they were collected before removing them to the Museum and Archeological Regional Storage facility (MARS), Lanham, Maryland. Photo by author.

Figure 88. Duery Felton, a National Park Service curator, with one of the thousands of items in Vietnam Veterans Memorial Collection at MARS. Photo by author.

who left them at the memorial.[71] For this reason, the objects have generally been exhibited without individual explanatory labels, but this curatorial diffidence has had a paradoxical result: even more meaning concentrates in the relatively few words that the curators do provide—the exhibitions' titles, the brief wall-mounted texts describing the exhibitions as a whole, and the accompanying brochures. These texts reproduce the conventional commemorative script with repeated references to the powerful discourse of "healing." For example, the subtitle of the Smithsonian exhibition is "The Healing of a Nation"; a text panel in the Museum of Our National Heritage exhibition refers to the "healing effects of the Wall"; a Gerald R. Ford Museum brochure states that the memorial "is meant to be a place of national reconciliation and healing" and that the museum exhibition "brings a small part of this tale of sorrow, grief and healing" to the museum. The references to "healing" come full circle at the Ford Museum because, as the title of his 1979 memoir *A Time for Healing* suggests, Ford was one of the early advocates of post–Vietnam War and post–Watergate reconciliation at about the time the VVMF were beginning their work.[72]

In some instances, though, materials exhibited in the museums have a historical significance, even if the motives of the individual who left them are unknown. A bank of "MIA bracelets" and the replica "tiger cage" in the Smithsonian exhibition evoked the controversy over the supposed presence of American MIAs, years after the end of the war, in Southeast Asia. The Museum of Our National Heritage displayed a model of a prison-camp watch tower and two vitrines of other MIA-related artifacts. No labels explained the historical or political significance of these artifacts.

The Smithsonian did give the media background information on some of the objects, but it tended to center on "human interest" stories, while providing limited historical interpretation. No interpretation was provided about some of the exhibition's gruesome contents.[73] The notches on the stock of an M-14 rifle in a Smithsonian vitrine were a tally of those killed by the bearer of the weapon or by his unit. A more explicit "kill count" of dead "gooks" was displayed on the side of a helmet cover (although slightly averted from the viewer's sight). Both objects reference the "body counts" and "kill ratios" that disillusioned the American public and brutalized Americans in the field, but it is unlikely that, in the absence of explanatory labels, audience members other than Vietnam veterans were aware of their significance.

Because some of the offerings were notes and letters, though, they required no interpretive labeling to speak to the public. They demonstrate the inadequacy of "healing" as a comprehensive description of public responses to the memory of the war. These artifacts offer us glimpses of uncontainable grief, ambivalence that refuses easy resolution, and political protest. Charles Liteky was awarded the Medal of Honor, the nation's highest military decoration, for his valor in saving wounded men while serving as a chaplain in Vietnam. He left his medal at the Vietnam Veterans Memorial in 1986 (as members of Vietnam Veterans Against the War had once returned their medals at the Capitol), renouncing the award in protest against Reagan's support of the *contras* in Nicaragua. Liteky was offended by the destruction being meted out by the *contras* and he expressed dismay that Reagan had called them "freedom fighters," "the moral equal of our Founding Fathers."[74] In an open letter to Reagan, which was displayed in the Smithsonian alongside the medal and adjacent to Reagan's 1988 note, Liteky writes, "In the name of freedom, national security, national interest, and anti-communism you have tried to justify crimes against humanity of the most heinous sort. You have made a global bully of the United States."[75] His words resist assimilation into the anodyne discourse of "healing," or its Reaganite variant of national strength and reunification.

A second person left a Medal of Honor at the memorial on Veterans Day in 1992, a few days after Liteky's was put on display in the Smithsonian exhibition. Terry Anderson, giving a speech at the ceremony at the memorial later that day, admitted that he did not know why the two had left their medals. He knew what the act meant to him, though: "It says that this is a fitting place for the nation's highest honor and that honor should be shared by everybody listed on that Wall."[76] Anderson's was a generous and appealing sentiment—but also an utter misinterpretation of Liteky's act of political protest and renunciation, which Anderson assimilated into the standard discourse of recognition and honor. This misinterpretation should not be dismissed as a simple "mistake." Whenever ideologically driven, inattentive, or—in this case—unaware speakers overlooked anomalous thoughts and resorted automatically to received ideas, the power of the dominant discourse spoke through them. The discourse's domination of a tradition of commemoration relies, therefore, not on a simple logic of repetition and dissemination but on millions of tiny—or huge—"mistakes" such as Anderson's whose cumulative effect is to crowd out alternative ways of seeing the world.

Other offerings bespeak irremediable pain that cannot be compensated by recognition or assuaged by the promised comforts of "healing." A note left at the memorial accompanied a wedding band and engagement ring and explained that the widow of a young man who died in Vietnam no longer wanted to keep the rings when she remarried.[77] The young man's mother buried them at his grave, but when rain washed them to the surface, a friend brought the rings to the memorial, explaining in his note that the soldier's widow "chooses to forget this part of her life." He did not know where else to take them. This story tells us something about the work to which the memorial has been put, as the final resting place for objects and feelings that have no home. The relinquishing of the rings, symbols of the promise of lives unlived, was the more tragic because of all that it left unsaid: Did the young widow give up the rings because she ceased to care about her dead husband or because she cared too much to be reminded of him?

A marine sergeant left another wedding ring at the wall, with a note explaining that it had belonged to a young Viet Cong fighter killed by the marines in May 1968. "I wish I knew more about this young man. I have carried this ring for 18 years and it's time for me to lay it down. This boy is not my enemy any longer."[78] How many other offerings at the memorial are surrounded by these complex feelings—the wish to shed part of the past while ensuring that it not be allowed simply to disappear, as though it had never existed? Leaving things at the memorial can constitute a complex gesture of simultaneously releasing and preserving the past. Interpreting the offerings is thus, as the exhibition curators recognized, a challenging task: Can we assume that the thousands of MIA bracelets left at the memorial were an attempt to ensure that the plight of those missing in action in Southeast Asia is not forgotten? How many were left there when their owners became convinced that there were no living MIAs, or otherwise abandoned hope for their return?[79]

A donation to the Pennsylvania Military Museum in Boalsburg, Pennsylvania, provides a clue to the difficult relationship people sometimes have to Vietnam War–related artifacts and may give us an insight into the motives of some of those who leave offerings at the memorial. William Peberdy served as a second lieutenant in Vietnam. A helmet cover that he wore at the time records the "kills" that Peberdy's platoon, under pressure from his company commander to achieve a high "body count," recorded. For each "kill," he drew a cartoon image of a head wearing a Vietnamese peasant's conical hat. At first, Peberdy's men mutilated the bodies of the dead but when he found that his Vietnamese enemy treated American bodies with more respect, Peberdy put a stop to the mistreatment of the enemy dead and began to feel ambivalent about the grisly scorecard he wore on his helmet. Peberdy also brought back an SKS automatic weapon whose stock was covered with the blood of a guerrilla his men killed. A "silent veteran," Peberdy did not speak to his wife about the war but knew that the cache of objects made her uncomfortable. Whether because of the morbid traces these objects bore or because of other memories they carried, she wanted him to get rid of them. Yet he did not feel right about simply dumping them in the trash; they were, after all, objects with some historical significance. So he donated them to the museum, where they were put on display, helmet cover, weapon, and all.[80] Some of those who leave things at the memorial perform a similar act of surrender and conservation.

Sometimes, leaving an object at the memorial signifies a transition in the life of the donor. Tom Allen, who composed a photographic book based on the Vietnam Veterans Memorial Collection, remarked that the number of teddy bears and other toys left at the wall increased in the 1990s. Perhaps the first example, with the attendant publicity, encouraged others to leave the same sort of offering. Allen speculated, though, that it may be that the parents of the dead were themselves dying or reaching the age of impending mortality, and that they or their heirs were finding a final repository for toys that once belonged to loved ones who died in the war—and therefore taking things from their own attics to place them in a vaster national attic, knowing that objects left at the memorial are carefully archived.[81] Such acts signify a generational transition but not necessarily emotional or political "healing." Despite the frequent use of the concept in news stories, museum labels, and institutional discourses about the memorial, many of the offerings signify its elusiveness. As a photographer who spent many hours taking pictures of people at the memorial said, "So many people came to the memorial to make closure—to say goodbye, to release guilt, make an end—and a lot of them can't find it."[82] Jan Scruggs anticipated as much before the memorial was built. He said, "Perhaps there have been some unrealistic expectations for this memorial in the minds of some people who viewed it as a way to finally 'make everything o.k.' for those who went to Vietnam. It cannot do that."[83] The facile talk of "healing" may indeed be a means of wishing away the truth that some pain is not easily consoled.

The desire to transform responses to the memorial into articulate, comprehensible human stories has proven irresistible to the writers of the numerous photographic books about the memorial. These books are revealing because of the ways that writers and publishers have mediated, packaged, and marketed the memorial experience to the public. Some books take a conventional documentary approach by providing captions for photographs, describing ceremonies and individual behaviors at the wall, and offering commentaries on the memorial's effects on its visitors.[84] The majority, though, infuse the pictures with human interest stories that provide narrative connections to the memorial. Michael Katakis juxtaposed his photographs of visitors hugging each other, crying, and touching the wall with quotations from notes or snippets of interviews that connected with the pictures. Duncan Spencer and Lloyd Wolf carried extended personal narratives of visitors adjacent to photographs posed in front of the wall. Other authors juxtaposed photographs of visitors and offerings at the memorial with quotations from letters left there.[85]

Sal Lopes combined images and text with powerful effect. In his book, despite the absence of any biographical link between individual photographs and the writings that appear alongside them, they connect implicitly. We see, for example, a woman's hand holding a photograph of a pilot next to his name; on the opposite page, we read, "I remember your elation on the night we graduated from high school together in 1960. . . . You gave your life for us. Now I'm just a middle-aged woman working daily with people whose youthful dreams have been shattered by life."[86] It is all too easy to be deceived into associating the woman who wrote the note with the woman holding up the photograph—until we recognize that the woman in the photograph is the same one described in another volume as the pilot's mother.[87] Lopes's book claims to evoke the "magic of the memorial," capturing "spontaneous outpourings of emotion." Yet the powerfully suggestive juxtapositions are anything but spontaneous—they are the products of editorial artifice.

The book from which Lopes borrows the quotations is the most evocative telling of the story of the offerings, the work of the journalist Laura Palmer.[88] Palmer visited the Vietnam Veterans Memorial for the first time on New Year's Day 1986. Like millions of visitors before her, Palmer was struck by the things left there; she then dedicated her research skills to tracking down some of those who had left notes. Crisscrossing the country to visit their homes, she found them eager to tell their stories, which she published in a book titled *Shrapnel in the Heart*. The book was about "breaking the silence." "Nothing I can write, no story I can tell," Palmer said, "will erase anyone's pain, but it can, I hope, crack the isolation which is the tyranny of grief." Although Palmer had worked as a reporter in Saigon in the early 1970s, she was moved during her visit to the memorial "simply as a mother." She wrote, "Name one child, your own, and each of the . . . names on the wall will break your heart."[89]

Each of *Shrapnel*'s chapters centers on one of the letter writers and tells the story of his or her relationship with someone who died in Vietnam. There one can read Anne Pearson's words to Eddie Lynn Lancaster: "Dearest Eddie Lynn, I'd give anything to have you shell just one more pecan for me on Grandma's porch. All my love, Your cousin Anne."[90] The simple sentiment and folksy image conjure up a peaceful time, transcending politics, that was shattered by the tragedies of war. Perhaps its evocativeness explains why this message was quoted several times—in Lopes's book, in one of the museum exhibitions, and in an article by Palmer.[91] In *Shrapnel in the Heart*, one can also find Sheri Masterson's letter to her father, Michael, listed as missing in action: "I have dreamed of the day you'll come home and finally be my *Dad*." One can read Carole Ann Page's note to her first love, Richard Ewald, who never returned from Vietnam: "I'm still trying to say goodbye. I never managed that very well with us, did I?" These human stories reveal the reservoir of emotion stretching out from the thousands who died to all those who suffered their loss. *Shrapnel in the Heart*, like the photographic books of visitors to the memorial, makes clear the human costs of the war but it divorces them from any critical consideration of history and politics; in this sense it logically extends the Vietnam Veterans Memorial's stated goal of "apolitical" commemoration.[92]

Some of those whose stories are featured in *Shrapnel in the Heart* met and formed a community, geographically dispersed across the country but united by their connection to the wall and their collective presence between the covers of the book. From their sense of connectedness emerged a newsletter, *From the Heart*, which helped them stay in touch with one another. Although Palmer's book concerns people who lost friends and loved ones in Vietnam, the newsletter devoted much attention to veterans' postwar experiences and emotional needs. The first issue, published in January 1988, includes poetry about the memorial, recollections of the war, and tributes from Vietnam veterans and family members thanking Palmer for telling the unaware about the anguish that veterans suffered.[93]

In a section of the April 1988 issue titled "Fred Few . . . Talks Healing," a Vietnam veteran writes in gratitude to Palmer: "I bought your book and have read it twice and cried and laughed and cried some more. Because of you, dear lady, I think I can now go to Washington and say goodbye to my friends." The From the Heart network tied Americans together with cords of emotion but allowed patriotic sentiments to bleed through. Side by side in the second issue of the newsletter are these statements: "I'm very proud to say I'm from these United States when there are great American patriots such as those who served and died for our country in Vietnam." "I am not a Vietnam vet, but in my heart I feel like one because I care."[94] "Caring" became the admission ticket to the community of feeling responding to the war's losses. The people featured in *Shrapnel in the Heart* periodically met at the memorial; eventually they decided to start a Web site to stay in touch with each other and to allow readers of *Shrapnel in the Heart* to direct questions to the people featured in the book. Visitors to the Web site are asked to submit a letter, about the book or about the war—a digital extension of leaving letters at the memorial.[95]

Among the stories in *Shrapnel in the Heart* is that of Eleanor Wimbish, who left a letter to her son, Billy Stocks, shortly after the 1982 dedication and wrote over two dozen more, leaving them at the memorial on his birthday, at Christmas, on Memorial Day, Veterans Day, and Valentine's Day.[96] She called the other people in *Shrapnel in the Heart* her "second family" and said that although people grieved with them, very few wanted to hear about the deaths they mourned. "We suffered a second kind of pain—rejection and lack of understanding. The Wall is also helping with that pain."[97] The act of leaving letters to Billy Stocks always stirred up painful memories for Wimbish, but she was willing to endure the emotional turmoil because of the letters' cathartic effect for others. Breaking through silence and incomprehension, comforting and being comforted by other survivors, was her contribution to the "healing." Wimbish was also aware that the letters were being preserved in an archive. "I think it's a great idea, especially for my children and grandchildren," she said. "I think it means part of the love I still feel for Billy will live on."[98]

On Veterans Day 1993, Eleanor Wimbish left another letter for Billy. It is headed, "William R. Stocks / 32 West Line 29," as though that is Billy's address. The body of the letter reads:

Dear Bill,

Today is Veterans Day, 1993. Here we are again, Bill, your family, who love you and will never forget you. We were all here 11 years ago, when they dedicated this memorial. We were here, last year, at the reading of the names on the wall and every year in between.

We are here today to honor the Vietnam Nurses. Those wonderful women who shared your living and your dying. They went to Vietnam to take care of you guys and came home to a country filled with more hate than love for them. Then they had to fight for a statue to recognize them. God Bless each and every one of them.

When the helicopter you were riding in crashed, you were still alive but un-conscious and taken to a hospital. For 24 years I have carried in my mind a picture that one of these nurses was there with you and you did not die alone. Maybe she was holding your hand, rubbing your brow or maybe she was even holding you. And as I hug these Vietnam nurses, I wonder, "Could she be the one?"

Through her letters, her contacts with veterans, and, not least, the publication of *Shrapnel in the Heart*, Wimbish became well known, particularly to the community interested in and knowledgeable about the memorial. Regular visitors made a point of stopping at panel 32W on ceremonial occasions to see if there was another letter from Wimbish. When no letter appeared, these visitors expressed concern about her medical problems, which sometimes made her visits to the memorial difficult. In the early 1990s, when I took a group of university students to visit the Maryland Vietnam Veterans Memorial, unprompted, they came upon a letter that Wimbish had left by Billy Stocks's name (he was from Glen Burnie, Maryland) and they rec-ognized its writer and subject.

One of her letters to Billy appears near the end of *Dear America*, a film based largely on letters written home by GIs stationed in Vietnam.[99] The letters featured in the film were chosen from among those solicited from the public to form the inscriptions on the New York Vietnam Veterans Memorial. They are read by off-screen actors, to the accompaniment of documentary footage.[100] An actor reads a letter home by David Westphall about the hardships of infantry life, and the comradeship of those who endured it together. Some of the other writers of the letters, like Westphall, did not survive the war, so it is as if we hear their voices from beyond the grave. Wimbish's letter to one of those who died seems to complete a dialogue between those separated by death. Palmer had said that Wimbish's voice became for her "the voice of every mother" who lost a child in Vietnam. In an emotional reading, the actress Ellen Burstyn brings that voice to life in the film.[101] The audience hears Burstyn as Billy's mother speak of how lucky she feels to have known him. She recounts how his friends say that, unlike some of his comrades, he never developed a mean streak. He remained the happy-go-lucky boy she always remembered, her voice lilting at the instant she recalls how hard it was to scold him. She tells Billy that she has heard that her letters bring comfort to others and hopes that this is so, because—and here, her voice, which has remained just short of a sob, cracks—there is so much pain left over from the war. The camera show Billy's photo on the wall, just above his name. After a pause, the film's closing sequence begins with the foot-age of the dedication parade of the Vietnam Veterans Memorial in Washington and the strains of Bruce Springsteen's "Born in the USA."[102]

In telling Wimbish's story in *Shrapnel in the Heart*, Palmer says, "The writing that began to bring her closer to Bill has brought her closer to others. She writes regu-larly to veterans she has met at the memorial and in the parades she marches in for Bill. She talks, listens, and cries with them. She loves them and they love her back. One told her, 'Maybe God took Billy so you could help all the rest of us.'"[103] Just as veterans had treated Victor Westphall as a symbolic father, they found in Wimbish a maternal figure. Palmer's account of hurt veterans and a grieving mother comforting one another is touching, irresistibly so. Yet even as one is drawn into sympathy with the emotional bond between the unnamed veteran and Wimbish, a key figure in the folklore that grew up around the memorial, one can also recognize a strand of the official discourse of commemoration: affecting, concerned with pain, compassionate, and ameliorative.

The emotion-laden narratives about the war and the stereotype of the Vietnam veteran became so powerfully imprinted in American culture that "wannabes"— people who never served in Vietnam—adopted the identity of veterans of that war. These fake veterans could compel the attention of listeners to their war stories, often filled with horror and emotionally charged incident; they could aggrandize themselves by claiming a part in important historical events; and they could explain away any shortcomings in their lives, transforming ordinary failure into something tragic. Palmer unwittingly transformed someone who had never served in Vietnam into a mouthpiece for the experiences of in-country nurses when she tracked down "Dusty," who had left a moving poem at the wall about sitting up with David, a dying soldier. "I will stay with you," the poem reads, "and watch your life flow through my fingers into my soul. I will stay with you until you stay with me."[104] The narrator tells of giving the dying man pain-killing medication, and after describing herself as the last person he will ever see, the last one who loves him, she asks, "Who will give me something for my pain?" The poem sums up the despair of nurses who could not save all those they cared for, and who are haunted by the memory of deaths in Vietnam. It was anthologized and became famous. Vice President Al Gore read it during the dedication ceremony of the Vietnam Women's Memorial in November 1993.[105]

Dana Shuster, who wrote the "Dusty" poem, became a member of the From the Heart network, meeting other members at reunions at the memorial. (They used her nickname Dusty interchangeably with Dana, and she published poems referring to her time in Vietnam under both names.) Shuster, however, turned out never to have been in the military and never to have served in Vietnam, although she based a large part of her identity and life story on the two years she said she had served as a nurse there.[106] Dusty's case demonstrates that responses to the wall had become sufficiently conventional that, by adhering to the cultural script, those attuned to matters of loss and grief could emote and write convincingly. Dusty carried off the role for two decades, a period in which her poetry moved thousands and crystallized the experience of nurses in Vietnam and in their difficult homecoming.[107]

As more Vietnam veterans memorials were built around the country the practice of leaving offerings, now part of a commemorative tradition, spread from the national Vietnam Veterans Memorial to these monuments. Offerings were evident when the author visited many of these commemorative sites in the 1980s, 1990s, and 2000s.[108] They are indistinguishable in kind from the materials that visitors leave at the memorial in Washington, DC and—apart from specific responses to statues—do not vary according to the type of memorial: whether at sculptures or inscribed walls, people leave notes and objects just the same. The remembrances have the same range, from public utterances and quasi-ceremonial gifts to personal, sometimes intimate, messages and gestures, some with enigmatic meanings. Vietnam veterans left their military decorations at the foot of the Vietnam Veterans Memorial statue in Eden Park, Cincinnati, and before the inscribed stone alcoves of the Oregon Vietnam Veterans Memorial in Portland.[109] Visitors left dog tags, notes, letters, and pictures at the Minnesota Vietnam Veterans Memorial in St. Paul, to be collected and catalogued by volunteers from the nearby Department of Veterans Affairs.[110] At the California Vietnam Veterans Memorial in Sacramento, visitors left a pair of women's bikini briefs (as someone also did at the memorial in Washington), a short-timer's calendar, an unopened can of beer, dog tags, and GI can openers. The sister of a Californian who died in Vietnam brought her children to see the inscribed name of the uncle they never knew and she left a note addressed to David telling him of the visit and ending, "I love you and always will. In your memory, Cyndi, 1989." In Dallas, someone left a photograph of a man who apparently died after the war. Inscribed on the back of the photograph are the words, "Larry Casey—Seabee. The bullets didn't get him but the Agent Orange did. Thanks Larry, Love Jimmy." A sister wrote a card to her brother whose name is inscribed on the Dallas memorial: "I never told you how much I loved you, Scottie. You were so young, but so pure of heart."[111] Three-dimensional objects are left there, too, just as they are in Washington, DC: a teddy bear, a POW/MIA headband, a Gold Star Mothers' banner, a camouflage cap, a can of Budweiser beer.[112]

Visitors take rubbings at state or local memorials wherever there are walls inscribed with names. In Sacramento, pieces of paper cut to the size of a name inscribed on the California Vietnam Veterans Memorial are made available. They have inscriptions at the top-right and lower-left corners worded with the prologue and epilogue of the Vietnam Veterans Memorial, except for the insertion of the word "California" instead of "our nation." The phenomenon of the offerings and the taking of rubbings around the country is imitative of the pattern of response in Washington, but its spread also suggests that the scale and intensity of public response to the national Vietnam Veterans Memorial was not a reaction to a uniquely evocative design; Vietnam memorials of any description seem to open up the same rich seam of emotion and this suggests that a national memorial of any kind that met a baseline of acceptability might well have brought forth the same response.[113]

Some offerings have been collected and displayed at sites away from Washington, becoming an extension of the commemoration. A helmet, combat boots, and dog tags left in front of the Oklahoma City Vietnam War memorial plaque were displayed at the Oklahoma Historical Society.[114] Artifacts left at the North Carolina Vietnam Veterans Memorial were displayed nearby in the state capitol in Raleigh. Along with dog tags, military decorations, and photographs was an elaborate framed composition that included a plastic model of a U.S. reconnaissance aircraft, a photograph of its pilot, and a map showing where it was shot down over North Vietnam in 1965.[115] In Sacramento, the display of remembrances included a map of the theater of conflict, a POW/MIA flag, an olive wreath, and a pair of combat boots. Offerings left at the Washington Vietnam Veterans Memorial, in the state capital, Olympia, include a bottle of beer, a Jimi Hendrix record, a gearshift knob from a 1957 Chevy, a high-school graduation invitation, and a bamboo cross wrapped in barbed wire. These and other objects and letters left at the memorial are gathered in the state archives and occasionally put on display.[116]

On May 14, 1989, at the Kentucky Vietnam Veterans Memorial, Tim Lynch left a poem dedicated to his brother, Michael Henry Lynch, who had died in Vietnam twenty-one years earlier to the day: "I wanted to leave him something," Lynch said. "It was just a personal thing. I figured someone would pick it up later and toss it." Lynch did not know, though, that Tom Fugate, curator at the Kentucky Military History Museum, had been visiting the memorial and picking up offerings left there, saving them in the museum's storage room.[117] In 1992, when the author visited the Kentucky memorial during the "LZ Bluegrass" Vietnam veterans gathering in Frankfort, some of these offerings appeared in a display case. Veterans at the Kentucky Vietnam Veterans Memorial drank a toast to their buddies and left a crumpled beer can during the Memorial Day ceremonies there in 1992. Within a few days, that beer can was also on display at LZ Bluegrass.

In the small exhibition, one could also find a visitor's hand-written transcription of Michael O'Donnell's poem describing the "gentle heroes" who fought in Vietnam, which became famous after being inscribed on the New York Vietnam Veterans Memorial and published in the book *Dear America*. Kentucky was just one of many places where the poem was reproduced. It enjoins, "Save for them a place / inside of you" and admonishes, "In that time / when men . . . feel safe / to call the war insane, / take one moment to embrace / those gentle heroes you left behind." The whole poem was written out by hand and left at the Vietnam Veterans Memorial by a marine veteran of the Khe Sanh hill fights with a note to "Don." The poem was also transcribed and left in 1992 at the California Vietnam Veterans Memorial, and a large, homemade sign someone else left there admonished, "Please do not forget the gentle heroes we left behind." (In a publication about the California memorial, a photo of that sign was juxtaposed with another of a display of MIA photos captioned "Abandoned!"). In a VVMF publication, a high school student added his own lines to the first seven by O'Donnell, saying they came "from [his] heart." The poem was excerpted in an inscription on the California Vietnam Veterans Memorial in Sacramento and appeared in *Hamburger Hill*, a feature film that begins by a rapid horizontal camera movement scanning the names on the Vietnam Veterans Memorial, which dissolves into a shot, traveling at the same pace, of a casualty being evacuated from the fighting for Ap Bia mountain. The poem's words among the film's final credits appear to offer a kind of closure. The poem's significance was recognized when Ronald Reagan quoted it in his 1988 speech at the Vietnam Veterans Memorial, in which he referred to the "gentle heroes" Americans remember each Veterans Day. The appropriation of the poem in these different discursive registers—vernacular writings, mass mediated and monumental forms, and a presidential address—signifies the elaboration of a public culture of commemoration with its own distinctive language and commonplaces going beyond the abstractions of healing and reconciliation.[118]

People bring gifts to memorial statues. Because the statues do not usually portray specific individuals but are intended as representative figures, dressing them and bringing them flowers signifies a tribute to all who served. At the 1987 dedication of the Vietnam Veterans Memorial in Sacramento, the central, seated figure of a GI wore garlands of flowers and a special forces' beret on its head, placed there by visitors. Some of these offerings, including the beret, were later cast in bronze and placed in two of the bas-relief panels lining the memorial's interior walls, making the offerings a permanent part of the memorial. Visitors to the Sacramento memorial regularly place bouquets on the near-horizontal body of a casualty rendered in bronze that projects from the sculptural quadrant devoted to scenes of wounding and medical treatment.[119]

When the Vietnam Women's Memorial was dedicated, it was festooned with so many bouquets and wreaths—conventional markers of mourning and chivalrous tributes to female recipients—that large parts of it were not visible. Someone placed an MIA bracelet around the wrist of one of the female figures, a type of offering that can frequently be found decorating life-sized commemorative statuary of the Vietnam War. The female figure leaning over the casualty wore an orange ribbon on her wrist, a symbol of the sickness caused by Agent Orange. Alongside was a Native American prayer feather, its quill decorated with beads in red, yellow, and green formed into stripes resembling the Vietnam Service Ribbon. Beads of the same colors were strung around the neck of the male figure, the casualty.

A touching gift was left at a less well-known memorial with far fewer visitors. When a heavy snowfall engulfed Reading, Pennsylvania, the first winter after the statue there was dedicated, someone draped a jacket over the lonely, seated figure of the GI as if to provide some comfort against the wind and cold.[120] (The statue wore only a sleeveless flak jacket to shield its back from the elements.) The same sort of symbolic care extended to a teddy bear left at the wall in Washington. According to park rangers, it was "left naked" at the wall. But throughout the day, visitors dressed it and added to its gear until it was garbed with a tee-shirt, a camouflage jacket, a dagger, a POW/MIA flag, the Stars and Stripes, and a belt with a canteen. The equipment connoted childhood games of "dressing up"; but metonymically, the clothing and other gifts are offered up to the men who died in Vietnam, recollected through the bear as youngsters playing with a beloved toy.[121] These second-order responses to an offering—gifts and embellishments brought to an offering—represent some of the key characteristics of the tradition of commemoration considered in this chapter: a tradition that is at once interactive, collaborative, sentimental, and tactile. The bear is accoutred for an afterlife in a Valhalla that is part playground, part battlefield, and the dagger it carries reminds us of the violence always already in prospect for the child who once played with the warm and fuzzy toy.

If you want to understand the values and knowledge to which a society subscribes, observe how it socializes and instructs its children. Adults, reflecting the society's sense of decorum, encourage quiet and nonboisterous comportment in young family members at the Vietnam Veterans Memorial. A young Boston father was heard to tell his rambunctious son near the wall, "Hush Timmy—this is like a church." Children are as fascinated as adults are by the offerings left at the wall, and although they are more ready than adults are to pick up the objects to examine them, they rarely need more than gentle admonition to treat the materials with respect. Young children can be both bewildered and transfixed by the memorial, asking questions there in hushed tones, but also having trouble grasping the purpose of the memorial and the scale of the losses. One little girl repeatedly asked about the names, "How many are dead?" "Mommy, is this one dead?" "This one?" "This one?" "This one?" Jack Wheeler observed that children ask the hard questions: Who are these people whose names are on the wall? How old were they? Why did they die?[122] Children's books respond to some of their questions with carefully composed answers. In these books, one can find a primer to all the lore, ritual, and decorum surrounding the Vietnam Veterans Memorial.

The Story of the Vietnam Memorial, in the Cornerstones of Freedom series published by the Children's Press, provides a history of the war itself before telling the behind-the-scenes story of how the memorial came to be built. Illustrated by a documentary photograph on every page or two, it gives the main lines of the well-known story. For example, using a film still from The Deer Hunter, it states, "One evening in 1979, [Jan] Scruggs went to a movie. The movie was The Deer Hunter. . . . That night, he could not sleep. He was stunned by the fact that the service and sacrifice of ordinary men, living and dead, continued to be forgotten. Scruggs made a decision that would affect millions: He would devote every extra minute to a memorial for Vietnam veterans." Clearly aimed at older children, the book gives the memorial's legislative history, a summary of the design controversy, and an account of the memorial's November 1982 dedication. It ends with a description of the "gifts" that people bring to the wall—and renders the near-obligatory story of the first item in that tradition, the Purple Heart placed in the wall's foundation.[123] Touching all the conventional topics, it provides a comprehensive précis of the story.

The Cornerstones of Freedom book on the Vietnam Women's Memorial is pitched at the same age group, with a similar mix of photographs and historical context, and describes the process by which the women's memorial came into being. It begins with a description of women's role in Vietnam, opening with the story of Hedwig Orlowski, one of the eight military nurses who died in Vietnam, recounting how Orlowski's mother received the telegram informing her that her daughter had been killed. It continues with statistics about American women in Vietnam during the war and then tells the story of Diane Carlson's arrival in Vietnam, her experience there, and how she came to lead the effort to create the Vietnam Women's Memorial. The book shows people touching the wall, leaving mementos there, and taking rubbings, and it shows a long-haired man in fatigues, wearing a headband, decorating the Vietnam Women's Memorial with a medal.[124]

Although the children's books are the products of private corporations, they cleave closely to the official "line" concerning the memorial. The books are not designed to be controversial but rather to provide basic information about national landmarks, hence socializing children into the core knowledge required for members of U.S. society. The Vietnam Veterans Memorial, for example, was published in PowerKids Press's Library of American Landmarks series. It is aimed at a younger reader and carries a full-page photograph on every other page but follows the same broad narrative line, beginning with a history of the war, including antiwar protests, and a description of the homecoming experience: "Instead of feeling welcome, many veterans felt unappreciated (un-uh-PREE-she-ay-ted)." It goes on to describe the idea of the memorial and the design controversy, referring to Jan Scruggs and Maya Lin by their first names, and ends by saying that many people believe that the addition of the Hart statue completes the memorial.[125]

Like the Library of American Landmarks books, *Vietnam Veterans Memorial*, in a series titled Discovery Library of American Landmarks, also provides basic information to younger children, along with the phonetic spelling of selected words. It carries a photograph of Gold Star Mothers bringing a wreath to the wall, and a photograph of the teddy bear dressed in the tee-shirt and camouflage jacket at the wall alongside the caption, "Visitors to the Wall leave tokens of love in fond memory." Describing the troops' homecoming, the book states, "American soldiers returned quietly. The nation did not celebrate their return. It seemed as if America just wanted to forget the war. But the soldiers couldn't forget. They had painful memories to deal with." The following page reads: "A memorial, Corporal Scruggs knew, could be a public place where some of the bitterness and sadness of the war could be left. And a memorial would finally recognize the service and sacrifice of Vietnam vets." The final page concludes that the memorial "has been a place for tears and a place for healing."[126] This reference to "healing" is the least controversial of all the elements of the narrative account of the memorial, simply reflecting a consensus about the memorial's function recorded, as we have seen, in dozens of other sources. Yet the absence of controversy and the apparent innocence of the remark do not remove it from the field of ideology. In the instruction of children regarding the material facts and social practices surrounding the memorial we can, indeed, see the way that ideology reproduces itself through its inculcation in the younger generation.

The father-and-daughter team of Brent and Jennifer Ashabranner followed up an earlier documentary book about the memorial with another that seems to be geared to adolescents. It touches on topics such as school visits to the memorial, the school days of those who fought and died in the war, and the lessons of Vietnam for future generations. Although it concentrates on personal stories of those who fought and those who visit the names on the wall, it also offers an ideological message: "We must not forget the lessons learned from the Vietnam War. One lesson is that we must resist being drawn into a war unless the security and well-being of the United States are clearly threatened." This lesson is a paraphrase of the most important of Caspar Weinberger's tenets governing the use of force. "And the most important lesson," the Ashabranners continue, "surely is that it is terribly wrong to send young men and women to war without giving them our country's total support." Republican politicians such as Senator John Warner and President Reagan had stressed this message time and again during ceremonies at the memorial and speeches elsewhere, and the Ashabranners' book disseminates their ideas not as political polemics but in the innocent guise of matter-of-fact lessons for the young.[127]

Margy Burns Knight's *Talking Walls* is the only children's book that would even slightly discomfit proponents of the official discourse about the memorial. Illustrated by a picture of a child reaching out to touch the memorial, it tells the story of the Vietnam Veterans Memorial along with those of thirteen other walls. Knight makes a similar point to the one Chris Burden makes in "The Other Vietnam Memorial" when she says that the Vietnam Veterans Memorial is "about 165 steps long" but that it would need another seven thousand giant steps if it included all the Vietnamese, Cambodians, and Laotians killed in the war.[128]

Eve Bunting's *The Wall*, unlike the factual books referred to earlier, tells the story of a fictional child taken to visit the memorial by his father to find the name of his grandfather, killed in Vietnam. The book is illustrated not by photographs but, as befits a children's storybook, by water color paintings. As the boy and his father encounter the wall, they meet a double amputee in a wheelchair, and a man comforting a crying woman, both of whom are of his grandfather's generation. "Flowers and other things," they notice, "have been laid against the wall. There are little flags, an old teddy bear, and letters, weighted down with stone so they won't blow away." They search through an ethnically diverse cluster of names until they find grandpa's. "Dad nods. 'Your grandpa.' His voice blurs. 'My dad. He was just my age when he was killed.'"

Father lifts the boy so that he can touch the name. Together, they make a rubbing. A group of girls in school uniforms arrives to place flags at the wall and one of them asks her teacher, "Is this the wall for the dead soldiers?" The teacher replies that the names are of the dead but that "the wall is for all of us." The boy's father takes out a photograph of the boy. They put it at the base of the wall and pile little stones on it so it won't blow away. The boy worries that grandpa won't know who he is, but father reassures him that grandpa will. "I move closer to him. 'It's sad here.' He puts his hand on my shoulder. 'I know. But it's a place of honor. I'm proud that my grandfather's name is on this wall.' 'I am, too.' I am."[129] The behaviors and sentiments in this children's book are a guide to the appropriate responses at the wall. Children reading it will know how they are expected to behave at the memorial; but more than that, they will know how they are expected to feel.

The younger generation learn about the wall outside of books, too. School groups regularly appeared at the memorial during the author's visits in the 1980s, 1990s, and 2000s, and school students are given assignments to write reports about it. The VVMF prepared "Echoes from the Mall," an activity guide for schoolchildren visiting the memorial, which it distributes to teachers leading school groups.[130] The Close-Up Foundation, a nonprofit, nonpartisan organization, takes groups of high school students around sites of national significance in Washington, DC. According to its literature, it "informs, inspires, and empowers people to exercise the rights and accept the responsibilities of citizens in a democracy."[131] In a typical program run by the foundation that focused on institutions of government, political issues, and citizenship, a group of high school juniors from Collierville High School, Memphis, visited the Smithsonian Institution and met elected representatives from their home state. They visited the Vietnam Veterans Memorial, where they observed the range of conventional practices that other visitors performed. They were initiated into the rituals when the group leader invited each one to make a rubbing of a name on the small sheets of paper provided for that purpose. One member of the group recalled that she thought that by taking a rubbing, she was keeping the person alive.[132]

In the 1990s, Chapter 227 of Vietnam Veterans of America, based in Arlington, Virginia, had a speakers bureau that addressed students of all ages, from elementary school to college. (Many other Vietnam veterans' groups continue to do the same.) The veterans took advantage of Arlington's proximity to the memorial to teach students there, where the veterans were able to confront their own memories. The veterans told the children about the memorial's design and used the *Three Infantrymen* statue and the Vietnam Women's Memorial as a starting point for discussions about their tours of duty and postwar experiences. The head of the speakers bureau stated that he was disturbed that the students' perceptions of the war have been shaped by movies like the *Rambo* films. The veterans, Vietnam Veterans of America's official publication says, were able to put "a human face on the war." The students, in turn, could "get a look at war through the eyes of those who have seen it up close" rather than having to rely on the "dry, impersonal" pages of a history book. The veterans tried to be "objective," even though they tended to have "strong opinions" about the war. Some shared their experiences through a booklet containing oral histories.[133]

Children's dramatic productions are a telling means of gauging what they learn from veterans. A group of students from Teague Middle School near Houston, Texas, researched and interviewed veterans to learn about the Vietnam War, and they created *Voices at the Wall* as a seventh-grade history project about "the destructive war and the healing effect of the Vietnam Veterans Memorial, the Wall." The fourteen-year-olds wrote the play and performed before veterans' groups, playing the parts of a soldier, a nurse, a grieving mother, and Maya Lin, while a black-robed spirit wandered through. In their performances, one could see the children internalizing all that they have heard about the nation's experience, refracted through emotions of loss, pain, and grief. The performance was highly attuned to the personal and psychological consequences of the war but lacked a critical purchase on politics and history—which is not to say that it was ideologically neutral. Veterans, whom the students had learned to admire and trust, imposed their own political agenda on the production. They appreciated the performance, thus validating the students' efforts: one gave the performance the highest accolade, telling a student performer, "You were me." In the face of this affirmation, how could the teenagers have refused the veterans' one request? A student said, "In the script, we had that we lost the war. . . . They [the veterans] asked that we change it."[134]

The Tabb High School (Yorktown, Virginia) Historical Drama Team devised and performed a play titled *Carved in Stone* based on their visits to the Vietnam Veterans Memorial, their research about the war, and conversations with Vietnam veterans. Their teacher, Paul Kirby, a Vietnam veteran, took them to meet members of two chapters of Vietnam Veterans of America.[135] The students and veterans began to correspond in a historical role-play, taking on the roles of civilians in the United States (the students) and GIs on active duty in Southeast Asia (the veterans) in 1968. The play grew out of the students' work with the veterans.

The performance of *Carved in Stone* began with a student's rendition of "The Star-Spangled Banner." With a stage set comprising large photographs of the memorial, and a rudimentary mock-up of the wall nearby, the students played characters confronting the names. In the play a grieving veteran from New York says that since he returned from Vietnam "every day's been hell for me." An angry veteran complains about the way he and his fellow troops were treated when they returned from Vietnam and questions why anyone who was not in Vietnam visits the wall. Another veteran expresses guilt because he survived when his buddies died; as their platoon leader, he should have saved them. A widow steps forward to touch the wall. She was only nineteen and pregnant with his child when her husband was killed in Vietnam. She says, "Mike, I brought Jenny here today. You two would have been a dangerous pair." Jenny finds it hard to be there without feeling angry. She knows many things about her father yet does not know him.

A comparison of these dramatic characters with the discourse about Vietnam veterans' psychological troubles and their need for public recognition—the starting points of the Vietnam Veterans Memorial's work—reveals how fully these concepts had attained the status of truisms by the mid-1990s. If the work of ideology consists in the transformation of a set of particularistic ideas into natural facts, the schoolchildren's adoption of the familiar, sentimental orthodoxies about the aftermath of the war demonstrates the relative success of the plaintive narrative of veterans' travails compared with the other strands of discourse that twined around the memorials to the Vietnam War: the more partisan and triumphalist narrative that the Vietnam Veterans Leadership Program promoted, the theme of "vigilance" preferred here and there, and the "massive force" doctrine that Republican politicians avowed.

In the performance, the students express rage, grief, and guilt. A nurse reads "Dusty's" poem about the soldier, David, whose life slipped through her hands. Yet the drama also expresses hope for emotional resolution. Although the dead cannot be brought back to life, the survivors' pain can be made better at the memorial. As the narrator says in the performance's prologue, the "black stone represents healing." It "looks back on death and forward to life." A veteran urges the guilt-stricken platoon leader to overcome his guilt about the loss of his men: "You must live, not only for yourself, but for all of them." A veteran consoles Jenny, who never knew her father, saying that all veterans are her fathers. (The sentiment is echoed by a child who, through the Friends of the Vietnam Veterans Memorial's In Touch program was put in touch with several veterans who served with her father. "I may have lost my father in Vietnam," she said, "but I feel I've gained seven more.")[136]

There are also political messages embedded in the drama. A couple of students play the mother and brother of an airman missing in action after being shot down over Laos. They demand that the government "finally be honest with us" about the fate of the MIAs. "I promise to continue to fight for you, son. I love you." A student helps a veteran find a name on the wall. The veteran remarks that he was just about the student's age when he went to Vietnam. "I hope you never have to go through anything like this. . . . Tell your friends . . . never let this happen again." But what precisely "anything like this" consists of is left unclear: a war? The lack of a proper welcome for the veterans when they returned? Betrayal by the government? And how one could prevent "this" is also left up in the air. What the play does convey is the broad sense that a tragedy, or thousands upon thousands of tragedies, occurred in Vietnam; that they should be prevented from recurring; and that the wall helps us to "heal" from them. The play climaxes with a rendition of the song "The Wind Beneath My Wings."

At the end of one performance, the widow of a real-life soldier killed in Vietnam approached the student who had played "Dusty" and told her that the play had helped her envision an "angel" caring for her husband as he died. Thus, through the emotional work surrounding the memorial, a schoolgirl representing a woman who fantasized her history as a nurse in Vietnam provides imaginary comfort, projected backward in time, for the real, mortal losses of war. The performance, although a tissue of dramatic creation overlaid on fabrication, had the ring of truth: this represents the moment when the circle of ideology closes, to capture the seeming natural order of the world within its imaginary horizon. The students ratified the received truths about the war by adopting them in *Carved in Stone*, and the veterans in turn validated the enactment of these truths by approving the performance. The president of Vietnam Veterans of America Chapter 433 remarked that these students would "be educating the future" just as the veterans had educated them. "They put out exactly what we felt and what we're going through."[137]

Students elsewhere echoed the cultural script of emotional response to the legacy of the war. One high school student wrote about an imagined draftee who returned from the war in 1968 to find himself unappreciated and even "loathed" by the country that sent him to fight. The country, she says, went through "mass amnesia" but then came together to build the memorial. The former draftee, now a veteran, visits the granite wall and sees his reflection, while all around him people search for names in "silence and reverence." The wall, the student concludes, "reminds, heals, and teaches" those who visit it. Another high school student wrote that, for veterans, the wall "heals the gaping wound left in their soul since their return to a hostile society."[138]

A high school graduate's fictionalized visit to the memorial in Bobbie Ann Mason's novel *In Country* involves the full range of customary responses to the memorial. Sam Hughes never knew her father, who was killed in Vietnam. She tries to understand who he was and what he went through by talking to Vietnam veterans and by reading his letters home and his in-country diary. She is horrified, though, by the violent scenes his diary describes and declares that she hates him. Nevertheless she tries to discover what "humping the boonies" must have been like by camping out in a swampy wood, telling herself that she is "walking point" as if on patrol in Vietnam. Her uncle Emmett, a Vietnam veteran, finds her in the swamp, and she encourages him at last to share his memories of the war with her. Just as she has had to struggle with a void of incomprehension left by her absent father, Emmett admits, "There's something wrong with me. I'm damaged. It's like something in the center of my heart is gone and I can't get it back."[139] Yet Emmett cares enough for Sam that he has come to find her. Love and compassion will provide comfort, if not redemption, for these two lonely people; this development establishes the context for the final section of the novel, part 3, when three generations of the family travel to Washington to visit the memorial.

The scene there takes the reader step by step through the nation's emotional responses to the memorial, before and after its creation. When Sam, Emmett, and Sam's grandmother, Mamaw, first see the memorial, it is "massive, a black gash in the hillside": the phrase "a black gash" recalls Tom Carhart's description of the memorial, although Mason's reference removes the pejorative sting. Coming from the mining country of western Kentucky, the family sees it "like a vein of coal exposed and then polished with polyurethane." Mamaw is skeptical, just as some members of the public and veterans were when they first heard of the design: "It don't show up good," she says. "It's just a hole in the ground." When they approach the wall, though, they feel its power. Sam is overwhelmed: "Sam doesn't understand what she is feeling, but it is something so strong, it is like a tornado moving in her, something massive and overpowering. It feels like giving birth to this wall." Her uncle Emmett goes to find the names of the group of men who died around him. Sam gets a "flash" of the grief he has been feeling for fourteen years since his homecoming.[140]

Mason researched before writing *In Country* by reading oral histories and talking to Vietnam veterans.[141] It is no wonder, then, that the novel contains a checklist of all the veterans' postwar problems: Agent Orange, post-traumatic stress disorder, alienation, and readjustment difficulties. The novel also touches on virtually all the conventional behaviors at the wall. The party sees the flowers and messages that people have left there: one is a message of gratitude to the men of a company of the 1st Airborne Division who died at Dak To, "Because of their bravery I am here today." A handwritten note apologizes to one of those named on the wall for abandoning him in a firefight. They find Sam's father's name, Dwayne E. Hughes, high up on a panel. Mamaw immediately wants to touch it and they help her up a ladder to do so. They leave a potted geranium at the base of the wall. They take a photograph of Sam high up on the ladder, near her father's name. Mamaw says, "Coming up on this wall of a sudden and seeing how black it was, it was so awful, but then I came down it and saw that white carnation blooming out of that crack and it gave me hope. It made me know he's watching over us."[142]

All the essentials of that scene are incorporated in the feature film, *In Country*, with some elements added.[143] Sam takes a rubbing of her father's name and kisses it. Early in the film we have seen Sam's picture being taken at her high school graduation. Sam leaves her graduation photograph for her father alongside the other offerings at the base of the wall, among them a teddy bear and a Bronze Star. With the embellishments provided by the film (the rubbing, the leaving of her high school graduation photograph), we have a virtual compendium of the traditions of interaction with the wall. This could be simply observational and descriptive of what people do at the wall; but for an audience unfamiliar with responses to the wall, it codifies normative behavior; for others, it reinforces the broadly shared knowledge of how one is supposed to act and feel there.

After completing the film, Norman Jewison and the crew that made *In Country* left a reel of film and Sam Hughes's graduation photographs (featuring the actress

Emily Lloyd) at the Vietnam Veterans Memorial. The photographs eventually made their way into the museum display at the Smithsonian of offerings left at the memorial. During the press preview of the exhibition, as reporters, photographers, and television camera crews made notes and shot images of the offerings, one camera crew lit on the photos. The field producer pointed them out to the camera operator, excitedly remarking that these were the graduation photographs of a girl who had lost her father in Vietnam—a touching piece of human interest for the evening news. Unaware of the fact that the stills depicted an actress playing a fictional character, the camera operator dutifully shot the photographs of Lloyd as Sam in front of the wall. Thus, the norms of behavior at the memorial achieved the fullest state of maturity: reality and fiction had become so fully imbricated in the cultural script of responses to the memorial that there was no meaningful distinction between them.

The creation of the Vietnam Veterans Memorial led to imitative responses in the form of mobile replicas across the country. In November 1982, John Devitt, an unemployed Vietnam veteran from San Jose, California, came to the National Salute to Vietnam Veterans and attended unit reunions with his buddies. The former helicopter door gunner was an opponent of the Lin design. "I'd read that it was black," he said, "and that was a color for mourning. And that it was in the ground, and that's a sign of shame—as though they were trying to bury the whole thing. And it wasn't designed by a Vietnam vet." He changed his mind when he stood before the memorial. "I stood far back for a long time, and then I went down into it and I was hooked. I felt pride and it was a healing emotion." He saw other veterans at the memorial, "smiling, smiling from the inside." To him, there was no way anyone could avoid falling in love with the memorial. Devitt decided that he wanted other veterans to share in this feeling—which was also a re-experience of the camaraderie that he had felt in the field but which he no longer found in his civilian life. Not everyone could visit the memorial, though. Many disabled veterans who lived far away from Washington, DC—among them, amputees and paralyzed veterans—found it difficult to visit the wall because they were hampered by their physical injuries. A month after the National Salute, Devitt learned that the organizers of a Vietnam veterans fair in San Francisco had advertised a scale reproduction of the Vietnam Veterans Memorial. He became involved in the project and soon dedicated his whole life to it, giving up his apartment and living in his car so that he would not waste money on rent, putting every penny he raised into the memorial.[144]

Devitt and his veteran colleagues, organized in the sometimes fractious groups the Vietnam Veterans Project and Vietnam Combat Veterans, Ltd., displayed the half-scale replica of the memorial made from plexiglass mounted on wooden panels at the Peace Is Alive Vietnam Veterans Fair in San Francisco's civic auditorium. Initially they planned to display the replica at a fixed site. Then it occurred to them that the wall might be portable, and Devitt realized that he might be able to "bring the spirit of the original [memorial] to those who can't visit Washington." The concept of the "traveling wall," or, as it came to be known, the "moving wall," emerged. To make a mobile version, Devitt and his cohorts silk-screened the names of the dead onto wooden panels. The whole wall folded up for transport on a flatbed truck. When mounted, the wall was approximately 250 feet long, around half the size of the wall in Washington, DC. Two years later another two walls were constructed as replacements out of stronger materials—black formica panels on aluminum frames—because the original wooden frame warped. In 1988, to make it more durable still, the wall was reconstructed from allodined aluminum panels. In addition to the moving walls, a permanent replica has been created: the half-scale "Wall South" in Pensacola, Florida. A Vietnam veteran created still another replica wall: a ninety-six-foot version of the Vietnam Veterans Memorial in his backyard in Stephenson, Michigan.[145]

The moving walls continually toured, stopping at towns and cities large and small, and as early as 1987, their visitors numbered in the millions.[146] A moving wall was erected at the entrance to Grant Park, the terminus of the 1986 "Welcome Home" parade in Chicago.[147] Since 1986, the moving wall made annual stops at LZ Friendly, a private, nonprofit Vietnam veterans gathering in Georgia. By the beginning of 1992, moving walls had been displayed in 286 communities, from Alaska to Hawaii and throughout the continental United States, and in Puerto Rico. The moving walls stop for a few days or a week at each site. One wall's itinerary is typical: in June and July 1992, one of the two moving walls went from Marion, Indiana, to Leetonia, Ohio, and thence to Muncy, Pennsylvania; Hermitage, Pennsylvania; Norwalk, Connecticut; and Lake Placid, New York. By 2002, there were three moving walls with separate itineraries administered by Devitt. In the more than twenty years that they have been traveling, the walls have criss-crossed the country many times, at every stop allowing people unable to travel long distances to see something that resembles the wall in Washington (fig. 89).[148]

Journalists writing about visits by the moving walls use conventional language familiar from reports about the original memorial in Washington, DC—for example, referring to its "healing" effects.[149] A Gold Star Mother speaking of her son while visiting the moving wall in Boalsburg, Pennsylvania, said, "The wound heals, but the scar never goes away."[150] Thanking those who had helped bring the moving wall to Eugene, Oregon, members of the local Vietnam Veterans of America chapter wrote, "The Wall provided a coming together of community and veterans in an atmosphere of healing."[151] While the adoption of this terminology may not be surprising, what is extraordinary is that people touch the replica with the same intense emotion and reverence that attaches to the original. This is all the more striking because the moving wall is not as impressive as the one in the nation's capital. Its shape is not as graceful, because the panels are uniform in height; the names alone narrow along their length. In fact, some visitors can see over the wall, because it is less than six feet high. One does not, therefore, experience the sensation of being surrounded and engulfed by the names at the vertex, as at the memorial in Washington, DC.[152] The moving wall, however, brings forth the same kind of behaviors. The silk screening of the names using an epoxy-based paint raises the letters above the wall's surface, allowing visitors, like those in Washington, DC, to take rubbings from it (fig. 90).[153] People also leave offerings at the moving wall that are indistinguishable in kind from those left Washington.[154] When the moving wall was in Boalsburg, Pennsylvania,

Figure 89. The moving wall, a half-scale replica of the Vietnam Veterans Memorial, Lancaster, Pennsylvania, June 1994. Photo by author.

Figure 90. A visitor makes a rubbing of a name from the moving wall. Photo by author.

people took rubbings and left poems and pictures. Someone left a pair of boots and an upturned rifle, with its muzzle sticking in the ground and a helmet on its stock—an enduring symbol of wartime losses, also used in ceremonial musters to honor the dead in the field.[155] When the memorial came near his home, a veteran wrote that he would leave a fifth of Jack Daniels whiskey for a friend. "Bet him a case in back alley bridge and lost, but he died before I could deliver."[156] Without the National Park Service to take custody of them, the offerings simply pile up in a warehouse in San Jose in variously shaped boxes marked with the date and place where they were collected.[157] The boxes stack up ever higher on industrial shelving like so many exotic specimens in Citizen Kane's Xanadu, an uncatalogued and uncounted reminder of the vast reservoir of unstilled emotion left over from the Vietnam War (fig. 91).

The moving wall may have been half scale, but it brought forth the full-blown rhetoric of patriotic recollection tempered by "healing": calls for the anointing of wounds, the claim about a war effort untarnished by defeat on the battlefield, and a rallying cry for unity in an America that had learned to respect its Vietnam veterans. Lieutenant General James Link (U.S. Army, Ret.) marked the arrival of the moving wall in Huntsville, Alabama, with a speech that began unpromisingly with his admission that when he first heard of the Vietnam Veterans Memorial's design he had "recoiled" at the thought of a "ditch on the Mall." However, he said, he soon realized that the wall "transcended all things political." In visitors' reflections in the stone, "we are made one with the memorial, we join its essence, and are consumed by images behind the names. . . . It is the wound on our National Mall that never heals, but it does serve to soothe the deep scars on those of us who carry heavy emotions." Taking the replica wall's visit to Huntsville as an occasion for reflection, Link recalled the military history of the war. U.S. forces were "never defeated" in battle, he asserted, as George Price had during the dedication of the California memorial; the war was lost because of a lack of will at home, undermined by media reporting. He went on to criticize one "myth" after another, following the broad lines of the Vietnam Veterans Leadership Program's statistics about who served, what proportion enlisted, the demography of the casualties, and so on. The speech ended with an uplifting appeal: "I ask each of you to treat each other with the dignity and respect you have earned. Reach out and welcome a fellow Vietnam

Figure 91. John Devitt, administrator of the moving wall, with some of the boxes of offerings left at the moving wall, stored in a San Jose, California, warehouse. Photo by author.

veteran home. God bless each of you, and may God continue to bless this America we love and serve."[158]

Jan Scruggs, who has remained president of the VVMF since the completion of the memorial, associated himself with yet another half-scale replica of the wall, this one sponsored by Service Corporation International (SCI), the nation's largest funeral company. SCI originally approached Devitt in 1988 about the possibility that the corporation might sponsor an existing or an additional wall or two, offering to host them at its cemeteries around the country. When Devitt turned down this of-fer, SCI approached the VVMF, who approved SCI's creating and sponsoring a half-scale memorial similar to the moving wall. This new half-scale replica of Lin's wall was inaugurated on Veterans Day 1996. Referring to it as "The Wall That Heals," Scruggs endorsed it as an ongoing VVMF program. A VVMF publicity leaflet said of it, "Bringing the Wall home to communities throughout the country allows the souls enshrined on the Memorial to exist, once more, among family and friends in the peace and comfort of familiar surroundings." People take rubbings from this replica memorial and leave offerings there too. "This memorial is a place of healing," Scruggs said, when it was erected at Valley Forge Memorial Gardens, an SCI-owned cemetery in King of Prussia, Pennsylvania. In return for his sponsorship, SCI gave him a stipend of about a thousand dollars a month.[159]

When money is involved in commemorating the war, veterans instinctively be-come uneasy. Just as there was controversy about the memorial in Washington, DC, so there was a controversy about the SCI-sponsored replica. Because it was usually erected in SCI-owned cemeteries, critics claimed that the Houston-based company was using the memorial to help sell burial plots.[160] "We find that they are using this memorial as a fund-raiser and a private enterprise and are exploiting the lives and loves of those men and women," the founder of a Florida-based veterans associa-tion said. One critical article mocked the memorial's customary language with the subtitle, "To Heal Jan Scruggs."[161]

At one stage, two rival walls faced off against each other at the same time in Pinellas County in Florida, Devitt's moving wall in a St. Petersburg park and the SCI-sponsored Wall that Heals in a nearby SCI-owned cemetery. A local member of Vietnam Veterans of America complained that it is hard enough to visit a wall inscribed with the names of one's dead friends without having to go to a cemetery to view it. Other veterans complained that, unlike at Devitt's moving wall, there would be no psychiatric counselors on hand at the SCI wall. A supporter of Devitt's moving wall said that it was "the real traveling wall" and called the other "the money wall."

Scruggs, while admitting skepticism about the enterprise at first, declared him-self to be pleased with the SCI venture. SCI claimed to have no ulterior motives in erecting the memorial in cemeteries, said that the money paid to Scruggs was a "gift," and stated that they intended to raise money to meet the ongoing costs of the Vietnam Veterans Memorial in Washington.[162] The Devitt moving wall also, perhaps unintentionally, supported the fundraising activities of those who wanted to create state and local memorials, but these tended not to attract the same sort of criticism SCI faced and were expressly forbidden in moving wall documents.[163] By

Figure 92. A diorama of three Navy Seals carrying the body of a fourth past a miniature Vietnam
Veterans Memorial, left at the memorial in May 1992. Photo by author.

2007, the VVMF-affiliated Wall that Heals appeared no longer to have a relationship with SCI; adding to the bewildering proliferation of mobile scale models of
the Vietnam Veterans Memorial, an SCI corporate brand, Dignity Memorial, now
sponsored a three-quarter-scale "faux granite" replica Vietnam Wall that tours the
country, stopping at cemeteries.[164] At the time of writing, this means there are now
four mobile replicas: two moving walls, the VVMF-sponsored Wall that Heals, and
the Dignity Memorial Vietnam Wall.

Long after the moving wall departed from some of its temporary locations, it
was still possible to see traces of its presence. In Boalsburg, the replica memorial
was erected at the Pennsylvania Military Museum, site of the 28th Division Shrine.
When the moving wall left, flower beds were planted that replicated its chevron
shape on its former site. In Eugene, Oregon, a far more modest concrete marker,
again chevron-shaped, indicates the place where the memorial once stood. These
material afterimages of the memorial's presence evoke the resonance of acts of
remembering, echoing through the years. In another replication of the memorial's
design, in Washington Crossing, Pennsylvania, sixty thousand small Stars and Stripes
were laid out in the shape of the Vietnam Veterans Memorial to mark July 4, 1988.[165]

Hart's statue and the wall have also been reproduced in miniature. A six-inch high
model of the Hart statue was on display in the New York State Vietnam Veterans
Memorial Resource Center in Albany in the mid-1990s, along with a wooden panel
from the original moving wall. At the Vietnam Veterans Memorial in Washington,
DC, someone once left a diorama, showing a group of three Navy SEALs walking

next to a tiny replica of Lin's wall (fig. 92). One of the three hoists the body of a comrade on his shoulder, a pose that creates a narrative link between the Hart statue and the wall: here, it seems, is one of those named on the wall being carried past it or to it by figures whose number, three, is reminiscent of the Hart statue.[166] A mail-order company marketed a nine-and-a half-inch high sculpture showing a moustached veteran in fatigues, with a little girl at his side, standing in front of two panels of the memorial and reaching out to touch it. The sculpture itself is crudely executed, but the wall panels are reproduced in loving detail: each of the names on the two panels is legible in tiny letters and appears as it does on the memorial itself.[167] A small-scale model of the chevron-shaped wall carries the name of a Vietnam veteran whose family was convinced that he had died because of Agent Orange poisoning. Because he was not listed on the memorial, they created their own.[168]

Replicas of *Three Infantrymen* have appeared elsewhere, also echoing the memorial in Washington, DC. In Junction City, Kansas, a wall of names accompanies a partial portrayal of Hart's statue.[169] In Streator, Illinois, the Vietnam Veterans Memorial features a life-sized engraving of the statue.[170] During the September 1987 Bicentennial celebration in Philadelphia, a larger-than-life version of the Hart statue paraded through Center City (fig. 93).[171] A group in Kokomo, Indiana, used live figures to replicate the Hart statue, with a fog machine giving the effect of jungle heat.[172] Three characters in the ABC television series *China Beach*—Boonie Lanier (Brian Wimmer), Dodger Wimslow (Jeff Kober), and Sam Beckett (Michael Boatman)—struck the same pose as the Hart statue near the end of one episode: the familiar characters caught in a fleeting pose that lasted into immemorial time a world away (fig. 94). The fictional characters appropriated the memorial's gravitas, the cast bronze on the Mall dematerializing and, after a change of costume but with weapons intact, reforming in the imaginary past as pixels on the screen; in exchange, the fictional characters gave the three statuary figures a living "back story." On the twenty-fifth anniversary of the wall's dedication, a contingent of former South Vietnamese soldiers and marines marched in the parade. Three young Vietnamese Americans, wearing bronze make-up and bronze-stained clothing, adopted the poses of the Hart statue as they rolled along on a float, signifying their continued loyalty to the cause for which Americans had fought and died. The Franklin Mint invited readers of *Parade* magazine to buy something that, depending on one's taste, might be described as a collectible or as a piece of kitsch: a limited-edition eight-inch plate bordered in 24-Karat gold featuring a picture of the *Three Infantrymen*, with names from the wall and a stylized U.S. flag in the background. It then marketed a three-dimensional miniature porcelain replica of the statue, "showcased within a crystal-clear dome."[173] In 1991, Sterling High School in Somerdale, New Jersey, dedicated a plaque with the names of former students who served in Vietnam, alongside one of the miniature Hart statues by the Franklin Mint. As well as these statue-related collectibles, one can buy a "piece" of the wall itself: a small piece of polished black granite inscribed with one of the names on the wall in its distinctive Optima font.[174]

The simplest explanation of the motives underlying the successive iterations of the wall and the Hart statue is that these re-creations endorse the designs and the

Figure 93. Larger-than-life replica of the Frederick Hart statue *Three Infantrymen* at a Philadelphia parade marking the bicentennial of the U.S. Constitution, September 17, 1987. Photo by author.

memorial projects to which they are attached. Some of them become display items in the personalized shrines containing memorabilia of the war that some Vietnam veterans maintain in a corner of a room, office, or garage. The reproduction of the objects in different scales also suggests an effort to achieve psychological mastery over historical experience, as if being able to reproduce a memorial and scale it up or miniaturize it means that one can at will contain or exteriorize the memories it

Figure 94. Three of the regular characters in the ABC television series *China Beach* imitate the pose of Frederick Hart's *Three Infantrymen*.

evokes, to possess, not be possessed by them; the apparently endless proliferation of replica memorials, though, suggests that this mastery remains elusive. The yearning desire the miniatures bespeak, an emptiness that cannot be filled, endlessly reproduces itself with each new object.[175]

In the 1990s one could order a cardboard replica of the Vietnam Veterans Memorial, complete with fifty-eight thousand printed names, to arrive folded in a cardboard mailing tube.[176] Is that a sign that people revere the roster of the dead, or does the flimsy photographic replica connote disrespect? References to Vietnam War–related themes in animated television comedies in the 1990s signify that the memory of the Vietnam War, far from a taboo subject, is becoming commonplace, even trivial.[177] Today, cyber memorials exist that allow one to locate all the names inscribed on the Vietnam Veterans Memorial, electronic "memorials to the memorial." One can even print out a virtual rubbing of one of the names from a printer.[178] It is also possible to obtain a wallet-sized Vietnam Memorial Wall card, with all the names readable on a microform reader.[179]

The moving wall's organizers have stated that, when it has "fulfilled the needs for which it was created," a permanent landscaped site will be developed for it. All the artifacts that have been left on its travels will be displayed there, with the flags

Figure 95. Miniature of the Vietnam Veterans Memorial, left at the moving wall on one of its stops, in the San Jose warehouse where offerings left at the moving wall are preserved. Photo by author.

of each state that it visited.[180] The decision that the moving wall's work is complete will mark an epoch. When the objects are displayed at the permanent site for the moving wall, visitors will see that somebody left a smaller version of the memorial on one of its stops, several feet long and beautifully presented in a plexiglass case (fig. 95). And perhaps a visitor will still wonder at the insistent demand for the mate-rialization of one wall after another, in response to a hunger that will seem to have been, for a time, insatiable (fig. 96).

The moving wall will cease its travels when it no longer attracts sufficient visitors to justify the trouble and expense of maintaining, administering, and moving it. But this will also foreshadow the time when, instead of inspiring imitation after imitation to satisfy a far-flung public, Lin's wall itself becomes the sort of unremarked, unre-membered place that Robert Musil observes that monuments typically become—a response to a war that once compelled our arguments and emotions but that will one day appear distant, perhaps irrelevant.[181] During visits to state and local memo-rials, I already saw prefigurations of that desertion: memorials from which visitors were absent for long periods, and sites that were being put to uses other than the contemplation of the war and its dead.[182]

Lin had once imagined that when the initial "wound" created by the wall healed and grass again grew up to its verges, the site in Washington, DC, would become a garden and place of recreation. She described the area enclosed by the walls as a "grassy park" and said that the memorial should "remain a park for all to enjoy."[183] Scruggs imagined people playing Frisbee on the lawn after a few years.

Figure 96. Miniature figure kneeling and touching a black wall panel, New York State Vietnam Veterans Memorial Resource Center, Albany. Photo by author.

The memorial's success with the public confounded these expectations but Scruggs was not wrong; only premature.

You are walking in a park. Stepping into sunlight, you catch sight of a long, dark wall, ahead, down a slope. It rises at its center and tapers at its ends. As you approach across a lawn, the wall's vanishing points stretch to right and left. Your eyes follow the line of the wall at one side and you see the Washington Monument. Looking the other way, you find the Lincoln Memorial, screened by trees. Once you near the center of the wall, it rises above you, the black stone majestic in its silence. A solitary, dim reflection looks back, deserted by the multitude that once moved in its realm. There are inscriptions, which speak of the "Vietnam War," "those who gave their lives," and "courage," "sacrifice," "duty and country." A war, then. Dates and names, beyond all remembering and forgetting. Without words to frame the questions, you do not ask who was healed or who believed in the end that the war was noble. You gaze at the mass of names and wonder, and the walls stretch into the distance as you turn to leave.

CONCLUSION

A "Statute of Limitations": What "Healing" from the War Might Mean

★

If we forget what we did, we won't know who we are.
I'm warning of an eradication of the American memory that could result,
ultimately, in an erosion of the American spirit.

—RONALD REAGAN, President's Farewell Address to the Nation,
January 11, 1989

SINCE THE dedication of the Vietnam Veterans Memorial in Washington, DC, the most common forms of commemoration of the Vietnam War in the United States have been inscribed walls of names and bronze statues. After 1982, the rhetoric and ideology of commemoration around the country have also been consistent with the precedent of the national memorial: memorials elsewhere have almost universally been titled Vietnam veterans memorials, not Vietnam War memorials, and exclusively record the names of military personnel on inscribed walls. The roll call of the dead recalls the fate of those who served, rather than anything they did. The members of the armed forces were killed in the war or they were spared. Their relationship to the war is rendered in the passive, not the active voice: thus, the memorials recall the war as an experience undergone or suffered by those who served rather than as a matter of national policy involving decisions by the state, actions by the armed forces, and debates on the home front.

The memorials have been overwhelmingly America-centered, overlooking the names of allies, enemies, and the war's numerous civilian casualties. The concentration on military service is sustained in commemorative statuary, which largely restricts the field of representation to America's armed forces. The demographic range of representation in statuary is intended to suggest the ethnic and gendered inclusiveness of the American "family," but it underlines the memorials' exclusive concentration on U.S. uniformed personnel. Statuary and walls of inscribed names focus attention on common soldiers rather than commanders.

399

The Vietnam Veterans Memorial Fund (VVMF) set other precedents for commemorations around the country, restricting any attempt to endow the war with historical meaning: the Vietnam Veterans Memorial and the vast majority of those that followed it attempted political neutrality, avoiding justifications or condemnations of the United States' war aims or the conduct of the war. Maya Lin imagined a child who knew nothing about the war seeing the Vietnam Veterans Memorial in a hundred years' time and predicted that the child would see "just . . . the immense sacrifice. . . . It doesn't really tell you what is right, what is wrong."[1]

The memorial planners' rejection of moral and political criticisms of the war brought their efforts into line with the predilections of America's postwar political leaders. From the moment President Gerald Ford announced that the departure of U.S. personnel from Saigon closed a chapter in the American experience, the nation's leaders demonstrated a flight from critical judgments of the war. America's postwar presidents rejected the notion that the United States was morally culpable because of its actions in Vietnam. According to them, America had nothing to apologize or atone for. The first president elected after the war ended, Jimmy Carter, said that America owed no moral debt to Vietnam because "the destruction was mutual." Carter went on, "I don't feel that we ought to apologize or to castigate ourselves or to assume the status of culpability."[2] In his August 1980 speech to the Veterans of Foreign Wars, Carter's successor, Ronald Reagan, treated guilt and shame as inexplicable and unjustified impositions on U.S. veterans of the Vietnam War. Reagan saw "giving way" to shame or guilt as a sign of moral weakness that brought dishonor on the memories of those who died in the war and resulted in the poor treatment of veterans who returned.[3] Both Reagan and Carter therefore rejected the wartime testimony by antiwar veterans that the United States had acted wrongfully in the Vietnam War.

The efforts of the VVMF to gain recognition for those who served in Vietnam accorded with Reagan's view that the nation's Vietnam veterans and the casualties of the war had been denied the honor and respect they deserved. Reagan and the VVMF initially diverged, though, in their approaches to the war's moral and political meaning. In his 1980 speech, Reagan defined the war as a "noble cause." In contrast, the VVMF tried to avoid statements about the worthiness of the war and advocated "healing." Whereas Reagan's speech was polemical and divisive, the VVMF wanted the memorial to transcend the domestic political conflicts that the war had caused and to bring about a resolution of those divisions. In their statements of purpose, the memorial fund described veterans' psychological difficulties, exacerbated by their poor homecoming, as emotional "wounds," and the nation's political divisions as a social "wound." They argued that these wounds were connected: because the war had been unpopular and divisive, the nation had rejected its veterans as it sought to forget the war.

This way of talking about the war reflected the emerging knowledge about war-induced trauma: in the same year that Congress passed its legislation authorizing the VVMF to create a memorial, the American Psychiatric Association validated the condition known thereafter as post-traumatic stress disorder (PTSD). The cure that the VVMF proposed connected veterans' emotional wounds with society's wounds: the memorial fund hoped that people who agreed about little else would be able to set aside their differences in recognizing Vietnam veterans' service and the sacrifices of those who died. Human sympathy for veterans would trump politics and allow Americans of all stripes to support the memorial. Recognition by their fellow citizens would help the veterans "heal"; a society coming together for this purpose would "heal" its own divisions.

The Vietnam Veterans Memorial appears to have partly fulfilled the objective of "healing" by providing psychological comfort for veterans troubled by memories of the war. Lynda Van Devanter, who found that people did not want to hear about her experiences as a nurse in Vietnam, wrote, "For many of us, the pain that the wall brought back was more than we could bear. For more of us, the pain was finally approachable, touchable, reconcilable. It has been the catalyst for healing of the wounds that could not be seen or touched."[4] As PTSD became common knowledge and thousands of veterans visited the newly established vet centers, Van Devanter's statement about healing at the memorial became the conventional mode of talking about its effects. Rocky Alvarez, a Vietnam veteran being treated for PTSD, said that the memorial wall was "therapeutic." A National Park Service spokesman said the memorial served as part of the "healing process" after the Vietnam War.[5] Vet center clients came to the national memorial and others around the country.[6] The fact that veterans found "healing" at memorials comported with the prevailing mass-media discourse about the memorial and made for emotive human interest stories that began by posing a problem for which they provided resolution and closure.

The idea that the Vietnam Veterans Memorial furthered societal healing was problematic, though. To begin with, the VVMF's history shows us that their work was beset with conflict. Tom Carhart, H. Ross Perot, James Webb, and their congressional allies engaged in ideological combat to promote and defend their interpretation of the war. Advocates of the "noble cause" idea such as Carhart and Thomas Pauken objected to the concept of healing as a valid approach to the commemoration of the war. Their view was that the proper role of commemoration, sanctioned by Congress, was recognizing and honoring those who served in Vietnam, not "healing" the wounds of war. Veterans like them, proud of their service, rejected pain-filled accounts of war experiences such as Van Devanter's. They disliked the emphasis on healing because it reinforced the image of veterans as "sick puppies." (Jo Ann Webb, an army nurse in Vietnam and James Webb's wife, accused Van Devanter of being a "professional veteran" who, after the publication of her memoir *Home before Morning*, was making money out of her "exaggerated" recollections.)[7] The debates about the design of the Vietnam Veterans Memorial therefore posed a double challenge to the VVMF's goal of societal healing: the memorial stirred up conflict, and some of the right-wingers involved in the conflict rejected the talk of healing.

In their quest for the elusive goal of reconciliation—and for pragmatic political reasons reflecting the balance of political forces—the VVMF made concessions to their antagonists. These changed the physical composition of the Vietnam Veterans Memorial without any dramatic transformation of its ideological meaning. Whatever one's views of the merits of Frederick Hart's statue—whether one sees it as hack-neyed or moving, superfluous or necessary—it does not convey the ideological views that the proponents of a statue wished for. It merely satisfies the demand for bronze statuary made by those to whom the United States Marine Corps War Memorial was the exemplar of a memorial that expresses pride. Hart's infantrymen are tired and bewildered, not triumphant or determined-looking. Whether in Washington or elsewhere, advocates of the "noble cause" idea never successfully imagined how to render the idea in visual and material form. Nowhere do we find a muscular as-sertion of the nobility of America's cause in Vietnam; with few exceptions, even the memorials in which right-wingers took the lead appear consistent with the VVMF's plaintive discourse of wounds and healing.

After the VVMF agreed to add a statue and flag, they fell out with their critics over the placement of these additions to the memorial. The memorial's overwhelming success with the public reduced the influence of their opponents, though, and the VVMF's narrative of societal healing proved irresistible. President Reagan had been the chief author and proponent of the "noble cause" idea but in 1984 he made his accommodation with the apologists for "healing." The convergence between the VVMF's and the White House's agendas can now be traced in the record of behind-the-scenes assistance rendered by the White House, but it was publicly declared by Reagan's November 1984 speech when the VVMF handed the memorial over to the federal government. Reagan adopted the VVMF's key term, "healing," and con-structed a narrative around the word in which wartime divisions were giving way to renewed unity and strength. His speech acknowledged that there were "moral and philosophical disagreements about the rightness of the war"; he accepted that "we cannot forget them because there is no wisdom to be gained in forgetting."[8] Reagan, however, provided no substantial description of what these moral and philosophical disagreements involved; they remained abstractions, a baseline against which the reunification he advocated and celebrated could count as progress. His assertion of the importance of memory was an empty rhetorical gesture: his own speech con-tradicted the principle that he proclaimed because it emptied the wartime debates of any meaningful content.

Americans, Reagan said, had learned to forgive one another and to forgive them-selves for whatever had been wrong in the war's conduct. Earnest in his desire to unite the nation in order to face the foreign policy challenges of the 1980s, he said that it was time to move on. Yet this approach to forgiveness was narcissistic and self-serving, the sentiment of a self-help book rather than of a moral leader. Before forgiveness can be sought, even from oneself, there must be some honest acknowledgment of wrongdoing; otherwise self-forgiveness is simply a euphemism for absent-minded irresponsibility. "Healing" gave a new and superficially attractive cast to the consistent policy of America's postwar leaders, which was to refuse to consider anything to do with U.S. culpability.

"Healing" the nation, as defined by the VVMF, involved the overcoming of social antagonisms. This sounds like a benign purpose; but ending division required the silencing of debate and dissent. The cost of accepting "healing" as a valid goal of commemoration was sidelining criticism of U.S. policies and actions in Vietnam. The Vietnam War provoked a powerful stream of criticism of America's foreign and military policies, engaged the energies of a broad-ranging opposition, and prompted moral questioning and self-examination. The results included attempts to correct abuses of executive authority (such as passage of the War Powers Act) and the mobilization of an opposition to American imperialism and militarism. This broad stream of dissent was set aside in the name of "healing."

The VVMF's attempt to still the divisive debates about the war succeeded in silencing only one side. After early opposition to the memorial voiced by some anti-war critics, all the criticism came from far-right, militarist ideologues. The debate about the commemoration of the Vietnam War was confined to a restricted spectrum: one group of unrepentant veterans and politicians insisted on asserting the nobility of America's cause, casting off any hint of shame or dishonor, while another group of veterans and politicians wanted to suspend political and moral judgments altogether, in the name of "healing." Contrary to the suspicions of the right-wingers, the antiwar movement was simply absent from the argument; no members of the organized opposition to the war played an effective part in the debates about the memorial's design. At the points that this concluding chapter touches on political and moral criticisms of the war, readers will recognize that such views were missing from the debates about the Vietnam Veterans Memorial and those that followed. Instead, difficult moral issues left over from the war, such as the American forces' targeting of civilians, were not articulated or addressed.

A zone of silence billowed from around the memory of My Lai and expanded to cover the terrain of Vietnam in the nation's memories. Few Americans recalled the name of twelve-year-old Do Thi Nguyet, whom their troops raped and killed on March 16, 1968. After the antiwar-veterans movement declined in numbers, hardly anyone in America spoke of Truong Tho, seventy-two years old, whom the Americal Division soldiers beat and threw into a well, killing him by dropping a grenade after him. His was not one of the names that an American veteran ached to recall and mobilized the nation to remember. Shrouded in the same oblivion was the killing of Vo Thi Phu, whom the troops of Charlie Company shot before heaping straw on her body and setting light to it, burning her along with her year-old baby. The silence encircled the world and gathered most densely at the epicenter of American commemoration; there, on the Washington Mall, it solidified in hard, black, polished granite. Hardly anyone, though, appeared to notice the constitutive absences in the Vietnam Veterans Memorial, a monument that the public acclaimed and that, once the objections of right-wingers were accommodated, won near-universal praise from commentators and critics.

Yet a truism about commemoration—and about history—is that, to learn from the past, one must first face up to it. As Maya Lin said, "In the design of the [Vietnam Veterans] Memorial, a fundamental goal was to be honest about death, since we must accept that loss in order to begin to overcome it."[9] If the memorial did bring its visitors to a stark confrontation with a roster of the dead, we find no comparable honesty about American wrongdoing in Vietnam: not in the memorial's founding rationale, not in the monument itself, and not in the speechmaking surrounding it.

In 1989, at the end of a decade in which numerous memorials around the country provided veterans with the recognition they demanded, some Vietnam veterans expressed concern that the Vietnam War was somehow being made "better" in Americans' recollections. A conscientious objector who served as a medic in Vietnam said, "I'm afraid of what kids are learning about Vietnam. They're learning this idea of welcoming home the Vietnam veteran, which I see as a lot of garbage. I have a sense that what's happening in the country now is that the war is being made 'better,' it's no longer this horrendous thing everybody participated in; now it's becoming a jingoistic kind of situation. And, people are going to forget. People are going to rewrite the history of Vietnam and it's going to happen again."[10] The poet W. D. Ehrhart, a Vietnam veteran, suggested that when most people tossed around the "high-sounding terms" "healing" and "reconciliation," they meant "that we ought to forget the past, or worse, transform it into a kind of national mythology devoid of truth."[11] Harry Maurer, the author of an oral history of Vietnam veterans, worried about the same problem of forgetting, made more attractive by being couched in the language of "healing." "What, exactly, does 'healing the wounds' mean? Is it actually a code phrase for forgetting, for painting history in prettier colors? . . . If healing means, as some would have it, that the U.S. should 'leave Vietnam behind' and 'regain its confidence,' then we are not listening to the people who were there."[12] Maurer presses onto our attention the ambiguity of the metaphor "healing," which is open to a number of definitions, depending on how one understands the "wound."

The VVMF borrowed from the psychiatric discourse about PTSD in making the case that Vietnam veterans needed societal recognition and that this would improve their emotional well-being. Yet what eventually emerged was a bowdlerized and simplistic concept of healing, especially in the words of overenthusiastic journalists, such as the one who asserted that "merely to touch" the Vietnam Veterans Memorial was to be healed.[13] War traumas are not so easily treated by quick fixes.

At the American Lake Veterans Administration PTSD treatment center, groups of about a dozen Vietnam veterans at a time participated in emotionally demanding therapy in the 1980s and 1990s in which they relived their memories of Vietnam. After an initial period of group therapy, they went out "on patrol" in the Washington state countryside and talked through the traumatic memories that these walks brought to the surface; the thirteen-week program culminated in a flight aboard a Huey helicopter, which carried strong associations with combat and the evacuation of casualties. Their completion of the program was marked by a graduation ceremony. Ray Scurfield, the director of the center, compared the desire for smooth, pain-free societal "healing" to attending such a graduation ceremony without having first gone through the program.[14]

My suggestion, counterintuitive though this might seem, is that all the talk of "healing" at the memorial neglected and foreclosed a more morally satisfactory and hence psychologically effective resolution of memories of the war. The superficial reconciliation and closure that "healing" promises prevent a serious scrutiny of issues that remain vital irrespective of their long neglect; in this sense the discourse of "healing" may not be simply irrelevant to the problem it purports to address, but actually counterproductive. As Marilyn Young has argued, the United States' post–Vietnam War divisions "need to be faced and thought about, and any other kind of healing is just a sealing over and a making things go away. . . . What was the wound? The wound was the Vietnam War itself, the reasons it was fought, the way it was fought, and the way no senior political leader has ever confronted that even for a nanosecond."[15]

Healing is, however, such a rhetorically powerful term that it is difficult to resist. Recovering from the war might bring Americans that new birth that their orators, in one idiom or another, have often proclaimed. The promise of "healing" resonates for the many who, whether or not they have been directly affected by the Vietnam War, suffer loneliness, sadness, or pain. "Healing" appeals to all who yearn to have their broken places made whole. Its promise may have a particular appeal in a society where the feeling of comity is always jeopardized by atomization and where community is endlessly undermined by competitive individualism. Rituals of collective grief, real and manufactured, may therefore be about more than the Vietnam War: lamentations for an imagined prelapsarian unity whose loss Vietnam War–induced divisions symbolize. A vague, amorphous "healing" may also, ironically, be the inadequate spiritual prescription for a society in which the brute fact of social deprivation denies many that most basic social good: actual medical care.

Yet, for all its blandishments, the achievement of a morally contentless post–Vietnam War "healing" can hardly be satisfactory for a society the majority of whose members believed that crimes such as the My Lai massacre were widespread and that they were sanctioned by higher officers. The commemorations of the Vietnam War considered in this book made no effort to address these beliefs or to contend with the events that underlay them. In memorials that provide textual narratives, such as the Vietnam veterans memorials in Portland, Oregon, Indianapolis, and New York City, the absences are particularly stark, but in all the others the silence, though less clearly marked, speaks through each stone, each bronze, and each planting. Abuses of authority, presidential deceit, the support of corrupt, repressive, and unrepresentative governments in South Vietnam, and the indiscriminate or deliberate use of violence against civilians: these are crucial to the moral legacy of the Vietnam War. Yet the whole history of post–Vietnam War commemoration in the United States has involved the marginalization of moral and political questioning of the war. The VVMF's requirement that their memorial be apolitical and promote "healing" by avoiding mention of divisive matters—an approach also pursued by subsequent memorial efforts around the country—meant that Americans commemorated the war while ignoring its most troubling aspects. Far from promoting remembrance of the past, therefore, the memorial's emphasis on "healing" elevates into its prime commemorative principle a strategy of historical denial.

We live in the epoch of the apology, a time when governments apologize to others, and sometimes to their own people, for crimes committed in the recent and distant past.[16] Both Bill Clinton and George W. Bush came close to apologizing for the enforced servitude of African Americans, without quite saying sorry.[17] Southern legislatures and the U.S. House of Representatives have been less reticent and have apologized for slavery.[18] The failure to apologize for other past misdeeds has been seen as a badge of shame. When Japanese history textbooks ignored the Rape of Nanjing or the Japanese government denied that its army forced so-called comfort women into sexual slavery in World War II, Japanese institutions and politicians became the subjects of international reproof.[19] As well as demanding apologies, advocates for the victims of state crimes have sought justice, years after the crimes took place. Determined Nazi hunters remain committed to bringing the last surviving perpetrators of World War II's crimes to court, and these processes continue six decades after the end of that war.[20] International tribunals demand judicial redress for the victims of persecution in Bosnia and Rwanda. Yet amid the festival of regret and restorative justice, no American government has apologized for the crimes that the United States perpetrated in Vietnam. Politicians like Senator John Warner and President Reagan said "never again," but they were not repudiating the massacre of civilians. They meant never again would America's leaders exercise restraint in their use of the destructive power of the U.S. armed forces.

The uncovering of the activities of the U.S. "Tiger Force" in Vietnam and the later discovery of the declassified reports of the Vietnam War Crimes Working Group demonstrated what had long been claimed: that the My Lai massacre was no isolated event.[21] A U.S. Army investigator established that the Tiger Force had engaged in a seven-month campaign of murder in Vietnam, during which they killed everyone they encountered in a free-fire zone, mutilated corpses, and kept strings of ears as souvenirs. Summaries of the investigation reached the offices of the secretary of defense and the secretary of the army, but there was no political will to prosecute the crimes: despite the ample evidence of American-perpetrated murders, the Pentagon decided that "nothing beneficial or constructive could result [from] prosecution at this time."[22] Years later, reporters for the *Toledo Blade* discovered the evidence of the crimes and the thwarted investigation. The Pentagon initially responded to their Freedom of Information requests and sent the reporters documents but then stopped cooperating and sealed the records from the public.[23] Similarly, after initially allowing *Los Angeles Times* reporters to see the records of the Vietnam War Crimes Working Group, which documented seven U.S.-perpetrated massacres of civilians among hundreds of other unpunished crimes, government officials removed the working group reports from the National Archives' public shelves.[24] Thus, rather than belatedly making up for the earlier failures of military justice, U.S. government actions perpetuated the official cover-ups of American crimes in Vietnam, carrying them through to the present. No public outcry rose against this official tolerance of murders by U.S. forces. In contrast to its closing the case on these crimes, the U.S. government was relentless in hunting down a former marine private accused of deserting the military during the Vietnam War—an unmistakable reminder for currently serving troops about the sort of crimes U.S. justice would never forgive.[25] The treatment of John Kerry during his 2004 election campaign demonstrates that, for some Americans, the greater crime was not committing atrocities but trying to shine the light of public scrutiny on them.[26]

The steps that were missing from American commemorations of the Vietnam War in the 1980s and after were an honest acknowledgment of wrongdoing, and respect for the principle of accountability for crimes committed during the war. The approach taken by Americans followed a different course. The nation's judicial processes failed properly to apportion responsibility for wartime crimes: the courts-martial following the My Lai massacre allowed most of the guilty to walk free; cover-ups ensured that other crimes did not come to light for years and never came to trial.[27] Because the cover-up of the My Lai massacre delayed the start of the inspector general's investigation of the crime for over a year, most of the perpetrators had resumed civilian status by the time it began. The Defense and Justice Departments decided that efforts to prosecute former servicemen would be dropped because, out of uniform, they could no longer be tried by courts-martial, and civilian courts had no jurisdiction over events that occurred overseas.[28] By failing to create a legal framework within which veteran suspects could be tried, the U.S. government ignored its obligation to enforce international law. Because it allowed most of the perpetrators impunity, the state made itself complicit in their crimes. Phillip Jessup, a former justice of the World Court, said that responsibility for the My Lai massacre should have been pinned up the line "to those who have the authority to forbid, to prevent, or to punish, but who actually directed, sanctioned, approved, acquiesced in, condoned, or tolerated" war crimes in Vietnam. The institutions of military justice did not, however, address the question of command responsibility for the massacre, focusing instead on commanders' role in the cover-up.[29] Judicial failures left a residue of unallocated responsibility for wrongdoing that attached generally—and hence unfairly—to all Vietnam veterans. When veterans complained about being called "baby killers," they expressed outrage at the misplaced accusation—but this ignored the greater and logically prior outrage: the institutional failure to identify and try most of the guilty. Veterans who recounted the "baby killer" story raised the bar against any talk of American-perpetrated crimes in Vietnam.[30] When their fellow citizens eventually perceived that veterans had been misjudged and mistreated on their return to the United States, they compensated for this injustice by participating in commemorations that recognized and honored the veterans. Although veterans like Jan Scruggs complained about having to organize commemorations that might appropriately have been led by the government, one could inflect the point in a different way by noting that the commemorations were self-serving. As Kendrick Oliver has stated, "For the most part, Vietnam veterans have not functioned as custodians of the conflict's moral memory; they have tended to seek the redemption only of the moral debts that were owed to themselves."[31]

In its form, the pattern of events appeared to correct an injustice and thus resolve a problem: veterans were badly treated; society and the veterans were reconciled when the nation recognized and honored the veterans. But this formal resolution of one injustice never reached the larger pattern of wrongdoing that lay behind it. If we define social divisions and the mistreatment of veterans as the only wrongs that needed to be corrected, the VVMF's work and the commemorations that followed might have provided an adequate cure for the Vietnam "wound." But this definition of the problem requires us to forget what the memorials ignored: the images of unarmed civilians killed by American troops. As long as we do remember the My Lai photographs and recall the events they depict and the other crimes to which they link, the apolitical (and hence all-too-political) "healing" promoted by the Vietnam Veterans Memorial may provide a measure of comfort to some, but it can never be morally satisfactory and, for that reason, it cannot provide psychological closure except at the cost of an atrophied conscience.

The repeated proposals for memorials including Vietnamese children appear, in this light, a symptom of Americans' persistent moral misgivings about the war. The complex image of the Vietnamese child concentrated in itself inconsistent ideas: both the official image of America helping its "offspring" in South Vietnam and the contradictory image of U.S. forces inflicting harm on innocent civilians. The child imagery in memorial designs signifies the failure of psychological and historical denial in the commemorative sphere, and the skirmishes about whether the figure of a child should be allowed in a memorial demonstrate how the boundary between the allowable and the forbidden in the field of representation was policed.

Although, apart from attempting justifications of the war, politicians have largely ignored its moral legacy, they have been obliged to attend closely to its political repercussions. In the 1980s and beyond, a recurrent preoccupation has been the nation's struggles with the "Vietnam syndrome": its leaders' hesitancy in the use of force, and the mutual mistrust of the nation's leaders and citizenry in the event of an armed conflict. Tom Carhart, Thomas Pauken, Representative John Ashbrook, and Senator Paula Hawkins saw the relevance of commemoration to the Vietnam syndrome. They thought that, depending on the form it took, commemoration might bolster or weaken the nation's defenses. But the relationship between memories of the Vietnam War and subsequent U.S. foreign policy and geopolitical events is reciprocal: if commemorations that improved the image of the Vietnam War could help, as the right-wingers believed, to secure American military preparedness, post–Vietnam War geopolitical events (such as the collapse of the Soviet Union) helped to endow the Vietnam War with novel, retrospective meaning. An unambiguous military triumph would accordingly do more to cure Americans of the Vietnam syndrome than a thousand "healing" memorials; another "quagmire" would ensure that the warning embodied in the Vietnam War experience seemed as relevant as ever. Each postwar U.S. military success or failure has thus affected how salient the lessons and legacy of Vietnam appear. To understand the durability of the Vietnam syndrome as a check on militarism, we must therefore examine not just the commemorative context but the arena of foreign policy and international affairs with which commemoration interacts.

Memories of Vietnam were invoked in the United States every time the "lessons" of Vietnam were applied to other settings, or when politicians disavowed the possibility that some new theater of conflict (such as Central America in the 1980s) would become "another Vietnam." The presidency of George H. W. Bush saw a continuation of the effort to leave behind the divisions of the Vietnam War, although an odd turn of phrase in his inaugural address seemed to betray the government's bad conscience over its forces' actions. Referring to mistrust, division, and partisanship in Congress, he said, "It's been that way since Vietnam. That war cleaves us still." Instead of calling for "healing," though, he declared, "But, friends, that war began in earnest a quarter of a century ago, and surely the statute of limitations has been reached." This was a striking phrase, because the "statute of limitations" refers to criminal acts. There is no statute of limitations for murder or war crimes. In one of the more elegant phrases in the speech, Bush said that the "final lesson" of the Vietnam War is that "no great nation can long afford to be sundered by a memory." He asked for unity rather than partisan bickering, as much in the domestic sphere as in foreign policy.[32]

Bush's insistence that the 1991 Gulf War would not be "another Vietnam" underlined the extent to which the specter of Vietnam haunted U.S. foreign and military policy two decades after the revelation of the My Lai massacre, the invasion of Cambodia, and the collapse of public support for the war in Indochina. The "quagmire" of Vietnam was a persistent reference point in discussions of "Operation Desert Storm" in 1991. During the build-up to the military campaign, *Newsweek* commented that "Vietnam hangs in the collective subconscious like a bad dream, a psychic wound that leaves the patient forever neurotic."[33] Everywhere there were admonitions to do it right this time, cautions against the mistakes that the United States had made in Vietnam.[34] Bush repeatedly stated that the 1991 war would not be "another Vietnam," meaning that it would be an overwhelming victory achieved quickly, and that American forces would not be forced to fight "with one hand tied behind their backs." He recited the orthodoxies embodied in Caspar Weinberger's principles governing the use of force, adopted as the tenets of the "Powell Doctrine": the United States would use massive force to achieve a quick and definite victory and would then promptly withdraw its combat troops.[35] Bush said, "In our country, I know that there are fears about another Vietnam. Let me assure you: should military action be required, this will not be another Vietnam; this will not be a protracted, drawn-out war. . . . If there must be war, we will not permit our troops to have their hands tied behind their backs. . . . If one American soldier has to go into battle, that soldier will have enough force behind him to win, and then get out as soon as possible."[36] And Americans determined that, once the war was over, the troops should be properly welcomed, a corrective to the poor welcome that all by now agreed that troops returning from Vietnam had received.[37] In the aftermath of victory, Bush triumphantly "buried" the memory of the Vietnam War, saying "by God, we've kicked the Vietnam syndrome once and for all" and the "specter of Vietnam has been buried forever in the desert sands of Kuwait."[38]

On June 8, 1991, a massive parade of Gulf War veterans, replete with tanks and other military hardware, passed along Constitution Avenue in Washington, DC, en route to the Pentagon. Afterward some of the troops, still in their desert camouflage uniforms, visited the memorial wall (fig. 97). A marine corporal left his Silver Star and citation at the memorial with a simple note saying, "To Dad, Love your son." Someone else left a cry of vindication at the memorial, a note declaring triumphantly, "Guys, This time we won!!!"[39]

Triumphalism in post–Desert Storm speeches at the Vietnam Veterans Memorial flew in the face of the claim that the memorial promoted apolitical commemoration. In May 1991, Chairman of the Joint Chiefs of Staff Colin Powell, glowing in the aftermath of victory, spoke at the Memorial Day ceremony at the wall. He said

Figure 97. A Gulf War veteran makes a rubbing of a name at the Vietnam Veterans Memorial after the June 1991 victory parade along Constitution Avenue. Photo by author.

that when the nation went to war, "you must do it right. You've got to be decisive. You've got to go in massively. You've got to fight in a way that minimizes casualties. You've got to fight to win."[40] This may have been a statement of the "common sense" expressed in the Powell Doctrine, but was this "apolitical"? Hardly. Senator Charles Hagel (R., Nebraska) said at another early 1990s ceremony at the memorial: "If this war taught us anything, it is that our nation must make a total commitment to victory whenever we commit our fighting men and women."[41] Victory in the Gulf, in a war prosecuted in line with Weinberger and Powell's "massive force" doctrine, underlined the Vietnam War "lesson" that the United States must fight all-out for victory, once it sends its troops into combat. It tied in with the Vietnam War hawks' claim that the Vietnam War could have been won and was lost only because U.S. forces fought "with one hand tied behind their backs." The record of speeches over the years at the memorial demonstrates that its custodians have repeatedly hosted speeches making this point (from John Warner's statement in 1982 that "we should never again ask our men and women to serve in a war that we do not intend to win" to Reagan's near-identical 1988 statement at the memorial: "Young people must never be sent to fight and die unless we are prepared to let them win"). This repeated recitation of the "massive force" doctrine against the backdrop of the memorial reinforced the belief that what was wrong with the Vietnam War was that the United States had not fought hard enough.

The public was not convinced, though, that America had "kicked" the Vietnam syndrome. Asked, in the flush of victory, whether success in the Gulf War would put the memory of Vietnam behind them, half the Americans who were asked disagreed.[42] Wartime divisions, suspicions, and fears persisted. Some worried that, in the flush of victory, America might become overly aggressive and "trigger-happy."[43] But somehow victory in the Gulf did not exorcise the ghost of Vietnam. Because of its brevity, the 1991 Gulf War did not bring about a reorganization of Americans' mental maps of the world and therefore did not dislodge the Vietnam War as a precedent and analogy for other possible military actions. And because the Gulf War was fought according to the "overwhelming force" doctrine proposed by Weinberger and Powell, it tended to confirm and reinforce the notion that long, drawn-out wars, unconventional wars, or nation-building campaigns were dangerous and should be avoided.[44] Justifying the decision to withdraw U.S. troops quickly rather than occupy Iraq, Bush said that "the United States is not going to intervene militarily in Iraq's internal affairs and risk being drawn into a Vietnam-style quagmire."[45] Fears of another Vietnam therefore continued to shape American policy—or were invoked to explain policy—even at the moment of victory in the Gulf. And the continued vitality of the specter appeared to be confirmed, not denied, by Bush's rhetoric about "kicking" the Vietnam syndrome (another of his odd metaphors, implying that the syndrome was addictive) and burying the specter of Vietnam in the sand, which reminded listeners of the very thing Bush wanted them to forget.

Approaching his campaign for re-election in 1992, Bush was forced to confront another legacy of the Vietnam War: the belief among some Americans that the federal government had not done enough to obtain a full accounting from the

Vietnamese government of Americans who had been listed as missing in action (MIA) at the end of the Vietnam War. Spurred by American businessmen eager to trade with and invest in Vietnam, the Bush administration announced a "road map" to the normalization of relations between the two countries, dependent on political moves by the Vietnamese and on their helping the United States to achieve a full accounting of its missing service personnel.[46] Bush said that there was no hard evidence that any Americans lost during the Vietnam War remained captive, and he condemned those who made fraudulent claims that kept alive the hopes of families that their loved ones still lived.[47] But conservative groups successfully lobbied him to maintain a trade embargo and he did not establish normal diplomatic relations with Vietnam—which simply gave America's commercial competitors a chance to steal a march in the developing Vietnamese market. Different definitions of "healing" were in contention: the establishment of friendly relations between the two countries would stand as one kind of healing; but counterposed against it was the sense of incompleteness felt by those who believed that American prisoners were still held in Southeast Asia. As Bush, despite interruption by hecklers, told a meeting of an MIA advocacy group, "The wounds won't heal, the American family will not be whole, as I said earlier, so long as the brave men remain missing."[48] This sort of statement pandered to the MIA lobby even as the administration took tentative steps toward rapprochement with Vietnam.

The U.S. government had created a monster. Fostered by the Nixon administration in the early 1970s as a justification for keeping the war going, the MIA lobby now stood in the way of the normalization of relations between the two countries, regarding any move by the government to settle the status of the missing by declaring them dead as part of a sinister and deceitful plot to abandon the men. The theory was that, once the government had knowingly left behind members of its armed forces in Southeast Asia, it could not admit this and so had to continue to weave a tissue of lies to cover up its original deception.[49] The accusation rang true for those who had learned to mistrust the government because of the deceptions of the Vietnam and Watergate eras, which continued in the Reagan presidency because of the Iran-Contra scandal and the numerous ethical and legal violations by members of his administration. In 1990, the majority of Americans—62 percent of the general public and 84 percent of Vietnam veterans—believed that there were still Americans held captive in Southeast Asia, a substantial obstacle to the repair of U.S. relations with Vietnam.[50] This belief, and the charge that Bush was somehow complicit in abandoning the MIAs, threatened to cost Bush votes in the 1992 election.

The VVMF's implacable enemy in the early 1980s returned to the scene as Bush's nemesis in 1992. As an independent candidate for the presidency in 1992 Ross Perot took every opportunity to confront the Bush administration about the POW/MIA [prisoner of war/missing in action] issue, which formed the cornerstone of Perot's political support.[51] Perot's candidacy seems to have been motivated in part by a personal vendetta against Bush. The author of a study of Perot's life and times has suggested that his hostility to Bush had its origins in their opposed stances regarding the Vietnam Veterans Memorial—but this assumes that Perot found out about

Bush's role in the matter of the statue and flag. Perot's antipathy for Bush deepened after President Reagan appointed Perot as a special investigator into the POW/MIA issue. Perot blamed Bush for blocking his efforts in 1986 to find American prisoners in Southeast Asia, and Bush's own administration was thought by the POW/MIA families who were Perot's allies on the issue "not [to be] eager for the truth" about live American captives in Indochina. If Perot was, as many suspected, motivated by a grudge, this development seems to validate the reluctance of Reagan White House principals like James Baker openly to oppose Perot in the arguments about the Vietnam Veterans Memorial, knowing, as they did, Perot's combativeness and his propensity to nurture, and act on, grudges.[52]

For a time Perot's anti-Washington message, his beady-eyed pugnacity, and his simple prescriptions for the nation's ills appealed to the electorate, and he looked in mid-1992 to be mounting a serious threat to Bush's re-election. In mid-May, a Time/CNN poll put Perot's support five points ahead of Bush's, with Bill Clinton trailing in third place; in late May, a Gallup poll put Perot's and Bush's popular support neck and neck, with Clinton ten points behind. Perot's popularity and the need to neutralize the POW/MIA conspiracy theories as an electoral issue explain why Bush was forced into the humiliating position of having to pretend that he believed that there might still be American captives in Southeast Asia, or at least to hint that he did. On Memorial Day 1992, President Bush made a point of recognizing the Americans who died in Vietnam "fighting for freedom or [who] are still unaccounted for as a result of that noble cause." No one was impressed, though, when Bush parroted Reagan's "noble cause" rhetoric or referred to those still "unaccounted for" as though he believed they were anything but dead. A few days after this speech, a new Gallup poll put Perot eight points ahead of Bush, with Clinton still trailing.[53]

In October 1992, after Perot's candidacy was weakened by his bizarre, temporary withdrawal from the campaign, Bush attempted further to undercut Perot's base of support by welcoming a supposed breakthrough in obtaining MIA data from the Vietnamese government. Bush announced to a bemused public, "Today, I am convinced that we can begin writing the last chapter of the Vietnam War."[54] "Begin" writing the last chapter of a war that had already been buried? How many "last chapters," epilogues, and addenda would be required before the war could safely be "put behind" the nation and Americans could move forward, "in unity and with resolve"? Perhaps Bush's wish to play down the significance of the Vietnam War—as the source both of a "syndrome" he was determined to "kick" and of the POW/MIA issue that seemed to have a life of its own—explains why until late in his presidency he did not visit the Vietnam Veterans Memorial, which had reportedly moved him to tears in 1983. On the tenth anniversary of the wall's dedication, shortly after he had lost his bid for re-election as president and could follow his predilections without any regard for political repercussions, Bush returned to the memorial—but not to make a Veterans Day speech. Instead, he made an unannounced visit to the wall shortly after midnight as the fifty-eight thousand names were being read, as they had been at the National Cathedral ten years earlier. He joined in reading some of them.[55]

In contrast to Bush, Bill Clinton, who early in his presidency antagonized military officers by proposing easing the ban against homosexuals' serving in the military, took the first opportunity after his election—Memorial Day 1993—to make a ceremonial visit to the memorial. His political opponents suggested that someone who had dodged the draft should not appear at the memorial, despite his status as commander in chief of the armed forces. Yet both Vietnam veterans and the general public were, in the main, capable of distinguishing his wartime avoidance of service with his ceremonial role as president. (More veterans had voted for him than for George Bush in the November 1992 presidential election.) In May 1993 a large majority (two-thirds in one opinion poll, three-quarters in another) agreed that it was appropriate for Clinton to participate in the Memorial Day ceremony.[56] The majority of the audience at the ceremony greeted Clinton's speech respectfully, although the speech was also peppered by heckling. Some veterans turned their backs on Clinton as he spoke but others praised his courage for having attended the ceremony.[57] The license given to right-wing revisionist histories in speeches at the wall was not matched, though, by any antiwar rhetoric from figures such as George McGovern, Kerry, and Clinton. When they spoke at the memorial, they tactfully avoided any criticism of the war that they had once opposed. Both Colin Powell, who introduced the president, and Clinton himself quoted Lincoln's second inaugural address, saying that it was time for Americans to set their differences aside and to "bind up the nation's wounds." Clinton even recited a version of the Weinberger/Powell doctrine: "If the day should come when our servicemen and women must again go into combat, let us all resolve they will go with the training, the equipment, the support necessary to win, and most of all, with a clear mission to win."[58]

The moves to normalize relations with Vietnam continued under Clinton. The co-chairs of a Senate Select Committee on POW/MIAs, Senators Kerry and John McCain, both Vietnam veterans, one a former protester, the other a former POW in North Vietnam, gave Clinton political cover by leading congressional calls for normalization.[59] Clinton ended the trade embargo against Vietnam in February 1994 and began first low-level and then full diplomatic relations, marked by the opening of a U.S. embassy in Hanoi in August 1995. In pursuing this policy, Clinton proved willing to bear some political costs, including complaints by the highly committed MIA lobby, resistance by congressional Republicans, and caviling by veterans' service organizations such as the American Legion and Vietnam Veterans of America.[60] The search for MIAs gave way to the recovery, with Vietnamese assistance, of the remains of U.S. casualties. U.S. tourism to Vietnam vastly increased and trade agreements led to a normalization of economic relations between the countries.[61]

The normalization of relations with Vietnam provides another meaning for "healing." In the 1980s, "healing the wounds of war" had meant the reconciliation of a divided America, the nation's embrace of its veterans, and their psychological recovery. But a new twist on a forgotten definition emerged in the 1990s. Article 21 of the 1973 Paris Peace Accords, which brought the U.S. fighting in Vietnam to an end, said that the United States would contribute to "healing the wounds of war" by aiding the postwar reconstruction of the Democratic Republic of Vietnam and other parts of Indochina, but the United States did not fulfill its commitment.[62] Diplomatic reengagement was the means by which Vietnam's economic development was eventually assisted in the 1990s, because it opened the door to trade and investment. Vietnam's foreign minister, Nguyen Co Thach, eager for improved ties between the countries, had adopted the metaphor of wounds and healing to describe the diplomatic situation at the beginning of the decade: "It is time to heal the wounds of war," he said. "I don't mention the physical or the mental wounds, but the moral ones. As long as the state of abnormal [diplomatic] relations drags on, the moral wounds will bleed." Kerry said that normalizing diplomatic relations with Vietnam would "close the book on the pain and anguish of the war and heal the wounds of the nation and help us to put it behind us once and for all."[63]

As the normalization of relations between the countries proceeded, journalists and commentators discussed the process using the same language as Nguyen and Kerry—the war was a "scar on the national psyche"; it was time for "healing" from old "wounds."[64] In the waning days of his presidency, Clinton marked the establishment of friendly relations with Vietnam by visiting the country, the first sitting U.S. president to do so since the war years. His successor, George W. Bush, visited Vietnam six years later.[65] During Bush's presidency, the two former enemies began to cooperate militarily.[66]

With the improvement in relations, an increasing number of American veterans revisited Vietnam and saw their old battlefields. Some were amazed that the Vietnamese who had once borne arms against them in the "American War" seemed to bear them no animosity.[67] This attitude comported with that of the Vietnamese government, which wished to develop trade and inward investment and end the nation's diplomatic isolation. A U.S. veteran who had lost his sight because of a wartime injury said, "I wasn't here to cure my blindness but to heal the scars in my heart. And I think that's happened."[68] A veteran participating in the Veterans' Vietnam Restoration Project, through which he planned to return to Vietnam to build a health clinic, said, "It's going to be such a good healing process for me—working in a humanitarian way instead of trying to kill each other."[69] In this statement, "healing" means the reconciliation of the former belligerents, with emotional benefits for the veteran himself.[70]

Over the years, there have been numerous articles about Vietnam veterans' return visits to Vietnam, which are always written about as emotional as well as physical journeys. Typically, the veterans encounter the people whom they had once fought and find they have more in common with their former enemies than they have with their nonveteran compatriots; they try to find the places where they served, and sometimes they find emotional resolution.[71] For example, Paul Critchlow, a member of the VVMF's corporate board, describes the journey to Vietnam that he and several veteran business executives made as a "mission of reconciliation." He meets the commander of the North Vietnamese army regiment against which he was fighting when he was wounded and evacuated. Returning to the battlefield, he finds answers to questions that had troubled him since the war. "It all makes perfect sense. The ghosts are evaporating. . . . The word *closure* is a contemporary cliché, but I was feeling what that word tries to express."[72]

The Clinton administration never repudiated the Weinberger/Powell doctrine, but U.S. commitment to it eroded in the 1990s. Under Clinton, the United States engaged in peace-keeping operations, limited warfare, and nation building, none of which conformed to the tenets of the Weinberger/Powell orthodoxy; the Clinton administration determined that it would not use the "overwhelming force" principle as a doctrinal template.[73] Anthony Lake, Clinton's first-term national security adviser, suggested that the "selective but substantial" use of force could be more effective than massive force.[74] Lake argued for the validity of humanitarian and nation-building missions, the sort of "fuzzy" missions against which the Joint Chiefs of Staff, conditioned by the "lessons" of Vietnam and the Somalia debacle, recoiled. In 1993, Chairman of the Joint Chiefs of Staff Colin Powell balked at sending troops to Bosnia without having a "clear mission," as his doctrine demanded. Clinton's ambassador to the United Nations, Madeleine Albright, chided Powell (just as George Shultz had once challenged Secretary of Defense Caspar Weinberger), "What's the point of having this superb military that you're always talking about, if we can't use it?"[75] The Clinton administration challenged the Weinberger/Powell doctrine in another significant respect, occasionally ignoring its requirement for a clear congressional mandate for a military intervention.[76] However, two of the tenets of the Weinberger/Powell doctrine, and hence two artifacts of the Vietnam War's "lessons," remained important: the emphasis on having an "exit strategy" and an aversion to "mission creep" (the gradual expansion of the armed forces' responsibilities once they were deployed, making it difficult to extricate them). Despite the apparent erosion of the Weinberger/Powell principles in the Clinton presidency, the Vietnam syndrome remained alive in another principle governing the use of force: a supposition, implicit throughout the Clinton years, that the U.S. public would not countenance any military action that risked large numbers of U.S. casualties.[77] The principle was implicit in the rules of engagement governing the use of American forces in the former Yugoslavia, in the preference for aerial attacks and missiles to ground troop deployments, and in the reluctance to send ground troops into combat against well-armed enemies.[78]

While the salience of the foreign policy "lessons" of the Vietnam War was being subjected to these limited tests in the 1990s, during the same decade the VVMF sponsored two ceremonies at the Vietnam Veterans Memorial that at last remembered the civilian victims of American arms. Kim Phuc, the Vietnamese child whom millions knew from Nick Ut's photograph, now an adult, visited and was honored at the Vietnam Veterans Memorial in 1996 (fig. 98). She came, she said, not to blame her American audience but to lay a wreath at the memorial, a gesture that the *New York Times* described as "an act of reconciliation and forgiveness." Kim laid the wreath accompanied by an air force veteran who had been a POW in North Vietnam. A veteran in the audience said, "It's important to us that she's here, part of the healing process. . . . For her to forgive us personally means something."[79] Unexpectedly,

Figure 98. Kim Phuc, standing before the vertex of the walls, during the November 11, 1996, ceremony at the Vietnam Veterans Memorial when her presence was recognized. Photo by author.

after the wreath-laying ceremony, Kim met a man claiming to be the American air controller who had called in the air strike that injured her. She embraced him as he repeated, "I'm so sorry." "It's okay," she said. "I forgive, I forgive."[80] Memorials erected by Americans featuring their own dead and wounded signify a turning inward of attention, a fixation on the self or on an extension of the self. Kim's visit to the memorial reminded the audience of others' wounds and bespoke another kind of healing, in which compassion extends from the self to others. Yet there was also a sting in this gesture of forgiveness, because forgiveness presupposes that there was harm done; otherwise there is nothing to forgive. Whenever former citizens of South Vietnam, remembering the war, forgive Americans for their actions, thank the Americans for having helped their country, or express sympathy for the suffering that Americans underwent, the message is always double-edged: they also obliquely remind Americans of the harm that the Vietnamese people suffered, that the Americans abandoned the country they were assisting, and that those Americans who suffered did so in vain.[81]

On the thirtieth anniversary of the atrocity at My Lai, Americans recalled the victims of the massacre at the Vietnam Veterans Memorial, when Hugh Thompson and two of his comrades were honored there for their actions in saving some Vietnamese civilians. On March 16, 1968, Thompson, a helicopter pilot, was horrified by what he saw after American troops entered My Lai. He saw a large number of bodies, of old men, women, and children, no one who looked like a combatant. Whenever he saw wounded civilians, he marked them with green smoke and requested assistance; when he flew over the same places later, he saw that the civilians had been killed. Finally, he realized what was happening when he saw a U.S. Army captain shoot a wounded woman Thompson had marked with smoke.[82] His crew then saw American troops firing at a group of civilians gathered in a ditch. The next time Thompson saw several Vietnamese civilians, who were fleeing to a make-shift bunker, he landed his helicopter and confronted the pursuing U.S. infantrymen who were about to attack them. The lieutenant in charge of the infantry said that he planned to get the civilians out of the bunker by using hand grenades.[83] Thompson insisted on talking to the Vietnamese first, managed to coax them out of the bunker, and arranged to fly them to safety in other helicopters. His crew chief, Glenn Andreotta, later pulled an eight-year-old boy, covered in blood, from a ditch full of dead civilians, and Thompson flew the boy to safety in his own helicopter. Thompson informed his commander of what he had seen and continued to complain until the battalion, brigade, and divisional commanders were made aware of his allegations.[84]

In the midst of trying to save the civilians in the bunker action, Thompson had ordered his crew to "open up on" the American infantry if they attacked the Vietnamese.[85] Gunner Lawrence Colburn turned his weapon on the American troops but they did not fire on the Vietnamese; whether Colburn would have obeyed Thompson's order was not put to the test. Afterward, whether because of this order or because of his participation in the investigation of the massacre, Thompson's fellow officers shunned him. His commanders placed him in life-threatening situations by withdrawing the gunship escorts for his observation helicopter—he was shot down five times while serving in Vietnam and broke his back in the last crash.[86] Congressmen grilled Thompson about having threatened his fellow soldiers; he received anonymous death threats.[87]

Thompson, Colburn, and Andreotta were awarded the Soldier's Medal during the March 1998 ceremony at the Vietnam Veterans Memorial. (Andreotta, who had died in a helicopter crash three weeks after the massacre, was awarded the medal posthumously.)[88] The memorial was selected as the site for the award ceremony after a protracted debate resulting from senior army officials' strong resistance to awarding the medals in public: Thompson's award was approved in August 1996 but the army took a year and a half to agree to a public ceremony. Army officers were still embarrassed about the massacre's effect on the service's reputation and worried about the likely media impact of the "ugly, controversial and horrible" story.[89] The decision to use the memorial as the stage for this ceremony was therefore an important political act, and the army used the occasion to declare how far it had come since My Lai.

Soon after the massacre, Thompson had been awarded the Distinguished Flying Cross and his comrades received Bronze Stars—but these are decorations for combat, which should not have been awarded for actions when there was no enemy fire.[90] Thompson's citation said fraudulently that he had rescued a child caught in crossfire, of which there was none. The original citations were therefore consistent with the military's cover-up of the massacre. The Soldier's Medal, in contrast, is the highest award a soldier can receive for action when not facing enemy fire. The citation signed by the secretary of the army and read out at the wall left no uncertainty about what had happened at My Lai, stating that Thompson and his crew had saved the lives of at least ten Vietnamese civilians "during the unlawful massacre of noncombatants by American forces at My Lai, Quang Ngai Province, South Vietnam."[91] The event was significant both in relation to the nation's coming to terms with the reality of the crime committed by American troops, and in relation to the history of the Vietnam Veterans Memorial itself: for the first time, the words "My Lai" were uttered in an official ceremony at the wall.

Along with the decoration came another kind of recognition from the armed services: Thompson was called on to lecture on military ethics at the elite service academies where officers are trained: the Air Force Academy, the Naval Academy at Annapolis, and the United States Military Academy at West Point. After he gave a similar talk at the marine base at Quantico, Virginia, a marine officer said, "I didn't know a lot about the story. . . . And I was devastated when Mr. Hugh spoke. I felt very proud for what he did."[92] Although Thompson clearly deserved to be honored for what he did at My Lai, there was something self-serving about the American military's belated discovery of the hero of the massacre—Thompson's actions now gave Americans another way of narrating the events of March 16, 1968, focusing on the good American whose moral make-up meant that he resisted the atrocity. Kendrick Oliver writes, "To award medals to Hugh Thompson and his crew was to emphasize that good people did serve in Vietnam, even at My Lai (4), and that the army had changed and learned lessons from its past."[93] "He was the guy who by his heroic actions gave a morality and dignity to the American military effort," Douglas Brinkley, a Tulane history professor, said.[94] Somehow, it seems typical of the American remembrance of the war that the most notorious atrocity committed by U.S. forces could now be recalled through a hero who gave the armed forces "morality and dignity."

We have seen no corresponding institutional repentance of the crimes committed at My Lai, and no effort to establish how and why the majority of perpetrators went unpunished. The U.S. government has never apologized to the inhabitants of My Lai or the citizens of Vietnam for the massacre. And, intent on normalizing diplomatic relations with the United States to enhance trade and inward investment, the Vietnamese government has not pressed the issue. In 1993, a senior Vietnamese government official said, "We regard [the massacre] as history, something that happened a long time ago."[95] It has been left to private citizens and organizations to make symbolic gestures of restitution. Private contributions funded a hospital and clinic near the massacre site.[96] The My Lai Loan Fund, based on the Grameen Bank concept, provided small amounts of privately donated capital to poor women and war widows.[97] Twenty-five years after the massacre, Earl Martin, a Mennonite churchman, went to My Lai and apologized on behalf of the American people for letting the massacre take place. He assured the relatives of those who had been killed that Americans would "never, never, never" allow such an event to be repeated anywhere in the world.[98] A local official said that the villagers felt better when they realized that the American people understood their suffering. But Martin may have exaggerated the strength of American awareness and resolve; why, if they were so strong, was it only he who apologized? Five years later, the Madison, Wisconsin, Society of Friends (Quakers) co-sponsored My Lai Peace Park along with Vietnamese civic organizations. The Mennonites and Quakers, who had opposed the war in Vietnam, owed the Vietnamese no moral debt. As Primo Levi remarked in a different context, "The innocent, not the guilty, repent: it's absurd—it's so human."[99]

A week after the award ceremony at the Vietnam Veterans Memorial, on the thirtieth anniversary of the massacre, a ground-breaking ceremony took place for the My Lai Peace Park. Thompson was there, along with Colburn, and the reporter Mike Wallace with a CBS television news crew—but there was no official U.S. representation.[100] Thompson and Colburn met some of the people they had saved on March 16, 1968, and a woman who had been wounded and covered by the bodies of others in the ditch from which they had pulled the young boy. Thompson apologized for not having rescued her.[101] U.S. Ambassador Douglas Peterson declined the opportunity to attend, writing that "neither the policy objectives of the United States nor the current relations between the United States and the Socialist Republic of Vietnam would be served by Embassy participation."[102] Wallace telephoned Peterson to ask him why he was not present and the ambassador responded that he had not been invited. (According to CNN, the ambassador's excuse was false.)[103] Three years later, Thompson and Colburn returned and met Do Hoa, the boy they had rescued from the ditch, who had been in jail for petty theft during their 1998 visit. Colburn's eight-year-old son, Connor, accompanied his father and Thompson. Do Hoa formally asked permission to be his older brother and Connor agreed. This gesture created a new family for Do Hoa, who had lost all his relatives in the massacre, because Thompson and Colburn told him that he now had two fathers.[104]

Important as the deaths at My Lai are in themselves, the massacre's moral significance radiates beyond the particular crimes committed on March 16, 1968. Michael Walzer argues that, once it became so difficult to distinguish South Vietnamese civilians from enemies that both were subjected to the same treatment, if the guerrillas could not be isolated from the people, then "the anti-guerrilla war can . . . no longer be fought—and not just because, from a strategic point of view, it can no longer be won." Under those conditions, it is no longer an anti-guerrilla but an anti-social war, a war against an entire people.[105] For Walzer, the civilian status of the victims establishes a legal limit to a society's right to make war. The crossing point has been reached "whenever ordinary soldiers . . . become convinced that old men and women and children are their enemies. For after that, it is unlikely that the war can be fought except by setting out systematically to kill civilians or to destroy their society and culture."[106] Or, as one of Tim O'Brien's characters says, if the whole rural population, including old men and women, is a potential enemy "you'd have to waste all the civilians in Vietnam, everyone" in order to "win."[107] The American troops' identification of the civilian inhabitants of Quang Ngai province with the enemy thus impugns the legitimacy of the whole American military enterprise in Vietnam. Although the medal ceremony at the Vietnam Veterans Memorial did not fully draw out the moral significance of the massacre, it met the first condition of working through its meaning: acknowledging the historical facts.

The two ceremonies at the Vietnam Veterans Memorial were not, however, typical of a newly self-critical trend in commemoration. In 1996, the same year that Kim was recognized at the Vietnam Veterans Memorial in Washington, a new state Vietnam Veterans Memorial was dedicated in Indiana. An inscribed wall of the memorial in Indianapolis, like the New York memorial, includes excerpts from letters home from GIs in Vietnam and provides a narrative summary of the Vietnam War's history. It says, "The Vietnam War was the most controversial war in America's history, but the objective, to save Southeast Asia from communist tyranny, was a noble one."[108] So the war was a "noble cause," after all. At the end of the decade, the American public's persistent moral misgivings about the war registered a small but measurable decline. In 2000, five years after the last poll on this question, pollsters again asked the public whether the Vietnam War was a "noble cause" or "wrong and immoral" (see Introduction, Table 2). For the first time, the "noble cause" respondents constituted a plurality narrowly edging out those who thought the war was "wrong and immoral." Was this a sign that the war's wounds had begun to "heal"? If so, rather than an indication that Americans had changed their minds, since opinions about the war seemed so durable, it was probably a mark of the inevitable generational shift as those who lived through the war years died. As a new generation took their place, the nation was beginning to forget.[109]

The September 11, 2001, attacks on the twin towers of the World Trade Center and on the Pentagon precipitated a renewed turning inward of attention to American victims, America's losses. A "new solidarity" seemed momentarily to repair all the cultural and political divisions left over from the Vietnam War.[110] The "war on terror" connected with memories of the Vietnam War in the rededication of the New York Vietnam Veterans Memorial in November 2001 (figs. 99 and 100). The ceremony was originally to have taken place in October but was postponed because of the attacks on the World Trade Center on September 11, which disrupted planning for the event. It was rescheduled to take place on November 9: the date 11/9 serving as the mirror image of 9/11. The ceremony was a symbol of the revival of downtown after the September 11 attack.[111] Speakers drew parallels between those who fought in Vietnam and the emergency responders—police and fire crews—who died during the September 11 attacks on the Twin Towers and the Pentagon.[112] After 9/11, the brief discursive opening at the Vietnam Veterans Memorial in Washington that was marked by the presence of Kim and by the 1998 medal ceremony shut down. With the new "war on terror" and troops once again in the field, the emphasis of commemorations has shifted back from contemplation of others to a concentration on America's own. Welcoming the veterans home and "healing" again began to dominate the discourse of Vietnam War commemoration.[113]

In the invasion of Iraq in 2003, the administration of George W. Bush shifted away from the Weinberger/Powell doctrine.[114] The concept of preemptive attack contradicted the Weinberger/Powell principle that military means should be a last resort. While the United States prepared to invade Iraq, the majority of the public favored giving UN weapons inspectors more time to do their work. However, Defense

Figure 99. The New York Vietnam Veterans Memorial, Manhattan; Peter Wormser, William Britt Fellows, Joseph Ferrandino, designers, dedicated May 7, 1985; rededicated November 9, 2001. The memorial consists of glass blocks inscribed with letters sent home by service personnel in Vietnam. Photo by author.

Figure 100. A row of inscribed tablets added to the New York Vietnam Veterans Memorial before the rededication on November 9, 2001. The addition of the inscribed names of New Yorkers killed in Vietnam brings the memorial in line with most others around the country. Photo by author.

Secretary Donald Rumsfeld's new guidelines for the use of the armed forces contemplated a military commitment for which there was initially weak public support, saying that leaders must be willing to invest political capital to sustain support for the period required.[115] The invasion contradicted the Weinberger/Powell doctrine in other ways. Definitions of the national interest in going to war shifted, and there was no clear exit strategy. Violating the "massive force" concept, the invaders were less numerous than the 1991 invasion force, relying on "shock and awe," mobility, "vertical envelopment" using helicopters, leadership decapitation, and high-tech military capabilities to achieve victory. In seeking to make Iraq the center of a new wave of democratization in the Middle East, the Bush administration indulged in an ambitious nation-building exercise unrealizable by military means. All of these features of the invasion repudiated the doctrine associated with Powell, secretary of state at the time.

Analogies between the occupation of Iraq and the Vietnam "quagmire" appeared increasingly in commentaries as the occupation dragged on with no successful end in sight.[116] The antiwar protester Cindy Sheehan, whose son had been killed in Iraq, conducted a vigil outside George W. Bush's ranch in Crawford, Texas, holding a sign that read, "Iraq is Arabic for Vietnam," reminiscent of the protests against Reagan's Central America policy that said that El Salvador was Spanish for Vietnam.[117] As Iraq descended into factional conflict, with no clear "exit strategy" and a lengthening roster of American casualties, the "lessons" of Vietnam appeared to some more pertinent than ever.[118] As one observer wrote in 2003, "Nostalgia for the Powell doctrine; cautious, conservative and based on the use of 'overwhelming force,' as in 1991, is rife."[119] The thinking in the Pentagon registered a surprising shift, though: in 2008, the army drafted a new operations manual that emphasized counterinsurgency and "stability operations" just as much as conventional warfare. The extent to which the experience of warfare in Iraq and Afghanistan would reinscribe the post–Vietnam War doctrinal orthodoxy remained, therefore, a matter of debate.[120]

Bush, however, attempted to recast the analogy between Vietnam and Iraq, asserting that the only thing wrong with the Vietnam War was that the United States had withdrawn prematurely. For him, the "lesson" of the Vietnam War was a warning against the "allure of retreat."[121] As Bush told the Veterans of Foreign Wars convention in August 2007, innocents suffered in Vietnam because the U.S. armed forces left them to their fate, and this proved that American troops should stay the course in Iraq. Commentators were unimpressed by the analogy.[122] Bush said that the troops had "one question: will their elected leaders in Washington pull the rug out from under them" just as they were beginning to succeed—an updating of the claim that American troops were forced to fight with "one hand tied behind them" in Vietnam and that their government refused to "let them win" that war. In fact that was not the only thought on the troops' minds: just four days earlier, U.S. noncommissioned officers and an enlisted man had questioned the premises on which the occupation of Iraq was proceeding, criticizing the "America-centered" perspective that, in Iraq as in Vietnam, produced false measures of "progress."[123]

In the current decade Vietnamese adult figures were finally allowed a place in American memorials to the Vietnam War, in representations of the armed forces of America's South Vietnamese ally. A Vietnamese American sculptor created a statue of an American and a South Vietnamese soldier in Westminster, California, dedicated in 2003; and members of the local Vietnamese American community were instrumental in the creation of the Central Minnesota Vietnam War Memorial, a black granite monument featuring engravings of a similar pair of soldiers, dedicated in downtown St. Cloud four years later. Rather than an indication of Americans' willingness to countenance the commemoration of people other than their own troops, the memorials are a measure of the mobilization of the Vietnamese community that fled South Vietnam to take residence in the United States.[124] The recollection of America's alliance with its anti-Communist junior partner signifies a complex set of ideas: a statement of solidarity and remembered friendship; a declaration of a common allegiance to the anti-Communist cause that was America's official creed for half a century; a reminder that America abandoned its ally; and a hint that there are still former South Vietnamese citizens who have not accepted the outcome of the war and who wish to reclaim Vietnam from a government that was once America's enemy as well as their own.

The Vietnamese Americans' wish to commemorate South Vietnam's alliance with its American patron sets off a disturbing chain of associations, though. As we recall from Chapter 1, Ronald Reagan traduced the history of the birth of South Vietnam to legitimize the U.S. effort to support that nation. Reagan claimed that the two Vietnams, North and South, were sovereign states, and that the United States was defending South Vietnam against "invasion" so that South Vietnam could attain "all the things that go with being an independent state."[125] However, at the height of the war Robert Komer, the head of U.S. pacification programs in South Vietnam, exploded the myth of South Vietnamese sovereignty and independence: "Hell, with half a million men in Vietnam, we are spending twenty-one billion dollars a year, and we're fighting the whole war with the Vietnamese watching us; how can you talk about national sovereignty?"[126] An independent South Vietnam was the premise for the American military enterprise; it was what the United States purported to be defending. Yet paradoxically, the more energy the United States exerted in its support, the more the illusion of independence was falsified.

This predicament constitutes a moral and legal problem, not just the practical problem that the United States' war aims were unattainable and its efforts self-defeating. A South Vietnamese state whose principal purpose was to serve U.S. geopolitical interests by requesting and receiving U.S. aid had no legitimate claim to rule its people; and U.S. intervention premised on requests for assistance from such a state had no just basis. A foreign power cannot justifiably install a friendly government in another country as a pretext for going to its defense. A war fought on behalf of such a client is no less unjust than a more blatant invasion. For Reagan, though, these were unthinkable thoughts. The idea that South Vietnam was an American creature, willed into existence by American interests, financed by American money, sustained by American arms, and prevented from sinking by American tenacity leads directly to the conclusion that Daniel Ellsberg found unavoidable: that U.S. policy was responsible for all the deaths on both sides of the war.[127] Part of the purpose of memorials to the alliance between South Vietnam and the United States was no doubt retrospectively to shore up the doubtful legitimacy of the American war effort. The memorials' strained attempt to sustain the wartime alliance unintentionally reminds us, though, that when the United States rolled the dice in a wager that its wealth and power could somehow invent an anti-Communist bulwark in South Vietnam, the stakes with which it was gambling were human lives—and that this was a roll of the dice that it did not cease making and losing, day by day and year by year, until thousands of its own people and millions of Asians lay dead.

A full accounting of the injuries the U.S. policies caused in Southeast Asia would include not only those killed during the period of combat but also those who have succumbed from various causes since the end of hostilities. A succession of annual ceremonies at the Vietnam Veterans Memorial commemorated those whose deaths were not included in the official count of the war's casualties.[128] In 1995, the sister of a pilot who died of cancer attributed to Agent Orange exposure began an effort to obtain recognition for Vietnam veterans who returned home but died as a result of their service, sometimes long after their time in Vietnam. On June 14, 2000, President Clinton signed into law a bill authorizing the creation of a plaque in the vicinity of the memorial recognizing these postwar casualties, and the American Battle Monuments Commission collected money to help fund it.[129] The plaque was dedicated in November 2004, adjacent to the paved plaza where the *Three Infantrymen* statue is found. It reads, "In memory of the men and women who served in the Vietnam War and later died as a result of their service. We honor and remember their sacrifice."[130] Present at the dedication were supporters of the "Quilt of Tears" with panels of the quilt dedicated to Americans who died as a result of exposure to Agent Orange in Southeast Asia.[131] Because it does not list any names, the plaque can represent anyone whose death is believed to have resulted from the war—whether as a result of suicide years later, the delayed effects of Agent Orange, or any other cause ultimately attributable to service in Vietnam. Soon after its dedication, though, visitors began to complain that because the plaque was flush with the ground, it was hard to find and was sometimes covered by leaves and ground water.[132] In 2007, an organization of people affected by Agent Orange began a campaign to protect the plaque, claiming that the inscription was eroding because of visitors' walking and standing on it. Just as the conservative veterans had once complained that the memorial was being hidden from sight, Agent Orange victims were frustrated by the "less than honorable" condition of the plaque.[133] Despite the 1984 out-of-court settlement, Agent Orange remains a live issue. Because some illnesses did not come to light for years after exposure to the chemical and some veterans did not hear about the earlier lawsuit in time to join it, the Supreme Court in June 2003 opened the way for a new class-action lawsuit by U.S. plaintiffs against the chemical companies. In March 2005, in contrast, a federal judge dismissed a lawsuit filed on behalf of the millions of Vietnamese exposed to Agent Orange poisoning, which sought compensation for the illnesses they had suffered and financial assistance to clean up the Vietnamese countryside blighted by the defoliant's effects. A federal circuit court upheld that decision in February 2008.[134] The long train of American irresponsibility continues, now with the federal courts' sanction.

At the time of writing, the VVMF is leading the effort to create a $100 million education center adjacent to the Vietnam Veterans Memorial, which will provide video testimony and photographs showing those who fought and died in the Vietnam War and other wars, as well as serving as a repository for a display of the offerings left at the memorial.[135] Predictably, as with every other phase of the design, construction, and elaboration of the memorial, this one has been surrounded by controversy. The *New York Times* said that it was "unnecessary" and would provide a "sanitized" glimpse of the war.[136] As when the original design for the memorial was contemplated, one of the objections to the education center was that it would intrude on the Mall, with a National Park Service official referring to the proposed addition as an "atrocity."[137] The trivialization of the meaning of the word *atrocity* is particularly inapt in the context of a plan to represent the history of the Vietnam War. If we were to forget the word's principal meaning—the outrages committed in war—as the Park Service official appears to have done, our language would be impoverished and our capacity to oppose such acts would correspondingly diminish. The realization of the memorial fund's plan will disclose whether the education center itself redoubles or counters this vitiation of historical meaning.

George H. W. Bush, the first retired or sitting American president to visit Vietnam since the war, gave a backhanded justification of America's war effort there during a visit to Hanoi: there was "no point," he said, in trying to convince his listeners of the rectitude of America's actions, as if the audience's reaction would be merely a reflection of parochial biases; then, in a refrain to which all Americans have now become accustomed, Bush added, "There is no point in opening old wounds."[138] A psychological "statute of limitations" barred serious consideration of what his nation has done, as if a near-perfect record of official failure to confront the deliberate or indiscriminate violence his nation's forces had inflicted on Vietnamese civilians, the millions of tons of bombs and artillery shells rained down on the country, the plane-loads of chemical defoliants that had poisoned its forests and fields, meant that these events never took place. Commemorations in the 1980s passed over any reference to crimes committed by Americans in Vietnam, perhaps because the recent events were too controversial and divisive; thirty years after the war, it appeared that the events were too distant for the cases to be re-opened. Somehow, it was never the right moment for Americans to come to grips with their nation's wrongdoing, and the events passed from raw immediacy to oblivion without even a half-step in between.[139]

Benjamin Ferencz, a chief prosecutor at the post–World War II Nuremberg Tribunal told the U.S. Congress, "We thought it was 'Never Again,' but it has been again and again—over and over again—ever since. . . . Ever since Nuremberg, the innocent have been massacred and the perpetrators have walked away scot free."[140] He might have added that, ever since the United States, along with the victorious allies, produced a new standard of international justice at Nuremberg, it has frequently held other nations to this ideal but failed to apply the Nuremberg standard to perpetrators who were within its unique jurisdiction—its own commanders in Vietnam.

Indeed, the U.S. government has expended considerable energy in ensuring that international law will not apply to its citizens and armed forces. Just as U.S. justice showed extraordinary leniency toward the perpetrators of the My Lai massacre, the government of George W. Bush attempted to remove U.S. officials and troops from the reach of international law. In May 2002 Bush formally renounced the Rome Treaty that established the International Criminal Court (ICC).[141] Congress passed a law (nicknamed the "Hague Invasion Act") empowering the president to send in the U.S. military to rescue any American soldiers held for prosecution at the ICC headquarters in the Hague, the Netherlands.[142] The Bush administration sought immunity for its own troops in UN peacekeeping operations and selectively cut off military and development assistance to any nation that refused to guarantee Americans immunity from prosecution at the tribunal.[143] The U.S. government opposed the ICC on the grounds that a "rogue" prosecutor might, for ideological reasons, mischievously seek to place U.S. troops in the dock.[144] A more serious danger for the United States is that the court might order well-founded prosecutions of its officials and troops, in cases where the United States did not conduct investigations and order prosecutions itself. As Anthony Lewis writes, "Instead of a country committed to law, the United States is now seen as a country that proclaims high legal ideals and then says that they should apply to all others but not to itself."[145] This asymmetry in the international legal order has its counterpart in the discourse of commemoration of the Vietnam War; in both domains, Americans have exempted themselves from all adverse judgments.

Some suggest that, in setting itself above the law, the United States has acted as the very thing it purports to oppose: a "rogue nation." But in insisting on its own exceptional status, as the sole nation to which the law does not apply, the United States demonstrates the vital qualification of a despotic law giver: military power that removes it to an echelon beyond the reach of others. The immunity the United States reserves for its own leaders and troops, however, undermines the foundations of legitimacy under the edifice of international law that the United States, as much as any other nation, established in the half century after World War II. That the most powerful military force in the world breaks the law with impunity shatters the concept that the laws of war and international human rights law are universal, binding on all nations. When a nation has accumulated so much power that it can establish rules for the rest of the world while exempting itself and its own from those rules, a general cynicism about the rule of law will follow, as well as a widespread resentment of *Pax Americana*.

U.S. disdain for international law was evident in the Bush administration's "anything goes" approach in the "war on terror." The CIA created a string of sites in foreign countries, where prisoners could be secretly kept in indefinite detention and interrogated under torture.[146] The administration created a legal "black hole" for Al Qaeda and Taliban suspects in the U.S. military base at Guantánamo Bay, Cuba, where they could be imprisoned, at first supposedly outside the jurisdiction of any court, with only limited rights to challenge the often secret evidence providing the grounds for their captivity.[147] The government's top lawyers worked hard to narrow the definition of *torture*, creating an idiosyncratic standard that excludes many actions that are internationally recognized as torture, to immunize its citizens against prosecution for abusing prisoners. The administration decreed that Common Article 3 of the Geneva Conventions did not apply to prisoners it suspected of being members of Al Qaeda or the Taliban.[148] The decision to deny the prisoners Geneva Convention protections was intended to preempt the prosecution of government officials under the 1996 War Crimes Act.[149] The denial of these protections to prisoners and the atmosphere of impunity surrounding detention-related activities by U.S. interrogators and guards led to the torture of prisoners.[150] Soldiers believed that they were doing the nation's work in abusing the prisoners that their commanders or members of the "intelligence community" identified as "enemy combatants."[151]

At Abu Ghraib prison in Iraq, U.S. military guards subjected prisoners to rape, torture, and sexual humiliation.[152] These illegal acts, and the fact that the guards' superiors had tolerated, if not sanctioned, them, reminded observers of American-perpetrated crimes in Vietnam and raised the question whether the U.S. armed forces had been purged of a propensity to treat enemies and neutrals without the respect demanded by international law. "The prison scandal," Christian Appy writes, "raises the same important questions as My Lai. To wit, how widespread have war crimes been in Iraq, how far up the chain of command does responsibility for them go, and what impact will their revelation have on already dwindling public support for American policy?"[153] At first, the White House and the Pentagon rationalized the torture at Abu Ghraib as "high jinks" committed by a few bad apples.[154] An independent report commissioned by the Pentagon found that the abuses were more than a failure of a few individuals to adhere to proper standards, and more than the negligence of a few commanders in enforcing the rule of law: "There is both institutional and personal responsibility at higher levels."[155]

Retired Brigadier General John H. Johns, who had served on the Vietnam War Crimes Working Group, pointed out the consequences of ignoring the lessons learned about U.S. armed forces' crimes. "If we rationalize it as isolated acts, as we did in Vietnam and as we're doing with Abu Ghraib and similar atrocities, we'll never correct the problem."[156] (Robert J. Lifton took a position that might have been predicted from his stance on crimes in Vietnam, exculpating individual perpetrators from responsibility for the prison abuse, and instead blaming the abuse once again on an "atrocity-producing situation.")[157] William Eckhardt, the chief military prosecutor of the My Lai cases, said before the uncovering of prisoner abuse in Iraq, Afghanistan, and elsewhere, that as a result of the lessons learned in Vietnam, "the Army set about creating a training program that has become the model for the rest of the world."[158] Yet whatever this training in international law was supposed to inculcate, the lessons had clearly not spread throughout the armed forces. In 2005, a Marine Corps unit killed twenty-four unarmed Iraqis, including women and children, in revenge for a roadside bombing in Haditha.[159] Sounding remarkably like the members of the Americal Division who explained the reasons for their hostility to Vietnamese civilians in Quang Ngai, Specialist Jeff Englehardt of Grand Junction, Colorado, said, "I guess while I was there, the general attitude was, A dead Iraqi is just another dead Iraqi. . . . You know, so what? . . . The soldiers honestly thought we were trying to help the people and they were mad because it was almost like a betrayal. Like here we are trying to help you, here I am, you know, thousands of miles away from home and my family, and I have to be here for a year and work every day on these missions. Well, we're trying to help you and you just turn around and try to kill us."[160] An investigation by the Pentagon found that senior Marine Corps commanders in Iraq showed a routine disregard for the lives of Iraqi civilians that contributed to a "willful" failure to investigate the massacre.[161] The unpublished report found, "All levels of command tended to view civilian casualties, even in significant numbers, as routine and as the natural and intended result of insurgent tactics. . . . [Commanders' statements] suggest that Iraqi civilian lives are not as important as U.S. lives, their deaths are just the cost of doing business, and that the marines need to get 'the job done' no matter what it takes."[162] In 2007, a U.S. armed forces mental health advisory team survey found that fewer than half of the soldiers and marines in Iraq believed that noncombatants should be treated with dignity and respect.[163] According to Waleed Mohammed, a lawyer, Iraqis expected the marines would receive light sentences in U.S. courts-martial, because, like the Vietnamese civilians in Quang Ngai province in 1968, "Iraqis have become like dogs in the eyes of Americans."[164] *Time* magazine commented, "What happened in Haditha is a reminder of the horrors faced by civilians caught in the middle of war—and what war can do to the people who fight it." The same refrain as in Vietnam, a form of words that disavows agency and hence responsibility: this is not what *they did*; this is what war did *to them*.[165]

It would be difficult to demonstrate that the U.S. failure to confront the history of criminal actions by its forces in Vietnam led to the crimes committed in Iraq and elsewhere in the name of the "war on terror." But it is also difficult, in the aftermath of the revelations about Abu Ghraib and Haditha, to avoid recalling Jonathan Schell's warning of the "alteration" that the nation would undergo if it failed to examine itself after the My Lai massacre. Imagine a nation that had repudiated unjust wars, repented of attacks against civilians, and demanded that commanders stringently enforce international law, rather than winking at—or ordering—its violation. Would such a nation have set about the systematic violation of the right of prisoners to humane treatment, set aside the Geneva Conventions, and claimed the right to practice torture as a matter of national policy? Whatever we imagine a morally rehabilitated United States might be like, the self-examination that Schell advocated in 1969 is no less urgent for being long overdue.

In an essay titled "Our Exceptional Innocence," Michael Kazin writes, "What does set the United States apart is that so many of its citizens believe in its moral superiority. The conviction began with the nation itself. 'We fight not to enslave, but to set a country free,' wrote Tom Paine during the Revolutionary War, 'and to make room upon the earth for honest men to live in.'" Kazin observes that "in their innocence," millions of Americans believe it is both their right and their duty "to spread the creed of democracy and liberty around the world."[166] As an enduring legacy of their most treasured political traditions, Americans pride themselves on being a nation that is not just strong but also virtuous. This conviction has resulted in a paradox. Instead of insisting that their nation behave virtuously, some Americans have found it difficult to cope with the idea that their nation is capable of behaving in any other way and have thrust aside historical facts and judgments that do not gibe with their assumptions. The unquestioning conviction that the nation is virtuous allows, indeed *requires*, state crimes to go unjudged, because accountability for past crimes would tarnish the nation's image of innocence.

The Vietnam Veterans Memorial disavowed politics and avoided judgments of the Vietnam War. The suspension of judgment meant that contemplation of the moral significance of the Vietnam War had, by default, to take place elsewhere. Because the memorial avoided consideration of the moral quandaries that soldiers had faced in Vietnam, it remained irrelevant to what Peter Marin has described as veterans' moral pain. The Vietnam veteran Robert McGowan said, "A lot of us, having done America's dirty work, and having brutalized the Vietnamese people, carry an additional burden. America has never addressed itself as a nation to the appalling damage done to the Vietnamese people and the land of Vietnam. We carry the burden alone."[167] In the absence of a national project that addressed the whole history of the war, including the parts that Americans were most reluctant to confront, veterans were left to struggle by themselves, or in small therapy groups, with the legacy of the armed forces' conduct.

Marin said that Vietnam veterans had achieved a certain moral depth and seriousness through their encounter with the human capacity for error and evil. After the war they simply wanted "justice to exist, for there to be justice in the world." But Marin may have been overgeneralizing from the veterans whom he knew. Or perhaps his observation reflects his own wish for there to be justice in the world, a wish that would come closer to realization if Vietnam veterans shared it. Anyway, his own formulation leaves unclear the important issue that Kendrick Oliver raised: justice for whom?[168] Most Americans, including the veterans who led commemoration projects, ignored Victor Westphall's appeal honorably to face up to what that unflinching moralist called the nation's shame; none of the memorials that followed the one in Angel Fire raised the ethical questions that his work so insistently did.

One of George W. Bush's aides said, "We're an empire now, and when we act, we create our own reality."[169] There are no limits to the dreams of empire, and they expand not just territorially but across time. The authors of empire project a future of America-defined freedom imposed, if necessary, at the point of a gun;[170] they also conjure up a bright past unsullied by moral doubts, in which recognition of the veterans and honor to those who died are sufficient to bring closure and to gird the nation up for new battles. As Walter Benjamin warned, even the dead are not safe from those who want to appropriate their memory as a tool of the powerful.[171] He might have said, especially the dead.

Ronald Reagan called on the nation to "move on" from the war, "in unity and with resolve," with the resolve to stand "for freedom, as those who fought did."

Reagan repeatedly said that the lesson of Vietnam was that the American govern-ment should never again be afraid to let its forces win; George W. Bush said that, in Vietnam, the United States should have stayed the course to victory. These bold assertions make the past into a theater of ideological warfare; but the frontal assault on the citadel of history is not the most effective right-wing strategy because it makes every American's memory a redoubt to be conquered—and therefore a potential point of resistance. The militarist cause advances farther by means of more insidious insults to history and memory: the moral blindness, obfuscation, and complacency that permit anyone to suppose that "healing," as defined by the VVMF, might be an adequate goal of commemoration.

Ronald Ray, with whose casualty call on the Westphall family this book began, was right about the need for a clear historical and moral reckoning. Ray was not alone in his conviction that commemorating the war demanded an ethical and didactic response. Victor Westphall, as well as some of Ray's cohorts in the Vietnam Veterans Leadership Program, shared this belief. And such a response is not solely the con-cern of those who served in war and those who mourn the ones who died. After visiting the memorial at Angel Fire, a place where she found serenity and a feeling of closure, Diane Carlson Evans said, "War affects all of us. War is not an issue for only those who go to war." She added, wisely, memorials "are not just for healing . . . they're for education."[172]

We make judgments about the past not to settle scores or exact vengeance but to learn from experience, to meet the demands of truth and justice, and to preserve the integrity of the values that we live by and wish others to observe. Each time we commemorate the past, we recall for posterity who we are and what we stand for. As Maya Lin says, memorials are our way of talking to the future about the past, "talking across time."[173] Our judgments about the past, or our lack of them, define the kinds of acts—by ourselves as well as others—that are acceptable tomorrow and in the days to come. Marin argues, "In the end, what we owe the dead (whether our own or the Vietnamese), what we owe the vets and what we owe ourselves is the same thing: the resumption of the recurrent conversation about moral values, the sources and meaning of conscience, and the roots of human generosity, solidarity and community."[174]

Americans have a long-destined, long-postponed appointment to confront and begin working through their own difficult memories of the Vietnam War. The com-memorations they have produced so far have advanced the recognition of their own losses, but, like the reflex exoneration of the therapist, they have arrested a more morally meaningful contemplation of the past—one that would be psychologically costly but would allow those costs to be shared by others, not borne solely by veter-ans. If Americans embark on this renewed encounter with the past, they might recall that there is a value to moral witnessing even, perhaps especially, when it unsettles people's minds; that the repudiation of criminal conduct and of misuses of power is deeply rooted in the history of dissent against the war, which brought credit to America's citizenry; and that the domestic debates that the VVMF's competition rules proscribed from representation are not an unwarranted intrusion on the field of commemoration but are a product of America's own democratic traditions. Knowing this, Americans might recognize that the achievement of unity and strength is not a paramount value—and that the health of the republic does not therefore lie in "the healing of a nation."

No one can compel Americans into a renewed encounter with the history of American wrongdoing in Vietnam, just as, while the United States retains unsurpassed military power, no one can force it to allow its citizens to submit to the judgment of international courts. Only Americans can decide about that. Their decisions will be, as so often in the American past, an object lesson for all. John Winthrop saw America as a city on a hill, with the eyes of all people upon it: "a story and a by-word through the world," an example to be emulated or scorned.[175] Here is what Americans, through their action or inaction, will demonstrate: Can the citizens of a great power whose institutions have not been overturned and whose territory remains intact scrutinize their own nation's actions with the same clarity that their government exercises in judging the acts of the deposed leaders and fighters of defeated and occupied enemies? A good deal hinges on the answer to this question.[176] It is not only, as Jonathan Schell once said, Americans' souls that are at stake, but the moral order of the world. Americans' decisions about how to remember the Vietnam War will help determine whether we live in a world where justice is possible or a world where the powerful forgive themselves anything, and then, without shame, move on. America remains a city upon a hill: the world is still watching.

ABBREVIATIONS

AFP: Angel Fire Papers, correspondence, newsletters, flyers, and meeting minutes related to the Vietnam Veterans Peace and Brotherhood Chapel, Angel Fire, New Mexico, collected at the visitors center at the memorial, to which the author was given access by Victor Westphall and Bob Lenham.

APP: John Woolley and Gerhard Peters. The American Presidency Project Database. University of California, Santa Barbara.

LBP: The Landau/Burkett Papers, a collection of documents related to the Vietnam Veterans Leadership Program to which the author was given access by Marcia Landau and Zack Burkett in a private residence in Virginia.

PPP: *Public Papers of the Presidents of the United States.*

RC: Roper Center for Public Opinion Research, University of Connecticut, Storrs.

Reagan Library: The National Archives and Records Administration, Ronald Reagan Presidential Library, Simi Valley, California.

VVM-DPP: Vietnam Veterans Memorial Collection, Division of Prints and Photographs, Library of Congress. This collection includes the slide documentation of the memorial's design competition.

VVMF-MD: Vietnam Veterans Memorial Fund Collection, Manuscript Division, Library of Congress. This collection includes the memorial fund's administrative records.

NOTES

Introduction

1. William E. Schmidt, "One Man's Memorial: Father Builds Chapel for His Son and All Vietnam War Dead," *Dallas Morning News*, November 14, 1982.

2. Paul Logan, "A Man, a Memorial, an Obsession," *Impact: Albuquerque (NM) Journal Magazine*, May 22, 1984; Alice Bullock, "Peace and Brotherhood Symbolized in Chapel," *Santa Fe Pasatiempo*, October 25, 1970; Sis and Eric Braun to Victor Westphall, March 1, [1973], AFP; Tad Bartimus, "Monument to Son Killed in Vietnam Consumes Father," *Sunday Oregonian*, April 25, 1982. For a full description of the building, see Victor Westphall, "The DAV [Disabled American Veterans] Vietnam Veterans National Memorial: A Brief History," *News from DAV Vietnam Veterans National Memorial*, November 1990, 4.

3. Corinne Brown, *Casualty* (New York: W. W. Norton, 1981), 50–51.

4. Victor Westphall built a construction business from scratch during the Great Depression, while obtaining a Ph.D. in history. At Milwaukee Teachers' College, where he obtained his B.A., he was the light heavyweight champion in boxing and wrestling, and a star in football. He published several works about New Mexico history and was the president of the New Mexico Historical Society in the 1960s. "Albuquerque Home Builder Uses Spare Time to Win PhD in History," *Albuquerque Tribune*, June 9, 1956; biographical clippings file at the Albuquerque, New Mexico, Public Library.

5. Victor Westphall, "Report Addendum," November 30, 1984; Victor Westphall, *David's Story: A Casualty of Vietnam* (Springer, NM: Center for the Advancement of Human Dignity, 1981), 5, 149–50, AFP.

6. William E. Schmidt, "On Barren Hill, a Father's Memorial to Son Killed in Vietnam," *New York Times*, November 13, 1982.

7. Brown, *Casualty*, 207; "Father of Fallen Marine Builds Memorial to All U.S. Casualties," *West Texas Livestock Weekly*, September 10, 1970; "Hippies Build Chapel to Slain Marine," *Binghamton (NY) Sun-Bulletin*, May 22, 1971; Patrick Lamb, "N.M. Father Honors Vietnam War Victim with Chapel Dedicated to Peace," *El Paso Herald-Post*, May 22, 1971.

8. Westphall was a record-breaking weight-lifter who also held a national time trials bicycle-racing title for his age range. These feats demonstrate the determination and drive with which Westphall approached everything. See, e.g., "The Man behind the Vietnam Memorial," *Sangre de Cristo* (Angel Fire, NM) *Chronicle*, May 22, 1986; "Westphall Wins Three Golds at World Senior Olympics," *Raton (NM) Range*, March 25, 1988.

9. Betty Burroughs, "Once Upon Paper," *Wilmington (DE) Morning News*, November 26, 1970.

10. Victor Westphall to President Nixon, November 29, 1970; Mark O. Hatfield, U.S. senator from Oregon, to Victor Westphall, September 17, 1970, Westphall personal files; Richard Nixon to Victor Westphall, July 15, 1971, quoted in Victor Westphall, *Vietnam: The Hinge of Destiny* (1972) (self-published pamphlet in AFP), ii. Westphall's personal files in AFP contain copies of his correspondence with U.S. political leaders.

11. Laura Palmer, *Shrapnel in the Heart: Letters and Remembrances from the Vietnam Veterans Memorial* (New York: Vintage, 1987), xv.

12. Victor Westphall, *What Have THEY Done to MY World* (East Brunswick, NJ: Cornwall Books, 1981), 141–44, 150–52.

13. Denise Kusel, "Like a Bridge over Troubled Water," *Santa Fe Reporter*, "Santa Fe Style" section, May 25, 1983.

14. Richard L. Schoenwald, "Dying for Nothing," essay accompanying a letter to Victor Westphall, June 22, 1972; Victor Westphall, "The Vietnam Veterans Peace and Brotherhood Chapel," [December 1971], AFP; Dick McAlpin, "Vietnam Memorial in Moreno Valley," *Albuquerque Tribune*, April 29, 1971.

15. Westphall, *David's Story*, 27, 51, 55; Victor Westphall, interview by the author, July 29, 1992.

16. Linda Vaughan, interview by the author, July 23, 1992; Westphall, interview.

17. In a television interview, Victor Westphall tearfully recited his son's writings, revealing that he spoke them to himself every day. The last two lines of the poem, inscribed at the entrance to the Angel Fire Memorial, "So man learned to shed the tears / With which he measures out his years" are very different when spoken in Victor Westphall's voice, for they remind one of his decades-long vigil in his son's memory. When the interviewer said to him, "You must have been very close," Westphall took the pronoun *you* to be singular, not plural as the interviewer must have intended it, and replied, "Yes, I was," whereas the logical response would have been, "Yes, we were." Larry Woods, "Across America," CNN cable newscast about the memorial at Angel Fire, February 3, 1992. The odd response, in which Victor, the individual, takes the place of Victor and David, father and son, is symptomatic of the way in which the devotee subsumed the object of his devotion.

18. Westphall, *David's Story*, 71–73; David Westphall to Douglas Westphall, May 15, 1968, Westphall personal files.

19. In Vietnam, the war is referred to as the "American War," to distinguish it from the "French War" of 1945–54. Heonik Kwon, *After the Massacre: Commemoration and Consolation in Ha My and My Lai* (Berkeley: University of California Press, 2006), 33. In this book, I use "Vietnam War" in keeping with common usage in English. For the same reason, I spell *Vietnam* as a single word, although it is arguably correct to spell it *Viet Nam*.

20. Letters to Victor Westphall cited here are from Jon A. Longerbore, April 21, 1970; John C. MacLean, Cambridge, MA, March 17, 1977; Sylvia Brugh, Troutwick, VA, March 4, 1977; M. E. Smith, Sioux Falls, SD, November 12, 1979. All are in AFP.

21. I have documented the existence of 461 memorials; others may have escaped my attention.

22. Thirty-four memorials dedicated to the Vietnam War or jointly to Vietnam and Korea were dedicated between 1966 and the fall of Saigon in 1975. Jerry L. Strait and Sandra S. Strait, *Vietnam War Memorials* (Jefferson, NC: McFarland, 1988), 11, 12, 18, 19, 21, 51, 53, 67, 71, 77, 83, 88, 91, 94, 103, 121, 139, 143, 150, 161, 169, 179, 182, 202–3, 205, 209; Gloria Emerson, *Winners and Losers: Battles, Retreats, Gains, Losses and Ruins from the Vietnam War* (New York and London: Harcourt, Brace, Jovanovich, 1976), 113; John Leykam, "A Forgotten Memorial for a War We Try So Hard to Forget," *Contra Costa Times* (Walnut Creek, CA), May 25, 1980; David Murray, "Two Vets Fight an Old War in a Daily Ritual," *Contra Costa Times*, May 31, 1982; Lawrence Muhammad, "Vietnam Veteran Mourns Sad State of Jefferson Monument," *Louisville Courier-Journal*, March 11, 1988; Gary Ford, unpublished research for his article in *Southern Living* (May 1995), sent to the author June 27, 1996.

23. A peace memorial was created in Lake Charles, Louisiana, in 1968. Gary Ford, unpublished research. Other "memorials" proposed or created by the visual artists Robert Morris (*War Memorial: Infantry Archive*, 1970) and Edward Kienholz (*The Non-War Memorial*, 1970) during the war years conveyed a distinctly antiwar sensibility. The Vietnam veterans memorials in Kansas City; Portland, Oregon; and New Orleans, dedicated in the 1980s, all refer to the antiwar movement.

24. "Veterans Chapel Dedicated," clipping from a Santa Fe newspaper, publication information erased, memorial clippings file, Albuquerque Public Library; Patrick Lamb, "Viet Veterans Peace Chapel Dedicated in New Mexico," *Albuquerque Journal*, May 23, 1971; Victor Westphall, "Music Was Meaningful," *Albuquerque Journal*, July 6, 1971; Gloria Emerson, "Chapel, a Father's Memorial, Honors More Than Vietnam Dead," *New York Times*, June 15, 1972; Michael Satchell, "One Man's Shrine to All Who Fell in Vietnam," *Parade*, November 4, 1979, 24.

25. Kenneth Fox, telephone interview by the author, May 13, 1995; Vonette Fontaine, "Unlit Statue Irks Its Creator," *Auburn (CA) Journal*, January 27, 1991; Vonette Fontaine, "County to Check Out Relighting Memorial," *Auburn Journal*, January 24, 1991. I am grateful to Michael Kelley for drawing my attention to this memorial, to Anita Yoder, the Placer County public information officer, for sending me relevant documents, and to Vonette Fontaine Buck of the *Auburn Journal* for sending me news clippings.

26. Fox, interview; *Placer Gold*, October 18, 1972, clipping provided by Anita Yoder.

27. Fox, interview; William S. Murphy, "Dentist Turned Artist Sculpts Concrete Giants," *Los Angeles Times*, July 11, 1979.

28. Westphall, *Vietnam*, i.

29. Jerry L. Chambers to Victor Westphall, May 6, 1973; Grace Rockwell to Victor Westphall, October 8, 1974, AFP.

30. "Services at Eagle Nest Memorial Saturday Denotes Ending of War," *Albuquerque Journal*, February 2, 1973; Michael Seiler, "Postscript: One Man's Memorial to Victims of Vietnam War," *Los Angeles Times*, June 1, 1977; "Fort Native Builds Vietnam Memorial," *Jefferson Union* (Fort Atkinson, WI), January 11, 1977.

31. See, e.g., Loren Baritz, *Backfire: A History of How American Culture Led Us into Vietnam and Made Us Fight the Way We Did* (Baltimore: Johns Hopkins University Press, 1998), 15. Philip Caputo says that the country "longed" for amnesia, in his memoir *A Rumor of War* (New York: Ballantine, 1977), 213.

32. "America Must Not Forget Sen. Domenici Tells Crowd," *Sangre de Cristo Chronicle* (Angel Fire, NM), June 9, 1977.

33. U.S. Rep. Manuel Lujan Jr. (R, NM) to Victor Westphall, August 21, 1975; copy of U.S. Rep. Benjamin A. Gilman (R, NY) to Otto A. Drechsel, September 1, 1976, sent to Victor Westphall by Drechsel, AFP; "National Parks Reject Vietnam Chapel," *Sangre de Cristo Chronicle*, November 11, 1976, 1; *CBS Evening News with Walter Cronkite*, February 14, 1977; Bob Duke, "Memorial to Honor Vietnam Warriors," *Albuquerque Tribune*, May 3, 1980.

34. Westphall, *David's Story*, 139; Tom Tiede, "Shrine Honors Vietnam Dead of Both Sides," *Rocky Mountain News*, May 26, 1980; Satchell, "One Man's Shrine," 24; Donald P. Batchelder, North Reading, MA, to Victor Westphall, November 4, 1979, AFP.

35. The letter to Ho, dated September 3, 1969, was attached to a letter to William P. Rogers, the U.S. secretary of state, for transmission through diplomatic channels. (There is no evidence that the letter was delivered, and there was no reply.)

36. Copies of the hostile reactions were not to be found in the memorial's records but are referred to in *Vietnam Veterans Chapel Bulletin*, December 1979.

37. Grace Rockwell, Los Angeles, to Victor Westphall, March 23, 1973; Julie V. Urban, Watertown, MA, to Victor Westphall, November 6, 1979, AFP.

38. The New Mexico senators' efforts are mentioned in *Vietnam Veterans Chapel Bulletin*, September 1980, box 31, VVMF-MD.

39. Russell E. Dickenson, director, U.S. Department of Interior, letter to the editor, *Stars and Stripes: The National Tribune*, December 1, 1983, clipping in box 31, VVMF-MD.

40. Joint Resolution to Authorize the Vietnam Veterans Memorial Fund, Inc., to Establish a Memorial, S.J. Res. 119, 96th Cong., 2d sess., July 1, 1980; Public Law 96-297, *Statutes at Large* 94 (1980): 827.

41. Leah Leach, "Vietnam War Dead to Be Honored," *Albuquerque Journal*, May 23, 1982. After Victor Westphall's death on July 22, 2003, the state of New Mexico adopted the memorial, assuming responsibility for its upkeep. It was rededicated as the Vietnam Veterans Memorial State Park on November 11, 2006. Tom Turnbull, administrator at the memorial, telephone interview by the author, February 1, 2007. In the intervening years, the memorial had been adopted by the Disabled American Veterans, as discussed in chapter 6.

42. Mary C. Bounds, "Ideals Imbue Angel Fire Memorial," *Dallas Morning News*, February 26, 1984.

43. Olga Curtis, "The Chapel Built by Grief," *Denver Post*, August 16, 1970; R. H. Ring, "One Man's Monument to Victims of War Rose Out of Grief," *The Star* (Tucson, AZ), October 31, 1983; Westphall, *David's Story*, 141.

44. "Vietnam Veterans Peace and Brotherhood Chapel, Inc.," April 30, 1973, AFP.

45. Howell Raines, "Reagan Calls Arms Race Essential to Avoid a 'Surrender' or 'Defeat,'" *New York Times*, August 19, 1980.

46. For definitions of the Vietnam syndrome, see Noam Chomsky, "Visions of Righteousness," in *The Vietnam War and American Culture*, ed. John Carlos Rowe and Rick Berg (New York: Columbia University Press, 1991), 28; Stewart M. Powell, "Reagan Legacy on Defense Is Good, Bad," *San Antonio Light*, December 26, 1988; Michael T. Klare, *Beyond the "Vietnam Syndrome": U.S. Interventionism in the 1980s* (Washington, DC: Institute for Policy Studies, 1981), 1.

47. Jimmy Carter, "Energy and National Goals Address to the Nation," July 15, 1979, APP, www.presidency.ucsb.edu/ws/?pid=32596 (accessed December 3, 2006). Neo-conservatives were former "cold war" Democrats who defected from the party and aligned themselves with the Republicans because of their disaffection with the Democrats' foreign policy positions after the McGovernite wing of the party achieved prominence in the 1970s.

48. Arnold R. Isaacs, *Vietnam Shadows: The War, Its Ghosts, and Its Legacy* (Baltimore: Johns Hopkins University Press, 1997), 4.

49. Nancy Zaroulis and Gerald Sullivan, *Who Spoke Up? American Protest against the War in Vietnam, 1963–1975* (Garden City, NY: Doubleday, 1984), 148; Andrew E. Hunt, *The Turning: A History of Vietnam Veterans against the War* (New York: New York University Press, 1999), 143, 195.

50. For the breakdown of the foreign policy consensus following the Vietnam War, see Ole R. Holsti and James Rosenau, "Consensus Lost: Consensus Regained? Foreign Policy Beliefs of American Leaders, 1976–1980," *International Studies Quarterly* 30, no. 4 (December 1986): 375–409; idem, *American Leadership in World Affairs: Vietnam and the Breakdown of Consensus* (London: Allen and Unwin, 1984); Eugene R. Wittkopf, "On the Foreign Policy Beliefs of the American People: A Critique and Some Evidence," *International Studies Quarterly* 30, no. 4 (December 1986): 444.

51. Walter H. Capps, *The Unfinished War: Vietnam and the American Conscience*, 2nd ed. (Boston: Beacon Press, 1990), 146, 160. The expression "Don't futz around with Uncle Sam" presumably means "don't

mess around with Uncle Sam," but the sound of *futz* more strongly suggests "Don't fuck with Uncle Sam." The original expression makes no sense without such a translation, since "futz around" means "dither."

52. Ronald Reagan, "Address at Commencement Exercises at the United States Military Academy," May 27, 1981, APP, www.presidency.ucsb.edu/ws/?pid=43865 (accessed December 7, 2006).

53. Editorial, *Denver Post*, August 26, 1980, in *Editorials on File* 11, no. 16 (August 16–31, 1980): 996; editorial, *Arizona Republic*, August 21, 1980, in ibid., 993; "Vietnam Syndrome," *Wall Street Journal*, August 20, 1980.

54. Editorials, *Miami Herald*, August 20, 1980, *Idaho Statesman*, August 22, 1980, *Chicago Sun-Times*, August 21, 1980, in *Editorials on File* 11, no. 16 (August 16–31, 1980): 996, 991, 992, respectively. For other criticisms of Reagan's stance on the war, see, in ibid., 997, editorials from *Milwaukee Journal*, August 19, 1980; *Des Moines Register*, August 20, 1980; *Hartford Courant*, August 21, 1980.

55. Los Angeles Times poll, March 15–19, 1995; data provided by RC.

56. Gallup Organization poll for Chicago Council on Foreign Relations, October 15–November 10, 1998; data provided by RC.

57. Keith Beattie, *The Scar That Binds: American Culture and the Vietnam War* (New York: New York University Press, 1998), 13; Fred Turner, *Echoes of Combat: The Vietnam War in American Memory* (New York: Anchor Books, 1996), 15.

58. See, e.g., Ronald Reagan, "Freedom vs. Anarchy on Campus," in *Takin' It to the Streets: A Sixties Reader*, ed. Alexander Bloom and Wini Breines (New York: Oxford University Press, 1995), 345–47. For Reagan's pro-war record as governor of California, see also Seth Rosenfeld, "The Governor's Race," *San Francisco Chronicle*, June 9, 2002.

59. Antonio Gramsci, *Selections from the Prison Writings*, ed. and trans. Quintin Hoare and Geoffrey Nowell Smith (New York: International Publishers, 1971), 10–15, 175–82; idem, "Hegemony, Relations of Force, Historical Bloc," in *A Gramsci Reader*, ed. David Forgacs (London: Lawrence and Wishart, 1988), 189–245.

60. Ronald Reagan, "Remarks on Presenting the Medal of Honor to Master Sergeant Roy P. Benavidez," February 24, 1981, APP, www.presidency.ucsb.edu/ws/?pid=43454 (accessed June 16, 2007).

61. Although the Disabled American Veterans (DAV) took it over, the Westphall family's story remained central to the memorial. "A Place Where the Spirit Soars," fundraising flyer for DAV Vietnam Veterans National Memorial, n.d. Victor Westphall remained on site as the resident director in living quarters adjacent to the visitors' center, though he often clashed with Bob Lenham, the DAV-appointed executive director. Susan Knutson, an administrator of the memorial, interview by the author, July 29, 1992.

62. Peter Kornbluh, "Nicaragua: U.S. Proinsurgency Warfare against the Sandinistas," in *Low Intensity Warfare: Counterinsurgency, Proinsurgency, and Antiterrorism in the Eighties*, ed. Michael T. Klare and Peter Kornbluh (New York: Pantheon Books, 1988), 137, 151. See also Richard A. Melanson, *Writing History and Making Policy: The Cold War, Vietnam, and Revisionism* (Lanham, MD: University Press of America, 1983), 199. The polls, dating between March 1981 and July 1984, are discussed in detail in Patrick Hagopian, "The Social Memory of the Vietnam War" (Ph.D. diss., Johns Hopkins University, 1993), 97–103.

63. U.S. Congress, House, "Veterans' Testimony on Vietnam—Need for Investigation," 92nd Cong., 1st sess., April 6, 1971, *Congressional Record*, E 9947–10055; Vietnam Veterans Against the War, *The Winter Soldier Investigation: An Inquiry into American War Crimes* (Boston: Beacon Press, 1972).

64. Philip Rieff, *The Triumph of the Therapeutic: Uses of Faith after Freud* (Chicago: University of Chicago Press, 1987); T. J. Jackson Lears, *No Place of Grace: Antimodernism and the Transformation of American Culture, 1880–1920* (Chicago: University of Chicago Press, 1994); Keith Beattie, *The Scar That Binds: American Culture and the Vietnam War* (New York: New York University Press, 1998), 26.

65. Kirk Savage, *Standing Soldiers, Kneeling Slaves: Race, War, and Monument in Nineteenth-Century America* (Princeton: Princeton University Press, 1997), 210.

1. "Never Again"

1. Myra MacPherson, *Long Time Passing: Vietnam and the Haunted Generation* (New York: Signet Books, 1985), 240.

2. In 1971 a presidential commission and Lyndon Johnson concluded that the Vietnam War was the most divisive conflict in the United States since the Civil War. Stanley Karnow, *Vietnam: A History* (New York: Viking Press, 1983), 625–26; Lyndon Baines Johnson, *The Vantage Point: Perspectives of the Presidency* (New York: Holt, Rinehart and Winston, 1971), 553.

3. Norman Podhoretz justified America's war aims, and Guenter Lewy defended the conduct of the war against charges of immorality. Podhoretz, *Why We Were in Vietnam* (New York: Simon and Schuster, 1984), 200; Lewy, *America in Vietnam* (New York: Oxford University Press, 1978); Lewy, "The Question

of American War Guilt," in *Light at the End of the Tunnel: A Vietnam War Anthology*, ed. Andrew J. Rotter (New York: St. Martin's Press, 1991), 374.

4. Many veterans held the view that the United States could have won the war if it had not been restricted militarily. See, e.g., Don Parrish in the documentary *The Long Road Back*, prod. Britt Davis (Office of Instructional Resources, University of Kentucky, n.d., ca. 1985); Mark Berent, in Al Santoli, *To Bear Any Burden: The Vietnam War and Its Aftermath in the Words of Americans and Southeast Asians* (New York: Ballantine Books, 1985), 141. Others disagreed. See, e.g., statement by Charles Cobb in Wallace Terry and Janice Terry, "The War and Race," in *The Wounded Generation: America after Vietnam*, ed. A. D. Horne (Englewood Cliffs, NJ: Prentice-Hall, 1981), 181; Frank Delgado in Charley Trujillo, *Soldados: Chicanos in Vietnam* (San Jose, CA: Chusma House Publications, 1990), 28.

5. Gen. John Arick, interview by Richard Burks Verrone, April 16, 2003, Virtual Vietnam Archive at Texas Tech University, stable URL, www.vietnam.ttu.edu/star/images/oh/oh0268/OH0268-4.pdf.

6. Kim Willenson, *The Bad War: An Oral History of the Vietnam War* (New York: New American Library, 1987), 407.

7. Thomas J. Knock, "'Come Home, America': The Story of George McGovern," in *Vietnam and the American Political Tradition: The Politics of Dissent*, ed. Randall B. Woods (Cambridge: Cambridge University Press, 2003), 108.

8. Joan Morrison and Robert K. Morrison, *From Camelot to Kent State* (New York: Times Books, 1987), 145. See also Morris Dickstein, *Gates of Eden: American Culture in the Sixties* (New York: Basic Books, 1977), 271.

9. George C. Herring, *America's Longest War: The United States and Vietnam, 1950–1975*, 2nd ed. (New York: McGraw-Hill, 1986), 256.

10. In February 1967, 65 percent of a national Gallup Organization poll sample thought that the Johnson administration was not telling them "all they should know" about the war. In February 1971, two years into Nixon's first term, Gallup found that 69 percent of a national poll sample thought the same. "Doubt on Vietnam Reported in Poll," *New York Times*, March 7, 1971.

11. Roy Rosenzweig, "'Washington . . . Is No Father to Me': National History and Its Audiences" (paper presented at the NYU-OAH conference "Where Is America?" July 6–8, 1998, Villa La Pietra, Florence), 10–11. The research was conducted in 1994, so the two respondents cited here must have been born about 1945 and 1949.

12. The poll was conducted between December 10 and 13, 1988, by Market Opinion Research for Americans Talk Security; data provided by RC.

13. From the start, the administration doubted that the second attack on U.S. naval vessels in the Tonkin Gulf, one of the incidents that triggered passage of the resolution, took place at all but did not express these doubts to congressional leaders. McNamara recommended that President Johnson tell Congress and the American people that the U.S. naval vessels suffered an unprovoked attack while in international waters rather than reveal that these vessels were operating in concert with South Vietnamese raids on North Vietnamese coastal installations, and he repeated the lie himself. Senator J. William Fulbright (D., Arkansas), who was kept in the dark about the administration's plans for an aerial bombing campaign, shepherded the Tonkin Gulf Resolution through the Senate after receiving administration assurances that the president would consult Congress before using the sweeping military authority it had granted him. Members of Congress later complained that they were hoodwinked into a war. Michael R. Beschloss, ed., *Taking Charge: The Johnson White House Tapes, 1963–1964* (New York: Simon and Schuster, 1997), 509; Joseph C. Goulden, *Truth Is the First Casualty* (Chicago: Rand McNally, 1969), 40; Randall Bennett Woods, *J. William Fulbright, Vietnam, and the Search for a Cold War Foreign Policy* (Cambridge: Cambridge University Press, 1998), 76–78, 86; Robert S. McNamara, with Brian VanDeMark, *In Retrospect: The Tragedy and Lessons of Vietnam* (New York: Times Books, 1995), 141; "The Gulf of Tonkin 'Incidents' and Resolution," in *Vietnam and America: A Documented History*, ed. Marvin E. Gettleman, Jane Franklin, Marilyn B. Young, and H. Bruce Franklin, 2nd ed. (New York: Grove Press, 1995), 248–52.

14. U. S. G. Sharp, *Strategy for Defeat: Vietnam in Retrospect* (Novato, CA: Presidio Press, 1998), 70; Woods, *Fulbright, Vietnam*, 76; Paul Hendrickson, *The Living and the Dead: Robert McNamara and Five Lives of a Lost War* (London: Macmillan, 1997), 163–72, 262–64; Larry Berman, *Planning a Tragedy: The Americanization of the War in Vietnam* (New York: W. W. Norton, 1982), 57.

15. "Remarks in Memorial Hall, Akron University," October 21, 1964, APP, www.presidency.ucsb.edu/ws/?pid=26635 (accessed April 13, 2007). The Johnson administration tried to make Barry Goldwater, Johnson's Republican opponent in the 1964 election, appear like a warmonger who would escalate the fighting in Vietnam. Fredrik Logevall, *Choosing War: The Lost Chance for Peace and the Escalation of War in Vietnam* (Berkeley: University of California Press, 1999), 149, 237.

16. Nixon never actually said that he had a "secret plan" to end the war but allowed this statement to

stand uncorrected when it was reported by the media. Robert B. Semple Jr., "Nixon Withholds His Peace Ideas; Says to Tell Details of Plan Would Sap His Bargaining Position if He's Elected," *New York Times*, March 11, 1968. On campaign stops, Nixon boasted that, as Dwight D. Eisenhower's vice president, he had been part of an administration that ended the Korean War and kept the nation out of other wars for eight years. E. W. Kenworthy, "Nixon Is Found Hard to Fathom on Basis of Public Statements," *New York Times*, October 26, 1968.

17. H. R. McMaster, *Dereliction of Duty: Lyndon Johnson, Robert McNamara, the Joint Chiefs of Staff, and the Lies that Led to Vietnam* (New York: HarperCollins, 1997), 175; Earl Tilford, "Crosswinds: Cultural Imperative of the Air War," in *America, France, and Vietnam: Cultural History and Ideas of Conflict*, ed. Phil Melling and Jon Roper (Aldershot, UK: Avebury, 1991), 114. Senators Richard Russell (D., Georgia) and John Stennis (D., Mississippi) supported an all-out bombing campaign against North Vietnam. Woods, *Fulbright, Vietnam*, 94, 114.

18. Lou Cannon, *President Reagan: The Role of a Lifetime* (New York: PublicAffairs, 2000), 163. Reagan was contemplating a run for the office of governor of California, which he won the following year. When running for the presidency in 1968, Reagan urged an intensification of the war "in order to win as quickly as possible." "Summary of Views on Vietnam War by Leading Presidential Candidates," *New York Times*, August 2, 1968.

19. Sharp, *Strategy for Defeat*, 107–24; McNamara, *In Retrospect*, 111, 227.

20. Johnson, *Vantage Point*, 66–67, 149.

21. The term *quagmire* was already in use in 1964, when David Halberstam first published his account of the 1962–63 period, *The Making of a Quagmire* (New York: Ballantine Books, 1989). The term is still in use as shorthand for a military stalemate that sucks in more and more forces that cannot be easily extricated when victory proves elusive.

22. Louis Harris quoted in McNamara, *In Retrospect*, 252; Adam Garfinkle, *Telltale Hearts: The Origins and Impact of the Antiwar Movement* (London: Macmillan, 1995), 16.

23. The Gallup Organization periodically asked national adult samples of the public to say whether they approved or disapproved of the president's "handling of the situation in Vietnam." Beginning in December 1966, a plurality consistently disapproved of Johnson's handling of the war. In July 1967 this became the majority view and from then until May 1968, the last such poll conducted during Johnson's presidency, the number who disapproved of his handling of the war exceeded those who approved of it. Data from Gallup polls (American Institute of Public Opinion [AIPO]) conducted June 1965 through May 1968 provided by RC.

24. Melvin Small, *The Presidency of Richard Nixon* (Lawrence: University Press of Kansas, 1999), 66. The Gallup Organization asked national adult samples the following question numerous times between August 1965 and January 1973: "In view of the developments since we entered the fighting in Vietnam, do you think the U.S. made a mistake sending troops to fight in Vietnam?" In October 1967 for the first time a plurality thought that entering the war had been a mistake but this reverted to a minority view in December. In February 1968 a plurality once again considered that entering the war had been a mistake and this view continued thereafter to be espoused by a plurality and, from August 1968 on, a majority of those polled. Gallup poll data provided by RC.

25. The Gallup Organization periodically asked national adult samples of the public to identify themselves as "hawks" or "doves." In the poll taken between February 1 and 6, 1968, in the immediate aftermath of the start of the Tet Offensive, the number of hawks peaked at 60 percent, with only 24 percent identifying themselves as doves. The public therefore became more "hawkish" at the same time that, in the "mistake" question, a plurality agreed that entering the war had been a mistake. In polls conducted in April and October 1968, the public was split, with roughly the same numbers identifying themselves as hawks and doves. Gallup poll data provided by RC.

26. Charles DeBenedetti and Charles Chatfield, *An American Ordeal: The Antiwar Movement of the Vietnam Era* (Syracuse, NY: Syracuse University Press, 1990), 113–14, 126–28, 129; Donald W. White, *The American Century: The Rise and Decline of America as a World Power* (New Haven: Yale University Press, 1996), 365; Carl Oglesby, "Carl Oglesby Denounces the 'Liberals' War'" (November 1965 speech at a Washington, DC, protest), in *Major Problems in the History of the Vietnam War*, ed. Robert McMahon, 3rd ed. (Lexington, Mass.: D.C. Heath, 2003), 429–31; Gerald Gioglio, *Days of Decision: An Oral History of Conscientious Objectors in the Military during the Vietnam War* (Trenton, NJ: Broken Rifle Press, 1989); James W. Tollefson, *The Strength Not to Fight: An Oral History of Conscientious Objectors of the Vietnam War* (Boston: Little, Brown, 1993); Larry G. Waterhouse and Mariann G. Wizard, *Turning the Guns Around: Notes on the GI Movement* (New York: Delta Books, 1972).

27. Robert D. Johnson, "The Progressive Dissent: Ernest Gruening and Vietnam," in Woods, *Vietnam and the American Political Tradition*, 72, 75.

28. A Gallup Organization poll found that Americans favored Nixon's policy of withdrawing U.S. troops while training more and more South Vietnamese troops by a 2 to 1 margin over the policies of his Democratic Party rivals for the presidency. This "de-Americanization" plan would later be renamed "Vietnamization." "Poll Rates Nixon Best at Handling War," *New York Times*, August 25, 1968. Humphrey, as a loyal vice president, was hamstrung by his association with Johnson's Vietnam policy.

29. Jeffrey Kimball, *Nixon's Vietnam War* (Lawrence: University Press of Kansas, 1998), 174–75.

30. In December 1972, only 38 percent of a poll sample agreed that the United States should sign any agreement that could be worked out with North Vietnam, regardless of the consequences for South Vietnam, as long as the agreement ended the U.S. part in the war and secured the release of American prisoners of war. Fifty-two percent of the sample disapproved of such a proposal, which sums up the main elements of the Paris Peace Accords signed the following month. Opinion Research Corporation, telephone poll of a national adult sample conducted for Richard Nixon, December 4–5, 1972; data provided by RC.

31. Kimball, *Nixon's Vietnam War*, 166; Gallup Organization polls of national samples, August and September 1969; data provided by RC. The Nixon administration was extremely attentive to the polls and did its best to cultivate and manipulate the pollsters.

32. George Gallup, "Shift from Hawk to Dove Is Almost Exact Reversal," *Washington Post*, November 13, 1969.

33. Richard Nixon, "Address to the Nation on the War in Vietnam," November 3, 1969, APP, www.presidency.ucsb.edu/ws/?pid=2303 (accessed December 11, 2006); Gallup Organization poll of a national adult sample conducted November 3, 1969; data provided by RC; William Borders, "Many in U.S. Back Nixon War Stand on Veterans Day," *New York Times*, November 12, 1969; Melvin Small, *Covering Dissent: The Media and the Anti–Vietnam War Movement* (New Brunswick, NJ: Rutgers University Press, 1994), 124–25. A postwar poll established that 5 percent of respondents had participated in antiwar demonstrations and 3 percent had participated in demonstrations in support of the war. Gallup Organization poll of a national adult sample conducted March 15–18, 1990. Data provided by RC.

34. William M. Hammond, *Reporting Vietnam: Media and Military at War* (Lawrence: University Press of Kansas, 1998), 175; Kimball, *Nixon's Vietnam War*, 175. Paradoxically, the public's antipathy to antiwar protesters increased even though public support for the administration's policies declined. Garfinkle, *Telltale Hearts*, 17–18.

35. John E. Mueller, *War, Presidents, and Public Opinion* (New York: Wiley, 1973), 81–98. In Gallup Organization polls of national adult samples conducted December 12–15, 1969, and May 21–26, 1970, Americans were asked whether they favored an early withdrawal of troops, sending more troops and stepping up the fighting, or taking as many years to withdraw the troops as necessary to turn the war over to the South Vietnamese. The last option—essentially, the "Vietnamization" policy—had the support of 39 percent of the public in December 1969, but this figure declined to 30 percent in May 1970, with corresponding increases in the number favoring an early withdrawal or escalation. Data provided by RC.

36. Richard Nixon, "Address to the Nation on the Situation in Southeast Asia," April 30, 1970, APP, www.presidency.ucsb.edu/ws/?pid=2490 (accessed December 11, 2006).

37. "Gallup Poll Finds 57% Support President on Cambodian Policy," *New York Times*, May 10, 1970. The survey was conducted immediately after Nixon gave his April 30, 1970, speech explaining the reasons for the invasion.

38. Andrew E. Hunt, *The Turning: A History of Vietnam Veterans Against the War* (New York: New York University Press, 1999), 43.

39. Marilyn Young, *The Vietnam Wars, 1945–1990* (New York: HarperCollins, 1991), 248; Richard Nixon, *RN: The Memoirs of Richard Nixon* (London: Book Club Associates, 1978), 454–56; Walter Isaacson, *Kissinger: A Biography* (Boston: Faber and Faber, 1992), 270.

40. Gallup Organization poll of a national adult sample conducted May 21–26, 1970; data provided by RC.

41. Woods, *Fulbright, Vietnam*, 225; Herring, *America's Longest War*, 238–39.

42. Kimball, *Nixon's Vietnam War*, 227.

43. Eighty-four percent agreed with the policy in March 1971. Louis Harris and Associates poll of a national adult sample, conducted in March 1971; data provided by RC. For the first time, in March 1971 a Gallup Organization poll found that a plurality (46 percent) disapproved of Nixon's handling of the "Vietnam situation" while 41 percent approved. "Doubt on Vietnam Reported in Poll," *New York Times*.

44. Louis Harris and Associates poll of a national adult sample conducted in January 1971; data provided by RC. The following month, an identical 61 percent said that the United States should withdraw its troops by the end of the year, "regardless of what happens there after U.S. troops leave." Gallup Organization, poll of a national adult sample conducted between February 19 and 22, 1971; data provided by RC.

45. Renewing the bombing while withdrawing forces from Vietnam was not as illogical a course as it might sound. Aircraft based on aircraft carriers off Vietnam's shores and in neighboring Thailand, and B-52s based as far away as the island of Guam could continue the aerial campaign in Vietnam without any U.S. forces' being based in South Vietnam. Beginning in March 1966, the Gallup Organization asked a sample of the public to respond to a multipart plan that involved UN-sponsored elections in North and South Vietnam and the withdrawal of all its soldiers from the mainland of Vietnam, along with the stationing of ships and planes offshore, "to be ready to bomb any or all parts of North Vietnam." In a series of polls up to June 1969, substantial majorities favored such a plan. Data provided by RC.

46. Drew Middleton, ed., *Air War—Vietnam* (New York: Arno Press, 1978), 275–76. The polarization of public opinion about the merits of the bombing was registered by an April 1972 poll, reporting that 45 percent of respondents favored the stepped-up bombing of North Vietnam but the same number opposed it. Gallup Organization poll of a national adult sample conducted April 21–24, 1972; data provided by RC. Once the bombing started, though, the familiar "rally-round-the-flag" phenomenon occurred: the president's pollster found that 60 percent of the public favored continuing to bomb North Vietnam while the Communist forces were killing South Vietnamese and Americans in South Vietnam. Opinion Research Corporation, poll of a national adult sample conducted for Richard Nixon, April 27–29, 1972; data provided by RC.

47. Isaacson, *Kissinger*, 467, 470.

48. For a critical discussion of that proposition, see Earl H. Tilford Jr., *Setup: What the Air Force Did in Vietnam and Why* (Maxwell AFB, AL: Air University Press, 1991), 289; John T. Smith, *The Linebacker Raids: The Bombing of North Vietnam, 1972* (London: Arms and Armour Press, 1988), 173. For a less critical view, see Sharp, *Strategy for Defeat*, 255.

49. Isaacson, *Kissinger*, 471.

50. Louis Harris and Associates, poll of a national adult sample conducted January 14–17, 1973; data provided by RC.

51. Woods, *Fulbright, Vietnam*, 266.

52. Mary Hershberger, *Jane Fonda's War* (New York: New Press, 2005), 116, 124.

53. Robert Timberg, *The Nightingale's Song* (New York: Simon and Schuster, 1995), 226.

54. James R. Wilson, *Landing Zones: Southern Veterans Remember Vietnam* (Durham: Duke University Press, 1990), 77. The Chicano veteran Frank Delgado, though, said, "If people like Jane Fonda had come earlier, there would have been less guys killed in Nam. I go along with what she did." Trujillo, *Soldados*, 27.

55. Henry Mark Holzer and Erika Holzer, *"Aid and Comfort"* (Jefferson, NC: McFarland, 2002). Jane Fonda was burned in effigy at a rally coinciding with the dedication of the New York Vietnam Veterans Memorial. Sam Rosensohn, "Jane Fonda Dummy Torched," *New York Post*, May 8, 1985. On Veterans Day 1992, the author observed "Hanoi Jane" burned in effigy at the Vietnam Veterans Memorial in Washington, DC.

56. "CACCF [Combat Area Casualties Current File] Record Counts by Year of Death or Declaration of Death (as of 12/98)," National Archives Statistical Information about Casualties of the Vietnam Conflict, www.archives.gov/research/vietnam-war/casualty-statistics.html#year (accessed June 15, 2007).

57. Paul M. Kattenburg, *The Vietnam Trauma in American Foreign Policy, 1945–1975* (New Brunswick, NJ: Transaction, 1982), 316.

58. Young, *Vietnam Wars*, 279. Years after the end of the war, the argument about the accords continued. Gettleman et al., *Vietnam and America*, 431; Lewis Sorley, *A Better War: The Unexamined Victories and Final Tragedy of America's Last Years in Vietnam* (New York: Harcourt Brace, 1999), 357–59.

59. Dennis M. Drew, *Rolling Thunder 1965: Anatomy of a Failure* (Maxwell AFB, AL: Air University Press, 1986), 45; Tilford, *Setup*, 289; John B. Nichols and Barrett Tillman, *On Yankee Station: The Naval Air War over Vietnam* (Annapolis: Naval Institute Press, 1987), 131; Douglas Pike, quoted in Mackubin Thomas Owens, "A Winnable War" (review of Mark Moyar, *Triumph Forsaken*, in the *Weekly Standard*, January 17, 2007), posted on History News Network, hnn.us/roundup/entries/36786.html (accessed March 26, 2007).

60. The *Dolchstoss* ("stab in the back") legend "attributed Germany's defeat [in 1918] to the betrayal of an undefeated army by a cowardly home front led by traitorous leftists." James Diehl, *The Thanks of the Fatherland: German Veterans after the Second World War* (Chapel Hill: University of North Carolina Press, 1993), 19. See also Jerry Lembcke, *The Spitting Image* (New York: New York University Press, 1998), 84–91; Jeffrey P. Kimball, "The Stab-in-the-Back Legend and the Vietnam War," *Armed Forces and Society* 14, no. 3 (Spring 1988): 433–58.

61. Jonathan Shay, *Achilles in Vietnam: Combat Trauma and the Undoing of Character* (New York: Touchstone, 1995), 8.

62. Louis Harris and Associates, *Myths and Realities: A Study of Attitudes toward Vietnam Era Veterans* (Washington, DC: Veterans Administration, 1980), 60, table III-4.

63. The War Powers Act required the president to report to Congress when forces were sent into combat and to seek congressional approval for such a commitment of forces after a sixty-day period. Gettleman et al., *Vietnam and America*, 489–95.

64. Young, *Vietnam Wars*, 285.

65. Podhoretz, *Why We Were in Vietnam*, 164.

66. Gerald Ford, press conferences of April 3, 16, and 21, 1975, in *Ford 1975*, bk. 1, *PPP* (1977), 420–21, 505, 544.

67. Herring, *America's Longest War*, 265–66. Soon after the signing of the Paris Peace Accords, 71 percent of the respondents to a poll said that the United States should not resume bombing if North Vietnam tried to take over South Vietnam. Gallup Organization telephone poll of a national adult sample, conducted January 23, 1973; data provided by RC.

68. Nixon, "Address to the Nation on the War in Vietnam"; Arnold R. Isaacs, *Without Honor: Defeat in Vietnam and Cambodia* (Baltimore: Johns Hopkins University Press, 1983), 500.

69. Gerald Ford, press conference, April 16, 1975, 505; Richard Nixon, *The Real War* (London: Sidgwick and Jackson, 1980), 130–31; Richard Nixon, *No More Vietnams* (New York: Arbor House, 1985), 165, 202; Nixon, *RN*, 889; William Turley, *The Second Indochina War: A Short Political and Military History, 1954–1975* (New York: New American Library, 1987), 183; Karnow, *Vietnam*, 667; Young, *Vietnam Wars*, 291.

70. Ronald Reagan, Speech on Indochina, April 1975, in *Reagan, in His Own Hand*, ed. Kiron K. Skinner, Annelise Anderson, and Martin Anderson (New York: Free Press, 2001), 49.

71. Larry Engelmann, *Tears before the Rain: An Oral History of the Fall of South Vietnam* (New York: Oxford University Press, 1990), 144.

72. Gloria Emerson, *Winners and Losers: Battles, Retreats, Gains, Losses, and Ruins from the Vietnam War* (New York: Harcourt Brace Jovanovich, 1976), 366.

73. Gerald Ford, Address at a Tulane University Convocation, April 23, 1975, APP, www.presidency.ucsb.edu/ws/?pid=4859 (accessed December 11, 2006).

74. Ron Nessen, "Surreal Surrender in Vietnam," *International Herald Tribune*, April 23, 1995.

75. Gerald Ford, "Statement Following the Evacuation of United States Personnel from the Republic of Vietnam," April 29, 1975, APP, www.presidency.ucsb.edu/ws/?pid=4874 (accessed December 11, 2006).

76. Gerald Ford, "The President's News Conference, May 6, 1975," in *Ford 1975*, bk. 1, *PPP* (1977), 645.

77. Paul Seabury, "The Moral and Strategic Lesson of Vietnam," in *The Vietnam Debate: A Fresh Look at the Arguments*, ed. John Norton Moore (Lanham, MD: University Press of America, 1992), 13.

78. MacPherson, *Long Time Passing*, 5.

79. Gerald Ford, *A Time to Heal: The Autobiography of Gerald Ford* (New York: Harper and Row, 1979), 24, 179, 196.

80. James Reston, *Sherman's March and Vietnam* (New York: Macmillan, 1984), 202.

81. Sylvia Sachs, "Amnesty: Haunting Puzzle," *Pittsburgh Press*, May 13, 1973.

82. Amnesty became a campaign issue in 1972, when George McGovern's opponents said his platform was "Amnesty, Acid and Abortion." Lawrence M. Baskir and William M. Strauss, *Chance and Circumstance: The Draft, the War, and the Vietnam Generation* (New York: Vintage Books, 1978), 209.

83. Gerald Ford, "Memoranda on Vietnam-Era Selective Service Discharges," January 19, 1977, APP, www.presidency.ucsb.edu/ws/?pid=5576 (accessed June 25, 2007); Baskir and Strauss, *Chance and Circumstance*, 221; Emerson, *Winners and Losers*, 132–33.

84. Peter N. Carroll, *It Seemed Like Nothing Happened: America in the 1970s* (New Brunswick, NJ: Rutgers University Press, 1990), 163.

85. Emerson, *Winners and Losers*, 48.

86. Podhoretz, *Why We Were in Vietnam*, 210.

87. Robert Elegant, "How to Lose a War," *Encounter* 57 (August 1981): 73–90; Peter Braestrup, *Big Story: How the American Press and Television Reported and Interpreted the Crisis of Tet 1968 in Vietnam and Washington* (Boulder, CO: Westview Press, 1977).

88. David Culbert, "Television's Vietnam and Historical Revisionism in the United States," *Historical Journal of Film, Radio and Television* 8, no. 3 (1988): 253–67. A number of scholars have refuted the claim that the media were responsible for the defeat. See, e.g., Mueller, *War, Presidents, and Public Opinion*, 60–62; Daniel C. Hallin, *The "Uncensored War": The Media and Vietnam* (Berkeley: University of California Press, 1989); William M. Hammond, *Public Affairs: The Military and the Media, 1962–1968* (Washington, DC: U.S. Army Center of Military History, 1988).

89. Hanson Baldwin, foreword to Sharp, *Strategy for Defeat*, xvii.

90. Jimmy Carter, "University of Notre Dame—Address at Commencement Exercises at the University," May 22, 1977, APP, www.presidency.ucsb.edu/ws/?pid=7552 (accessed December 7, 2006).

91. Jimmy Carter, "Inaugural Address of President Jimmy Carter Following His Swearing In as the 39th President of the United States," January 20, 1977, APP, www.presidency.ucsb.edu/ws/?pid=6575 (accessed December 7, 2006). See also Jimmy Carter, "United Nations—Address before the General Assembly," March 17, 1977, APP, www.presidency.ucsb.edu/ws/?pid=7183 (accessed December 7, 2006); Zbigniew Brzezinski, *Power and Principle: Memoirs of the National Security Adviser 1977–1981* (London: Weidenfeld and Nicolson, 1983), 124.

92. Brzezinski, *Power and Principle*, 154–56; John Lewis Gaddis, *The United States and the End of the Cold War: Implications, Reconsiderations, Provocations* (New York: Oxford University Press, 1992), 60, 120; Richard A. Melanson, *American Foreign Policy since the Vietnam War*, 2nd ed. (Armonk, NY: M. E. Sharpe, 1996), 101; Cyrus Vance, *Hard Choices: Critical Years in America's Foreign Policy* (New York: Simon and Schuster, 1983), 421; Richard C. Thornton, *The Carter Years: Toward a New Global Order* (New York: Paragon House, 1991), 6.

93. Carter, "Address at Commencement Exercises."

94. Cyrus Vance, "Meeting the Challenges of a Changing World," May 1, 1979, quoted in Richard A. Melanson, *Writing History and Making Policy: The Cold War, Vietnam, and Revisionism* (Lanham, MD: University Press of America, 1983), 181.

95. Thornton, *Carter Years*, 491.

96. James M. Scott, *Deciding to Intervene: The Reagan Doctrine and American Foreign Policy* (Durham: Duke University Press, 1996), 114; Thornton, *Carter Years*, 140, 168, 202.

97. Brzezinski, *Power and Principle*, 398.

98. Jimmy Carter, "President's News Conference, January 17, 1979," APP, www.presidency.ucsb.edu/ws/?pid=32324 (accessed June 2, 2007). A coup in neighboring Afghanistan brought Communists to power there, another setback for U.S. influence in Southwest Asia. Thornton, *Carter Years*, 189.

99. Carter's failure to support the shah in Iran and the Somoza dictatorship in Nicaragua were the key offenses with which Jeane Kirkpatrick charged his administration in an influential essay. Kirkpatrick, "Dictatorships and Double Standards," *Commentary* 68, no. 5 (November 1979): 34–35.

100. Jimmy Carter, "Energy and National Goals Address to the Nation," July 15, 1979, APP, www.presidency.ucsb.edu/ws/?pid=32596 (accessed December 3, 2006). The address has come to be known as the "malaise" speech. Although Carter did not use that term himself, it was used soon afterward by journalists in references to the speech. See, e.g., Colin Campbell, "The Editorial Notebook 'Confidence': Mr. Carter's Word Was Bound to Have an Underside," *New York Times*, July 21, 1979; Francis X. Clines, "About Chautauqua: The Circuit Is Gone but Not the Oratory," *New York Times*, August 2, 1979. The most frequently recurring term in the speech was "confidence," with references at key points to the "American spirit" and a "crisis of the spirit."

101. Mark Pinsky, "Lessons of a Bad War," *New York Times*, July 11, 1979; Jay Winik, *On the Brink: The Dramatic, Behind-the-Scenes Saga of the Reagan Era and the Men and Women Who Won the Cold War* (New York: Simon and Schuster, 1996), 110–11; Kirkpatrick, "Dictatorships and Double Standards," 41–42; Melanson, *American Foreign Policy*, 123–24.

102. Reston, *Sherman's March and Vietnam*, 253; Keith Beattie, *The Scar That Binds* (New York: New York University Press, 1998), 13.

103. Baskir and Strauss, *Chance and Circumstance*, 231.

104. Robert Timberg, *The Nightingale's Song* (New York: Simon and Schuster, 1995), 257.

105. See, e.g., Pinsky, "Lessons of a Bad War."

106. MacPherson, *Long Time Passing*, 450. Even a strong supporter of the morality of America's war effort respected those who went to jail. See James Webb, "The Invisible Vietnam Veteran," *Washington Post*, August 4, 1976; James Webb, *Fields of Fire* (New York: Pocket Books, 1978), 401.

107. In a Louis Harris and Associates telephone poll of a national adult sample conducted between February 1 and 8, 1977, the respondents were asked whether they agreed or disagreed with the following statement: "By giving a pardon, President Carter is making those who refused to serve admit that they did wrong, whereas amnesty would have been the right thing to do." Thirty-one percent agreed and 46 percent disagreed. Data provided by RC.

108. Arthur Egendorf, Andrea Remez, and John Farley, *Dealing with the War: A View Based on the Individual Lives of Vietnam Veterans*, vol. 5 of Arthur Egendorf, Charles Kadushin, Robert S. Laufer, George Rothbart, and Lee Sloan, *Legacies of Vietnam: Comparative Adjustment of Veterans and Their Peers* (Washington, DC: U.S. Government Printing Office, 1981), 728.

109. Timberg, *Nightingale's Song*, 257–58.

110. In August 1979, Pentagon and CIA representatives at a White House meeting won approval for the resumption of military aid to El Salvador and Guatemala, which had been interrupted as a result of human rights violations in those countries. Allan Nairn, "Opening Gambits—Black versus White," *NACLA Report on the Americas*, May/June 1984, 20.

111. Scott, *Deciding to Intervene*, 154; Thomas Carothers, *In the Name of Democracy: U.S. Policy toward Latin America in the Reagan Years* (Berkeley: University of California Press, 1991), 80–81, 82; Nairn, "Opening Gambits," 20, 22; Jimmy Carter, "Peace and National Security Address to the Nation on Soviet Combat Troops in Cuba and the Strategic Arms Limitation Treaty," October 1, 1979, APP, www. presidency.ucsb.edu/ws/?pid=31458 (accessed December 7, 2006).

112. Brzezinski, *Power and Principle*, 429.

113. Vance, *Hard Choices*, 394.

114. Melanson, *Writing History*, 184.

115. Jimmy Carter, "'Meet the Press' interview by Bill Monroe, Carl T. Rowan, David Broder, and Judy Woodruff," January 20, 1980, APP, www.presidency.ucsb.edu/ws/?pid=33060 (accessed December 7, 2006).

116. Brzezinski, *Power and Principle*, 499.

117. The Harris survey registered a 66 percent approval rating in mid-December 1979 and a 65 percent disapproval rating in April 1980. Gallup Organization polls registered a 77 percent approval rating in mid-December and a 49 percent disapproval rating in April. Thornton, *Carter Years*, 495.

118. Melanson, *American Foreign Policy*, 118.

119. Thornton, *Carter Years*, 480.

120. Hedrick Smith, "Carter's On-Job Rating Falls in Poll Because of Foreign Policy Concerns," *New York Times*, March 18, 1980; Daniel Madar, *Reagan's Foreign Policy: Emerging Organization and Themes, Behind the Headlines* (Toronto: Canadian Institute of International Affairs, 1981), 1–2.

121. Jerry Falwell, "Future-Word: An Agenda for the Eighties," in *The Fundamentalist Phenomenon: The Resurgence of Conservative Christianity*, ed. Jerry Falwell with Ed Dobson and Ed Hinson (Garden City, NY: Doubleday, 1981), 213; Lewis Walt, *The Eleventh Hour* (New York: Caroline House, 1979), xi, xii, quoted in ibid.

122. Donald S. Spencer, *The Carter Implosion: Jimmy Carter and the Amateur Style of Diplomacy* (New York: Praeger, 1988), 7.

123. Ronald Reagan, Speech at the Chicago Council on Foreign Relations, March 17, 1980, quoted in Nairn, "Opening Gambits," 23 (for a draft of the speech, see Skinner, Anderson, and Anderson, *Reagan, in His Own Hand*, 471–79); Lou Cannon, "Reagan: 'Peace through Strength,'" *Washington Post*, August 19, 1980; Cannon, *President Reagan*, 7, 11; Ronald Reagan, Speech at the Republican National Convention, July 17, 1980, millercenter.virginia.edu/scripps/diglibrary/prezspeeches/reagan/rwr_1980_0717.html (accessed December 7, 2006).

124. Howell Raines, "Reagan Calls Arms Race Essential to Avoid 'Surrender' or 'Defeat,'" *New York Times*, August 19, 1980; Ronald Reagan, "Peace," in Skinner, Anderson, and Anderson, *Reagan, in His Own Hand*, 481.

125. Rick Perlstein, *Nixonland: The Rise of a President and the Fracturing of America* (New York: Scribner, 2008), xii.

126. Cannon, "Reagan: 'Peace through Strength.'" As the 1979 Louis Harris poll revealed, Reagan's final sentence accorded with the view of the vast majority of Vietnam veterans.

127. Isaacs, *Without Honor*, 488.

128. Perlstein, *Nixonland*, 91; Cannon, *President Reagan*, 290; Ronald Reagan, "'State of the Union' Speech," in Skinner, Anderson, and Anderson, *Reagan, in His Own Hand*, 479; for later iterations of the pledge, see, e.g., *Reagan 1981*, PPP (1982), 155; Ronald Reagan, press conference, April 18, 1985, in *Reagan 1985*, bk. 1, PPP (1986), 454.

129. In an October 1980 Gallup Organization poll 52 percent picked Carter and 23 percent Reagan as the candidate best able to keep America out of war. Everett Carll Ladd, "The Brittle Mandate: Electoral Dealignment and the 1980 Presidential Election," *Political Science Quarterly* 96, no. 1 (Spring 1981): 23.

130. James L. Sundquist, "Whither the American Party System?—Revisited," *Political Science Quarterly* 98, no. 4 (Winter 1983–84): 587.

131. Mark P. Lagon, *The Reagan Doctrine: Sources of American Conduct in the Cold War's Last Chapter* (Westport, CT: Praeger, 1994), 86.

132. Winik, *On the Brink*, 56.

133. Ronald Reagan, President's News Conference, January 29, 1981, APP, www.presidency.ucsb. edu/ws/?pid=44101 (accessed December 6, 2006). Reagan had denounced détente as an "illusion" in his March 17, 1980, speech at the Chicago Council on Foreign Relations. Steven V. Roberts, "Reagan in Chicago Speech, Urges Big Increases in Military Spending," *New York Times*, March 18, 1980.

134. Ronald Reagan, "Address at Commencement Exercises at the United States Military Academy" May 27, 1981, APP, www.presidency.ucsb.edu/ws/?pid=43865 (accessed December 7, 2006). See also Melanson, *Writing History*, 205.

135. Alexander M. Haig Jr., *Caveat: Realism, Reagan, and Foreign Policy* (London: Weidenfeld and

Nicolson, 1984), 27; William LeoGrande, *Our Own Backyard: The United States in Central America, 1977–1992* (Chapel Hill: University of North Carolina Press, 1998), 81 (for recurrent instances where the specter or lessons of Vietnam impinged on debate about Central America policy, see 81–103).

136. Nixon, *Real War*, 37; Michael Lind, *Vietnam: The Necessary War; A Reinterpretation of America's Most Disastrous Military Conflict* (New York: Touchstone Books, 1999), 25; Scott, *Deciding to Intervene*, 16; Lagon, *Reagan Doctrine*, 44–46.

137. Engelmann, *Tears before the Rain*, 221.

138. Dario Moreno, *U.S. Policy in Central America: The Endless Debate* (Miami: Florida International University Press, 1990), 82.

139. Jeane J. Kirkpatrick, *The Reagan Doctrine and U.S. Foreign Policy* (Washington, DC: Heritage Foundation and the Fund for an American Renaissance, 1985), 6, 8; Winik, *On the Brink*, 299–300.

140. Gaddis, *United States and the End of the Cold War*, 121; Joseph Smith, *The Cold War, 1945–1991*, 2nd ed. (Oxford: Blackwell, 1998), 124–26, 132; Cannon, *President Reagan*, 132–33.

141. Helga Haftendorn, "Toward a Reconstruction of American Strength: A New Era in the Claim to Global Leadership?" in *The Reagan Administration: A Reconstruction of American Strength?* ed. Helga Haftendorn and Jakob Schissler (Berlin, NY: de Gruyter, 1988), 3.

142. Melanson, *Writing History*, 192, 199.

143. Nairn, "Opening Gambits," 26. Nairn quotes Kirkpatrick from the *Boston Globe*, February 23, 1981.

144. Jeff McMahan, *Reagan and the World: Imperial Policy in the New Cold War* (London: Pluto Press, 1984), 103. Carter had suspended "non-lethal" military aid following the killing of four American churchwomen by a rightist death squad but resumed it after forty days, when the Christian Democrat José Napoleón Duarte assumed the position of head of the governing junta. Nairn, "Opening Gambits," 25.

145. Allan Nairn, "The Middle Game," *NACLA Report on the Americas*, May/June 1984, 36; idem, "The Pieces on the Board," *NACLA Report on the Americas*, May/June 1984, 31; Piero Gleijeses, "Guatemala: Crisis and Response," in *SAIS Papers No. 7: Report on Guatemala; Findings of the Study Group on United States–Guatemalan Relations* (Boulder, CO: Westview Press, with the Foreign Policy Institute, School of Advanced International Studies, Johns Hopkins University, 1985), 58–60.

146. Raymond Bonner, "The Thousand Small Escalations of the Vietnam War," *Washington Post*, September 16, 1984.

147. Carothers, *In the Name of Democracy*, 83; Donald E. Schulz and Deborah Sundloff Schulz, *The United States, Honduras, and the Crisis in Central America* (Boulder, CO: Westview Press, 1994), 152–53.

148. Scott, *Deciding to Intervene*, 160; LeoGrande, *Our Own Backyard*, 143–46.

149. Martin Tolchin, "House Panel Bars Aid for the CIA against Nicaragua," *New York Times*, May 4, 1983.

150. Haftendorn, "Toward a Reconstruction of American Strength," 3; George Shultz, *Turmoil and Triumph: Diplomacy, Power, and the Victory of the American Ideal* (New York: Charles Scribner's Sons, 1993), 625.

151. In 1982 a Chicago Council on Foreign Relations survey found that only 54 percent of the public believed that the United States should take an active part in world affairs. Eugene R. Wittkopf, "On the Foreign Policy Beliefs of the American People: A Critique and Some Evidence," *International Studies Quarterly* 30, no. 4 (December 1986): 434.

152. Jenny Pearce, *Under the Eagle: U.S. Intervention in Central America and the Caribbean*, 2nd ed. (Boston: South End Press, 1982), 270–71; Christian Smith, *Resisting Reagan: The U.S. Central America Peace Movement* (Chicago: University of Chicago Press, 1996), 90–97.

153. Nairn, "Opening Gambits," 26.

154. William LeoGrande and Philip Brenner, "The House Divided: Ideological Polarization over Aid to the Nicaraguan 'Contras,'" *Legislative Studies Quarterly* 18, no. 1 (February 1993): 113, 123–24; Moreno, *U.S. Policy in Central America*, 113–14.

155. Cannon, *President Reagan*, 153; John H. Kessel, "The Structures of the Reagan White House," *American Journal of Political Science* 28, no. 2 (May 1984): 256. See also David Greenberg, "Five Myths about Ronald Reagan," History News Network, hnn.us/articles/5605.html (accessed June 16, 2004).

156. Sundquist, "Whither the American Party System?—Revisited," 579–83; Pamela Johnston Conover, "The Mobilization of the New Right: A Test of Various Explanations," *Western Political Quarterly* 36, no. 4 (December 1983): 632–49.

157. For tensions between traditional Republicans and "movement conservatives," see Tom Pauken, "ACTION: The Times They Are a-Changin'," in *Steering the Elephant: How Washington Works*, ed. Robert Rector and Michael Sanera (New York: Universe Books, 1987), 185; Morton Blackwell, "Building a Conservative Governing Majority," in ibid., 30–36; Sidney Blumenthal, "Quest for Lasting Power," *Washington Post*, September 25, 1985.

158. Moreno, *U.S. Policy in Central America*, 87.

159. Haig, *Caveat*, 130, 144. Haig named Vice President Bush, Defense Secretary Caspar W. Weinberger, Director of Central Intelligence William J. Casey, National Security Adviser Richard V. Allen, and the senior White House advisers Edwin Meese, James Baker, and Michael Deaver as all fearing "another Vietnam." Bernard Gwertzman, "Haig Cites Advice to Press Havana," *New York Times*, March 25, 1984.

160. Winik, *On the Brink*, 261; LeoGrande, *Our Own Backyard*, 82; Haig, *Caveat*, 123, 125; Melanson, *Writing History*, 203.

161. Lagon, *Reagan Doctrine*, 48.

162. Bob Woodward, *Veil: The Secret Wars of the CIA, 1981–87* (London: Headline Publishing, 1987), 124; Moreno, *U.S. Policy in Central America*, 89.

163. Moreno, *U.S. Policy in Central America*, 101; Haig, *Caveat*, 128; LeoGrande, *Our Own Backyard*, 197; Roy Gutman, *Banana Diplomacy: The Making of American Policy in Nicaragua, 1981–1987* (New York: Simon and Schuster, 1988), 277; Drew Middleton, "U.S. Generals Are Leery of Latin Intervention," *New York Times*, June 21, 1983; Richard Halloran, "U.S. Army Chief Opposes Sending Combat Forces to Aid El Salvador," *New York Times*, June 10, 1983.

164. Associated Press, "Senator Warns of Risk of a Wider Latin War," *New York Times*, June 8, 1983. Critics of U.S. policy saw "strong parallels" between U.S. support of El Salvador and the early stages of U.S. involvement in Vietnam. Charles Mohr, "Salvador and Vietnam," *New York Times*, August 10, 1983.

165. For a description of Baker's, Deaver's, and Meese's relationships with Reagan, see Robert Dallek, *Ronald Reagan: The Politics of Symbolism* (Cambridge, MA: Harvard University Press, 1999), 75–77. For their White House role, see Cannon, *President Reagan*, 149, 152, 264. For the troika arrangement, see Edwin Meese, *With Reagan: The Inside Story* (Washington, DC: Regnery Gateway, 1992), 78–81. During Reagan's first term, Baker, Deaver, and Meese breakfasted together at 7:30 every workday, ironing out any discord arising from rival policy proposals. They then met Reagan for his first meeting of the day, along with Vice President Bush. Kessel, "Structures of the Reagan White House," 243, 252, 253; Edwin Meese, "The Reagan Presidency" in *Leadership in the Reagan Presidency, Part II: Eleven Intimate Perspectives*, ed. Kenneth W. Thompson (Lanham, MD: University Press of America, 1993), 232; Michael Deaver with Mickey Herskowitz, *Behind the Scenes* (New York: William Morrow, 1987), 128.

166. Cannon, *President Reagan*, 56; LeoGrande, *Our Own Backyard*, 194; Scott, *Deciding to Intervene*, 25; Gutman, *Banana Diplomacy*, 90; Deaver, *Behind the Scenes*, 170.

167. Peggy Noonan, *What I Saw at the Revolution: A Political Life in the Reagan Era* (New York: Fawcett Columbine, 1990), 239.

168. Kessel, "Structures of the Reagan White House," 233.

169. Moreno, *U.S. Policy in Central America*, 97.

170. Quoted in LeoGrande, *Our Own Backyard*, 84.

171. K. Larry Storrs and Nina Serafino, "The Reagan Administration's Efforts to Gain Support for Contra Aid," in *Public Opinion in U.S. Foreign Policy: The Controversy over Contra Aid*, ed. Richard Sobel (Lanham, MD: Rowman and Littlefield, 1993), 126; Richard Sobel, "Public Opinion about U.S. Intervention in Nicaragua: A Polling Introduction," in Sobel, *Public Opinion in U.S. Foreign Policy*, 57–58n5; Mark Hertsgaard, *On Bended Knee: The Press and the Reagan Presidency* (New York: Farrar Straus Giroux, 1988), 20; Noonan, *What I Saw at the Revolution*, 249; Deaver, *Behind the Scenes*, 88, 125. Wirthlin had been Reagan's pollster off and on since 1968.

172. Richard Reeves, *President Reagan: The Triumph of the Imagination* (New York: Simon and Schuster, 2005), 133; Hertsgaard, *On Bended Knee*, 184; Moreno, *U.S. Policy in Central America*, 114.

173. LeoGrande, *Our Own Backyard*, 140.

174. Gallup Organization telephone poll, sponsored by *Newsweek*, of a national sample of the subpopulation that knew which side the United States was backing in El Salvador, conducted February 17–18, 1982; data provided by RC.

175. CBS/*New York Times* telephone poll of a national adult sample, conducted March 11–15, 1982; Louis Harris and Associates telephone poll of a national adult sample, conducted March 12–16, 1982; Yankelovich, Skelly and White telephone poll, sponsored by *Time, Inc.*, of a national sample of registered voters, conducted March 16–18, 1982. All data provided by RC.

176. Francis X. Clines, "Reagan, in New York, Defends Curbs on Disclosures," *New York Times*, April 28, 1983; David Bird, "Kissinger's Office Site of Protest," *New York Times*, January 13, 1984; Associated Press, "Reagan Foes Say Their Rights Were Violated," *New York Times*, September 16, 1984. Such slogans appear on posters in the collection of the Center for Political Graphics in Los Angeles and the AOUON [All of Us or None] Archive in Berkeley. Lapel buttons also carried such slogans; "El Salvador is Spanish for Vietnam" appears on a button collected by the author ca. 1982.

177. Winik, *On the Brink*, 254, 304, 479. In Abrams's State Department office, his staff referred to congressional opponents as "the Cong," reminiscent of the Communist Viet Cong.

178. Low-intensity conflict is defined according to its place on a "conflict spectrum," ascending from civil disorders through warfare with conventional weapons to nuclear war. It combines military means with political, economic, and psychological warfare. Sara Miles, "The Real War: Low Intensity Conflict in Central America," *NACLA Report on the Americas*, April/May 1986, 19; Tom Barry, *Low Intensity Conflict: The New Battle in Central America* (Albuquerque, NM: The Inter-Hemispheric Resource Center, 1986), 1–2; Peter Kornbluh and Joy Hackel, "Low-Intensity Conflict: Is It Live or Is It Memorex?" *NACLA Report on the Americas*, June 1986, 8–11.

179. George Shultz's memoir shows that the internal conflicts about the administration's Central America policy continued after he replaced Haig as secretary of state. The Department of State worked at cross purposes with the Pentagon and the national security adviser. Shultz, *Turmoil and Triumph*, 314–16, 321–22. For the pragmatists' moderating effect on Reagan's anti-Soviet policy, see Lagon, *Reagan Doctrine*, 107.

180. Moreno, *U.S. Policy in Central America*, 103; Winik, *On the Brink*, 261.

181. The policy was dubbed the "Reagan Doctrine" by the neo-conservative commentator Charles Krauthammer in his response to Reagan's 1985 State of the Union Speech, although it had already been outlined in various speeches and policy documents between 1982 and 1984. Winik, *On the Brink*, 457–58. See also Kirkpatrick, *Reagan Doctrine*, 10–11.

182. Scott, *Deciding to Intervene*, 22.

183. LeoGrande, *Our Own Backyard*, 96–97, 130–34, 208; Nairn, "Middle Game," 35, 37–38.

184. Peter Kornbluh, *Nicaragua: The Price of Intervention* (Washington, DC: Institute for Policy Studies, 1987), 137–39; LeoGrande, *Our Own Backyard*, 95; Nairn, "Middle Game," 38.

185. LeoGrande, *Our Own Backyard*, 201.

186. Martin Tolchin, "Reagan Being Warned against Bypassing Congress on Salvador Aid," *New York Times*, March 4, 1983.

187. LeoGrande, *Our Own Backyard*, 455.

188. Martin Tolchin, "Congress Is Skeptical on Salvadoran Aid," *New York Times*, March 12, 1983.

189. Ronald Reagan, *An American Life* (London: Hutchinson, 1990), 479.

190. Kornbluh, *Nicaragua*, 159.

191. Ronald Reagan, "Remarks at the Annual Washington Conference of the American Legion," February 22, 1983, APP, www.presidency.ucsb.edu/ws/?pid=40955 (accessed December 9, 2006).

192. Ronald Reagan, "Remarks and a Question-and-Answer Session with Members of the Commonwealth Club of California in San Francisco," March 4, 1983, APP, www.presidency.ucsb.edu/ws/?pid=41002 (accessed December 9, 2006).

193. Ronald Reagan, "Remarks on Central America and El Salvador at the Annual Meeting of the National Association of Manufacturers," March 10, 1983, APP, www.presidency.ucsb.edu/ws/?pid=41034 (accessed December 9, 2006).

194. Ronald Reagan, "Address before a Joint Session of the Congress on Central America," April 27, 1983, APP, www.presidency.ucsb.edu/ws/?pid=41245 (accessed December 9, 2006).

195. Kornbluh, *Nicaragua*, 160. The Central America Policy Outreach Group tried to rally the president's conservative supporters; and the State Department's Office of Public Diplomacy built support among foreign officials and U.S. and foreign media. Sara Miles, "Real War," *NACLA Report on the Americas*, April/May 1986, 28.

196. LeoGrande, *Our Own Backyard*, 215–16.

197. Carothers, *In the Name of Democracy*, 86.

198. LeoGrande, *Our Own Backyard*, 214. Reagan made the same point in a press interview the day before his address to Congress: "There is no comparison whatsoever in this situation [Central America] and Vietnam." "Interview with USA Today," April 26, 1983, APP, www.presidency.ucsb.edu/ws/?pid=41240 (accessed June 3, 2007).

199. LeoGrande, *Our Own Backyard*, 201–2, 213.

200. Reagan, "Interview with USA Today."

201. "Final Declaration of the Geneva Conference," July 21, 1954, in Gettleman et al., *Vietnam and America*, 75.

202. Reeves, *President Reagan*, 207; Ronald Reagan, "The President's News Conference," February 18, 1982, APP, www.presidency.ucsb.edu/ws/?pid=42183 (accessed June 3, 2007). President Eisenhower's advisers had told him that Ho Chi Minh would win 80 percent of the vote in a nationwide election, if one had been held. Dwight D. Eisenhower, *Mandate for Change: 1953–1956* (London: Heinemann, 1963), 337–38, 372. See also Mark Green and Gail MacColl, *There He Goes Again: Ronald Reagan's Reign of Error* (New

York: Pantheon Books, 1983), 32–34; H. Bruce Franklin, *Vietnam and Other American Fantasies* (Amherst: University of Massachusetts Press, 2000), 28–31, for further discussion of Reagan's misrepresentation of the relevant history.

203. Defenders of the U.S. war effort in Vietnam have sometimes resorted to the argument that the United States did not sign the Geneva Accords but took note of them in a separate protocol. This point is irrelevant to criticisms of subsequent U.S. actions, though. The U.S. nation-building campaign in South Vietnam was wrong not because it violated an international agreement but because it was designed to thwart the will of the Vietnamese people, who would have elected Ho Chi Minh as their president if they had been allowed the chance to do so.

2. "Something Rather Dark and Bloody"

1. Larry G. Waterhouse and Mariann G. Wizard, *Turning the Guns Around: Notes on the GI Movement* (New York: Delta Books, 1971), 91.

2. When the war ended in 1975, veterans drifted away from activism or undertook other kinds of missions that initially complemented and ultimately superseded the goal of ending the war: some agitated to draw attention to the damage inflicted on veterans, their offspring, and Vietnamese people, by Agent Orange, a chemical defoliant the United States used in Vietnam; some campaigned for the release of American prisoners they believed were still held captive in Southeast Asia; others advocated amnesty for deserters and draft resisters. Richard Stacewicz, *Winter Soldiers: An Oral History of Vietnam Veterans against the War* (New York: Twayne, 1997), 387–93; H. Bruce Franklin, *M.I.A. or Mythmaking in America* (New Brunswick, NJ: Rutgers University Press, 1993); John Hagan, *Northern Passage: American Vietnam War Resisters in Canada* (Cambridge, MA: Harvard University Press, 2001), 164–79.

3. On civilian attitudes toward the veterans of other American wars, see Richard Severo and Lewis Milford, *The Wages of War: When America's Soldiers Came Home: From Valley Forge to Vietnam* (New York: Simon and Schuster, 1989), 16, 189–227, 261–63, 290–93, 334–41; David M. Kennedy, *Over Here: The First World War and American Society* (Oxford: Oxford University Press, 1980), 363; William M. Tuttle, *Race Riot: Chicago in the Red Summer of 1919* (New York: Atheneum, 1970).

4. Eric T. Dean Jr., *Shook over Hell: Post-Traumatic Stress, Vietnam, and the Civil War* (Cambridge, MA: Harvard University Press, 1997), 10.

5. Andrew E. Hunt, *The Turning: A History of Vietnam Veterans against the War* (New York: New York University Press, 1999), 116–19.

6. They dubbed the demonstration "Operation Dewey Canyon III: A Limited Incursion into the Country of Congress" as a parody of Dewey Canyons I and II, the U.S. incursion into Cambodia and a planned invasion of Laos (hastily renamed when VVAW borrowed the name Dewey Canyon). John Kerry and Vietnam Veterans Against the War, *The New Soldier*, ed. David Thorne and George Butler (New York: Macmillan, 1971), 31, 152–53; Gerald Nicosia, *Home to War: A History of the Vietnam Veterans Movement* (New York: Three Rivers Press, 2001), 98–157.

7. Kerry and Vietnam Veterans Against the War, *New Soldier*, 12–24; John Kerry, "Testimony to Congress," in *Peace Is Our Profession*, ed. Jan Barry (Montclair, NJ: East River Anthology, 1981), 154–57; "Fulbright Panel Hears Antiwar Vet," *Washington Post*, April 23, 1971.

8. "Returning War Medals to Congress," in Barry, *Peace Is Our Profession*, 152–53; Stacewicz, *Winter Soldiers*, 249.

9. Richard Moser, *The New Winter Soldiers: GI and Veteran Dissent during the Vietnam Era* (New Brunswick, NJ: Rutgers University Press, 1996), 117; Stacewicz, *Winter Soldiers*, 279.

10. Robert J. Lifton, *Home from the War: Vietnam Veterans neither Victims nor Executioners* (New York: Simon and Schuster, 1973), 31.

11. Adam Garfinkle, *Telltale Hearts: The Origins and Impact of the Vietnam Antiwar Movement* (Basingstoke, UK: Macmillan, 1985), 197.

12. Charles DeBenedetti and Charles Chatfield, *An American Ordeal: The Antiwar Movement of the Vietnam Era* (Syracuse, NY: Syracuse University Press, 1990), 310.

13. Patrick J. Buchanan, memorandum to H. R. Haldeman, April 21, 1971, in *From the President: Richard Nixon's Secret Files*, ed. Bruce Oudes (New York: Harper and Row, 1989), 240.

14. Quoted in A. D. Horne, ed., *The Wounded Generation: Americans after Vietnam* (Englewood Cliffs, NJ: Prentice-Hall, 1981), 116.

15. Leonard Sykes Jr., "Vietnam: A Horror Story Unfairly Told," *Lake Sun (IL) News-Sun*, November 20–21, 1982.

16. Myra MacPherson, *Long Time Passing: Vietnam and the Haunted Generation* (New York: New American Library, 1984), 590.

17. Telford Taylor points out that the designation of the hamlet where the majority of killings took place as My Lai is incorrect: the central target of the attack was a subhamlet Xom Lang in the hamlet Tu Kung, labeled My Lai (4) on American maps. Taylor, *Nuremberg and Vietnam* (Chicago: Quadrangle Books, 1970), 127–28. In keeping with the conventional usage in the United States, I refer to the massacre site as My Lai. "Americal" was a contraction of "American" and "New Caledonia," the Pacific island where the 23rd Infantry Division was formed during World War II. The division was reactivated in Vietnam in 1967 and was generally referred to by the name "Americal" rather than its number.

18. Michael Bilton and Kevin Sim, *Four Hours in My Lai: A War Crime and Its Aftermath* (New York: Penguin, 1993), 3, 74, 128–34.

19. Seymour Hersh, *Cover-Up: The Army's Secret Investigation of the Massacre at My Lai 4* (New York: Vintage Books, 1973), 34; Taylor, *Nuremberg and Vietnam*, 128; W. R. Peers, *The My Lai Inquiry* (New York: W. W. Norton, 1979), 230. Calley told the psychiatrics producing a trial report that he considered the Vietnamese like animals with whom one could not speak or reason. Bilton and Sim, *Four Hours in My Lai*, 336.

20. Bilton and Sim, *Four Hours in My Lai*, 80–82, 375; Taylor, *Nuremberg and Vietnam*, 150–52; Philip Caputo, *A Rumor of War* (New York: Ballantine, 1977), 160; Patience Mason, *Recovering from the War* (New York: Penguin Books, 1990), 145; James S. Olson and Randy Roberts, *Where the Domino Fell: America and Vietnam, 1945–1990* (New York: St. Martin's Press, 1991), 145; Peers, *My Lai Inquiry*, 208; James S. Olson and Randy Roberts, *My Lai: A Brief History with Documents* (Boston and New York: Bedford Books, 1998), 113–32. As one officer remarked about Americal Division procedures, "I think that the general feeling over there was that anything that was shot was VC [Viet Cong]." Hersh, *Cover-Up*, 48.

21. The cover-up was widespread and incriminating information was destroyed. Michal Belknap, *The Vietnam War on Trial: The My Lai Massacre and the Court-Martial of Lieutenant Calley* (Lawrence: University Press of Kansas, 2002), 83; Hersh, *Cover-Up*, 133–38, 162–69, 176–78, 204–5, 218; Bilton and Sim, *Four Hours in My Lai*, 300–304; U.S. Congress, House, 91st Cong., 2d sess., *Investigation of the My Lai Incident: Report of the Armed Services Investigating Subcommittee of the House of Representatives Committee on Armed Services*, July 15, 1970 (Washington, DC: U.S. Government Printing Office, 1970), 26, 34.

22. Associated Press, "Lt. Calley Convicted of Murder," *Indianapolis Star*, March 30, 1971.

23. Olson and Roberts, *My Lai*, 147–51.

24. Prior to the publication of the photographs, Wayne Greenhaw reported the charges in an article in the *Alabama Journal* (Montgomery) on November 12, 1969. Greenhaw, *The Making of a Hero: The Story of Lieutenant William Calley Jr.* (Louisville, KY: Touchstone, 1971), 40. The following day Dispatch News Service carried Seymour Hersh's report in the *Chicago Sun-Times*, among other newspapers. The story was also reported on the front pages of the *New York Times* and the *Washington Post*. On November 20, 1969, the *Cleveland Plain Dealer* published some of Ron Haeberle's photographs on its front page, and CBS News showed the paper's photo spread as the lead item of its nightly news broadcast. *Life* magazine published photographs of the massacre on December 5, 1969, shortly after the Army Commission of Inquiry (the Peers Inquiry) began taking testimony. The massacre was the cover story for *Time* on December 5, 1969, and *Newsweek* on December 8, 1969.

25. As the army psychologist David Grossman says, "The sheer horror of atrocity serves . . . to generate disbelief in distant observers." Gary D. Solis, *Son Thang: An American War Crime* (New York: Bantam Books, 1998), 173; Taylor, *Nuremberg and Vietnam*, 154–55; Edward M. Opton Jr. and Robert Duckles, *My Lai: It Never Happened and Besides, They Deserved It* (Berkeley, CA: Wright Institute, 1970); Opton and Duckles, "It Didn't Happen and Besides, They Deserved It," in *Crimes of War: A Legal, Social, and Psychological Inquiry into the Responsibility of Leader, Citizens, and Soldiers for Criminal Acts in War*, ed. Richard A. Falk, Gabriel Kolko, and Robert Jay Lifton (New York: Vintage Books, 1971), 441–44; Seymour Hersh, *My Lai 4: A Report on the Massacre and Its Aftermath* (New York: Vintage Books, 1970), 151–52; MacPherson, *Long Time Passing*, 589.

26. Belknap, *Vietnam War on Trial*, 188.

27. Apart from Calley, all those who faced courts-martial because of their direct participation in the massacre were acquitted or had the charges dropped before trial. A number of officers received administrative sanctions or demotions for failing to take proper action on the basis of what they learned about the massacre.

28. Peers, *My Lai Inquiry*, 289; Bilton and Sim, *Four Hours in My Lai*, 3; Severo and Milford, *Wages of War*, 350. The "normality" of Calley and his men seemed disquietingly to confirm the ordinary citizens' capacity for dispensing unreasoning lethal violence, which the psychologist Stanley Milgram's experiments demonstrated. Milgram, "Behavioral Study of Obedience," *Journal of Abnormal Psychology* 67, no. 4 (1963): 371–78; Milgram, *Obedience to Authority: An Experimental View* (New York: Harper and Row, 1974).

29. Kevin P. Buckley, "Pacification's Deadly Price," *Newsweek*, June 19, 1972, 42–43; Jonathan Schell,

The Real War: The Classic Reporting on the Vietnam War (New York: Pantheon Books, 1988); Philip Scribner Balboni, "What Every Vietnam Veteran Knows," *New Republic*, December 19, 1970, 13. Contemporaneous sources indicate that America's Vietnamese enemies did not regard the My Lai massacre as exceptional or unique. VC Notice, "Concerning the Crimes Committed by US Imperialists and Their Lackeys" (March 28, 1968), in Peers, *My Lai Inquiry*, 283; "Statement of the Spokesman of the Provisional Revolutionary Government of the Republic of South Viet Nam," in *The Son My Mass Slaying* (South Vietnam: Giai Phong Editions, 1969), 36.

30. Murray Polner, *No Victory Parades* (New York: Holt, Rinehart and Winston, 1971), 10, 135.

31. Chaim Shatan, "The Grief of Soldiers: Vietnam Combat Veterans' Self-Help Movement," *American Journal of Orthopsychiatry* 43, no. 4 (July 1973): 641; Robert B. Shapiro, "Working through the War with Vietnam Vets," *Group* 2, no. 3 (Fall 1978): 156–83; Wilbur Scott, *The Politics of Readjustment: Vietnam Veterans since the War* (New York: Aldine de Gruyter, 1993), 15; Judith Lewis Herman, *Trauma and Recovery* (London: Pandora, 1992), 27.

32. Quoted in Stacewicz, *Winter Soldiers*, 210. Muller went on to found Vietnam Veterans of America, the principal national organization of Vietnam veterans.

33. Scott, *Politics of Readjustment*, 17.

34. Robert Jay Lifton, "Oversight of Medical Care of Veterans Wounded in Vietnam," testimony before the U.S. Senate Subcommittee on Labor and Public Welfare, quoted in Polner, *No Victory Parades*, 154–55; Scott, *Politics of Readjustment*, 5–6.

35. U.S. Congress, Senate, "Veterans' Testimony on Vietnam—Need for Investigation," 92d Cong., 1st sess., April 6, 1971, *Congressional Record*, E 9977–88. See also *Winter Soldier* (Winterfilm and Vietnam Veterans Against the War, 1972); Vietnam Veterans Against the War, *The Winter Soldier Investigation: An Inquiry into American War Crimes* (Boston: Beacon Press, 1972). The phrase "winter soldier" borrows the revolutionary-era coinage of Tom Paine, who praised the soldiers who wintered with George Washington at Valley Forge while the "sunshine patriots" abandoned the revolutionary cause. Kerry and Vietnam Veterans Against the War, *New Soldier*, 8.

36. Scott, *Politics of Readjustment*, 12; "Veterans' Testimony on Vietnam," E 9948, 9949, 9952–54; John Helmer, *Bringing the War Home: The American Soldier in Vietnam and After* (New York: Free Press, 1974), 203–4; Hunt, *Turning*, 69.

37. Shatan, "Grief of Soldiers," 642; Scott, *Politics of Readjustment*, 16–18; Shapiro, "Working through the War," 164–65. Guenter Lewy raised doubts about the identity of some of the witnesses at the Winter Soldier investigation, because some later denied having participated. Lewy, *America in Vietnam* (New York: Oxford University Press, 1978), 317. It is possible, however, that their denials arose from a fear that they might be prosecuted or called as witnesses as a result of their testimony. All the veterans participating in the hearings had been required to produce their DD-214 discharge papers; according to Gerald Nicosia, the U.S. military never refuted the Winter Soldier testimony. Nicosia, *Home to War*, 87, 97.

38. Shatan, "Grief of Soldiers," 643; Herman, *Trauma and Recovery*, 27; Shapiro, "Working through the War," 159.

39. Robert Jay Lifton, "Advocacy and Corruption in the Healing Profession," in *Stress Disorders among Vietnam Veterans: Theory, Research, and Treatment*, ed. Charles R. Figley (New York: Brunner/Mazel, 1978), 214, 215.

40. Scott, *Politics of Readjustment*, 17–18.

41. Shatan, "Grief of Soldiers," 648; Scott, *Politics of Readjustment*, 27, 43; Ben Shephard, *A War of Nerves: Soldiers and Psychiatrists 1914–1994* (London: Jonathan Cape, 2000), 358; Tom Wicker, "The Vietnam Disease," *New York Times*, May 27, 1975.

42. Lifton, *Home from the War*, 127–28.

43. "Veterans' Testimony on Vietnam," E 9978.

44. Charles R. Figley, "A Postscript: Welcoming Home the Strangers," in *Strangers at Home: Vietnam Veterans since the War*, ed. Figley and Seymour Leventman (New York: Praeger, 1980), 363. For confirmation of the subtext of the debates about "post-Vietnam syndrome," see Richard Halloran, "Psychiatrist Says 'Brutalizing' Vietnam War Causes Problems for Ex-G.I.'s," *New York Times*, November 26, 1970.

45. Shephard, *War of Nerves*, 369, 370.

46. Sarah V. Haley, "When the Patient Reports Atrocities: Specific Treatment Considerations of the Vietnam Veteran," *Archives of General Psychiatry* 30 (1974): 191–96.

47. Nicosia, *Home to War*, 188–95.

48. American Psychiatric Association, *Diagnostic and Statistical Manual of Mental Disorders*, 1st ed. (Washington, DC: American Psychiatric Association, 1952).

49. American Psychiatric Association, *Diagnostic and Statistical Manual of Mental Disorders*, 2nd ed. (Washington, DC: American Psychiatric Association, 1968); Figley, introduction to *Stress Disorders among*

Vietnam Veterans, xvii; John O. Lipkin, Raymond M. Scurfield, and Arthur S. Blank, "Post-Traumatic Stress Disorder in Vietnam Veterans: Assessment in a Forensic Setting," *Behavioral Sciences and the Law* 1, no. 3 (Summer 1983): 53.

50. Arthur S. Blank Jr., "Irrational Reactions to Post-Traumatic Stress Disorder," in *The Trauma of War: Stress and Recovery in Viet Nam Veterans*, ed. Stephen M. Sonnenberg, Arthur S. Blank Jr., and John A. Talbott (Washington, DC: American Psychiatric Press, 1985), 74; Joel Osler Brende and Erwin Randolph Parson, *Vietnam Veterans: The Road to Recovery* (New York: Plenum Press, 1986), 175; Sarah Haley, "Treatment Implications of Post-Combat Stress Response Syndromes for Mental Health Professionals," in Figley, *Stress Disorders among Vietnam Veterans*, 257–58; Scott, *Politics of Readjustment*, 63.

51. Allan Young, *The Harmony of Illusions: Inventing Post-Traumatic Stress Disorder* (Princeton, NJ: Princeton University Press, 1995), 109–10; Shephard, *War of Nerves*, 366; Scott, *Politics of Readjustment*, 59–61. In 1975, Congress mandated the first large-scale study of the needs of Vietnam veterans. The VA funded the study, published as Arthur Egendorf, Charles Kadushin, Robert S. Laufer, George Rothbart, and Lee Sloan, *Legacies of Vietnam: Comparative Adjustment of Veterans and Their Peers*, 5 vols. (Washington, DC: U.S. Government Printing Office, 1981).

52. Lifton, *Home from the War*, 16; Robert Jay Lifton, *Death in Life: Survivors of Hiroshima*, rev. ed. (1968; repr., Chapel Hill: University of North Carolina Press, 1991), 479.

53. Shephard, *War of Nerves*, 361.

54. Scott, *Politics of Readjustment*, 59–66; Figley, introduction to *Stress Disorders among Vietnam Veterans*, xix.

55. American Psychiatric Association, *Diagnostic and Statistical Manual of Mental Disorders*, 3rd. ed. (Washington, DC: American Psychiatric Association, 1980), 236–39.

56. Patricia B. Sutker, Madeline Uddo-Crane, and Albert N. Allain Jr., "Clinical and Research Assessment of Posttraumatic Stress Disorder: A Conceptual Overview," *Psychological Assessment* 3, no. 4 (1991): 524; Rachel Yehuda and Alexander C. McFarlane, "Conflict between Current Knowledge about Posttraumatic Stress Disorder and Its Original Conceptual Basis," *American Journal of Psychiatry* 152, no. 12 (December 1995): 1706–7. For further criticisms of PTSD's intellectual foundations and for a defense of the concept, see Young, *Harmony of Illusions*, 115–16, 124; Blank, "Irrational Reactions to Post-Traumatic Stress Disorder," 78–79.

57. Dean, *Shook over Hell*, 15; Young, *Harmony of Illusions*, 129. In August 2006, a re-examination of the data in the 1988 National Vietnam Veterans Readjustment Study (one of two large-scale studies of Vietnam veterans' readjustment problems) reduced the lifetime rate of PTSD among Vietnam veterans from around 30 percent to 18.7 percent. Bruce P. Dohrenwend et al., "The Psychological Risks of Vietnam for U.S. Veterans: A Revisit with New Data and Methods," *Science* 313, no. 5789 (August 18, 2006): 979–82; Benedict Carey, "Review of Landmark Study Finds Fewer Vietnam Veterans with Post-Traumatic Stress," *New York Times*, August 18, 2006.

58. American Psychiatric Association, *Diagnostic and Statistical Manual of Mental Disorders*, 3rd ed., 238.

59. Chaim Shatan, "Have You Hugged a Vietnam Veteran Today? The Basic Wound of Catastrophic Stress," in William E. Kelly, ed., *Post-Traumatic Stress Disorder and the War Veteran Patient* (New York: Brunner/Mazel, 1985), 18. Shatan had first made the comparison in 1971 as a result of "similar clinical symptoms and findings" about Vietnam veterans and the survivors of death camps and concentration camps.

60. Lifton, *Home from the War*, 436.

61. "Veterans' Testimony on Vietnam," E 9978, 9982, 9979. Jonathan Schell concurred, writing in his introduction to "The Military Half," that all Americans must share the responsibility for the war, not just those who bear arms. Schell, *Real War*, 192.

62. Dean, *Shook over Hell*, 183. For relevant discussions of international law and the law of war, see Taylor, *Nuremberg and Vietnam*; Michael Walzer, *Just and Unjust Wars: A Moral Argument with Historical Illustrations* (New York: Basic Books, 1977); Sidney Axinn, *A Moral Military* (Philadelphia: Temple University Press, 1989).

63. Seventy-nine percent agreed that the sentence was "too harsh." Question R3, Gallup Organization poll of a national adult sample conducted by telephone for *Newsweek* magazine in April 1971; data provided by RC.

64. Question R2, ibid.

65. Question R17A, Louis Harris and Associates, poll of a national adult sample conducted in February 1971; data provided by RC.

66. Michael Sallah and Mitch Weiss, *Tiger Force: A True Story of Men and War* (Boston: Little, Brown, 2006); Nick Turse and Deborah Nelson, "Civilian Killings Went Unpunished," *Los Angeles Times*, August 6, 2006; Deborah Nelson and Nick Turse, "A Tortured Past," *Los Angeles Times*, August 20, 2006; Nicholas

Turse, "'Kill Anything That Moves': United States War Crimes and Atrocities in Vietnam, 1965–1973" (Ph.D. diss., Columbia University, 2005); Deborah Nelson, *The War behind Me* (New York: Basic Books, 2008).

67. Question R29A asked respondents to agree or disagree with the statement, "It is unfair to find Lt. Calley guilty and not put higher-ups on trial who gave Calley his orders?" Harris survey, April 1971, data provided by RC.

68. "Calley Verdict: Who Else Is Guilty?" *Newsweek*, April 12, 1971; "The Clamor Over Calley: Who Shares the Guilt?" *Time*, April 12, 1971, www.time.com/time/magazine/article/0,9171,904957-11,00.html (accessed April 11, 2007); Greenhaw, *Making of a Hero*, 189–90.

69. Belknap, *Vietnam War on Trial*, 195; Bilton and Sim, *Four Hours in My Lai*, 340; W. L. Calley, *Body Count: Lieutenant Calley's Story as Told to John Sack* (London: Hutchison, 1971), 15–16; Jep Cadou, "'I May Be Guilty'—Whitcomb," *Indianapolis Star*, April 2, 1971; Greenhaw, *Making of a Hero*, 191–93.

70. Rowland Evans Jr. and Robert D. Novak, *Nixon in the White House: The Frustration of Power* (New York: Random House, 1971), 394.

71. Belknap, *Vietnam War on Trial*, 213; Kendrick Oliver, *The My Lai Massacre in American History and Memory* (Manchester: Manchester University Press, 2006), 110.

72. Peter P. Mahoney, "Calley and That Old Bitterness," in Barry, *Peace Is Our Profession*, 104.

73. Quoted in James Reston Jr., *Sherman's March and Vietnam* (New York: Macmillan, 1984), 168. See also Nancy Zaroulis and Gerald Sullivan, *Who Spoke Up? American Protest against the War in Vietnam, 1963–1975* (Garden City, NY: Doubleday, 1984), 355.

74. Transcript of the National Educational Television documentary *Nuremberg and Vietnam: Who Is Guilty?* 23, box 6, Executive Producers Series, "Nuremberg and Vietnam" folder, Vietnam: A Television History Collection, Joseph P. Healey Library, University of Massachusetts, Boston.

75. "Clamor Over Calley," 3.

76. Zaroulis and Sullivan, *Who Spoke Up?* 356. Kerry and most of the VVA leadership opposed this move, thinking that if the veterans were arrested (for a public-order offense, not for war crimes) it would damage VVAW's positive public image. Nicosia, *Home to War*, 126–27.

77. Nicholas Turse, "Swift Boat Swill: From the National Archives: New Proof of Vietnam War Atrocities," available under "Swift Boat Swill" at www.villagevoice.com/ (accessed November 2, 2006).

78. Kerry/O'Neill Debate, *The Dick Cavett* Show, ABC television, June 30, 1971, transcript, ice. he.net/~freepnet/kerry/index.php?topic=KerryONeill (accessed January 19, 2007).

79. Neil Sheehan, "Taylor Says by Yamashita Ruling Westmoreland May Be Guilty," *New York Times*, January 9, 1971. For further discussion, see Patrick Hagopian, "The Social Memory of the Vietnam War" (Ph.D. diss., Johns Hopkins University, 1994), 141–218.

80. This legal standard is set out in the 1956 U. S. Army Field Regulations and is consistent with international law and the precedents set in the post–World War II tribunals. Taylor, *Nuremberg and Vietnam*, 53, 182; Axinn, *Moral Military*, 129. A fuller explication of the content and relevance of the 1956 field regulations can be found in Col. Jared B. Schopper, "Lessons from My Lai," U.S. Army War College essay, Carlisle Barracks, April 14, 1973, 3–4.

81. In late 1967, Jonathan Schell told Secretary of Defense McNamara of what he had learned about U.S. forces' abuse of civilians in Quang Ngai province. McNamara arranged for Schell to read his handwritten manuscript into a Dictaphone to be transcribed by Pentagon typists. Ambassador Ellsworth Bunker showed the typescript to William Westmoreland in December 1967. (Schell's reporting was later published in the *New Yorker* and republished as "The Military Half," in Schell, *Real War*, 189–398.) Jonathan Schell, personal communication with the author; William Westmoreland, *A Soldier Reports* (New York: Da Capo, 1989), 288. Westmoreland was sufficiently concerned about the article's content that he asked the U.S. Embassy in Saigon to conduct an investigation, which established that Schell's report was "exaggerated" but contained "truth enough" for concern. For a summary of the findings of the investigation by the embassy official James Hataway, see Research File—Individuals; Bunker, Ellsworth—Notes; Neil Sheehan Papers, Manuscript Division, Library of Congress, Washington, DC.

82. Westmoreland, *Soldier Reports*, 288. Westmoreland's conclusion that "it was inevitable that some crimes of violence against civilians would occur" seems horribly correct under the circumstances (ibid.). In the documentary film *Hearts and Minds*, dir. Peter Davis (1974), Westmoreland states that, in Vietnam, "life is plentiful; life is cheap." This was not a slip of the tongue. Responding to a criticism that he cherry-picked the quotation, the director Peter Davis said that he shot three takes of the interview and Westmoreland made the same remark each time. Derrick Z. Jackson, "The Westmoreland Mind-Set," *International Herald Tribune*, July 22, 2005.

83. Quoted in Oliver, *My Lai Massacre*, 137, 139.

84. The approval rating for Nixon's handling of the Vietnam War had peaked at 77 percent after the November 1969 "silent majority" speech and had remained above 60 percent until January 1970. By

April 1970, it had slid to 46 percent. Gallup Organization polls of national adult samples, November 1969, January 1970, and April 1970; data provided by RC.

85. "General Thoughts on Presidential Intervention" and "Uniform Code of Military Justice," unsigned reports in "Tom Pauken" file, John W. Dean III, box 92, Staff Member and Office Files, White House Special Files, National Archives Nixon Presidential Materials Project, National Archives, College Park, MD; John Dean, memorandum for John Ehrlichman and H. R. Haldeman, April 1, 1971, "Calley—April–May '71" file, box 14, National Archives Nixon Presidential Materials Project; Tom Pauken, memorandum to John Dean, May 11, 1971, "War Crimes Study [Calley]," John W. Dean III, box 15; Perlstein, *Nixonland*, 556.

86. Richard Nixon, *RN: The Memoirs of Richard Nixon* (London: Book Club Associates, 1978), 500; Bilton and Sim, *Four Hours in My Lai*, 342–46; Belknap, *Vietnam War on Trial*, 193–208. For Nixon's attempts to block investigations of alleged crimes by U.S. personnel in Vietnam, see Richard Reeves, *President Nixon: Alone in the White House* (New York: Simon and Schuster, 2001), 217–18.

87. Opinion Research Corporation, telephone surveys of national adult samples conducted April 1, 1971, and April 5–6, 1971. The privately commissioned polls bore out the findings of publicly released Harris polls. Louis Harris and Associates survey of a national adult sample conducted April 1971; data provided by RC. Reeves, *President Nixon*, 307–8; Oliver, *My Lai Massacre*, 162; Scott Shane, "A Quest to Unmask the 'Brilliant, Devious' Duo," *International Herald Tribune*, April 19, 2007; Belknap, *Vietnam War on Trial*, 251; Olson and Roberts, *My Lai*, 162.

88. Quoted in John Helmer, *Bringing the War Home: The American Soldier in Vietnam and After* (New York: Free Press, 1974), 204n55.

89. For an account of what went wrong with the prosecution of Calley's superior Captain Ernest Medina, see Bilton and Sim, *Four Hours in My Lai*, 348–49; Belknap, *Vietnam War on Trial*, 229–32. They cite the skills of Medina's defense team, bias by the judge, and poor preparation of the prosecution case. For the prosecutor William Eckhardt's account of the trial, see David L. Anderson, *Facing My Lai: Moving Beyond the Massacre* (Lawrence: University Press of Kansas, 1998), 43–46.

90. Scott, *Politics of Readjustment*, 19.

91. Steven M. Silver, "Post-Traumatic Stress and the Death Imprint: The Search for a New Mythos," in Kelly, *Post-Traumatic Stress Disorder*, 45, 48.

92. Jim Goodwin, "The Etiology of Combat Related Post-Traumatic Stress Disorders," in *Vietnam: The Battle Comes Home; A Photographic Record of Post-Traumatic Stress with Selected Essays*, ed. Nancy Howell-Koehler, with photos by Gordon Baer (Dobbs Ferry, NY: Morgan and Morgan, 1984), 18.

93. Reston, *Sherman's March and Vietnam*, 185.

94. Ghislaine Boulanger, "Predisposition to Post-Traumatic Stress Disorder," in *The Vietnam Veteran Redefined: Fact and Fiction*, ed. Ghislaine Boulanger and Charles Kadushin (Hillsdale, NJ: Lawrence Erlbaum Associates, 1986), 50; Richard A. Kulka, William E. Schlenger, John A. Fairbank, Richard L. Hough, B. Kathleen Jordan, Charles R. Marmar, Daniel S. Weiss, and David A. Grady, *Trauma and the Vietnam War Generation: Report of Findings from the National Vietnam Veterans Readjustment Study* (New York: Brunner/Mazel, 1990), 84.

95. Robert H. Stretch, James D. Vail, and Joseph P. Maloney, "Posttraumatic Stress Disorder among Army Nurse Corps Vietnam Veterans," *Journal of Consulting and Clinical Psychology* 53, no. 5 (1985): 704–8; Robert H. Stretch, "Posttraumatic Stress Disorder among U.S. Army Reserve Vietnam and Vietnam–Era Veterans," *Journal of Consulting and Clinical Psychology* 53, no. 6 (1985): 935–36; Brende and Parson, *Vietnam Veterans*, 43–63. Parson coined the term *dysreception* to describe veterans' negative homecoming experiences. Erwin Randolph Parson, "The Reparation of the Self: Clinical and Theoretical Dimensions in the Treatment of Vietnam Combat Veterans," *Journal of Contemporary Psychotherapy* 14 (1984): 4–51, cited in Brende and Parson, *Vietnam Veterans*, 134.

96. Shephard, *War of Nerves*, 201, 244–45.

97. Shatan, "Grief of Soldiers," 643.

98. Lipkin, Scurfield, and Blank, "Post-Traumatic Stress Disorder in Vietnam Veterans," 54.

99. Shephard, *War of Nerves*, 348; Dean, *Shook over Hell*, 40; "Dividend from Vietnam," *Time*, October 10, 1969, www.time.com/time/magazine/article/0,9171,839053,00.html (accessed March 1, 2007).

100. Ronald Bitzer, "Caught in the Middle: Mentally Disabled Veterans and the Veterans Administration," in Figley and Leventman, *Strangers at Home*, 306; Ghislaine Boulanger, introduction to *Long Term Stress Reactions: Some Causes, Consequences, and Naturally Occurring Support Systems*, by Charles Kadushin, Ghislaine Boulanger, and John Martin, vol. 4 of Egendorf et al., *Legacies of Vietnam*, 479.

101. Jim Goodwin, *Readjustment Problems among Vietnam Veterans* (Cincinnati: Disabled American Veterans, [1971]), 6–10; Shatan, "Grief of Soldiers," 645.

102. Nicosia, *Home to War*, 200; Ronald H. Spector, *After Tet: The Bloodiest Year in Vietnam* (New York: Vintage Books, 1993), 277.

103. Arthur Egendorf, *Healing from the War: Trauma and Transformation after Vietnam* (Boston: Houghton Mifflin, 1985), 25; Hunt, *Turning*, 52; U.S. Air Force veteran Charles Booth in the documentary *The Long Road Back*, prod. Britt Davis (Office of Instructional Resources, University of Kentucky, n.d., ca. 1985).

104. Figley, introduction to *Stress Disorders among Vietnam Veterans*, xxii.

105. William Broyles Jr., "Remembering a War We Want to Forget," *Newsweek*, November 22, 1982, 83.

106. Christian G. Appy, *Working-Class War: American Combat Soldiers and Vietnam* (Chapel Hill: University of North Carolina Press, 1993), 303. For other examples of the parable of social rejection, see Bob Greene, *Homecoming: When the Soldiers Returned from Vietnam* (New York: Ballantine, 1989). For a critical response to these stories as an "urban legend," see Jerry Lembcke, *The Spitting Image* (New York: New York University Press, 1998), 71–82.

107. James R. Wilson, *Landing Zones: Southern Veterans Remember Vietnam* (Durham: Duke University Press, 1990), 27, 52.

108. U.S. Congress, Senate, 92d Cong., 2d sess., Committee on Veterans' Affairs, *A Study of the Problems Facing Vietnam Era Veterans on Their Readjustment to Civilian Life* (Washington, DC: U.S. Government Printing Office, January 31, 1972), 10–13, table 5; Louis Harris and Associates, *Myths and Realities: A Study of Attitudes Toward Vietnam Era Veterans* (Washington, DC: Veterans Administration, 1980), 22–24, tables I-5d–g.

109. Louis Harris and Associates, *Myths and Realities*, 77, table III-11.

110. Brende and Parson, *Vietnam Veterans*, 58.

111. *Study of the Problems Facing Vietnam Era Veterans*, 18.

112. Ibid., 6, table 3.

113. Louis Harris and Associates, *Myths and Realities*, 91, table IV-5.

114. MacPherson, *Long Time Passing*, 70.

115. Robert Brewin, "TV's Newest Villain: The Vietnam Veteran," *TV Guide*, July 19, 1975, 5. See also Charles Moskos, "Surviving the War in Vietnam," and Paul Camacho, "From War Hero to War Criminal: The Negative Privilege of the Vietnam Veteran," in Figley and Leventman, *Strangers at Home*, 83 and 269–70.

116. Silver, "Post-Traumatic Stress," 48; Victor J. DeFazio, "Dynamic Perspectives on the Nature and Effects of Combat Stress," in Figley, *Stress Disorders among Vietnam Veterans*, 32; Elizabeth M. Norman, "The Victims Who Survived," *American Journal of Nursing* 82, no. 11 (November 1982): 1696.

117. Jason Katzman, "From Outcast to Cliché: How Film Shaped, Warped, and Developed the Image of the Vietnam Veteran, 1967–1990," in *The United States and the Vietnam War: Significant Scholarly Articles*, ed. Walter L. Hixson (New York: Garland, 2000)," 221. See also Dane Archer and Rosemary Gartner, "The Myth of the Violent Veteran," *Psychology Today*, December 1976, 94–96; Tim O'Brien, "The Violent Vet," *Esquire*, December 1979, 96–104. Desmond Ryan wrote, "For years, the Vietnam veteran was the first resort of any hack screenwriter who needed a motive for a deranged killer or just an all-purpose psychopath." "How Hollywood Fought the War," *Philadelphia Inquirer Magazine*, January 13, 1988.

118. Seymour Leventman, "Epilogue: Social and Historical Perspectives on the Vietnam Veteran," in Figley, *Stress Disorders among Vietnam Veterans*, 294.

119. Brewin, "TV's Newest Villain," 6.

120. As Jason Katzman shows, in feature films from 1975 to 1979, the Vietnam veteran "became a shameful character, a man itching for the chance to do something violent." This period overlapped with a subsequent phase, from 1977 to 1984, when veterans garnered more sympathy. Katzman, "From Outcast to Cliché," 219.

121. *Taxi Driver*, dir. Martin Scorsese (1976).

122. *Apocalypse Now*, dir. Francis Ford Coppola (1979).

123. *Coming Home*, dir. Hal Ashby (1978). Nicosia, *Home to War*, 321; Lembcke, *Spitting Image*, 163, 172. For the background to the commissioning of the script, see Thomas Kiernan, *Jane Fonda* (London: Granada, 1983), 352–54; Jane Fonda, *My Life So Far* (London: Ebury Press, 2005), 360–61, 367–68.

124. *The Deer Hunter*, dir. Michael Cimino (1978). Bruce Franklin suggests that this is one of a number of scenes that invert well-known images of the war: in this case, Eddie Adams's photograph of General Loan shooting a Viet Cong suspect. Franklin, *M.I.A. or Mythmaking in America*, 135. For further discussion of this photograph, see Patrick Hagopian, "Vietnam War Photography as a Locus of Memory," in *Locating Memory: Photographic Acts*, ed. Annette Kuhn and Kirsten McAllister (New York: Berghahn Books, 2006).

125. Figley, "Postscript," 365.

126. Tim O'Brien, *If I Die in a Combat Zone* (New York: Delacorte, 1973); Caputo, *Rumor of War*; Ron Kovic, *Born on the Fourth of July* (New York: Pocket Books, 1977).

127. Louis Harris and Associates, *Myths and Realities*, 304.

128. Donald E. Johnson, the head of the VA, testified before Cranston's subcommittee that "the Vietnam veteran generally did not come home in a peculiar state of mind" and that there were fewer psychiatric patients in the Vietnam War than in other wars. Halloran, "Psychiatrist Says 'Brutalizing' Vietnam War Causes Problems."

129. Richard B. Fuller, "War Veterans' Post-Traumatic Stress Disorder and the U.S. Congress," in Kelly, *Post-Traumatic Stress Disorder,* 5. Cranston's VFW speech is quoted in Polner, *No Victory Parades,* 143.

130. Fuller, "War Veterans' Post-Traumatic Stress Disorder," 6.

131. Memorandum signed by the chair of the Board of Veterans Appeals, August 18, 1978, published as "Appendix to Chapter 16," in Figley and Leventman, *Strangers at Home,* 321–23.

132. Jill Moyer, "Whatever Happened to G.I. Joe?" *Pittsburgh Magazine,* October [1979], 38, clipping in "Pittsburgh War Activities, Vietnam," Pennsylvania Room, Carnegie Library, Pittsburgh (year of publication, incorrectly inscribed; inferred from internal evidence).

133. Scott, *Politics of Readjustment,* 37–39, 70–71.

134. Paul Starr, *The Discarded Army: Veterans after Vietnam* (New York: Charterhouse, 1973), 97.

135. VA staff had found that black Vietnam veterans tended to avoid the VA hospital system. Horowitz and Solomon, "Delayed Stress Response Syndromes in Vietnam Veterans," 271.

136. W. Peter Sax, "Establishing a Post-Traumatic Stress Disorder Inpatient Program," in Kelly, *Post-Traumatic Stress Disorder,* 237.

137. R. Carl Sipprelle, "A Vet Center Experience: Multievent Trauma, Delayed Treatment Type,"in *Treating PTSD: Cognitive-Behavioral Strategies,* ed. David W. Foy (New York: Guilford Press, 1992), 13, 27.

138. Young, *Harmony of Illusions,* 221–22.

139. Peter Marin, "Living in Moral Pain," in *The Vietnam Reader,* ed. Walter Capps (New York: Routledge, 1991), 45; Shephard, *War of Nerves,* 374.

140. Shapiro, "Working through the War," 179.

141. John Russell Smith, "Individual Psychotherapy with Viet Nam Veterans," in Sonnenberg, Blank, and Talbott, *Trauma of War,* 153.

142. Nicosia, *Home to War,* 516, 527.

143. Ibid., 531–55.

144. Blank, "Irrational Reactions to Post-Traumatic Stress Disorder," 87.

145. As of May 2008, there were 232 vet centers around the country, serving the needs of veterans of the wars in Iraq and Afghanistan as well as Vietnam veterans. www.vetcenter.va.gov/ (accessed May 31, 2008).

146. Nicosia, *Home to War,* 536–38.

147. Chester Paul Adams and Jack McCloskey, "Twice Born Men," in *Beyond Clinic Walls,* ed. A. B. Tulipan and C. L. Attneave (Tuscaloosa: University of Alabama Press, 1974), cited in Brende and Parson, *Vietnam Veterans,* 180.

148. Stacewicz, *Winter Soldiers,* 217.

149. Jimmy Carter, "Remarks at a White House Reception, May 30, 1979," APP, www.presidency.ucsb.edu/ws/?pid=32409 (accessed June 16, 2007).

150. Stacewicz, *Winter Soldiers,* 98.

151. Nicosia, *Home to War,* 540–50.

152. Ibid., 512, 528–29, 550–55.

153. Gloria Emerson noted early on that "trauma of Vietnam is a popular expression, a convenient one for writers in magazines and newspapers." Emerson, *Winners and Losers: Battles, Retreats, Gains, Losses, and Ruins from the Vietnam War* (New York: Harcourt Brace Jovanovich, 1976), 112. For a critique of the popular discourse of "healing" and "closure," see Ellen Goodman, "Let's Drop the Jargon of Efficient Mourning," *International Herald Tribune,* January 7, 1998.

154. Robert D. Heinl, "The Collapse of the Armed Forces," *Armed Forces Journal,* June 7, 1971; reprinted in *Vietnam and America: A Documented History,* ed. Marvin E. Gettleman, Jane Franklin, Marilyn B. Young, and H. Bruce Franklin, 2nd ed. (New York: Grove Press, 1995), 326–35; quotation on p. 330.

155. Paul M. Kattenburg, *The Vietnam Trauma in American Foreign Policy, 1945–75* (New Brunswick, NJ: Transaction Books, 1982).

156. Peter N. Carroll, *It Seemed Like Nothing Happened: America in the 1970s* (New Brunswick, NJ: Rutgers University Press, 1990), 72.

157. Joan A. Furey, "For Some, the War Rages On," *American Journal of Nursing* 82, no. 11 (November 1982): 1696.

158. Linda Kay Vandenberg, "Amnesty," in Barry, *Peace Is Our Profession,* 203.

159. Lifton, *Home from the War,* 447.

160. Howard Wolinsky, "Draft Resister Looks Back, Too," *Chicago Sun-Times,* June 14, 1986.

161. Jeffrey Jay, "After Vietnam: In Pursuit of Scapegoats," *Harper's*, July 1978, quoted in Nicosia, *Home to War*, 382.

162. Louis Harris and Associates, *Myths and Realities*, 49.

163. Egendorf et al., *Legacies of Vietnam*, quoted in John Wheeler, *Touched with Fire: The Future of the Vietnam Generation* (New York: Avon Books, 1984), 185–86.

164. Harry Wilmer, "The Healing Nightmare: A Study of the War Dreams of Vietnam Combat Veterans," in *Unwinding the Vietnam War: From War into Peace*, ed. Reese Williams (Seattle: Real Comet Press, 1987), 73.

165. Carl A. Trocki, "Why Remind Ourselves of the Vietnam War?" in Howell-Koehler, *Vietnam*, 11.

166. Sax, "Establishing a Post-Traumatic Stress Disorder Inpatient Program," 247.

167. Francis Ford Coppola answered political criticism of *Apocalypse Now* by saying he was "cauterizing old wounds." Ryan, "How Hollywood Fought the War," 34. See also Reston, *Sherman's March and Vietnam*, 5.

168. Shatan, "Have You Hugged a Vietnam Veteran Today?" 27.

169. Appy, *Working-Class War*, 8–9.

170. *Fortunate Son: The Autobiography of Lewis B. Puller Jr.*, excerpted in Olson and Roberts, *My Lai*, 187.

171. "Viet Nam: The Soldier in the Field" (panel discussion at "Viet Nam 20 Years After: Voices of the War" conference at Hampden-Sydney College, VA, September 17, 1993). For a discussion of the panel, see Theodore M. Lieverman, "When the Truth Is Found," *Viet Nam Generation* 6, nos. 1–2 (1995): 71–73.

172. See, e.g., David Anderson, ed., *Facing My Lai: Moving beyond the Massacre* (Lawrence: University Press of Kansas, 1998), 126.

173. MacPherson, *Long Time Passing*, 369.

174. Jeremiah Murphy, "A Type Some Say Is Overlooked: The Well-Adjusted Vietnam Vet," *Boston Globe*, August 6, 1983.

175. A journalist found that a number of Vietnam veteran interviewees said that Calley had been scapegoated for following orders. One of them said (in her paraphrase), "There, but for fortune, were any of the grunts who slogged through the rice paddies, following orders and doing the admittedly horrible business of war." Abby Mendelson, "Coming Home as the Deer Hunter," *Pittsburgh*, July 1979, 41.

176. Message from smtp%vwar-l@ubvm.cc.buffalo.edu to Multiple recipients of list VWAR-L, posted March 6, 1996. Print-out in possession of the author.

177. Ibid., posted March 3, 1996.

178. See, e.g., Anderson, *Facing My Lai*; Lawrence A. Tritle, *From Melos to My Lai: War and Survival* (New York: Routledge, 2000); Oliver, *My Lai Massacre*; Heonik Kwon, *After the Massacre: Commemoration and Consolation in Ha My and My Lai* (Berkeley: University of California Press, 2006); Claude Cookman, "An American Atrocity: The My Lai Massacre Concretized in a Victim's Face," *Journal of American History* 94, no. 1 (June 2007): 154–62.

179. Brende and Parson, *Vietnam Veterans*, 99.

180. Many Vietnam veterans today would dispute this claim. See, e.g., B. G. Burkett and Glenna Whitley, *Stolen Valor: How the Vietnam Generation Was Robbed of Its Heroes and Its History* (Dallas: Verity Press, 1998), 305–8.

181. Marin, "Living in Moral Pain," 45.

182. Ibid., 44.

183. Dean, *Shook over Hell*, 199–200.

184. Richard Moser, *The New Winter Soldiers: GI and Veteran Dissent during the Vietnam Era* (New Brunswick, NJ: Rutgers University Press, 1996), 127; Stacewicz, *Winter Soldiers*, 346–93; Hunt, *Turning*, 157–65.

185. Lifton, *Home from the War*, 447.

3. The Discourse of Healing and the "Black Gash of Shame"

1. References to the *DSM-III* definition of PTSD began to appear in scholarly periodicals early in 1980. See, e.g., Mardi J. Horowitz, Nancy Wilner, Nancy Kaltreider, and William Alvarez, "Signs and Symptoms of Posttraumatic Stress Disorder," *Archives of General Psychiatry* 37, no. 1 (January 1980): 85–92.

2. The most well-known example was the long-delayed memorial to Franklin Delano Roosevelt. Nan Robertson, "Roosevelt Panel Abandons Design," *New York Times*, January 22, 1965; Grace Glueck, "Roosevelt Memorial: Finally, a Plan Is Set," *New York Times*, July 18, 1978. The VVMF were well aware of the problems experienced by the FDR memorial. "Information on Other Competitions," a document prepared before the VVMF's press conference of May 6, 1981, box 67, VVMF-MD. The VVMF's founder was aware of an unsuccessful effort to create a Vietnam War memorial in 1973, when authorizing legislation passed in the Senate but failed in the House of Representatives. "Vietnam Monument Voted," *Washington*

Post, April 13, 1973; Library of Congress Thomas, thomas.loc.gov/cgi-bin/bdquery/D?d093:45:./list/bss/d093SJ.lst:@@@R (accessed February 28, 2007); Jan Scruggs to H. Ross Perot, February 13, 1980, box 30, VVMF-MD.

3. Chris Buckley, "The Wall," *Esquire*, September 1985, 64, 68; Elisabeth Bumiller, "The Memorial, Mirror of Vietnam," *Washington Post*, November 9, 1984; Tom Wolfe, "Art Disputes War: The Battle of the Vietnam Veterans Memorial," *Washington Post*, October 13, 1982. Another writer describes Scruggs as "the son of a waitress and a milkman, . . . an Army enlisted man out of Bowie, Maryland," who, after the war, had "drifted for a while, put himself through college, then got a job with the Labor Department." Robert Timberg, *The Nightingale's Song* (New York: Simon and Schuster, 1995), 308. See also Tom Morganthau and Mary Lord, "Honoring Vietnam Veterans—At Last," *Newsweek*, November 22, 1982, 81; Kurt Andersen and Jay Branegan, "A Homecoming at Last," *Time*, November 22, 1982, 45; Philip Geyelin, "The Vietnam Memorial (Cont'd.?)," *Washington Post*, January 11, 1983. A rare exception to the general parroting of the official line that Scruggs was an ordinary "grunt" appears in Robin Wagner-Pacifici and Barry Schwartz, "The Vietnam Veterans Memorial: Commemorating a Difficult Past," *American Journal of Sociology* 97, no. 2 (September 1991): 390–91.

4. Lydia Fish, *The Last Firebase: A Guide to the Vietnam Veterans Memorial* (Shippensburg, PA: White Mane, 1987), 2.

5. Jan C. Scruggs and Joel L. Swerdlow, *To Heal a Nation: The Vietnam Veterans Memorial* (New York: Harper and Row, 1985), 7.

6. Keith Beattie, *The Scar That Binds: American Culture and the Vietnam War* (New York: New York University Press, 1998), 46; Fred Turner, *Echoes of Combat: The Vietnam War in American Memory* (New York: Anchor Books, 1996), 171–72. See also Elizabeth Hess, "Vietnam: Memorials of Misfortune," in *Unwinding the Vietnam War*, ed. Reese Williams (Seattle: Real Comet Press, 1987), 262–80, 263.

7. Scruggs and Swerdlow, *To Heal a Nation*, 7–10. This story was frequently repeated, as a sign of the memorial's early struggles and the inexperience of its leaders. See, e.g., the untitled editorial in the *Des Moines Register*, November 11, 1982; Rick Atkinson, "Viet Veterans Memorial under Fire," *Kansas City Star*, December 16, 1981; Bumiller, "Memorial"; Buckley, "The Wall," 66; Gerald Posner, *Citizen Perot: His Life and Times* (New York: Random House, 2006), 140; Jenny Edkins, *Trauma and the Memory of Politics* (Cambridge: Cambridge University Press, 2003), 74.

8. Jan C. Scruggs, "We Were Young. We Have Died. Remember Us," *Washington Post*, November 11, 1979. The article's title is borrowed from Archibald MacLeish's frequently quoted poem "The Young Dead Soldiers."

9. Jan Scruggs, testimony, minutes of the Commission of Fine Arts meeting, October 13, 1981, 49, records of the Commission of Fine Arts, Washington, DC.

10. Scruggs, "We Were Young." The tale of the scorned amputee is an often-repeated story complaining of the unfairness of public disdain for returning veterans. It originally appeared in the preface to Fred Downs, *The Killing Zone* (New York: Berkley Books, 1983), [xi].

11. Jan Scruggs, remarks following "Memorials and Remembrance" panel, at a conference titled "Vietnam Legacies: Twenty Years after the Fall of Saigon," University of California, Davis, April 26, 1995; Jan Scruggs, interview by Steve Roberts, *The Diane Rehm Show*, National Public Radio, May 29, 1995; Jan Scruggs, interview in the documentary *Vietnam Veterans Memorial: The Last Landing Zone*, prod. Bob Muller (All-American Video Productions, Inc., 1994); Jan C. Scruggs, foreword to *The Wall: A Day at the Vietnam Veterans Memorial*, by Peter Meyer and the editors of *Life* (New York: St. Martin's Press, A Thomas Dunne Book, 1993), 5; Jan Scruggs, draft of June 24, 1982, speech to Vietnam Veterans of New Mexico, box 53, VVMF-MD; "Vietnam Veterans Memorial Fund, Inc.," publicity flyer, n.d., VVMF-MD; Scruggs, testimony, Commission of Fine Arts, October 13, 1981.

12. Margaret W. Freivogel, "Vietnam War Memorial 'Rescued,'" *St Louis Post-Dispatch*, February 14, 1982.

13. Scruggs, foreword to Meyer et al., *The Wall*, 5.

14. Scruggs, U.C. Davis conference remarks; Jan C. Scruggs, Alan L. Berman, and Carole Hoage, "The Vietnam Veteran: A Preliminary Analysis of Psychosocial Status," *Military Medicine* 145 (April 1980): 267–69. Scruggs presented testimony based on an earlier version of the paper before the Senate Subcommittee on Health and Readjustment on June 22, 1977. An unpublished version of the paper is cited in Ronald Bitzer, "Caught in the Middle: Mentally Disabled Veterans and the Veterans Administration," in *Strangers at Home: Vietnam Veterans since the War*, ed. Charles R. Figley and Seymour Leventman (New York: Praeger, 1980), 313, 320n37.

15. Gerald Nicosia, *Home to War: A History of the Vietnam Veterans' Movement* (New York: Three Rivers Press, 2001), 383.

16. Jan Craig Scruggs, "Forgotten Veterans of 'That Peculiar War,'" *Washington Post*, May 25, 1977.

See also Scruggs, "The Building of the Vietnam Memorial," op ed column distributed by Newspaper Enterprise Association, March 25, 1985.

17. Scruggs, UC Davis conference remarks.

18. Charles R. Figley, quoted in Tom Wicker, "The Vietnam Disease," *New York Times*, May 27, 1975.

19. Charles R. Figley, "A Postscript: Welcoming Home the Strangers," in Figley and Leventman, *Strangers at Home*, 365.

20. Figley and Leventman, *Strangers at Home*, xxv.

21. Jimmy Carter, "Vietnam Era Veterans: Message to the Congress, October 10, 1978," in *Carter, 1978*, bk. 2, *PPP* (1979), 1737.

22. Laura Palmer, "The Wall," *GQ* 57, no. 7 (July 1987): 140. Although Scruggs made this statement to a number of journalists, only Laura Palmer, a writer highly attuned to the dynamics of post-traumatic experience, reported it.

23. *Statement of the Vietnam Veterans Memorial Fund, Inc., before the National Capital Memorial Advisory Committee*, October 24, 1979, 2, box 33, VVMF-MD.

24. Most of the ceremonies were local events. The first troops withdrawn under the Vietnamization program were greeted by a ticker-tape parade in Seattle, with a crowd yelling "Thank you," flags waving, and women pressing roses into the men's hands. "Joy in Seattle; Troops Withdrawn from Vietnam," *Time*, July 18, 1969, 15, cited in Eric T. Dean Jr., *Shook over Hell: Post-Traumatic Stress, Vietnam, and the Civil War* (Cambridge, MA: Harvard University Press, 1997), 9. See also "Vietnam Veterans Honored Upstate," *New York Times*, October 18, 1970; and the local New Jersey event honoring the returning prisoner of war George Croker, shown in the documentary *Hearts and Minds*, dir. Peter Davis (1974).

25. In appealing to sentiment, Scruggs repeatedly stressed the youth of those who served in Vietnam: innocents sent into battle by a government and society that did not care enough for their young to give them due recognition when they returned from the war. Scruggs, "Our Purposes and Objectives," in a VVMF fund-raising brochure, n.d, in the author's possession. See also Rick Atkinson, *The Long Gray Line: From West Point to Vietnam and After; The Turbulent Odyssey of the Class of 1966* (New York: Pocket Books, 1989), 564.

26. VVMF, "Tribute to Honor: A History," in *Program Souvenir, National Salute to Vietnam Veterans, November 10–14, 1982, Washington, DC* (McLean, VA: Tyl Associates, [1982]), 5.

27. Wagner-Pacifici and Schwartz, "Vietnam Veterans Memorial," 386.

28. Jimmy Carter, "Vietnam Veterans Week: Remarks at a White House Reception," May 30, 1979, APP, www.presidency.ucsb.edu/ws/?pid=32409 (accessed June 16, 2007).

29. Scruggs and Swerdlow, *To Heal a Nation*, 8–10; *Vietnam Veterans Memorial: The Last Landing Zone*.

30. Mary McLeod, "The Battle for the Monument: The Vietnam Veterans Memorial," in *The Experimental Tradition: Essays on Competitions in Architecture*, ed. Hélène Lipstadt (New York, 1989), 116.

31. R. W. Doubek to Lewis Belcher Jr., February 18, 1980, 1. The letter was in the files of the Washington State Department of Veterans Affairs, Olympia, when the author visited in July 1991; a photocopy is in the author's possession.

32. Wheeler's first name is John, although he frequently appears in documents as Jack. For consistency's sake, he appears throughout this narrative as Jack, except in citations of his publications, where his name appears as on the title page. Wheeler was politically well-connected, having helped to organize the Jimmy Carter inaugural. Atkinson, *Long Gray Line*, 565.

33. Statement by Jack Wheeler, Council of Vietnam Veterans, Inc., "Vietnam Veterans and Their Supporters Describe the Nation's Lack of Response," June 28, 1978, 2, document sent by Stuart F. Feldman to Richard G. Darman, assistant to the president, November 8, 1982, casefile 111189, Reagan Library. Feldman was counsel to the Council of Vietnam Veterans, a precursor to Vietnam Veterans of America.

34. See the pen portraits in Timberg, *Nightingale's Song*, 309; Atkinson, *Long Gray Line*, 444–49. For further sketches of significant personalities involved in the argument about the memorial's design, see Bumiller, "Memorial"; R. Horowitz, "The Memorial—A Year Later," *Baltimore Sun*, November 14, 1983; Atkinson, *Long Gray Line*, 563–603. Jack Wheeler was exhausted and sank into depression after helping to create the memorial. John Wheeler, "Offerings at the Wall," *Washington Post*, September 13, 1992.

35. Atkinson, *Long Gray Line*, 162.

36. Tom Carhart, *The Offering* (New York: Warner Books, 1987), 49–78; Michael Sallah and Mitch Weiss, *Tiger Force: A True Story of Men and War* (New York: Little, Brown, 2006), 249, 373. Carhart commanded the force after the period of atrocities and other crimes covered by Sallah and Weiss.

37. Bumiller, "Memorial." Carhart later regretted the statement and said that it had been taken out of context. "'The Memorial, The Mirror': A Reply," letter to the editor, *Washington Post*, November 12, 1984.

38. Carhart, *Offering*, 57, 63, 109, 143, 271–72; Atkinson, *Long Gray Line*, 328–30, 341–45, 357–59, 577.

39. Atkinson, *Long Gray Line*, 564.

40. Buckley, "The Wall," 65.

41. Gary D. Solis, *Son Thang: An American War Crime* (New York: Bantam, 1998), 320.

42. Timberg, *Nightingale's Song*, 256–57; James Webb, *Fields of Fire* (New York: Pocket Books, 1978), 308, 392.

43. James H. Webb, "The Invisible Vietnam Veteran," *Washington Post*, August 4, 1976.

44. Timberg, *Nightingale's Song*, 256.

45. Atkinson, *Long Gray Line*, 579.

46. Ibid., 170, 350, 364, 373–74, 453, 588; Carhart, *Offering*, 79, 165.

47. John Wheeler, *Touched with Fire: The Future of the Vietnam Generation* (New York: Avon Books, 1984), 4, 108.

48. Atkinson, *Long Gray Line*, 554.

49. John Wheeler, memorandum, October 24, 1983, 7, VVMF-MD. Wheeler produced this narrative of his involvement in the Vietnam Veterans Memorial to assist Scruggs and Swerdlow with the research for their book *To Heal a Nation*.

50. Wheeler, memorandum, October 24, 1983, 7.

51. Scruggs and Swerdlow, *To Heal a Nation*, 15.

52. Atkinson, "Memorial under Fire."

53. "Senate Approves Memorial to Honor Vietnam Veterans," *Dallas Morning News*, May 4, 1980.

54. Scruggs and Swerdlow, *To Heal a Nation*, 39.

55. Atkinson, *Long Gray Line*, 575.

56. James Webb, "When a One-Armed Man Is Not a Loser," *Parade*, November 21, 1982, 27.

57. A. D. Horne, ed., *The Wounded Generation: America after Vietnam* (Englewood Cliffs, NJ: Prentice-Hall, 1981), 119–20.

58. Buckley, "The Wall," 65.

59. Scruggs and Swerdlow, *To Heal a Nation*, 17, 18, 36, 39; Atkinson, *Long Gray Line*, 573; Webb, "Invisible Vietnam Veteran."

60. John Dreyfuss, "In the Wake of Controversy: Vietnam Memorial Launched," *Los Angeles Times*, March 26, 1982; Jimmy Carter, "Vietnam Veterans Memorial Bill: Remarks on Signing S.J. Res. 119 into Law, July 1, 1980," in *Carter, May 24, 1980 to January 26, 1981, PPP* (1982), 1268–69.

61. Philip Caputo, *A Rumor of War* (New York: Ballantine, 1977), 212–13.

62. Horace, *Odes* 3.2, 13. The sentiment in Horace encourages soldiers to stand and fight, since death can seize hold of even those who flee.

63. Owen's poem describes the horrifying death of a soldier caught in a gas attack without his mask. *The Poems of Wilfred Owen*, ed. Edmund Blunden (London: Chatto and Windus, 1971), 66.

64. Carter, "Vietnam Veterans Week."

65. Carter, "Vietnam Veterans Memorial Bill," 1269.

66. Wheeler, *Touched with Fire*, 65. President Reagan, also echoing Caputo, said that veterans "were greeted by no parades, no bands, no waving of the flag they so proudly served." Ronald Reagan, "Remarks on Presenting the Medal of Honor to Master Sergeant Roy P. Benavidez," February 24, 1981, APP, www.presidency.ucsb.edu/ws/?pid=43454 (accessed June 16, 2007).

67. Scruggs and Swerdlow, *To Heal a Nation*, 40. Apparently going to the original source for the quotation rather than the presidential records, Scruggs quotes the passage from Caputo without Carter's omissions. Scruggs dates the event in May 1980, although the presidential records indicate that it took place the previous year.

68. Caputo, *Rumor of War*, 306, 309, 317, 325.

69. Scruggs, "We Were Young."

70. The 1990 public opinion poll asked, "Thinking of the American soldiers who lost their lives in the Vietnam War, do you think they died in vain or not?" Fifty-one percent believed they had died in vain; 41 percent believed they did not die in vain; 7 percent did not know, and 1 percent refused to respond. Gallup Organization poll, March 15–18, 1990; data provided by RC.

71. Jan Scruggs, letter to the editor, *Washington Star*, January 4, 1981.

72. Sandie Fauriol, "One Man's Dream Builds Nation's Tribute to Vietnam War Vets," *Fundraising Management*, November 1982, 24.

73. Scruggs and Swerdlow, *To Heal a Nation*, 49.

74. The other six elements were, "Trees and a spacious garden setting, inviting and hospitable to passers-by; a suitable size, approximately two acres; a system of chimes . . . to create an aural effect, but no visual disruptions; a display of the names of all of the 57,000 who died in Vietnam . . . ; artistic unity

throughout the entire memorial; good taste." All but the chimes survived in later elaborations of the concept. *Statement of the Vietnam Veterans Memorial Fund, Inc.*, October 24, 1979, 1–2.

75. J. Carter Brown, "The Vietnam Memorial Decision: 'Part of the Healing,'" *Washington Post*, October 16, 1982; Scruggs and Swerdlow, *To Heal a Nation*, 133.

76. *The Vietnam Veterans Memorial Design Competition: Design Program* (Washington, DC: VVMF, 1980). The jury members were the architects Pietro Belluschi and Harry Weese; the landscape architects Garrett Eckbo and Hideo Sasaki; the sculptors Richard Hunt, Constantino Nivola, and James Rosati; and Grady Clay, editor of *Landscape Architecture* magazine.

77. Atkinson, *Long Gray Line*, 582.

78. Paul Spreiregen, interview by the author, June 4, 1992; Grady Clay, "Discovery," *Harvard Magazine*, July–August 1985, 56D; McLeod, "Battle for the Monument," 118; "Information on Other Competitions," 4.

79. The readings for competition entrants were "After Vietnam: Voices of a Wounded Generation," *Washington Post*, May 25, 1980 (republished as Horne, *Wounded Generation*); Michael Charlton and Anthony Moncrieff, *Many Reasons Why: The American Involvement in Vietnam* (New York: Hill and Wang, 1978); Caputo, *Rumor of War*; Webb, *Fields of Fire*; Tim O'Brien, *Going after Cacciato* (New York: Dell, 1979); Tim O'Brien, *If I Die in a Combat Zone* (New York: Dell, 1974); Peter Braestrup, *Big Story: How the American Press and Television Reported and Interpreted the Crisis of Tet in 1968 in Vietnam and Washington* (New York: Doubleday, 1978); the works are listed in *Design Competition* (Washington, DC: Vietnam Veterans Memorial Fund, November 24, 1980), 6. At least three of the readings on this list were included in the "extensive list" for jurors. Scruggs, "Process for Selecting Design for National Vietnam Veterans Memorial," 3.

80. *Design Program*, 7, 16, 5.

81. Scruggs and Swerdlow, *To Heal a Nation*, 54.

82. Horne, *Wounded Generation*, 145.

83. "Draft General Secretaries' Statement on National Day of Reconciliation," November 20, 1980, document attached to National Conference of Catholic Bishops to Rabbi Bernard Mandelbaum, executive vice president of the Synagogue Council of America, and Claire Randall, general secretary of the National Council of Churches, November 20, 1980, box 48, VVMF-MD. The statement was drafted by Robert Doubek.

84. Clay, "Discovery," 56F.

85. *The Vietnam Veterans Memorial Design Competition: Questions and Answers* (Washington, DC: VVMF, February 10, 1981), 15, box 65, VVMF-MD.

86. Ibid., 3, 6, 7, 8.

87. Robert Doubek to Walter D. Westphall, August 2, 1980, 2, box 31, VVMF-MD. This was a fairly accurate prediction of the eventual appearance of the memorial when Frederick Hart's statue was added to Lin's wall, although Doubek had no way of foreseeing the circuitous and argument-filled course that led to this outcome.

88. For the design of the Mall, see Richard Longstreth, ed., *The Mall in Washington, 1791–1991* (Hanover, NH: University Press of New England; London: National Gallery of Art, 1991); and John W. Reps, *Monumental Washington: The Planning and Development of the Capital Center* (Princeton: Princeton University Press, 1967). For a brief but useful discussion of Constitution Gardens, see J. Carter Brown, "The Mall and the Commission of Fine Arts," *Studies in the History of Art* 30 (1991): 251–53.

89. The phrase "bewildering variety" is from a critic who reviewed the process through which the design jury selected the competition winner. Wolf Von Eckhardt, "Of Heart and Mind: The Serene Grace of the Vietnam Memorial," *Washington Post*, May 16, 1981.

90. Allen Freeman, "An Extraordinary Competition," *AIA Journal*, August 1981, 47.

91. Slides of almost all of the 1,421 entries to the design competition, including the winning entry, are in VVM-DPP. McLeod, "Battle for the Monument," provides an excellent account of the competition.

92. Competition entry no. 260, submitted by Charles Atherton, VVM-DPP.

93. Competition entry no. 235, submitted by Henry Arnold, Richard Benjamin, M. Khandvala, Warren Gran, and Mary Pat Hogan, VVM-DPP; Freeman, "Extraordinary Competition," 50, fig. 1.

94. Competition entry no. 703, submitted by W. Kent Cooper (team leader), Edward Corr, Julia Craighill, and Jeffrey Howard, VVM-DPP; Freeman, "Extraordinary Competition," 49, fig. 3. Kent Cooper's firm, Cooper-Lecky Partnership, became the architect of record charged with construction of the memorial.

95. "Artist Creates Memorial Sculpture," *Daily Texan*, November 12, 1979; S. Davis, "Design for Memorial Stirs Monumental Spat," *Dallas Morning News*, December 24, 1979; Laurence Jolidon, "War Memorial Controversy Ends with Both Sides Winning," *Austin American-Statesman*, January 4, 1980;

S. Davis, "Compromise Settles Feud: Two Austin Monuments to Vietnam Soldiers Planned," *Dallas Morning News*, January 7, 1980; "Ground Broken for War Dead Memorial," *Austin American-Statesman*, May 4, 1980; Jim Halbrook, Austin Parks and Recreation Department, interview by the author, July 17, 1996.

96. James Webb, untitled narrative of his involvement in the VVMF, 3, sent to Jan Scruggs, January 17, 1984, box 32, VVMF-MD.

97. Maya Lin, quoted in Joel Swerdlow, "To Heal a Nation," *National Geographic*, May 1985, 557. Lin had conceived the design in a class on funerary architecture. Before she submitted the design to the competition, her studio teacher and classmates persuaded her to remove a sculptural representation of a row of falling dominoes that she originally placed in front of the wall. Her teacher suggested that the names be placed in chronological order. McLeod, "Battle for the Monument," 120; Scruggs and Swerdlow, *To Heal a Nation*, 59.

98. Maya Lin, "Making the Memorial," *New York Review of Books*, November 2, 2000, 34.

99. VVMF, *Program Souvenir, National Salute to Vietnam Veterans*, 9; Grady Clay, *Comments by the Jurors: Vietnam Memorial Competition, Andrews Air Force Base, MD., April 26–29, 1981*, 3, box 62, VVMF-MD.

100. Clay, *Comments by the Jurors*, 3; Paul Spreiregen, Pietro Belluschi, Grady Clay, Garrett Eckbo, Richard H. Hunt, Constantino Nivola, James Rosati, Hideo Sasaki, and Harry M. Weese, *Report of the Vietnam Veterans Memorial Design Competition* (May 1, 1981); an unnamed juror, quoted in Eckhardt, "Of Heart and Mind."

101. Clay, *Comments by the Jurors*, 2.

102. Scruggs and Swerdlow, *To Heal a Nation*, 64–65; Timberg, *Nightingale's Song*, 312. The support of the VVMF at this stage was crucial, because only they had the legal authority to take the memorial to the federal government agencies for approval. Scruggs, "Process for Selecting Design," 4.

103. Clay, *Comments by the Jurors*, 2.

104. Scruggs and Swerdlow, *To Heal a Nation*, 66, 68, 87.

105. Ibid., 73; McLeod, "Battle for the Monument," 122.

106. Minutes of the Commission of Fine Arts meeting, July 7, 1981, 20–21, 23, records of the Commission of Fine Arts.

107. Scott Brewer, "Statement Delivered before the Commission of Fine Arts," Exhibit A-1, in ibid.

108. Paul Gapp, "Clouds of Doubt Engulf Viet Nam War Memorial," *Chicago Tribune*, June 28, 1981, sec. 6.

109. Raymond Coffey, "America's Neglected War Vets," *Chicago Tribune*, May 22, 1981.

110. One problem that the design's detractors did not notice was that the estimated cost was more than double the $3 million that the VVMF originally budgeted. "Information on Other Competitions."

111. For an astute discussion of the inscriptions, see Kirk Savage, "Trauma, Healing, and the Therapeutic Monument," in *Terror, Culture, Politics: Rethinking 9/11*, ed. Daniel Sherman and Terry Nardin (Bloomington: University of Indiana Press, 2006), 107–8.

112. Scruggs and Swerdlow, *To Heal a Nation*, 375.

113. Swerdlow, "To Heal a Nation," 571. One can see the designer's statement, as well as Lin's account of the creation of the memorial, in Maya Lin, *Boundaries* (New York: Simon and Schuster, 2000), 4:05–4:17.

114. Lin said, "I played very dumb for the first nine months of the Vietnam project. I played very quiet and naive. I knew nothing about the war, its history and politics. But although one of my strong choices was not to read anything on that war, I also didn't tell them I had spent three months researching, coming to grips with the whole definition of a memorial in general, just so I could get specific." Quoted in Peter Tauber, "Monument Maker," *New York Times Magazine*, February 24, 1991.

115. Scruggs and Swerdlow, *To Heal a Nation*, 110. Lin said, "The fund has always seen me as female—as a child. I went in there when I first won and their attitude was—okay, you did a good job, but now we're going to hire some big boys—boys—to take care of it." "An Interview with Maya Lin," in Williams, *Unwinding the Vietnam War*, 271.

116. Freivogel, "Vietnam War Memorial 'Rescued.'"

117. "Stop that Monument," *National Review*, September 18, 1981, 1064. See the replies by James Kilpatrick and Robert Doubek defending the memorial in letters to the editor, *National Review*, October 16, 1981, 1170–71. See also Daphne Berdahl, "Voices at the Wall: Discourses of Self, History, and National Identity at the Vietnam Veterans Memorial," *History and Memory* 6, no. 2 (Fall 1994): 92.

118. Quoted in James Webb, "Reassessing the Vietnam Veterans Memorial," *Wall Street Journal*, December 18, 1981, clipping in box 32, VVMF-MD.

119. Atkinson, *Long Gray Line*, 588.

120. Morton C. Blackwell, "Building a Conservative Governing Majority," in *Steering the Elephant: How Washington Works*, ed. Robert Rector and Michael Sanera (New York: Universe Books, 1987), 36. As special assistant in the White House Office for Public Liaison, Blackwell had responsibilities for liaison

with veterans, along with conservative organizations, religious groups, fraternal organizations, and Native Americans.

121. VVMF call report on meeting between Donald Schaet, VVMF executive vice president, Morton Blackwell, and Joe Coors, September 24, 1981, box 48, VVMF-MD.

122. Donald Schaet to Morton Blackwell, March 30, 1981; Jan Scruggs to Morton Blackwell, July 20, 1981, box 48; Jan Scruggs to Elliot Richardson, January 18, 1982, box 33, VVMF-MD.

123. Minutes of the Commission of Fine Arts meeting, October 13, 1981, 33–43. Carhart's testimony at the Fine Arts Commission meeting is excerpted as Tom Carhart, "Insulting Vietnam Vets," *New York Times*, October 24, 1981, 7. The story was distributed by the New York Times News Service and Associated Press and was widely reported. See, e.g., L. Parker, "Vet Protests Memorial Design—in Vain," *Army Times*, October 26, 1981; Associated Press, "Veteran Calls Vietnam Memorial 'Black Gash of Shame and Sorrow,'" *Arkansas Gazette* (Little Rock), October 14, 1981; Tom Carhart, "A Black Gash of Shame and Sorrow," *Commercial Appeal* (Memphis, TN), October 27, 1981.

124. "VVMF Press Conference December 21, 1981 Questions and Answers," 2, box 5, VVMF-MD.

125. Minutes of the Commission of Fine Arts meeting, October 13, 1981, 39–41. Proud of his service, Carhart said he refused to stand idly by while the dead were commemorated by a "black shaft of shame thrust into the earth" (42). See also the discussion in Atkinson, *Long Gray Line*, 590–91; Atkinson quotes Carhart as saying the memorial was like an open urinal.

126. Competition entry no. 658, VVM-DPP; Atkinson, *Long Gray Line*, 584.

127. Carhart, *Offering*, 145.

128. Larry Heinemann, *Paco's Story* (New York: Penguin Books, 1987), 157. Heinemann confirmed that he had Carhart's design in mind when he wrote those words, concerned about the "rush to sentimentalize" that he was afraid would emerge in commemorations of the Vietnam War. Heinemann, e-mail message to the author, August 30, 2007.

129. Minutes of the Commission of Fine Arts meeting, October 13, 1981, 42, 41; "Lest We Forget," *60 Minutes*, CBS News, October 10, 1982; James Webb, "Remarks of James Webb, Press Conference of 4 November 1982," 3, box 32, VVMF-MD.

130. Allan Young, *The Harmony of Illusions: Inventing Post-Traumatic Stress Disorder* (Princeton: Princeton University Press, 1995), 220.

131. Quotation from the documentary *Vietnam Memorial*, prod. Steve York and Foster Wiley (WGBH, Boston, 1983).

132. For discussions of the design conflict, see Hess, "Vietnam"; Buckley, "The Wall," 61–73; Karal Ann Marling and Robert Silberman, "The Statue Near the Wall: The Vietnam Veterans Memorial and the Art of Remembering," *Smithsonian Studies in American Art* 1, no. 1 (Spring 1987): 5–29; Catherine Howett, "The Vietnam Veterans Memorial: Public Art and Politics," *Landscape* 28, no. 2 (1985): 1–9; Wagner-Pacifici and Schwartz, "Vietnam Veterans Memorial"; McLeod, "Battle for the Monument"; and J. Dreyfuss, "In the Wake of Controversy: Vietnam Memorial Launched," *Los Angeles Times*, March 26, 1982.

133. Deborah Sutton brought this memorial, completed in 1966 in Kuala Lumpur, Malaysia's capital, to the author's attention.

134. Quotations from John Bodnar, *Remaking America: Public Memory, Commemoration, and Patriotism in the Twentieth Century* (Princeton: Princeton University Press, 1992), 6.

135. Initially, the Marine Corps League expressed their opposition to the design quite mildly, asking that a flag be included or that a new design be selected by a jury including Vietnam veterans. C. L. Kammeier, executive director of the Marine Corps League, to Bob Doubek, September 10, 1981, box 62, VVMF-MD. After the denunciations by Carhart and Webb, the league's rhetoric escalated. "Veterans Fault Vietnam War Memorial Plans," *Washington Post*, December 8, 1981; Timberg, *Nightingale's Song*, 313.

136. Ted Bell, "Viet Memorial Criticized as 'Monstrosity,'" *Sacramento Bee*, December 28, 1981.

137. Scruggs, "Forgotten Veterans."

138. Representatives Philip Crane (R., Illinois), Bill Dickinson (R., Alabama), Samuel Scratton (D., New York), Ed Derwinski (R., Illinois), Robert Livingston (R., Louisiana), and Daniel Lungren (R., California) to James G. Watt, November 20, 1981, box 30, VVMF-MD.

139. Timberg, *Nightingale's Song*, 312–13; James Webb to Jan Scruggs, December 2, 1981, box 63, VVMF-MD; Webb, "Remarks," November 4, 1982; Webb, untitled narrative, 7.

140. Webb, untitled narrative, 3, 5.

141. Webb to Scruggs, December 2, 1981.

142. Associated Press, "Vietnam Memorial Inappropriate, Millionaire Sympathizer Protests," *Newport News (VA) Times-Herald*, December 17, 1981.

143. Robert Doubek to Garrett Eckbo, November 16, 1981, box 62, VVMF-MD; Buckley, "The Wall," 66–67; Robert Doubek, "The Story of the Vietnam Veterans Memorial," *Retired Officer*, November 1983, 21.

144. Charles Colson, memorandum to John Dean, May 31, 1972, in *From the President: Richard Nixon's Secret Files*, ed. Bruce Oudes (New York: Harper and Row, 1989), 460.

145. Patrick J. Buchanan, "Memorial Does Not Honor Vietnam Vets," *Moline (IL) Dispatch*, December 27, 1981; "Memorial Ditch on the Mall," *Eureka (CA) Times Standard*, January 14, 1982.

146. Entry under December 3, 1981, "Chronology of Events: Involvement of Secretary of Interior in Approval of Design," box 62, VVMF-MD.

147. Robert Doubek to Garrett Eckbo, November 16, 1981; handwritten notes by VVMF staff and photocopies of Eckbo testimony and statements, box 62, VVMF-MD.

148. Manuscript notes of conversation between Garrett Eckbo and a staff member of VVMF, November 18, 1981; Garrett Eckbo to Robert Doubek, November 18, 1981, box 62, VVMF-MD.

149. Handwritten notes headed "Richard Hunt" and "Grady Clay," Jury Criticism file, box 62, VVMF-MD.

150. "VVMF Press Conference December 21, 1981," 2.

151. Manuscript, signed "Don" [presumably for Donald Schaet], February 2, 1982, box 62, VVMF-MD.

152. James Webb to Jan Scruggs, November 24, 1981, box 63, VVMF-MD; Webb, untitled narrative, 11.

153. Jan Scruggs, VVMF call report of conversation with Cooper T. Holt, December 3, 1981, box 32, VVMF-MD.

154. Webb, "Reassessing the Vietnam Veterans Memorial."

155. Ibid.

156. James Webb to Grady Clay, November 16, 1981, 1, 2, box 62, VVMF-MD.

157. Grady Clay to James Webb, December 2, 1981, 1, ibid.

158. "VVMF Press Conference December 21, 1981," 1.

159. Bob Doubek, memorandum to design competition jurors and Paul Spreiregen re: "New Developments and Jim Webb article in *Wall Street Journal*," December 19, 1981, box 62, VVMF-MD.

160. Susan Baer, "When Fiction Nears Truth: Webb's War Novel Poses Predicament," *Baltimore Sun*, February 13, 1991.

161. Perry Pendley, deputy assistant secretary for energy and minerals, memorandum to Secretary Watt, December 14, 1981, box 33, VVMF-MD.

162. Senators Steve Symms (R., Idaho), Jesse Helms (R., North Carolina), John P. East (R., North Carolina), and Jeremiah Denton (R., Alabama) to James G. Watt, January 11, [1982], box 30, VVMF-MD.

163. Doubek, memorandum to jurors and Paul Spreiregen, December 19, 1981.

164. Donald Schaet to Morton Blackwell, March 30, 1981; Gregory J. Newell, special assistant to the president, to Jan Scruggs, April 8, 1981; Donald E. Schaet to Ann Wrobleski, director of special projects, Office of the First Lady, April 13, 1981; Jan Scruggs to George Bush, April 29, 1981, box 48, VVMF-MD.

165. Sandie Fauriol, VVMF campaign director, to Ann Wrobleski, director of special projects, Office of the First Lady, July 31, 1981, box 48, VVMF-MD. "Message from Mrs. Nancy Reagan for VMF Radiothon, May 8–10, 1981," casefile 023809, Reagan Library.

166. Elizabeth H. Dole, assistant to the president for public liaison, to Jan Scruggs, July 30, 1981, box 48, VVMF-MD. The President's Schedule, July 17, 1981; Morton Blackwell, memorandum to Mary Powers, July 17, 1981; Ronald Reagan to Jan Scruggs, November 9, 1981, casefile 047184, Reagan Library.

167. Tom Carhart, "Coming out of the Shadows of Vietnam," unpublished manuscript, box 29, VVMF-MD.

168. Minutes of the Commission of Fine Arts meeting, October 13, 1981, 46–47; statement by Harold Burson, ibid., 54, 56.

169. James J. Kilpatrick, "Finally, We Honor the Vietnam Dead," *Washington Post*, November 11, 1981.

170. Charles McC. Mathias and John W. Warner to Ronald Reagan, October 27, 1981; note, November 24, [1981], casefile 046293, Reagan Library.

171. Webb, untitled narrative, 9–10.

4. A "Dangerous Political Issue"

1. Richard Cohen, "A Touch Unhinged," *Washington Post*, October 27, 1992; Gerald Posner, *Citizen Perot: His Life and Times* (New York: Random House, 1996), 92–94, 202, 212, 215, 296, 327–28.

2. Robert Dallek, *Ronald Reagan: The Politics of Symbolism* (Cambridge, MA: Harvard University Press, 1999), 86.

3. Edwin Meese III, telephone interview by the author, September 4, 2007.

4. Rick Atkinson, "Viet Veterans Memorial under Fire," *Kansas City (MO) Times*, December 16, 1981; Jan C. Scruggs and Joel L. Swerdlow, *To Heal a Nation: The Vietnam Veterans Memorial* (New York: Harper and Row, 1985), 68; VVMF call report of conversation between Jan Scruggs and Ross Perot, May 18, 1981; Jan Scruggs to Ross Perot, May 21, July 8, and July 21, 1981, box 30, VVMF-MD.

5. Scruggs reported that Perot said, "Your design is great for the 57,000 who died, but not for the 2 million who came home. I've enjoyed helping you but I'm folding my tent now. I'm not coming to DC on Memorial Day to speak [in response to a VVMF invitation] because if somebody in the press asks me I'll tell them I don't like it. I never lie but I'll never tell anyone but you that I don't like this memorial." VVMF call report of conversation with Ross Perot, May 13, 1981, box 30, VVMF-MD. Perot sought Carhart's phone number in November 1981, saying he disliked the design more each day. Jan Scruggs, VVMF call report of conversation with Ross Perot, November 5, 1981, box 30, VVMF-MD.

6. Henry Allen, "Perot Doesn't Pity You," *Washington Post*, June 28, 1992. On the "therapeutic society," see Philip Rieff, *The Triumph of the Therapeutic: Uses of Faith after Freud* (Chicago: University of Chicago Press, 1987); T. J. Jackson Lears, *No Place of Grace: Antimodernism and the Transformation of American Culture, 1880–1920* (Chicago: University of Chicago Press, 1994).

7. On Perot's taste in art and monuments, see Michael Kelly, "Where Perot Exhibits a Lifetime of Memories," *New York Times*, June 20, 1992; Lawrence Wright, "The Man from Texarkana," *New York Times Magazine*, June 28, 1992; Peter Applebome, "Perot, the 'Simple' Billionaire, Says Voters Can Force His Presidential Bid," *New York Times*, March 19, 1992; Mimi Swartz, "Mythomania," *New York Times*, June 21, 1992.

8. Michael K. Deaver with Mickey Herskowitz, *Behind the Scenes* (New York: Morrow, 1987), 43; Perot, interview by Morley Safer in "Lest We Forget," *60 Minutes*, CBS News, October 10, 1982.

9. VVMF call reports of conversations between Jan Scruggs and Ross Perot, May 13 and July 17, 1981, box 30, VVMF-MD; "Watt Raises Obstacle on Vietnam Memorial," *New York Times*, January 13, 1982; "Perot Dislikes Design of Vietnam Memorial," *Cincinnati Enquirer*, December 17, 1981.

10. Jan Scruggs, VVMF call report of conversation with a representative of Associated Press, December 15, 1981, box 30, VVMF-MD; Associated Press, "Vietnam Memorial Inappropriate, Millionaire Sympathizer Protests," *Newport News (VA) Times-Herald*, December 17, 1981.

11. Jan Scruggs, VVMF call report of conversation with Ross Perot, December 11, 1981, box 30, VVMF-MD; "The Chronology of Events Listed Below Is a History of the Involvement of Mr. H. Ross Perot with the Vietnam Veterans Memorial Fund," 3, box 30, VVMF-MD.

12. Atkinson, "Viet Veterans Memorial under Fire."

13. Jan Scruggs to Charles Mathias, December 4, 1981, box 47, VVMF-MD; Donald Schaet, VVMF call report of conversation with Chuck Hagel, December 10, 1981, box 29, VVMF-MD.

14. Fuller was assistant to the president and director of cabinet affairs. Along with the "troika," he was a prime coordinator of the communication flow in the White House. Cribb, like Blackwell, was a "movement conservative," and his involvement signals the interest of his boss, Edwin Meese. John H. Kessel, "The Structures of the Reagan White House," *American Journal of Political Science* 28, no. 2 (May 1984): 239; Sidney Blumenthal, "Quest for Lasting Power," *Washington Post*, September 25, 1985.

15. Frederick R. Daly to Mike Deaver, November 25, 1981, casefile 051450, Reagan Library; Kenneth Cribb Jr., note to Morton Blackwell, December 8, 1981, box 33, VVMF-MD; Office of Cabinet Affairs: Action Tracking Worksheet first signed November 25, 1981, circulated until February 3, [1982], casefile 051450, Reagan Library.

16. Dallek, *Ronald Reagan*, 76.

17. Bob Giuffra, memorandum to Morton C. Blackwell re: "Present Status of Vietnam Veterans Memorial," December 11, 1981, box 33, VVMF-MD. A copy is in casefile 051450, Reagan Library. The manuscript annotation "I pick option # 2," with an added manuscript comment, "In Deaver's hand," is found on a note from Craig L. Fuller to Mike Deaver, December 19, 1981, box 33, VVMF-MD.

18. Giuffra, memorandum to Blackwell re: "Present Status."

19. Entry under December 18, 1981, "Chronology of Events: Involvement of Secretary of Interior in Approval of Design," box 62, VVMF-MD; letter quoted in "Watt Raises Obstacle on Vietnam Memorial," *New York Times*, January 13, 1982.

20. Rep. Henry Hyde and thirty other U.S. representatives to Ronald Reagan, January 12, 1982, box 30, VVMF-MD.

21. Margaret W. Freivogel, "Vietnam War Memorial 'Rescued,'" *St. Louis Post-Dispatch*, February 14, 1982.

22. "Lawmakers Decry Viet Memorial," *San Diego Tribune*, January 22, 1982; "Politics Threatens to Engulf Vietnam Memorial Design," *AIA Journal*, February 1982.

23. "Senior Staff Meeting Action Items (1-18-82)," casefile 061324, Reagan Library; Jan Scruggs to Elliot Richardson, January 18, 1982, Box 33, VVMF-MD; Donald Schaet, VVMF call report of conversation with Tom Shull, January 25, [1982], box 50, VVMF-MD.

24. VVMF call report of conversation between Republican National Committee member and VVMF political consultant Charles Bailey and James Watt, January 18, 1982, box 33, VVMF-MD.

25. Rep. John M. Ashbrook to Ronald W. Reagan, January 27, 1982, casefile 057761, Reagan Library.

26. Jan Scruggs mentions the pledge by Westmoreland in a letter to the editor, *Washington Star*, January 4, 1981.

27. Ellsworth Bunker to James Watt, January 26, 1982; Stanley R. Resor to James Watt, January 21, 1982; Charles McC. Mathias to James Watt, January 20, 1982; George McGovern to James Watt, January 22, 1982, box 33, VVMF-MD; VVMF call report of conversation between Tom Shull and Donald Schaet, January 19, [1982], box 50, VVMF-MD; Scruggs and Swerdlow, *To Heal a Nation*, 97; Tom Shull, telephone interview by the author, September 13, 2007.

28. Bill Peterson, "Conservatives Get Administration Glad Hand," *Washington Post*, March 21, 1981; idem, "For Reagan and the New Right, the Honeymoon Is Over," *Washington Post*, July 21, 1981.

29. Edwin Meese III, *With Reagan: The Inside Story* (Washington, DC: Regnery Gateway, 1992), 315.

30. Morton C. Blackwell, "Building a Conservative Governing Majority," in *Steering the Elephant: How Washington Works*, ed. Robert Rector and Michael Sanera (New York: Universe Press, 1987), 32–33, 36.

31. Bill Peterson, "Abortion Aid Faces Further Cuts," *Washington Post*, March 20, 1981.

32. "Watt Raises Obstacle on Vietnam Memorial."

33. Scruggs to Richardson, January 18, 1982.

34. Entry under January 22, 1982, "Chronology of Events: Involvement of Secretary of Interior in Approval of Design."

35. Ibid.; Scruggs and Swerdlow, *To Heal a Nation*, 96, 99; Craig Howes, *Voices of the Vietnam POWs: Witnesses to Their Fight* (New York: Oxford University Press, 1993); S. Baer, "Texas Billionaire Poised to Be Election-year Savior," *Baltimore Sun*, April 5, 1992.

36. Monika Jensen-Stevenson and William Stevenson, *Kiss the Boys Goodbye: How the United States Betrayed Its Own POWs in Vietnam* (New York: Plume, 1991), 80. The operation became the basis for Ken Follett's bestseller *On Wings of Eagles* (New York: New American Library, 1990).

37. Elizabeth Hess, "Vietnam: Memorials of Misfortune," in *Unwinding the Vietnam War: From War into Peace*, ed. Reese Williams (Seattle: Real Comet Press, 1987), 265.

38. The American Legion, with 2.6 million members, claimed 600,000 Vietnam veterans among its members. Thomas J. Haynes to Tom Carhart, October 29, 1981, box 29, VVMF-MD; total membership figures come from William H. Sloan, assistant director, internal affairs and membership, American Legion, e-mail message to the author, March 6, 2007. The VFW, with 1.9 million members, said that a quarter of them, or roughly half a million, were Vietnam veterans. Arthur J. Fellwock, national commander-in-chief, Veterans of Foreign Wars of the United States, telegram to James G. Watt, January 29, 1982, box 5, VVMF-MD.

39. "Vietnam Veterans Memorial Meeting, January 27, 1982; 3:30–8:15 pm," attendance sheet on U.S. Senate letter-head, attached to Jim Cicconi (special assistant to Baker, 1981–85), memorandum to Craig L. Fuller, January 28, 1982, casefile 063219, Reagan Library (also in box 62, VVMF-MD); "Kathy," memorandum to Morton [Blackwell], January 28, 1982, casefile 051450, Reagan Library.

40. Voice-over narration by Rocky Bleier in *Vietnam Veterans Memorial: The Last Landing Zone*, prod. Bob Muller (All-American Video Productions, Inc., 1994). The documentary was made with Scruggs's and Wheeler's cooperation.

41. Associated Press, "Compromise Reached in Vietnam Memorial Plans," *Leesburg (FL) Commercial*, February 2, 1982.

42. *Vietnam Veterans Memorial: The Last Landing Zone*.

43. Chris Buckley, "The Wall," *Esquire*, September 1985, 67.

44. Brig. Gen. George Price, interview in *Vietnam Veterans Memorial: The Last Landing Zone*.

45. "Statement of the Vietnam Veterans Memorial Fund Regarding Compromise Agreement," December 14, 1982, box 62, VVMF-MD.

46. Scruggs to Richardson, January 18, 1982; Kent Cooper, interview by the author, August 11, 1994; Rick Atkinson, *The Long Gray Line: From West Point to Vietnam and After; The Turbulent Odyssey of the Class of 1966* (New York: Pocket Books, 1989), 594.

47. "Vietnam Veterans Memorial Meeting, January 27, 1982." The attendance sheet tallies with every other account of who was at the meeting. It records that fifty-six people were present at the meeting. Of these, thirteen can be confidently identified as critics and their associates; eighteen were officers or supporters of VVMF and their associates. Some, such as observers from the White House and the National

Park Service, can be considered neutral, and some are not easily identifiable with any camp. There is no reason to suppose that all the unidentified attendees were critics, so it is perfectly possible that the VVMF and their supporters were in fact in the majority. Tom Shull, present at the meeting, confirms that there were no more than the fifty-six people present, and he does not believe that the supporters of the VVMF were outnumbered. Shull, interview.

48. Scruggs and Swerdlow, *To Heal a Nation*, 100.

49. Jan Scruggs to Meg Greenfield, editorial page editor, *Washington Post*, July 12, 1982, box 50, VVMF-MD.

50. Scruggs and Swerdlow, *To Heal a Nation*, 99.

51. Brig. Gen. George Price, "My Involvement with the Wall: The Most Rewarding Experience of My Life," in *Veterans Day at the Wall* [25th anniversary ceremony booklet] (Washington, DC: VVMF, 2007), 9. Although Price is alone in recalling the prior decision to add a statue, the fact that his statement appeared in the VVMF's own publication lends it authority.

52. Shull, interview.

53. Lance Gay, "Message, Statue, Flag Are Planned at Viet Memorial," *Rocky Mountain News*, February 5, 1982.

54. Tom Shull, memorandum to Jim Cicconi re: "Vietnam Veterans Memorial Design," January 28, 1982, box 33, VVMF-MD (copy in casefile 063219, Reagan Library). See also Scruggs and Swerdlow, *To Heal a Nation*, 102; entry for January 27, 1982, in "Chronology of Events: Involvement of Secretary of Interior in Approval of Design"; Shull, interview.

55. Shull's recommendation was sent up the White House hierarchy. Cicconi, memorandum to Craig L. Fuller, January 28, 1982.

56. Scruggs and Swerdlow, *To Heal a Nation*, 101.

57. William LeoGrande, *Our Own Backyard: The United States in Central America, 1977–1992* (Chapel Hill: University of North Carolina Press, 1998), 193; Edwin Meese, "The Reagan Presidency," in *Leadership in the Reagan Presidency, Part II: Eleven Intimate Perspectives*, ed. Kenneth W. Thompson (Lanham, MD: University Press of America, 1993), 223–24; Kessel, "Structures of the Reagan White House," 252.

58. "Note for Judge Clark," January 27, 1982, National Security Council casefile 563/White House casefile 060083, Reagan Library.

59. Mike Wheeler, memorandum to Tom Reed, January 27, 1982, National Security Council casefile 563/White House casefile 060083.

60. Richard T. Childress, memorandum to William P. Clark, January 28, 1982, White House casefile 060083.

61. Morton Blackwell, memorandum to Elizabeth Dole, January 29, 1982, casefile 051450, Reagan Library.

62. Meese, interview. GHJ [Harris Jordan], memorandum re: Vietnam Veterans Memorial to PMC [Rep. Philip Crane] and DA, November 17, 1981, box 30, VVMF-MD.

63. Arthur J. Fellwock, national commander-in-chief, Veterans of Foreign Wars of the U.S., telegram to James G. Watt, January 29, 1982, White House casefile 060083; also in box 5, VVMF-MD.

64. George Ricker, committee chairman, VFW Post 8317, Benton, PA, open letter to Ronald Reagan, n.d., received by White House February 20, 1982, casefile 062358, Reagan Library.

65. Carroll Campbell to Ronald Reagan, February 1, [1982], casefile 048724, Reagan Library.

66. Unnumbered document [Resolution by Coronado Republican Women, February 10, 1982], Reagan Library.

67. "Minutes of Management Meeting," February 8, 1982, casefile 060843, Reagan Library; "Kathy," memorandum to Morton [Blackwell], January 28, 1982.

68. "Kathy," memorandum to Morton [Blackwell], February 4, 1982, casefile 066679, Reagan Library; "Senior Staff Meeting Action Items (2-8-82)," casefile 061335, Reagan Library; VVMF call report of conversation between Donald Schaet and Deputy Under Secretary of the Interior Bill Horn, February 24, 1982; VVMF call report of conversation between Robert Doubek and Bill Horn, February 25, 1982, box 33, VVMF-MD; James G. Watt to J. Carter Brown, February 25, 1982, box 30, VVMF-MD; "Secretary Watt Delays Start on Revised Vietnam Veterans Memorial," *St Louis Post-Dispatch*, February 28, 1982.

69. "Current Developments and Alternative Courses of Action regarding Secretary Watt's Failure to Approve Design as of March 1, 1982," document attached to "Chronology of Events: Involvement of Secretary of Interior in Approval of Design."

70. Scruggs and Swerdlow, *To Heal a Nation*, 104.

71. Morton C. Blackwell, memorandum to Veterans and Service-Related Groups re: "Vietnam Veterans Memorial," March 2, 1982, box 33, VVMF-MD.

72. Helen M. Scharf, chairman, National Capital Planning Commission, to James Watt, March 9, 1982,

box 62, VVMF-MD; J. Carter Brown, "The Mall and the Commission of Fine Arts," *Studies in the History of Art* 30 (1991): 258; J. Carter Brown to James C. Watt, March 9, 1982, box 5, VVMF-MD.

73. The VVMF had gone down the list of attendees at the January 27 meeting, vetting the names to establish which ones should be invited again. "Invitation List: March 11th Meeting," box 62, VVMF-MD.

74. Tom Carhart reports that Perot sent the VVMF the poll results on February 23. Carhart, "Poll Shows Most Viet-Vets Against Memorial Design," *Washington Times*, October 12, 1982.

75. Scruggs and Swerdlow, *To Heal a Nation*, 106. James Webb, untitled narrative of his involvement with the VVMF, sent to Jan Scruggs, January 17, 1984, box 32, VVMF-MD, 13.

76. Scruggs and Swerdlow, *To Heal a Nation*, 105. See also Buckley, "The Wall," 66–67; Robert Doubek, "The Story of the Vietnam Veterans Memorial," *Retired Officer*, November 1983, 21.

77. "Proposed Agenda: Vietnam Veterans Memorial Design Issues, March 11, 1982," document attached to Senator John W. Warner to Tom Shull, March 3, 1982, copied and sent to the author by Shull, September 18, 2007.

78. William P. Lecky to Senator John Warner, March 15, 1982, box 62, VVMF-MD.

79. Scruggs and Swerdlow, *To Heal a Nation*, 102. See also Thomas J. Haynes, director of internal affairs of the American Legion, to Tom Carhart, explaining his organization's commitment to the memorial fund, October 29, 1981, box 29, VVMF-MD.

80. See, e.g., in the Reagan Library, Max E. Julian, department commander, American Legion, Department of Indiana, to Ronald Reagan, March 8, 1982, casefile 078538; Else Daniels, national vice president, Northwestern Division, American Legion Auxiliary, to Ronald Reagan, March 12, 1982, casefile 078546; U.S. Rep. Carroll Hubbard (D., Kentucky) to Ronald Reagan, March 19, 1982, casefile 067346; Alabama state senator Mike Weeks to Ronald Reagan, March 18, 1982, casefile 067100.

81. Shull, interview; Scruggs and Swerdlow, *To Heal a Nation*, 107.

82. John Wheeler, memorandum to Fred Ryan and Sandra Warfield, June 9, 1988, casefile 616912, Reagan Library. Ryan was special assistant to the president and director of appointments and scheduling. Wheeler said, "But for Tom [Shull], there would be no Memorial." Jack Wheeler to National Security Adviser Robert C. McFarlane, November 30, 1984. A photocopy of the letter, on VVMF stationery, was sent by Tom Shull to the author on September 18, 2007. Scruggs and Wheeler publicly thanked Reagan for overruling Watt during a ceremony at the memorial. Michael York, "Reagans Pay Emotional Visit to the Vietnam Veterans Wall," *Washington Post*, November 12, 1988. Edwin Meese confirmed that, although the decision to allow groundbreaking was formally credited to Reagan, it is likely that, on the basis of the president's support for the memorial, the decision was made by one of his aides. Meese, interview.

83. James G. Watt to Jan C. Scruggs, March 11, 1982, box 4, VVMF-MD; Jean White, "Watt Okays a Memorial Plan," *Washington Post*, March 12, 1982; U.S. Congress, House, Henry J. Hyde, "Vietnam Veterans Memorial," 97th Cong., 2d sess., March 25, 1982, *Congressional Record*, E 1276; "Senior Staff Meeting Action Items (3-25-82)," casefile 068556, Reagan Library; "Senior Staff Meeting Action Items (3-26-82)," casefile 068557, Reagan Library; New York Times News Service, "Work Starts on Viet War Memorial," *San Diego Union*, March 27, 1982.

84. Scruggs and Swerdlow, *To Heal a Nation*, 49, 115; "Vietnam Veterans Memorial Fund Selects Frederick Hart to Design Statue," press release, 2nd draft, [1982], box 51, VVMF-MD; VVMF call report of conversation between Jan Scruggs and Gen. [Mike] Davison, February 2, 1982, box 30, VVMF-MD.

85. "Work Starts on Viet War Memorial," *San Diego Union*, March 27, 1982.

86. Timberg, *Nightingale's Song*, 316.

87. Webb, untitled narrative, 14.

88. Hart said that he became close friends with many veterans and drank with them in bars. Hess, "Vietnam," 274.

89. Marling and Silberman report that Hart used Webb's boots as the model for those worn by one of the figures. Karen Ann Marling and Robert Silberman, "The Statue Near the Wall: The Vietnam Veterans Memorial and the Art of Remembering," *Smithsonian Studies in American Art* 1, no. 1 (Spring 1987): 16.

90. Jay Hall Carpenter, telephone interview by the author, June 3, 2008. Carpenter was Hart's assistant and created the mock-up of the statue. Charles Krauthammer, "Washington Diarist," *New Republic*, November 29, 1982, 42 (Krauthammer reports on discussions that took place in July 1982); Richard E. Radez (a director of VVMF), memorandum for the record, July 12, 1982, box 30, VVMF-MD; Kelly, "Where Perot Exhibits a Lifetime of Memories," main photograph by Mark Perlstein for the *New York Times*; "Viet Memorial Designer, AIA Strongly Denounce Alterations," *AIA Journal*, August 1982, 9; VVMF call report of conversation between Jan Scruggs and "Ciconi" [James Cicconi], July 16, 1982, box 48, VVMF-MD.

91. Charles Fishman, "Memorial's First Names Unveiled," *Washington Post*, July 22, 1982. The VVMF began inscribing the names on June 24, 1982. Jan Scruggs, speech to Vietnam Veterans of New Mexico, June 24, 1982, box 53, VVMF-MD.

92. Rick Horowitz, "Maya Lin's Angry Objections," *Washington Post*, July 7, 1982.

93. "Transcript of Maya Lin Interview on the 'Today' Show, Monday July 12, 1982," box 33, VVMF-MD; Maya Ying Lin to VVMF, September 20, 1982, box 33, VVMF-MD.

94. Hess, "Vietnam," 271–74.

95. Scruggs and Swerdlow, *To Heal a Nation*, 120–21, 132; "Back Talk: The Memorial Conflict Cont'd," *Washington Post*, July 28, 1982.

96. Ross Perot, interview by Gerald Posner, quoted in Posner, *Citizen Perot*, 147.

97. VVMF call report of conversation with Tom Bettag of CBS's *60 Minutes*, May 4, 1982; Jan Scruggs, VVMF call report of conversation with Ross Perot, May 4, 1982; Jan Scruggs to Paul Thayer of LTV Corporation, May 26, 1982, box 30, VVMF-MD.

98. Jan Scruggs to Tom Bettag, May 19, 1982, box 30, VVMF-MD.

99. VVMF call report of conversation with Ed DeBolt, February 1, 1982; [Jan Scruggs], VVMF call report of conversation between [VVMF director George] Sandy Mayo and Perot's legal representative, May 7, 1982; Jan Scruggs to Elliot Richardson, May 11, 1982; Jan Scruggs to Paul Thayer of LTV Corporation, May 26, 1982; Richard E. Radez, memorandum for the record, July 16, 1982; Jan Scruggs, VVMF call report of conversation with Cyrus Vance, July 6, 1983, box 30, VVMF-MD.

100. VVMF call report of conversation between Sandy Mayo and Ross Perot's legal representative, May 7, 1982, box 30, VVMF-MD.

101. Jan Scruggs's remarks following "Memorials and Remembrance" panel, at conference titled "Vietnam Legacies: Twenty Years after the Fall of Saigon," University of California, Davis, April 26, 1995, recorded by the author. Jan Scruggs to Elliot Richardson, May 11, 1982; Jan Scruggs, VVMF call report of conversation with Charles Bailey, box 30, VVMF-MD; John Wheeler, "Perot Showed Much about Himself in War against 'Wall,'" *Dallas Morning News*, June 8, 1992; John Mintz, "Perot's War: Viet Vets' 'Tombstone,'" *Washington Post*, July 7, 1992; Atkinson, *Long Gray Line*, 583; Posner, *Citizen Perot*, 139.

102. Jan Scruggs, VVMF call report of conversation with Gen. Mike Davison re: "Call to Ross Perot," February 2, 1982, box 30, VVMF-MD. The quoted phrases are Scruggs's annotations.

103. "The Chronology of Events Listed Below Is a History of the Involvement of Mr. H. Ross Perot with the Vietnam Veterans Memorial Fund," 1; Jan Scruggs to Paul Thayer of the LTV Corporation, May 26, 1982, 2, box 30, VVMF-MD.

104. VVMF call report of conversation with Elliot Richardson, May 10, 1982; VVMF call report of conversation between Richard Radez and Sandy Mayo, May 11, 1982, box 30, VVMF-MD.

105. Scruggs, VVMF call report of conversation with Davison, February 2, 1982.

106. "Overheard," *Newsweek*, July 6, 1992, 15; John Wheeler, "Perot's War against the Vets," *Baltimore Evening Sun*, June 8, 1992; Jan C. Scruggs to Lloyd Unsell, Independent Petroleum Association, September 8, 1982, box 13, VVMF-MD; Jan C. Scruggs, memorandum to Independent Audit Committee, July 1, 1983; Jan C. Scruggs to Elliot Richardson, July 15, 1983, box 30, VVMF-MD; Terry O'Donnell, telephone interview by the author, September 10, 2007.

107. VVMF call report of conversation with Gen. Mike Davison, March 11, 1982; VVMF call report of Jack Wheeler's conversation with Ross Perot, May 5, 1982; VVMF call report of Gen. Mike Davison's conversation with Ross Perot, May 17, 1982; Jan Scruggs to Paul Thayer of LTV Corporation, May 26, 1982, box 30, VVMF-MD.

108. Jan Scruggs to Paul Thayer, May 26, 1982, 2; Jan Scruggs to Ross Perot, June 11, 1982; Scruggs to Thayer, June 11, 1982, box 30, VVMF-MD.

109. VVMF call report of conversation with Sandy Mayo, May 7, 1982; Ross Perot to Jack Wheeler, May 7, 1982; Perot to Wheeler, June 2, 1982; VVMF call report of Gen. Mike Davison's conversation with Ross Perot, June 7, 1982; Radez, memorandum for the record, July 12, 1982; Ross Perot to Board of Directors, VVMF, July 23, 1982; Jan C. Scruggs, memorandum to VVMF's Independent Audit Committee, September 21, 1982; Jan Scruggs, VVMF call report of conversation between Paul Thayer and Ross Perot, October 4, 1982; VVMF call report of conversation between Elliot Richardson and Joe Allbritton (of the Independent Audit Committee), October 29, 1982; Jan C. Scruggs, memorandum for the record, November 1, 1982, box 30, VVMF-MD.

110. Posner, *Citizen Perot*, 95. All the while Perot hired private investigators or encouraged government probes of his business rivals, political opponents, and employees, he accused others of conspiring against him. See, e.g., ibid., 274, 290; Michael Wines, "The 1992 Campaign: White House, Bush Aides Try to Paint Perot as a Threat to Liberties," *New York Times*, June 23, 1992; David Jackson, "As Accuser or Accused, Perot Has a History of Links to Conspiracy Theories," *Dallas Morning News*, October 27, 1992; Bob Woodward, "Perot Launches Investigations of Bush," *Washington Post*, June 21, 1992.

111. Perot to Wheeler, May 7, 1982; Steven M. Umin, of Williams and Connolly (VVMF's lawyers) to Richard P. Shlakman, vice president of EDS, September 17, 1982; Shlakman to Umin, September 28, 1982; Jan Scruggs, memorandum to the Independent Audit Committee, September 21, 1982; VVMF call

report of conversation between Dick Radez and [George] Sandy Mayo, May 11, 1982; John [Jack] Wheeler to Perot, June 8, 1982; Jan Scruggs to Ross Perot, June 11, 1982, box 30, VVMF-MD.

112. VVMF call report of conversation with Davison, March 11, 1982; Jan C. Scruggs to Elliot Richardson, June 14, 1982, box 30, VVMF-MD.

113. Radez, memorandum for the record, July 16, 1982.

114. See the extensive correspondence between Scruggs and Richardson between May and July 1982 in box 30, VVMF-MD.

115. Lou Cannon, *President Reagan: The Role of a Lifetime* (New York: PublicAffairs, 2000), 89; Ronald Brownstein and Nina Easton, *Reagan's Ruling Class* (New York: Pantheon Books, 1983), 647; Shull, interview.

116. VVMF call report of conversation between Gen. Mike Davison and Ross Perot, March 11, 1982, box 30, VVMF-MD.

117. John Mintz, "Perot Regarded by Nixon Aides as a Man Who Broke His Promises," *Washington Post*, May 24, 1992.

118. H. Bruce Franklin, *M.I.A. or Mythmaking in America* (New Brunswick, NJ: Rutgers University Press, 1993), 57–60, 190–91; Fred Powledge, "H. Ross Perot Pays His Dues," *New York Times*, February 28, 1971; "Game Plan for the President's Pursuit of Peace Speech," in *From the President: Richard Nixon's Secret Files*, ed. Bruce Oudes (New York: Harper and Row, 1989), 65–69; Posner, *Citizen Perot*, 76–78; Catherine S. Manegold, "Perot Faces Same Questions He Left Hanging," *Oregonian*, October 4, 1992.

119. Robert Fitch, "H. Ross Perot: America's First Welfare Billionaire," *Ramparts*, November 1971, 42–51, quoted in Franklin, *M.I.A.*, 190.

120. R. P. Bourland, director of administration, Texas Blue Shield, to H. Ross Perot, May 17, 1962; Perot to Bourland, June 15, 1962, and other correspondence in "EDS" files, John W. Dean III, box 31, National Archives Nixon Presidential Materials Project, White House Special Files, Staff Member and Office Files, National Archives, College Park, MD; U.S. General Accounting Office, *Report to the Congress: Improvements Needed in Processing Medicare Claims for Physicians' Services in Texas*, report no. B-164031 (4), December 31, 1970, 2, 35, 37–41; U.S. Congress, House, Committee on Government Operations, 92d Cong., 1st sess., *Administration of Federal Health Benefit Programs*, pt. 3, *Data Processing. Hearings*, September 28, 30, November 9, December 1, 1971; Stuart Auerbach, "U.S. Paid Texas Millionaire Perot Computer Fee It Called 'Exorbitant,'" *Washington Post*, October 1, 1971; Peggy Simpson, "Hill Perot Inquiry Arouses Dispute," *Washington Post*, December 2, 1971; Dan Thomason, "Nixon Fan Got No-Bid U.S. Plum," *Washington Daily News*, January 17, 1972; Posner, *Citizen Perot*, 34–72, 239–40. See also documentation in "Ross Perot" files, Charles W. Colson, box 98, National Archives Nixon Presidential Materials Project.

121. Mintz, "Perot Regarded by Nixon Aides"; Posner, *Citizen Perot*, 70.

122. VVMF call report of conversation between Jan Scruggs and Elliot Richardson, May 10, 1982, box 30, VVMF-MD. See also Susan Baer, "Texas Billionaire Poised to Be Election-Year Savior," *Baltimore Sun*, April 5, 1992.

123. Elliot Richardson to Jan Scruggs, May 7, 1982; VVMF call report of Richardson's views regarding Perot's latest demand, June 7, 1982, box 30; VVMF call report regarding Perot, June 17, 1982, box 47, VVMF-MD; VVMF call report of conversation with Cy[rus] Vance, re: "Briefing on Ross Perot," June 9, 1982, box 30, VVMF-MD.

124. Diagram with proposals by Cooper-Lecky Partnership, Henry Arnold, and the Sculpture Committee; W. Kent Cooper to John P. Wheeler, September 9, 1982, box 7, VVMF-MD; James Watt to Jan C. Scruggs, September 29, 1982; James Watt to J. Carter Brown, October 4, 1982, box 62; VVMF call report of conversation between Jan Scruggs and James Watt, October 4, 1982, box 33; Sandie Fauriol, VVMF campaign director, VVMF call report of conversation with Gordon Mansfield, September 23, 1982, box 5, VVMF-MD.

125. VVMF call report of conversation between Jack Wheeler and James Webb, August 3, 1982, box 32, VVMF-MD. The continuing antagonism between the VVMF and their critics is captured in the "follow-up action" added to the call report in Scruggs's handwriting: "Concrete boots for Carhart's Tidal Basin tour."

126. Bob Carter, VVMF executive vice president, VVMF call report of conversation with Tom Carhart, August 23, 1982, box 29, VVMF-MD.

127. Tom Carhart, letter to the editor, *Washington Times*, October 6, 1982.

128. Carhart, "Poll Shows Most Viet-Vets against Memorial Design."

129. "Senior Staff Meeting Action Items (10-13-82)," casefile 107478, Reagan Library.

130. "Proposed Viet Sculpture Shown as Architects Fight Additions," *AIA Journal*, October 1982, 22; Robert M. Lawrence, president of the American Institute of Architects [AIA], to J. Carter Brown, July 15, 1982, box 33, VVMF-MD; "AIA Defends Design and Competition for Vietnam Veterans Memorial,"

Memo: Newsletter of the American Institute of Architects, July 30, 1982; "Viet Memorial Designer, AIA Strongly Denounce Alterations," 9.

131. Associated Press, "Most Ex-POWs Polled Dislike Vietnam War Memorial Design," *Washington Post*, October 12, 1982.

132. "Lest We Forget."

133. Enclosure 2, Robert A. Carter to Secretary Watt, September 23, 1982, box 29, VVMF-MD. See also Webb, untitled narrative, 16.

134. "Proposed Viet Sculpture Shown as Architects Fight Additions," *AIA Journal*, October 1982, 22, 27.

135. Robert Doubek, VVMF call report, November 1, 1982, box 62, VVMF-MD; Benjamin Forgey, "Vietnam Memorial Changes Clear Last Major Hurdle," *Washington Post*, October 14, 1982; Jan Scruggs, VVMF call report of conversation with Frederick Hart, October 30, 1982, box 62, VVMF-MD.

136. Forgey, "Vietnam Memorial Changes Clear Last Major Hurdle"; J. Carter Brown, "The Vietnam Memorial Decision: 'Part of the Healing,'" *Washington Post*, October 16, 1982.

137. "Statement of the Vietnam Veterans Memorial Fund Regarding Compromise Agreement"; Jan Scruggs to Secretary Watt, December 8, 1982, box 62; Robert Doubek, testimony at Commission of Fine Arts meeting, February 8, 1983, 95–96, box 29; Charles McC. Mathias and John W. Warner to Ronald Reagan, October 27, 1981, box 48, VVMF-MD.

138. *Nightline* (ABC News), October 14, 1982, transcript by Radio-TV Monitoring Service. The number of respondents referred to by Perot, 324, is unexplained, since the original report of the poll stated that only 265 of the 587 former POWs had responded to the poll. Associated Press, "Most Former War Prisoners Dislike Vietnam Memorial," *Home News* (New Brunswick, NJ), October 12, 1982.

139. Editorial, *Richmond (VA) Times-Dispatch*, October 20, 1982, in *Editorials on File* 13, no. 21 (November 1–15, 1982): 1286; *Dayton (OH) Journal Herald*, October 22, 1982, 10, clipping in box 33, VVMF-MD.

140. Senators Steve Symms, James A. McClure (R., Idaho), John P. East (R., North Carolina), Chuck Grassley (R., Iowa), Representatives Don Bailey, Larry E. Craig (R., Idaho), Phil Crane (R., Illinois), and Henry Hyde to James G. Watt, October 15, 1982, box 29, VVMF-MD.

141. Don Bailey, press conference statement of November 4, 1982, box 29, VVMF-MD; "Bailey Bills for Vietnam Memorial Pass House in Final Hours," December 20, 1982, press release by Rep. Don Bailey, box 62, VVMF-MD; Thomas Ferraro, "Vietnam Memorial," *Dallas Morning News*, November 10, 1982.

142. Hess, "Vietnam," 269.

143. Lucy Lippard, *A Different War: Vietnam in Art* (Bellingham and Seattle, WA: Whatcom Museum of History and Art and Real Comet Press, 1990) contains several graphic antiwar statements, including proposals for memorials. Some local pieces of public art did convey an antiwar message, such as *The Veterans Lobby* by Richard Posner (see the cover of Williams, *Unwinding the Vietnam War*), and various designs for a memorial at Kent State University.

144. K. Andersen and J. Branegan, "A Homecoming at Last," *Time*, November 22, 1982, 45.

145. Hess, "Vietnam," 273; Frederick Hart, letter to the editor, *Art in America*, November 1983, 6.

146. Tom Wolfe, "Art Disputes War: The Battle of the Vietnam Memorial," *Washington Post*, October 13, 1982. This article elaborates the critique of architectural modernism Wolfe articulates in *From Bauhaus to Our House* (New York: Farrar, Straus, Giroux, 1981).

147. Keri Guten, "Viet Memorial Art's 'Beauty' in Eye of Beholder," *San Antonio Light*, November 10, 1982.

148. J. E. Nelson, telegram to Ronald Reagan, November 7, 1982; Ronald Reagan to J. E. Nelson, December 6, 1982, casefile 114540, Reagan Library.

149. Edwin Meese recalled that the fundamental issue was that the statue and flag were to be added, not their location. Meese, interview.

150. John Bodnar, *Remaking America: Public Memory, Commemoration, and Patriotism in the Twentieth Century* (Princeton: Princeton University Press, 1992), 3–9.

151. James Webb, James Stockdale, and Ross Perot, all opponents of the Lin design, were graduates of the U.S. Naval Academy; Jack Wheeler, Richard Radez, Art Mosley, and Tom Shull were graduates of the U.S. Military Academy; and Mike Davison and William Westmoreland were former superintendents at West Point. Shull, interview.

152. Sandie Fauriol, "National Salute to Vietnam Veterans: Major Donors," *Program Souvenir, National Salute to Vietnam Veterans, November 10–14, 1982, Washington, DC* (McLean, VA: Tyl Associates, [1982]), 13. Of the veterans' organizations, the American Legion donated $1 million, the VFW improved on their initial pledge of $180,000 by donating $250,000, and AMVETS contributed $37,000. Lloyd Unsell of the Independent Petroleum Association raised $500,000 and Paul Thayer, president of LTV Corporation, raised $1 million more. Scruggs, "The Building of the Vietnam Memorial," op-ed column distributed by Newspaper Enterprise Association, March 25, 1985.

153. "Tribute to Honor: A History," *Program Souvenir, National Salute to Vietnam Veterans*, 34; Lydia Fish, *The Last Firebase: A Guide to the Vietnam Veterans Memorial* (Shippensburg, PA: White Mane, 1987), 2.

154. Jack A. Kelley, to VVMF, n.d.; Joan Gooding to VVMF, October 21, 1982; these and other similar letters from small donors asking for refunds are in box 62, VVMF-MD.

155. Shelton said that Scruggs had done a wonderful job and was proud that his $360 donation went to complete the wall. John Shelton to Jan Scruggs, October 26, 1982, box 62, VVMF-MD.

5. "Home to America's Heart"

1. "Quotelines," *USA Today*, November 12, 1982; Phil McCombs, "Veterans Honor the Fallen, Mark Reconciliation," *Washington Post*, November 14, 1982; Kurt Andersen and Jay Branegan, "A Homecoming at Last," *Time*, November 22, 1982, 46.

2. Thomas Ferraro, "Vietnam Memorial," *Dallas Morning News*, November 10, 1982; McCombs, "Veterans Honor the Fallen"; Stan Federman, "Vietnam Vets Seek Funding for D.C. Trip," *Oregonian*, October 28, 1982; Jan C. Scruggs and Joel L. Swerdlow, *To Heal a Nation: The Vietnam Veterans Memorial* (New York: Harper and Row, 1985), 140; Francis X. Clines, "Tribute to Vietnam Dead: Words, Wall," *New York Times*, November 11, 1982; Associated Press, "Pride in Ranks as Vietnam Veterans March and Dedicate Monument," *Kansas City Star*, November 14, 1982.

3. Scruggs and Swerdlow, *To Heal a Nation*, 139, 140.

4. Ed Bruske and Kenneth Bredemeier, "Vietnam War Dead's Names Read, Remembered," *Washington Post*, November 11, 1982.

5. "Find the Cost of Freedom," Stephen Stills (1970). The song was popularized by Crosby, Stills, Nash, and Young and was the B-side of the single release of Neil Young's "Ohio" (1971), which protested the killings at Kent State.

6. Kenneth Bredemeier, "Diverse Crowd Is Unanimous in Homage to Vietnam Veterans," *Washington Post*, November 14, 1982; William Broyles Jr., "Remembering a War We Want to Forget," *Newsweek*, November 22, 1982, 83.

7. Phil McCombs and Neil Henry, "Whole Again," *Washington Post*, November 15, 1982.

8. Anna Madrzyk, "Vietnam Vets' Long Wait for Honor Is Nearly Over," *Chicago Herald*, November 11, [1982].

9. McCombs, "Veterans Honor the Fallen."

10. *Vietnam Memorial*, prod. Steve York and Foster Wiley (WGBH, Boston, 1983).

11. *To Heal a Nation*, dir. Michael Pressman, 1988. The film is based on Scruggs and Swerdlow, *To Heal a Nation*; Scruggs and Swerdlow are credited as consultants. Scruggs actually made the remark two years later, when the statue was dedicated.

12. Mary McGrory, "It May Have Been the Best Idea Vietnam Veterans Ever Had," *Washington Post*, November 16, 1982.

13. Lynn Rosellini, "Salute Opening for Vietnam Veterans," *New York Times*, November 10, 1982.

14. Tom Morganthau and Mary Lord, "Honoring Vietnam Veterans—At Last," *Newsweek*, November 22, 1982, 80, 86.

15. Editorial, *Minneapolis Star and Tribune*, November 11, 1982, in *Editorials on File* 13, no. 21 (November 1–15, 1982): 1288; editorial, *Chattanooga Times*, November 11, 1982, in ibid., 1285.

16. Editorial, *Gary Post-Tribune*, November 9, 1982, in ibid., 1288 (presumably the editor meant *perpetrators*, not *provocateurs*); Jeff Levine and Kathleen O'Dell, "Emotions of War Still Run High," *USA Today*, November 9, 1982; editorial, "'Nam Revisited," *Dallas Morning News*, November 11, 1982.

17. Kip Cooper, "Memorial, or Hole in Ground?" *San Diego Union*, [November 1982], in *Vietnam Veterans Leadership Program Press Coverage: The Program's Second Year, October 1982–October 1983*, 247, LBP; Jan Scruggs to Ronald Reagan, June 23, 1982, casefile 103524, Reagan Library; Jan Scruggs to Elizabeth Dole, July 15, 1982, box 48, VVMF-MD; Jan Scruggs to Ronald Reagan, October 20, 1982, casefile 105352, Reagan Library.

18. Jan Scruggs to Sen. Alan J. Dixon (D., Illinois), July 27, 1982, casefile 092920; Jan Scruggs to Sen. Alfonse D'Amato (R., New York), July 27, 1982, casefile 094938; Jan Scruggs to Sen. John Tower (R., Texas), July 28, 1982, casefile 092300, Reagan Library.

19. E.g., Rep. Gillespie V. (Sonny) Montgomery (D., Mississippi) to President and Mrs. Ronald Reagan, July 19, 1982, document no. 088516; Sen. S. I. Hayakawa (R., California) to Ronald Reagan, July 26, 1982, document no. 090215; Elizabeth H. Dole, memorandum for Michael K. Deaver, August 3, 1982, casefile 103524; Orrin G. Hatch to Nina Wormser, scheduling director for the first lady, September 29, 1982, casefile 106189, Reagan Library.

20. Senator George J. Mitchell to Ronald Reagan, August 6, 1982, casefile 093458; Sen. Paula Hawkins

to Ronald Reagan, August 16, 1982, casefile 094574, Reagan Library. Hawkins was often classed as a "New Right" politician. "The New Right Senators," *Washington Post*, January 17, 1982.

21. Allan A. Myer, memorandum for William P. Clark, November 4, 1982, casefile 111168; hand-written annotation dated November 6, 1982, on letter to the president from Al Keller Jr., national commander, American Legion, October 29, 1982, casefile 107677, Reagan Library.

22. Lou Cannon, *President Reagan: The Role of a Lifetime* (New York: PublicAffairs, 2000), 130.

23. VVMF call report of conversation with Morton Blackwell, October 7, [1982], box 48, VVMF-MD; VVMF call report of conversation with an unnamed "White House Insider," October 21, 1982, box 48, VVMF-MD.

24. Scruggs and Swerdlow, *To Heal a Nation*, 128; Lou Cannon, "White House Team No Longer Pulling Together in the Traces," *Washington Post*, November 15, 1982; William K. Sadleir, director, presidential appointments and scheduling, to Jan Scruggs, October 6, 1982, box 50, VVMF-MD; Ronald Reagan and Nancy Reagan to VVMF, October 28, 1982, casefile 107308, Reagan Library; VVMF, *Program Souvenir, National Salute to Vietnam Veterans, November 10–14, 1982, Washington, DC* (McLean, VA: Tyl Associates, [1982]), 31.

25. Chris Buckley, "The Wall," *Esquire*, September 1985, 69.

26. Milt Copulos, "An Effort to Victimize Vietnam Vets One Last Time," *Washington Times*, November 12, 1982.

27. Jan C. Scruggs to Edmund T. Pratt Jr., April 14, 1983; minutes of the VVMF independent audit committee meeting, April 29, 1983, box 30, VVMF-MD; *Program Souvenir, National Salute*, 13; McCombs, "Veterans Honor the Fallen."

28. Myer, memorandum to William P. Clark, November 4, 1982.

29. "Drafts of a Proclamation and Radio Address that Are Being Offered for Consideration for the Vietnam Veterans Memorial," November 5, 1982, casefile 111161, Reagan Library.

30. Bruske and Bredemeier, "Vietnam War Dead's Names"; Andersen and Branegan, "Homecoming at Last"; editorial, *Sacramento Bee*, November 11, 1982, in *Editorials on File* 13, no. 21 (November 1–15, 1982): 1287.

31. Scruggs and Swerdlow, *To Heal a Nation*, 142.

32. Broyles, "Remembering a War." Jerome Brondfield wrote about the ethnic diversity of the names on the wall, and those of his little league baseball team, as a "perfect American counterpoint." Brondfield, "The Little Leaguer I'll Never Forget," *Reader's Digest*, August 1983.

33. Peggy Noonan, *What I Saw at the Revolution: A Political Life in the Reagan Era* (New York: Fawcett Columbine, 1990), 30; John Wheeler, Jan Scruggs, and Robert Doubek to Ronald Reagan, January 27, 1983, casefile 276100, Reagan Library; Andersen and Branegan, "Homecoming at Last."

34. Bruske and Bredemeier, "Vietnam War Dead's Names"; "Quotelines"; Robin Wagner-Pacifici and Barry Schwartz, "The Vietnam Veterans Memorial: Commemorating a Difficult Past," *American Journal of Sociology* 97, no. 2 (September 1991): 378.

35. *Art in America*, November 1983, 26; Gerald Nicosia, *Home to War: A History of the Vietnam Veterans' Movement* (New York: Three Rivers Press, 2001), 102. The Nixon administration was so concerned about the reading of the names of the dead in the 1969 demonstration that it considered taking out an injunction against the use of the names. "Game Plan for the President's Pursuit for Peace Speech," in *From the President: Richard Nixon's Secret Files*, ed. Bruce Oudes (New York: Harper and Row, 1989), 66.

36. "The Faces of the American Dead in Vietnam: One Week's Toll," *Life*, June 27, 1969, 20–32.

37. Peggy Borsay, "Memories from the Wall [November 11, 1982]," in Jan Scruggs, with Kim Murphy, *The Wall That Heals* (Washington, DC: VVMF, 1992), 19; there is footage of Sandie Fauriol of the VVMF reading names in the documentary *Vietnam Memorial*.

38. In some memorials in the South created during the Jim Crow era, there were separate listings for white and "colored" troops. The author is grateful to Chris Appy for pointing this out.

39. Ellen Syvertson, "Rudy Lujan," *Del Sol* (New Mexico), July 1983, 50.

40. Robert W. Doubek, memorandum to VVMF executive staff re: "Treatment of Names of Unaccounted For," October 1, 1981, box 2, VVMF-MD.

41. Ann Mills-Griffith, National League of Families of American Prisoners and Missing in Southeast Asia, telephone interview by the author, November 16, 2006; Lisa Gough, VVMF, e-mail message to the author, November 21, 2006.

42. Jan Scruggs, *Writings on the Wall: Reflection on the Vietnam Veterans Memorial* (Washington, DC: VVMF, 1994), 56.

43. VVMF, the Virtual Wall, www.vvmf.org//index.cfm?SectionID=110&Wall_Id_No=200003 (accessed August 17, 2007); Clay Marston, "Name of USAF Technical Sergeant Richard Bernard Fitzgibbon to Be Added to the Vietnam Veterans Memorial," the Virtual Wall, www.vvmf.org//index.cfm?SectionID=110&anClip=173176 (accessed August 17, 2007).

44. Several families asked that the name of their relative be omitted from the wall, and their wishes were respected. Datalantic, Inc., to Robert Doubek, January 25, 1982, box 7, VVMF-MD. Clerical errors in military record keeping meant that the names of fourteen people who survived the war were inscribed on the memorial. The errors could be corrected if and when a panel was damaged and needed to be replaced. "A Memorial Lists Living as the Dead," *New York Times*, February 11, 1991.

45. Stories of soldiers who died long after the war from injuries received in combat or who died outside the combat zone and whose families successfully petitioned to have their names added to the wall appear in Zita Arocha, "A Snowy Remembrance Day at Vietnam Wall, Arlington," *Washington Post*, November 12, 1987. Another such story is recorded in White House correspondence: Mary E. Brazen to Joseph M. Gaydos, November 16, 1982; Joseph M. Gaydos to the president, November 18, 1982; Kenneth M. Duberstein, assistant to the president, to Joseph M. Gaydos, January 31, 1983, casefile 110384, Reagan Library. Josephine Gimble, letter to the editor, *Washington Post*, November 20, 1982, tells the story of a young man who suffered irreversible brain damage because of an adverse reaction to the anesthetic administered following a minor shrapnel wound. He died without recovering but his name was left off the wall.

46. A former Agency for International Development (AID) worker proposed that a memorial be constructed for the AID personnel, journalists, and International Voluntary Service advisers who were killed in Vietnam. Michael Benge, letter to the editor, *Washington Post*, March 5, 1988. William E. Colby, head of CORDS, complained that the CORDS workers who died in Vietnam were not recognized on the wall. Colby to John P. Wheeler III, June 27, 1983; William E. Colby to the Office of the Assistant Secretary of Defense for Public Affairs, June 27, 1983; Jan Scruggs to William E. Colby, July 8, 1983, box 4, VVMF-MD. Others complained about the absence of civilian names from the memorial. Jan Scruggs, VVMF call report of conversation with George Esper, May 26, 1983, box 50, VVMF-MD.

47. Robert Nogle, quoted in Ken Ringle, Keith B. Richburg, and Kenneth Bredemeier, "Voices from a War," *Washington Post*, November 13, 1982.

48. On the names added since the unveiling of the wall, see Scruggs and Swerdlow, *To Heal a Nation*, 415; David Stout, "Six New Names in a Wall of Granite Recall Cost of Vietnam," *International Herald Tribune*, May 26, 2003; VVMF, "Additions Since the Dedication," www.vvmf.org/index.cfm?sectionID=402 (accessed February 19, 2007); VVMF, "Three Names to Be Added to Vietnam Veterans Memorial," press release dated April 27, [2007], www.vvmf.org/index.cfm?SectionID=554 (accessed May 24, 2007).

49. Chris Burden, *Beyond the Limits*, ed. Peter Noever (Ostfildern, Germany: Cantz Verlag, 1996), 150–51. Burden created "The Other Vietnam Memorial" in 1991.

50. Robert D. Heinl, "The Collapse of the Armed Forces," *Armed Forces Journal*, June 7, 1971; reprinted in *Vietnam and America: A Documented History*, ed. Marvin E. Gettleman, Jane Franklin, Marilyn B. Young, and H. Bruce Franklin, 2nd ed. (New York: Grove Press, 1995), 327.

51. The term *fragging* comes from the weapon of choice in such attacks, fragmentation grenades, which left no forensic evidence that could identify the attacker. For an account of incidents of mutiny, combat refusal, and fraggings, see David Cortright, *Soldiers in Revolt: GI Resistance during the Vietnam War* (Chicago: Haymarket Books, 2005), 35–39, 44. Fragging attempts ran to 435 between 1969 and 1971, resulting in 85 deaths. Given the mortality rate of those who served in Vietnam—approximately one in 50 died there in 1969, consistent with the casualty rate in the course of the war—it is plausible to suppose that one or more of the perpetrators must, in turn, have died in Vietnam.

52. Associated Press, "Pride in Ranks"; Philip M. Boffey, "Vietnam Veterans' Parade a Belated Welcome Home," *New York Times*, November 14, 1982; *Program Souvenir, National Salute*, 20; editorial, *Bismarck (ND) Tribune*, November 11, 1982, in *Editorials on File* 13, no. 21 (November 1–15, 1982): 1286; photo by Nick Sebastian in Scruggs and Swerdlow, *To Heal a Nation*, following p. 144; photo by Gordon Baer, in Nancy Howell-Koehler, *Vietnam: The Battle Comes Home* (New York: Morgan and Morgan, 1984), 99. Bloom quoted in Morganthau and Lord, "Honoring Vietnam Veterans," 82; Campbell and Pennsylvania veteran quoted in Bredemeier, "Diverse Crowd Is Unanimous."

53. Bredemeier, "Diverse Crowd Is Unanimous"; McCombs, "Veterans Honor the Fallen"; photo of hand-lettered signs by Richard Hofmeister, in *Reflections on the Wall: The Vietnam Veterans Memorial*, photographs by the Smithsonian Institution's Printing and Photographic Services, introduction and narration by Edward Ezell (Harrisburg, PA: Stackpole Books, 1987), 31; *Vietnam Memorial*; Associated Press, "Pride in Ranks"; Keith Walker, *A Piece of My Heart: The Stories of Twenty-Six American Women Who Served in Vietnam* (New York: Ballantine, 1985), 178–79.

54. McGrory, "It May Have Been the Best Idea"; Scruggs and Swerdlow, *To Heal a Nation*, 150; photo of a placard by Jeff Tinsley, in Ezell, *Reflections on the Wall*, 30; Boffey, "Vietnam Veterans' Parade"; *Vietnam Memorial*; Associated Press, "Pride in Ranks."

55. Scruggs and Swerdlow, *To Heal a Nation*, 150; McGrory, "It May Have Been the Best Idea."

56. Boffey, "Vietnam Veterans' Parade." The author met Poccia at an antidraft protest in New York in the summer of 1980 and remembers Poccia's hospitality then with gratitude.

57. Footage in *Vietnam Memorial* and the documentary *All the Unsung Heroes*, prod. Roger Peterson (Heritage America Group, 1990); Scruggs and Swerdlow, *To Heal a Nation*, 149; Bredemeier, "Diverse Crowd Is Unanimous"; Boffey, "Vietnam Veterans' Parade"; U.S. Congress, House, Don Lassen, "The Sad Facts," *Static Line*, October 1982, 98th Cong., 1st sess., February 15, 1983, *Congressional Record*, E 472. During the Civil War, local recruitment meant that there was a strong correlation between service in a particular military unit and citizenship of a state, but this connection had been largely broken by the time of the Vietnam War except in reserve and National Guard units, few of which were mobilized.

58. Photos by Dane A. Penland and Jeff Tinsley, in Ezell, *Reflections on the Wall*, 33; *Vietnam Memorial*; McCombs, "Veterans Honor the Fallen"; McGrory, "It May Have Been the Best Idea." This affectionate description of the ragged army of marchers strongly resembles the appreciation by a retired general for the men who have organized a fundraiser for his failing hotel in the film *White Christmas*, dir. Michael Curtiz (1954). Christian Appy has pointed out the similarity between Sullivan's statement and the general's, as examples of what he aptly terms "sentimental militarism." See Christian G. Appy, "'We'll Follow the Old Man': Strains of Sentimental Militarism in Popular Films of the Fifties," in *Rethinking Cold War Culture*, ed. Peter J. Kuznick and James Burkhart Gilbert (Washington, DC: Smithsonian Institution Press, 2001).

59. McGrory, "It May Have Been the Best Idea"; Myra MacPherson, *Long Time Passing: Vietnam and the Haunted Generation* (New York: New American Library, 1984), 77; banner photo by Larry Ford in Scruggs and Swerdlow, *To Heal a Nation*, following p. 144.

60. Scruggs and Swerdlow, *To Heal a Nation*, 150.

61. McCombs, "Veterans Honor the Fallen"; Rosellini, "Salute Opening for Vietnam Veterans."

62. Scruggs and Swerdlow, *To Heal a Nation*, 149; banner photo by Dane A. Penland, in Ezell, *Reflections on the Wall*, 32; *Vietnam Memorial*.

63. McCombs, "Veterans Honor the Fallen, Mark Reconciliation."

64. Renata Adler, *Reckless Disregard: Westmoreland v. CBS et al.; Sharon v. Time* (New York: Knopf, 1986); Burton Benjamin, *Fair Play: CBS, General Westmoreland, and How a Television Documentary Went Wrong* (New York: Harper and Row, 1988). For the background to the lawsuit, see Sam Adams, *War of Numbers: An Intelligence Memoir* (South Royalton, VT: Steerforth Press, 1994).

65. Ezell, *Reflections on the Wall*, 39, with photo by Richard Hofmeister.

66. Brewin and Shaw, *Vietnam on Trial*, 43; Michael Clark, "Remembering Vietnam," in *The Vietnam War and American Culture*, ed. John Carlos Rowe and Rick Berg (New York: Columbia University Press, 1991), 178.

67. McGrory, "It May Have Been the Best Idea."

68. See, e.g., Larry Levy, "We Licked 'Em: Westmoreland Addresses Viet Vets," *Arizona Republic*, February 9, 1984.

69. Ringle, Richburg, and Bredemeier, "Voices from a War."

70. McCombs, "Veterans Honor the Fallen."

71. Stephen Weiss, Clark Dougan, David Fulghum, Denis Kennedy, and the editors of the Boston Publishing Company, *The Vietnam Experience: A War Remembered* (Boston: Boston Publishing Company, 1986), 164.

72. Wallace Terry, *Bloods: An Oral History of the Vietnam War by Black Veterans* (New York: Ballantine, 1984), 14.

73. John Bodnar, *Remaking America: Public Memory, Commemoration, and Patriotism in the Twentieth Century* (Princeton: Princeton University Press, 1992), 7.

74. As well as fig. 13, see American Servicemen's Life Insurance, photograph following p. 144, in Scruggs and Swerdlow, *To Heal a Nation*.

75. Footage in *All the Unsung Heroes*; McCombs, "Veterans Honor the Fallen."

76. McCombs, "Veterans Honor the Fallen."

77. Footage of the speech in *Vietnam Memorial*. The Vietnam veteran Lily Adams recalls that, at that line of the speech, "everyone went nuts" with cheering. Walker, *Piece of My Heart*, 405.

78. Quoted in Scruggs and Swerdlow, *To Heal a Nation*, 152.

79. McCombs, "Veterans Honor the Fallen."

80. Scruggs and Swerdlow, *To Heal a Nation*, 152.

81. Quotations from *Vietnam Memorial*; Bredemeier, "Diverse Crowd Is Unanimous."

82. Scruggs, *Wall That Heals*, 22–23.

83. Lydia Fish, *The Last Firebase: A Guide to the Vietnam Veterans Memorial* (Shippensburg, PA: White Mane, 1987), 25; footage of the dedication ceremony appears in the documentaries *All the Unsung Heroes*;

Vietnam Memorial; and *Vietnam Veterans Memorial: The Last Landing Zone*, prod. Bob Muller (All-American Video Productions, Inc., 1994).

84. Associated Press, "Pride in Ranks."

85. Scruggs and Swerdlow, *To Heal a Nation*, 154. The feature film *To Heal a Nation* dramatizes the scene. Christopher Buckley reports that scenes such as that of veterans searching for each other's names but encountering each other instead did take place—but not necessarily during the dedication. Buckley, "The Wall," 61; Paul Weingarten, "The Black Wall," *Chicago Tribune*, April 21, 1985.

86. Kevin Cook, "Notes to Dead Heroes Gone, Not Forgotten," *Washington Times*, May 27, 1985; Eleanor Wimbish, "Letters to Billy," *McCall's*, June 1985, 27, 141. Wimbish's symbolic role is discussed further in chapter 11.

87. Marcia Hynes Amos, letter to the editor, *Washington Post*, November 20, 1982. The letter is reproduced in Scruggs and Swerdlow, *To Heal a Nation*, 140–41.

88. Veterans quoted in Keri Guten, "Viet Memorial Art's 'Beauty' in Eye of Beholder," *San Antonio Light*, November 10, 1982; Rosellini, "Salute Opening for Vietnam Veterans"; Douglas Turner, "Vietnam War Memorial Evokes Dark Memories for Area Vets," *Buffalo News*, November 12, 1982; Becky Pietz quoted in Kathryn Marshall, *In the Combat Zone: Vivid Personal Recollections of the Vietnam War from the Women Who Served There* (New York: Penguin, 1987), 106.

89. Ringle, Richburg, and Bredemeier, "Voices from a War."

90. Morganthau and Lord, "Honoring Vietnam Veterans," 81.

91. Fish, *Last Firebase*, 69.

92. Behan's visit took place in 1983, the year after the salute and before the Frederick Hart statue was added. *Wall of Tears: Vietnam Confronted*, prod. Allan M. Perkal and Judith Montell (Vietnam Veterans Video Production Co., 1985).

93. Leonard Sykes Jr., "Vietnam: A Horror Story Unfairly Told," *Lake County (IL) News-Sun*, November 20–21, 1982.

94. Don Norville, "Welcome Home," *Montana Vietnam Veterans' Memorial* (Missoula: Montana State Vietnam Memorial Committee, 1988), 8; this souvenir magazine of the 1988 dedication of the Montana Vietnam Veterans Memorial was found in AFP.

95. Levine and O'Dell, "Emotions of War Still Run High"; Marshall, *In the Combat Zone*, 228; McGrory, "It May Have Been the Best Idea"; *From Vietnam to Washington, D.C., and Beyond*, prod. Carlos Ricketson (Vietnam Veterans of Oregon Memorial Fund, 1984); Scruggs, *Wall That Heals*, 6; Walker, *Piece of My Heart*, 65; Diane Carlson Evans, speaking in the documentary *Not on the Front Line*, prod. Janet Nearhood (University of Nebraska, Lincoln, ETV Network, KUON, 1991); "Veteran Observers," *Newsweek*, November 8, 1987, 13. For more on the therapeutic visits to the memorials by veterans suffering from PTSD, see, e.g., John S. Lang, "A Memorial Wall that Healed Our Wounds," *U.S. News and World Report*, November 21, 1983, 70; Aphrodite Matsakis, *Vietnam Wives: Women and Children Surviving Life with Veterans Suffering Post Traumatic Stress Disorder* (Kensington, MD: Woodbine House, 1988), 141; John Russell Smith, "Individual Psychotherapy with Viet Nam Veterans," in *The Trauma of War: Stress and Recovery in Viet Nam Veterans*, ed. Stephen M. Sonnenberg, Arthur S. Blank Jr., and John A. Talbot (Washington, DC: American Psychiatric Press, 1985), 138, 161–62.

96. Editorial, *Chattanooga Times*, November 11, 1982, in *Editorials on File* 13, no. 21 (November 1–15, 1982): 1285; editorial, *Deseret News*, November 10–11, 1982, in ibid., 1292; editorial, "The Vietnam Memorial," *Washington Post*, November 13, 1982. See also, e.g., editorial, *Wisconsin State Journal*, November 12, 1982, in *Editorials on File* 13, no. 21 (November 1–15, 1982): 1284; Weingarten, "Black Wall." "Vietnam Memorial Gathering Its Own Art Exhibit," *New York Times*, November 10, 1991.

97. Michael Miller, Board of Directors of Oregon Vietnam Veterans Leadership Program, and Robert Hunter, chairman, Oregon Vietnam Veterans National Salute to "Dear Fellow Oregonian," October 1982, in the records of the Vietnam Veterans of Oregon Memorial Fund, made available to the author by Jerry Pero.

98. *From Vietnam to Washington, D.C., and Beyond*.

99. Walker, *Piece of My Heart*, 178–79.

100. McGrory, "It May Have Been the Best Idea." Margaret Hamilton, telegram to Ronald Reagan, November 13, 1982; Lynne Burgess to Ronald Reagan, November 11, 1982; Keith Hazen to Ronald Reagan, November 12, 1982, casefile 108268, Reagan Library.

101. *Program Souvenir, National Salute*, 36. Shull's name is misspelled as "Schull."

102. *Vietnam Veterans Memorial: The Last Landing Zone*.

103. *Vietnam Memorial*.

104. Maguire, letter to the editor, *Washington Post*, November 20, 1982.

105. Ronald Reagan, "Remarks on Presenting the Presidential Citizens Medal to Raymond Weeks at a Veterans Day Ceremony," November 11, 1982, in *Reagan 1982*, bk. 2, *PPP* (1983), 1445–46.

106. Harry Haines, "'What Kind of War?': An Analysis of the Vietnam Veterans Memorial," *Critical Studies in Mass Communication* 3, no. 1 (March 1986): 3.

107. Ronald Reagan, "Address to the Nation on Strategic Arms Reduction and Nuclear Deterrence," November 22, 1982, in *Reagan 1982*, bk. 2, *PPP* (1983), 1505.

108. Sen. Alfonse D'Amato to Ronald Reagan, August 18, 1982, casefile 094938, Reagan Library.

109. Broyles, "Remembering a War," 83.

6. "In Unity and with Resolve"

1. Jan Scruggs and Joel Swerdlow, *To Heal a Nation* (New York: Harper and Row, 1985), 120, 122, 127.

2. Jan Scruggs to James Watt, December 8, 1982, box 62, VVMF-MD; Robert Martin, national commander of AMVETS, to James Watt, December 15, 1982, casefile 122911, Reagan Library (a copy of the letter appears in box 5, VVMF-MD). AMVETS claimed two hundred thousand members, an unspecified number of whom were Vietnam veterans.

3. VVMF, *Statement Regarding Legislative Initiative on Memorial Design*, November 4, 1982, box 62, VVMF-MD. Rep. Morris Udall (D., Arizona), chairman of the House Interior Committee, introduced the bill on Bailey's behalf. U.S. Congress, House, H.J. Res. 636, Directing Completion of Vietnam Veterans Memorial in West Potomac Park in the District of Columbia, 97th Cong., 2d sess., December 20, 1982, *Congressional Record*, H 10511; "Bailey Bills for Vietnam Memorial Pass House in Final Hours," press release for Don Bailey (December 20, 1982), box 62, VVMF-MD; VVMF call report of conversation with Mark Trautwein, Udall's legislative assistant, December 21, 1982, box 29, VVMF-MD; "House Maneuver on Memorial Fails but Controversy Continues," *AIA Journal*, February 1983, 11; VVMF call report of conversation with Andy Walquist, assistant to Sen. John Warner, December 21, 1982, box 29, VVMF-MD; Philip Geyelin, "The Vietnam Memorial (Cont'd.?)," *Washington Post*, January 11, 1983.

4. The meeting took place on December 14, 1982. Jan C. Scruggs to Elliot Richardson, January 26, 1983, box 30, VVMF-MD.

5. VVMF call report of conversation with Andy Walquist, December 21, 1982, box 29, VVMF-MD. See also Phil McCombs, "Arts Beat," *Washington Post*, January 5, 1983.

6. Gary C. Blyer, White House memorandum to Becky Norton Dunlop, January 10, 1983, casefile 117823, Reagan Library. Dunlop, a "movement conservative," was special assistant to the president and director of the Office of Cabinet Affairs.

7. Geyelin, "Vietnam Memorial (Cont'd.?)."

8. Jim Cicconi, memorandum to Craig L. Fuller, January 11, 1983, casefile 117823, Reagan Library. Cicconi, special assistant to James Baker, circulated Geyelin's article to other staff members, and the comment was his annotation.

9. Charles Mathias and John Warner to James Watt, January 11, 1983, box 13, VVMF-MD; a copy is in casefile 126865, Reagan Library. VVMF call report of conversation with Monica Healy, an aide to Sen. Mathias, concerning Mathias's call to Michael Deaver, January 20, 1983, box 48, VVMF-MD. Mathias followed up with a note to Michael Deaver "supplementing our conversation," attaching the letter he and John Warner wrote to Watt on January 11, 1983, casefile 126865, Reagan Library.

10. Jan Scruggs, VVMF call report of conversation with Dick Munro, January 19, 1982; and J. Richard Munro to James A. Baker III, January 25, 1983, box 30, VVMF-MD.

11. Terrence O'Donnell to Byron Cavaney, deputy assistant to the president, January 14, 1983, box 7, VVMF-MD; Terrence O'Donnell to Byron Cavaney, January 19, 1983, box 30, VVMF-MD; Scruggs to Richardson, January 26, 1983.

12. Site plan attached to Robert A. Carter, VVMF executive vice president, to James Watt, January 14, 1983, box 13; VVMF call report of conversation between Jack Wheeler and Sen. Mathias, January 17, 1983, box 30; VVMF call report of conversation with Dan Smith of the Department of the Interior, January 25, 1983, box 30, VVMF-MD.

13. Scruggs to Elliot Richardson, January 26, 1983.

14. Judith Miller, "Reagan Certifies Salvador for Aid: Hails Progress Despite 'Obstacles,'" *New York Times*, January 22, 1983.

15. Dario Moreno, *U.S. Policy in Central America: The Endless Debate* (Miami: Florida International University Press, 1990), 94, tables 3 and 4.

16. "Decertify Hypocrisy on Salvador," *New York Times*, January 24, 1983.

17. Martin Tolchin, "Reagan Being Warned against Bypassing Congress on Salvador Aid," *New York Times*, March 4, 1983.

18. Bernard Weinraub, "Congress Renews Curbs on Actions against Nicaragua," *New York Times*, December 23, 1982; James M. Scott, *Deciding to Intervene: The Reagan Doctrine and American Foreign Policy* (Durham: Duke University Press, 1996), 163. The amendment to the Intelligence Authorizing Act of 1983

was named for Rep. Edward P. Boland (D., Massachusetts), chairman of the Permanent Select Committee on Intelligence.

19. William LeoGrande, *Our Own Backyard: The United States in Central America, 1977–1992* (Chapel Hill: University of North Carolina Press, 1998), 303.

20. John B. Oakes, "Central American Folly," *New York Times*, November 26, 1982.

21. Bernard Weinraub, "Rumor and Bickering on U.S. Salvador Policy," *New York Times*, February 11, 1983; "Around the World; Salvadoran Rebels Raid Army's Biggest Barracks," *New York Times*, January 28, 1983; UPI [United Press International], "Salvadoran City Seized by Rebels," *New York Times*, February 1, 1983; Lydia Chavez, "City's Fall Called Blow to Salvador," *New York Times*, February 2, 1983.

22. Phil McCombs, "Watt Stalls Addition to Vietnam Memorial," *Washington Post*, January 29, 1983. At a Chamber of Commerce briefing, Watt said, "I will be resolved in the next 12–15 months. We had a consensus and I am not willing to break from that until we have a new consensus." Mary Jo Malone, memorandum to Those Concerned with Vietnam Veterans Memorial, January 28, 1983, box 30, VVMF-MD.

23. James Watt to J. Carter Brown, February 1, 1983, box 29, VVMF-MD.

24. Phil McCombs, "Watt's Memorial Turnabout," *Washington Post*, February 2, 1983; M. Sullivan, "Watt Opts for 'Peace with Honor' on the Mall," *Washington Times*, February 3, 1983.

25. Morgan S. Ruph, national executive director, AMVETS, to Edwin Meese III, January 31, 1983, casefile 122911; Morgan S. Ruph to Michael Deaver, White House deputy chief of staff, January 31, 1983, casefile 124217, Reagan Library.

26. According to Doubek, he helped draft the letters. Doubek, VVMF call report of conversation with Cooper Holt and [Thorne H.] "Tip" Marlow of the Veterans of Foreign Wars, January 26, 1982, box 5, VVMF-MD; Cooper Holt, executive director, Veterans of Foreign Wars, to James Watt, January 26, 1983; and Cooper Holt to George Bush, January 27, 1983, box 48, VVMF-MD.

27. Robert Dallek, *Ronald Reagan: The Politics of Symbolism* (Cambridge, MA: Harvard University Press, 1999), 84–85. Ronald Brownstein and Nina Easton, *Reagan's Ruling Class* (New York: Pantheon, 1983), 118–25.

28. Edwin M. Yoder Jr., "Watt's Forked Tongue," *Washington Post*, January 26, 1983; Associated Press, "Two Indian Groups Ask for Watt Resignation," *Washington Post*, January 28, 1983.

29. Jan Scruggs, VVMF call report of conversation with Jack Wheeler III, January 26, [1983], box 30, VVMF-MD.

30. Jan Scruggs to Edwin Meese III, January 26, 1983; and Jan Scruggs to George Bush, January 26, 1983, box 48, VVMF-MD.

31. John Wheeler, Jan Scruggs, and Robert Doubek to Ronald Reagan, January 27, 1982, casefile 276100; William K. Sadleir, director, presidential appointments and scheduling to John Wheeler, February 7, 1983, casefile 276100, Reagan Library.

32. Jan Scruggs to Jennifer Fitzgerald, assistant to the vice president for appointments and scheduling, January 26, 1982, box 48, VVMF-MD.

33. Cooper Holt to George Bush, January 27, 1983, box 48, VVMF-MD.

34. VVMF call report of conversation with Bill Eckert, January 28, 1983, box 30; Doubek, VVMF call report of conversation with Cooper Holt and "Tip" Marlow, January 26, 1983, box 5, VVMF-MD.

35. VVMF call report of conversation between Jack Wheeler and Margaret Tutwiler, assistant to James Baker, January 31, 1983; VVMF call report of conversation with Michael Deaver's secretary, January 31, 1983; VVMF call report of conversation with Monica Healy, of Sen. Mathias's staff, January 31, 1983; and VVMF call report of conversation with Terry O'Donnell, February 2, 1983, box 48, VVMF-MD.

36. VVMF call report of conversation with O'Donnell, February 2, 1983.

37. Reagan established a "hands-off" management style, setting the policy or strategy and then leaving it to his aides to implement it. John Patrick Diggins, *Ronald Reagan: Fate, Freedom, and the Making of History* (New York: W. W. Norton, 2007), 309; Edwin Meese III, telephone interview by the author, September 4, 2007. Reagan's diary gives no hint that he was aware of the machinations about the placement of the statue and flag during the relevant weekend. Ronald Reagan, *The Reagan Diaries*, ed. Douglas Brinkley (New York: HarperCollins, 2007), 128–29.

38. Doubek, VVMF call report of conversation with Holt and Marlow, January 26, 1983; VVMF call report of conversation between Robert Carter and Milt Copulos, October 12, 1982, box 29, VVMF-MD; Mark A. Peterson, "The Presidency and Organized Interests: White House Patterns of Interest Group Liaison," *American Political Science Review* 80, no. 3 (September 1992): 620; John H. Kessel, "The Structures of the Reagan White House," *American Journal of Political Science* 28, no. 2 (May 1984): 251; Juan Williams, "President Courting Conservatives, but They Remain Cool," *Washington Post*, April 13, 1984.

39. VVMF call report of conversation with O'Donnell, February 2, 1983. The White House wanted to keep its name out of the story because "there were well-intentioned people on both sides" of the argument.

Terry O'Donnell, telephone interview by the author, September 10, 2007. Tom Shull also speculates that the White House wanted to keep a low profile so that it would not become "a target for either side"—those who supported and opposed the VVMF. Shull, telephone interview by the author, September 13, 2007.

40. Jan C. Scruggs to Elliot Richardson, February 4, 1983, box 30, VVMF-MD.

41. Kirk Savage, "The Politics of Memory: Black Emancipation and the Civil War Monument," in *Commemorations: The Politics of National Identity*, ed. John R. Gillis (Princeton: Princeton University Press, 1994), 135.

42. Benjamin Forgey, "The Memorial's Moment of Truce," *Washington Post*, February 9, 1983; Phil McCombs, "Flag, Statue Approved for 'Front Door' of Lin's Vietnam Design," *Washington Post*, February 9, 1983; Kent Cooper, "A Proposal for Locating a Flag and Sculpture on the Grounds of the Vietnam Veterans Memorial" (text), and Cooper-Lecky Partnership, EDAW, and Frederick Hart, "Proposal for Locating Flag and Sculpture" (diagram of the plan), December 6, 1982, box 7, VVMF-MD.

43. John Wheeler, statement before the Commission of Fine Arts, February 8, 1983, casefile 276100, Reagan Library.

44. Jack Koczela, letter to the editor, *Washington Post*, February 5, 1983.

45. Benjamin Forgey, "A Mood Is Built," *Washington Post*, November 13, 1982.

46. Steven M. Silver, testimony, minutes of the Commission of Fine Arts meeting, February 8, 1983, 85–89, box 29, VVMF-MD.

47. James Webb, untitled narrative of his involvement in the VVMF sent to Jan Scruggs, January 17, 1984, 16, box 32; VVMF call report of conversation with Dean Phillips, January 21, 1983, box 30, VVMF-MD.

48. Minutes of the Commission of Fine Arts meeting, February 8, 1983, 71–73, 93–95. VVMF call report of conversation with Dan Smith, November 18, 1982; "Placement Poll Taken at the Dedication of the Vietnam Veterans Memorial"; Richard L. Lobb of DCM Group to Jan Scruggs, December 1, 1982, box 62, VVMF-MD.

49. Minutes of the Commission of Fine Arts meeting, February 8, 1983, 30, 35, 41–42; McCombs, "Flag, Statue Approved for 'Front Door' of Lin's Vietnam Design." Henry Hyde also set great store by the press release that Sen. Warner issued on March 24, 1982, stating that the flag would be at the apex of the walls and the statue in front of them. Henry Hyde, "Hyde Calls for American Flag at Vietnam Veterans Memorial," press release, February 7, 1983, box 30, VVMF-MD.

50. U.S. Congress, House, 98th Cong., 1st sess., February 15, 1983, *Congressional Record*, E 472; Michael K. Deaver to Morgan S. Ruph, national executive director, AMVETS, February 9, 1983, casefile 124217; Craig L. Fuller, memorandum for Michael K. Deaver, February 9, 1983, annotated, "Warner, Sen. John W., Mathias, Sen. Charles," casefile 126865; Michael K. Deaver to Jan C. Scruggs, February 9, 1983, casefile 124218, Reagan Library.

51. Ronald Reagan, "Remarks at the Conservative Political Action Conference Dinner," February 18, 1983, APP, www.presidency.ucsb.edu/ws/?pid=40948 (accessed June 22, 2008).

52. VVMF call report of conversation between Kimberly Timmons and Robert Doubek, February 16, 1983; and VVMF call report of conversation between Kimberly Timmons and Jan Scruggs, February 17, 1983, box 48, VVMF-MD.

53. Reagan, "Remarks at the Conservative Political Action Conference Dinner."

54. Lou Cannon, *President Reagan: The Role of a Lifetime* (New York: PublicAffairs, 2000), 290; Robert Timberg, *The Nightingale's Song* (New York: Simon and Schuster, 1995), 17.

55. *Uncommon Valor*, dir. Ted Kotcheff (1983); *Missing in Action*, dir. Joseph Zito (1984); *Rambo: First Blood, Part II*, dir. George Pan Cosmatos (1985). Desmond Ryan, "How Hollywood Fought the War," *Philadelphia Inquirer Magazine*, January 31, 1988.

56. VVMF call report of conversation between Timmons and Scruggs, February 17, 1983.

57. John Wheeler to Edwin Meese III, February 19, 1983, box 48, VVMF-MD.

58. Jan Scruggs to Nancy Reagan, July 14, 1983, annotated "Suggest we do privately?" by AW [Ann Wroblenski, director of projects, Office of the First Lady]; Ann Wroblenski to Jan Scruggs, August 22, 1983; and James S. Rosebush, memorandum to Michael K. Deaver, July 18, 1983, casefile 159036, Reagan Library.

59. VVMF call report of conversation with Meralee Williams, assistant to Edwin Meese, March 21, 1983, box 48, VVMF-MD; communications regarding the presidential visit to the wall, casefile 121213, Reagan Library.

60. Reagan, *Reagan Diaries*, 149.

61. Robert Doubek to Robert F. Cairo, June 10, 1982, box 33, VVMF-MD; Craig Howes, *Voices of the Vietnam POWs: Witnesses to Their Fight* (New York: Oxford University Press, 1993), 8; Gloria Emerson, *Winners and Losers: Battles, Retreats, Gains, Losses and Ruins from the Vietnam War* (New York and London:

Harcourt Brace Jovanovich, 1976), 36. A few years later, the Khe Sanh graffito was inscribed on the Philadelphia Vietnam Veterans Memorial.

62. *The Vietnam Veterans Memorial Fund Report to Congress*, September 1983, 11, casefile 171823, Reagan Library.

63. Jan Scruggs to Elliot Richardson, March 9, 1983; Richardson to Scruggs, March 14, 1983, box 30, VVMF-MD.

64. Roy Cohn to Terrence O'Donnell, March 29, 1983; and Gerald W. Thomas [investigator for GAO], record of phone conversation with Bill Stensland, San Antonio VVLP, January 31, 1984, re: "The 'Roy Cohn' Situation," box 30, VVMF-MD; John Baines, telephone interview by the author, February 5, 2007. At various times, Cohn said that Baines was his client but that Perot was footing the bill, that he was representing both of them, or that Baines was his nominal client but that he was following Perot's instructions. Extensive correspondence and reports of conversations among Scruggs, Cohn, O'Donnell, and the VVMF's advisers can be found in box 30, VVMF-MD.

65. James Webb to Jan Scruggs, January 17 and 27, 1984, box 32, VVMF-MD. Jan Scruggs, memorandum to the file, November 2, 1983, box 32, VVMF-MD. According to Baines, Webb and Perot asked him to act as their "front" in hiring Cohn, during a three-way conference call. William Stensland stated that Webb told him about the argument between Perot and Scruggs regarding the VVMF's financial records. Baines, interview; Thomas, record of phone conversation with Stensland.

66. James Webb, *A Sense of Honor* (Annapolis, MD: Bluejacket Books, 1995); Baines, interview; Reed Harp, "S[an] A[ntonio] Man Leads Fight to Improve Viet Vet's Image," *San Antonio Light*, [November 1981], in *Vietnam Veterans Leadership Program Press Coverage: The Program's First Year, September 1981–September 1982*, LBP; William Stensland, "We Owe Viet Vets Respect," "Viewpoint" section, *San Antonio Light*, March 7, 1982; Keri Guten, "Viet Memorial Art's 'Beauty' in the Eye of the Beholder," *San Antonio Light*, November 10, 1982.

67. Baines, interview; Jan Scruggs, VVMF call report of conversation with Cyrus Vance, July 6, 1983, box 30, VVMF-MD.

68. "Controversy over the Vietnam Memorial," *Eyewitness News*, WDVM TV, November 7, 1983, transcript by Radio-TV Monitoring Service, Inc., Washington, DC, 1; Phil McCombs, "Battle of the Wall," *Washington Post*, November 8, 1983; Christopher Buckley, "The Wall," *Esquire*, September 1985, 70–71. James Webb to Jan Scruggs, January 17, 1984; Scruggs to Webb, January 24, 1984; and Jan Scruggs, memorandum to the file, November 2, 1983, box 32, VVMF-MD. David Christian reported that Sherwood was an ally of Webb and Carhart's in an extensive correspondence with Scruggs in box 31, VVMF-MD. David A. Christian, "Statement," September 23, 1983, sworn and notarized document, box 29, VVMF-MD.

69. "Vietnam Memorial: A Broken Promise, Part III," *Eyewitness News*, WDVM television, November 9, 1983, transcript by Radio-TV Monitoring Service, Inc., Washington, DC, 3–4.

70. A VVMF press release announcing that it formed "to raise funds for a Vietnam memorial in Washington, D.C. and for the New Mexico Chapel" was incorporated in "It's a Capitol Idea," *The Word: The Journal of the Marine Corps Reserve Officers Association*, October 1979, 3. Documentation for the VVMF's intentions and Douglas Westphall's break with the VVMF appears in box 31, VVMF-MD, and includes minutes of the VVMF Board of Directors meeting, November 15, 1979, 2; Walter D. Westphall (Douglas, chairman of the Vietnam Veterans Chapel Board of Trustees) to Jan Scruggs, June 18, 1980; *Vietnam Veterans Chapel Bulletin*, December 1980, box 31, VVMF-MD.

71. "Controversy over the Vietnam Memorial," 1–2.

72. *Vietnam Veterans Chapel Bulletin*, December 1980; "Investigation into Vietnam Memorial Fund Continues," *Eyewitness News*, WDVM television, November 10, 1983, transcript by Radio-TV Monitoring Service, Inc., Washington, DC, 4.

73. John Fales, interview by Carlton Sherwood, "Controversy over the Vietnam Memorial," transcript, 2; "Disabled American Veterans Support Chapel," *Sangre de Cristo Chronicle* (Angel Fire, NM), June 9, 1977, 1; "Vietnam Veterans Peace and Brotherhood Chapel," *DAV Magazine*, July 1977, 12–13; *Vietnam Veterans Chapel Bulletin*, July 1977, AFP; VVLP, *An American Sunrise: A History of ACTION's Three-Year Veterans' Initiative: Technical Report*, attachment 9, "Highlights of Techniques Being Used to Project a Positive Image to the American Public," 5, LBP; "National Gift to Veterans Chapel," *New Mexico Magazine*, July 1983. VVMF call report of conversation between Jan Scruggs and [Charles] Butch Joeckel, assistant national legislative director of the DAV, March 9, [1983]; Jan Scruggs, memorandum, "Conversation with Ray Grace [president of a fundraising organization] Regarding the Disabled American Veterans," March 9, 1983; VVMF call report of conversation between Jan Scruggs and Bill Stensland, March 14, 1983; and VVMF call report of conversation between Jan Scruggs and Denvel Adams, national adjutant and executive director of the DAV, March 15, 1983, box 30, VVMF-MD. Donald E. Schaet to [Denvel] Dale Adams, June 19, 1981; Denvel Adams to Jan Scruggs, June 28, 1983; Scruggs to Adams, July 15, 1983; and VVMF call

report of conversation between Jan Scruggs and Ray Grace concerning Grace's conversation with Butch Joeckel, June 1, 1983, box 31, VVMF-MD.

74. David Christian, a friend of Sherwood's, writes that Sherwood used the words when questioning Christian's support for the VVMF. David Christian and William Hoffer, *Victor Six* (New York: McGraw-Hill, 1990), 201.

75. "Vietnam: A Broken Promise," transcript, 1–2; Rick Atkinson, *The Long Gray Line: From West Point to Vietnam and After; The Turbulent Odyssey of the Class of 1966* (New York: Pocket Books, 1989), 670.

76. Lois Romano, "Veterans and the Memorial Flap," *Washington Post*, November 9, 1983.

77. John S. Lang, "A Memorial Wall That Healed Our Wounds," *U.S. News and World Report*, November 21, 1983, 68. See also Patrice Gaines-Carter, "It Looks Like the Wall Is Crying," *Washington Post*, November 12, 1986.

78. The statement and the first draft of letters to VVMF officers were prepared by National Security Council staff. Untitled statement signed by Ronald Reagan, November 7, 1983, casefile 184445, Reagan Library.

79. Marcia A. Slacum, "Ceremonies Held at Vietnam Memorial," *Washington Post*, November 12, 1983; Charlotte Porter, "Nation Remembers Honored Veterans," *Oregonian*, November 12, 1983.

80. VVMF, "Carlton Sherwood's Series on the Vietnam Memorial: A Miscarriage of Investigative Journalism" 37-page rebuttal document, sent to Edwin Pfeiffer, WDVM-TV, December 21, 1983, box 31, VVMF-MD.

81. Jacquelyn Trescott, "GAO to Audit Vets Fund," *Washington Post*, December 17, 1983. Reps. G. V. "Sonny" Montgomery (D., Mississippi), Duncan Hunter (R., California), John McCain (R., Arizona), Thomas Carper (D., Delaware), David O'B. Martin (R., New York), Thomas Ridge (R., Pennsylvania) to Charles A. Bowsher, comptroller general, GAO, November 18, 1983; Jan Scruggs to the Hon. Charles A. Bowsher, comptroller general, GAO, November 20, 1983; Jan Scruggs, memorandum to Independent Audit Committee, November 28, 1983, box 4, VVMF-MD.

82. Jan Scruggs, VVMF call report of conversation with Giemarso (assistant to Rep. John Murtha of Pennsylvania, a VVMF supporter), January 19, 1984, box 14, VVMF-MD. Giemarso said that Sonny Montgomery would assist Murtha in handling Hunter.

83. Terrence O'Donnell to National Personnel Record Center, St. Louis, Missouri, October 28, 1983; O'Donnell to the Veterans Administration, November 14, 1983; O'Donnell to Kathleen Buck, assistant general counsel, the Pentagon, December 8, 1983; Buck to O'Donnell, April 13, 1984; and Jan C. Scruggs, memorandum to the file, February 24, 1984, box 13, VVMF-MD.

84. Jacquelyn Trescott, "GAO Clears Vet Fund," *Washington Post*, May 19, 1984.

85. *Report by the Comptroller General of the United States: The Vietnam Veterans Memorial Fund's Financial Operations Were Properly Accounted For and Reported* (Washington, D.C.: General Accounting Office, 1984), 61–62.

86. Jan C. Scruggs to H. Ross Perot, June 7, 1984, box 30, VVMF-MD.

87. Jonathan Friendly, "Reporter's Project Ruins His Career," *New York Times*, July 17, 1984.

88. Dave Pearce, WDVM news director, "Memorial Fund Found to Be Commendably Conducted," *Eyewitness News*, WDVM, TV, November 7, 1984, transcript by Radio-TV Monitoring Service, Inc. Washington, DC.

89. Rupert Welch, "Congressman Calls GAO Audit of Viet Memorial 'Inaccurate,'" *Washington Times*, May 23, 1984.

90. Phil McCombs, "No Medals for Memorial," *Washington Post*, June 12, 1986.

91. Jay Winter, *Sites of Memory, Sites of Mourning: The Great War in European Cultural History* (Cambridge: Cambridge University Press, 1995), 27–28.

92. Caspar Weinberger, memorandum to the president re: "Selection and Interment of an Unknown Serviceman from the Vietnam Era," March 16, 1984, casefile 19781955, Reagan Library.

93. Rick Atkinson, "Battle Still Being Fought for Vietnam's Unknown Soldiers," *Kansas City Times*, November 11, 1981. See also Robin Wagner-Pacifici and Barry Schwartz," The Vietnam Veterans Memorial: Commemorating a Difficult Past," *American Journal of Sociology* 97, no. 2 (September 1991): 385.

94. William M. Hammond, *The Unknown Serviceman of the Vietnam Era* (Washington, DC: United States Army Center of Military History, 1985), 5; Allan A. Myer, National Security Council staff member, memorandum to Becky Norton Dunlop, director, Office of Cabinet Affairs, re: "Meeting with National Service Organization Leaders," February 3, 1983, casefile 123146, Reagan Library; David Stout, "Unknown Soldier May Soon Be Known," *International Herald Tribune*, January 21, 1998; "Unknown Vet to Be Exhumed," *International Herald Tribune*, May 8, 1998; "No Longer an 'Unknown,'" *International Herald Tribune*, July 1, 1998; "A Decoration Lost," *International Herald Tribune*, August 24, 1998; *CBS Evening News*, broadcast in the UK on the Sky News channel, January 21, 1998.

95. Associated Press, "Unknown Soldier Begins Journey," *Oregonian*, May 18, 1984. Footage of the procession of the caisson and of President Reagan's speech at the interment ceremony is shown in *Missing in Action 2: The Beginning*, dir. Lance Hool (1985).

96. Michael Blassie grew up in St. Louis. He was single and childless, and his father worked as a meatcutter. Stout, "Unknown Soldier May Soon Be Known."

97. White House, Office of the Press Secretary, "Remarks of the President at Memorial Day Ceremony Honoring Vietnam Unknown Soldier," May 28, 1984, box 48, VVMF-MD.

98. J. Thomas Burch Jr. to Ronald Reagan, June 3, 1984, casefile 230626, Reagan Library.

99. Frederick J. Ryan Jr., director, Presidential Appointments and Scheduling, to Jan Scruggs, May 17, 1984, box 48, VVMF-MD.

100. Scott, *Deciding to Intervene*, 26; David E. Bonior to James Baker, April 25, 1984, box 48, VVMF-MD (a copy of the letter appears in casefile 228547, Reagan Library).

101. Manuscript annotation of National Security Council document routing sheet, casefile 235827, Reagan Library.

102. Robert M. Kimmitt, schedule proposal to Frederick J. Ryan, May 22, 1984, casefile 235827, Reagan Library.

103. Scott, *Deciding to Intervene*, 163–64; Kathryn Roth and Richard Sobel, "Chronology of Events and Public Opinion," in *Public Opinion in U.S. Foreign Policy: The Controversy over Contra Aid*, ed. Richard Sobel (Lanham, MD: Rowman and Littlefield, 1993), 23.

104. Dallek, *Ronald Reagan*, 158.

105. Ronald Reagan, *An American Life* (London: Hutchinson, 1990), 471, 479.

106. Mark Hertsgaard, *On Bended Knee: The Press and the Reagan Presidency* (New York: Farrar Straus Giroux, 1988), 271; Ronald Reagan, "Remarks at the Annual Convention of the National Association of Evangelicals in Orlando, Florida," March 8, 1983, APP, www.presidency.ucsb.edu/ws/?pid=41023 (accessed July 15, 2008).

107. Combat losses in Grenada are cited in Bill Keller and Joel Brinkley, "U.S. Military Is Termed Prepared for Any Move against Nicaragua," *New York Times*, June 4, 1985.

108. Colin Powell, with Joseph E. Persico, *A Soldier's Way: An Autobiography* (London: Hutchinson, 1995), 292.

109. The poll was conducted in September 1983. Hedrick Smith, "Reagan's Crucial Year," *New York Times*, October 16, 1983.

110. Steven R. Weisman, "Reagan Rides the Crest of an Anti-Soviet Wave," *New York Times*, September 25, 1983.

111. George Shultz, *Turmoil and Triumph: Diplomacy, Power, and the Victory of the American Ideal* (New York: Charles Scribner's Sons, 1993), 345.

112. The phrase "Win quickly or get out quickly" was an interpretation of the administration's lessons from Vietnam by William Schneider of the conservative think tank the American Enterprise Institute. "The Legacy of Grenada: Messages to Foes, Allies," *New York Times*, October 26, 1984.

113. Cannon, *President Reagan*, 301, 302.

114. Weinberger presented his tests in a November 28, 1984, speech at the National Press Club; they were later republished as Caspar Weinberger, "The Uses of Military Power," *Defense Issues* 2, no. 44 [1986]. According to Colin Powell, the White House's "political operatives" delayed the public enunciation of Weinberger's six principles until after the November 1984 election. Powell, *A Soldier's Way*, 303.

115. Cannon, *President Reagan*, 302.

116. Timberg, *Nightingale's Song*, 342; Shultz, *Turmoil and Triumph*, 650.

117. Richard Halloran, "U.S. Will Not Drift into a Latin War, Weinberger Says," *New York Times*, November 29, 1984.

118. Wayne S. Smith, "Lies about Nicaragua," *Foreign Policy* 67 (Summer 1987): 88.

119. Roy Gutman, "America's Diplomatic Charade," *Foreign Policy* 56 (Fall 1984): 15–17.

120. LeoGrande, *Our Own Backyard*, 314–18; Peter Kornbluh, "Nicaragua: U.S. Proinsurgency Warfare against the Sandinistas," in *Low Intensity Warfare: Counterinsurgency, Proinsurgency, and Antiterrorism in the Eighties*, ed. Michael T. Klare and Peter Kornbluh (New York: Pantheon Books, 1988), 147; Lydia Chavez, "Reagan's Man in Honduras Hearing Some Back Talk," *New York Times*, July 22, 1984; William Rogers, "The United States and Latin America," *Foreign Affairs: America and the World 1984*, 564; Philip Taubman, "Casey and His CIA on the Rebound," *New York Times*, January 16, 1983.

121. Jeff McMahan, *Reagan and the World: Imperial Policy in the New Cold War* (London: Pluto Press, 1984), 140.

122. Roy Gutman, *Banana Diplomacy: The Making of American Policy in Nicaragua, 1981–1987* (New York: Simon and Schuster, 1988), 140–44; Kornbluh, "Nicaragua," 143–46.

123. Gutman, "America's Diplomatic Charade," 17; McMahan, *Reagan and the World*, 138–41; Kornbluh, "Nicaragua," 136, 142; Shirley Christian, "Nicaragua Police Criticized on Rights," *New York Times*, April 5, 1985; Sara Miles, "Preparing the Battlefield," *NACLA Report on the Americas*, April/May 1986, 35; LeoGrande, *Our Own Backyard*, 314.

124. Louis Harris and Associates telephone poll of a national adult sample, conducted August 18–22, 1983; data provided by RC.

125. Steven R. Weisman, "Reagan Denies Aim Is Bigger Presence in Latin Countries," *New York Times*, July 27, 1983; "President's News Conference on Foreign and Domestic Matters," *New York Times*, July 27, 1983.

126. LeoGrande, *Our Own Backyard*, 195; Shultz, *Turmoil and Triumph*, 961.

127. Shultz, *Turmoil and Triumph*, 311.

128. Steven V. Roberts, "House Backs Halt in Covert Aid to Sandinista Foes," *New York Times*, July 29, 1983.

129. LeoGrande, *Our Own Backyard*, 239–40; Scott, *Deciding to Intervene*, 165.

130. Kornbluh, "Nicaragua," 154; Richard Reeves, *President Reagan: The Triumph of the Imagination* (New York: Simon and Schuster, 2005), 219.

131. LeoGrande, *Our Own Backyard*, 347; Frank J. Fahrenkopf Jr., "Reagan as Political Leader," in *Leadership in the Reagan Presidency, Part II: Eleven Intimate Perspectives*, ed. Kenneth W. Thompson (Lanham, MD: University Press of America, 1993), 26–27.

132. "The State of Things as Seen from State," *New York Times*, April 22, 1984. Eagleburger was the under secretary of state for political affairs.

133. Shultz, *Turmoil and Triumph*, 317.

134. LeoGrande, *Our Own Backyard*, 338–39; Gutman, "America's Diplomatic Charade," 21.

135. Louis Harris and Associates, sponsored by Business Week, telephone poll of a national adult sample conducted between July 7 and 12, 1984; data provided by RC.

136. Joel Brinkley, "Playing by the Wrong Book on Nicaragua," *New York Times*, October 21, 1983; editorial, "The CIA's Murder Manual," *Washington Post*, October 21, 1984; LeoGrande, *Our Own Backyard*, 321, 364; Philip Taubman, "House Votes to Deny Help to Nicaraguan Insurgents," *New York Times*, August 3, 1984. For a discussion of Boland II, see Haynes Johnson, *Sleepwalking through History: America in the Reagan Years* (New York: Anchor Books, 1992), 280; LeoGrande, *Our Own Backyard*, 343–46.

137. Peter Kornbluh, *Nicaragua: The Price of Intervention* (Washington, DC: Institute for Policy Studies, 1987), 193.

138. Lawrence Walsh, *Firewall: The Iran-Contra Conspiracy and Cover-Up* (New York: W. W. Norton, 1997), 7, 60–61, 82, 119. See also Timberg, *Nightingale's Song*, 416; LeoGrande, *Our Own Backyard*, 502; Moreno, *U.S. Policy in Central America*, 115; Shultz, *Turmoil and Triumph*, 414–15.

139. Reeves, *President Reagan*, 227.

140. Fred Hiatt and Joanne Omang, "Details on Honduras Maneuvers Delayed," *Washington Post*, May 16, 1984; Adam Clymer, "Long-Range Hope for Republicans Is Found in Poll," *New York Times*, November 11, 1984; Richard J. Meislin, "New U.S. Exercises Seen in Honduras," *New York Times*, November 17, 1984.

141. VVMF, "America's Veterans—One and All; Tentative Schedule of Events," September 20, 1984; Edward V. Hickey Jr., memorandum to Michael K. Deaver, October 19, 1984, casefile 278319, Reagan Library. Hart himself never gave the sculpture a title. It is referred to variously as the *Three Servicemen*, *Three Fightingmen*, and so forth; these terms are used to avoid the more obvious Three Soldiers, which many marines would regard as a slight. Reagan was not the first president present at the dedication of a Vietnam Veterans Memorial. Gerald Ford was present at the dedication of the El Paso Vietnam Veterans Memorial, although presidential records do not indicate that he gave a speech. Jerry L. Strait and Sandra S. Strait, *Vietnam War Memorials: An Illustrated Reference to Veterans Tributes throughout the United States* (Jefferson, NC: McFarland, 1988), 188–90.

142. Ronald Reagan, "Remarks at Dedication Ceremonies for the Vietnam Veterans Memorial Salute," November 11, 1984, APP, www.presidency.ucsb.edu/ws/?pid=39414 (accessed June 27, 2008).

143. Ronald Reagan to Ray Michael Reed, November 29, 1984, casefile 278322, Reagan Library.

144. Reagan, "Remarks at Dedication Ceremonies"; Arthur S. Brisbane, "President Leads Tribute to Vietnam Veterans: Reconciliation Theme Voiced in Mall Ceremony," *Washington Post*, November 12, 1984. Various drafts of the speech can be found in casefile 8408323l, Reagan Library. The version Reagan gave is marked at the top "Noonan," suggesting that it was written by Peggy Noonan, of all his speech writers the one with the most rhapsodic gifts.

145. Peter J. Rusthoven, associate counsel to the president, memorandum to Richard G. Darman, November 9, 1984, casefile 276946, Reagan Library.

146. Reagan, "Remarks at Dedication Ceremonies."

147. Courtland Milloy, "Brass, Vietnam Veterans Mend Rift: Generals Attend Reunion of 82nd Airborne Paratroopers," *Washington Post*, November 11, 1984.

148. Brisbane, "President Leads Tribute."

149. Arthur S. Brisbane, "Black Vets Spurn Memorial Events," *Washington Post*, November 18, 1984. Holcomb is one of the narrators in Wallace Terry, *Bloods: An Oral History of the Vietnam War by Black Veterans* (New York: Ballantine, 1984).

150. Charles E. Wheeler, "After the War, the Fight Continues," *Washington Times*, November 12, 1984.

151. Elisabeth Bumiller, "The Memorial, Mirror of Vietnam," *Washington Post*, November 9, 1984.

152. Charles E. Wheeler, "Soldiers of Bronze Stand by Memorial," *Washington Times*, October 30, 1984.

153. "Statue of Three GIs Unveiled, Ending Viet Memorial Battle," *Sacramento Bee*, November 10, 1984.

154. Charles Atherton, secretary of the Commission of Fine Arts, presentation at a VVMF symposium, National Building Museum, Washington, DC, November 6, 1992. Karal Ann Marling and Robert Silberman discuss the figures' appearance of vulnerability in "The Statue Near the Wall: The Vietnam Veterans Memorial and the Art of Remembering," *Smithsonian Studies in American Art* 1, no. 1 (Spring 1987): 5–29.

155. Scruggs and Swerdlow, *To Heal a Nation*, 129.

156. Laura Palmer, *Shrapnel in the Heart: Letters and Remembrances from the Vietnam Veterans Memorial* (New York: Random House, 1987), 185.

157. Ira Hamburg, "The President's Corner: A Little Piece of Memorial Folklore," *Among Friends: News of the Friends of the Vietnam Veterans Memorial* 5, no. 1 (Spring 1991): 3.

158. Paul Weingarten, "The Black Wall," *Chicago Tribune*, April 21, 1985.

159. See "House Maneuver on Memorial Fails but Controversy Continues," *AIA Journal*, February 1983, 11; U.S. Congress, House, 100th Cong., 1st sess., November 10, 1987, *Congressional Record*, H 9925–27, in which Robert Dornan introduces HR 1600 mandating a flag at the apex of the memorial; and K. Swisher, "Arts Beat," *Washington Post*, March 13, 1989, which indicates that Dornan was still periodically introducing the bill.

160. *Congressional Record*, H 9926.

161. The VVMF closed their offices on January 25, 1985, but remained in existence at first in a reduced role, organizing ceremonies at the wall, and more recently in an expansive role, running educational programs and fundraising for a visitors' center. Jan Scruggs remains in charge. Patrice Gaines-Carter, "Viet Memorial Fund Closes," *Washington Post*, January 26, 1985.

162. Jan Scruggs, VVMF call report of conversation with Bill Jayne, May 3, 1982; Jan Scruggs, VVMF call report of conversation with Sgt. Quinto Gesiotto of the Park Police, May 7, 1982, box 5, VVMF-MD; Gerald Nicosia, *Home to War: A History of the Vietnam Veterans' Movement* (New York: Three Rivers Press, 2001), 493.

163. Jan Scruggs, call report of conversation with Jim Roderick of Vietnam Veterans Against the War, September 8, 1982, box 5, VVMF-MD.

164. "Vietnam Vets Leadership Group Forming Color Guard Contingent," *Albuquerque Journal*, September 1, 1983. The count of 2,500 MIAs was higher than the Defense Department's and the VVMF's count of 1,350. The higher number appears to include those listed as "killed in action/body not recovered" among the MIAs.

165. Minutes of the VVMF Board of Directors meeting, March 9, 1983, 4, box 1, VVMF-MD.

166. Linda Wheeler, "Vietnam Veterans Quit Vigil, Claiming U.S. 'Double Cross,'" *Washington Times*, July 24, 1985; "Stand Watch for POW/MIAs," *VFW*, February 1984, 24, 64–65; Weingarten, "Black Wall," 37; William M. Welch, "$85,000 in Royalties for Memorial Sculpture," *Washington Post*, November 11, 1987; "Vietnam Veterans of America Baltimore Maryland Chapter 451 News," [March 1989], newsletter, in the author's possession; Stephen Goldstein, "Statue Sculptor Sues over Use of Image," *Washington Times*, November 28, 1991; Jan Scruggs, "Seedy Side of the Memorial," *USA Today*, July 13, 1993; "History of the Last Firebase," www.lastfirebase.com/lfb_story2.htm (accessed November 16, 2006); Linda Wheeler, "Park Rule to Stamp Out Sales of Tee-shirts on Mall," *Washington Post*, April 6, 1995; Linda Wheeler, "Sale of Tee-shirts on Mall to End, Park Service Says; Self-Described Protesters Lose Ruling," *Washington Post*, August 19, 1997; David G. Young, "25 Years after the Vietnam War, Time Has Come to Rid Mall of Shacks," *Washington Post*, October 5, 2000; Ted Sampley, "Embattled Last Firebase POW/MIA Vigil Braces for Another Assault," www.usvetdsp.com/lfb_story.htm (accessed July 31, 2002).

167. A flyer for the event was headlined, "Stop the U.S. War against Central America and the Caribbean," with the subheadings, "No More Viet Nam Wars" and "$$ for Jobs, Equality, and Human Needs," box 48, VVMF-MD.

168. Peter Perl, "Old Soldiers in Conflict," *Washington Post*, July 2, 1983.

169. David J. Passamaneck, national legislative director of AMVETS, to Robert A. Carter, VVMF, June 7, 1983, box 5, VVMF-MD.

170. Jan Scruggs, VVMF call report of conversation with Milt Copulos, June 14, 1983, box 48, VVMF-MD.

171. Jan Scruggs, VVMF call report of a conversation with Fran Garth of the National Park Service, June 3, 1983, box 50; Scruggs, VVMF call report of a conversation with Peter Kahn of Williams and Connolly, VVMF's lawyers, June 21, 1983, box 48; Scruggs, VVMF call report of conversation with Ron Kovic, June 29, 1983, box 48, VVMF-MD.

172. Peter Perl and Caryle Murphy, "Opposing Groups Air Latin America Views and Vietnam Memorial," *Washington Post*, July 3, 1983.

173. Ibid.

174. Perl, "Old Soldiers in Conflict."

175. U.S. Congress, House, 98th Cong., 1st sess., October 19, 1983, *Congressional Record*, E 5001.

176. "Volunteer News," August 19, 1983; and Jan Scruggs to Lowell V. Sturgill of the National Park Service, n.d., box 4, VVMF-MD; Kevin Cook, "Pilots' Children Want End to Their War, *Washington Times*, June 15, 1985; Mark Vane, "Park Service, Vets Argue over Incident," *Washington Times*, July 25, 1989. The buffer zone recognized since 1984 comprises the area enclosed by the line south from 20th Street, the inner edge of the north Reflecting Pool walk, Constitution Avenue, Lincoln Memorial Drive, and Henry Bacon Drive. Edward Sargent, "Park Service Proposes Curbing Demonstrations at Vietnam Memorial," *Washington Post*, April 5, 1984; Charles E. Wheeler, "Possibility of Living MIAs Can't Be Ruled Out," *Washington Times*, November 5, 1984; "Leafletting OK'd at Vietnam Memorial," *Washington Times*, May 24, 1992.

177. Chris Black, "Kerry Faces Defection among Veterans over Campaign Ad," *Boston Globe*, September 4, 1984.

178. Gaines-Carter, "It Looks Like the Wall Is Crying."

179. Thomas J. Knock, "'Come Home, America': The Story of George McGovern," in *Vietnam and the American Political Tradition*, ed. Randall B. Woods (Cambridge: Cambridge University Press, 2003), 88; Memorial Day Ceremony at the Vietnam Veterans Memorial, May 25, 1992, observations by the author. See also Charles Babington, "Remembering Those Who Didn't Return," *Washington Post*, May 26, 1992.

180. The figure is the aggregate of the 20 percent who thought this outcome was "very likely" and the 20 percent who thought it "somewhat likely." Telephone survey of a national adult sample conducted on December 1–2, 1990, by the Gordon S. Black Corporation for USA Today; data provided by RC.

181. The figure aggregates the 32 percent who said they were "very worried" and the 22 percent who were "somewhat worried." Telephone survey of a national adult sample conducted on January 14, 1991, by Black; data provided by RC.

182. "Shedding Tears against the Wall," *Washington Times*, January 3, 1991; "New Senator Pleads for Peace," *Washington Post*, January 3, 1991; Helen Dewar and Tom Kenworthy, "Congress Opens Debate on Using Force in Gulf," *Washington Post*, January 11, 1991; Eleanor Clift, John McCormick, and Todd Barrett, "Crashing the Capitol Club," *Newsweek*, January 14, 1991, 26.

183. H. Bruce Franklin, *M.I.A. or Mythmaking in America* (New Brunswick, NJ: Rutgers University Press, 1993), 56; Mary McGrory, "The McCain Mutiny," *Washington Post*, April 30, 1995.

184. Ben A. Franklin, "Vietnam War an Increasing Focus for Nation's Veterans Day Observances," *New York Times*, November 12, 1986.

185. Ronald Reagan, "Remarks at a Memorial Day Ceremony at Arlington National Cemetery in Virginia," May 26, 1986, APP, www.presidency.ucsb.edu/ws/?pid=37350 (accessed November 25, 2006); W. Dale Nelson, "Reagan Hails Vets of 'Thankless' War," *Sacramento Union*, May 27. The previous month, a plurality of respondents, 46 percent, agreed with the statement, "The United States is increasing its involvement in Nicaragua—just like in Vietnam—and will probably end up sending American troops there." Forty-one percent disagreed. Yankelovich Clancy Shulman telephone poll of a national adult sample with an oversample of thirty- to forty-year-olds, conducted April 15–17, 1986. Another poll that same month found 62 percent responding that they were "afraid the United States will get involved in Nicaragua the way it did in Vietnam." CBS News/New York Times telephone poll of a national adult sample, conducted April 6–10, 1986; data provided by RC.

186. Everett Carll Ladd, "The 1988 Elections: Continuation of the Post-New Deal System," *Political Science Quarterly* 104, no. 1 (Spring 1989): 1.

187. Veterans Day Ceremony at the Vietnam Veterans Memorial, November 11, 1988, observations by the author; Cablecast on C-SPAN, November 11, 1988; Michael York, "Reagans Pay Emotional Visit to Vietnam Veterans Wall," *Washington Post*, November 12, 1988; Ronald Reagan, "Remarks at the Veterans

Day Ceremony at the Vietnam Veterans Memorial," November 11, 1988, APP, www.presidency.ucsb. edu/ws/?pid=35155 (accessed November 25, 2006).

188. Photo by Jack Kightlinger, in *Images of War*, by Julene Fischer and the picture staff of Boston Publishing Company (Boston: Boston Publishing Company, 1986), 133.

189. Veterans Day ceremony at the Vietnam Veterans Memorial, November 11, 1988, observations by the author; cablecast on C-SPAN, November 11, 1988; York, "Reagans Pay Emotional Visit."

190. Myra MacPherson, "What Did It Cost, Our Vietnam War? Here Is the Price . . . ," *Washington Post*, May 27, 1984.

191. Colman McCarthy, "The Wall and Scars Unhealed," *Washington Post*, November 20, 1988.

192. George L. Mosse, *Fallen Soldiers: Reshaping the Memory of the World Wars* (New York: Oxford University Press), 7.

193. A few audience members heckled Reagan on Veterans Day 1988, but they were demanding an accounting of POW/MIAs, not questioning Reagan's historical judgment or recommendations for military strength and national resolve. Larry Ryckman, "America Honors Its Veterans," *Sacramento Union*, November 12, 1988.

7. "No Shame or Stigma"

1. The organization has almost entirely escaped the attention of other scholars; this chapter begins to redress that neglect. The papers of the national VVLP organization I examined are privately held, in LBP. A search in 1995 revealed that the National Archives held no VVLP papers. Further queries in 2007 about the disposition of the VVLP's papers found no evidence that they have been reposed in a publicly accessible archive. Although I informed the National Archives about how I had located the LBP collection, up to the time of writing the archives' efforts to locate these materials have been inadequate to the task. Wherever responsibility for this situation lies, with the former officers and staff of ACTION and the VVLP, or with the National Archives' staff, there is a danger that the activities of this historically significant organization funded by the federal government will be lost to history.

2. The quotation is from Arthur Egendorf's summary of the study's findings in *Healing from the War: Trauma and Transformation after Vietnam* (Boston: Houghton Mifflin, 1985), 2. The study itself appeared the same year the VVLP began. Arthur Egendorf, Charles Kadushin, Robert S. Laufer, George Rothbart, and Lee Sloan, *Legacies of Vietnam: Comparative Adjustment of Veterans and Their Peers*, 5 vols. (Washington, DC: U.S. Government Printing Office, 1981). Vol. 5 of the study, *Dealing with the War: A View Based on the Individual Lives of Vietnam Veterans*, by Egendorf, Andrea Remez, and John Farley, found that half of all Vietnam veterans had "unresolved" war experiences, and a further one-fifth had forestalled inner conflict "through emotional avoidance" (711).

3. Thomas W. Pauken, *The Thirty Years War: The Politics of the Sixties Generation* (Ottawa, IL: Jameson Books, 1995), 199.

4. "Lest We Forget," *60 Minutes*, CBS News, October 10, 1982.

5. Thomas Pauken, telephone interview by the author, August 27, 2007.

6. Pauken, *Thirty Years War*, 199. Pauken regarded the Vietnam War as the defining experience of his generation, creating dividing lines between right and left that shaped American politics in the years after the war. Pauken, telephone interview by the author, March 10, 1995.

7. Pauken, *Thirty Years War*, 119, 200.

8. Tom Pauken, "ACTION: The Times They Are a-Changin'," in *Steering the Elephant: How Washington Works*, ed. Robert Rector and Michael Sanera (New York: Universe Books, 1987), 185–86; Lou Cannon, "Appointments by White House Take Right Turn," *Washington Post*, June 18, 1981.

9. "Wikipedia" entry on Morton Blackwell, en.wikipedia.org/wiki/Morton_Blackwell (accessed November 29, 2006); Pauken, interview, August 27, 2007; Pauken, *Thirty Years War*, 53–63.

10. Scott Armstrong, "Nomination of Pauken as Director of Action Is Postponed in Senate," *Washington Post*, May 1, 1981; Thomas Pauken, resumé, provided to the author by Pauken; Pauken, *Thirty Years War*, 1, 10–15. For the conflict in the villages and the Phoenix Program, see, e.g., Ronald H. Spector, *After Tet: The Bloodiest Year in Vietnam* (New York: Vintage Books, 1993), 282, 287–88; David Chanoff and Doan Van Toai, *Portrait of the Enemy* (New York: Random House, 1986), 107–9; Stuart A. Herrington, *Stalking the Vietcong* (Novato, CA: Presidio Press, 1997), 31–32; Zalin Grant, *Facing the Phoenix* (New York: W. W. Norton, 1991), 291–98; Lewis Sorley, *A Better War* (New York: Harcourt, Brace, 1999), 67, 145–47. The degree to which Operation Phoenix was an "assassination program" is disputed. See, e.g., James W. Trullinger, *The Village War* (Stanford, CA: Stanford University Press, 1994), 173; James William Gibson, *The Perfect War: The War We Couldn't Lose and How We Did* (New York: Vintage Books, 1988), 298–303; Felix Belair Jr., "U.S. Aide Defends Pacification Program in Vietnam Despite Killings of Civilians," *New*

York Times, July 20, 1971. Pauken denied having participated in the Phoenix Program. Pauken, interview, August 27, 2007.

11. "State of the War: An Intelligence Report," *U.S. News and World Report*, October 27, 1969, 36–37; Pauken, *Thirty Years War*, 14–15.

12. Pauken, interview, August 27, 2007.

13. Pauken, *Thirty Years War*, 3, 69–70.

14. The description of Pauken's return at the airport appears in Susan Katz Keating, "Vietnam Veterans Helping Themselves: VVLP in Action," *VFW*, May 2005, www.vfw.org/index.cfm?fa=news .magDtl&dtl=1&mid=2513 (accessed December 8, 2006).

15. UPI [United Press International], "Reagan Names Ex-Aide to Post in Health Department," *New York Times*, February 4, 1981.

16. Adam Cohen describes Colson as "the quintessential Watergate-era hatchet man," in Cohen, "Charles Colson and the Mission That Began with Watergate," *New York Times*, July 25, 2005. Pauken also describes him as a "hatchet man." *Thirty Years War*, 112.

17. Pauken, *Thirty Years War*, 103.

18. Tom Pauken, memorandum to John W. Dean re: "Intelligence Evaluation Committee Report of February 1, 1971," February 8, 1971; White House Daily Intelligence Summary (n.d.) covering October 2–7, 1970, marked "Pauken FYI"; John Dean, memorandum to Tom Pauken, September 21, 1970; all in "Tom Pauken" file, John W. Dean III, box 92, Staff Member and Office Files, White House Special Files, National Archives Nixon Presidential Materials Project, National Archives, College Park, MD.

19. Tom Pauken, memorandum to John W. Dean re: "Formation of a Task Force on Contingency Planning for Mass Demonstrations, Disruptions, and Domestic Violence," February 8, 1971, in ibid.

20. Tom Pauken, memorandum to Richard Burress re: "Human Events Interview with Bryce N. Harlow," October 2, 1970, in ibid.

21. Pauken, *Thirty Years War*, 74, 88.

22. Quoted in John Wheeler, *Touched with Fire: The Future of the Vietnam Generation* (New York: Avon Books, 1984), 173; Pauken expressed the same sentiments in Pauken, "ACTION," 195, and repeated them in his March 10, 1995 interview.

23. Keating, "Vietnam Veterans Helping Themselves."

24. Pauken, *Thirty Years War*, 87.

25. Gerald Nicosia, *Home to War: A History of the Vietnam Veterans' Movement* (New York: Three Rivers Press, 2001), 211.

26. Pauken, *Thirty Years War*, 88.

27. Christopher Andrew, *For the President's Eyes Only: Secret Intelligence and the American Presidency from Washington to Bush* (London: HarperCollins, 1995), 366–68; *The Senate Watergate Report* (New York: Dell Books, 1974), 54–55; Pauken, *Thirty Years War*, 104; Rick Perlstein, *Nixonland: The Rise of a President and the Fracturing of America* (New York: Scribner, 2008), 130, 403.

28. U.S. Senate Select Committee to Study Governmental Operations with Respect to Intelligence Activities, *Final Report: Intelligence Activities and the Rights of Americans*, bk. 2, 94th Cong., 2d sess. (Washington, DC: U.S. Government Printing Office, 1976), 141.

29. Andrew, *For the President's Eyes Only*, 369; Pauken, *Thirty Years War*, 105; Keith W. Olson, *Watergate: The Presidential Scandal That Shook America* (Lawrence: University Press of Kansas, 2003), 17; Steve Weissman, "Tom Huston's Plan," in *Big Brother and the Holding Company: The World Behind Watergate*, ed. Weissman (Palo Alto, CA: Ramparts Press, 1974), 52, 59.

30. Pauken, *Thirty Years War*, 104.

31. Ibid., 106; Olson, *Watergate*, 17; John Dean, *Blind Ambition* (New York: Simon and Schuster, 1976), 37.

32. Senate Select Committee, *Final Report: Intelligence Activities*, 115; Melvin Small, *The Presidency of Richard Nixon* (Lawrence: University Press of Kansas, 1999), 56; *Senate Watergate Report*, 64–65, 223–33; Olson, *Watergate*, 43–59; Stanley I. Kutler, ed., *Watergate: The Fall of Richard M. Nixon* (St. James, NY: Brandywine Press, 1996), 43–45, 217–26; Ronald Brownstein and Nina Easton, *Reagan's Ruling Class* (New York: Pantheon Books, 1983), 673.

33. Pauken, *Thirty Years War*, 121; UPI, "Reagan Names Ex-Aide to Post in Health Dept."

34. Although "ACTION" is usually capitalized and therefore the agency's name looks like an acronym, the initials do not stand for anything. For background on the agency, see Jack Rosenthal, "New-Agency Plan Drops VISTA Aides," *New York Times*, May 23, 1971.

35. Charles DeBenedetti and Charles Chatfield, *An American Ordeal: The Antiwar Movement of the Vietnam Era* (Syracuse: Syracuse University Press, 1990), 249–50.

36. Sam Brown, "The Legacy of Choices," in *The Wounded Generation*, ed. A. D. Horne (Englewood Cliffs, New Jersey: Prentice Hall, 1981), 186.

37. Pauken, *Thirty Years War*, 136.

38. Nancy Gibbs, "The Currie Riddle," *Time*, April 27, 1998, 39.

39. Myra MacPherson, *Long Time Passing: Vietnam and the Haunted Generation* (New York: Signet Books, 1985), 337; Pauken, *Thirty Years War*, 138–39; Gary Ronberg, "He Urges Vets to Enlist in ACTION," *Philadelphia Inquirer*, November 24, 1981; Bill Jayne, telephone interview by the author, March 10, 1995, regarding the "ugly charges"; Scott Armstrong, "Nomination of Pauken as Director of Action Is Postponed in Senate," *Washington Post*, May 1, 1981. Although President John F. Kennedy ordered the CIA not to use the Peace Corps as cover, former ACTION director Sam Brown stated that the CIA had "assured" him that it had not used the Peace Corps for cover since 1975—tantamount to an admission that it had done so before that date. Sandy Smith, "The Peace Corps: Benign Development?" *Multinational Monitor* 7, no. 13 (September 1986), multinationalmonitor.org/hyper/issues/1986/09/smith.html (accessed November 22, 2006).

40. "Director of Peace Corps Warns Against Using Workers as Spies," *New York Times*, January 15, 1981; Armstrong, "Nomination of Pauken"; Pauken, *Thirty Years War*, 140, 145; Pauken, "ACTION," 186–88; Rowland Evans and Robert Novak, "Percy: Whose Side Is He On?" *Washington Post*, June 3, 1981; Judith Miller, "Senators Slash Reagan's Request for Foreign Aid by $949 Million," *New York Times*, May 7, 1981; "The Senate Foreign Relations Committee Voted Six to Zero," *Washington Post*, May 7, 1981. Alan Cranston confirmed that the Peace Corps was removed from the ACTION umbrella to keep it free of the taint of an "intelligence connection." Alan Cranston, letter to the editor, *New York Times*, December 16, 1981.

41. Council on Hemispheric Affairs, "News and Analysis," November 25, 1986, www.coha.org/Press%20Release%20Archives/1986/032.pdf (accessed December 10, 2006).

42. Pauken, *Thirty Years War*, 156, 170–71; Marjorie Miller, "New Chief Alters Course of ACTION," *San Jose Mercury*, August 28, 1981; John Rees, "An Exclusive Interview with the Conservative Administrator of One Great Society Agency Reveals Changed Policies," *Review of the News* 19, no. 2 (January 12, 1983). Under Pauken, ACTION eliminated funding for any "community organizing" project inconsistent with its new ethos of "self-sufficiency and non-dependency." It did not give proper notice of this decision, which a federal district court found illegal. General Accounting Office (GAO), "Statement of Robert A. Peterson before the Subcommittee on Select Education, Committee on Education and Labor, House of Representatives, on ACTION's Policies and Practices," April 19, 1983," 27, archive.gao.gov/d40t12/121136.pdf (accessed December 10, 2006).

43. ACTION used "Schedule B" appointments (where the appointee has special skills or the appointment is constrained by special circumstances making it impossible to use the competitive hiring process) to avoid hiring career civil servants, and it had more noncareer employees than the House and Senate Appropriations Committees would have liked. The GAO considered that ACTION's use of "Schedule B" hiring for ACTION positions assigned to the VVLP was inappropriate. GAO, "ACTION's Hiring and Use of Certain Noncareer Employees and Other Personnel Matters," September 4, 1984, GAO/HRD-84-57, 3, Appendix I, 2, 4, 10–11, 17, archive.gao.gov/d6t1/125104.pdf (accessed December 10, 2006). Pauken later expressed irritation at career employees who did not toe the Reaganite line. Pauken, "ACTION," 191.

44. Pauken, "ACTION," 189.

45. Bill Keller, "Action's Not Dull with Tom Pauken," *Dallas Times Herald*, April 15, 1983. For other accounts of the VVLP's travails with public relations and Congress, see Wheeler, *Touched with Fire*, 132–33; Dan Cragg, "Pauken's Penchant for Action," *Washington Times*, May 18, 1983. The GAO studied VISTA volunteer projects, including ones in which seventy-one VISTA volunteers were assigned to VVLP programs. The VVLP projects were granted supervisory grants seven times higher than those given to the other VISTA projects. "Statement of Robert A. Peterson before the Subcommittee on Select Education," 15.

46. Rees, "Exclusive Interview"; VVLP, *An American Sunrise: A History of ACTION's Three-Year Veterans' Initiative, Technical Report*, 2, LBP.

47. Small-scale self-help projects were launched in Philadelphia, Wichita, and San Francisco under the supervision of the National Institutes of Mental Health. Ford H. Kuramoto, "Federal Mental Health Programs for the Vietnam Veteran," in *Strangers at Home: Vietnam Veterans since the War*, ed. Charles R. Figley and Seymour Leventman (New York: Praeger, 1980), 299–300.

48. Jo Mannies, "Congress Skirted in Plan to Aid Vietnam Veterans," *St. Louis Post-Dispatch*, September 7, 1982.

49. Wheeler, *Touched with Fire*, 52. Susan Katz Keating writes that there were forty-seven "franchise" operations in forty-nine states. The precise number of local VVLPs varied, however, through the three years of federal funding. Keating, "Vietnam Veterans Helping Themselves."

50. Dennis Rhoades, quoted in Nicosia, *Home to War*, 578; Keller, "Action's Not Dull with Tom

Pauken"; "Biographical Information: James Webb," *VVLP News*, n.d., LBP. Webb was a "lifelong Democrat" until Jimmy Carter proposed a pardon for draft resisters; he switched again to win one of Virginia's Senate seats as a Democrat in 2006. Robert Timberg, *The Nightingale's Song* (New York: Simon and Schuster, 1995), 256; Michael D. Shear, "Reagan Navy Secretary Will Run for U.S. Senate," *Washington Post*, February 8, 2006. Ronald Reagan appointed Timperlake as director of Mobilization Planning and Requirements at the Department of Defense. VVLP, *American Sunrise*, 7; "Nomination of Edward T. Timperlake to Be an Assistant Secretary of Veterans Affairs," June 14, 1989, APP, www.presidency.ucsb. edu/ws/?pid=17150 (accessed November 25, 2006). Ronald Reagan appointed Ray as the deputy assistant secretary of defense for reserve affairs, Ray was the Kentucky finance co-chairman of George H. W. Bush's presidential campaign, and he considered running as a Republican candidate for the U.S. Senate. Ronald D. Ray, 2-page biography given by Ray to the author in 1992; Bob Johnson, "Louisville Lawyer Says He May Run against Ford," *Louisville Courier-Journal*, January 19, 1986.

51. Craig Howes, *Voices of the Vietnam POWs: Witnesses to Their Fight* (New York: Oxford University Press, 1993), 11; *Vietnam Veterans Leadership Program: Chairmen and Program Directors, July 1983* and *November 1983*, LBP; Sally Bixby Defty, "Veterans Program Here Has Four Aims," *St. Louis Post-Dispatch*, September 7, 1982; John Baines, telephone interview by the author, February 7, 2007; Jeff Benkoe, "Vietnam Program Aims to Find Work for Florida Vets," *Miami News*, n.d., in *Vietnam Veterans Leadership Program [VVLP] Press Coverage: The Program's Second Year, October 1982–October 1983*, 86, LBP; "Eight Vietnam Vets Who Came Out Winners," *U.S. News and World Report*, March 29, 1982, 45–46. Keating describes Hagel as a member of the VVLP leadership, although she does not specify what role he filled. Keating, "Vietnam Veterans Helping Themselves."

52. Presidential statement about VVLP, August 12, 1983, sent to Jerry Naylor, Agoura, CA; Leo K. Thorsness to Michael K. Deaver, July 11, 1983; Colonel R. J. Affourtit, Office of the Secretary of Defense, memorandum to Dodie Livingstone, director, Office of Special Presidential Messages, August 19, 1983, casefile 154962, Reagan Library.

53. Ronald Reagan, "Remarks at a Ceremony Commemorating the Initiation of the Vietnam Veterans Leadership Program," November 10, 1981, in Reagan *1981*, PPP (1982), 1028. Excerpts of the speech and ceremony can be seen in the documentary *When Their Country Called*, dir. Zack Burkett (VVLP, sponsored by ACTION, n.d., ca. 1983); a videocassette copy was donated to the author by Zack Burkett.

54. Reed Harp, "S[an] A[ntonio] Man Leads Fight to Improve Viet Vet's Image," *San Antonio Light*, [November 1981], in *Vietnam Veterans Leadership Program, Press Coverage: The Program's First Year, September 1981–September 1982*, LBP. As mentioned in chapter 6, Baines was Roy Cohn's nominal client in the matter of the Vietnam Veterans Memorial Fund audit.

55. VVLP, *American Sunrise*, 18.

56. "Vietnam Veterans Leadership Program (VVLP)," 1 (n.d.), 6-page typescript found in the VVLP papers of Ronald Ray.

57. VVLP, *American Sunrise*, 19.

58. Paula Hawkins's letter is quoted in chapter 5; Caspar Weinberger's Veterans Day speech at Arlington National Cemetery is quoted in Ben A. Franklin, "President Accepts Vietnam Memorial," *New York Times*, November 12, 1984.

59. Pauken, *Thirty Years War*, 171; Colman McCarthy, "Thomas Pauken's Penchant for Underestimating Action," *Washington Post*, May 1, 1983; Tom Pauken, "Character Assassination," *Washington Post*, May 14, 1983; Cragg, "Pauken's Penchant for Action." "Background Information," *VVLP News*, n.d., 3, LBP; Kevin Krajick, "The Separate Peace of White-Collar Veterans," *Across the Board: The Conference Board Magazine* 21, no. 6 (June 1984): 7.

60. Pauken, *Thirty Years War*, 163–64; *VVLP: Vietnam Veterans Leadership Program: The Program at Mid-Term, March 1983*, 6, LBP (hereafter cited as *VVLP Mid-Term*). For a chronicle of a particularly sustained period of ineffectiveness by a local VVLP, see the files on the "living memorial" organized as part of the New York Vietnam Veterans Memorial: New York Vietnam Veterans Memorial Commission Records, box 14, folders 11 and 12, New York City Municipal Archives.

61. MacPherson, *Long Time Passing*, 337; Keller, "Action's Not Dull with Tom Pauken"; "Statement of Robert A. Peterson before the Subcommittee on Select Education," 12–13; VVLP, *American Sunrise*, 3–4.

62. *VVLP Mid-Term*, 5; Lanita Gardner, "Vietnam Veterans Program Forms Volunteer Advisory Panel," *Tennessean*, February 7, 1982.

63. Krajick, "Separate Peace of White-Collar Veterans" 10.

64. VVLP, *American Sunrise*, 63.

65. Linda Sarrio, "Vietnam Veterans Leadership Program: Windowdressing or a Job-Finding Plan?" *San Antonio Light*, March 30, 1983.

66. VVLP, *American Sunrise*, attachment 15, "Reports on Goals and Priorities for the Next Five Years," 5.

67. "Proclamation 4841—National Day of Recognition for Veterans of the Vietnam Era," April 23, 1981, in *Reagan 1981, PPP* (1982), 381.

68. "Biographical Information (Kip Becker, Ph.D.)," *VVLP News*, n.d., LBP.

69. "Trench War over Vista," *Wall Street Journal*, August 17, 1982.

70. "Vietnam Veterans Deserve Better Image—Broadcaster," *Greensboro, N.C. Daily News*, April 11, 1984; Ralph Blumenthal, "Veterans Accept $180 Million Settlement on Agent Orange," *New York Times*, May 8, 1984.

71. Tom Carhart, "Don't Pity This Vietnam Veteran," *Hartford Courant*, May 13, 1984.

72. Patrick K. Lackey, "Letters from Lackey," *Des Moines Register*, November 1, 1983.

73. "Meet the Leaders of the Vietnam Veterans Leadership Program: The Honorable Thomas Weir Pauken, Director, ACTION," *Stars and Stripes—The National Tribune*, July 29, 1982.

74. Rees, "Exclusive Interview."

75. David Wharton, "Vets Seek Help from Each Other," *Los Angeles Times*, January 2, 1983, part 2.

76. Chuck Green, "Operation Outreach to Aid Vietnam Vets," *Lake County (IN) Star*, September 15, 1983.

77. Mark Mogensen, "Vets Helping Vets; Targeting Self-Esteem," *Lewiston* ([title incomplete)], April 29, 1984, in *Vietnam Veterans Leadership Program Press Coverage: The Program's Third Year*, LBP (hereafter cited as *VVLP Third Year*).

78. David Miller, "Viet Vets Marched Home to No Hurrahs," *Jeffersonian*, February 8, 1984.

79. Keating, "Vietnam Veterans Helping Themselves."

80. Cragg, "Pauken's Penchant for Action."

81. Richard Kolb, telephone interview by the author, March 16, 1995. Before Kolb's work, others had used statistics to question the prevailing stereotypes about the disadvantages Vietnam veterans faced. See, e.g., Abby Mendelson, "Coming Home as the Deer Hunter," *Pittsburgh*, July 1979, 25–26, 41.

82. Vietnam Veterans Leadership Program of Houston, Inc., *Education Kit: Myths versus Realities: A Teaching Guide to the Vietnam War and Its Veterans*, comp. Richard Kolb (Houston: VVLP, [1984]), 2–3; idem., *The Vietnam War in Historical Perspective*, comp. Richard Kolb (Houston: VVLP, n.d.), 2–3. Copies of these documents were given to the author by Richard Kolb.

83. Wallace Terry, "Bloods: The Black Experience of the Vietnam War," presentation at the University of Pennsylvania, November 4, 1987. In fact, at the start of the war, 31 percent of all combat troops were black, and in 1965 blacks accounted for 24 percent of all army combat deaths; a higher proportion of blacks than whites was drafted, partly because of poor health care and education, which denied them the exemptions on medical or educational grounds that some of their white peers enjoyed. Those who volunteered were more likely to obtain a safer billet in the U.S. Air Force, Navy, or National Guard. Fewer than 1 percent of the reserves and National Guard were black. Michal R. Belknap, *The Vietnam War on Trial: The My Lai Massacre and the Court-Martial of Lieutenant Calley* (Lawrence: University Press of Kansas, 2002), 26. Over time, the proportion of African American casualties declined. For the class composition of the armed forces who fought in Vietnam, see also Egendorf et al., *Legacies of Vietnam*, 105–8, 142–44. Men with blue-collar backgrounds, from low-income parental families, and with lower education levels were more likely to have served in Vietnam than men with professional and managerial backgrounds, from higher-income families, and with higher levels of education.

84. The education kit carried seventy-two footnotes drawn from several dozen sources.

85. Jackson M. Andrews, "Readers' Views: Vets 'Productive' Citizens," *Louisville Courier-Journal*, November 21, 1983.

86. Richard Kolb, letter to the editor, *Time*, February 11, 1991 (a copy of the letter was given to the author by Richard Kolb); Richard Kolb, letter to the editor, *Wall Street Journal*, March 4, 1991; James Webb, "Viet Vets Didn't Kill Babies, and They Aren't Suicidal: The Myth of the Viet Vet," *Washington Post*, April 6, 1986.

87. B. G. Burkett and Glenna Whitley, *Stolen Valor: How the Vietnam Generation Was Robbed of Its Heroes and Its History* (Dallas: Verity Press, 1998), 305–8; Michael Kelley, "One Vet's Mission to Set the Record Straight," *Washington Post*, August 15, 1999; Michael Kelley, "The Three Walls behind the Wall," unpublished essay, sent to the author by Michael Kelley.

88. Kolb, interview; "Vietnam Warriors: A Statistical Profile," *VFW*, March 1993, 3.

89. U.S. Congress, House, 97th Cong., 2nd sess., October 1, 1982, *Congressional Record*, E 4642.

90. VVLP, *American Sunrise*, 26, 58.

91. Ernie Hernandez, "Vietnam Veterans Finally Get Their Parade," *Indiana Post-Tribune*, July 12, 1984; Robert L. Koenig, "Vigil Honors 206 Here Killed in Vietnam," *St. Louis Post-Dispatch*, November 1983; Larry Levy, "We Licked 'Em: Westmoreland Addresses Viet Vets," *Arizona Republic*, February 9, 1984; Ozzie St. George, "Vietnam-Era Veterans Will Meet for Special Tribute Next Weekend," *St. Paul*

Pioneer Press, September 18, 1983; editorial, *Pine Bluff (AR) Commercial*, October 1, 1983, all in *VVLP Third Year*.

92. The Pentagon provided an estimated million dollars' worth of assistance in the making of the pro-war film *The Green Berets*, dir. John Wayne and Ray Kellogg (1968). Leo Cawley argues that the promise of Pentagon assistance has influenced film scripts. "The result of this gold thumb on the scales has permitted the production of a whole clutch of propagandistic films that would have otherwise been strangled in the cradle by the magic of the marketplace." Cawley, "The War about the War: Vietnam Films and American Myth," in *From Hanoi to Hollywood*, ed. Linda Dittmar and Gene Michaud (New Brunswick, NJ: Rutgers University Press, 1990), 74.

93. *First Blood* dir. Ted Kotcheff, (1982). Marcia Landau, telephone interview by the author, March 10, 1995.

94. Keating, "Vietnam Veterans Helping Themselves."

95. Rees, "Exclusive Interview," 23; *Coming Home*, dir. Hal Ashby (1978). The film was made before the VVLP came into existence, so the issue of vetting for government support was not relevant.

96. Kathryn Tolbert, "YAF [Young Americans for Freedom] Convention Lauds Veterans of Vietnam," *Boston Globe*, August 23, 1981.

97. *Frank: A Vietnam Veteran*, dir. Fred Simon (Boston, WGBH, 1981).

98. "Free the Veterans," *Wall Street Journal*, November 11, 1981.

99. Kurt Andersen and Jay Branegan, "A Homecoming at Last," *Time*, November 22, 1982, 46.

100. Luther Young, "Vietnam Vets: Creating a More Positive Image," *Baltimore Sun*, July 1, 1982.

101. George Arnold, "This Man Wants Your Respect," *El Dorado (AR) News-Times*, April 4, 1984.

102. Carolyn Hayes-Knoll, "Recognition of Vietnam Vets," *Madison [County] (TN) Messenger*, May 23, 1984.

103. Lackey, "Letters from Lackey."

104. Quoted in ibid.

105. Edward G. Galian to VVLP, March 1, 1983, in *VVLP Mid-Term*, 52.

106. The series was co-produced by WGBH, Boston, Associated Television (ATV) in Britain, and the French Antenne Deux. The administrative records, interview transcripts, film footage of the televi-sion series, and an extensive correspondence among the series' producers and academic advisers can be found in the Executive Producers files in the collection of the Joseph P. Healey Library, University of Massachusetts, Boston. See also IMDb movie database, www.imdb.com/title/tt0185129/combined (ac-cessed November 27, 2006).

107. Richard Ellison, Question 5, untitled document with seventeen questions and answers about the series, March 17, 1981, "Vietnam Development" folder, Executive Producers files, box 3. Visitation figures appear in a VVMF press release, September 23, 1983, box 29, VVMF-MD.

108. Statement by Richard Ellison quoted in David O. Ives, president, WGBH Educational Foundation, to "Dear Colleague," [1982], Executive Producers files.

109. Dick Ellison, memorandum to Peter McGhee and Sam Tyler, March 12, 1981, ibid.

110. Ellison, Question 1, untitled document, March 17, 1981.

111. "Comments by E. Deane on General Approach and Narrative," [1982], "Homefront USA Memo/Comments" folder, Executive Producers files.

112. Ellison, Question 14, untitled document, March 17, 1981; Richard Ellison, memorandum to Nancy England re: "Pew [Charitable Trust] Request," March 8, 1982, Executive Producers files.

113. Summary by "LWL" (Lawrence Lichty) to Richard Ellison, March 3, 1982, of taped comments at the Boston review session of January 4, 1981, ibid.

114. Richard Ellison, memorandum to TVP [the Vietnam Project] Staff, Stanley Karnow, Lawrence Lichty, and Peter McGhee, January 28, 1982, ibid.

115. The unsigned and undated document appears to have been written by Lawrence Lichty to Richard Ellison and Stanley Karnow in response to a September 1, 1982, memorandum by Richard Ellison, "Homefront USA Memo/Comments" folder, ibid.

116. Richard Kolb, "A Viet Vet Looks at 'Vietnam: A Television History," *Human Events*, June 16, 1984, 12–14. From 1948 to 1950 Karnow wrote for the "progressive" newsweekly *National Guardian* before he began to work for *Time*, published by the arch-conservative Henry Luce. A few years later, Karnow had to swear an oath at the American Embassy in Paris that he was not and never had been a Communist. Stanley Karnow, *Paris in the Fifties* (New York: Twelve Rivers Press, 1999), 21, 64.

117. Don Grigg, "TV Makes U.S. Effort Appear Less than Noble," *Arkansas Gazette*, November 6, 1983; Bill Jayne, "Polemic? Yes. History? No," *Washington Times*, November 15, 1983; Shamus Maloney, "Viet 'Fairy Tales,'" *Pittsburgh Press*, January 1, 1984.

118. Stephen J. Morris, "'Vietnam,' a Dual-Vision History," *Wall Street Journal*, December 20, 1983,

enclosed with Tom Pauken to Vietnam Veterans Leadership Program chairmen and program directors, December 20, 1983, LBP.

119. William R. Black Jr., of Paducah, KY, to Stephen J. Morris, December 31, 1983. A copy of the letter was given to the author by William Black.

120. *Television's Vietnam: The Real Story*, 1–3, 5, 10, 14, 15, transcript in "Office File: Accuracy in Media," Healey Library; Don Kowet, "PBS Official Balks at Debate with AIM," *Washington Times*, August 12, 1986; clipping provided to the author by Accuracy in Media, Inc.

121. Elbridge Durbrow to Richard Ellison, March 2, 1979, Executive Producers files.

122. *Television's Vietnam*, 16–17.

123. Ibid., 28. This is not to say that the series escaped criticism from the left. J. William Gibson wrote a critical review in *In These Times* pointing out, among other things, that the series followed the perspective of commanders for most of the time, concentrated on images of military hardware in line with the "technowar" ethos, and was reticent in showing the physical costs of war in dead and wounded bodies. Personal communication with Gibson, February 19, 2007.

124. *Television's Vietnam*, 21–22.

125. Minutes of the Kentucky Vietnam Veterans Memorial Fund Design Committee meeting, September 8, 1984, 3. The author was given access to Kentucky VVMF and VVLP papers at Ronald Ray's law offices in Louisville and to Kentucky VVMF papers at the Boone Center, Division of Veterans Affairs, Frankfort. At the time of writing, Ray has reposed some of the papers with the Kentucky Vietnam Veterans Memorial Fund, Inc., location unknown; James Halvtagis has custody of the papers previously at the Boone Center.

126. VVLP, *American Sunrise*, attachment 9, "Highlights of Techniques Being Used to Project a Positive Image to the American Public," 2.

127. *Vietnam Vets: A St. Louis Profile* (KETC/Channel 9, broadcast January 2, 1984); "TV Special Spotlights 110,000 Area Vietnam Vets," *Webster-Kirkwood Times* (Missouri), December 19, 1983.

128. In the documentary, Pauken says, "The overwhelming majority of Vietnam veterans look back with pride on their military service." James Webb also appeared as a "talking head" in another documentary, *Vietnam: The 10,000 Day War*, prod. Ian McLeod (Canadian Broadcasting Company, 1980; broadcast in the United States in 1982).

129. *Vietnam*, prod. Zack Burkett (Nevada VVLP, 1986). A videocassette copy was donated to the author by Zack Burkett.

130. Jayne, interview.

131. Press release, February 15, 1980, signed by G. William Jayne, director of public relations, Vietnam Veterans Memorial Fund, box 48, VVMF-MD.

132. Jan Scruggs, speech given to Vietnam Veterans of New Mexico, June 24, 1982, 4, box 53, VVMF-MD.

133. VVLP, *American Sunrise*, 30; Carol Dobbs, "Kolb Speaks for Vietnam Vets at Memorial," *North Freeway Leader* (Houston), November 1982, in *VVLP Press Coverage: The Program's Second Year*, 219–20.

134. Luther Young, "Vietnam Vets: Creating a More Positive Image," *Baltimore Sun*, July 1, 1982.

135. "Biographical Information (Edward T. Timperlake)," *VVLP News*, n.d., LBP.

136. Jerry Harkavy, "Group Seeks Better Image for Viet Vets," *Kennebec Journal* (Augusta, ME), February 7, 1984.

137. William Fagginger-Auer, "Now Vets Should Work for Communities," *Burlington Free Press*, May 30, 1983.

138. Joy Horowitz, "Vietnam Vets' Support Group Stages a Benefit," *Los Angeles Times*, November 14, 1983.

139. VVLP, *American Sunrise*, 63.

140. Jack Wheeler, memorandum to "Each Participant in the Vietnam Veterans Leadership Program" re: "New National Director," June 14, 1982, VVMF-MD.

141. Pauken, *Thirty Years War*, 145.

142. Mary Gugliuzza, "Valley Veterans Remembered," *Valley Morning Star News*, May 18, 1984, in *VVLP Third Year*; attendance list of January 27, 1982, meeting in the U.S. Senate's Russell Building, with handwritten annotation "Invitation List: March 11th Meeting," box 62, VVMF-MD; "Controversy over the Vietnam Memorial," *Eyewitness News*, WDVM TV, November 7, 1983, transcript by Radio-TV Monitoring Service, Inc., Washington, DC, 2.

143. "Sgt. Shaft" [John Fales], *Stars and Stripes—The National Tribune*, December 1, 1983, in box 31, VVMF-MD. The irony, previously noted, is that the memorial fund retained Terrence O'Donnell of Williams and Connolly only because of the campaign of harassment against them.

144. See, e.g., "Sergeant Shaft," *Stars and Stripes—The National Tribune*, May 24, 1984, in box 30, VVMF-MD.

145. Jan Scruggs, "Setting the Record Straight," *Stars and Stripes—The National Tribune*, August 16, 1984; "Sergeant Shaft," *Stars and Stripes—The National Tribune*, August 16, 1984, in box 30, VVMF-MD.

146. Jan Scruggs to John Lewis Smith III of *Stars and Stripes*, August 22, 1984.

147. "Sergeant Shaft," *National Vietnam Veterans Review*, April 1984; Jan Scruggs, "Setting the Record Straight," *National Vietnam Veterans Review*, April 1984, 24–25, 32; Jan Scruggs to Chuck Allen of the *National Vietnam Veterans Review*, September 24, 1984, box 30, VVMF-MD.

148. Terrence O'Donnell to Fred F. Fielding, August 9, 1984, box 30, VVMF-MD.

149. Pauken, *Thirty Years War*, 192, 204.

150. *The A Team* was broadcast on the NBC network from 1983 to 1986. *Magnum P.I.* was broadcast on CBS from 1980 to 1988. The A Team are former special forces troops who act as soldiers of fortune, although invariably on the side of good. They operate outside the law, having escaped from jail after being convicted of a crime in which they were acting under orders. Magnum (played by Tom Selleck) is a former U.S. Navy SEAL ("Sea, Air and Land" troops), the Naval Special Forces, who served in Vietnam but now works as a private detective in Hawaii, sometimes with the assistance of former comrades in arms. Both shows portray Vietnam veterans struggling successfully with the psychological aftereffects of their wartime service, not snapping or turning to crime, as in the 1970s television shows that Brewin complained about.

151. William E. Geist, "About New York: The Ticker-Tape Parade They Finally Got," *New York Times*, May 8, 1985; "Welcome Home! New York's Ticker-Tape Salute to Viet Vets," *New York Post*, May 7, 1985; "Vietnam Vets: Parade America Almost Forgot," *U.S. News and World Report*, May 20, 1985.

152. Peter Goldman and Tony Fuller, *Charlie Company: What Vietnam Did to Us* (New York: Ballantine, 1983), 104.

153. "Wars are only fought over property, really. And the war in Vietnam was basically about economics." Robert E. Holcomb, quoted in Wallace Terry, *Bloods: An Oral History of the Vietnam War by Black Veterans* (New York: Ballantine 1984), 202. "They had us naïve, young, dumb-ass niggers believin' that this war was for democracy and independence. It was fought for money. All those big corporations made billions on the war, and then America left." Arthur E. "Gene" Woodley, quoted in ibid., 257.

154. The poet W. D. Ehrhart, a Vietnam veteran, responded to the parade more critically. He suggested that any self-respecting vet would give the middle finger to a parade ten years and more too late: "yet there they were: the sad / survivors, balding, overweight / and full of beer, weeping, grateful / for their hour come round at last." Ehrhart, "Parade Rest," in *The Vietnam War in American Culture*, ed. John Carlos Rowe and Rick Berg (New York: Columbia University Press, 1991), 257.

155. Tom Conroy and Kris Colt, *Vietnam Veterans Parade Chicago—1986* (Santa Fe, NM: Nam Vets Publishing Company, 1987), 6, 79, 94, 101; Ronald Reagan, "Remarks at a White House Briefing for Supporters of United States Assistance for the Nicaraguan Democratic Resistance," June 16, 1986, *Reagan 1986*, bk. 1, *PPP* (1988), 772.

156. *Rambo: First Blood Part II*, dir. George Pan Cosmatos (1985); *Platoon*, dir. Oliver Stone (1986).

157. Bernard Weinraub, "39 American Hostages Free after 17 Days; Go from Lebanon to Syria and Head Home," *New York Times*, July 1, 1985; Peggy Noonan, *When Character Was King: A Story of Ronald Reagan* (New York: Penguin Books, 2002), 257.

158. Michael McAfee, quoted in Tom Sabulls, "'Platoon' Hits Close to Home," *Dallas Times Herald*, January 17, 1987. For other testimonies to *Platoon*'s authenticity, see David Kleinberg, "Why 'Platoon' Rings True," *San Francisco Chronicle*, March 31, 1987; Lorraine Adams, "For Veterans, Movie Is Hauntingly Authentic," *Dallas Morning News*, January 23, 1987. *Time* said the film showed Vietnam "as it really was," implicitly endorsing the grunt's point of view as the core experience of the war. Richard Corliss, "Platoon: Vietnam as It Really Was," *Time*, January 26, 1987.

159. Pat Aufderheide, "Oliver Stone as Pulp Artist," *Cineaste* 15 (1987): 5; Sabulls, "'Platoon' Hits Close to Home."

160. Susan Katz Keating, "A 'Long Way Home' for the Truth about Vietnam Veterans," *VFW*, March 2003.

161. Norman Podhoretz, "'Platoon' Sullies Vietnam Veterans," *Insight*, January 19, 1987, 65.

162. Quoted in Richard Corliss, "Platoon: Vietnam as It Really Was," *Time*, January 26, 1987.

163. Joe Logan, "Outcry over 'Platoon,'" *Philadelphia Inquirer*, March 1, 1987; Clyde Taylor, "The Colonialist Subtext in *Platoon*," *Cineaste* 15 (1987): 8–10.

164. Sabulls, "'Platoon' Hits Close to Home"; Burkett and Whitley, *Stolen Valor*, 74–86, 254–308.

165. Barnes is played by Tom Berenger, Bunny by Kevin Dillon, Chris by Charlie Sheen, and Elias by Willem Dafoe.

166. The phenomenon of "Viet guilt" was heralded by a much-cited and -anthologized article: James Fallows, "What Did You Do in the Class War, Daddy?" *Washington Monthly* (October 1975), 5–20. For other statements of guilt or envy of those who served in Vietnam, see James Fallows, "Why the Country Needs

It," *Atlantic Monthly*, April 1980; Todd L. Newmark, "A Parade Won't Heal the Divisions over Vietnam," *Wall Street Journal*, November 10, 1982; Bob Greene, "Guilt Trip about Not Going to Vietnam Beginning to Show," *Dallas Morning News*, August 22, 1983; Chris Buckley, "Viet Guilt," *Esquire* 100 (September 1983): 68–72; Vermont Royster, "Thinking Things Over: Those Who Were There," *Wall Street Journal*, September 14, 1983; Edward Tick, "Apocalypse Continued," *New York Times Magazine*, January 13, 1985; John Wheeler, "Coming to Grips with Vietnam," *Foreign Affairs* 63, no. 4 (Spring 1985): 751; Peter Conn III, "Coping with Vietnam," *New York Times*, February 17, 1985; Bryan K. Grigsby, "20 Years of Vietnam," *Philadelphia Inquirer Magazine*, January 31, 1988, 13; Richard Cohen, "Watching the Vietnam War Left Questions and Guilt," *International Herald Tribune*, August 13, 1997; Pat Conroy, "My Heart's Content," *Forbes ASAP*, www.forbes.com/asap/00/1002/112.htm (accessed September 28, 2000); P. J. O'Rourke, *Give War a Chance* (London: Picador, 1992), v.

167. The description of the war as an "ordeal" the veterans "underwent"—rather than an act of policy the U.S. government and its armed forces deliberately engaged in—is highly problematic and is not to be regarded as an adequate description of service in Vietnam. It is, rather, my critical account of the way *Platoon* represents the war.

168. At the time that it published Kolb's statistics, *VFW* magazine had a circulation of 2.1 million and an estimated readership three times as large. The Vietnam Veterans Memorial Fund subsequently used an offprint of "Vietnam Warriors: A Statistical Profile" for educational purposes, included in the 16-page "Vietnam War Combat Chronology" distributed to thousands of educators. Richard Kolb, editor-in-chief of *VFW* magazine, e-mail messages to the author, June 8, 2007.

8. "A Confrontation between Faiths"

1. See Jerry L. Strait and Sandra S. Strait, *Vietnam War Memorials: An Illustrated Reference to Veterans Tributes throughout the United States* (Jefferson, NC: McFarland, 1988); Project on the Vietnam Generation, *Report on the Survey of Vietnam Veterans Memorials Nationwide* (Fairfax, VA: Indochina Institute, George Mason University, 1986). As stated in the introduction, I have identified 461 Vietnam memorials, using these sources, local newspapers, Web sources, data gathered by Vietnam Veterans of America, listings in the organization's *VVA Veteran* magazine, unpublished research by Pegi Donovan, and research conducted by Gary Ford of *Southern Living* magazine. Vietnam veterans memorials continue to be created and dedicated at the time of writing.

2. Howard Wilkinson, "Vietnam Memorial Dedicated," *Cincinnati Enquirer*, April 9, 1984.

3. "Groups Begin Drive to Build Three Memorials to Vietnam Veterans in County," *Houston Post*, November 20, 1982.

4. *Minnesota Vietnam Veterans Memorial Design Selection: Staff Report and Competition Jury Report*, June 1990, sent to the author by Teresa Vetter, president of the Minnesota Vietnam Veterans Memorial, Inc., Board of Directors.

5. "Vietnam Veterans Memorial Details," www.sos.arkansas.gov/virtual_tour_02/popups/grounds/vietnam/vietnam_details.html#design (accessed December 5, 2006); Robert Waechter to Claude Dorsey, [1984], letter made available to the author by Waechter. Waechter, a Vietnam veteran, worked at the Kansas City vet center and was a member of Vietnam Veterans and Friends, which organized fundraising for the Kansas City Vietnam Veterans Memorial.

6. New York Vietnam Veterans Memorial Commission documents, including competition rules and the names and credentials of those who voted for the winning design, are collected in folder 4, box 7, New York Vietnam Veterans Memorial Commission Records, New York City Municipal Archives.

7. See, e.g., Richard Borreca, "Two Wars May Scar Our Capitol," *Honolulu Star-Bulletin*, February 8, 1991; Gregg K. Kakesoko, "Plans over War Vets Memorial Trigger Strife," *Honolulu Star-Bulletin*, January 8, 1992. A step-by-step outline of the controversy can be traced through articles in the *Honolulu Advertiser* and *Honolulu Star-Bulletin* between January 1991 and July 1994, when the memorial was dedicated. The author is grateful for the assistance of Libby Hatch, project director of the Vietnam Veterans Memorial Fund, and Roland F. Perkins and Neal Hatayama of the Hawaii Public Library System for identifying news sources about the memorial controversy.

8. *New York Vietnam Veterans Memorial Commission Records, 1963–1990* (New York: City of New York Department of Records and Information Services, n.d.), 5, 9.

9. Tim Ghianni, "Vietnam Vets Seek to Bring War 'Out of Closet,'" *Paducah Sun*, December 2, 1983.

10. Fundraising letter addressed to "Dear Friend," signed by John W. Saputo, president of the North Carolina Vietnam Veterans Memorial Committee, n.d., referred to as "our first fund raising letter" and attached to letter from Steve Acai, vice president and publicity director of the committee, to Bernard Edelman, December 31, 1982, box 14, New York Vietnam Veterans Memorial Commission Records.

11. Bill East, "Triad Veterans Give Okay to Plans for N.C. Memorial," n.d., ca. 1984 (no bibliographical reference available), in *Vietnam Veterans Leadership Program [VVLP] Press Coverage: The Program's Third Year*, LBP.

12. Project on the Vietnam Generation, *Report*, 79; Ghianni, "Vietnam Vets"; Lena H. Sun, "Vietnam Generation Honors Its Own . . . ," *Washington Post*, November 6, 1986; Larry Ligtenberg, Brown County Vietnam Veterans, to Bernard Edelman, n.d. [received September 22, 1988], box 14, New York Vietnam Veterans Memorial Commission Records; Rusty Marks, "Memorial Wars," *Charleston Gazette-Mail*, December 16, 1990.

13. *Montana State Vietnam Veterans' Memorial, Dedication* (Missoula, November 11, 1988), booklet found in AFP.

14. *New Art Examiner*, January 1990, 60; *Minnesota Vietnam Veterans Memorial*, dedication ceremony brochure, September 26, 1992, 4. A copy of the brochure was sent to the author by Teresa Vetter.

15. Edward Colimore, "March Will Help Build a Memorial to Area Men Who Died in Vietnam," *Philadelphia Inquirer*, January 18, 1987. For a discussion of the Minnesota memorial, see Patrick Hagopian, "Vietnam Veterans Memorials as Places of Commemoration," in *Places of Commemoration: Search for Identity and Landscape Design*, ed. Joachim Wolschke-Bulmahn (Washington, DC: Dumbarton Oaks Research Library and Collection, 2001), 362–64.

16. Joan Burke, to the Pittsburgh-Allegheny County Vietnam Veterans Monument Fund (n.d.), copy sent to the author by T. J. McGarvey, president of the Pittsburgh/Allegheny County Vietnam Veterans Monument Committee.

17. See, e.g., Harry G. Summers, *On Strategy: A Critical Analysis of the Vietnam War* (Novato, CA: Presidio Press, 1982); Andrew F. Krepinevich, *The Army and Vietnam* (Baltimore: Johns Hopkins University Press, 1986); Bruce Palmer, *The 25-Year War: America's Military Role in Vietnam* (New York: Touchstone, 1985).

18. Brewin and Shaw, *Vietnam on Trial*, 42–43.

19. Westmoreland also participated in the dedication ceremonies of the Vietnam Veterans Memorials at Pittsburgh; Eufaula, Alabama; and Newport News, Virginia. He was present when the names of the Vietnam War dead were added to the war memorial in Richmond, Virginia. He served on the "blue ribbon committee" of the California Vietnam Veterans Memorial. Jerry Strait and Sandra Strait, *Vietnam War Memorials* (Jefferson, NC: McFarland, 1988), 5, 23, 171, 178; Margie Romero, "Vietnam Remembered: Pittsburghers Build Salute to All Veterans—Survivors and Casualties," press clipping, publication information deleted, sent to the author by T. J. McGarvey; J. P. Furst, "Northland Vets Pay Off Debt for Local Vietnam Memorial," *Duluth News-Tribune*, September 24, 1992; Michael Shain, Amy Pagnozzi, and Maralyn Matlick, "10 Years Later, We Remember," *New York Post*, May 7, 1985; Anita Lewis Hisley, "Date Set for Vietnam Memorial Dedication," *Lexington (KY) Herald Leader*, December 25, 1986; Gary Ford's notes for his article, "In the Name of Glory," *Southern Living*, May 1995, generously donated to the author; Kay Harvey, "Minnesotans Have 'a Coming Home,'" *St. Paul Pioneer Press*, September 27, 1992; Gil Dominguez, "Vietnam Veterans Memorials of San Antonio," 1, grunt.space.swri.edu/satexmem.htm (accessed September 11, 2005); Evelyn Barbour in the *From the Heart* newsletter, April 1988, 9.

20. VVLP, *An American Sunrise: A History of ACTION's Three-Year Veterans' Initiative: Technical Report*, attachment 9, "Highlights of Techniques Being Used to Project a Positive Image to the American Public," 4, LBP.

21. Quotation from the documentary *From Vietnam to Washington, D.C., and Beyond*, prod. Carlos Ricketson (Vietnam Veterans of Oregon Memorial Fund, 1984).

22. The quotation is from Doug Wood, "Vietnam Veterans Memorial Speech," November 11, 1987, attached to materials sent by John Deering, the sculptor of the Arkansas memorial, to Jack McKinley of the Vietnam Veterans Memorial Fund of Texas, found in the latter's records to which the author was given access by B. G. Burkett.

23. *California Vietnam Veterans Memorial, December 10, 1988*, dedication ceremony program, 3. A photograph of Woods at the dedication ceremony of the national memorial can be found in Sal Lopes, *The Wall: Images and Offerings from the Vietnam Veterans Memorial* (New York: Collins, 1987), 41.

24. Project on the Vietnam Generation, *Report*, 18.

25. Ibid., 93; "Louisiana Artist Wins Memorial Design Contest," *Louisiana Legionnaire*, August 1983, 1–2; Susan Feeney, "Bronze Figure at Dome to Honor Vietnam Vets," *New Orleans Times-Picayune*, October 12, 1983.

26. VVLP, "Highlights of Techniques Being Used," 5.

27. Marc Leepson, "531 Names Etched into Eternity," *VVA Veteran*, June/July 2000, 12–13. The Sacramento memorial had Leo Thorsness, a VVLP officer, on its board; the North Carolina and western New York memorials are listed among the VVLP-led projects in Project on the Vietnam Generation, *Report*, 18n1.

28. "Louisiana Artist Wins Memorial Design Contest," 1–2.

29. Ted Cohen, "Vietnam Memorial Selected," *Portland (ME) Press Herald*, January 18, 1985.

30. Lisa Leff, "Md. [Maryland] Breaks Ground on Memorial," *Washington Post*, November 12, 1986.

31. "Never Again," editorial, *Pine Bluff Commercial*, October 1, 1983.

32. The wall is pictured in Strait and Strait, *Vietnam War Memorials*, 13. For a history of the Arkansas memorial and its inscription, see the on-line history "Vietnam Veterans Memorial Details."

33. For photographs by Andy Richmond of front and rear views of the statue designed by John William Deering, see grunt.space.swri.edu/images/vn/deanna/ark9.jpg; and grunt.space.swri.edu/images/vn/deanna/ark7.jpg (accessed December 5, 2006). The program of the statue's dedication ceremony says, "The artist worked closely with the Vietnam Veterans Memorial Committee to ensure the authenticity of the equipment and details of the figure." "Arkansas Vietnam Veterans Memorial: 'The Statue'; Unveiling Ceremony," November 11, 1987, dedication ceremony booklet, found in the records of the Vietnam Veterans Memorial Fund of Texas. Like one of Hart's figures in Washington, DC, the foot soldier has a towel draped around his neck.

34. For a graphic description of the literal and emotional load that grunts carried, see Tim O'Brien, *The Things They Carried* (New York: Penguin, 1990), 3–25.

35. Quoted in Marc Leepson, "Distinction and Valor," *VVA Veteran*, July 2004, 43.

36. Jayne Merkel, "Proposed War Monument: Emotions, Aesthetics at Issue," *Cincinnati Inquirer*, March 9, 1983.

37. Leepson, "Distinction and Valor," 43; Carolyn Hayes-Knoll, "Recognition of Vietnam Vets," *Madison Messenger* (Madison County, TN), May 23, 1984.

38. Bruce M. Smith, "Memorial Planned for Vietnam Veterans," *Columbia, South Carolina, State*, February 18, [1984]; and Merle D. Kellerhals Jr., "Monument Planned in North Charleston for Vietnam Veterans," *News and Courier* (Charleston, SC), n.d. [1984], in *VVLP Press Coverage: The Program's Third Year*; Bonnie Jordan, "Design Selected for Proposed Veterans Monument," *News and Courier*, June 18, 1984; Bonnie Jordan, "Monument to Honor S.C. Vietnam Veterans," *News and Courier*, June 18, 1984.

39. Ronald Ray, interviews by the author, April 10 and May 14, 1992; Ronald D. Ray to Victor Westphall, February 28, 1990; Ronald D. Ray to Walter Douglas Westphall, April 18, 1990. (Ray's role as the local chairman of the VVLP and a Republican Party activist is mentioned in chapter 7.) Ray's correspondence and the Kentucky VVLP and Kentucky Vietnam Veterans Memorial Fund papers are found in the document collections described in chapter 7, n125. Unless otherwise indicated, the materials related to the Kentucky Vietnam Veterans Memorial were found there.

40. Ray, interview, May 14, 1992.

41. Lucie Blodgett, "Vietnam Winners Make the News," *Louisville Skyline*, September 5, 1983.

42. Robert Timberg, *The Nightingale's Song* (New York: Simon and Schuster, 1995), 13–14, 396.

43. Ronald Ray, resumé, provided to the author by Ronald Ray; U.S. General Accounting Office (GAO), *Central America: U.S. National Guard Activities* (Washington, DC: General Accounting Office, July 1988), document GAO/NSIAD-88-195, 6; Tom Barry, *Low-Intensity Conflict: The New Battlefield in Central America* (Albuquerque, NM: The Inter-Hemispheric Education Resource Center, 1986), 21; Sara Miles, "Preparing the Battlefield," *NACLA Report on the Americas*, April/May 1986, 30–32; Bill Keller and Joel Brinkley, "U.S. Military Is Termed Prepared for Any Move against Nicaragua," *New York Times*, June 4, 1985; Allan Nairn, "Endgame," *NACLA Report on the Americas*, May/June 1984, 19.

44. Miles, "Preparing the Battlefield," 32; Nairn, "Endgame," 29.

45. Keller and Brinkley, "U.S. Military Is Termed Prepared."

46. Peter Kornbluh, "Nicaragua: U.S. Proinsurgency Warfare against the Sandinistas," in *Low Intensity Warfare: Counterinsurgency, Proinsurgency, and Antiterrorism in the Eighties*, ed. Michael T. Klare and Peter Kornbluh (New York: Pantheon Books, 1988), 148–50; GAO, *Central America*, 1.

47. "Executive Order 12513—Prohibiting Trade and Certain Other Transactions Involving Nicaragua," May 1, 1985, APP, www.presidency.ucsb.edu/ws/?pid=38582 (accessed December 3, 2006).

48. Miles, "Preparing the Battlefield," 31.

49. Karl E. Cocke, *Department of the Army: Historical Summary Fiscal Year 1985*, ed. Marilee S. Morgan (Washington, DC: U.S. Army Center for Military History, 1995), 32–33, www.army.mil/cmh/books/DAHSUM/1985/ch03.htm (accessed November 27, 2006). The quoted phrase describes all field exercises undertaken during the year. The specific purpose of Big Pine ("Ahuas Tara") III and Universal Trek exercises was to "continue the U.S. presence in Central America, reassure friendly Caribbean nations, and deter aggression."

50. GAO, *Central America*, 1.

51. Comptroller General of the United States, "Decision B-213137, Appropriations—Defense Department—Honduras Military Exercises—Operations and Maintenance Funds—Availability," June 22,

1984, *Decisions of the Comptroller General of the United States*, vol. 63, *October 1, 1983 to September 30, 1984*, 422–47; Kornbluh, "Nicaragua," 49, 149, 156; William LeoGrande, *Our Own Backyard: The United States in Central America, 1977–1992* (Chapel Hill: University of North Carolina Press, 1998), 317, 400–408; Harry Stoffer, "Central America Sites for Guards Opposed," *Pittsburgh Post-Gazette*, February 27, 1988; Center for Defense Information, "The Nuts and Bolts of the U.S. Military Presence in Honduras," in Peckenham and Street, *Honduras*, 303; Haynes Johnson, *Sleepwalking through History: America in the Reagan Years* (New York: Anchor Books, 1992), 284–89. Allan Nairn agrees that the 1983 exercises were "a pretext for leaving behind equipment and facilities" for the use of the *contras*. Nairn, "The United States Militarizes Honduras," in *Honduras: Portrait of a Captive Nation*, ed. Nancy Peckenham and Annie Street (New York: Praeger, 1985), 296. Peter Kornbluh concurs. Kornbluh, telephone interview by the author, December 6, 2006.

52. Scott Anderson and Jon Lee Anderson, *Inside the League* (New York: Dodd, Mead, 1986), 240; "United States Military Assistance and Training," in *Honduras: A Country Study*, ed. Tim Merrill (Washington, DC: Federal Research Division, Library of Congress, 1993), www.country-data.com/cgi-bin/query/r-5731.html (accessed July 29, 2008). Associated Press, "U.S. National Guard to Help Honduran Military Build Road," *New York Times*, December 6, 1985; Kornbluh, "Nicaragua," 149; Keller and Brinkley, "U.S. Military Is Termed Prepared."

53. The results of the CBS/New York Times poll, published on April 15, 1986, are reported in Allan Nairn, "Low-Intensity Conflict: One Hit, Two Misses," *NACLA Report on the Americas*, June 1986, 4; Associated Press, "Reagan Considers Change for Guard," *New York Times*, April 26, 1986.

54. Babbitt, "If Guardsmen Go to Honduras," *New York Times*, September 16, 1986.

55. Associated Press, "Reagan Considers Change for Guard"; "White House Drops Proposal on Control of National Guard," *New York Times*, May 6, 1986.

56. James Webb, letter to the editor, *New York Times*, October 7, 1986.

57. Nairn, "Low-Intensity Conflict," 5. This correlation does not imply causation. When asked to volunteer reasons for opposing *contra* aid, only 2 percent mentioned "another Vietnam" and the danger of escalation. David K. Shipler, "Poll Shows Confusion on Aid to Contras," *New York Times*, April 16, 1986.

58. Ronald Reagan, *The Reagan Diaries*, ed. Douglas Brinkley (New York: HarperCollins, 2007), 308.

59. Ronald D. Ray to Alexander Solzhenitsyn, April 6, 1984, 1–2. The records of correspondence do not indicate whether Solzhenitsyn replied.

60. Ronald Ray, "Vietnam as a Noble Cause," lecture presented to a class on the Vietnam War at the University of Louisville, April 8, 1983, 7. Ronald D. Ray to Millard Cox III, March 28, 1983.

61. Richard Nixon, "Address to the Nation on the Situation in Southeast Asia," April 7, 1971, APP, www.presidency.ucsb.edu/ws/?pid=2972 (accessed July 15, 2008).

62. In a letter to Richard N. Pfeiffer, September 2, 1982, Ray argued these points, expressing his strong agreement with the arguments of the neo-conservative Norman Podhoretz in *Why We Were in Vietnam* (New York: Simon and Schuster, 1982).

63. For example, at the 1988 dedication of a local memorial in Kentucky, Rep. Jim Bunning said, "When their nation called, they went. . . . When they returned, they never received the heroes' welcome they so deserved. This is one of the things this memorial can correct." Bonnie Winters, "A Memorial to Those Who Fell: Kenton County Pays Respect to Vietnam Vets," *Kentucky Post*, October 17, 1988.

64. "Ronald D. Ray Memorial Statement: *Symbol and Metaphor*," submission to Kentucky VVMF design committee, 4, attached to Ronald D. Ray to Jim Lundgard, November 2, 1984.

65. Ronald D. Ray, letter with the salutation "Dear Friend," September 7, 1984.

66. Remarks of Ronald D. Ray at the dedication of the Vietnam Veterans Flagpole and Memorial Plaque, Louisville, KY, November 19, 1983.

67. Leslie Ellis, "Vietnam Vets to be Honored on Belvedere," *Louisville Courier-Journal*, September 24, 1983.

68. Minutes of the Kentucky VVMF design committee meeting (hereafter cited as Design Committee minutes), September 8, 1984, 1, 2.

69. Minutes of the Kentucky VVMF memorial committee meeting, November 20, 1984; "Organization and Operating Plan, Kentucky Vietnam Veterans Memorial Fund, Vietnam Veterans Leadership Program of Kentucky, Inc.: Draft," November 5, 1985, 1–2.

70. Commonwealth of Kentucky, General Assembly, Regular Session 1984, House Joint Resolution No. 7, March 23, 1984.

71. Jim Halvatgis, executive director of the Kentucky VVMF, interview by the author, April 10, 1992. The eventual cost of completing the memorial was about $750,000, most of it raised through private donations. Helm Roberts, interview by the author, April 16, 1992. Official memorial fund documents state that over a million dollars was raised to meet construction and other costs.

72. Ronald D. Ray to Kentucky Vietnam Veterans Memorial Advisory Board members, May 10, 1984;

Associated Press, "Model of Vietnam Memorial Displayed," *Louisville Courier-Journal*, March 20, 1984; Berry Craig, "Vietnam Veterans Gather to Share Stories, Memories," *Paducah Sun*, March 11, 1984.

73. Design Committee minutes, September 8, 1984, 3, 5, 12; Ronald Ray, interviews by the author, April 13 and 14, 1992.

74. The statement of the committee's responsibility for the design is in Ronald D. Ray to Fellow Advisory Board Members, May 10, 1984, 2.

75. Design Committee minutes, September 8, 1984, 12.

76. Keith Lawrence, "Monument Model, Ceremony Honor Vietnam Soldiers," *Owensboro (KY) Messenger-Inquirer*, April 19, 1984.

77. Ray and Chase had met at the National Defense School, Florida, in February 1984 and they corresponded about the memorial the following month. Design Committee minutes, September 8, 1984, 2.

78. Design Committee minutes, September 8, 1984, 12.

79. Ray, resumé.

80. Ray, "Vietnam as a Noble Cause," 6–7. Other VVLP supporters took issue with what they saw as equivocation about the Hué killings in *Vietnam: A Television History* (see chapter 7).

81. Jack Chase to Ronald D. Ray, March 7, 1984, 1, 2.

82. Ibid., 1; Ronald Ray to David Barten, April 6, 1984; Bill Black, notes of a July 20, 1984, telephone conversation with Ray, in the possession of the author; Ronald Ray to Bill Black, August 24, 1984; Design Committee minutes, September 8, 1984, 4.

83. The stylized female figure buries her face in her hands. Her torso is fashioned from bullet casings. A picture of the sculpture appears at www.jackchase.com/wargal/grief1.htm (accessed December 5, 2006).

84. A picture and details of *Bondage* appeared in Chase's Web site, www.jackchase.com/wargal/bondage1.htm; and www.jackchase.com/wargal/bondage2.htm (accessed December 5, 2006).

85. Chase to Ray, March 7, 1984, 2.

86. Ronald D. Ray to William R. Black Jr., August 24, 1984, 2, and March 9, 1984.

87. Ronald D. Ray to William Black Jr., August 30, 1983; copy provided to the author by Black.

88. Donna Rains, "Purchase Vietnam Veterans Plan Massive Gathering Saturday," *Paducah Sun*, March 7, 1984.

89. Design Committee minutes, September 8, 1984, 2, 11; William Black Jr., interview by the author, May 29, 1992. Jack Chase's Web site displays a picture labeled as the maquette for the Kentucky Vietnam Veterans Memorial, www.jackchase.com/wargal/1kyvvmem3.htm (accessed December 5, 2006). Black explained the term "true believer," one who single-mindedly follows an ideology, by referring to Eric Hoffer, *The True Believer: Thoughts on the Nature of Mass Movements* (New York: Harper Perennial, 2002).

90. Bill Black, memoranda to Design Committee, June 25 and July 12, 1984; "Trip to Cincinnati: Design Committee," July 21, 1984, Kentucky VVMF planning document; Bill Black to Jack Chase, July 2, 1984; Design Committee minutes, September 8, 1984, 6–7, 11, and December 1, 1984, 5; Black, interview.

91. Whittaker Chambers was the former Communist who became a radical Christian and right-wing Republican and testified at the House Un-American Activities Committee in 1948 that both he and the State Department's Alger Hiss had been spies for the Soviet Union. Ray's faith was tied to his commitment to create the memorial. George Morrison, "Memorial Project Has Unforeseen Faith Ties," *The Record: Louisville Archdiocesan Newspaper*, January 12, 1989. It was also strongly connected to his political worldview. In a letter to David Barten, April 6, 1984, he wrote, "It is imperative that the Judeo-Christian world view prevail" in the "worldwide intellectual and propaganda struggle for the minds of the people."

92. Ronald Reagan, "Remarks at the Annual Convention of the National Association of Evangelicals in Orlando, Florida," March 8, 1983, APP, www.presidency.ucsb.edu/ws/?pid=41023 (accessed July 15, 2008).

93. Ronald Ray to Bill Black, August 24, 1984. Ray enclosed the introduction to Whittaker Chambers's autobiography, *Witness*, with this letter.

94. John Canaday, "Our National Pride: The World's Worst Sculpture," *New York Times*, July 25, 1965. The author identified the article, attached to the Design Committee minutes, September 8, 1984, without title or bibliographical details, thanks to the extraordinary efforts of Elizabeth Helm of the National Sculpture Society.

95. Design Committee minutes, September 8, 1984, 2–5; Ray reiterated these points in an interview by the author, May 19, 1992.

96. Design Committee minutes, September 8, 1984, 5.

97. Ibid., 6, 7.

98. Ronald Ray, interviews by the author, April 13 and May 19, 1992. Ronald Ray, "Vietnam Veterans Memorial Dedication Speech," November 12, 1988, 4. Ray condemns relativism in his April 6, 1984, letter

to Barten: "Truth and true are ugly words in our universities and seminaries." For the proposition that "a man fights for the man next to him," and an application of that thesis to U.S. servicemen in Vietnam, see S. L. A. Marshall, *Men against Fire: The Problem of Battle Command* (New York: Morrow, 1968), 161; Albert Auster, "'Reflections of the Way Life Used to Be': *Tour of Duty, China Beach,* and the Memory of the Sixties," in *Historical Memory and Representations of the Vietnam War,* ed. Walter L. Hixson (New York: Garland, 2000), 331.

99. "Ronald D. Ray Memorial Statement: *Symbol and Metaphor,*" 6–7.

100. Minutes of the Kentucky VVMF design committee, parameters subcommittee meeting, December 15, 1984, 8.

101. Ibid., 3.

102. *Outline of Request for Proposal for Kentucky Vietnam Veterans Memorial,* attached to parameters subcommittee, memorandum to design committee members, December 31, 1984.

103. "Statement" adopted by design committee, October 27, 1984; *Outline of Request for Proposal for Kentucky Vietnam Veterans Memorial,* 4, 8; design committee minutes, December 1, 1984, 2–4; Black, interview.

104. Ronald Ray to William R. Black Jr., January 30, 1985, 1.

105. Design committee minutes, July 21, 1984, 3; design statements by ten committee members discussed at the October 27, 1984, design committee meeting and appended to its minutes.

106. Minutes of the Vietnam Veterans Leadership Program of Kentucky, Inc., Board of Directors meetings, February 13 and March 19, 1985.

107. Design committee minutes, September 8, 1984, 14 (on the new members), and April 13, 1985.

108. Ronald Ray to Bill Black, June 28, 1985.

109. Al McKnight, "Comments and Response to November 5th Draft of the Organization and Operating Plan for KVVMF," November 8, 1985; Black, interview. W. K. Gregory to Bill Black, November 20, 1985; Albert E. McKnight to Bill Black, November 26, 1985. Gregory and McKnight resigned from the VVLP as well as from the design committee. Bill Black forwarded the letters to Ronald Ray along with his own resignation from the design committee. Bill Black to Ronald Ray, January 7, 1986. Bill Black made copies of these letters available to the author.

110. Ronald Ray to William Black, August 27, 1985.

111. Wick Gregory to Ronald Ray, November 21, 1985.

112. *Kentucky Vietnam Veterans Memorial Fund Guidelines for Design Submission and Memorial Design Selection Process,* January 15, 1987. The quotation from the design criteria appears on the "History of the Memorial" plaque at the memorial's entry area. The text is reproduced in *Kentucky Vietnam Veterans Memorial Directory of Names* (Frankfort: Kentucky Vietnam Veterans Memorial Fund, Inc., 1988), 6. Helm Roberts, "Kentucky's Vietnam Veterans Memorial," *Cadence,* June 1989, 45.

113. Thomas H. Meeker to William H. Mook, January 12, 1987. A fundraising letter by Ronald Ray to Bertram W. Klein, September 10, 1986, also used the phrase, "This is a way to reconcile and heal old wounds."

114. Jim Halvatgis, interview by the author, May 18, 1992; Associated Press, "Tentative Site Chosen for Vietnam Memorial," *Louisville Courier-Journal,* April 17, 1987; James C. Burch, mayor of the city of Frankfort to Gordon C. Duke, secretary, Finance and Administration Cabinet, March 10, 1987; "Memorial Design Unveiled," *Frankfort State Journal,* July 1, 1987.

115. "Sundial Shows War's Shadow on State," *Lexington Herald-Leader,* November 11, 1980; Helm Roberts, interview by the author, May 16, 1992.

116. Helm Roberts, *Kentucky Vietnam Veterans Memorial, Submission 2,* sheet 1 of 3. Architect's concept and plan, a copy of which was given to the author by Helm Roberts.

117. Roberts, interview, May 16, 1992. Eunice Ray, Ronald Ray's wife, described herself and Ronald as "born again" Christians. Eunice Ray, interview by the author, May 15, 1992. Ray's spiritual journey after his return from Vietnam had led to his discovery of Thomas Merton, St. Thomas Aquinas, and other Roman Catholic theologians, leading to his conversion to Catholicism. Morrison, "Memorial Project Has Unforeseen Faith Ties."

118. "Remarks of Ronald D. Ray, Chairman, Kentucky Vietnam Veterans Memorial Fund, Inc., at the Dedication of the Kentucky Vietnam Veterans Memorial," November 12, 1988, 2–4.

119. Script of welcoming remarks and speeches by Jim Halvatgis.

120. Ted Sloan, "Solemn Dedication Planned," *Frankfort State-Journal,* November 11, 1988; Bill Weronka, "Shadows of Memory," *Louisville Courier-Journal,* November 13, 1988.

121. Andrea Orzoff, "State Remembers Its Vietnam Dead," *Lexington Herald-Leader,* May 29, 1989.

122. Associated Press wire report, "Kentucky Vietnam Veterans' Memorial Being Dedicated," November 12, 1988.

123. "Remarks of Ronald D. Ray, Chairman, Kentucky Vietnam Veterans Memorial Fund, Inc., at the Dedication of the Kentucky Vietnam Veterans Memorial," November 12, 1988, 2.

124. Ronald Ray, interview by the author, May 13, 1992.

125. Bob Deitel, "Veterans Memorial Is a Pointed Reminder of Vietnam Casualties," *Louisville Courier-Journal*, October 31, 1988.

126. Anne Pardue, "Campaign Seeks Funds for a State Memorial to the Vietnam War," *Louisville Courier-Journal*, August 6, 1986; Jack Brammer, "State Memorial Planned for Vietnam War Dead," *Lexington Herald-Leader*, August 6, 1986.

127. Associated Press, "Vets' Memorial Sundial Shadow Is Far-Reaching," *Louisville Courier-Journal*, November 13, 1989; Kevin Nance, "Honoring the Fallen: Ceremony Marks Anniversary of State's Vietnam Memorial," *Lexington Herald Leader*, November 12, 1989.

128. Ronald D. Ray, "Topic: Veterans Day and Vietnam," *Louisville Courier-Journal*, [November 11, 1986], clipping attached to Ronald Ray to Larry Hayes, November 26, 1986.

129. LeoGrande, *Our Own Backyard*, 475.

130. Dan Morgan, "Iran Report Accuses Administration of 'Disdain for Law,'" *Washington Post*, November 19, 1987; LeoGrande, *Our Own Backyard*, 500; Johnson, *Sleepwalking through History*, 287; Lawrence Walsh, *Firewall: The Iran-Contra Conspiracy and Cover-Up* (New York: W.W. Norton, 1997), 60–61, 193.

131. George Shultz, *Turmoil and Triumph: Diplomacy, Power, and the Victory of the American Ideal* (New York: Charles Scribner's Sons, 1993), 968, 969; Michael Dobbs, "Slavic Republics Declare Soviet Union Liquidated," *Washington Post*, December 9, 1991; Stephen Cohen, "The Break-Up of the Soviet Union Ended Russia's March to Democracy," *Guardian*, December 13, 2006.

132. Results of a Gallup Organization telephone poll of a national sample conducted between March 15 and 18, 1990, data provided by RC. According to the U.S Department of Defense, 116,516 Americans died in World War I, 405,399 died in World War II, 36,574 died in the Korean War, and 58,209 died in the Vietnam War. U.S. Department of Defense, *Principal Wars in which the United States Participated U.S. Military Personnel Serving and Casualties* siadapp.dior.whs.mil/personnel/CASUALTY/WCPRINCIPAL. pdf (accessed December 14, 2006).

133. Bill McCloud, "What Vietnam Should Teach Us," *Washington Times*, August 25, 1988; videotape of the dedication ceremony of the California Vietnam Veterans Memorial, in the author's possession.

134. Speech by Brig. Gen. Julius Berthold, May 16, 1992; author's observations.

135. Lee Byrd, "A Country Honors Its Veterans," *Philadelphia Inquirer*, November 12, 1989.

136. George H. W. Bush, "Remarks at the Dedication Ceremony for the Vietnam Veterans Memorial in Dallas, Texas," November 11, 1989, in *Bush, 1989, PPP*, bk. 2 (1990), 1502–3.

137. "Address before a Joint Session of the Congress on the State of the Union," January 28, 1992, APP, www.presidency.ucsb.edu/ws/?pid=20544 (accessed September 12, 2007).

138. Author's observation of the Veterans Day ceremony at the Vietnam Veterans Memorial, November 11, 1992.

139. Col. Harry G. Summers quoted in Jan Scruggs, *Reflections on the Vietnam Veterans Memorial* (Washington, DC: VVMF, 1994), 43.

140. C. Ray Hall, "Of Monuments and Memories," *Louisville Courier-Journal Magazine*, May 28, 1989, 6–7, 8.

141. Ibid., 8–9.

142. Fourteen questionnaires, administered face to face between May 17 and May 20, 1992; in the author's possession. Comments by a thirty-eight-year-old, white, male, non–Vietnam veteran, employed as an emergency medical services adviser, who had two friends whose deaths are recorded on the memorial; a thirty-seven-year-old white, male, non–Vietnam veteran police officer; and a forty-one-year-old, white, non–Vietnam veteran, housewife, with no friends or relatives named on the memorial, and with a brother and distant cousin who were Vietnam-era veterans.

143. Gallup Organization poll of March 15–18, 1990. The overwhelmingly favorable opinion of Vietnam veterans stands apart from the ratings of Congress, Lyndon Johnson, wartime military leaders, Richard Nixon, Henry Kissinger, Jane Fonda, and George McGovern.

144. The comments quoted in the text are from a thirty-six-year-old white, nonveteran man, employed as an emergency medical services adviser, whose cousin and a friend were remembered in the Kentucky memorial's roster of the dead; a forty-six-year-old white, male Vietnam veteran of the brown-water navy, currently employed as a dentist, with no friends or relatives recorded on the memorial; a fifty-three-year-old white, non–Vietnam veteran woman, employed as a clothing manufacturing quality controller, with no friends or acquaintances recorded on the memorial; a twenty-one-year-old white, non-

veteran man, employed as a school bus driver, with the names of a distant relative and a neighbor recorded on the Kentucky memorial, and an uncle who served in Vietnam and survived the war.

Although the size of the sample is too small to be statistically significant, the number of Kentucky memorial visitors who agreed with the "noble cause" idea is larger than would be predicted from the national polls (see Introduction, Table 2), in which only a third of respondents in 1985 and 1995 thought the war a "noble cause." The Kentucky responses are also markedly different from those of respondents to an equivalent questionnaire administered face-to-face by the author at the California Vietnam Veterans Memorial. (Eighteen questionnaires, administered face-to-face between April 7 and April 9, 1991, in the author's possession.) There, nine of the eighteen respondents agreed that the war was "more than a mistake, it was fundamentally wrong and immoral." The higher proportion of "noble cause" respondents in Kentucky makes their overall skepticism about the lessons of the war all the more striking.

9. "Today, We Are One People"

1. Competition entry no. 658, VVM-DPP.

2. This ideological subtext is also signified by the subtitle of a book about Vietnam veterans: Peter Goldman and Tony Fuller, *Charlie Company: What Vietnam Did to Us* (New York: Ballantine Books, 1983).

3. For examples of writings that look at these memorials, see Lena H. Sun, "Vietnam Generation Honors Its Own . . . ," *Washington Post*, November 6, 1986; Karal Ann Marling and John Wetenhall, "The Sexual Politics of Memory: The Vietnam Women's Memorial Project and 'The Wall,'" *Prospects: An Annual of American Cultural Studies* 14 (1989): 341–72.

4. Karen Ann Marling and Robert Silberman, "The Statue Near the Wall: The Vietnam Veterans Memorial and the Art of Remembering," *Smithsonian Studies in American Art* 1, no. 1 (Spring 1987): 16. Typically, grunts would wear one dog tag around their neck and one around a boot so that they could still be identified in case of "traumatic amputation" of their head or a limb.

5. Russell E. Dougherty, Air Force Association, to Jan Scruggs, June 5, 1984, box 35, VVMF-MD.

6. Joe White, president of the National War Dogs Memorial Project, Inc., quoted in Dale Russakoff, "Monumental Obsessions," *Washington Post*, February 23, 1989. For the stories of two efforts to establish war dog memorials, neither of which was successful at the time of this writing, see www.uswardogs.org/id3.html; and www.nationalwardogsmonument.org/default.asp (accessed June 20, 2007).

7. Jay Hall Carpenter, telephone interview by the author, June 3, 2008.

8. Juan Hipolito, American GI Forum, Department of California, to Robert Doubek, Vietnam Veterans Memorial Fund project director, October 25, 1982, box 35, VVMF-MD.

9. Jane Addams Allen, "Vietnam Memorial Gets a Spanish Face," *Washington Times*, May 25, 1984.

10. Statement by Jan Scruggs, president of Vietnam Veteran Memorial Fund, May 8, 1984. The statement and the correspondence about what a Latino figure should look like are in box 35, VVMF-MD. For a picture of a typical Latino sent in by one of the correspondents, see Patrick Hagopian, "America's Offspring: Infanticide and the Iconography of Race and Gender in Commemorative Statuary of the Vietnam War," *Prospects: An Annual of American Cultural Studies* 26 (2002): 546.

11. Allen, "Vietnam Memorial Gets a Spanish Face"; Marling and Silberman, "Statue Near the Wall," 18. Hart's assistant, Jay Hall Carpenter, claims German, Swedish, and Dutch ancestry. Carpenter, interview.

12. Complaints about the absence of Native Americans came in a letter from Shirley Jones, of Albuquerque, NM, to Jan Scruggs, [1984], box 35, VVMF-MD; and from Charlotte Kugler in a letter to President Reagan, November 16, 1984, casefile 283813, Reagan Library. Complaints about the absence of Asian Americans came in letters from Henry Woon, of Oakland, CA, to Vietnam Veterans Memorial Fund, November 10, 1982, and Rep. Norman Mineta (D., California) to Jan Scruggs, July 13, 1984, box 35, VVMF-MD.

13. Allen, "Vietnam Memorial Gets a Spanish Face."

14. Jan C. Scruggs to Norman Mineta, August 3, 1984, box 35, VVMF-MD.

15. Marling and Silberman, "Statue Near the Wall," 18.

16. Mary Lou Grier, deputy director, U.S. Department of the Interior, to Charlotte Kugler, January 30, 1985, casefile 283813, Reagan Library.

17. Rep. Tom Daschle (D., South Dakota) to J. Carter Brown, July 9, 1985, records of the Commission of Fine Arts, Washington, DC. For *The Highground*'s Native American memorial, see www.thehighground.org/tributes/nnavvm/ (accessed June 21, 2007).

18. Doug Wood, "Vietnam Veterans Memorial Speech [concerning the Arkansas memorial]," November 11, 1987, found in the records of the Vietnam Veterans Memorial Fund of Texas, Dallas, to

which the author was given access by B. G. Burkett; "Reliable Source: Veteran Sculpts Tribute to Fallen Comrades," *The Torch* (Smithsonian Institution), no. 87-3 (March 1987): 4. In addition to the statues in Reading, Pennsylvania; Little Rock, Arkansas; St. Paul, Minnesota; Salt Lake City, Utah; and Pierre, South Dakota described in this chapter and chapter 8, the single-figure statues are found in Fort Lauderdale, Florida (dedicated 1972); Longview, Texas (dedicated November 1983); Spokane, Washington (dedicated November 1985); Massillon, Ohio (dedicated 1985); and Council Bluffs, Iowa, where Strait and Strait report a statue was planned. Jerry L. Strait and Sandra S. Strait, *Vietnam War Memorials: An Illustrated Reference to Veterans Tributes throughout the United States* (Jefferson, NC: McFarland, 1988), 67, 96, 191–92, 205; records of Vietnam Veterans of America, made available to the author by Mark Leepson at VVA's Washington, DC, office; photograph of the Inland Northwest Vietnam Veterans Memorial (Spokane) at www.way-marking.com/gallery/image.aspx?f=1&guid=669810cb-1db6-4aee-83b2-8c24aaad638c (accessed June 26, 2007); e-mail message from Neina Kennedy of the Gregg County, Texas, Historical Museum, August 4, 2008. In addition to the statues of single male figures, there are three memorials depicting single female figures, the statue of Sharon Lane discussed in this chapter and the two smaller models mentioned in n102.

19. "Vietnam Veterans Memorial Planned for Capitol Grounds," *The Capitol Crowd*, capitolcrowd.blogspot.com/2008_05_01_archive.html (accessed August 9, 2008). The memorial, a bronze statue by Duke Sundt approved by the state legislature in 2005, is scheduled for completion in 2010.

20. Barbara Brueggebors, "Vietnam Vet Honors Comrades," *Centre Daily Times*, July 3, 1988, reprinted in the inside back cover of *Reflections of Those Who Served: The Men, The Women, Their Families, Their Friends* (n.p. [Boalsburg, PA]: Moving Wall Regional Committee, [June 1989]).

21. The Glens Falls memorial was dedicated in 1985 and the Missoula memorial in 1988. Strait and Strait, *Vietnam War Memorials*, 148; www.ci.missoula.mt.us/mayor/public_art.htm (accessed June 26, 2007). A photograph of the Missoula memorial can be found at photos1.blogger.com/photoInclude/blogger/7811/793/640/DCP_0738.0.jpg (accessed August 20, 2008).

22. Joe Smith, "Veteran Plans March to Fund New Memorial," *Albuquerque (NM) Journal*, April 9, 1983; Norman Oder, "Former S.C. Man's Work of Art Has Profound Effect on Veterans," *Charleston (WV) Gazette*, July 3, 1985; Vickie L. Walton, "KU's Fallen to Stand Again in Bronze," *Kansas City Star*, May 27, 1984; Terry Steel to James Lundgard II of the Louisville, Kentucky, VVLP, January 25, 1985. For the disposition of the Steel–Lundgard correspondence and other papers of the Kentucky VVMF and VVLP ("Kentucky papers"), see chapter 7, n125. As noted in chapter 3, slides of most of the entries to the Vietnam Veterans Memorial's design competition are in VVMF-DPP.

23. For further discussion of post–Vietnam War uses of the metaphor of healing, see Kevin Beattie, *The Scar That Binds: American Culture and the Vietnam War* (New York: New York University Press, 1998), 11–57.

24. John Eckberg, "Vietnam Statue Survives Battle," *Cincinnati Enquirer*, March 10, 1983; Tim Fitzpatrick, "Vets' Statue Ready to Be Unveiled," *Salt Lake City Tribune*, [October 1989]; Marc Leepson, "South Dakota Memorial Dedication: A Rousing Welcome Home," *VVA Veteran*, November/December 2006, 25.

25. Strait and Strait, *Vietnam War Memorials*, 126–27. Brodin is quoted in "Monument to the Living," brochure advertising miniature bronze of the St. Paul, Minnesota, memorial sent to the author by Brodin.

26. The sculpture by the local artist Charles Parks is located in a park in Wilmington, Delaware. Strait and Strait, *Vietnam War Memorials*, 35–36; Stephen Weiss, Clark Dougan, David Fulghum, Denis Kennedy, and the editors of the Boston Publishing Company, *The Vietnam Experience: A War Remembered* (Boston: Boston Publishing Company, 1986), 9.

27. Leo Steinberg, *The Sexuality of Christ in Renaissance Art and in Modern Oblivion* (London: Faber and Faber, 1984), 35. Steinberg refers here to Madonna-and-Child paintings, but the point could also apply to the Pietà, where the Christ is often barely clothed.

28. For other twentieth-century secular versions of the Pietà and Lamentation, see Mario De Micheli, Attilio Pizzigoni, Elvira Cassa Salvi, and Marco Rosci, *Monumenti Alla Resistenza in Europa* (Milan: Vangelista, 1985), 61, 91, 95.

29. Vonette Fontaine Buck, telephone interview by the author, May 19, 1995; Gus Thomson, "Creator of Memorial Statue Has Questions," *Auburn Journal*, February 6, 1991.

30. Vonette Fontaine, "County to Check Out Relighting Memorial," *Auburn Journal*, January 24, 1991; idem, "Statue May Get Moved," *Auburn Journal*, February 15, 1991; idem, "Gulf Clash Rekindling Old Debate," *Auburn Journal*, February 18, 1991.

31. Jon Engellenner, "Controversy over Auburn War Memorial Resurfacing," *Sacramento Bee*, February 20, 1991.

32. Vonette Fontaine, "Statue Readied for Homecoming," *Auburn Journal*, March 22, 1991.

33. Marc Leepson, "Distinction and Valor," *VVA Veteran*, July 2004, 43.

34. Minutes of the Kentucky Vietnam Veterans Memorial Fund design committee, parameters sub-committee meeting, December 15, 1984, 7, 9–10, in Kentucky papers.

35. Cary Johnson, "Viet Memorial Designs Viewed," *Portland (ME) Press Herald*, November 17, 1984.

36. Strait and Strait, *Vietnam War Memorials*, 108–9; Pegi Donovan, unpublished "handbook" on Vietnam Veterans Memorials [hereafter cited as Donovan handbook], unpaginated [17–18]. Donovan's interim findings, based on questionnaire research, consist of forty-six pages of closely typed notes about memorials nationwide. Completion of the project was prevented by her untimely death. A copy of the handbook is reposed among Vietnam Veterans of America's documents about Vietnam War memorials, to which the author was kindly given access by Marc Leepson, an exceptionally knowledgeable source for information about Vietnam War–related material.

37. Gary D. Ford, research notes for his article, "In the Name of Glory," *Southern Living*, May 1995, 134–39; Weiss et al., *Vietnam Experience*, 164.

38. Some caution should be used in generalizing from the memorial commission and memorial fund members whom I met, since my conclusions are based on research at only a limited number of sites and I did not meet all the members of the memorial commissions and memorial funds in every location. The research is corroborated, though, by coverage of memorial projects in local newspapers that appears to confirm that there were hardly any African Americans involved in creating the memorials.

39. Robert Timberg, *The Nightingale's Song* (New York: Simon and Schuster, 1995), 317.

40. During the Korean War, although manpower shortages led to the rapid integration of fighting units, the armed services had not fully integrated. Morris J. MacGregor, *Integration of the Armed Forces, 1940–1965* (Washington, DC: United States Army Center of Military History, 1985), chap. 16, table 8B, chap. 18, table 11, and chap. 19, www.history.army.mil/books/integration/IAF-18.htm (accessed August 20, 2008).

41. A picture of the maquette appears in Strait and Strait, *Vietnam War Memorials*, 185.

42. Ibid., 21–22, 105–6; Weiss et al., *Vietnam Experience*, 9; Donovan handbook, [3–4]. In a telephone interview by the author, July 30, 2007, Joe Pollocino, Albany County Veterans Committee (sponsor of the memorial), said that the sculptor of the Albany memorial, Merlin Szasz, who had a "free hand" in the design, decided on the race of the two figures.

43. John Mullen, a member of the Rensselaer County Vietnam Memorial Committee, Inc., interview by the author, May 8, 1995. The author also saw references to the original designer spelled Risendorf and was unable to establish which spelling is correct.

44. Gil Dominguez, "Vietnam Veteran [sic] Memorials of San Antonio," grunt.space.swri.edu/satex-mem.htm (accessed September 11, 2005). A photograph of the memorial is located at grunt.space.swri.edu/images/vn/billm/satex1s.jpg (accessed January 3, 2006).

45. Austin Deuel, e-mail message to the author, January 30, 2007. A photograph of *For What* and a brief description of the artist's involvement in the exhibition are found in Austin Deuel, *Even God Is Against Us* (Escondido, CA: Impressions West, 1988), 114–15.

46. Donovan handbook, [39]. The description, "It is from a moment of battle in Khe Sanh, April 30, 1967" suggests that the sculpture is based on an eyewitness account or news photograph. The scene in fact resembles a photograph by Catherine Leroy of one of the 1967 Khe Sanh Hill battles, although Deuel says that he witnessed the incident himself. The photograph is reproduced in Julene Fischer and the picture staff of Boston Publishing Company, *Images of War* (Boston: Boston Publishing Company, 1986), cover, 77.

47. Ray Stubbe, narrative of the Khe Sanh hill battles, www.geocities.com/Pentagon/4867/hillbatt.html (accessed January 3, 2007), originally published as Ray Stubbe, "The 1967 Hill Battles," *Khe Sanh Veterans Newsletter; Special Issue: 30th Anniversary of the Hill Battles at Khe Sanh* 39 (May 1997): 6–46; Ray Stubbe, telephone interview by the author, January 3, 2007.

48. Strait and Strait, *Vietnam War Memorials*, 193–94.

49. Scott Huddleston, "Vietnam Memorial Turns 20," *Express-News* (San Antonio), November 10, 2006.

50. John Baines, telephone interview by the author, February 5, 2007. In e-mail exchanges with the author (January 30, 31, February 1, 2, 2007), Austin Deuel declined to answer direct questions about how he decided to make the mortally wounded figure an African American, and whether Baines influenced this decision. Baines did not recall how the decision was made. "This is about all of us," he said, not just the two men whom Deuel witnessed during the battle. Baines, interview.

51. "North Carolina Vietnam Veterans Memorial Fact Sheet," [1983], document attached to Steve Acai, vice president and publicity director of the North Carolina Vietnam Veterans Memorial Committee, to Bernard Edelman, December 31, 1982; New York Vietnam Veterans Memorial Commission Records, box 14, New York City Municipal Archives.

52. "Heroes and Heroines on Union Square: The Statues and Monuments on Union (Capitol) Square at Raleigh, North Carolina," n.d., in the possession of the author.

53. North Carolina Vietnam Veterans Memorial, Inc., "North Carolina Vietnam Veterans Memorial" (1989), 4 (7-page information sheet sent to the author by Stephen Acai Jr.).

54. Arthur Egendorf, Andrea Remez, and John Farley, *Dealing with the War: A View Based on the*

Individual Lives of Vietnam Veterans, vol. 5 of Arthur Egendorf, Charles Kadushin, Robert S. Laufer, George Rothbart, and Lee Sloan, *Legacies of Vietnam: Comparative Adjustment of Veterans and Their Peers* (Washington, DC: U.S. G.P.O., 1981), 727. See also Christian Appy, *Working-Class War: American Combat Soldiers and Vietnam* (Chapel Hill: University of North Carolina Press, 1993), 11–12; Lawrence M. Baskir and William A. Strauss, *Chance and Circumstance: The Draft, the War, and the Vietnam Generation* (New York: Vintage Books, 1978), 6–10; Wallace Terry, *Bloods: An Oral History of the Vietnam War by Black Veterans*, 2nd ed. (New York: Ballantine, 1992), xvi–xvii.

55. Charles Kadushin, Ghislaine Boulanger, and John Martin, *Long Term Stress Reactions: Some Causes, Consequences, and Naturally Occurring Support Systems*, vol. 4 of Egendorf et al., *Legacies of Vietnam*, 498. Ghislaine Boulanger qualifies this finding by reporting that it is not statistically significant.

56. Sun, "Vietnam Generation Honors Its Own."

57. David Glassberg, personal communication, October 28, 1994.

58. Strait and Strait, *Vietnam War Memorials*, 21–22.

59. James E. Westheider, *Fighting on Two Fronts: African Americans and the Vietnam War* (New York: New York University Press, 1997), 113–15.

60. Terry, *Bloods*, 12, 38, 57, 99; *The Bloods of Nam*, dir. Wallace Terry (WGBH, Boston, 1986).

61. Westheider, *Fighting on Two Fronts*, 32–33, 146–49; Weiss et al., *Vietnam Experience*, 164.

62. Kadushin, Boulanger, and Martin, *Long Term Stress Reactions*, 523, 533, 546. Egendorf, Remez, and Farley, *Dealing with the War*, 812–22.

63. Cf. Keith Beattie's reading of the evocation of a transcendent unity that overcomes racial and class differences in the film *Grand Canyon* (1992). Beattie, *The Scar that Binds: American Culture and the Vietnam War* (New York: New York University Press, 1998), 148–49.

64. According to the Vietnam Women's Memorial Project, 265,000 women served in the armed forces during the Vietnam War era. Approximately 11,000 uniformed women served in country, 90 percent of whom were nurses. "Statement of the Vietnam Women's Memorial Project, Inc.," [November 1993], document distributed with dedication press packet.

65. Diane Carlson Evans, statement at Washington Project for the Arts panel discussion, "Commemorative Public Sculpture: The Politics of Memory," November 5, 1987, 10. The author, who was in the audience, was given access to a transcript by Philip Brookman and Susan Ades of the Washington Project for the Arts. The transcript is now in the Archives of American Art, Smithsonian Institution, Washington, DC. See also the testimony of women veterans in the television documentary *Not on the Frontline*, prod. Janet Nearhood (Nebraska ETV Network, 1991).

66. Al Jenkins to Jan Scruggs, May 16, 1984, box 5, VVMF-MD.

67. See, e.g., Lynda Van Devanter, with Christopher Morgan, *Home before Morning: The True Story of an Army Nurse in Vietnam* (New York: Warner Books, 1984), 259, 312–13.

68. Weiss et al., *Vietnam Experience*, 41–43. Other nurses describe having special soldiers who stayed in their minds. See, e.g., Judy Elbring in the documentary *The Long Road Back*, prod. Britt Davis (Office of Instructional Resources, University of Kentucky, n.d., ca. 1985).

69. National Geographic Explorer series, *Vietnam: The Women Who Served*, prod. Mitch Wood (TBS channel, June 12, 1994); Kathryn Marshall, *In the Combat Zone* (New York: Viking Penguin, 1987), 225–26.

70. Diane Evans, "Getting Cold" (1990), 2, 4–7; unpublished narrative found in AFP.

71. Van Devanter, *Home before Morning*, 113–16, 199, 259, 271. Van Devanter, who was women's director of Vietnam Veterans of America, wrote the book in part so that other former nurses who had undiagnosed PTSD would be able to recognize that they were not alone and not crazy. For an account of how the first publicly reported narratives by female Vietnam veterans served this function, see Patrick Hagopian, "Oral Narratives: Secondary Revision and the Memory of the Vietnam War," *History Workshop Journal* 32 (Autumn 1991): 145.

72. See, e.g., Keith Walker, *A Piece of My Heart: The Stories of Twenty- Six American Women Who Served in Vietnam* (New York: Ballantine, 1985), 201.

73. *The Vietnam Women's Memorial National One-Step Open Design Competition Program, Design Standards, Rules, and Procedures* (Washington, DC: Vietnam Women's Memorial Project, 1990), 5.

74. Laura Palmer, "How to Bandage a War," *New York Times Magazine*, November 7, 1993, 40, 41. See also Lily Lee Adams in Walker, *Piece of My Heart*, 403.

75. Vietnam Women's Memorial Project, *Invisible Veterans: A Legacy of Healing and Hope* (Minneapolis: Vietnam Women's Memorial Project, n.d.), records of the Commission of Fine Arts.

76. B. T. Collins, letter to the editor, *California Nursing Review*, November/December 1988, reproduced in *Celebration of Patriotism and Courage: Dedication of the Vietnam Women's Memorial, November 10–12, 1993* (Washington, DC: Vietnam Women's Memorial Project, 1993), 75.

77. Walker, *Piece of My Heart*, 132.

78. See, e.g., the poem "The Friendship Only Lasted a Few Seconds" by Lily Lee Adams, in *Visions of War, Dreams of Peace: Writings of Women in the Vietnam War*, ed. Lynda Van Devanter and Joan Furey (New York: Warner Books, 1991), 38–39.

79. Marine Corps Community for U.S. Marine Corps Veterans Web site, "Women Soldiers and Sailors," www.leatherneck.com/forums/archive/index.php/t-13474.html (accessed August 5, 2008); Strait and Strait, *Vietnam War Memorials*, 48.

80. Ted Kozlowski and Richard Haring of Westchester County, New York, Parks Department, telephone interviews by the author, June 22, 2007. I am grateful to Rebecca Shapiro for drawing my attention to this memorial.

81. Danny Griffin, president of Vietnam Veterans of America Westchester County Chapter 49, telephone interview by the author, July 23, 1998.

82. Kozlowski, interview.

83. For discussion of this photograph, see Patrick Hagopian, "Vietnam War Photography as a Locus of Memory," in Annette Kuhn and Kirsten McAllister, ed., *Locating Memory: Photographic Acts* (New York: Berghahn Books, 2006); and the television documentary *Decisive Moments: Photographs that Made History* (BBC2), broadcast November 1, 1997.

84. For photographs of the memorial, see Rodney S. Anderson, *Most Hallowed Ground: The California Vietnam Veterans Memorial* (North Highlands, CA: Andersonville Publishing, 1992). The information in the captions for figs. 45–46 is from *California Vietnam Veterans Memorial*, n.d., the California Vietnam Veterans Memorial Commission commemorative dedication booklet; and Robert D. Salgado, "California Vietnam Veterans Memorial Commission," unpublished description of the sources of the sculptures and bas-reliefs in the memorial. Both documents were donated to the author by Don Drumheller and Michael Kelley.

85. The U.S. Marine Corps photograph on which the sculpture was based became famous when it was used as the cover illustration for Terry's *Bloods*; it also appears on the cover of Nick Mills, *Combat Photographer* (Boston: Boston Publishing Company, 1986). The bas-reliefs include one based on Larry Burrows's photograph of a weary soldier weighed down by equipment and ammunition. See Larry Burrows, *Vietnam* (London: Jonathan Cape, 2002), 145. It is also published in Fischer, *Images of War*, 11.

86. The sculpture is based on a photograph by David Douglas Duncan.

87. The photograph (#3873) is available from www.popasmoke.com/ (accessed January 6, 2007). Eugene McCarthy said that the publication of this photograph marked a turning point of the war because it brought home the cost of the war to the public. Patrick J. Sloyan, "The War You Won't See," *Washington Post*, January 12, 1991.

88. See Burrows, *Vietnam*, 123, 164–65. The Burrows photographs are discussed in the television documentary *Vietnam: The Camera at War* (BBC2), broadcast November 7, 1997.

89. The letter is intended to be legible to visitors. Its text is reproduced in the commemorative dedication booklet *California Vietnam Veterans Memorial*, 12.

90. *Vietnam War Fact Sheet*, n.d., compiled by Gary Rousch of the Vietnam Helicopter Pilots Association (in the author's collection), claims that the average age of infantrymen in Vietnam was twenty-two. The same claim is made by B. G. Burkett and Glenna Whitley, *Stolen Valor: How the Vietnam Generation Was Robbed of Its Heroes and Its History* (Dallas: Verity Press, 1998), 47.

91. A letter with a similar ending—this one actually written by a mother to her son in Vietnam—is inscribed on the Vietnam Veterans Memorial in New York City and printed in *Dear America: Letters Home from Vietnam*, ed. Bernard Edelman (New York: W. W. Norton, 1985), 36.

92. The problem of paternal abandonment of African American families was elevated to national attention in the 1965 "Moynihan Report," Daniel Patrick Moynihan, *The Negro Family: A Case for National Action*, www.dol.gov/oasam/programs/history/webid-meynihan.htm (accessed July 26, 2008).

93. S. Webb, "Welcome Home (at Last)," *Pittsburgh*, November 1987, 12. See also Eric Heyl, "Schools Recruited to Help Vietnam Vet Memorial," *Pittsburgh Progress*, May 6, 1987; Joanne Veto, "Vietnam Memorial Planned," *Pittsburgh Progress*, May 20, 1987.

94. According to *Vietnam: The Women Who Served*, sixty-two American women died in Vietnam. This figure includes Red Cross workers and other civilians.

95. Marling and Wetenhall, "The Sexual Politics of Memory," 351. This article provides a thorough treatment of the early design history the Vietnam Women's Memorial. As J. Carter Brown said, "What the scheme did accomplish was to open the door to other groups not incorporated in Hart's realistic sculpture, which we recognized from the beginning as a flaw in the idea of adding *any* sculpture." Brown, "The Mall and the Commission of Fine Arts," *Studies in the History of Art* 30 (1991): 260.

96. Terrie Claflin, "Monumental Achievement," *Ms.*, November/December 1993, 87.

97. Diane Carlson Evans to Jan Scruggs, July 3, 1984, box 35, VVMF-MD.

98. Vietnam Women's Memorial Project, *Invisible Veterans*, 6.

99. Ibid., 4.

100. See, e.g., Jan Scruggs to Arnold Garay III, December 10, 1984, box 1, VVMF- LC; and Kara Swisher, "Action on the Women's Memorial," *Washington Post*, June 22, 1988.

101. Benjamin Forgey, "Women and the Wall," *Washington Post*, October 22, 1987.

102. Transcript and minutes of the Commission of Fine Arts meeting, October 22, 1987, records of the Commission of Fine Arts. In 1992, one of the thirty-six-inch models of Brodin's *The Nurse* was added to *The Highground*, the Wisconsin Vietnam Veterans Memorial. The most recent sculptural memorial to the Vietnam War is a similar-sized model of a servicewoman added to the Monroe County, Michigan, Vietnam Veterans Memorial and dedicated in May 2008. "Memorial Mission Is Complete," *VVA Veteran*, July/August 2008, 39. In another sign that women's contributions in Vietnam are regarded as worthy of representation, a three-person statue of a wounded man being supported at left and right by a soldier and a nurse was dedicated in May 2004 as the Cole Land Transportation Vietnam Veterans Memorial, in Bangor, Maine. Cole Land Transportation Museum Web site, www.colemuseum.org/warmemorials. cfm (accessed August 5, 2008).

103. Diane Carlson Evans, "Moving a Vision: The Vietnam Women's Memorial," www.vietnam-womensmemorial.org/pages/pdf/dcevans.pdf (accessed December 15, 2006); Karen K. Johnson, quoted in James R. Wilson, *Landing Zones: Southern Veterans Remember Vietnam* (Durham: Duke University Press, 1990), 254.

104. Editorial, "Leave the Vietnam Memorial Alone," *Washington Post*, February 27, 1988.

105. David Corn and Jefferson Morley, "Beltway Bandits: The War on the Wall," *Nation*, June 4, 1988, 780.

106. Panel discussion, "Commemorative Public Sculpture: The Politics of Memory," Washington Project for the Arts, November 5, 1987.

107. Maya Lin and J. Carter Brown, witness statements, U.S. Congress, Senate, Subcommittee on Public Lands, National Parks, and Forests of the Committee on Energy and Natural Resources, *Hearings on S. 2042, to Authorize the Vietnam Women's Memorial Project, Inc., to Construct a Memorial in Honor and Recognition of the Women of the United States Who Served in the Vietnam Conflict*, 100th Cong., 2d sess., February 23, 1988, 16–17, 122.

108. Evans, "Moving a Vision"; *Celebration of Patriotism and Courage*, 12.

109. PL 100-660 authorizing the women's memorial was signed by President Reagan on November 15, 1988; Kara Swisher, "Reagan Signs Bill for Vietnam Women's Memorial," *Washington Post*, November 17, 1988. Seventeen of the twenty-three respondents to the author's face-to-face questionnaire administered at the Vietnam Veterans Memorial between November 1990 and March 1991 agreed that it was appropriate to add a statue of a nurse to the memorial.

110. Kara Swisher, "Arts Beat: Vietnam Statue Clears Hurdle," *Washington Post*, May 16, 1988; Phil McCombs, "Senate Backs Women's Memorial," *Washington Post*, June 15, 1988.

111. After the secretary of the interior had approved the addition of the statue to the Vietnam Veterans Memorial, the "Sense of the Congress" provision included in PL 100-660 was strengthened by Congressional Joint Resolution 207, approving the location of the memorial in "Area I" designated by the Commemorative Works Act of November 14, 1986.

112. Minutes of the Commission of Fine Arts meetings, April 19, 1990, 8, and, September 19, 1991, 4, records of the Commission of Fine Arts.

113. Unsigned, undated 1-page typewritten statement under the letterhead of the Vietnam Women's Memorial Project, Inc., Minneapolis. Copied for the author by Rodger Brodin.

114. Diana Hellinger, executive director of the Vietnam Women's Memorial Project, telephone interview by the author, June 6, 1995.

115. *Vietnam Women's Memorial National One-Stage Open Design Competition Program, Design Standards, Rules and Procedures*; undated press release, under the letterhead of R. M. Brodin Studios, Inc., titled, "Design Competition May Have Excluded the Original Artist, But It Can't Stop Him from Finishing What He Set Out to Do—Honor the Women Veterans of Vietnam," sent to the author by Rodger Brodin.

116. Cheryl Nicol, a supporter of the Vietnam Women's Memorial Project, interview by the author, June 27, 1991.

117. J. B. Johnson, "Design Picked for Women Vets' Memorial, *Minneapolis Star-Tribune*, November 20, 1990. Slides of the Barry and Desmond designs can be found in the Vietnam Women's Memorial Project's documentation of the competition and in the records of the Commission of Fine Arts. A sculpture by Eileen Barry similar to the VWMP competition entry, a uniformed figure holding her helmet in her left hand, was dedicated in Veterans Memorial Plaza, Rockaway Beach, New York, in 1989.

118. Statement by Glenna Goodacre, minutes of the Commission of Fine Arts meeting, September 19, 1991, 2; Glenna Goodacre, interview by the author, July 17, 1992. It has been suggested that the kneel-

ing figure might represent an Asian American. Sabine Behrenbeck, "Versailles and Vietnam: Coming to Terms with War," in *America, the Vietnam War, and the World: Comparative and International Perspectives*, ed. Andreas W. Daum, Lloyd C. Gardner, and Wilfried Mausbach (Cambridge: Cambridge University Press, 2003), 145.

119. Evans, "Moving a Vision."

120. Minutes of the Commission of Fine Arts meeting, April 19, 1990, 7.

121. George Dickie, landscape architect for the Vietnam Women's Memorial Project, interview by the author, July 30, 1993; planning diagram of alignment of Glenna Goodacre's statue copied for the author by George Dickie.

122. *Vietnam Women's Memorial Dedication, November 11, 1993*, videocassette (Vietnam Women's Memorial Foundation, Washington, DC, 1993).

123. Diane Carlson Evans, "Welcome from the Founder and Chair," *Celebration of Patriotism and Courage*, 6.

124. *Vietnam Women's Memorial Dedication, November 11, 1993*.

10. "Our Offspring"

1. Elizabeth Kutsche of Richland, MI, to Vietnam Veterans Memorial Competition organizers, March 2, 1981, box 64, VVMF-MD.

2. Daniel E. Lamber, state adjutant, American Legion, Department of Maine, to Jan Scruggs, March 23, 1982, box 4, VVMF-MD.

3. Competition entry no. 627, submitted by Timothy Patrick Ward (the quoted reference to the war's "innocent victims" is from the designer's statement accompanying the submission); no. 721, submitted by a team led by Robert W. Raymond; no. 906, submitted by a team led by John Evan Korhonen, VVM-DPP.

4. Competition entry no. 1283, submitted by Garth E. Bute; no. 805, submitted by a team led by Michael D. Rich, VVM-DPP. The other designs featuring Vietnamese children are nos. 151, 158, 188, 360, 577, 1126, 1296, VVM-DPP.

5. Rodger Brodin, one of two veterans on the Minnesota design competition jury, telephone interview by the author, August 14, 1991.

6. Established networks such as the Vietnam Veterans Leadership Program and Vietnam Veterans of America spread the word about concepts they admired. Syndicated news reports of memorials in different parts of the country helped make their example known in other localities. See, e.g., Prentice Palmer, "Georgia to Erect Statue in Honor of Its Vietnam Vets," *Atlanta Constitution*, May 27, 1987.

7. John F. Kennedy, "America's Stake in Vietnam, the Cornerstone of the Free World in Southeast Asia," *Vital Speeches of the Day* 22, no. 17 (June 15, 1956): 618.

8. *Why Vietnam?* (U.S. Directorate for Armed Forces Information and Education, 1965).

9. *The Green Berets*, dir. John Wayne and Ray Kellogg (1968).

10. *Hearts and Minds*, dir. Peter Davis (1974).

11. The National Archives and the photographic collections of the U.S. Army contain numerous examples of such official photographs. For published examples, see Julene Fischer and the picture staff of Boston Publishing Company, *Images of War* (Boston: Boston Publishing Company, 1986), 52, 53; Nick Mills, *Combat Photographer* (Boston: Boston Publishing Company, 1986), 82, 83; William Westmoreland, *A Soldier Reports* (New York: Da Capo Press, 1989), photograph section between 326 and 327. For examples of combat art, see Noel Daggett, *Gifts for the Children of An Phong Orphanage*, and Apollo Dorian, *Vietnamese Girls with Gifts from Coast Guardsman*, in *Combat Art of the Vietnam War*, ed. Joseph F. Anzenberger Jr. (Jefferson, NC: McFarland, 1986), 85, 97; Cliff Young, *The "Other" War*, and Capt. John T. Dyer Jr., *Saigon Street Scene*, in *Vietnam Combat Art*, by Henri Raymond (New York: Cavanagh and Cavanagh, 1968), unpaginated. See also the 1965 U.S. State Department photograph of a foreign service worker with Vietnamese children, and Stephen H. Randall's *Two Medics* (1968), in Patrick Hagopian, "America's Offspring: Infanticide and the Iconography of Race and Gender in Commemorative Statuary of the Vietnam War," *Prospects: An Annual of American Cultural Studies* 26 (2002): 538–539.

12. According to Tom Englehardt the image of U.S. forces as perpetrators of crimes in Vietnam "robbed Americans of their inheritance" as liberators of Europe in World War II. Englehardt, *The End of Victory Culture: Cold War America and the Disillusioning of a Generation* (New York: Basic Books, 1995), 254.

13. Rick Perlstein, *Nixonland: The Rise of a President and the Fracturing of America* (New York: Scribner's, 2008), 206; *Tour 365*, Spring/Summer 1968, 16, 32–33; Richard Slotkin, *Gunfighter Nation: The Myth of the Frontier in Twentieth-Century America* (Norman: University of Oklahoma Press, 1998), 522. I am grateful to Shelley Morgan for bringing the passage by Slotkin to my attention. Christina Klein has usefully illuminated the adoption metaphor in relations between the United States and Southeast Asian countries. Klein,

"Family Ties and Political Obligation: The Discourse of Adoption and the Cold War Commitment to Asia," in *Cold War Constructions*, ed. Christian G. Appy (Amherst: University of Massachusetts Press, 2000).

14. Spec. 5 Thomas Pellaton to his college roommate and best friend, John Niles, in *Dear America: Letters Home from Vietnam*, ed. Bernard Edelman (New York: W. W. Norton, 1985), 243–44.

15. Al Santoli, *To Bear Any Burden: The Vietnam War and Its Aftermath in the Words of Americans and Southeast Asians* (New York: Ballantine, 1985), 320.

16. For examples of narratives, see Eunice Splawn, in Kathryn Marshall, *In the Combat Zone: Vivid Personal Recollections of the Vietnam War from the Women Who Served There* (New York: Penguin, 1987), 97; Reginald "Malik" Edwards, in Wallace Terry, *Bloods: An Oral History of the Vietnam War by Black Veterans* (New York: Ballantine, 1984), 6; Thomas Bird, David Ross, Karl Phaler, and Lynda Van Devanter, in Al Santoli, *Everything We Had: An Oral History of the Vietnam War by Thirty Three Americans Who Fought It* (New York: Ballantine, 1981), 35, 48, 55, 163–64.

17. Ronald Reagan, "Remarks on Presenting the Medal of Honor to Master Sergeant Roy P. Benavidez," February 24, 1981, APP, www.presidency.ucsb.edu/ws/?pid=43454 (accessed June 16, 2007).

18. Leonard Sykes Jr., "Vietnam: Horror Story Unfairly Told," *News-Sun* (Lake County, Illinois), November 20–21, 1982.

19. Dana Gower, "Vietnam Vets Begin Telling Experiences," *Laurel (MI) Leader Call*, [1984], in *Vietnam Veterans Leadership Program Press Coverage: The Program's Third Year*, LBP.

20. Otto J. Lehrack, *No Shining Armor: The Marines at War in Vietnam: An Oral History* (Lawrence: University Press of Kansas, 1992), 206.

21. Neil Sheehan, *A Bright, Shining Lie: John Paul Vann and America in Vietnam* (New York: Random House, 1988), 520.

22. *Good Morning, Vietnam*, dir. Barry Levinson (1987).

23. PFC George Williams to his mother, April 1967, in Edelman, *Dear America*, 105.

24. Barry Dornfeld, "*Dear America*: Transparency, Authority, and Interpretation in a Vietnam War Documentary," in *From Hanoi to Hollywood*, ed. Linda Dittmar and Gene Michaud (New Brunswick, NJ: Rutgers University Press, 1990), 288. The original letter (L-202), held in New York Vietnam Veterans Memorial Commission Records, New York City Municipal Archives, appears almost verbatim, with only spelling errors corrected, in Edelman, *Dear America*, 105. The version read out in the documentary, *Dear America: Letters Home from Vietnam*, dir. Bill Couturie (1987), is abbreviated. A still shorter excerpt is inscribed on the New York Vietnam Veterans Memorial.

25. Murray Polner, *No Victory Parades: The Return of the Vietnam Veteran* (New York: Holt, Rinehart and Winston, 1971), 156.

26. PFC Dan Bailey to his mother, September 6, 1966, inscribed on the New York Vietnam Veterans Memorial and printed in Edelman, *Dear America*, 110.

27. Keith Walker, *A Piece of My Heart: The Stories of Twenty-Six American Women Who Served in Vietnam* (New York: Ballantine, 1985), 225.

28. "The War Orphans," *Time*, March 25, 1974. Marilyn Young says that there were 879,000 orphans. Young, *The Vietnam Wars 1945–1990* (New York: HarperCollins, 1991), 302.

29. Robert Jay Lifton, *Home from the War: Vietnam Veterans neither Victims nor Executioners* (New York: Simon and Schuster, 1973), 206.

30. By his own account, Calley was as much a failure in his effort to do good works as he was in his role as a platoon commander. W. L. Calley, *Body Count: Lieutenant Calley's Story as Told to John Sack* (London: Hutchison, 1971), 139–44.

31. Capt. John Ripley, in Lehrack, *No Shining Armor*, 146–67.

32. Jerry L. Strait and Sandra S. Strait, *Vietnam War Memorials: An Illustrated Reference to Veterans Tributes throughout the United States* (Jefferson, NC: McFarland, 1988), 169–70.

33. Reed May Sr., telephone interview by the author, February 2007. May is a Gold Star Father whose son was killed in Vietnam, and who was instrumental in getting the memorial built. The inscription on the front of the pedestal reads "Vietnam," while inscriptions on the sides refer to other wars.

34. Bill Henry, secretary of Vietnam Veterans of America Chapter 279 and chairman of Omaha's Vietnam Peace Memorial Restoration Committee, letter and photograph to the author, February 27, 1996.

35. James C. Keith, "Korea–Vietnam Memorial History and Future Plans," August 4, 1995, faxed to the author by James C. Keith, June 27, 1996; Keith, fax to the author, June 21, 1996.

36. Margaret Clancy Keith, "War Vet Memorial to Be Unveiled Sunday," *Omaha World-Herald*, May 26, 1976.

37. "Memorial Park: A Reminder to the Living," *Omaha World-Herald*, May 30, 1976.

38. Bill Henry, telephone interview by the author, June 4, 1996.

39. Keith, "Korea–Vietnam Memorial History and Future Plans."

40. Minutes of the Kentucky VVMF annual meeting, June 16, 1984, 2. These minutes and other documents concerning the Kentucky memorial, unless otherwise indicated, are from the Kentucky papers described in chapter 7 n125.

41. Minutes of the Kentucky VVMF design committee, parameters subcommittee meeting, December 15, 1984.

42. Minutes of the Kentucky VVMF design committee meeting, October 27, 1984, 2; minutes of the Kentucky VVMF design committee, parameters subcommittee meeting, December 15, 1984, 7, 8.

43. Leon R. Timmons to Bill Black, October 22, 1984, copied to the author by Bill Black.

44. Michael Stebbins, "Viet Nam Memorial Design Statement," submitted for consideration at the Kentucky VVMF design committee meeting, October 27, 1984.

45. "Over and over they repeated it, these men in their late thirties now: 'Ask not what your country can do for you, ask what you can do for your country. . . .' Always they say it with a sense of emotion, as if it were a message meant for each alone, like the lyrics of a love song. It is, they say, the single most memorable sentence of their lives." Myra MacPherson, *Long Time Passing: Vietnam and the Haunted Generation* (New York: New American Library, 1984), 47.

46. The antiwar veteran Bobby Muller said that Kennedy's address summed up "a time when we had a common sense of purpose and pride in who we are and what we stand for." Then the Vietnam War "shattered our common sense of purpose, our common sense of pride." *Phil Donahue Show*, WGN-TV, Chicago, December 3, 1979. Philip Caputo writes, "In the patriotic fervor of the Kennedy years, we had asked, 'What can we do for our country?' and our country had answered, 'Kill VC.'" Caputo, *A Rumor of War* (New York: Ballantine, 1986), 218.

47. The Roswell Vietnam War Memorial Committee, Inc., *The Faces of War*, brochure marking the memorial's dedication on May 29, 1995; donated to the author by the City of Roswell, Georgia, Legal Department.

48. Godfrey Hodgson, *America in Our Time* (New York: Vintage Books, 1978), 344.

49. A transcript of the CBS interview was published in the *Washington Post* and the *New York Times*, November 25, 1969. Seymour Hersh, *My Lai 4: A Report on the Massacre and Its Aftermath* (New York: Random House, 1970), 201. A copy of the original Art Workers Coalition poster is in the AOUON [All of Us or None] Archive, Berkeley, CA; copies of both versions are in the antiwar poster collection of the Center for the Study of Political Graphics, Los Angeles, and the poster collection of the Division of Politics and Reform, National Museum of American History, Smithsonian Institution, Washington, DC.

50. H. Bruce Franklin, *Vietnam and Other American Fantasies* (Amherst: University of Massachusetts Press, 2000), 73.

51. The same photograph, by Felix Green (Associated Press/Wide World), appears on the cover of James William Gibson, *The Perfect War: The War We Couldn't Lose and How We Did* (New York: Vintage Books, 1988).

52. Judith Butler, *Precarious Life: The Powers of Mourning and Violence* (New York: Verso, 2004), 150.

53. AOUN. Numerous other posters featuring dead and injured Vietnamese children exist in archives of antiwar posters in AOUON; Center for the Study of Political Graphics, Los Angeles; and Division of Politics and Reform, National Museum of American History. See also David Kunzle, *Posters of Protest: A Graphic Dossier of U.S. Vietnam War Crimes*, catalogue of the exhibition at the Wight Art Gallery, University of California, Los Angeles, 1991; and Maurice Berger, *Representing Vietnam, 1965–1973: The Antiwar Movement in America*, catalogue of an exhibition at the Bertha and Karl Leubsdorf Art Gallery, Hunter College, New York, 1988.

54. In the Philippine-American War that began in 1899, troops wrote home about atrocities against civilians, including women and children, and these allegations became the subject of anti-imperialist agitation; similarly in the U.S. Marines' occupation of Haiti that began in 1915, American journalists, politicians, and others protested against atrocities the marines perpetrated against civilians. Such reports had largely been forgotten by the 1960s, overshadowed by images of World War II, the "good war," so the evidence of atrocities in Vietnam, highlighted by graphic antiwar propaganda posters, was all the more shocking to the public.

55. Mark Baker, *Nam: The Vietnam War in the Words of the Soldiers Who Fought There* (New York: Berkley Books, 1983), 157–58, 177, 179, 292; Emmanuel J. Holloman in Terry, *Bloods*, 83; Debbie Wong (alias) and Jeanne Christie, in Marshall, *In the Combat Zone*, 23, 180.

56. Harold O. (pseudonym), in Gerald Gioglio, *Days of Decision: An Oral History of Conscientious Objectors in the Military During the Vietnam War* (Trenton, NJ: Broken Rifle Press, 1989), 128. Some of the stories published in oral histories are unverifiable because of the anonymity of their tellers. All the narrators in Baker's *Nam* are anonymous, and Harold O's anonymity is preserved. For the purposes of our

argument, the important fact is that the tales of atrocities against Vietnamese children were circulated as fact—the "gut truth" of the war, as the jacket blurb of Baker's *Nam* says. Bob Clark told essentially the same story of troops on trucks' using cans of food as a weapon in his Winter Soldier testimony: U.S. Congress, Senate, "Veterans' Testimony on Vietnam—Need for Investigation," 92nd Cong., 1st sess., April 6, 1971, *Congressional Record*, E 9972.

57. Interview in *Remember My Lai*, prod. Michael Bilton and Kevin Sim (Yorkshire Television and PBS, 1989).

58. Martin Gershen, *Destroy or Die: The True Story of Mylai* (New Rochelle, NY: Arlington House, 1971), quoted in Lifton, *Home from the War*, 45.

59. Interview in *Remember My Lai*.

60. Lawrence F. Daly, "The Vet," *Montana Vietnam Veterans Memorial* (Missoula, MT, 1988), 16; dedication souvenir booklet found in AFP.

61. Denise Chong, *The Girl in the Picture* (London: Simon and Schuster, 2000), 55–67.

62. *Kim Phuc*, dir. Manus van de Kamp (1984).

63. Michael Carlebach, in *From Camelot to Kent State*, ed. Joan Morrison and Robert K. Morrison (New York: Times Books, 1987), 96–97.

64. Lucy Lippard, *A Different War: Vietnam in Art* (Bellingham and Seattle, WA: Whatcom Museum of History and Art and Real Comet Press, 1990), 105.

65. Floyd was a member of Vietnam Veterans Against the War. He testified at the Detroit Winter Soldier hearing under the name "Jon Floyd" but was identified as Randy Floyd by another witness, Howard Zinn. "Veterans Testimony on Vietnam—Need for Investigation," 9994–95, 9999.

66. Hugh Thompson said of a child he rescued during the My Lai massacre (whose name, he later learned, was Do Hoa), "[I was] thinking, 'It could be your kid.' . . . It still hurts to think about us doing things like that." Interview in *Remember My Lai*. See also Robert Santos, in Santoli, *Everything We Had*, 116.

67. Copies of both posters are in AOUON. The first is a double-page foldout from *World* magazine, August 5, 1972; the second advertises a November 12 march on Washington. See also the appropriations of Kim's image by the artists Jerry Kearns and Juan Sanchez in Lippard, *Different War*, 78, 79. Kim's image appears in a quilt amid the faces of three African American troops, framed by the repeated words, "Tomorrow return." The quilt, created by Penny Sisto in 1990, was displayed at the LZ Bluegrass Vietnam veterans' gathering in Frankfort, Kentucky, in May 1992.

68. Minutes of the Kentucky VVMF design committee meeting, September 8, 1984, 9. The reference to Eddie Adams's photograph of General Loan is garbled but unmistakable—the minutes refer to a "colonel" shooting a "North Vietnamese soldier" but there is no well-known photograph other than Adams's that comes close to matching this description.

69. Heidi Mae Bratt, "Vietnam Vets Honored," *Detroit News*, September 10, 1991.

70. Fred Sepelak, telephone interview by the author, September 21, 1994. In a letter to the author, September 26, 1994, Sepelak says that his primary motivation in building the memorial was to "relieve a terrible guilt complex I developed" and to remind visitors of the "terrible tragedy" that affected individuals, friends, and families in both countries.

71. The Florence Pietà is found in Florence's Museo Dell'Opera del Duomo.

72. Eve Sinaiko, ed., *Vietnam: Reflexes and Reflections; The National Vietnam Veterans Art Museum* (New York: H. N. Abrams, 1998), 146. Although Page does not specify the photographer, he must mean Don McCullin's famous photograph of a marine at Khe Sanh. McCullin, *Unreasonable Behaviour* (London: Vintage, 1992), 110.

73. Anzenberger, *Combat Art of the Vietnam War*, 126.

74. Baker, *Nam*, 193. Douglas Anderson made a similar statement, in almost identical phrases, in Santoli, *Everything We Had*, 69.

75. Baker, *Nam*, 138–9, 173–4; Terry, *Bloods*, 110; Walker, *Piece of My Heart*, 73, 83; Marshall, *In the Combat Zone*, 40; U.S. Army veteran Bob Watters, in *The Long Road Back: Vietnam Remembered*, prod. Britt Davis for Office of Instructional Resources, University of Kentucky (n.d., ca. 1985); Charley Trujillo, *Soldados: Chicanos in Vietnam*, (San Jose, CA: Chusma House, 1990), 6, 141.

76. Mike Soliz, in Trujillo, *Soldados*, 87.

77. "America in Vietnam," one-hour preview of the series *Vietnam: The 10,000 Day War*, prod. Ian McLeod (Canadian Broadcasting Company, 1980; broadcast in the United States in 1982).

78. *Tour of Duty* (CBS television; rebroadcast on the FX channel over Sky satellite in November 2006).

79. *Interviews with My Lai Veterans*, dir. Joseph Strick (1970).

80. Chaim F. Shatan, "Stress Disorders among Vietnam Veterans: The Emotional Content of Combat Continues," in *Stress Disorders among Vietnam Veterans: Theory, Research, and Treatment*, ed. Charles R. Figley (New York: Brunner/Mazel, 1978), 50.

81. John O. Lipkin, Arthur S. Blank, and Raymond Monsour Scurfield, "Forensic Assessment of Post-Traumatic Stress Disorder in Viet Nam Veterans," in *The Trauma of War: Stress and Recovery in Vietnam Veterans*, ed. Stephen M. Sonnenberg, Arthur S. Blank Jr., and John A. Talbott (Washington, DC: American Psychiatric Press, 1985), 423.

82. John P. Wilson, "Towards an Understanding of Post-Traumatic Stress Disorders among Vietnam Veterans," Testimony before the U.S. Senate Subcommittee on Veteran Affairs, May 21, 1980, 4; document found among the papers of the Paducah (Kentucky) Vietnam Veterans Group.

83. Quoted in Santoli, *To Bear Any Burden*, 61.

84. Gary D. Solis, *Son Thang: An American War Crime* (New York: Bantam Books, 1997), 163. Michael Walzer argues that such stories might function in a self-serving way in *Just and Unjust Wars: A Moral Argument with Historical Illustrations* (New York: Basic Books, 1977), 189. See also Englehardt, *End of Victory Culture*, 254, on the rendering of the My Lai perpetrators as "victims."

85. Psychiatric counselor at American Lake Veterans Administration Hospital, Washington, interview by the author, June 26, 1991.

86. For one such story, see Ron Nessen, "Surreal Surrender in Vietnam," *International Herald Tribune*, April 23, 1995. For an account of the tragic deaths of "orphans" Americans tried to save during "Operation Babylift," see Hagopian, "America's Offspring," 541–42.

87. Walker, *Piece of My Heart*, 83.

88. Both Vietnam Women's Memorial Competition entries 119 and 272 show multifigure groups in which one woman ministers to a Vietnamese child whose head is clasped tenderly in her hands. Diana Hellinger and Diane Carlson Evans of the Vietnam Women's Memorial Project graciously gave the author permission to copy the slides documenting the 317 competition entries, which were held at the Memorial Project's Washington, DC, office.

89. Quoted in Melanie Howard, "Vietnam Memorial to Women Gets the Nod," *Washington Times*, September 20, 1991.

90. Terrie Claflin, "Monumental Achievement," *Ms.*, November/December 1993, 88.

91. Cheryl Nicol, a regional coordinator for the Vietnam Women's Memorial Project, interview by the author, June 27, 1991; Glenna Goodacre, interview by the author, July 16, 1992; Diana Hellinger, executive director of the Vietnam Women's Memorial Project, interviews by the author, July 26, 1991, and June 6, 1995. Wayne Smith, an employee of Vietnam Veterans of America and an organizer of the tenth anniversary commemoration of the dedication of the national Vietnam Veterans Memorial, had heard that the child in the original design was wounded, and that it therefore would have evoked the "baby-killer" stereotype. Smith, interview by the author, January 8, 1993.

92. *Vietnam Women's Memorial Dedication, November 11, 1993*, videocassette (Vietnam Women's Memorial Foundation, Washington, DC, 1993).

93. "Vietnam Veterans Memorial Commission Announces a Competition for the State of California," administrative records of the California Vietnam Veterans Memorial Commission, California Department of Veterans Affairs, Sacramento (hereafter cited as CVVMC).

94. James C. Daniels, executive director, Veterans Assistance Center, Berkeley, to California Vietnam Veterans Memorial Commission, August 27, 1984, CVVMC.

95. Trinda Pasquet, "Vietnam Veterans Lambast Proposed Memorial," *Sacramento Union*, February 13, 1985.

96. Leo K. Thorsness to Hon. Richard E. Floyd, Sept. 28, 1984, CVVMC.

97. The commission defended the original idea while stating that "it was not concrete that children would be included." Minutes of the Memorial Commission meeting, September 18, 1984, 1–2, CVVMC.

98. Minutes of the Memorial Commission meeting, October 25, 1984, 1, CVVMC.

99. A photograph of this design was among those in a photographic display of California Vietnam Veterans Memorial design competition entries at the California Department of Veterans Affairs, Sacramento, in April 1991.

100. Michael Kelley, the entrant who submitted the third-placed submission, personal communication with the author.

101. The successive designs of the California memorial were found in CVVMC and in the architect Michael Larson's San Francisco office in 1991. The main sculptures in the California Vietnam Veterans Memorial do not have official titles. In referring to *The Nurse* and *The Action Panel* here and in the captions for figs. 45, 46, and 73, I follow the titles used in Robert Salgado, "California Vietnam Veterans Memorial," October 24, 1989, CVVMC.

102. The photograph was taken by Phil Schutzer for *Life* magazine. The action was "Operation Piranha," conducted in November 1965. Salgado, "California Vietnam Veterans Memorial."

103. For an astute discussion of an earlier contest over the limits of commemorative representation,

see Kirk Savage, *Standing Soldiers, Kneeling Slaves: Race, War, and Monument in Nineteenth-Century America* (Princeton: Princeton University Press, 1997). See also Michele Bogart, "The Rise and Demise of *Civic Virtue*," in *Critical Issues in Public Art: Content, Context, and Controversy,* ed. Harriet F. Senie and Sally Webster (New York: HarperCollins, 1992).

11. "The Wall Is for All of Us"

1. Competition entry no. 1026, VVM-DPP. The original drawings do not show the current pagelike arrangement.

2. Joel Swerdlow, "To Heal a Nation," *National Geographic* 167, no. 5 (May 1985): 557.

3. "Building a Memorial," *Program Souvenir, National Salute to Vietnam Veterans, November 10–14, 1982, Washington, DC* (McLean, VA: Tyl Associates, [1982]), 33.

4. The largest panels have 137 lines of names; the shortest 1 line. On every second panel, every tenth line has a marker in the margin to facilitate counting the lines. (The location of each name in the directory is identified by panel and line number.)

5. Maya Lin, "Statement of Winning Designer, Maya Ying Lin," box 65, VVMF-MD.

6. The VVMF's design program states that the names should be readable by observers at ground level. "Requirements of the Memorial Design," *Vietnam Veterans Memorial Design Competition; Design Program* (Washington, DC: VVMF, 1980), 16; *The Vietnam Veterans Memorial Design Competition* (Washington, DC: VVMF, November 24, 1980), 7. A later instruction suggested alphabetical ordering to facilitate finding individual names. *The Vietnam Veterans Memorial Design Competition: Questions and Answers* (Washington, DC: VVMF, February 10, 1981), 10.

7. Some reports placed it second to the Lincoln Memorial and, early in the memorial's history, visitation at the National Air and Space Museum was reckoned for a time to be higher.

8. John S. Lang, "A Memorial Wall That Healed Our Wounds," *U.S. News and World Report*, November 21, 1983, 68.

9. VVMF, "Press Advisory—Not for Publication: May 19, 1983, Vietnam Veterans Memorial, Memorial Day Weekend Events," box 4, VVMF-MD.

10. Gallup Organization poll for CNN and USA Today, conducted February 23 to 25, 1996; Gallup Organization poll, conducted November 13–15, 2000. Data provided by RC.

11. Copies of the artist's representations are in VVM-DPP. The American Institute of Architects' journal attributes the unsigned drawings to Steve Oles. A. Freeman, "An Extraordinary Competition," *AIA Journal*, August 1981, 47.

12. Minutes of the Commission of Fine Arts meeting, April 13, 1983, 26, records of the Commission of Fine Arts, Washington, DC. Of all the members of the commission, Netsch was the most committed to maintaining the purity of Lin's original design.

13. The added features are pictured and described in *Vietnam Veterans Memorial*, a brochure produced by the VVMF after the design was selected but before the memorial was completed; (Washington, DC, n.d.), box 62, VVMF-MD.

14. A photograph of the model accompanies J. Dreyfuss, "Vietnam Memorial Launched," *Los Angeles Times*, March 26, 1982. The artist's impressions and the architectural model can be seen in Jan C. Scruggs and Joel L. Swerdlow, *To Heal a Nation* (New York: Harper and Row, 1985), VVMF photograph between pp. 80 and 81.

15. Paul Goldberger, "Vietnam War Memorial Captures Anguish of a Decade of Doubt," *New York Times*, June 6, 1981.

16. It is possible to see this turf abutting the wall in chapter 5, fig. 14, and in the photographs in Edward C. Ezell, *Reflections on the Wall: The Vietnam Veterans Memorial* (Harrisburg, PA: Stackpole Books, 1987), 64–66.

17. Robert Campbell, "An Emotive Place Apart," *AIA Journal*, May 1983, 151.

18. Kent Cooper, testimony, and J. Carter Brown comments, minutes of the Commission of Fine Arts meeting, February 8, 1983, 24–25, 103, box 29, VVMF-MD; Lang, "Memorial Wall That Healed Our Wounds," 68; Phil Gailey and Warren Weaver Jr., "Memorial Mud Problem," *New York Times*, December 9, 1982. Joshua Lowenfish, an architect, had been warning the VVMF for some time about the dangers of creating a "sinkhole saturated with ground water." Joshua D. Lowenfish to Robert Doubek, [December 1982], box 62, VVMF-MD; Robert Doubek, testimony, minutes of the Commission of Fine Arts meeting, April 13, 1983, 28; Joe Brown of EDAW landscape architects, testimony, ibid., 24.

19. William Lecky, testimony, minutes of the Commission of Fine Arts meeting, September 13, 1983, 70, records of the Commission of Fine Arts.

20. Minutes of the Commission of Fine Arts meeting, April 13, 1983, 24, 28.

21. An enlarged walkway was installed in 1983, lighting was added in 1984, and the walkway was rebuilt in 1992. Jan Scruggs, *Writings on the Wall: Reflections on the Vietnam Veterans Memorial* (Washington, DC: VVMF, 1994). A photograph by J. Burns appears on the VVMF brochure *Vietnam Veterans Memorial*. According to Kent Cooper, of Cooper-Lecky Partnership, architect of record, Lin disapproved of all the pathways added to the site. Kent Cooper, interview by the author, August 11, 1994.

22. Lin, "Statement of Winning Designer."

23. Footsteps on the snow also provide a record of the commonest avenues of approach. See the photograph in Sal Lopes, *The Wall: Images and Offerings from the Vietnam Veterans Memorial* (New York, 1987), 120–21; and Brent Ashabranner and Jennifer Ashabranner, *Always to Remember: The Story of the Vietnam Veterans Memorial* (New York, 1988), 53, 82.

24. VVMF, *Vietnam Veterans Memorial* contains the locations of the casualties listed month by month. The names of those who died in May 1968 occupy the panels from 53E to 62W.

25. Paul Weingarten, "The Black Wall," *Chicago Tribune*, April 21, 1985.

26. Campbell describes the experience in "An Emotive Place Apart," 150.

27. "CACCF [Combat Area Casualties Current File] Record Counts by Year of Death or Declaration of Death (as of 12/98)," National Archives Statistical Information about Casualties of the Vietnam Conflict, www.archives.gov/research/vietnam-war/casualty-statistics.html#year (accessed August 6, 2008).

28. Maya Lin, "Making the Memorial," *New York Review of Books*, November 2, 2000, 34; author's observations of visitors at the site. One competition juror said that the design, with the walls receding at each end, "is symbolic of the slow start and the ending of the Vietnam War and the casualties." Grady Clay, *Comments by the Jurors: Vietnam Memorial Competition, Andrews Air Force Base, MD., April 26–29, 1981*, 2, box 62, VVMF-MD. Another said that the design "shows the evolution of the war." Scruggs and Swerdlow, *To Heal a Nation*, 63. Sergiusz Michalski writes, "The height of the black walls rises to correspond with the increasing number of deaths in the late 1960s." Michalski, *Public Monuments: Art in Political Bondage 1870–1997* (London: Reaktion Books, 1998), 189. Arthur C. Danto, "The Vietnam Veterans Memorial," *The Nation*, August 31, 1985, 154.

29. Statement by George Dickie, the Vietnam Women's Memorial Project's landscape architect, *Celebration of Patriotism and Courage* (Washington, DC: Vietnam Women's Memorial Project 1993), 20; George Dickie, interview by the author, July 30, 1993.

30. For a photograph of the newly surfaced path to the women's memorial, see Patrick Hagopian, "The Commemorative Landscape of the Vietnam War," in *Places of Commemoration: Search for Identity and Landscape Design*, ed. Joachim Wolschke-Bulmahn (Washington, DC: Dumbarton Oaks Research Library and Collection, 2001), 345.

31. Scruggs and Swerdlow, *To Heal a Nation*, 123; Charles Fishman, "Memorial's First Names Unveiled," *Washington Post*, July 22, 1982; Phil Garlington, "1st Viet Vet Memorial Names Unveiled," *Washington Times*, July 22, 1982.

32. Levern Neely, in the newsletter *From the Heart: News from and for Families and Friends of "Shrapnel in the Heart,"* January 1988, 11.

33. See, e.g., Mark Graham's photograph accompanying William A. Scott, "Hello Carrie: A Combat Veteran Writes Home," *Dallas Times Herald*, November 12, 1989; and the cover photographs for Peter Meyer and the editors of Life, *The Wall: A Day at the Vietnam Veterans Memorial* (New York: Thomas Dunne, 1993); for Lopes, *The Wall*; and for the Smithsonian Institution's brochure for the exhibition, Personal Legacy: The Healing of a Nation, October 1992–September 2003, collected by the author at the National Museum of American History, Smithsonian Institution, Washington, DC, in October 1992.

34. Sharon LaFraniere and Priscilla Painton, "Ex-Soldiers Search for Familiar Faces," *Washington Post*, November 12, 1984.

35. Lee Teter, *Reflections* (1988) marketed by Vietnam Veterans of America Chapter 172 (Cumberland, MD). It was advertised for sale as a print and an image adorning a clock in *VVA Veteran*, November/ December 2005, [2]. The image was found at www.vietnamreflections.com, where in addition to the various other forms, it is offered printed on a tee-shirt (accessed February 27, 2007).

36. Quoted in Laura Palmer, *Shrapnel in the Heart: Letters and Remembrances from the Vietnam Veterans Memorial* (New York: Random House, 1987), 73–74.

37. Friends of the Vietnam Veterans Memorial brochure, offering a sixteen-by-twenty-inch reproduction of *A Touching Moment* for sale, collected by the author at the LZ Bluegrass gathering, Frankfort, Kentucky, May 1992. Kendall made the work to record his reaction to the death in Vietnam of a friend from the small Kentucky town where they both grew up.

38. Valerie Chow Bush, "Strangers United by Loss," *Washington Post*, June 29, 1990; Friends of the Vietnam Veterans Memorial, *In Touch*, brochure, n.d., photographs by John Holman and Sal Lopes;

collected by the author at the memorial site in May 1993; Sue Ann Presley, "Vietnam's Loose Ends," *Washington Post*, May 29, 1990.

39. It is not clear precisely when the practice of taking rubbings started; a *New York Times* reporter who interviewed Park Service volunteers at the memorial called the practice "new" in August 1983. Phil Gailey, "Vietnam Memorial, Touching, Tears, Roses, and Rain," *New York Times*, August 30, 1983. In November 1986, a teacher made a rubbing for a schoolgirl, so she could take it back to her father, whose best friend's name was on the wall. Patrice Gaines-Carter, "It Looks Like Wall Is Crying," *Washington Post*, November 12, 1986.

40. Friends of the Vietnam Veterans Memorial, *In Touch*.

41. For a discussion of the Philadelphia and New Jersey last patrols, see Hagopian, "Commemorative Landscape of the Vietnam War," 354–55.

42. John Hall, "A 'Last Patrol' to Recall Those Lost in Vietnam," *Philadelphia Inquirer*, April 30, 1988; Bob Charlanza, "Memorable Parade Unites Vets, Viewers," *Reading Eagle*, September 25, 1988.

43. Scruggs and Swerdlow, *To Heal a Nation*, 124.

44. See, e.g., Mike McIntyre, "Gifts of Grief," *San Diego Union*, May 14, 1989; Howard G. Chua-Eoan and Deborah Papier, "Along the Wall, Gifts from the Heart," *People*, June 1, 1992, 110; Charles Harbutt, "The Things They Leave Behind," *New York Times Magazine*, November 12, 1995; Thomas B. Allen, *Offerings at the Wall: Artifacts from the Vietnam Veterans Memorial Collection* (Atlanta: Turner, 1995), 10; *Beyond the Wall: Stories Behind the Vietnam Wall*, DVD (Magnet Interactive Studios; distributed by Twentieth Century Fox Home Entertainment, Inc., 1995).

45. Scruggs, *Writings on the Wall*, 57; idem, *Wall That Heals*, 111.

46. Jennifer Locke, National Museum of American History, interview by the author, June 17, 1992. Examples of "spontaneous" materials from the period 1984 to 1986 include items x.344, x.378, and x.612 (an identification system that apparently preceded the current system of accession numbers), copies of which were made available to the author by Pamela Beth West, regional curator of the national capital region, National Park Service. Such spontaneous materials became rare beginning in the late 1980s.

47. Lopes, *The Wall*, 67; Myra MacPherson, "What Did It Cost, Our Vietnam War? Here Is the Price," *Washington Post*, May 27, 1984; Peter Carlson and Carol Guzy, "Back to the Wall," *Washington Post Magazine*, November 6, 1988, 37.

48. Those that are sealed are left that way by the Park Service curators.

49. Joan Mower, "Gifts for the Names in Black Marble [*sic*]," *Washington Times*, November 12, 1984; A. Cheree Carlson and John E. Hocking, "Strategies of Redemption at the Vietnam Veterans' Memorial," *Western Journal of Speech Communication* 52 (Summer 1988): 213. See also Kristin Ann Hass, *Carried to the Wall: American Memory and the Vietnam Veterans Memorial* (Berkeley: University of California Press, 1998).

50. The beer can and the note, once displayed in the exhibition Personal Legacy, are in a virtual exhibition associated with the exhibition Price of Freedom: Americans at War, National Museum of American History, americanhistory.si.edu/militaryhistory/exhibition/flash.html?path=12.4.r_465 (accessed February 22, 2007).

51. Objects displayed in the exhibition Personal Legacy.

52. Laura Palmer, "The Wall," *GQ* 57, no. 7 (July 1987): 141; idem, *Shrapnel in the Heart*, 21–22.

53. See, e.g., Co Rentmeester's photograph in *Images of War* by Julene Fischer and the picture staff of Boston Publishing Company (Boston: The Boston Publishing Company, 1986), 78–79.

54. Author's observations; Barbara Ornelas and Sierra Ornelas, interview by the author at the Vietnam Veterans Memorial, May 30, 1994.

55. John Wheeler, "Offerings at the Wall," *Washington Post*, September 13, 1992.

56. Carlson and Guzy, "Back to the Wall," 37.

57. See, e.g., Bill Outlaw, "The Wall Carries a Message for All Who Care to Visit," *Washington Times*, September 12, 1983; Stewart Powell, "A Sacred Place on the Potomac," *U.S. News and World Report*, November 10, 1986, 16–18; Gelareh Asayeh, "Items Left at Vietnam Memorial Tell a Powerful Story," *Baltimore Sun*, June 4, 1989; Muriel Dobbin, "Pieces of a Troubled Past Turn Vietnam Wall into a Living Memorial," *Sacramento Bee*, November 29, 1991; Delia M. Rios, "Guard Duty," *Dallas Morning News*, April 4, 1992.

58. David Guynes, a curator of the Vietnam Veterans Memorial Collection at the National Park Service's Museum and Archeological Regional Storage Facility, interview by the author, November 4, 1991.

59. The broadcasts include a *Nightline* episode broadcast May 26, 1986, cited by Carlson and Hocking, "Strategies of Redemption," 214; and "Vietnam Memorial Exhibit," WRC [Washington, DC] Television, News Four broadcast, October 27, 1992, transcript by Radio-TV Monitoring Service, Washington, DC.

60. Daphne Berdahl, "Voices at the Wall: Discourses of Self, History, and National Identity at the Vietnam Veterans Memorial," *History and Memory* 6, no. 2 (Fall 1994): 115.

61. Ronald Reagan, *The Reagan Diaries*, ed. Douglas Brinkley (New York: HarperCollins, 2007), 665.

62. Scruggs, *Wall That Heals*, 40–41; Lopes, *The Wall*, photograph by Wendy Watriss, 48–49; *Program Souvenir, National Salute to Vietnam Veterans*, 18; "Vietnam Dead Hailed on Father's Day," *New York Times*, June 22, 1992; Corky Condon, "Sons and Daughters in Touch," [1993], 3-page letter announcing the second annual Father's Day Weekend observance, in the possession of the author; Joe Allessie, "Sons and Daughters in Touch: The Story Behind the Name," *VVA Veteran*, February/March 1997, 14; "Father's Day at the Wall," *VVA Veteran*, June/July 2000, 17. In addition to Memorial Day, Veterans Day, and Father's Day events, the VVMF also sponsors Mother's Day and In Memory Day ceremonies.

63. Patrice Gaines-Carter, "Depressed Veteran Shoots Himself," *Washington Post*, January 16, 1985.

64. William Broyles Jr., "Remembering a War We Want to Forget," *Newsweek*, November 22, 1982, 83; personal communication with Duery Felton, a curator of the Vietnam Veterans Memorial Collection at the National Park Service's Museum and Archeological Regional Storage Facility.

65. "Apparent Suicide Victim Found at War Monument," *Washington Times*, September 17, 1984; Weingarten, "Black Wall."

66. Kevin Cook, "Police, Vigil-Keepers Foil Vet Suicide at Memorial," *Washington Times*, January 16, 1985; Patrice Gaines-Carter, "Viet Vet's Inner Scars Slow to Heal," *Washington Post*, January 26, 1985.

67. Carlson and Guzy, "Back to the Wall," 36; McIntyre, "Gifts of Grief."

68. The Museum and Archeological Regional Storage Facility (MARS), Lanham, MD, is a vast warehouse containing a substantial number of National Park Service collections, including that of the Vietnam Veterans Memorial.

69. Carlson and Hocking, "Strategies of Redemption," 204; Laura Palmer, "The Wall," *GQ*, July 1987, 138; Carlson and Guzy, "Back to the Wall"; "Left at the Wall," *Economist*, October 31, 1992, 28; VVMF and National Park Service, "Number of Offerings Left at the Vietnam Veterans Memorial Tops 100,000," press release, December 6, 2006, www.vvmf.org/index.cfm?SectionID=518 (accessed April 19, 2007); Jennifer Locke Jones, telephone interview by the author, February 22, 2007. Tony Porco, a curator of the MARS collection, estimated that in 1994, 10 to 20 percent of the collection had been catalogued. Porco, interview by the author, December 12, 1994. Duery Felton estimated the size of the collection in 2002 as sixty-six thousand objects. In the four years from 2002 to 2006 the collection therefore grew by considerably more than it did in the eight years from 1994 to 2002. Felton, interview by the author, November 11, 2002.

70. In addition to the exhibitions discussed in this chapter, Duery Felton said that exhibitions had taken place or were planned at the Lewis and Clark National Historical Park in Oregon and Washington states; the Jersey Explorers Children's Museum, in East Orange, New Jersey; departments of veterans affairs exhibits in the District of Columbia, New York City, Louisiana, and Houston; the Imperial War Museum, London; and an unnamed site in New Zealand. Felton, interview. An exhibition took place at the Interior Museum, U.S. Department of the Interior, Washington, DC, from November 2007 to May 2008, author's observation.

71. Patrick Hagopian, "Personal Legacy: The Healing of a Nation; Gathered at the Wall: America and the Vietnam Veterans Memorial," *Journal of American History* 82, no. 1 (June 1995): 158–64.

72. Author's observations of Personal Legacy; and Gathered at the Wall: America and the Vietnam Veterans Memorial, Museum of Our National Heritage, Lexington, MA, October 1994–May 1995; *A Place of Tribute: The Vietnam Veterans Memorial*, brochure accompanying an exhibition with the same title (May 1995–January 1996), Gerald R. Ford Museum, Ann Arbor, MI, sent to the author by Donna Lehman, archives technician at the Gerald R. Ford Presidential Library; Gerald R. Ford, *A Time to Heal: The Autobiography of Gerald Ford* (New York: Harper and Row, 1979).

73. Duery Felton, "Background on Selected Objects from the Vietnam Veterans Memorial Collection," in the press packet distributed at the media preview of Personal Legacy, October 27, 1992; in the author's possession.

74. Ronald Reagan, "Remarks at the Annual Dinner of the Conservative Political Action Conference," March 1, 1985, APP, www.presidency.ucsb.edu/ws/?pid=38274 (accessed October 9, 2007).

75. "Veteran Returns Medal to Protest U.S. Policy," *Washington Post*, July 30, 1986. Liteky's letter can also be found in Reese Williams, ed., *Unwinding the Vietnam War* (Seattle: The Real Comet Press, 1987), 283–86; the medal and letter are shown in Allen, *Offerings at the Wall*, 70–71.

76. Terry Anderson, "Time to Put Divisions Aside," in *Voices from the Wall*, ed. Jan C. Scruggs (Washington, DC: VVMF, 1998), 5.

77. The rings and the note were in Personal Legacy and can also be found in Allen, *Offerings at the Wall*, 126.

78. Palmer, *Shrapnel in the Heart*, 184.

79. For an account of the phenomenon of the MIA bracelets, see H. Bruce Franklin, *M.I.A., or Mythmaking in America* (New Brunswick, NJ: Rutgers University Press, 1993), 54–57.

80. William Peberdy, interviews by the author, July 1993; author's observations at the Pennsylvania Military Museum, Boalsburg, July 1993.

81. Tom Allen, interview by the author, July 12, 1994.

82. Michael Katakis, quoted in Mike Capuzzo, "Remembering Those Who Cannot Forget," *Philadelphia Inquirer*, November 11, 1988.

83. Jan Scruggs to Ross Perot, November 9, 1981, 2, box 30, VVMF-MD.

84. Ezell, *Reflections on the Wall*. Consistent with the official discourses about the memorial, the authors described the themes of the book's text as "reconciliation, catharsis, healing, and homecoming." Edward Ezell and Jim Wallace, director of the Office of Printing and Photographic Services, Smithsonian Institution (whose photographers supplied the pictures), interview by the author, May 17, 1991.

85. Michael Katakis, *The Vietnam Veterans Memorial* (New York: Crown, 1988); Duncan Spencer and Lloyd Wolf, *Facing the Wall: Americans at the Vietnam Veterans Memorial* (New York: Collier Books, 1986). For further examples, see Thomas F. Morrissey, *Between the Lines: Photographs from the National Vietnam Veterans Memorial* (Syracuse, NY: Syracuse University Press, 2000); Larry Powell, *Hunger of the Heart: Communion at the Wall* (Dubuque, IO: Islewest, 1995).

86. Lopes, *The Wall*, 98–99. An editor's note in the front matter denying any specific relationship between texts and photos is easily overlooked.

87. Ezell, *Reflections on the Wall*, 62.

88. For example, the passages in Lopes, *The Wall*, 32, 56, 58, 77, 85, 92, 103, 114 come from Palmer, *Shrapnel in the Heart*, 107, 132, 25, 189, 176, 35, 149, 69. Lopes made minor modifications in some of the wording of the passages, crediting their authors in a listing of "friends, advisers, and consultants" (128). Laura Palmer is not included in the list. The passage about the 1960 high school graduation is borrowed from *Shrapnel in the Heart*, 207.

89. Palmer, *Shrapnel in the Heart*, xii, xiii.

90. Ibid., 3. The letter, with the accession number 8-11-85 2230, is one of several items in the Vietnam Veterans Memorial archival collection that National Park Service staff made available to the author, as to other scholars.

91. The letter from Anne Pearson to Eddie Lynn Lancaster was quoted in the Place of Tribute exhibition; Lopes, *The Wall*, 112; and Palmer, "The Wall," 166.

92. Palmer, *Shrapnel in the Heart*, 45, 101. David Guynes said that Laura Palmer did not pick out a representative sample of letters but instead selected those most laden with emotional content. Guynes, interview.

93. *From the Heart*, January 1988, 3, 4, 5, 12. Carole Page kindly gave me an extensive run of back issues of the newsletter. The last such issue is dated March 1994 and the newsletter ceased appearing then or soon after, giving way to the Shrapnel in the Heart Web site.

94. *From the Heart*, April 1988, 3, 5.

95. Marilyn Knapp Litt, e-mail message to the author, March 30, 1998.

96. Palmer, *Shrapnel in the Heart*, 122.

97. *From the Heart*, April 1988, 11.

98. Barbara Carton, "Vietnam Mementos," *Washington Post*, July 8, 1985.

99. *Dear America: Letters Home from Vietnam*, dir. Bill Couturie (1987).

100. A selection of the letters is collected in Bernard Edelman, ed., *Dear America: Letters Home from Vietnam* (New York: Norton, 1985).

101. Quotation from Shrapnel in the Heart Web site, www.users.interport.net/m/k/mklweb/illyria. com/www.illyria.com/shrapnel.html (accessed July 27, 2008). In *From the Heart*, April 1988, 11, Wimbish states that Burstyn read the letter.

102. Bruce Springsteen, "Born in the USA," Columbia Records, 1984. The song, despite its rousing rhythm and melody, tells the hard-luck story of a Vietnam veteran betrayed by the American Dream.

103. Palmer, *Shrapnel in the Heart*, 122.

104. Ibid., 128.

105. The author, who had been introduced to Dusty by members of the From the Heart network, was with her in the audience as she listened impassively to Gore reading her poem. Dusty was a welcoming member of the From the Heart "family" and the author recalls her solicitude with appreciation.

106. Laura Palmer to Diane Carlson Evans, September 20, 2006, www.vietnamwomensmemorial. org/pages/frames/dusty.html (accessed March 18, 2007). For further discussion of the "wannabe" phenomenon, see Patrick Hagopian, "Voices from Vietnam: Veterans' Oral Histories in the Classroom," *Journal of American History*, 87, no. 2 (September 2000): 594–95; B. G. Burkett and Glenna Whitley, *Stolen Valor: How the Vietnam Generation Was Robbed of Its Heroes and Its History* (Dallas, TX: Verity Press, 1998).

107. Laura Palmer said that, invented or not, Dusty's writings brought recognition to what real nurses

underwent when serving in Vietnam. Diantha Parker, "Celebrated Military Nurse, Poet Revealed as a Fraud," *All Things Considered*, National Public Radio, September 30, 2006, www.npr.org/templates/story/story.php?storyId=6173681 (accessed March 18, 2007).

108. There were offerings on view during the author's visits to the memorials in Philadelphia; Baltimore; New York City; Frankfort, KY; Dallas, TX; Holmdel, NJ; Sacramento, CA; Angel Fire, NM; and Kansas City, MO.

109. Howard Wilkinson, "Vietnam Memorial Dedicated," *Cincinnati Enquirer*, April 9, 1984; Don Hamilton, "Remembrance Blooms at Memorial to State's War Dead," *Sunday Oregonian*, April 3, 1988.

110. "Vietnam Memorial Items Collected," *Minneapolis Star Tribune*, October 5, 1992; Richard Marshall, photo of mementoes at the base of the memorial wall, accompanying Kay Harvey, "Minnesotans Have 'a Coming Home,'" *St. Paul Pioneer Press*, September 27, 1992.

111. Item numbers 88-200-54, 88-200-60, 88-200-77, 88-200-180, 89-200-238, 89-200-250, California Vietnam Veterans Memorial Collection, California State Archives, Sacramento; box 2, Texas Vietnam Veterans Memorial Collection, Dallas Municipal Archives; Chris Buckley, "The Wall," *Esquire*, September 1985, 63.

112. Item numbers 91-132/00017, 91-132/00024, 91-132/00074, 91-132/00076, 91-132/00084, Dallas Municipal Archives.

113. I owe this insight to Catharine Clark; personal communication.

114. Edward Connie Shoemaker, director, Library Resources Division, Oklahoma Historical Society, to the author, January 6, 1994, along with a text by Max J. Nichols, "One for the Oklahoma History Book," [n.d.].

115. Observation during the author's visit in December 1991.

116. News release by Secretary of State March Fong Eu, November 8, 1989, California Vietnam Veterans Memorial Collection, California State Archives; Richard Seven, "State to Display Remembrances of Vietnam Dead: Memorial in Olympia Attracts Letters, Photos, Other Reminders," *Seattle Times*, May 20, 1997.

117. Associated Press, "Museum Keeps Mementos Left at State's Memorial," *Lexington Herald-Leader*, November 12, 1991.

118. For the text of O'Donnell's poem, see Edelman, *Dear America*, 29. Item no. x.1378, Vietnam Veterans Memorial Collection, made available to the author by Pamela Beth West; item no. 93-200-067A in the California Vietnam Veterans Memorial Collection, California State Archives; Rodney S. Anderson, *Most Hallowed Ground: The California Vietnam Veterans Memorial* (North Highlands, CA: Andersonville Publishing, 1992), 24–25; James Miller, "Standing Vigil," in *Voices from the Wall*, 71; *Let Us Remember: The Vietnam Veterans Memorial* (Washington, DC: Parks and History Association, 1986); *Reflections of Those Who Served: The Men, The Women, Their Families, Their Friends* ([Boalsburg, PA]: Moving Wall Regional Committee, [June 1989]); *Hamburger Hill*, dir. John Irvin (1987); Ronald Reagan, "Remarks at the Veterans Day Ceremony at the Vietnam Veterans Memorial," November 11, 1988, APP, www.presidency.ucsb.edu/ws/?pid=35155 (accessed November 25, 2006). The poem appears on the "Vietnam Veterans Memorial Wall" home page (not the official home page of the VVMF), thewall-usa.com/ (accessed March 19, 2007).

119. In a photographic book about the memorial, several photographs are devoted to the offerings left there (although not the ones left during the dedication). Anderson, *Most Hallowed Ground*.

120. Photograph by Ron Romanski accompanying "Snowstorm of Four Inches Coats Berks," *Reading Eagle*, January 7, 1989, 2; Tony Giuffreda, interview by the author, March 8, 1993.

121. The bear was displayed at Gathered at the Wall. Photographs showing it at the wall are in Allen, *Offerings at the Wall*, 152; Powell, *Hunger of the Heart*, 53.

122. Children's behavior, based on author's observations between 1987 and 2007; Kurt Andersen, "Hush, Timmy—This Is Like a Church," *Time*, April 15, 1985, 61; William W. Pollock, "The Wall," *VFW* magazine, January 1990, 56; Weingarten, "The Black Wall"; Brent Ashabranner and Jennifer Ashabranner, *Their Names to Live: What the Vietnam Veterans Memorial Means to America* (Brookfield, CT: Twenty-First Century Books, 1998), 53.

123. David K. Wright, *The Story of the Vietnam Memorial* (Chicago: Children's Press, 1989), 10, 30–31.

124. Deborah Kent, *The Vietnam Women's Memorial* (Chicago: Children's Press, 1995), 3, 15, 28.

125. Patra McSherry Sevastiades, *The Vietnam Veterans Memorial* (New York: Rosen Publishing Group's PowerKids' Press, 1997), 12, 16, 19, 21.

126. Jason Cooper, *Vietnam Veterans Memorial* (Vero Beach, FL: Rourke Corporation, 1999), 19, 20, 22.

127. Ashabranner and Ashabranner, *Their Names to Live*, 52.

128. Margy Burns Knight, *Talking Walls* (Gardiner, ME: Tilbury House, 1995), reviewed in Steve Sherman, "Every Wall Tells a Story," *Publishers Weekly*, April 27, 1992, 31.

129. Eve Bunting, illustrated by Ronald Himler, *The Wall* (New York: Clarion Books, 1990), unpaginated.

130. Author's observations. Students and parents have sent requests for information to assist in school reports to ATPM "Vietnam Memorial," www.atpm.com/7.01/washington-dc/vietnam-memorial. shtml (accessed March 4, 2007); "Echoes from the Mall," VVMF activity guide, www.vvmf.org/index. cfm?SectionID=8 (accessed March 18, 2007).

131. *Preparing for Close Up, 2000 Edition* (Alexandria, VA: Close Up Foundation, 1999), donated to the author by Louisa Medhurst.

132. Louisa Medhurst, interview by the author, March 15, 2002.

133. Charles Hand, "Telling It Like It Was," *VVA Veteran*, March 1994, 31–32.

134. Roberta Thisdell, "'Voices of the Wall' Play Speaks to Veterans," *Virginian-Pilot and Ledger-Star*, August 6, 1993.

135. Chapter 48 of Vietnam Veterans of America (VVA), based in Norfolk, VA, and Chapter 433, based in Newport News; the groups' members allowed the author to attend several meetings between 1993 and 1995, some of which included performances of the play. The author also viewed the performances at the "Vietnam Revisited" reenactment at Forest Glen Middle School, Suffolk, VA, August 6 and 7, 1994.

136. Corky Condon, "In Touch—The Healing Legacy," *Among Friends: News of the Friends of the Vietnam Veterans Memorial* 8, no. 1 (Spring 1994): 5.

137. "Eighth Annual Vietnam Revisited," *Colonial Times* (VVA Chapter 433) 1, no. 43 (September 1994): 7–8.

138. Jennifer Huggins, "I Can Only Imagine," in *Voices from the Wall*, 45–47; James Miller, "Standing Vigil," in ibid., 69.

139. Bobbie Ann Mason, *In Country* (New York: Harper and Row, 1985), 225.

140. Ibid., 239, 240–41.

141. Eric Schroeder, *Vietnam, We've All Been There: Interviews with American Writers* (Westport, CT: Praeger, 1992), 170.

142. Mason, *In Country*, 242–45.

143. *In Country*, dir. Norman Jewison (1989).

144. Adam Rome, "The Moving Walls," *East Texas Entertainment Guide*, [October 1990], 11 (the article was originally published in the *Wichita Eagle-Beacon* and has been reproduced in materials related to the moving wall); Project on the Vietnam Generation, *Report on the Survey of Vietnam Veterans Memorials Nationwide* (Fairfax, VA: George Mason University, 1986), 1; Lydia Fish, *The Last Firebase: A Guide to the Vietnam Veterans Memorial* (Shippensburg, PA: White Mane, 1987), 68–69; John Devitt, telephone interview by the author, June 1992; Leo Mullen, "A Journey of Healing Is Viet Vet's Objective," *Bellingham (WA) Herald*, May 10, 1990; John Devitt to VVMF, August 22, 1983, box 5, VVMF-MD; Rome, "Moving Walls."

145. Jan Scruggs, memorandum for the record, concerning his May 1983 trip to California, n.d., box 5, VVMF-MD; Bill Morris, "Vietnam Veterans Memorial Replica Visits LV Aug. 5–12," *Las Vegas Sun*, July 27, 1986; "Dedication of Vietnam Veterans Memorial 'The Moving Wall' Saturday October 20, Teague Park, Longview," *East Texas Entertainment Guide*, [October 1990], 7; Devitt, interview; *The Moving Wall Vietnam Veterans Memorial Sponsor Handbook* (1987; repr., San Jose: Vietnam Combat Veterans, Ltd, 1991), 10; *The Moving Wall Vietnam Veterans Memorial: A Guide to Scheduling* (1988; repr., San Jose: Vietnam Combat Veterans, Ltd., 1991), unpaginated [12]; Richard Danielson, "Pasco Bid for Memorial to Emphasize Veterans," *Pasco Times*, October 15, 1991; "The Wall South," www.pensacolawallsouth.org/page1.html (accessed February 18, 2007); "Membership Notes," *VVA Veteran*, January/February 2006, 38.

146. By August 1987, when John Devitt tallied the visitor numbers at each site, the total came to 3.5 million. Devitt, interview.

147. Tom McNamee and Andrew Herrmann, "A Big Thank You!" *Chicago Sun-Times*, June 14, 1986; Tom Conroy and Kris Colt, *Vietnam Veterans Parade Chicago—1986* (Santa Fe, New Mexico: Nam Vets Publishing Co., 1987).

148. *L.Z. Friendly Eighth Annual Campout*, brochure produced by LZ Friendly; in the collection of the author; *Guide to Scheduling*, [12]; *The Moving Wall 1992, Schedule "A" and Schedule "B,"* document provided to the author by John Devitt of Vietnam Combat Veterans, Ltd; Dennis Johnson of "Operation Just Cause" (a POW/MIA advocacy group), "The Moving Wall," ojc.org/NL/march/dennisa398.htm (accessed August 8, 2002).

149. David H. Morrissey, "'The Wall' Source of Healing for Veterans," *Albuquerque Journal*, October 8, 1987.

150. *The Moving Wall*, dir. John Kepler (1989), documentary of the moving wall's visit to Boalsburg, videocassette viewed by the author at the Pennsylvania Military Museum in Boalsburg.

151. Irwin Noparstak, Ed Reiman, and Steve Tice, VVA Chapter 144, Eugene, OR, to [no addressee],

October 10, 1986; letter in an album of photographs, letters, and clippings about the moving wall's visit to Eugene made available to the author by members of VVA Chapter 144.

152. Photo by Matt Rose, accompanying Sandra Barbieri, "'Wall Brings War Memories Home," *New Orleans Times-Picayune*, November 2, 1987.

153. *East Texas Honors America's Veterans*, publicity brochure produced by Vietnam Veterans Foundation of Texas, Longview Event, Dallas.

154. Fish, *Last Firebase*, 70 The author observed people leaving offerings when visiting the wall in Lancaster, Pennsylvania, in June 1994, and Davis, California, in April 1995.

155. Barbara Brueggebors, "Wall's Names Move Visitors," *Centre Daily Times*, June 23, 1988; see also the photograph in Allen, *Offerings at the Wall*, 234.

156. Post to the Vietnam War list, vwar-l@listserv.acsu.buffalo.edu on March 28, 1997.

157. The author has visited the San Jose warehouse where the offerings are stored. See Linda Taylor, "Wall Items Saved in a Warehouse," *Centre Daily Times* (Centre County, PA), July 5, 1989.

158. James Link, "Vietnam Perspective," speech delivered at the breakfast marking the arrival of the moving wall in Huntsville, AL, reproduced in VVA Digest no. 3448, Vietnam Veterans of America Talklist, vva@talklist.com, posted July 12, 2001.

159. Kaylois Henry, "Vietnam Exhibit Sparks Debate," *St Petersburg Times*, April 1, 1991; "Scruggs Helps 'Ghouls' Hustle Cemetery Plots," *U.S. Veteran News and Report*, February/March 1992, 6; Jan C. Scruggs, foreword to Morrissey, *Between the Lines*, xi; *Vietnam Veterans Memorial Fund*, n.d., 14-page brochure describing the VVMF's commemorative programs; Larry Lewis, "Vietnam Memorial Pays a Visit; Replica Displayed at U[pper] Merion Cemetery," *Philadelphia Inquirer*, June 22, 1991; Rhonda Holifield, "Traveling Memorials Arouse Controversy," *St. Petersburg Times*, April 12, 1991.

160. Lewis, "Vietnam Memorial Pays a Visit; Replica Displayed at U[pper] Merion Cemetery"; Holifield, "Traveling Memorials Arouse Controversy"; "Replica of Vietnam Memorial Coming to Houston for Three Days," *Pasadena (TX) Citizen*, February 7, 1991.

161. "Scruggs Helps 'Ghouls' Hustle Cemetery Plots."

162. Holifield, "Traveling Memorials Arouse Controversy"; Henry, "Vietnam Exhibit Sparks Debate."

163. See, e.g., Rick Gill, "Texas Veterans of Vietnam War to Be Recognized as Two Memorials Go on Display in Dallas," *Irving (TX) News*, November 30, 1986; *Moving Wall Vietnam Veterans Memorial: A Guide to Scheduling*, [12].

164. A recent itinerary for the VVMF-linked Wall that Heals indicates no cemetery locations and no connection with SCI. VVMF, "Wall that Heals 2007 Tour Schedule," www.vvmf.org/index.cfm?SectionID=505 (accessed March 18, 2007).

165. *Channel 10 News*, Philadelphia, February 7, 1988.

166. Author's observations in Albany and Washington, DC.

167. Advertisement for a limited edition of ninety-five hundred copies of *Standing Tall Together* by Terry Jones, marketed by the Fleetwood Collection of Cheyenne, WY, in 1992. The sculpture reproduces panels 28E and 29E of the memorial.

168. Allen, *Offerings at the Wall*, 218.

169. Robin Wagner-Pacifici and Barry Schwartz, "The Vietnam Veterans Memorial: Commemorating a Difficult Past," *American Journal of Sociology* 97, no. 2 (September 1991): 413.

170. Strait and Strait, *Vietnam War Memorials*, 85–86.

171. Observations and photo documentation by the author.

172. Post by Carol Near, an associate member of VVA, June 8, 2003, VVA Digest, no. 7556, June 9, 2003.

173. Advertisements in *Parade*, April 19, 1992, 7, and July 30, 1995, 7.

174. Sandra Sardella, "Sterling to Honor Vietnam Veterans," *Philadelphia Inquirer*, New Jersey edition, November 10, 1991; the granite mementos are advertised for sale by mail order in Vietnam veteran–oriented publications. One of them, with David Westphall's name, is displayed in the Visitors' Center at the memorial at Angel Fire.

175. See Susan Stewart, *On Longing: Narratives of the Miniature, the Gigantic, the Souvenir, the Collection* (Durham, NC: Duke University Press, 1993).

176. "The Living Wall" by Steve Klein, a Vietnam Veterans Memorial replica, ordered from Klein's Designs of Ensino, California, and mailed to the author May 14, 1998.

177. The issue of the aftermath of the war was explored in the graffiti tribute–mall mob episode of MTV's Beavis and Butthead cartoon, in the Ned and Jimbo war story episode of Comedy Central's *South Park* and in the recurrent Armen Tamzarian/Principal Skinner story line of Fox Broadcasting Company's *The Simpsons*.

178. See the virtual wall at www.thevirtualwall.org (accessed June 26, 2007) and the Vietnam Wall, "a memorial to the memorial," www.vietnamwall.org/ (accessed June 26, 2007).

179. The American War Library, Gardena, CA, advertised the microfiche cards, which veterans could obtain if they sent a copy of their DD-214 discharge papers. VVA Digest #16333, March 6, 2007.

180. *Sponsor Handbook*, 10.

181. Robert Musil, *Posthumous Papers of a Living Author*, trans. Peter Wortsman (Hygiene, CO: Eridanos Press, 1987), 61–62.

182. Author's observations. See also John Leykam, "A Forgotten Memorial for a War We Try So Hard to Forget," *Contra Costa Times*, May 25, 1980; Justo Bautista, "Vandals Trash Vietnam Memorial," *Bergen (NJ) Record*, May 3, 1995.

183. Lin, "Statement of Winning Designer."

Conclusion

1. "The Wall," *Reading Rainbow*, prod. Ronnie Krauss (Lancit Media Productions, WNED-TV, and GPN, 1992). Lin's on-camera monologue follows a reading of Eve Bunting's storybook *The Wall*, which is discussed in chapter 11.

2. President's press conference of March 24, 1977, APP, www.presidency.ucsb.edu/ws/?pid=7229 (accessed March 28, 2007).

3. Reagan said, "We dishonored the memory of fifty thousand young Americans who died [in Vietnam] when we gave way to feelings of guilt as if we were doing something shameful, and we have been shabby in the treatment of those who returned." Howell Raines, "Reagan Calls Arms Race Essential to Avoid 'Surrender' or 'Defeat,'" *New York Times*, August 19, 1980; Ronald Reagan, "Peace," in *Reagan, in His Own Hand*, ed. Kiron K. Skinner, Annelise Anderson, and Martin Anderson (New York: Free Press, 2001), 481.

4. Lynda Van Devanter to Jan Scruggs, June 15, 1983, box 5, VVMF-MD.

5. Bill Outlaw, "The Wall Carries a Message for All Who Care to Visit," *Washington Times*, September 12, 1983.

6. Bob Waechter, a therapist at the vet center in Kansas City, Missouri, and a supporter of the Kansas City Vietnam Veterans Memorial, spoke of the therapeutic benefits of visits there. Interview by the author, January 22, 1992.

7. Sandra G. Boodman, "War Story: Ex-Army Nurse's Book on Horrors of Vietnam Renews Old Controversy," *Washington Post*, May 23, 1983.

8. Ronald Reagan, "Remarks at Dedication Ceremonies for the Vietnam Veterans Memorial Salute," November 11, 1984, APP, www.presidency.ucsb.edu/ws/?pid=39414 (accessed June 27, 2008).

9. Maya Lin, *Boundaries* (New York: Simon and Schuster, 2000), 4:10.

10. Stephan Gubar, in Gerald Gioglio, *Days of Decision: An Oral History of Conscientious Objectors in the Military during the Vietnam War* (Trenton, NJ: Broken Rifle Press, 1989), 287–88.

11. Quoted in Elizabeth Louise Kahn and Ellen Rocco, eds., *Reclaiming the Pieces: Changing Perspectives from the Vietnam Generation* (Ogdensberg, NY: Mr. Hubbard's Printing Service, 1989), 43.

12. Harry Maurer, *Strange Ground: An Oral History of Americans in Vietnam, 1945–1975* (New York: Avon Books, 1989), 17.

13. Peter Tauber, "Monument Maker," *New York Times Magazine*, February 24, 1991.

14. Ray Scurfield, interview by the author, June 26, 1991; Leslie Brown, "Rides in Helicopters Help Vietnam Vets Heal Mental Woes," *Oregonian*, November 19, 1988; Michael Wark, "Healing through Helicopters," *Evergreen State College Review* 10, no. 3 (April 1989).

15. Quoted in David L. Anderson, ed., *Facing My Lai: Moving beyond the Massacre* (Lawrence: University Press of Kansas, 1998), 181.

16. Russell Baker, "Mea Culpa Mania," *International Herald Tribune*, July 4, 1997; Miles Kington, "Sorry, je ne regrette rien," *Independent*, August 23, 1995.

17. Michael A. Fletcher, "Call for Official Apology on Slavery Rips Open Racial Wounds," *International Herald Tribune*, August 6, 1997; Peter Baker, "Clinton Weighs Apology for Slavery," *International Herald Tribune*, June 17, 1997; Derek Z. Jackson, " "Where Is the Apology for Slavery?" *Boston Globe*, July 11, 2003.

18. Gary D. Robertson, "North Carolina House Passes Slavery Apology," Associated Press, April 11, 2007; Jennie Jarvie, "Slavery Apologies Debated across U.S.," LATimes.com, March 19, 2007; "House Apologizes for Slavery, 'Jim Crow' Injustices," CNN.com, July 29, 2008, edition.cnn.com/2008/POLITICS/07/29/house.slavery/index.html (accessed August 1, 2008).

19. See, e.g., Abraham Cooper, "It's Time That Japan Acknowledged Its Wartime Atrocities," *International Herald Tribune*, April 12–13, 1997; Norimitsu Onishi, "Denial Reopens Wounds of Japan's Ex-Sex Slaves," *New York Times*, March 8, 2007; Clifford Coonan, "Why Are Relations between Japan and China So Poor, and Can They Be Improved?" *Independent*, April 12, 2007.

20. See, e.g., Ben Aris, "86-Year-Old Goes on Trial for Wartime Nazi Massacre," *Guardian*, September 10, 2004; Dale Fuchs, "Nazi War Criminal Escapes Costa Brava Police Search," *Guardian*, October 17, 2005; "Nazi Hunters Seeking Death Head Doctor," *Sydney Morning Herald*, November 7, 2007.

21. The series of articles published in the *Toledo Blade* began with "The Series: Elite Unit Savaged Civilians in Vietnam," October 22, 2003, www.toledoblade.com/apps/pbcs.dll/article?AID=/20031022/SRTIGERFORCE (accessed November 19, 2003). Col. David H. Hackworth, who organized the Tiger Force but was not its commander during the period covered by the articles, claimed that there were "hundreds of My Lais." John Kifner, "Report on Brutal Vietnam Campaign Stirs Memories," *New York Times*, December 28, 2003.

22. Michael Sallah and Mitch Weiss, *Tiger Force: A True Story of Men and War* (Boston: Little, Brown, 2006), 299, 306, 319.

23. Ibid., 311; Kifner, "Report on Brutal Vietnam Campaign"; Kendrick Oliver, *The My Lai Massacre in American History and Memory* (Manchester: Manchester University Press, 2006), 252.

24. Nick Turse and Deborah Nelson, "Civilian Killings Went Unpunished," *Los Angeles Times*, August 6, 2006. See also Nicholas Turse, "'Kill Anything that Moves': United States War Crimes and Atrocities in Vietnam, 1965–1973" (Ph.D. diss., Columbia University, 2005).

25. Julian Borger, "Vietnam War 'Deserter' Charged," *Guardian*, January 5, 2006. See also Bill Nichols, "Decades Later, Marines Hunt Vietnam-Era Deserters," *USA Today*, March 7, 2006; Paul von Zielbauer, "U.S. Army Clamps Down on Deserters," *International Herald Tribune*, April 9, 2007.

26. Kate Zernike and Jim Rutenberg, "Friendly Fire: The Birth of an Anti-Kerry Ad," *New York Times*, August 20, 2004.

27. Michael R. Belknap, *The Vietnam War on Trial* (Lawrence: University Press of Kansas, 2002), 221–22, 224, 230–32; Anderson, *Facing My Lai*, 43, 45.

28. Ninety percent of the perpetrators at My Lai were out of uniform by the time of the investigation. Civilian suspects could nevertheless have been tried by military commissions or in federal district courts, but the executive branch lacked the will to test the constitutional legitimacy of these courses of action. Belknap, *Vietnam War on Trial*, 112, 222. The 1996 War Crimes Act closed the loophole that allowed veteran suspects to avoid prosecution. William George Eckhardt, "My Lai: An American Tragedy" (2000), www.law.umkc.edu/faculty/projects/ftrials/mylai/ecktragedy.html#_ftnref45 (accessed April 28, 2007).

29. Transcript of the National Educational Television documentary *Nuremberg and Vietnam: Who Is Guilty?* 39, 42, 50, in box 6, Executive Producers Series, "Nuremberg and Vietnam" folder, Vietnam: A Television History Collection, Joseph P. Healey Library, University of Massachusetts, Boston.

30. A stream of invective greeted two contributors to the vwar Internet list when they attempted to initiate a discussion of wartime atrocities by Americans, and participants said that they were fed up with having been called "baby killer." Series of posts to vwar-l (VWAR-L@UBVM.cc.buffalo.edu), March 6, 1996. In the discussion, the word *atrocity* itself became so unacceptable that participants began to refer to it as "A" or "the A word."

31. Oliver, *My Lai Massacre*, 264.

32. "Transcript of Bush's Inaugural Address," *New York Times*, January 21, 1989.

33. Evan Thomas, John Barry, Ann McDaniel, and Douglas Waller, "No Vietnam," *Newsweek*, December 10, 1990, 24. Jack Germond and Jules Witcover also used the metaphor of the Vietnam experience as a "bad dream." Germond and Witcover, "Basking in the Gulf War's Warm Afterglow," *Baltimore Evening Sun*, March 8, 1991.

34. See, e.g., Tony Clifton, "This Time, a Winnable War," *Newsweek*, December 10, 1990, 30; Joseph J. Kane and Priscilla Painton, "A Long Hallucination of War," *Time*, December 10, 1990, 43; Tony Kornheiser, "Not Another Vietnam," *Washington Post*, January 20, 1991.

35. The doctrine was largely a rehashing of Weinberger's six tests, which codified ideas first articulated by Maxwell Taylor. "The Lessons of Vietnam: Exclusive Interview with Gen. Maxwell D. Taylor, USA (Ret.), Adviser to Three Presidents," *U.S. News and World Report*, November 27, 1972, 23–24. See Colin Powell, with Joseph E. Persico, *A Soldier's Way* (London: Hutchinson, 1995), 303; Michael R. Gordon, "Powell Delivers Resounding No on Using Military Force in Bosnia," *New York Times*, September 28, 1992; Colin Powell, "US Forces: Challenges Ahead," *Foreign Affairs* 71, no. 5 (Winter 1992–93).

36. "Excerpts from the President's News Conference," *New York Times*, December 1, 1990, 6. For Bush's repeated assurances that the Gulf War would be different from the one in Vietnam, see, e.g., "Text of Radio Address by President Bush," *New York Times*, January 6, 1991; President's Press Conference, February 5, 1991, APP, www.presidency.ucsb.edu/ws/?pid=19278 (accessed April 18, 2007).

37. While the war was still going on, citizens were preparing to give the Gulf War veterans a welcome they said the Vietnam veterans had not enjoyed. Alessandra Stanley, "War's Ribbons Are Yellow with Meaning of Many Hues," *New York Times*, February 3, 1991. After the cease-fire, Americans resolved to give the troops a proper welcome. George Bush asked communities around the country to make the

upcoming July 4 a day of celebration for the troops. President Bush, "Address before a Joint Session of the Congress on the Cessation of Hostilities in the Gulf Conflict," March 6, 1991, APP, www.presidency.ucsb.edu/ws/?pid=19364 (accessed April 20, 2007). Vietnam veterans showed remarkably little resentment at the enthusiastic reception of returning Gulf War veterans. They often made a point of demanding that their victorious successors should be properly honored, and the homecoming for the Gulf War veterans provided an occasion for retrospective appreciation of the Vietnam veterans. Phil McCombs, "Finally, the Maine Event," *Washington Post*, May 12, 1991; Jean Marbella, "Vets Remember Their Wars," *Baltimore Sun*, May 27, 1991; Sue Ann Presley, "Desert Storm Celebration Is Also a Parade of Tears," *Washington Post*, June 6, 1991; Susan Baer, "Desert Storm Takes N.Y.," *Baltimore Sun*, June 11, 1991. Art Fillmore of the Kansas City VVMF, chairman of the Desert Storm Homecoming in Kansas City, Missouri, interview by the author, January 24, 1992.

38. George H. W. Bush, "Remarks to the American Legislative Exchange Council," March 1, 1991, in *Bush 1991*, bk. 1, *PPP*, 197; "Radio Address to United States Armed Forces Stationed in the Persian Gulf Region," March 2, 1991, in *Bush 1991*, bk. 1, *PPP*, 207. Again, Bush may have said more than he realized. Students of Freud will recall that "burial in the sands" was one of his descriptions of the way that repressed memories are preserved intact and retain a capacity for effective action, submerged in the unconscious.

39. These two offerings were placed together in the final display, representing the years 1990–91, in Personal Legacy: The Healing of a Nation, exhibition at the National Museum of American History, Smithsonian Institution, Washington, DC.

40. Quoted in Ruben Castenada, "Quayle, Powell Honor Those Who Sacrificed," *Washington Post*, May 28, 1991.

41. Charles Hagel, "The Lessons of the War," in *Voices from the Wall*, by Jan C. Scruggs (Washington, DC: VVMF, 1998), 3.

42. Yankelovich Clancy Shulman poll for Time/CNN, March 7, 1991; Market Strategies poll for Americans Talk Security, March 19 to March 24, 1991; data provided by RC.

43. Anna Quindlen, "The Microwave War," *New York Times*, March 3, 1991. Ellen Goodman also worried about the "meaning of an 'easy' win." Goodman, "What Lessons from Easy Victory?" *Washington Post*, March 2, 1991.

44. Dan Balz and Ann Devroy, "For Bush, Persian Gulf War Was Transforming Moment," *Washington Post*, March 3, 1991. R. W. Apple, contemplating the lessons of victory in the Gulf, confirmed several of the Weinberger/Powell precepts: the need for a domestic consensus, clear objectives, and massive firepower. Apple, "Done. A Short, Persuasive Lesson in Warfare," *New York Times*, March 3, 1991.

45. Quoted in Elaine Sciolino, "Bigger Relief Plan," *New York Times*, April 17, 1991.

46. In 1988, the Vietnamese government agreed to allow Americans to search throughout Vietnam for the remains of those who remained missing in action. In 1991, the American representative and the Vietnamese foreign minister announced the creation of an MIA office in Hanoi. In 1992, the U.S. government created the Joint Task Force for a Full Accounting.

47. President's News Conference, August 2, 1991, APP, www.presidency.ucsb.edu/ws/?pid=19873 (accessed April 18, 2007).

48. George H. W. Bush, "Remarks to the National League of Families of American Prisoners and Missing in Southeast Asia in Arlington, Virginia," July 24, 1992, APP, www.presidency.ucsb.edu/ws/?pid=21263 (accessed April 17, 2007). For the perspective of the hecklers, see Mark Sauter and Jim Sanders, *The Men We Left Behind: Henry Kissinger, the Politics of Deceit, and the Tragic Fate of POWs after the Vietnam War* (Washington, DC: National Press Books, 1993), 19–21.

49. Sauter and Saunders, *Men We Left Behind*, 250–51, 307–8, 324.

50. Paul A. Witteman, "Nam 15 Years Later," *Time*, April 30, 1990, 20.

51. H. Bruce Franklin, *M.I.A., or Mythmaking in America* (New Brunswick, NJ: Rutgers University Press, 1993), 188.

52. Gerald Posner, *Citizen Perot: His Life and Times* (New York: Random House, 1996), 152, 201; Monika Jensen-Stevenson and William Stevenson, *Kiss the Boys Goodbye* (New York: Plume Books, 1991), 295, 337; Sauter and Saunders, *Men We Left Behind*, 251. Posner cites Craig Fuller's "instrumental" role in the matter of the statue and flag and points out that Fuller was Bush's chief of staff, but that seems to exaggerate Fuller's importance, given the intervention of the White House troika and Bush himself, and does not settle the issue of how Perot knew of Fuller's actions. Tom Shull speculates that James Baker wanted to keep his role in the matter of the statue and flag quiet because he did not want to cross his fellow Texan Perot. Shull, telephone interview by the author, September 13, 2007.

53. Carol J. Castaneda and Ron Prichards, "Nation Honors Its War Dead," *USA Today*, May 26, 1992. "The 1992 Campaign: On the Trail; Poll Gives Perot Clear Lead," *New York Times*, June 11, 1992; Posner, *Citizen Perot*, 259, 378.

54. Quoted in Barbara Crossette, "Hanoi Said to Vow to Give M.I.A. Data," *New York Times*, October 24, 1992.

55. Andrew Brownstein, "A Tolling of Voices at the Wall," *Washington Post*, November 9, 1992; Charles Babington, "Vietnam War Looms over Veterans Day," *Washington Post*, November 12, 1992. After the 1992 election, the Bush family blamed Perot for Bush's defeat, although it is doubtful that Perot's candidacy made a difference to the election's outcome. Although Perot won 19 percent of the vote, exit polls indicated that more of his voters would have voted for the winner, Bill Clinton, than for Bush had Perot not been running. R. W. Apple, "The 1992 Elections," *New York Times*, November 4, 1992; Allen R. Myerson, "The 1994 Campaign: Ross Perot; Richards Draws Perot's Backing in Tough Texas Governor's Race," *New York Times*, November 2, 1994.

56. Presidential election exit polls reported in ABC News, November 3, 1992; Richard Cohen, "A Monument to Healing," *Washington Post*, November 11, 1992. CBS News poll conducted May 26 and 27, 1993; Yankelovich Partners poll conducted on the same dates for Time, Inc., and CNN; data provided by RC.

57. Observations by the author; Ruth Marcus, "Jeers, Cheers Greet Clinton at the Wall," *Washington Post*, June 1, 1993; Thomas L. Friedman, "Clinton, in Vietnam War Tribute, Finds Old Wound Is Slow to Heal," *New York Times*, June 1, 1993. According to the *Washington Times*, some three hundred of the estimated eight thousand attending the ceremonies protested Clinton's presence. Janet Naylor, "Many Veterans Refuse to Hail the Chief," *Washington Times*, June 1, 1993.

58. "Disagree, If We Must, about the War, but Let Us Not Let It Divide Us," *Washington Post*, June 1, 1993.

59. John McCain, "Let's Normalize Relations with Vietnam," *Washington Post*, May 21, 1995; Mary McGrory, "Recognizing Vietnam—and China," *Washington Post*, June 27, 1995.

60. Thomas W. Lippman, "GOP-Controlled Foreign Policy Panels Would Reverse Several Clinton Stands," *Washington Post*, May 21, 1995; Carol Giacomo, "Christopher Formally Urges U.S.-Vietnam Normalization," *Washington Post*, June 14, 1995; Thomas W. Lippman, "Clinton at Bat; Vietnam Is Pitching," *Washington Post*, June 16, 1995; "Normalization of Relations Evokes Rapid Response," *VVA Veteran*, August/September 1995, 9.

61. Martin Sieff, "U.S. Quietly Opens Embassy in Vietnam," *Washington Times*, August 7, 1995; John Gittings, "U.S. and Vietnam Back in Business," *Guardian*, August 17, 1999.

62. "Agreement on Ending the War and Restoring Peace in Viet-Nam," in *Vietnam and America: A Documented History*, ed. Marvin E. Gettleman, Jane Franklin, Marilyn B. Young, and H. Bruce Franklin, 2nd ed. (New York: Grove Press, 1995), 479.

63. Stanley W. Cloud, "It's Time to Heal the Wounds," interview with foreign minister Nguyen Co Thach, *Time*, April 30, 1990, 25; Robert D. Schulzinger, *A Time for Peace: The Legacy of the Vietnam War* (New York: Oxford University Press, 2006), 53.

64. Virginia Foote, president of the U.S.–Vietnam Trade Council, said that the war was a "scar on the national psyche" that made the establishment of trade relations difficult. Robert Boyd and Mary Otto said, "The wounds of the bitter conflict that shadowed and twisted the lives of a generation are healing." Boyd and Otto, "Analysis: The Vietnam War; U.S. Is Ready to Let Wounds Heal, Start Over with North [*sic*] Vietnam," *Orange County Register*, July 8, 1995.

65. Seth Mydans, "Clinton in Vietnam: The Overview," *New York Times*, November 20, 2000; David E. Sanger and Helene Cooper, "Unlike Clinton, Bush Sees Hanoi in a Bit of a Hurry," *New York Times*, November 19, 2006.

66. "Vietnamese Pays Historic Visit to U.S.," *International Herald Tribune*, November 11, 2003; Ellen Nakashima, "Vietnam, U.S. to Improve Intelligence, Military Ties," *Washington Post*, June 17, 2005; Michael R. Gordon, "U.S. and Vietnam Agree to Broaden Military Ties," *International Herald Tribune*, June 6, 2006.

67. See, e.g., Henry Kamm, *Dragon Ascending: Vietnam and the Vietnamese* (New York: Arcade, 1996); W. C. O'Donovan, "Vietnam Revisited," *Williamsburg Magazine*, July 1993, 39; William Broyles Jr., "The Road to Hill 10," *Atlantic Monthly*, April 1985, 92; Keith Richburg, "Returning to Vietnam for Comfort—or Cash," *Washington Post*, April 27, 1995.

68. David Lambs, "Vietnam Trip Heals Old Wounds," *Boston Globe*, January 17, 1998.

69. Rex Graham, "Vietnam Veterans Going Back to Help People, Heal Wounds," *Albuquerque (NM) Journal*, February 13, 1992.

70. See, e.g., Brian Willson, "A Time for Healing," *Peace Work*, February 1995, 17–18; Gay-Winn Cooper, "Peace Trees, Vietnam," *Yes!*, Summer 1999, www.yesmagazine.com/article.asp?ID=751 (accessed April 20, 2007).

71. See, e.g., W. D. Ehrhart, "Going Back," *Philadelphia Inquirer Magazine*, March 16, 1986; William Broyles Jr., *Brothers in Arms: A Journey from War to Peace* (New York: Knopf, 1986); Joshua Hammer,

"Unfinished Business," *Washington Post Magazine*, October 18, 1987; Associated Press, "Veteran Shakes Vietnam Ghosts," *Hampton Roads Daily Press*, May 22, 1994; "Return to Kham Duc," *VVA Veteran*, March 1995, 19.

72. Paul Critchlow, "Hill 102," *American Heritage*, June/July 2003, 59, 62.

73. Interview with Richard Holbrooke, *Frontline*, Public Broadcasting System, [1999], www.pbs.org/wgbh/pages/frontline/shows/military/guys/holbrooke.html (accessed April 24, 2007). The possibility that military forces might be used in "operations other than war" (such as peacekeeping, humanitarian assistance, and support of domestic civil authorities) was recognized in the U.S. Army's statements of military doctrine early in the 1990s: see, e.g., *AirLand Operations: A Concept for the Evolution of AirLand Battle for the Strategic Army of the 1990s and Beyond*, U.S. Army Training and Doctrine Command/U.S. Air Force Tactical Air Command, TraDoc Pamphlet 525–5, August 1, 1991, 26.

74. Anthony Lake, "From Containment to Enlargement," Johns Hopkins School of Advanced International Studies, September 21, 1993, www.mtholyoke.edu/acad/intrel/lakedoc.html (accessed June 1, 2007); idem, "Defining Missions, Setting Deadlines: Meeting New Security Challenges in the Post–Cold War World," Remarks at George Washington University, March 6, 1996, www.pbs.org/wgbh/pages/frontline/shows/military/force/lake.html (accessed April 24, 2007).

75. Powell, *Soldier's Way*, 576.

76. William C. Banks and Jeffrey D. Straussman, "A New Imperial Presidency? Insights from U.S. Involvement in Bosnia," *Political Science Quarterly* 114 (1999): 215; Louis Fisher, "Congressional Checks on Military Initiatives," *Political Science Quarterly* 109 (1994–95): 739; Bruce W. Jentleson and Rebecca L. Britton, "Still Pretty Prudent: Post–Cold War American Public Opinion on the Use of Military Force," *Journal of Conflict Resolution* 42 (August 1998): 407.

77. Jentleson and Britton, "Still Pretty Prudent," 402–3; Edward N. Luttwak, "Where Are the Great Powers? At Home with the Kids," *Foreign Affairs*, July/August 1994; Michael Dobbs, "The 'Clinton Doctrine' of Scaled-Down Force," *International Herald Tribune*, November 18, 1996, 10; E. J. Dionne, "Modest Success in Bosnia for 'Clinton Doctrine,'" *International Herald Tribune*, December 31, 1997.

78. Michael McGwire, "Why Did We Bomb Belgrade?" *International Affairs* 76, no. 1 (January 2000): 18. For a skeptical discussion of the "casualty aversion" hypothesis, see James Burk, "Public Support for Peacekeeping in Lebanon and Somalia: Assessing the Casualties Hypothesis," *Political Science Quarterly* 114, no. 1 (1999): 53–78.

79. Elaine Sciolina, "From Napalm's Horror to Forgiveness for Vietnam," *International Herald Tribune*, November 13, 1996. Kim was once an icon of anti-imperialism, but her role has shifted. She left Cuba for a new home in Canada in 1992 and often speaks of reconciliation and forgiveness in media interviews. For her remarks at the ceremony at the memorial, see Kim Phuc, "Forgiveness," in Scruggs, *Voices from the Wall*, 31–32.

80. Captain John Plummer, the air controller, had been unable to shake off his guilt for putting in the air strike that injured Kim. Denise Chong, *The Girl in the Picture: The Remarkable Story of Vietnam's Most Famous Casualty* (New York: Simon and Schuster, 1999), 83, 361–63.

81. I am grateful to Grey Gundaker for alerting me to the complexity of gestures of apology, gratitude, and forgiveness. For stories of forgiveness, see, e.g., Karlyn Barker, "At the Wall, Sympathy and Sorrow," *Washington Post*, November 11, 1989; *From the Heart: News from and for the Families and Friends of Shrapnel in the Heart*, January 1989, 7; *From the Heart*, January 1990, 11–12. A refugee who came to the United States in 1975 thanks U.S. Vietnam veterans for sacrifices that his people will never forget but also describes America's abandonment of South Vietnam to totalitarianism. Toan Truong, "Hollywood's Vietnam, Not Mine," *New York Times*, February 19, 1990.

82. Michael Bilton and Kevin Sim, *Four Hours in My Lai* (New York: Penguin, 1993), 137; David Anderson, ed., *Facing My Lai: Moving Beyond the Massacre* (Lawrence: University Press of Kansas, 1998), 29.

83. The lieutenant Thompson encountered appears to have been William Calley, who recalls the same conversation. W. L. Calley, *Body Count: Lieutenant Calley's Story as Told to John Sack* (London: Hutchison, 1971), 114–18.

84. Bilton and Sim, *Four Hours in My Lai*, 177.

85. Ibid., 139.

86. "An American Hero: Vietnam Veteran Speaks Out about My Lai," *60 Minutes*, CBS News, May 9, 2004, transcript, www.cbsnews.com/stories/2004/05/06/60minutes/main615997.shtml?source=search_story (accessed April 9, 2007).

87. U.S. Congress, House, 91st Cong., 2d sess., *Investigation of the My Lai Incident: Report of the Armed Services Investigating Subcommittee of the House of Representatives Committee on Armed Services*, July 15, 1970 (Washington, DC: U.S. Government Printing Office, 1970), 16–20; "American Hero"; "My Lai Massacre Hero Dies at 62," BBC News, January 6, 2006, news.bbc.co.uk/2/hi/americas/4589486.stm (accessed April 8, 2007).

88. "United States," *Guardian*, March 7, 1998; David Montgomery, "30 Years after My Lai, Hard Truths and Heroism," *International Herald Tribune*, March 9, 1998.

89. Tom Bowman, "My Lai Still Causes Army to Flinch, Delaying a Medal," *Baltimore Sun*, November 14, 1997; Gregory L. Vistica, "The Brass Battles over Giving a Hero of My Lai a Medal," *Newsweek*, November 24, 1997; message from Captain Lawrence Rockwood of the My Lai Commemoration Campaign, forwarded by Randy Fertel, Tulane University, to the author, January 22, 1998.

90. Bilton and Sim, *Four Hours in My Lai*, 204–5.

91. David Montgomery, "30 Years Later, Heroes Emerge from Shame of My Lai Massacre," *Washington Post*, March 7, 19981; transcript of CNN coverage of the My Lai Medal Ceremony, March 6, 1998, www.174ahc.org/mylai-01.htm (Web site of the 174th Assault Helicopter Company) (accessed April 12, 2007); Eckhardt, "My Lai: An American Tragedy."

92. "Return to My Lai," *60 Minutes II*, CBS News, December 13, 1999, transcript, www.cbsnews.com/stories/1999/12/06/60II/main73270.shtml?source=search_story (accessed April 9, 2007).

93. Oliver, *My Lai Massacre*, 251.

94. "My Lai Hero Hugh Thompson Dies at 62," CBS News, January 6, 2006, transcript, www.cbsnews.com/stories/2006/01/06/national/main1185502.shtml (accessed August 1, 2008).

95. John Rogers, "Vietnamese Recall 1968 My Lai Massacre," *Philadelphia Inquirer*, March 17, 1993.

96. Oliver, *My Lai Massacre*, 259.

97. "A Commitment to Health, Education and Welfare at My Lai," part of the content of a flyer by the My Lai 30th Anniversary Project [1997], sent to the author by the project; Randy Fertel, "My Lai Peace Park and Anniversary Commemoration," *Indochina Interchange*, May 1997, 12; Mike Boehm, e-mail message to the author, May 18, 1997.

98. Rogers, "Vietnamese Recall."

99. Quoted in Ian Thomson, "The Good German," review section, *Guardian*, April 7, 2007.

100. "Cold War Chat: Hugh Thompson," CNN, edition.cnn.com/SPECIALS/cold.war/guides/debate/chats/thompson/ (accessed June 1, 2007).

101. "Return to My Lai."

102. The October 14, 1997, letter from Ambassador Peterson to Lawrence Rockwood of the My Lai Commemoration Campaign is quoted in a message by Rockwood e-mailed to the author in January 1998.

103. "Cold War Chat." Peterson, however, planted a tree and unveiled a plaque at the Vietnamese-American Peace Park near the Vietnamese capital, Hanoi, stating, "The Vietnamese-American Peace Park represents the exchange of love and mutual respect between the people of Vietnam and America." Circular sent to the author by Mike Boehm.

104. "A Celebration of Life! The Boy from the Ditch Reunited in My Lai with His Rescuers," "Mr. Long's Letter of Support for Do Hoa," "Do Hoa Writes to His Fathers," *Winds of Peace: Newsletter for Madison Friends' Projects in Vietnam*, April/May 2001, 3, 4.

105. Michael Walzer *Just and Unjust Wars: A Moral Argument with Historical Illustrations* (New York: Basic Books, 1977), 187.

106. Ibid., 195.

107. Tim O'Brien, *If I Die in a Combat Zone* (New York: Dell, 1974), 191.

108. Author's observations at Indiana War Memorial Plaza.

109. CBS News/New York Times poll conducted April 15–April 17, 2000; data provided by RC.

110. E. J. Dionne, "Sept. 11 Has Stilled the Post-Vietnam Battles," *International Herald Tribune*, September 11, 2002, 9. Ariel Dorfman said that America had "innocence" handed back to it as a result of the 9/11 attacks. Dorfman, "An Open Letter to America," *Observer*, September 8, 2002.

111. Glenn Collins, "Refurbished Vietnam Memorial Is Dedicated, 11/9/01," *New York Times*, November 10, 2001.

112. "Making of the Memorial 1985–2001," NewYorkVietnamVeteransMemorial.org, www.nyvietnamveteransmemorial.org/vvm/making.html (accessed April 16, 2007).

113. "Operation Homecoming 2005" in Branson, Missouri, in November 2005 was "the welcome home [Vietnam veterans] never received." "'Vietnam Homecoming' Documentary Filmed in Branson to Air Saturday on History Channel," news release, December 11, 2006. "Welcome Home" parades also took place in Las Vegas in 2005 and Antelope Valley, California, on Veterans Day 2006. Samantha L. Quigley, "America Supports You: California Parade Honors Vietnam Vets," American Forces Press Service, November 1, 2006, VVA Digest 15741, Vietnam Veterans of America Talklist, vva@vva2.talklist.com, posted November 2, 2006. Webcast of the November 11, 2006 ceremony at the Vietnam Veterans Memorial, www.tvworldwide.com/events/usvets/061111/default.cfm?id=7684&type=wmhigh (accessed November 13, 2006); webcast of the Memorial Day 2007 ceremonies at the Vietnam Veterans Memorial, www.tvworldwide.com/events/vvmf/070528/default.cfm?id=8543&type=wmhigh (accessed August 2, 2007).

114. Once President George W. Bush had spoken in favor of preemptive force, Secretary of State Powell expanded his doctrine to embrace the concept. Glenn Kessler and Peter Slevin, "Any Use of Preemptive Force Must Be 'Decisive,' Powell Says," *International Herald Tribune*, June 17, 2002.

115. "Guidelines When Considering Committing U.S. Forces," March 2001, www.defenselink.mil/news/Oct2002/d20021017guidelines.pdf (accessed June 1, 2007); Thom Shanker, "Rumsfeld Spells Out His Rules for Combat," *International Herald Tribune*, October 15, 2002; Michael R. Gordon, "A New Military Doctrine Is on Tap," *International Herald Tribune*, March 19, 2003; Julian Borger and Richard Norton-Taylor, "A Showcase for Rumsfeld's Grand Plan," *Guardian*, March 22, 2003.

116. See, e.g., Max Boot, "The Lessons of a Quagmire," *New York Times*, November 16, 2003; Todd S. Purdum, "Flashback to the 60s: A Sinking Sensation of Parallels Between Iraq and Vietnam," *New York Times*, January 29, 2005; "Kissinger Finds Parallels to Vietnam in Iraq," CNN.com August 15, 2005; Charles J. Hanley, "Analysis: Parallels between Iraq, Vietnam," *Jackson, Mississippi Clarion-Ledger*, May 26, 2006; Robert Brigham, *Is Iraq Another Vietnam?* (New York: PublicAffairs, 2006); M. Kenneth Campbell, *A Tale of Two Quagmires: Iraq, Vietnam, and the Hard Lessons of War* (Herndon, VA: Paradigm Press, 2007).

117. Reuters and *New York Times* news reports, "Bush Gets First Look at Antiwar Vigil in Texas," *International Herald Tribune*, August 13–14, 2005.

118. Mark Shields, "The Powell Doctrine: A Good Idea Whose Time Has Come . . . Again," *Cagle Post*, March 3, 2007, available at www.caglepost.com/ (accessed August 1, 2008).

119. Julian Coman, "'Not Everybody Wants to Be Seen Too Close to Don Rumsfeld Right Now,'" *Sunday Telegraph*, March 30, 2003.

120. Michael R. Gordon, "New Weight in Army Manual on Stabilizing War-torn Areas," *New York Times*, February 8, 2008.

121. Jim Rutenberg, Sheryl Gay Stolberg, and Mark Mazzetti, "'Free Iraq' Is within Reach, Bush Declares," *New York Times*, August 23, 2007.

122. The commentary on *NBC Nightly News*, *CBS Evening News*, and *Sky News* (broadcast via Sky satellite in Britain) was uniformly skeptical on August 22, 2007, as was commentary in the *New York Times* and the *Times* (London) the following day: Thom Shanker, "Historians Question Bush's Reading of Lessons of Vietnam for Iraq," *New York Times*, August 23, 2007; Bronwen Maddox, "An Imprudent Comparison that Undermines the American Case," *Times*, August 23, 2007.

123. Buddhika Jayamaha, Wesley D. Smith, Jeremy Roebuck, Omar Mora, Edward Sandmeier, Yance T. Gray, and Jeremy A. Murphy, "The War as We Saw It," *New York Times*, August 19, 2007.

124. Schulzinger, *Time for Peace*, 128; "Memorials," *VVA Veteran*, March/April 2007, 42, 48; "Memorials," *VVA Veteran*, July/August 2007, 40. Also, in 1987 the New Orleans Vietnamese American community dedicated an abstract memorial, a tall pyramid, "in memory of the American and allied armed forces who bravely fought and sacrificed during the Vietnam War." Vietnamese Americans raised funds for the California Vietnam Veterans Memorial in Sacramento and for the Mississippi Vietnam Veterans Memorial in Gulfport, a project that the Gulf Coast Vietnamese American community initiated. Author's observations in New Orleans; personal communication with Michael Kelley and Don Drumheller; *Design Program for the Mississippi Vietnam Veterans Memorial, Biloxi, Mississippi*, December 15, 1989, 3, of which the author was given a copy by members of the Mississippi Vietnam Veterans Memorial Committee.

125. Ronald Reagan, "Interview with USA Today," April 26, 1983, APP, www.presidency.ucsb.edu/ws/?pid=41240 (accessed August 22, 2008). As discussed in chapter 1, President Eisenhower was convinced that the Communist Ho Chi Minh would have won a presidential election had one been held throughout Vietnam, North and South, at the time of the Geneva Accords. This view was shared by the joint chiefs of staff and American intelligence services. Gareth Porter, ed., *Vietnam: A History in Documents* (New York: New American Library, 1981), 133, 163.

126. Quoted in Andrew F. Krepinevich Jr., *The Army and Vietnam* (Baltimore: Johns Hopkins University Press, 1986), 196.

127. Daniel Ellsberg, quoted in *Hearts and Minds*, dir. Peter Davis (1974). An estimated three million Vietnamese people (North Vietnamese armed forces, Viet Cong guerrillas, South Vietnamese armed forces, and civilians on both sides) are believed to have been killed during the period of U.S. warfare in Indochina. In addition there were numerous casualties among the citizens of Cambodia and Laos, and members of the armed forces of America's allies.

128. "VA Secretary Principi to Speak at Annual In Memory Ceremony at Vietnam Veterans Memorial," *VVA Digest* 2844, March 21, 2001.

129. Jim Doyle, "Communication at Ground Zero," *VVA Veteran*, June/July 2000, 11; "Veterans Day Vietnam War In Memory Plaque Project Newsletter—Veterans Day 2002," *VVA Digest* 6404, October 6, 2002.

130. Jim Belshaw, "In Memory Plaque," *VVA Veteran*, October 2004, 25, 43. See the "In Memory" plaque Web site, members.aol.com/vietwarmem/plaque.htm (accessed November 3, 2006).

131. "Agent Orange Victims and Widows Support Network" Web site, www.agentorangequiltoftears.com/ (accessed November 3, 2006).

132. "In Memory Plaque—Comments by a Visitor," VVA Digest 11126, November 10, 2004; "RE: In Memory Plaque—Comments by a Visitor," VVA Digest 11146, November 15, 2004.

133. Message from Gerry Fitzpatrick, president, Agent Orange Diabetic Victims, embedded in VVA Digest, June 13, 2007.

134. Gerson H. Smoger, "Knocking Down Windmills," Trial, July 2003, www.agentorangelaw.net/agent_orange_lawsuit.htm (accessed August 2, 2008); "Agent Orange Lawsuits Allowed," www.agent-orange-lawsuit.com/ (accessed August 2, 2008); William Glaberson, "Civil Lawsuit on Defoliant in Vietnam Is Dismissed," New York Times, March 11, 2005; "Court Rejects Vietnamese Victims' Agent Orange Suit," Los Angeles Times, February 23, 2008. The Department of Veterans Affairs lists prostate cancer, respiratory cancers, multiple myeloma, type II diabetes, Hodgkin's disease, non-Hodgkin's lymphoma, soft tissue sarcoma, chloracne, porphyria cutanea tarda, peripheral neuropathy, and spina bifida in children of veterans exposed to Agent Orange as effects of the herbicide on humans.

135. Mark Thompson, "The Vietnam Veterans Memorial," Time, June 4, 2007, 72.

136. Editorial, "An Unwelcome Visitors Center," New York Times, August 14, 2006.

137. "Vietnam Memorial Education Center," OAH Newsletter, May 2001, 10; Testimony of Daniel Smith of the National Park Service before the Senate Committee on Resources, Concerning S. 1076, to Authorize the Design and Construction of an Education Center at or near the Vietnam Veterans Memorial, June 3, 2003, energy.senate.gov/hearings/testimony.cfm?id=776&wit_id=618 (accessed June 9, 2003).

138. New York Times Service, "In Speech in Hanoi, Bush Defends the War," International Herald Tribune, September 7, 1995.

139. Kendrick Oliver reports that a recruit at Fort Benning, Georgia, where Calley had been confined during his court martial, told a reporter in March 1998 that he had never heard of the My Lai massacre. Oliver, My Lai Massacre, 251. My own visit to the military history museum at Fort Benning in 1993 found no mention of the My Lai Massacre there. The commanding general of Fort Jackson, South Carolina, largest center for basic infantry training for the U.S. Army, reported that recruits were given a week of training on the ethics and laws of combat. When asked by Thompson whether the recruits ever heard the words My Lai, he admitted that they did not. "Cold War Chat: Hugh Thompson, U.S. Army helicopter pilot at My Lai," CNN Interactive, edition.cnn.com/SPECIALS/cold.war/guides/debate/chats/thompson/ (accessed April 9, 2007). The interview with Thompson took place December 6, 1998.

140. Ed Vulliamy, "Why We Still Need a Nuremberg Court," Guardian, August 5, 1997.

141. Thomas W. Lippmann, "A Good Idea, but Not for Americans," International Herald Tribune, July 28, 1998; Associated Press, "US Renounces Treaty on War Crimes Tribunal," International Herald Tribune, May 7, 2002. With support from legislators, George W. Bush selectively cut off military aid to nations that ratified the Rome Treaty, which brought the court into being, and that refused to immunize U.S. citizens from prosecution. Daniel Benjamin, "Relaxing the Strong Arm," Time, September 10, 2001, 37; Elizabeth Becker, "U.S. Suspends Aid to 35 Countries over New International Court," New York Times, July 2, 2003; Christopher Marquis, "U.S. Stand Is Headache for Ally in Colombia," New York Times, July 17, 2003.

142. Adam Clymer, "Key House Panel Targets International Tribunal," International Herald Tribune, May 13, 2002; Hugo Young, "We Can't Allow US Tantrums to Scupper Global Justice," Guardian, July 2, 2002; "U.S.: 'Hague Invasion Act' Becomes Law; White House 'Stops at Nothing' in Campaign against War Crimes Court," Human Rights Watch Press Release, New York, August 3, 2002. www.hrw.org/press/2002/08/aspa080302.htm (accessed April 17, 2007).

143. Christopher Marquis, "US Takes New Tack to Bypass Tribunal," International Herald Tribune, August 8, 2002; Elizabeth Becker, "US Warns that Backers of Tribunal May Lose Aid," International Herald Tribune, August 12, 2002; Julian Borger, "Congress Threatens to Cut Aid in Fight over Criminal Court," Guardian, November 27, 2004; Nicholas D. Kristof, "Schoolyard Bully Diplomacy," International Herald Tribune, October 17, 2005.

144. See, e.g., John C. Yoo, memorandum to Alberto R. Gonzales, counsel to the president, August 1, 2002, in The Torture Papers: The Road to Abu Ghraib, ed. Karen J. Greenberg and Joshua L. Dratel (Cambridge: Cambridge University Press, 2005), 218, 221; "International Criminal Court—Rome Statute," updated April 24, 2004, U.S. State Department Web site, usinfo.state.gov/dhr/Archive_Index/rome_statute.html (accessed April 26, 2007).

145. Anthony Lewis, "A President Beyond the Law Sets a Bad Example," International Herald Tribune, May 8–9, 2004. As well as attempting to achieve for its own uniformed personnel and government officials de facto immunity against prosecution under international law, the United States has claimed, under an evolving doctrine of "extraterritoriality" and under "status of forces agreements," that other nations' domestic laws do not apply to its military personnel in those countries. James Petras and Morris Morley, Empire or Republic? American Global Power and Domestic Decay (New York: Routledge,

1995), 4; Chalmers Johnson, *The Sorrows of Empire: Militarism, Secrecy, and the End of the Republic* (London: Verso, 2004), 35–36.

146. Amnesty International, "Beyond the Radar: Secret Flights to Torture and 'Disappearance,'" April 5, 2006, Amnesty International report no. AMR 51/051/2006, web.amnesty.org/library/Index/ENGAMR510512006 (accessed April 30, 2007).

147. "Ability of Detainees in Cuba to Obtain Federal Habeas Corpus Review," *American Journal of International Law* 98, no. 1 (January 2004): 188–90; Joseph Margulies, *Guantánamo and the Abuse of Presidential Power* (New York: Simon and Schuster, 2006).

148. Alberto Gonzales, "Memorandum for the President," January 25, 2002, in Greenberg and Dratel, *Torture Papers*, 119; Jay Bybee, memorandum for Alberto Gonzales, January 22, 2002, ibid., 81–117; John Ashcroft, memorandum to the president, February 1, 2002, ibid., 126–27.

149. Michael Isikoff, "Memos Reveal War Crimes Warnings," *Newsweek*, May 19, 2004, www.msnbc.msn.com/id/4999734/ (accessed April 28, 2007); Johanna McGeary, "Pointing Fingers," *Time*, May 24, 2004, www.time.com/time/magazine/article/0,9171,994233-2,00.html (accessed April 24, 2007).

150. Evan J. Wallach, "The Logical Nexus between the Decision to Deny Application of the Third Geneva Convention to the Taliban and Al Qaeda and the Mistreatment of Prisoners in Abu Ghraib," *Case Western Reserve Journal of International Law* 36 (2004): 542.

151. Marcy Strauss, "The Lessons of Abu Ghraib," *Ohio State Law Journal* 66 (2005): 1279.

152. "Report of the International Committee of the Red Cross (ICRC) on the Treatment by the Coalition Forces of Prisoners of War and Other Protected Persons by the Geneva Conventions in Iraq During Arrest, Internment and Interrogation" (February 2004), in Greenberg and Dratel, *Torture Papers*, 383–404; The Taguba Report: Article 15–6 Investigation of the 800th Military Police Brigade" (March 2004), ibid., 405–50.

153. Christian Appy, "Ghosts of War," *Chronicle of Higher Education* 50 (July 9, 2004): B12–13.

154. Strauss, "Lessons of Abu Ghraib," 1275; McGeary, "Pointing Fingers."

155. James Schlesinger, *Final Report of the Independent Panel to Review DoD Detention Operations* (Arlington, VA: U.S. Department of Defense, 2004), 5.

156. Quoted in Deborah Nelson and Nick Turse, "A Tortured Past," *Los Angeles Times*, August 20, 2006.

157. Thane Peterson, "The Environment Creates the Atrocity," *Business Week Online*, May 18, 2004, www.businessweek.com/bwdaily/dnflash/may2004/nf20040518_9951_db028.htm (accessed August 2, 2008). See also Robert J. Lifton, "Conditions of Atrocity," *Nation* May 31, 2004, 4–5; Lawrence F. Kaplan, "Blame Worthy," *New Republic*, May 7, 2004.

158. Eckhardt, "My Lai."

159. Ellen Knickmeyer, "In Haditha, Memories of a Massacre," *Washington Post*, May 27, 2006.

160. Chris Hedges and Laila Al-Arian, "The Other War: Iraq Vets Bear Witness," *Nation*, July 13, 2007.

161. Paul von Zielbauer, "The Struggle for Iraq: Military Cites 'Negligence' in Aftermath of Iraq Killings," *New York Times*, April 22, 2007.

162. Josh White, "Report on Haditha Condemns Marines," *Washington Post*, April 21, 2007.

163. U.S. Army.Mil/News, "Defense Department Releases Mental Health Assessment Findings," May 7, 2007, www.army.mil/-news/2007/05/07/3005-defense-department-releases-mental-health-assessment-findings/ (accessed June 1, 2007).

164. Knickmeyer, "In Haditha." As of June 2008, charges had been dropped or courts-martial had resulted in acquittal for all but one of the U.S. suspects in the Haditha massacre.

165. Tim McGirk, "Collateral Damage or Civilian Massacre in Haditha?" *Time*, March 19, 2006, www.time.com/time/world/article/0,8599,1174649,00.html (accessed April 30, 2007).

166. Michael Kazin, "Our Exceptional Innocence," *U.S. News and World Report*, June 28, 2004, 72.

167. Quoted in Kahn and Rocco, *Reclaiming the Pieces*, 38. See also John F. Fergueson, "Can the Church Offer Vietnam Vets Its Forgiveness?" *Episcopalian*, July 1987, 15.

168. Peter Marin, "What the Vietnam Vets Can Teach Us," in *Vietnam: The Battle Comes Home; A Photographic Record of Post-Traumatic Stress with Selected Essays*, ed. Nancy Howell-Koehler, with photos by Gordon Baer (Dobbs Ferry, NY: Morgan and Morgan, 1984), 41.

169. Ron Suskind, "Without a Doubt," *New York Times Magazine*, October 18, 2004.

170. George W. Bush's second inaugural address pronounced the goal of advancing democratic institutions in every land, with the ultimate goal of eliminating "tyranny" throughout the world, an enormously far-reaching conception of America's international reach and responsibilities. George W. Bush, "Inaugural Address," January 20, 2005, APP, www.presidency.ucsb.edu/ws/?pid=58745 (accessed June 2, 2007).

171. Walter Benjamin, "Theses on the Philosophy of History," in *Illuminations*, ed. and trans. Hannah Arendt (New York: Schocken Books, 1969), 255.

172. Diane Evans, "Getting Cold" (1990), 9, unpublished narrative found in AFP.

173. "The Wall."

174. Marin, "What the Vietnam Vets Can Teach Us," 47.

175. John Winthrop, "A Modell of Christian Charity," in *The Heath Anthology of American Literature*, ed. John Lauter, 3rd ed. (Boston: Houghton Mifflin, 1998), 233.

176. Anticipating the inauguration of a new president, Ronald Dworkin said: "We desperately need, most of all, a renaissance of international law and order. The Bush administration has nearly destroyed international law; it has debased our moral as well as our fiscal currency. America cannot face the growing terrorist threat effectively, or the equally menacing terrors of climate degradation, unless the world creates new institutions and doctrines of international law with genuine power and authority." Ronald Dworkin, "A Fateful Election," *New York Review of Books*, November 6, 2008, reprinted in special pull-out section of *The Guardian*, October 25, 2008. Barack Obama, a former law professor and student of international affairs at Columbia University, has advocated adherence to "internationally agreed-upon standards of conduct"; his election therefore promises a new approach to foreign policy more mindful of international law. As a senatorial candidate in 2004, however, Obama responded equivocally to the question whether the United States should ratify the Rome Statute of the International Criminal Court by saying, "Yes[.] The United States should cooperate with ICC investigations in a way that reflects American sovereignty and promotes our national security interests." The qualifications about national interests and sovereignty carefully hedge the initial affirmative response. Global Solutions, "Candidate Questionnaire: 2004," http:// globalsolutions.org/politics/elections_and_candidates/questionnaire/2004?id=20 (accessed January 6, 2009). In his presidential campaign autobiography, although Obama speaks positively about international institutions and says that the United States should seek legitimacy in its foreign policy, he is silent about re-signing and ratifying the Rome treaty. Barack Obama, *The Audacity of Hope: Thoughts on Reclaiming the American Dream* (Edinburgh: Canongate, 2007), 289, 309, 310, 316, 320.

INDEX

Note: Page numbers in italics refer to illustrations.

531

PATRICK HAGOPIAN is lecturer in American studies
at Lancaster University.